Rick Steves'

EUROPE

THROUGH THE

BACK DOOR

2011

Thirty Years of Europe Through the Back Door

You are holding the lessons of a 30-year travel career distilled into 800 pages. I carefully update it every year, so your next trip will benefit from the latest I've learned, as well as the timeless travel truths I still swear by. Thanks for letting me, through this guidebook, share with you my love of European travel.

Clockwise from left: Rick Steves in the seventies at a 'back door' he's discovered; this book's first edition from 1980 (typewritten text, no photos, 192 pages, $4.95); and a decades-long parade of new editions since.

Rick Steves'
EUROPE
THROUGH THE
BACK DOOR
2011

AVALON
TRAVEL

CONTENTS

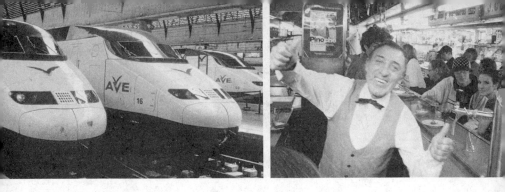

Preface to the 30th Anniversary Edition

This edition marks the 30th anniversary of *Europe Through the Back Door*. Thinking back over those three decades—plus 10 more years of trips preceding the first edition—has me reminiscing about what's changed in European travel... and what hasn't.

On my first visit to Europe, around 1970, there was little more than Arthur Frommer's *Europe on 5 Dollars a Day* to guide Americans. Back then, a cuckoo clock cost as much as a two-minute phone call to the States. Guest houses advertised "hot and cold," since hot running water wasn't a given. American Express offices were like way stations for wandering Yankee souls on pilgrimage. The autobahn was full of VW bugs. Travelers dressed up to fly, and made hotel reservations by letter. And one-legged reminders of the carnage of World War II gawked at a new age of tourists invading their homeland.

In spite of (or maybe because of) the challenges of European travel, I was hooked. As I went back to Europe again and again, each new trip was smoother than the last. It gradually became clear...I must be learning from my mistakes. And I saw people making the same mistakes I had made—mistakes costly in time, money, and experience. After I had a few trips under my belt, it occurred to me that if I could package the lessons I'd learned into a book, others could learn from my mistakes rather than their own. I could help fellow travelers enjoy a better, smoother trip. (And I'd have a good excuse to go back to Europe every summer to update my material.)

And so, in 1980, I began work on this book. I rented an IBM Selectric, and sweet-talked my girlfriend into typing it and my roommate into sketching the illustrations. I gingerly drove that precious first pile of pages to a small publishing house and, on my 25th birthday, returned to pick up 2,500 copies.

After the first edition of this book came out, Arthur Frommer had me on his TV show and introduced me as "the next Stephen Birnbaum, Temple Fielding, and Eugene Fodor of the travel publishing world." Hoping his faith in me wasn't misplaced, I've brought out a new edition of this book nearly each of the 30 years since to try to prove him right.

Travel has changed radically since this book's first edition. My staff and I work long and hard to keep the details right up-to-date and scoop any pending changes for travelers in the coming year. Flipping through copies of this book from the last 30 years, you can trace the advent of the Internet, smartphone apps, and e-books... and the demise of film cameras, travelers checks, and border checkpoints.

But as much as travel has changed, the fundamentals of enjoying "Europe Through the Back Door" are exactly the same. I saw it in 1980, and I see it in 2010: The average American traveler enters Europe through the front door. This Europe greets you with cash registers cocked, $10 cups of coffee, and service with a purchased smile. Now more than ever, it's critical that we venture beyond the constraints of mass tourism that shape the average American trip to Europe. Traveling through the back door, a warm, relaxed, personable Europe welcomes us as friends. We're part of the party—not part of the economy.

Traveling this way, we become temporary Europeans, members of the family—approaching Europe on its level, accepting and enjoying its unique ways of life. We'll demand nothing, except that no fuss be made over us.

This "Back Door–style" travel is better because of—not in spite of—your budget. Spending money has little to do with enjoying your trip. In fact, spending less money brings you closer to Europe. A lot of money forces you through Europe's grand front entrance, where people in uniforms greet you with formal smiles. But the back door is what keeps me in my wonderful European rut.

I'm just off the plane from the first of my 2010 trips, and I'm doing exactly what I've been doing since the 1970s—traveling with my teaching in mind, taking careful notes, making mistakes, ordering a margarita and ending up with pizza, and getting ripped off just to see what happens. This book, fully updated for its 30th anniversary edition, is my report to you.

My readers (many of whose grandkids warned them, "You shouldn't be doing this") are having great trips and coming home with money in the bank for next summer. I'm careful not to send people to Europe with too much confidence and not enough money, reservations, or skills. If I did, trips would suffer, and I'd hear about it. But judging from the happy gelato-stained postcards my "Road Scholars" send me, it's clear that those who equip themselves with good information and expect to travel smart, do.

The first half of this book covers the skills of Back Door European travel—packing, planning an itinerary, finding good hotels, getting around, and so on. The second half gives you keys to my favorite discoveries, places I call "Back Doors," where you can dirty your fingers in pure Europe—feeling its fjords and caressing its castles. So raise your travel dreams to their upright and locked positions, and let this book fly you away.

Happy travels!

Rick Steves' Back Door Travel Philosophy

Travel is intensified living—maximum thrills per minute and one of the last great sources of legal adventure. Travel is freedom. It's recess, and we need it.

Experiencing the real Europe requires catching it by surprise, going casual..."Through the Back Door."

Affording travel is a matter of priorities. (Make do with the old car.) You can eat and sleep—simply, safely, and enjoyably—anywhere in Europe for $120 a day plus transportation costs. In many ways, spending more money only builds a thicker wall between you and what you traveled so far to see. Europe is a cultural carnival, and time after time, you'll find that its best acts are free and the best seats are the cheap ones.

A tight budget forces you to travel close to the ground, meeting and communicating with the people. Never sacrifice sleep, nutrition, safety, or cleanliness to save money. Simply enjoy the local-style alternatives to expensive hotels and restaurants.

Connecting with people carbonates your experience. Extroverts have more fun. If your trip is low on magic moments, kick yourself and make things happen. If you don't enjoy a place, maybe you don't know enough about it. Seek the truth. Recognize tourist traps. Give a culture the benefit of your open mind. See things as different, but not better or worse. Any culture has plenty to share.

Of course, travel, like the world, is a series of hills and valleys. Be fanatically positive and militantly optimistic. If something's not to your liking, change your liking.

Travel can make you a happier American, as well as a citizen of the world. Our Earth is home to six and a half billion equally precious people. It's humbling to travel and find that other people don't have the "American Dream"—they have their own dreams. Europeans like us, but with all due respect, they wouldn't trade passports.

Thoughtful travel engages us with the world. In tough economic times, it reminds us what is truly important. By broadening perspectives, travel teaches new ways to measure quality of life.

Globetrotting destroys ethnocentricity, helping us understand and appreciate other cultures. Rather than fear the diversity on this planet, celebrate it. Among your most prized souvenirs will be the strands of different cultures you choose to knit into your own character. The world is a cultural yarn shop, and Back Door travelers are weaving the ultimate tapestry. Join in!

PART ONE
TRAVEL SKILLS

In Europe, life's very good—even if you're on a budget.

GETTING STARTED

1. Affording Europe

Europe Can Be a Sweet Deal...for Smart Travelers

A European adventure is a major investment of time and money. We've been through some challenging economic times lately, and some would-be travelers have put their trips on hold for one more year, just in case. But even through times of uncertainty, millions of globetrotters—who see exploring our world as a way of life—have stuck to their plans to keep on traveling.

It's difficult to put a price tag on the value of living life with abandon and filling it with vivid experiences. I can't recall anyone who traveled well and then regretted the expense of a European trip. You may need to crank up the budget focus, but you don't need to hold back when it comes to maximizing your experience. The true "value" of a trip isn't just a function of your cost, but your enjoyment. If everyone says, "Portugal is cheap," but your travel dreams are of the Swiss Alps, then *your* best value is in Switzerland...traveling smartly.

Let's be honest. Europe truly is expensive. In fact, in today's Europe, the nickel is the new penny. (Rich countries like Finland and the Netherlands have actually taken their one-cent and two-cent coins out of circulation.) Prices are high for locals—and even steeper for Americans. Yet regardless of the soaring cost of living, Europeans remain experts at living well. Even those who don't have much money manage plenty of *la dolce vita*. And savvy travelers can join them on the cheap.

The best travelers are not those with the thickest wallets, but those with a knack for connecting with locals and their culture. Before delving into the nitty-gritty of money-saving tricks, ponder how finding rich experiences can increase the value of your trip.

Between Sunday services at Paris' St. Sulpice Church, you can scamper like a sixteenth note up the spiral staircase into the organ loft, and literally sit on the bench next to Europe's greatest organist (Daniel Roth) as he plays one of Europe's finest pipe organs...and it doesn't cost a thing.

If you're wandering through Santiago de Compostela and hear music and dancers in a gym, pop in and observe. As you enjoy the Galician folk club practicing their traditional dance, you realize that northwest Spain is actually Celtic—where flamenco meets *Riverdance*.

In Helsinki, rather than sweat with a bunch of tourists in your hotel's sterile steam room, ride the public bus into a working-class neighborhood to a rustic-and-woody $14 sauna. Surrounded by milky steam, knotty wood, stringy blond hair, and naked locals, you'll have no idea which century you're in. But one thing is clear: You're in Finland.

Make your trip worth more by cranking up the experiences. Attending a sporting event anywhere in Europe—like this soccer match in Germany—puts you in touch with the local spirit for little money. If you're wearing a lei with colors, be sure you root for the right team. Auf geht's Deutschland!

Sporting events immerse you in the local scene affordably. Joining 60,000 Dubliners for a hurling match at Croke Park costs about $30. Taking your seat, you're among new Irish friends. On my last visit, they gave me a flag to wave and taught me who to root for, the rules of the game...and lots of new swear words.

Even in London—Europe's most expensive city—you can have a world-class experience for next to nothing. In Italy, it'll cost you a total of $50 to see Michelangelo's *Last Judgment*, Leonardo's *Last Supper*, and Botticelli's *Birth of Venus*; but in London, seeing the Tate Gallery, British Museum, and National Gallery won't cost you a pence. And when the seats at London's Royal Albert Hall are sold out, standing-room spots are often still available. For $8, you're part of the arts scene—up in the nosebleed section, with the students and struggling musicians. (The same strategy works at the opulent opera houses in Vienna and Budapest.)

When you stumble into a Barcelona square and see locals celebrating their Catalan heritage in the *Sardana* circle dance, join in. (A few generations ago, Franco would have locked you up.) Connect with the British expat community in Rome by going to the English-language Mass, and then hang around afterwards for coffee and cookies. Match your hobbies with a local in Helsinki's "Meet the Finns" program—and suddenly, you're searching out classic comics at the flea market with a new local friend.

Join the Scotsman who runs your B&B in a game of lawn bowling, the Frenchman who runs your *chambre d'hôte* in a game of *pétanque*, or the Greek who runs your *dhomatia* for a game of backgammon. Even if you don't know the rules, you'll end up with a memory that's easy to pack and costs nothing.

When I read over my past trip journals, I'm always impressed by how often the best experiences were free. Even more important than saving you money, these tips bring you rich experiences that become indelible memories...the kind of souvenirs you'll enjoy for a lifetime.

Seek Out Budget Alternatives

We Americans are simply not as rich as we have been conditioned to think we are. For a generation, insiders, politicians, and elites have goosed our economy—and now it just no longer responds to further goosing. We're far from poor. We just need to get real with the fact that rather than hopping into a taxi like a German, we'll stand in line for the bus with the Spaniards.

Budget travelers need to know their money-saving options, and take advantage of them: Ride the shuttle rather than the taxi in from the airport (saves $40 in Vienna). Order a carafe of house wine instead of a bottle of fine wine (saves $20 in Rome). Choose a two-star hotel rather than a three-star one (saves $60 per night in Paris). Buy the transit pass rather than individual tickets (saves $4 per ride on London's Tube). For making calls home to the US, buy a scratch-off phone card at a European newsstand, and you'll pay pennies rather than dollars per minute.

Your biggest budget challenges are accommodations: Hotels are pricey just about everywhere in Europe. But, equipped with good information, you can land some fine deals—which often come with the most memories, to boot. On recent visits, I slept well in a former medieval watchtower along Germany's Rhine River (Hotel Kranenturm, $85 double, www.kranenturm.com), a room in a private home on the Italian Riviera (Camere Fontana Vecchia in Vernazza, $100 double, m.annamaria@libero.it), and a welcoming guest house in Dubrovnik's Old Town (Villa Ragusa, $90 double, http://villaragusa.netfirms.com).

If you're willing to "rough it," you'll save even more. Consider the Norwegian YWCA in London ($42 beds, www.kfukhjemmet.org.uk), a renovated jail in Ljubljana (Hostel Celica, $30 for a bunk in a 12-bed dorm, www.hostelcelica.com), a schooner-turned-youth hostel moored in Stockholm's harbor (*Af Chapman*, $50 bunks, www.stfchapman.com), or a summer-only circus tent in Munich ($10 per mattress, www.the -tent.com).

When choosing a restaurant, look for small "mom & pop" places filled with enthusiastic local eaters. If a short, handwritten menu in one language is posted out front, that's a good sign. Daily specials, lunch deals, and early-bird dinners let you dine well for under $25 nearly anywhere in Europe.

Even in Scandinavia, Europe's priciest corner, locals are taking the high cost of living gracefully in stride: Norwegians "eat out" in the parks, barbecuing their groceries on disposable "one-time grills" ($4 in supermarkets). The last time I was in a restaurant in Oslo, 16 of 20 diners were drinking only tap water. While you'll see crowds of young people drinking beer

When young Norwegians "eat out," they drop by the grocery store for a disposable "one-time grill" and head for the park.

along Copenhagen's canals, that doesn't mean consumption is higher in Denmark—it's just that many young adults can't afford to drink in the bars, so they pick up their beer at the grocery store and party al fresco.

Eastern Europe is both a fine value and a new frontier for many travelers. While hotels are nearly as expensive as in the West, other items are a relative steal. A mug of Czech beer—the best in Europe—costs $2 (versus $5 in Britain or Ireland, or $8–10 in Oslo). A ticket for Mozart in a sumptuous Budapest opera house runs $20 (versus $65 in Vienna). And your own private Polish guide is $100 for half a day (versus $200 in London).

When you travel, time really *is* money. (Divide the complete cost of your trip by your waking hours in Europe, and you'll see what I mean. My cost: $20 per hour.) Don't waste your valuable time in lines. I queue

GETTING STARTED

as little as possible. (Speaking of IQ, I find there are two IQs of travelers in Europe: those who wait in lines, and those who don't.) In Europe's most crowded cities (especially Paris, Rome, and Florence), easy-to-make reservations and museum passes—which pay for themselves in four visits—let you skirt the long ticket-buying lines. If it costs $1 to use your mobile phone to confirm museum times, but it saves you trekking across town to discover the sight is closed, that's a buck very well spent. And sometimes, calculated "splurges" save both time and money: A taxi ride split by four people can cost less than four bus tickets.

Yes, you can travel affordably in Europe—if you travel "through the back door," using the budget tips you'll learn from this book. For added value, pump up the experiences.

2. Take a Tour or Be Your Own Guide?

From the start, you need to decide if you're taking a tour or going on your own.

Do you want the security of knowing that all your rooms are reserved and that a guide will take you smoothly from one hotel to the next? Do you require comfortable, American-style hotels? Will you forgo adventure, independence, and the challenge of doing it on your own in order to take the worry and bother out of travel-

Eight and forty tourists baked in a bus

ing? If you don't mind sitting on a bus with the same group of tourists and observing rather than experiencing, a tour may be just the right way for you to scratch your travel bug bites. There's a tour for just about every travel dream. Browse your options online, or ask a travel agent for advice.

Some tours deliver exactly what they promise.

For many people with limited time and money, tours are the most efficient way to see Europe. Without a tour, restaurant meals and big, modern hotel rooms can be very expensive. Large tour companies book thousands of rooms and meals year-round, and with their tremendous economic clout, they can get prices that no individual tourist can match. For instance, on a tour with Cosmos (one of the largest and cheapest tour companies in Europe), you will get fine rooms with private

Not all tours are as exciting as their brochures make them sound.

baths, some restaurant meals, bus transportation, and the services of a European guide—all for less than $150 a day. Considering that many of the hotel rooms alone cost around $150, that all-inclusive tour price is great.

Efficient and "economical" as tours may be, the tour groups that unload on Europe's quaintest towns experience things differently. They are treated as an entity: a mob to be fed, shown around, profited from, and moved out. If money is saved, it's at the cost of real experience. For me, the best travel values in Europe are enjoyed not by gazing through the tinted windows of a tour bus, but by traveling independently.

This book focuses on the skills necessary for do-it-yourself European travel. If you're destined for a tour, read on anyway (especially Chapter 33: Bus Tour Self-Defense). Even on a bus with 50 other tourists, you can and should be in control, equipped with a guidebook and thinking as an independent traveler. Your trip is too important for you to blindly trust an overworked, underpaid tour guide.

Being Your Own Guide

As this book has evolved with my experience as a tour guide, I find myself simply encouraging readers to approach their trip as thoughtfully as I would if you hired me to show you around. As a tour guide, I phone ahead to reconfirm reservations, ask at hotel check-in if there's any folk entertainment tonight, and call restaurants to confirm that they're open before I cross town. A good guide reads ahead. Use local entertainment periodicals and talk to other travelers. Ask questions or miss the festival.

Putting together a dream trip requires skills. Consider this book a do-it-yourself manual.

Traveling Alone

One of your first big decisions is whether to travel alone or with a friend. Consider the pros and cons of solo travel.

You have complete freedom and independence. You never have to wait for your partner to pack up. You never need to consider a partner's wishes when you decide what to see, where to go, how far to travel, how much to spend, or when to call it a day. You go where you want, when you want, and you can get the heck out of that stuffy museum when all the Monets start to blur together. If ad-libbing, it's easier for one to slip between the cracks than two.

You meet more people when you travel alone because you're more approachable in the eyes of a European, and because loneliness will drive you to reach out and make friends. When you travel with someone, it's easy to focus on your partner and forget about meeting Europeans.

Solo travel is intensely personal. Without the comfortable crutch of a friend, you're more likely to know the joys of self-discovery and the pleasures found in the kindness of strangers. You'll be exploring yourself, as well as a new city or country.

But loneliness can turn hotel rooms into depressing cells. And meals for one are often served in a puddle of silence. Big cities can be cold and ugly when the only person to talk to is yourself. Being sick and alone in a country where no one knows you is a sad and miserable experience—even in retrospect.

Fortunately, combating loneliness in Europe is easy. The continent is full of lonely travelers and natural meeting places. You're likely to find vaga-buddies in hostels, in museums, on half-day bus tours, and on trains. Travel as a student, whatever your age: Students have more fun, make more friends, and spend less money than most travelers. Board the train with a little too much of a picnic—and share it with others. Be lonely...or be bold.

For more pointers, see Chapter 27: The Woman Traveling Alone. (While this chapter is geared for female travelers, many of its tips work well for solo male travelers, as well.)

Traveling with a Partner

Having a buddy overcomes the disadvantages of solo travel. Shared experiences are more fun, and for the rest of your life there will be a special bond between you and your partner. The confident, uninhibited extrovert is better at making things happen and is more likely to run into exciting and memorable events. When I travel with a partner, it's easier for me to be that kind of "wild-and-crazy guy."

Traveling with a partner is cheaper. Rarely does a double room cost as much as two singles. If a single room costs $80, a double room will generally be about $100—a savings of $30 per night per person. Virtually everything is cheaper and easier when you share costs: picnicking, guidebooks, maps, magazines, taxis, storage lockers, and much more. Besides expenses, partners can share the burden of time-consuming hassles, such as standing in lines at train stations and post offices.

Traveling without a tour, you'll have the locals dancing with you—not for you.

Remember, traveling together greatly accelerates a relationship—especially a romantic one. You see each other constantly and make endless decisions. The niceties go out the window. Everything becomes very real; you're in an adventure, a struggle, a hot-air balloon for two. The experiences of years are jammed into weeks.

Consider a trial weekend together before merging dream trips. A mutual travel experience is a good test of a relationship—often revealing its ultimate course. I'd highly recommend a little premarital travel.

Your choice of a travel partner is critical. It can make or break a trip. Traveling with the wrong partner can be like a bad blind date that lasts for weeks. I'd rather do it alone. Analyze your travel styles and goals for compatibility. One summer I went to Europe to dive into as many cultures and adventures as possible. I planned to rest when I got home. My partner wanted to slow life down, get away from it all, relax, and escape the pressures of the business world. Our ideas of acceptable hotels and the purpose of eating were quite different. The trip was a near disaster.

You can get real close to traditional Europe... sometimes too close.

Many people already have their partner—for better or for worse. In the case of married couples, minimize the stress of traveling together by recognizing each other's needs for independence. Too many people do Europe as a three-legged race, tied together from start to finish. Have an explicit understanding that there's absolutely nothing selfish, dangerous, insulting, or wrong about splitting up occasionally. This is a freedom too few travel partners allow themselves. Doing your own thing for a few hours or days breathes fresh air into your togetherness.

Traveling with Two or More Companions

Traveling in a threesome or foursome is usually troublesome. With all the exciting choices Europe has to offer, it's often hard for even a twosome to reach a consensus. Unless there's a clear group leader, the "split and be independent" strategy is particularly valuable.

To minimize travel-partnership stress, go communal with your money. Separate checks and long lists of petty IOUs are a pain. Pool your resources, noting how much each person contributes, and just assume everything equals out in the long run. Keep track of major individual expenses, but don't worry about who got an extra postcard or cappuccino. Enjoy treating each other to taxis and dinners out of your "kitty," and after the trip, divvy up the remains. If one person consumed $50 or $60 more, that's a small price to pay for the convenience and economy of communal money. For example, a group of four often travels more cheaply in a shared taxi or rental car than by subway, bus, or train.

Travelers defending Caesar's empire atop Hadrian's Wall in Britain

If your group includes kids, see Chapter 30: Family Travel.

If You've Read This Far...

...you've got what it takes intellectually to handle Europe on your own. If you're inclined to figure things out, you'll find Europe well-organized and well-explained, usually in English. But some people are not inclined to figure things out on a trip. They figure things out to earn a living 50 weeks a year, and that's not their idea of a good vacation. These people should travel with a tour...or a spouse. But if you enjoy the challenge of tackling a great new continent—and of being your own guide—you can do it.

3. Gathering Information

Those who enjoy the planning stage as part of the experience invest wisely and reap tremendous returns. Study before you go. This kind of homework is fun. Take advantage of the wealth of material available: guidebooks, the Internet, magazines, classes, other travelers, TV and radio shows, and tourist information offices.

Guidebooks

Guidebooks are $25 tools for $4,000 experiences. Many otherwise smart people base the trip of a lifetime on a borrowed copy of a three-year-old guidebook. The money they save in the bookstore is wasted the first day of their trip, searching for hotels and restaurants long since closed. As a writer of guidebooks, I am a big believer in their worth. When I visit somewhere as a rank beginner—a place like Belize or Sri Lanka—I equip myself with a good, up-to-date guidebook and expect to travel smart. I travel like an old pro, not because I'm a super traveler, but because I have reliable information and I use it. I'm a connoisseur of guidebooks. My trip is my child. I love her. And I give her the best tutors money can buy.

Too many people are penny-wise and pound-foolish when it comes to information. I see them every year, stranded on street corners in Paris, hemorrhaging money. It's cascading off of them in €100 notes. Their vacations are disasters. Tourists with no information run out of money, fly home early, and hate the French. With a good guidebook, you can come into Paris for your first time, go anywhere in town for less than $2 on the subway, enjoy a memorable bistro lunch for $20, and pay $150 for a double room in a friendly hotel (with a singing maid) on a pedestrian-only street a few blocks from the Eiffel Tower—so French that when you step outside in the morning, you feel you must have been a poodle in a previous life. All you need is a good guidebook.

Never underestimate the value of an up-to-date guidebook.

Before buying a book, study it. How old is the information? (The cheapest books are often the oldest—no bargain.) Who wrote it? What's the author's experience? Does the book work for you—or for the tourist industry? Does it specialize in hard opinions—or superlatives? For whom is it written? Is it readable? It should have personality without chattiness and information without fluff.

Don't believe everything you read. The power of the printed word is scary. Most books are peppered with information that is flat-out wrong. (Incredibly enough, even this book may have an error.) Many "writers" succumb to the temptation to write guidebooks based on hearsay, travel brochures, other books, and wishful thinking. A writer met at the airport by an official from the national tourist board learns tips that are handy only for others who are met at the airport by an official from the national tourist board.

Europe is always changing, and guidebooks begin to yellow even before they're printed. It's essential to travel with the most up-to-date information in print. Most guidebooks get an update every two or three years, but a handful of titles (like many of mine) are actually updated in person each year. The rule of thumb: If the year is not printed on the cover, the guidebook is not updated annually (and you'll have to check the copyright information page—usually just inside the front or back cover—to see when it was most recently updated). When I'm choosing a guidebook for a trip, the publication date is usually the single most important factor in which one I buy.

While travel information is what keeps you afloat, too much information can sink the ship. I buy several guidebooks for each country I visit, rip them up, and staple the pertinent chapters together into my own personalized hybrid guidebook. Bring only the applicable pages. There's no point in carrying 120 pages of information on Scandinavia to dinner in Barcelona. When I finish seeing a country, I give my stapled-together chapter on that area to another traveler or leave it in my last hotel's lounge. (For other ideas on customizing your guidebook, see "Guidebooks: Small, Handy, and Hidden," on page 21.)

You can buy guidebooks at any major bookstore. But most large cities have at least one good bookstore that specializes in travel, with knowledgeable salespeople and a great selection. Ask around or search the Internet to find one near you.

Types of Guidebooks

There are as many types of guidebooks as there are types of travelers. Here are a few general guidelines to help you sort through the options.

Guidebooks differ in how they cover destinations. You'll find guides that specialize in **cities, regions within a single country** (such as Tuscany or the Loire Valley), **individual countries, combinations of two or three neighboring countries** (like Spain and Portugal), and sweeping **multi-country regions** (like Eastern Europe). Shop for guidebooks strategically. For example, if you're visiting only Venice and Florence, it can make sense to take two slim, in-depth city guides rather than lugging a hefty all-Italy book that covers far more (in far less depth) than you need.

Here are a few of the types of guidebooks you'll encounter:

Traditional Guidebooks: This is the industry standard—mostly text, with black-and-white maps for key destinations, generally a few glossy pages of color photos and maps, and sometimes black-and-white photos or illustrations throughout. My guidebooks—and most of those listed under "Guidebook Series," in the next section—follow this model.

Visual Guides: These guides feature high-tech, visually beautiful layouts with appealing color photos and illustrations (like cutaway cross-sections of important castles and churches). Visual learners and those who enjoy pretty pictures love this format. But the written information is scant and lacks depth, as it's mostly presented in blurbs short enough to squeeze between the pictures. I don't travel with these (they're printed on glossy paper, so they weigh a ton)—but if I ever need to locate, say, a Caravaggio painting in a church, I seek out a tourist with a copy and ask for a quick peek. **Eyewitness** (published by DK, http://traveldk.com) offers gorgeous guides covering London, Paris, Rome, Venice, Florence, Tuscany, Prague, Budapest, Athens, Vienna, Barcelona, Madrid, Dublin, and more, plus several regions and countries ($20–30 each, widely available in Europe).

"Lite" Guidebooks: These slim, pocket-sized books combine full-color maps and images with sightseeing information that's been distilled for maximum portability. Often these are a condensed version of a major series (such as **Eyewitness Top 10, Lonely Planet Encounter,** or my new **Rick Steves' Pocket** city guides—coming in 2011). Some are basically in-depth maps with some added guidebook-type content (such as **Moon Metro** or **Knopf MapGuides**).

Specialty Books: If you have a focus, there's a book written just for you—whether you're traveling with toddlers, pets, or grandparents. There are books for vegetarians, galloping gluttons, wine snobs, hedonists, cranky teens, nudists, pilgrims, bird-watchers, gay people, music lovers, potheads, campers, hikers, bikers, and motorcyclists. Some are for the rich and sophisticated; others are for the cheap and earthy. Visit a good travel bookstore and solicit the staff's help.

Digital Guidebooks: With the proliferation of iPhones, Black-Berrys, other smartphones, and wireless reading devices such as the

Kindle, Nook, Sony Reader, and iPad, technology developers and publishers are searching for the perfect way to sell guidebooks digitally. The technology is not refined yet, and results so far are mixed (you can't easily flip though e-books to find info, and the maps can be nearly illegible). That said, digital books are here to stay. Many guidebook series, including most of my guidebooks, are already available as e-books for the Kindle, and some are also available for the Sony Reader. (Note that to download titles directly to your Kindle in Europe, you need to have their Global Wireless service.) Meanwhile, Apple's iPhone App Store is finding creative new uses for travel resources, such as interactive guidebooks (including selections from my Paris and Rome guidebooks) and "talking phrase books." E-books allow you to really pack light, and eventually they'll offer other advantages impossible for traditional paper books—including customizing a book to cover precisely the destinations you want and linking maps to GPS technology so you'll never get lost. But until the perfect digital solution arrives, the most practical guidebook format remains the one you're holding in your hands.

Guidebook Series

Since most travelers prefer to take a traditional guidebook to Europe, that's what I'll focus on. Each of these series has its own area of specialization. Let's Go is the hosteler's bible, but you'll be disappointed if you try to use it to find fancy restaurants. If you're into fine cuisine, Michelin Red Guides can't be beat. History nuts seek out Cadogan, Blue Guides, and Rough Guides. Some guidebooks (like mine) are more opinionated and selective, choosing only the most worthwhile destinations in each country and really covering them in depth. These work perfectly for a quick trip to hit the highlights, but leave gaps if you're spending a lot of time in a single country—in which case, you should probably take along more than one guidebook anyway.

Here are some of my favorite series:

Lonely Planet (www.lonelyplanet.com): The worldwide standard for a solid guidebook, Lonely Planet guides cover most countries in Europe, Asia, Africa, and the Americas. They offer bricklike editions covering large swathes

A good guidebook allows you to play "tour guide" and brings Europe's museums to life.

of Europe (such as Western Europe and Mediterranean Europe), as well as books on individual countries, regions, and cities. The Lonely Planet guides offer no-nonsense facts, low- and mid-budget listings, and helpful on-the-ground travel tips. These guides' biggest strength is that they're extremely comprehensive—ideal for spending a long time in one country. Lonely Planet books are widely available in English editions throughout Europe. However, they are not updated annually; before you buy, check the publication date, and find out when the new edition is due out.

Rough Guides (www.roughguides.com): This British series includes books covering just about every country in Europe, as well as a fat all-Europe edition and several regional and city guides. These books are written by Europeans who understand the contemporary and social scene better than most American writers. While the Rough Guides' hotel listings can be skimpy and uninspired, the historical and sightseeing information tends to offer greater depth than their close competitor, Lonely Planet. Like Lonely Planet, Rough Guides are not updated annually—check the copyright date. When deciding between the two series, many travelers simply pick the one that was published more recently.

Let's Go (www.letsgo.com): Designed for young train travelers on tight budgets, Let's Go books are written and updated by Harvard students—making them refreshingly youthful and opinionated. Titles include the huge *Let's Go Europe,* as well as individual books on most countries and a few cities in Europe. As other formerly "budget" series are focusing more and more on mid-range travel, Let's Go has retained its super-low-budget approach and is the best resource for shoestring travelers (in many cities, they list only hostels and cheap hotels). With a hip student focus, Let's Go offers the best coverage on hosteling and the alternative nightlife scene. The series' biggest drawback is that nearly every young North American traveler uses it, and the flood of backpacker business it generates can overwhelm a formerly cozy village, hotel, or restaurant and give it a whopping Daytona Beach hangover. Most Let's Go guides to Europe are updated about every two years.

Frommer's Guides (www.frommers.com): Arthur Frommer's books are full of reliable and handy listings of hotels, restaurants, and sightseeing tips originally compiled by the father of independent budget travel himself. The guides cover individual countries, regions, and cities, giving good advice on which sights are essential when time is short. They're especially well-attuned to the needs of older travelers, but some readers may feel like they're being handled with unnecessary kid gloves. Though he's best known for the frugal-travel classic *Europe on 5 Dollars a Day,* Frommer's "Dollar-a-Day" guides are gradually being replaced by his daughter Pauline's budget travel series. The Pauline Frommer guides are part of a publishing behemoth that is generally good for the most important big cities but light on everything else—skipping some of my favorite places in Europe. Other series belonging to the Frommer's empire include the "Irreverent," "Unofficial," and "For Dummies" guides.

Michelin Green Guides (www.michelintravel.com): These famous, tall, green books are sort of a hybrid of traditional guidebooks and the newer visual breed: Printed on glossy paper and packed with full-color maps and photos, they offer more written content than most visual guides (such as Eyewitness). A French publisher, Michelin has English editions covering several regions of France and most countries of Europe. (The English editions are often available in Europe—especially in France—for lower prices than in the United States.) French-speakers will find more editions available. Each book includes small but encyclopedic chapters on history, lifestyles, art, culture, customs, and economy. Recent editions also contain information on hotels and restaurants. These practical books are a tour guide's best friend. All over Europe, tour leaders are wowing their busloads by reading from their Green Guides. ("And these are fields of sugar beets. Three-quarters of Austria's beet production lies along the banks of the Danube, which flows through 12 countries, draining an area the size of Sudan.") A wonderful and unique feature of the Green Guides is their handy maps, in which the prominence of a listed place is determined by its importance to the traveler, rather than its population. This means that a cute, visit-worthy village (such as Rothenburg, Germany) appears bolder than a big, dull city (like Dortmund). These books are filled with fine city maps and are designed for drivers...ideally on Michelin tires. The **Michelin Red Guides** are the hotel and restaurant connoisseur's bibles. But I don't travel with a coat and tie, and my taste buds weren't designed to appreciate $100 meals.

Blue Guides (www.blueguides.com): The Blue Guides (which have nothing to do with European brothels) take a dry and scholarly approach to the countries of Europe, and have begun to include more maps and color photos. They're ideal if you want to learn as much about history, art, architecture, and culture as you possibly can. With the Blue Guide to Greece, I had all the information I needed about any sight and never needed to hire a guide. Scholarly types actually find a faint but endearing personality hiding between the sheets of their Blue Guides. There are Blue Guides covering many of Europe's countries, cities, and regions. The Blue Guides publisher, Somerset, also produces two other series: the visually oriented "Visible Cities" and the "art/shop/eat" series, which covers...well, you know.

Cadogan Guides (www.cadoganguides.com): Cadogan (rhymes with "toboggan") guides are readable and thought-provoking, giving the curious traveler cultural insights into many regions. They're similar to Blue Guides, but more accessible to the typical traveler. The series includes country, city, and regional guides for destinations throughout Europe, as well as the "Flying Visits" series for quick trips, the "Take the Kids" series for parents, and the "Pick Your Brains About..." series for kids, filled with fun facts, puzzles, and cartoons. They're good pre-trip reading. If you're traveling alone and want to understand tomorrow's sightseeing, Cadogan gives you something productive to do in bed.

Time Out (www.timeout.com): This popular monthly entertainment guide, which originated in London, has parlayed its wealth of information about the scene in that grand city into a fine series of guidebooks. Time Out guides now have editions—readily available in Europe—covering nearly 40 European cities and regions, from Amsterdam to Zagreb. They cover sights, current events, entertainment, eating, and sleeping with an insider's savvy. Written with the British market in mind, they have a hard-hitting, youthful edge and assume readers are looking for the trendy scene. Their "Shortlist" series is pocket-sized and suitable for quick city jaunts.

Access Guides (www.accessguides.com): These creatively crafted guides offer sightseeing information on London, Paris, Rome, and Florence/Venice. They're organized by a city's neighborhoods, with text color-coded for sights, hotels, and restaurants.

Rick Steves' Guidebooks

The book you're holding is the foundation of a series of books—written and refined over the last three decades—that work together to help smooth your travels and broaden your cultural experience.

While *Europe Through the Back Door* teaches you the nuts and bolts of how to travel, *Europe 101: History and Art for the Traveler* (co-authored with Gene Openshaw) helps you achieve a deeper understanding of the story of Europe. Written for smart people who slept through their art history classes before they knew they were going to Europe, this full-color, easily readable manual is full of boiled-down, practical information that will enliven your sightseeing. After reading *Europe 101,* you can walk into a Gothic cathedral, excitedly nudge your partner, and marvel, "Isn't this a great improvement over Romanesque!"

The next step, *Travel as a Political Act,* illustrates how Americans who travel with an open mind and a curious spirit can have the time of their lives and come home smarter—with a keener appreciation for the interconnectedness of the world around them. Through a series of field reports from Europe, Central America, and the Middle East, I explain how you can turn travel into a life-changing experience.

This trilogy of books forms a pyramid—a kind of Abraham Maslow's "hierarchy of needs" for the thinking traveler. You start off with the basics: Pack light, stay safe, catch the train, and eat and sleep well. When those needs are met, you can enjoy the art, history, and culture. Finally you reach the pinnacle of travel: gaining a deeper understanding of our place on this delightful planet.

The above-mentioned trio of books is designed to be read before your trip, to give your travels a firm foundation. But once you're on the road, you need a blueprint for your actual trip. My take-along **country, city,** and **regional guidebooks** weave my favorite sights, accommodations, and restaurants into trip strategies designed to give you the most value out of every mile, minute, and dollar. As a guidebook writer, I focus on helping you explore and enjoy Europe's big cities, small towns, and regions, mixing must-see sights with intimate Back Door nooks and offbeat crannies. My books cut through the superlatives. Yes, I know you can spend a lifetime in Florence. But you've got a day and a half, and I've got a great plan. For travelers staying a bit longer in one place—whether in a thriving city (London, Paris, Rome) or an enticing region (Provence)—my city and regional guidebooks feature engaging, in-depth, self-guided tours of the top sights, highlighting the great art and history with photos and commentary.

If you plan to mix-and-match your way through Europe, try my **Snapshot** guides. These slim titles consist of chapters on some of my favorite destinations, excerpted from my larger country guidebooks. For example, if you're headed only to the Cinque Terre but not the rest of Italy, consider *Rick Steves' Snapshot Cinque Terre* (rather than the longer, more inclusive *Rick Steves' Italy* book).

Rick Steves' Best of Europe is a "greatest hits" compilation of the most popular destinations from my country guidebooks (including many of the Back Doors described in the last half of this book). If its table

Rick Steves' Guidebooks

Country Guides
Rick Steves' Best of Europe
Rick Steves' Croatia & Slovenia
Rick Steves' Eastern Europe
Rick Steves' England
Rick Steves' France
Rick Steves' Germany
Rick Steves' Great Britain
Rick Steves' Ireland
Rick Steves' Italy
Rick Steves' Portugal
Rick Steves' Scandinavia
Rick Steves' Spain
Rick Steves' Switzerland

City and Regional Guides
Rick Steves' Amsterdam,
   Bruges & Brussels
Rick Steves' Athens & the Peloponnese
Rick Steves' Budapest
Rick Steves' Florence & Tuscany
Rick Steves' Istanbul
Rick Steves' London
Rick Steves' Paris
Rick Steves' Prague & the Czech Republic
Rick Steves' Provence & the French Riviera
Rick Steves' Rome
Rick Steves' Venice
Rick Steves' Vienna, Salzburg & Tirol

Snapshot Guides
Excerpts from country guides, such as *Rick Steves' Snapshot Barcelona*, *Rick Steves' Snapshot Scotland*, and *Rick Steves' Snapshot Hill Towns of Central Italy*.

Pocket Guides (new in 2011)
Condensed, pocket-size, full-color guides to Europe's top cities, including Paris, London, and Rome.

More Books
Rick Steves' Europe 101: History and Art for the Traveler
Rick Steves' Europe Through the Back Door
Rick Steves' Travel as a Political Act
Rick Steves' European Christmas
Rick Steves' Postcards from Europe

of contents lists all of your destinations, *Best of Europe* is an all-in-one option that will serve your trip as well as (and cheaper than) several individual country guides.

What makes my guidebooks different from the competition? With the help of my research partners, I update my guidebooks lovingly and in person—many of them annually. In order to experience the same Europe that most of my readers do, I insist on doing my research in the peak tourist season—from April through September. And I'm stubbornly selective, writing about fewer destinations. For example, Italy has dozens of hill towns, but my Italy book zooms in on the handful that are truly worth the trip. I cover with more depth the places that make the cut—I base page count on a place's worthiness, rather than its population or fame.

Once in Europe, connecting with the culture is key. My **phrase books** for French, Italian, German, Spanish, Portuguese, and French/Italian/German are the only phrase books on the market designed by a guy who speaks just English. That's why they're so good. They're based on many years of experience struggling with other phrase books. These are both fun and practical, with a meet-the-people and stretch-the-budget focus. Mr. Berlitz knew the languages, but he never stayed in a hotel where he had to ask, "Where can I hang my laundry?"

And for some leisure reading laced with inspiration—think of it as a guidebook in disguise—consider my autobiographical book, **Rick Steves' Postcards from Europe**. In *Postcards*, I take you on a private tour of my favorite 2,000-mile loop through Europe: from Amsterdam through

If your taxi driver is going too fast, my phrase books will help you say, "If you don't slow down, I'll throw up."

Guidebooks: Small, Handy, and Hidden

As I travel in Europe, I meet lots of people with clever book treatments. The couple on the left was proud of the job they did in the name of packing light: cutting out only the pages they'd be using and putting them into a spiral binding. The couple on the right put the guidebook in a brown-paper-bag book cover so they wouldn't look so touristy (a smart move, I'll admit).

I love the ritual of trimming down the size of guidebooks I'll be using: Fold the pages back until you break the spine, then neatly slice out the sections you want with a utility knife, and pull them

out with the gummy edge intact. Reassemble the pieces you're keeping with a monster stapler to "rebind" the whole book. Finish it off with some clear, heavy-duty packing tape to smooth and reinforce the spine.

Whatever you do, get serious about both packing light and taking advantage of good information.

Germany, Italy, and Switzerland, with a grand finale in Paris. Shuffled among my *Postcards* are stories from my past, including my first trip to Europe (my parents forced me to go). Four decades later, I can't stop. The reasons are in *Postcards*.

My guidebooks are published by Avalon Travel (www.travelmatters .com); *Travel as a Political Act* is published by Nation Books (www.nation books.org).

Travel Literature

Consider some trip-related recreational reading. A book on the court of Louis XIV brings Versailles to life. Books such as James Michener's *Iberia* (for Spain and Portugal) or *Poland*, Irving Stone's *The Greek Treasure* for Greece and Turkey, William Wordsworth's poems for England's Lake District, and Leon Uris' *Trinity* for Ireland are real trip bonuses. After reading Stone's *The Agony and the Ecstasy*, you'll visit dear friends in Florence—who lived there 500 years ago.

Personal accounts are fun and vivid, such as *Notes from a Small Island* by Bill Bryson (on Britain), Peter Mayle's Provence books (on himself), and the Travelers' Tales series (on Ireland, France, Paris, Provence, Italy, Tuscany, Spain, Prague, Greece, and Turkey; www.travelerstales.com). Bibliotravel.com provides user-generated lists of suggested reading sorted by destination.

To get in an adventurous mood, start with Mark Twain's classic, witty travelogue, *The Innocents Abroad* (and follow it up with *A Tramp Abroad*, which takes you to Germany, Switzerland, and bits of France and Italy).

To glimpse life in Italy, consider Frances Mayes' *Under the Tuscan Sun*, Tim Parks' *Italian Neighbors*, Jan B. Kubik's *Piazzas and Pizzas*, or John Berendt's *The City of Falling Angels*. Christina Björk's *Vendela in Venice* is aimed at kids but is also enjoyable for adults.

For the flavor of France, try M. F. K. Fisher's *Two Towns in Provence*, Polly Platt's diplomatic *French or Foe?* and *Savoir-Flair*, Stephen Clarke's *Talk to the Snail* and *A Year in the Merde*, Thad Carhart's *The Piano Shop on the Left Bank*, Sarah Turnbull's *Almost French*, Ernest Hemingway's *A Moveable Feast*, Adam Gopnik's *Paris to the Moon*, or Carol Drinkwater's *The Olive Farm*. To sample Spain, consider *Driving Over Lemons* by Chris Stewart or *It's Not About the Tapas* by Polly Evans. For understanding the Basque region (divided between Spain and France), Mark Kurlansky's *The Basque History of the World* is essential.

Tony Hawks' *Round Ireland with a Fridge* affords a goofy look at the Irish, *The Emperor's New Kilt* by Jan-Andrew Henderson deconstructs the myths surrounding the tartan-clad Scots, and Susan Allen Toth's *My Love Affair with England* explores the country's charms and eccentricities.

For Germany, consider the travel memoir *The Bells in Their Silence: Travels through Germany*, by Michael Gorra. Marcus Zusak's award-winning novel, *The Book Thief*, follows a young German girl during and after World War II.

To get a sense of Greece, consider Patricia Storace's *Dinner with Persephone*, Tom Stone's *Summer of My Greek Taverna*, Henry Miller's

Colossus of Maroussi, or Gerald Malcolm Durrell's *My Family and Other Animals.* Travelers to Turkey might enjoy Alev Lytle Croutier's novel, *Seven Houses,* or Yashar Kemal's classic tale, *Memed, My Hawk.*

If you're a mystery fan, try the detective series by Anne Perry (Victorian London) or Lindsey Davis (Ancient Rome); Alan Furst's WWII spy novels; or Steven Saylor's Roma Sub Rosa historical mysteries. Dan Brown's popular thrillers, *The Da Vinci Code* and *Angels and Demons,* are set in modern times but deal with real historical figures.

History buffs recommend Ross King's *Brunelleschi's Dome* (on how the stunning dome of Florence's cathedral was built) and his *Michelangelo and the Pope's Ceiling* (the story behind the Sistine Chapel); Jan Morris' and H. V. Morton's books on Italy; Salley Vickers' *Miss Garnet's Angel* (Venice); Colleen McCullough's Masters of Rome series; Edward Rutherfurd's *London, Sarum, The Forest,* and *Dublin;* Nigel Tranter's trilogies (Scotland); and Ken Follett's *The Pillars of the Earth* (cathedral epic set in England).

The Diary of Anne Frank tells the story of a young Jewish girl hiding out from the Nazis in Amsterdam. Corrie Ten Boom's autobiography, *The Hiding Place,* offers another angle with the story of a Christian family caught hiding Jews from the Nazis in Haarlem (near Amsterdam). For a harrowing account of survival in a Nazi concentration camp, consider the much-lauded *Night* by Elie Wiesel.

For literature lovers, there's Victor Hugo's *The Hunchback of Notre-Dame,* set in medieval Paris; Voltaire's 18th-century French satire *Candide;* Czech existentialist Franz Kafka's disturbing *The Metamorphosis;* James Joyce's Irish odyssey, *Ulysses;* and the British classics by Jane Austen, Charles Dickens, the Brontë sisters, D. H. Lawrence, William Shakespeare, C. S. Lewis, and so on.

For more complete country-by-country lists of recommended reading (and viewing), see www.ricksteves.com/travelreading. You'll also find additional suggestions from fellow travelers in the "Recommended Novels for Your Travels" section at our Graffiti Wall (www.ricksteves .com/graffiti).

Paging through coffee-table books on places you'll be visiting (e.g., *Hill Towns of Tuscany, The French Café*) can give you some great, often untouristy, sightseeing ideas. If travel partners divide up their studying, they can take turns being "guide" and do a better job. Your local travel bookstore stocks good travel literature as well as guidebooks. And your hometown library has a lifetime of valuable reading on European culture. Wander over to nonfiction: Dewey gave Europe the numbers 914 and 940. Take your travel partner on a date to the library and start your trip early.

Maps

European travelers have needed good maps since the days of Alexander the Great. But with so many choices, it's hard to know where to start.

Maps and atlases are sold at European gas stations, bookshops, newsstands, and tourist shops. The only reason to buy a map before your trip is for general planning purposes. Once you get to Europe, compare maps side by side to choose your favorite. Many travelers prefer Michelin maps, but other quality European brands include Hallwag, Freytag Berndt, Marco Polo, Berndtson & Berndtson, AA (Britain's AAA-type automobile club), Road Editions (for Greece), Cappelens (for Norway), and Kod & Kam (for Croatia and Slovenia). The *Michelin 705* Europe map provides an excellent overall view of Europe. Many guidebook publishers (including Rough Guides, Lonely Planet, and Rick

My planning maps highlight what you want to see...not just the biggest cities.

Steves) make maps or combination map-guidebooks. For example, my European planning maps are designed to be used with my guidebooks.

Here are some tips for choosing and using a map:

Decide the scope of the map you need. Your main decision when choosing a map is its purpose. Do you want an overview, or a map of a specific region or city? Are you driving? Bicycling? Walking? Traveling by rail?

Understand the scale. European maps indicate their scale with a ratio (such as 1:100,000). The lower the second number on the ratio, the more detailed the map. A 1:100,000 scale means that one centimeter on the map equals 100,000 centimeters (or one kilometer) in real life. A basic all-Europe map, such as the *Michelin 705*, has a scale of 1:3,000,000—perfectly fine for overall route planning. But if you're exploring a specific region by car, you need something more detailed (such as 1:200,000). If you're biking, you could use even more detail (1:100,000 or 1:50,000). Obviously, the more detailed a map is, the more information it can show—but some overachiever maps are so crammed with detail that they become hard to read. Figure out the level of detail you need and purchase accordingly.

Drivers require first-class maps. The free maps you sometimes get from your car-rental company usually don't cut it. Drivers need detail, especially when focusing on a specific region. I like Michelin maps (various scales, about $10–12 each, cheaper in Europe). But the cost for these maps can add up, so consider the popular and relatively inexpensive Michelin road atlases for each country (1:200,000, about $22–25 each, with good city maps and detailed indexes). Though they can be heavy, atlases are compact, a good value, and easier for drivers to use than big fold-out maps. Sometimes the best regional maps are available locally. For example, if you're exploring your roots in the Norwegian fjord country, Cappelens 1:200,000 maps are detailed enough to help you find Grandpa Ole's farm.

Cyclists and walkers also need highly detailed maps. Maps at 1:200,000 scale may not show cyclists the off-the-beaten roads. Maps that have even more detail, at 1:100,000 or 1:50,000 (good for walkers), are more helpful but harder to find. Consider OS Ordnance Survey (Britain), Michelin (throughout Europe), IGN's Blue series (good for France), Touring Club Italiano (Italy), and Die Generalkarte (Germany).

Like me, this goat appreciates a good map.

Elevation gain and loss is a major concern for those traveling by two wheels or two feet. Make sure the map shows general elevation gain with contour lines and/or indicates the steepness of roads (sometimes with small Vs on the road). You'll be outdoors most of the time; maps are rarely waterproof, so keep yours in a plastic pouch.

Train travelers can get by with less-detailed maps. By train, you can usually wing it with the map that comes free with your railpass, though some more detailed rail-line maps are available.

Smart sightseers use city maps. For an extended stay in a sprawling city, I make a point of buying a good city map immediately upon arrival. While guidebooks come with black-and-white (and sometimes color) maps of big cities, they're generally small, and intended only to give you an overview of the place. A detailed, fold-out map can save you endless time and frustration. You can often get a decent map free or cheap at the local tourist office. Many city maps sacrifice important town-center detail by trying to show the entire city (including the suburbs, where you probably won't go). If choosing a city sightseeing map, make sure the city center is detailed enough, since that's where you'll be spending most of your time.

Look for clarity and durability. Choose a map that's clear and easy to read. The map should have crisp lines that don't bleed into one another. Size is another important factor: The bigger the map, the more chance for detail, but the harder it is to use and refold. Also consider durability. A map you plan on using for your entire trip should hold up to constant folding and unfolding (not to mention a few raindrops). A cardboard or plastic cover on the map will help it last longer, but adds weight.

Learn the legend. Spend half a traffic jam studying the map key. Each map has a legend that indicates navigational as well as sightseeing information, such as types of roads, scenic routes and towns, ruined castles, hostels, mountain huts, viewpoints, and so on. Good maps even include such specific details as tolls and opening schedules of remote mountain roads. When estimating how long a trip will take, figure you'll average 100 kilometers per hour on expressways (about the same as going 60 mph back home). Determining how much ground you can cover off the freeway is a crapshoot. I use a trick an Irish bus driver taught me: Figure a minute for every kilometer (covering 90 km will take you about an hour and a half). Double that for slow, curvy roads (such as in Italy's Dolomites or Amalfi Coast). Normally, the more digits the road number has, the smaller it is. In Britain, M-1 is a freeway, A-34 is a major road, and B-4081 is a secondary road. Roads are labeled on many maps with both national and European designations—for example, the same expressway from Madrid to Sevilla may be labeled A-4, E-5, or both. Since road numbers can change, it's often best to navigate by town names.

The Internet

The Internet is filled with free travel resources: global weather reports, news, travel advice, visa information, hotel and restaurant reviews, maps and route-planners, flight- and hotel-reservation services, and lots more.

I've listed helpful websites throughout this book, including the ones that my staff and I rely on when we're planning our own trips. The following list is our "greatest hits" to help get you started. (To browse a much more extensive list, visit www.ricksteves.com/links.)

General Resources

www.google.com—The best Web search engine and a good starting point for finding information on any topic (travel-related or otherwise);

also try www.bing.com

http://news.bbc.co.uk—The most informative site for European news, from Britain's premier news agency; also try www.iht.com *(International Herald Tribune)* and www.europeantimes.com

www.ricksteves.com/graffiti—One of many online message boards where travelers swap tips and tales; to ask and answer questions of fellow travelers, see www.ricksteves.com/helpline

Transportation

http://bahn.hafas.de/bin/query.exe/en—German Rail timetable, ideal for checking train schedules for anywhere in Europe

www.railfaneurope.net—Links to each country's own national rail website

www.eurolines.com—Europe's most extensive bus network

www.aferry.to—Ferry connections throughout Europe; also try www.youra.com/intlferries

www.viamichelin.com—Online maps for all of Europe, plus a reliable route planner with good estimates of driving time and distance for your journey; other good map sites include www.google.com/maps, www.theaa.com, and www.mappy.com

www.skyscanner.net—Search engine for tracking down cheap flights; also try www.wegolo.com and www.whichbudget.com

www.tsa.gov/travelers—The latest on rules and regulations for flights

www.worldtravelguide.net/airport—Arrival information for most of Europe's airports, including how to get into the city center

Practicalities

www.oanda.com—The best online currency conversion tool

www.countrycallingcodes.com—Instructions on how to dial any phone number in Europe; also see www.howtocallabroad.com

www.skype.com—Free long-distance calling over the Internet

www.towd.com—Tourism Offices Worldwide Directory, with contact information for tourist offices throughout Europe

www.travel.state.gov—The US State Department's official travel site, with foreign entry requirements, travel warnings, and more

www.google.com/language_tools—Helpful language translator

www.weather.com—Weather predictions for anywhere in the world; for general climate information, see www.weatherbase.com

www.whatsonwhen.com—Dates and details on European festivals and cultural events; also check tourist office websites per country (see www.towd.com)

GETTING STARTED

Ricksteves.com

With my website, www.ricksteves.com, this book becomes just the tip of an informational iceberg sharing the collective travel experience of my 70-person staff (logging well over 2,000 days of European travel each year) and legions of Back Door travelers—our true "Road Scholars."

Ricksteves.com is completely free, fast, and user-friendly. You'll find my latest guidebook updates (www.ricksteves.com/update), European country information, a monthly travel e-newsletter (easy and free to sign up), my personal travel blog, and scripts for my public-television programs. Look for the most recent version of our railpass guide. Listen to dozens of free, information-packed interviews about Europe from the archives of my weekly public-radio show (look for "Rick Steves Audio Europe"). The Press Room includes a sampling of newspaper articles about our work, and our fun and user-friendly online Travel Store covers all the travel gear, guidebooks, videos, railpasses, and tours we offer.

Our Graffiti Wall (www.ricksteves.com/graffiti) is one of the most popular corners of our site. It's an immense (yet well-groomed)

Travel Booking Sites (Hotels, Transportation, and More)

www.tripadvisor.com—Most useful for its extensive user reviews of hotels and restaurants, but can also be used to book hotels, flights, and rental cars

www.travelocity.com—One of many sites where you can search for and book accommodations and transportation; also see www.expedia.com, www.orbitz.com, www.kayak.com, and www.mobissimo.com

Sharing Your Trip

www.blogger.com—Create your own travel blog (online journal) here or at other free blogging sites

www.twitter.com—Popular host site for "micro-blogging" (posting brief minute-by-minute updates about what you're doing)

Scrawl on our Graffiti Wall.

collection of message boards where our Road Scholars share their personal experiences on the most important or perplexing travel issues of the day. As you read this book, remember that almost every chapter has a corresponding thread growing on our Graffiti Wall with hundreds of postings. With more than a hundred topics, there's something for everyone: Room-Finding Tricks, Best Walking Shoes, Cell Phone Tips, Best European Hostels, Tipping Tips, Chocoholics Unite!, Shopping Finds, iPod and Other MP3 Player Tips, Marijuana in Europe, Tourist Scam Alert, Staying Healthy, Accessible Europe, Leaping Language Barriers, Flying to and Within Europe, Driving Europe Crazy, Getting Married in Europe, Tricks for Packing Light, Photography in Europe, Travel with Kids, Women Travelers, Solo Travel, Savvy Seniors, Minority Travelers' Forum, European Travel Partners Wanted, and much more.

Our Travelers Helpline (www.ricksteves.com/helpline) lets you present a particular travel question or problem you are facing, and invite other readers to chime in with advice.

www.facebook.com—Social networking site that can be used for blogging and keeping in touch with friends

www.flickr.com—Tool for organizing and sharing photos from your trip; also try http://picasa.google.com, www.photobucket.com, or www.snapfish.com

Travel Magazines and Newsletters

While some magazines have gone all-digital (such as www.transitions abroad.com), many others are still available in print. Whether online, in print, or both, these can be a timely resource. My favorites devote more attention to practical travel advice than to breathless raves.

International Travel News, printed on newsprint in black and white, is packed with down-and-dirty travel news, industry announcements, reports from traveling readers, globetrotting personals, and advertisements from creative small-time travel operators (monthly, $24/year, www.intl travelnews.com, tel. 800-486-4968). *National Geographic Traveler* offers travel advice, trip ideas, and money-saving tips (eight issues annually, $10/year, www.nationalgeographic.com/traveler, tel. 800-647-5463). *Arthur Frommer's Budget Travel* is another glossy with a budget focus (10 issues annually, $12/year, www.budgettravel.com, tel. 800-829-9161). *Smithsonian* magazine combines beautiful photography with scholarly articles, often on travel-related topics (11 issues annually, $12/year, www .smithsonianmag.com, tel. 800-766-2149). *Abroad View* is geared toward college students studying overseas, with a focus on cultural awareness (2 issues annually, free on college campuses or by ordering online, www .abroadview.org). *The Nation* magazine offers a progressive—and more European—take on American politics (weekly, $32/year, check website for online deals, www.thenation.com, tel. 800-333-8536). *The Economist,* published in Britain, is best for an intellectual look at contemporary world events and politics (weekly, $127/year, www.economist.com).

Classes

The more you understand a subject, the longer it stays interesting. Those with no background in medieval architecture are the first to get "cathedraled out." Whether you like it or not, you'll be spending lots of time browsing through historic buildings and museums. Those who take trip-related classes beforehand have more fun sightseeing in Europe.

There are plenty of worthwhile classes on many aspects of Europe. Although you can get by with English, a foreign language—even a few survival phrases—can only make Europe more fun. A basic modern European history course brings Europe and its "dull" museums to life. A class in Eastern European studies shines some light on that complicated corner of the world.

Art history is probably the most valuable course for the prospective tourist. Don't go to Europe—especially Italy or Greece—without at least having read something on art and architecture.

Talk with Other Travelers

Both in Europe and here at home, travelers love to share the lessons they've learned. Learn from other tourists. Firsthand, fresh information can be good stuff. Keep in mind, however, that all assessments of a place's touristic merit are a product of that person's personality and experiences there. It could have rained on her parade, he could have shared an elevator with the town jerk, or she may have been sick in "that lousy, overrated city." Or he might have fallen in love in that "wonderful" village. Every year, I find travelers hell-bent on following miserable travel advice from friends at home. Except for those found in this book, treat opinions as opinions.

Take advantage of every opportunity (such as train or bus rides, or online discussion boards such as the Graffiti Wall at www.ricksteves .com/graffiti or the Travelers Helpline at www.ricksteves.com/helpline) to swap information with travelers you meet from other parts of the English-speaking world. This is particularly important when traveling beyond Western Europe.

Rick Steves' TV, Radio, Audio Tours, and Audio Europe

Public Television: Resources are available on the air. My public television series, *Rick Steves' Europe,* covers my favorite continent in 100 episodes (80 of them also available on DVD), and we're working on new shows every year. I've also done several TV specials, including *Rick Steves' European Christmas* and *Rick Steves' Iran,* a one-hour special on my visit to that proud if perplexing nation of 70 million people. For more on my TV shows, see page 737.

Public Radio: My weekly hour-long radio show, *Travel with Rick Steves,* is carried by more than 130 public radio stations across the US. I've interviewed the top experts on world travel. Guests have included European royalty, Irish politicians, and authors Salman Rushdie and David Sedaris—and I also take questions from Road Scholars like you. For details on my radio program, see page 738, and to download free podcasts of the show, see "Rick Steves Audio Europe," next page.

Audio Tours: At most major European museums, you can rent audioguides that offer a dry headphone commentary on the great works of art. If you prefer your art-history information in a light, easy-to-digest style, consider my free audio tours—a recorded version of what I'd tell you if I were your tour guide. In Paris, I lead you through the Louvre, Orsay, Versailles, and the historic core of the city. My five London audio tours take you on walks in The City and Westminster, and inside St. Paul's Cathedral, the British Museum, and the British Library. In Italy,

16 different audio tours cover the top sights of Venice, Florence, and Rome. To download the audio tours, see "Rick Steves Audio Europe" next.

Rick Steves Audio Europe: For a free, online library covering destinations in Europe, try Rick Steves Audio Europe, which contains hours of audio information: my public radio interviews on European travel, excerpts of my travel writing, and audio tours of major sights in Rome, Venice, Florence, Paris, and London. It's downloadable to your iPod, other MP3 player, or smartphone. With one click, you'll get interesting, useful information that will improve your trip. Rick Steves Audio Europe is at www.ricksteves.com (and also offered for free in iTunes).

Our free audio tours cover the top sights in Rome, Florence, Venice, Paris, and London.

Tourist Information Offices

Tourism is an important part of Europe's economy. Just about every European city has a tourist information office (abbreviated as **TI** in my books) located downtown

and loaded with maps and advice. This is my essential first stop upon arrival in any town. But you don't need to wait until you get to Europe. Each European country has its own **official tourism website**—a great first stop when you begin researching your trip. Many of these sites are packed with practical information, suggested itineraries, city guides, interactive maps, video and audio files, colorful photos, and free downloadable brochures. Some also allow you to order printed materials by snail mail (either for free or with a handling fee). For an even more extensive listing of tourist boards, see www.towd.com.

In addition, nearly every European country has a **national tourist office** in the United States that you can call with specific questions.

GETTING STARTED

European National Tourist Websites
Austrian National Tourist Office: www.austria.info, tel. 212/944-6880
Belgian Tourist Office: www.visitbelgium.com, tel. 212/758-8130
Croatian National Tourist Board: http://us.croatia.hr, tel. 212/279-8672
Czech Tourism Office: www.czechtourism.com, tel. 212/288-0830, ext. 101
Denmark (see Scandinavia)
Estonian Tourist Board: www.visitestonia.com, tel. 212/883-0636
Finland (see Scandinavia)
French Government Tourist Office: www.franceguide.com, tel. 514/288-1904
German National Tourist Board: www.cometogermany.com, tel. 212/661-7200
Great Britain Tourist Office: www.visitbritain.us, automated phone for requesting brochures only—tel. 800-462-2748 (US) or 888-847-4885 (Canada)
Greek National Tourist Organization: www.gnto.gr, tel. 212/421-5777
Hungarian National Tourist Office: www.gotohungary.com, tel. 212/695-1221
Tourism Ireland: www.discoverireland.com, tel. 800-742-6763
Italian Government Tourist Board: www.italiantourism.com, tel. 212/245-5618
Luxembourg National Tourist Office: www.visitluxembourg.com, tel. 212/935-8888
Netherlands Board of Tourism: www.holland.com, tel. 212/370-7360
Norway (see Scandinavia)
Polish National Tourist Office: www.poland.travel, tel. 201/420-9910
Portuguese National Tourist Office: www.visitportugal.com, tel. 646/723-0200
Scandinavian Tourist Boards: www.goscandinavia.com, tel. 212/885-9700
Slovenian Tourist Office: www.slovenia.info, Slovenian tel. 011-386-1-589-8550
Spain Tourist Office: www.spain.info, tel. 212/265-8822
Sweden (see Scandinavia)
Switzerland Tourism: www.myswitzerland.com, tel. 877-794-8037
Turkish Tourist Office: www.tourismturkey.org, tel. 212/687-2194

Middle Eastern and North African Tourist Offices
Egyptian Tourist Authority: www.egypt.travel, tel. 877-773-4978

Israeli Ministry of Tourism: www.goisrael.com, tel. 888-774-7723
Moroccan National Tourist Office: www.visitmorocco.com, Moroccan
tel. 011-212-537-674-013

4. Paper Chase

While going to Europe isn't all that complex, your trip will be smoother
if you consider these documents and details well before your departure
date.

Passports

In much of Europe, the only document a US or Canadian citizen needs
is a passport. (The new US "passport card" works only for those driving
or cruising to Canada, Mexico, Bermuda, and the Caribbean.) For most
travelers, the only time any customs official will look at you seriously is
at the airport as you re-enter the United States.

US passports, good for 10 years, cost $100 ($75 to renew). The fee
for minors under 16 (including infants) is $85 for a passport good for five
years (kids under 16 must apply in person with at least one parent and the
other parent's notarized permission). You can apply at some courthouses
and post offices, as well as municipal buildings such as your City Hall.
For details and the location of the nearest passport-acceptance facility,
see www.travel.state.gov or call 877-487-2778. Processing time varies; the
current wait is posted on the State Department website. During busier
periods, a one- or two-month wait is common. One or two weeks after
you apply, you can check the status of your passport application and its
estimated arrival date on the website.

If you need your passport faster than two months, tack on an additional $60 expediting fee (plus overnight shipping both ways), and you'll
get it by mail in two to three weeks (check the website for current processing times). If you're in a last-minute emergency situation, call the above
number and speak to a customer-service representative. If you can prove
that you have to leave within two weeks (by showing a purchased airline
e-ticket or a letter from work requiring you to travel overseas on short
notice), you may be able to receive a passport in a day or so. Make an
appointment to go in person to the nearest US Passport Agency and pay
the additional $60 fee. They'll issue your new passport in 24–72 hours.

Keep an eye on your passport's expiration date. Many European
countries—including the Czech Republic, Denmark, Germany,
Hungary, Norway, Portugal, Switzerland, and Ukraine—require that
your passport be valid for three to six months *after* your ticketed date of

---

European Borders (or the Lack Thereof)

Over the last decade, borders between European countries have faded away. Thanks to a series of treaties known as the Schengen Agreement, today there are no border checks between 25 countries in Western and Eastern Europe: Austria, Belgium, the Czech Republic, Denmark, Estonia, Finland, France, Germany, Greece, Hungary, Iceland, Italy, Latvia, Lithuania, Luxembourg, Malta, the Netherlands, Norway, Poland, Portugal, Slovakia, Slovenia, Spain, Sweden, and Switzerland.

Holdouts include the United Kingdom and the Republic of Ireland, as well as some Eastern European countries (such as Croatia, Bosnia-Herzegovina, Montenegro, Romania, Bulgaria, and Turkey). These non-Schengen countries still have border checks... for now. But for the most part, even in these places, the border crossing is generally just a quick wave-through for US citizens.

What does Schengen mean for you? When traveling between participating countries, you don't have to stop or show a passport—you'll simply blow past abandoned, forgotten border posts on the superhighway or high-speed train...souvenirs of an earlier, more complicated era of European travel. However, you still need to show your passport at your first point of entry into Europe, and to re-enter the US.

---

return to the United States. This means that even if your passport doesn't expire for a few months, you may still be denied entry to a country until you get a new passport issued. If necessary, get your passport renewed before you go. Other countries can have surprising entry requirements. For example, the Czech Republic and Poland require visitors to carry proof that they have medical insurance coverage (your health insurance card usually suffices). While it's virtually unheard-of that a border guard would actually request this, it's worth knowing about. For specific country-by-country entry requirements, see www.travel.state.gov.

As you travel, take good care of your passport, but relax when it comes to temporarily giving it up. When you sleep on an international night train to a non-Schengen country (see sidebar above), the conductor may take your passport so you won't be disturbed when the train crosses the border at 3 a.m. Hotels routinely take your passport "for the night" so they can register you with the police. This bookwork must be done for foreign guests throughout Europe. Receptionists like to gather passports and register them all at the same time when things are quiet. Although it's unreasonable to expect them to drop whatever they're doing to register me immediately, I politely ask if I can pick up my passport in two hours. I just don't like my passport in the top drawer all night long.

A passport works well for collateral in cases when you don't have the cash right now (hefty deposits on bike rentals, audioguides, and so on).

Losing your passport while traveling is a major headache. If you do, contact the police and the nearest US consulate or embassy right away. You can get a short-term replacement, but you'll earn it. A photocopy of your passport (and a couple of passport-type photos you've brought from home or have had taken in Europe) can make it much easier to get a replacement. Pack photocopies of important documents deep in your bag, and consider also leaving copies with a loved one back home (to be faxed to you in case of an emergency). Some people scan their documents and email them to a secure account that they can access from the road, although this does pose a potential security risk.

If you're a frequent international traveler, consider the US Customs' Global Entry Program, which lets you bypass passport control at major US airports ($100 fee, www.cbp.gov/travel).

Canadian citizens can refer to www.voyage.gc.ca for Canada-specific passport information.

Visas

A visa is a stamp placed in your passport by a foreign government, allowing you to enter their country. Visas are not required for Americans or Canadians traveling in Western Europe and most of the East (including the Czech Republic, Slovakia, Poland, Hungary, Slovenia, Croatia, Bosnia-Herzegovina, Montenegro, and the Baltic States).

Both Canadians and Americans need visas to visit **Turkey.** They're cheapest and easiest to get upon arrival at the border or airport. You can pay in US currency or euros (US residents pay $20 or €15; Canadians pay $60—US dollars, not Canadian—or €45). For more information, see www.disisleri.gov.tr (Turkish Ministry of Foreign Affairs), www.tourismturkey.org (Turkish tourism information offices in the United States), or www.turkishembassy.com (Turkey's embassy in Canada).

Americans can also get a Turkish visa in advance by money order through the Turkish embassy in Washington, DC (tel. 202/612-6700) or the Turkish consulates in New York (tel. 212/949-0160), Chicago (tel. 312/263-0644), Houston (tel. 713/622-5849), or Los Angeles (tel. 323/655-8832). For more information, see www.washington.emb.mfa.gov.tr.

For Canadians, the Turkish embassy in Ottawa sells single-entry, 90-day visas for $75 Canadian and multiple-entry visas for $178 Canadian

(197 Wurtemburg St., Ottawa, Ontario K1N 8L9, tel. 888-566-7656, www.turkishembassy.com).

Travelers to **Russia** also need visas. The process can be expensive, and you should begin several weeks in advance. Before applying for a visa, you must first get an official document called a "visa invitation" or a "visa support letter" (generally from a hotel or visa agency). It's smart to enlist an agency that specializes in steering your application through the process (Passport Visa Express is one of many, www.passportvisasexpress .com). The costs add up: The visa itself costs $131 (subject to change), visa agencies charge a service fee of about $50–85, and you'll also pay to ship your passport to the embassy and back (your passport must be valid for six months from the day your visit ends, and you must have a clean page free of any stamps). Figure about $250 total per person. For more details, see www.russianembassy.org (which lists Russian consulate locations in Washington, DC, New York, San Francisco, Seattle, and Houston). If you live near one of these consulates, you can save some money (but go through a lot of steps— see website) by applying for your visa in person at the consulate.

For **travel beyond Europe,** get up-to-date information on visa requirements from your travel agent or the US Department of State (travel.state.gov).

If you do need a visa, it's usually best to get it at home before you leave (unless you're going to Turkey). If you forget, just about every country has an embassy or consulate (which can issue visas) in the capital of every other European country.

Vaccinations

No vaccinations are required for travel in Europe. If you're traveling beyond Europe, check the inoculation requirements with your doctor or a travel-medicine clinic before you leave home. Countries "require" shots in order to protect their citizens from you and "recommend" shots to protect you from them. If any shots are recommended, take that advice seriously. (For more information, see Chapter 23: Staying Healthy.)

Student Cards and Hostel Memberships

The International Student Identity Card (ISIC), the only internationally recognized student ID card, gets you discounts on transportation, entertainment, and sightseeing throughout Europe, and includes some basic trip insurance. If you are a full-time student (and can prove it), get one. Your ISIC card can also be used as a prepaid phone card. Be aware that if you're older than 26, you might have trouble using the card in some places. Two other varieties of the card, offering similar discounts, are available, though they're often not honored: for teachers of any age (International Teacher Identity Card, or ITIC) and for non-student travelers under age 26 (International Youth Travel Card, or IYTC). Each of these cards costs $22 and is good for one year from the date of issue. Get yours on the ISIC website (www.myisic.com), through STA Travel (www.statravel.com), or from your university foreign-study office.

Travelers who know they'll be staying at least six nights in official HI hostels should get a hostel membership card from a local hostel or Hostelling International (www.hiusa.org, tel. 301/495-1240; for more information, see Chapter 16: Sleeping).

Railpasses and Car Rental

Most railpasses are not sold in Europe and must be purchased before you leave home. Car rental is usually cheaper when arranged before your trip (online or through your hometown travel agent). An International Driving Permit is required if driving in Spain, Italy, Austria, Greece, Poland, or Hungary (get it at AAA before your departure—for $15 plus tax and the cost of two passport photos, www.aaa.com). For specifics on railpasses and driving, see Chapters 10 and 11.

Travel Insurance—To Insure or Not to Insure?

Travel insurance is a way to minimize the considerable financial risks of traveling. These risks include accidents, illness, missed flights, canceled tours, lost baggage, emergency evacuation, and getting your body home if you die. Each traveler's risk and potential loss varies, depending on how much of your trip is prepaid, the refundability of the air ticket purchased, your state of health, the value of your luggage, where you're traveling, the financial health of the tour company or airline, and what coverage you already have (through your medical insurance, homeowners' or renters' insurance, or credit card).

For some travelers, insurance is a good deal; for others, it's not. What are the chances of needing it? How willing are you to take risks? What is peace of mind worth to you? The following information will help you understand your options and make an informed decision for your trip.

Types of Coverage

The insurance menu includes five main courses: trip cancellation and interruption, medical, evacuation, baggage, and flight insurance. Supplemental policies can be added to cover specific concerns, such as terrorism, identity theft, or political evacuation. The various types are generally sold in some combination—rather than buying only baggage, medical, or cancellation insurance, you'll usually purchase a package that includes all of them. If you want one type of coverage in particular—such as medical—ask for a policy that focuses on that coverage (though it might come with a little cancellation or baggage insurance, too). The most complete version is called "comprehensive insurance."

Insurance costs vary dramatically, but most packages are between 5 and 12 percent of the total trip cost. Two factors can increase this price: age at the time of purchase (rates go up dramatically for every decade over 50) and trip cost (more expensive trips cost more to insure). Coverage is generally inexpensive or even free for children 17 and under.

Travel agents should recommend that you get travel insurance, and they can provide information on options (in fact, they can be held liable for your losses if they don't explain insurance options to you). However, they are not insurance agents, and specific questions should always be directed to the insurance provider.

For extensive coverage, go with a big-name company (avoid buying insurance from a no-name company on the Web). Consider the package deals sold by K & K Consulting Services (www.betins.com, tel. 866-552-8834 or 253/238-6374), Access America (www.accessamerica.com, tel. 800-284-8300), Travelex (www.travelex-insurance.com, tel. 800-228-9792), Travel Guard (www.travelguard.com, tel. 800-826-4919), and Travel Insured International (www.travelinsured.com, tel. 800-243-3174). Insuremytrip.com allows you to compare insurance policies and costs among various providers (they also sell insurance; www.insuremytrip.com, tel. 800-487-4722). The $22 ISIC student identity card (mentioned earlier) includes very minimal travel insurance.

Some travel insurance, especially trip cancellation coverage, is reimbursement-only: You'll pay out-of-pocket for your expenses, then submit the paperwork to your insurer to recoup your money. Medical coverage is more likely to pay your hospital or doctor bills directly. Either way, if you have a problem, it's wise to communicate with your insurance company immediately to ask them how to proceed. Many major insurance companies are accessible by phone 24 hours a day—handy if you have problems in Europe.

Policies available vary by state. For example, Washington State strictly regulates insurers, so Washingtonians have fewer options than, say, Ohioans. Furthermore, not all insurance companies are licensed in every state. If you have to make a claim and encounter problems with a company that isn't licensed in your state, you don't have a case.

For each type of insurance that follows, I've outlined some of the key legalese. But be warned—these are only guidelines. Policies can differ, even within the same company. Certain companies and policies have different levels of coverage based on whether you purchase the car rental, hotel, or flight directly on your own or through a travel agent. Ask a lot of questions, and always read the fine print to see what's covered (e.g., how they define "travel partner" or "family member"—your great-aunt might not qualify).

Trip Cancellation or Interruption Insurance

This insurance covers the nonrefundable financial penalties or losses you incur when you cancel a prepaid tour or flight for an acceptable reason. These might include if:

1. You, your travel partner, or a family member cannot travel due to sickness, death, layoff, or a list of other acceptable reasons;
2. Your tour company or airline goes out of business or can't perform as promised;
3. A family member at home gets sick, causing you to cancel;
4. For a good reason (such as a car accident, inclement weather, or a strike), you miss a flight or need an emergency flight.

In other words, if you or your travel partner accidentally breaks a leg a few days before your trip, you can both bail out (if you both have trip cancellation insurance) without losing all the money you paid for the trip. And if, a day into your tour, you have an accident that prevents you from continuing with the group, you'll be reimbursed for the portion of the tour you haven't used.

This type of insurance can be used by people on an organized tour or cruise, as well as by people traveling independently (in which case, only the prepaid expenses—such as their flight and any nonrefundable hotel reservations—are covered). If you're taking a tour, it may come with some cancellation insurance. Understand exactly what's included before you consider buying additional coverage.

Note the difference: Trip *cancellation* is when you don't go on your trip at all, and is fully covered. Trip *interruption* is when you begin a journey but have to cut it short; in this case, you'll be reimbursed only for the portion of the trip that you didn't complete.

Some insurers won't cover certain airlines or tour operators. Many are obvious—such as companies under bankruptcy protection—but others can be surprising (including major airlines). Make sure your carrier is covered.

It's smart to buy your insurance policy within a week of the date you make the first payment on your trip. Policies purchased later than a designated cutoff date—generally 7–21 days, as determined by the insurance company—are less likely to cover tour company or air carrier bankruptcies, pre-existing medical conditions (yours or those of family members at home), or terrorist incidents. Mental health concerns are generally not covered.

Jittery travelers are fretful about two big unknowns: terrorist attacks and natural disasters. Ask your company for the details. You'll likely be covered only if your departure city or a destination on your itinerary actually becomes the target of a terrorist incident within 30 days of your trip. Even then, if your tour operator offers a substitute itinerary, your coverage may become void. As for natural disasters, you're covered only if your destination is uninhabitable (for example, your hotel is flooded or the airport is gone). A terrorist attack or natural disaster in your hometown may or may not be covered—ask. War or outbreaks of disease generally aren't covered.

You can avoid the question of what is and what isn't covered by buying a costly "any reason" trip cancellation policy. These offer at least partial reimbursement (generally 75 percent) no matter why you cancel the trip. But the premiums are so hefty that these policies appeal mostly to deep-pocketed nervous Nellies prepaying for extremely expensive trips.

Before purchasing this type of insurance, check with your credit-card issuer—yours may offer limited trip cancellation or interruption coverage for flights or tours purchased with the card.

The rugged, healthy, unattached, and gung-ho traveler will probably forgo trip cancellation coverage. I have skipped it for more than 70 trips, and my number has yet to come up. But if you're paying out a lot of up-front money for an organized tour (which is expensive to cancel), if you have questionable health, or if you have a loved one at home in frail health, you should probably get this coverage.

Medical Insurance

Before buying a special medical insurance policy for your trip, check with your medical insurer—you might already be covered by your existing health plan. While many US insurers cover you overseas, Medicare does not. Most additional coverage you buy is supplemental (or "secondary"), so it covers whatever expenses your primary coverage doesn't.

Travel medical insurance generally covers only emergencies. If this is the case, ask what happens after you are moved from the ER to a recovery room. The hospital will typically work directly with your insurer on billing, while a quick visit to a doctor will more likely be an out-of-pocket

GETTING STARTED

expense (you'll bring home documentation to be reimbursed). In some cases, you may have to contact your insurer for approval before seeking medical help.

Many pre-existing conditions are covered by medical and trip-cancellation coverage, depending on when you buy the coverage and how recently you've been treated for the condition. If you travel frequently to Europe, multi-trip annual policies can save you money. Check with your agent or insurer before you commit.

The US State Department periodically issues warnings about traveling to at-risk countries (see www.travel.state.gov). If you're visiting one of these countries, your cancellation and medical insurance will likely not be honored, unless you buy supplemental coverage.

Other Insurance

Evacuation insurance covers the cost of getting you to a place where you can receive appropriate medical treatment in the event of an emergency. (In the worst-case scenario, this can mean a medically equipped—and incredibly expensive—private jet.) This is usually not covered by regular medical insurance. Sometimes this coverage can get you home after an accident, but more often, it'll just get you as far as the nearest major hospital. "Medical repatriation"—that is, getting you all the way home—is likely to be covered only if it's considered medically necessary. Ask your insurer exactly what's covered before *and after* you get to the hospital.

Keep in mind that medical and evacuation insurance may not cover you if you're participating in an activity your insurer considers to be dangerous (such as skydiving, bungee jumping, scuba diving, or even skiing). Some companies sell supplementary adventure sports coverage.

Baggage insurance is included in most comprehensive policies, but it's rare to buy it separately. Baggage insurance puts a strict cap on reimbursement for such items as jewelry, eyewear, electronics, and photographic equipment—read the fine print. If you check your baggage for a flight, it's already covered by the airline (check with your airline for its luggage liability limit; if you have particularly valuable luggage, you can buy supplemental "excess valuation" insurance directly from the airline). Check if your homeowners' or renters' insurance covers baggage (with a "floater" supplement, if necessary, for international travel)—it may be cheaper, and you'll have coverage even after your trip. Travelers' baggage insurance will cover the deductibles and items excluded from your homeowners' policy. Double-check the particulars with your agent. If your policy doesn't cover railpasses, consider buying the $14–18 insurance deal sold with the pass.

Flight insurance ("crash coverage") is a statistical rip-off that heirs love. It's basically a life insurance policy that covers you when you're on the airplane. Since plane crashes are so rare (see "The Fear of Flying," page 100), there's little sense in spending money on this insurance.

Another important type of insurance—**collision coverage,** for rental cars—is covered on page 142. Collision insurance may be included in some comprehensive travel insurance plans or available as an upgrade on others.

Comprehensive plans can also cover expenses incurred if your trip is delayed, if you miss your flight, or if your tour company changes your itinerary.

The Final Word on Travel Insurance

If you think you might want insurance, do some homework. Look around the Internet or ask a travel agent to be sure you fully understand your options (including all the fine print). Consider how insurance fits your travel and personal needs, compare its cost to the likelihood of using it and your potential loss—and then decide.

5. Pack Light Pack Light Pack Light

The importance of packing light cannot be overemphasized, but, for your own good, I'll try. You'll never meet a traveler who, after five trips, brags: "Every year I pack heavier." The measure of a good traveler is how light she travels. You can't travel heavy, happy, and cheap. Pick two.

No matter your age, you can travel like college kids: light, mobile, and wearing your convertible suitcase/backpacks.

Limit yourself to 20 pounds in a carry-on–size bag. An unstructured 9" × 22" × 14" bag should fit under most airplane seats. It will certainly fit in the overhead bins. That's my self-imposed limit. At my company, we've taken tens of thousands of people of all ages and styles on tours through Europe. We allow only one carry-on bag. For many, this is a radical concept: 9" × 22" × 14"? That's my cosmetics kit! But they manage, and they're glad they did. And after you enjoy that sweet mobility and freedom, you'll never go any other way.

You'll walk with your luggage more than you think you will. Before leaving home, give yourself a test. Pack up completely, go into your hometown, and practice being a tourist for an hour. Fully loaded, you should enjoy window-shopping. If you can't, stagger home and thin things out.

When you carry your own luggage, it's less likely to get lost, broken, or stolen. (Some travelers claim that airline employees have stolen items from checked luggage.) Quick, last-minute changes in flight plans become simpler. A small bag sits on your lap or under your seat on the bus, taxi, and airplane. You don't have to worry about it, and, when you arrive, you can hit the ground running. It's a good feeling. When I land in London, I'm on my way downtown while everyone else stares anxiously at the luggage carousel. When I fly home, I'm the first guy the dog sniffs.

These days, you'll also save money by carrying your own bag: Many airlines charge a fee to check even one suitcase. These fees can add up if you check more than one bag.

Pack light...and pack smart. You can't bring anything potentially dangerous—such as knives, lighters, or large quantities of liquids or gels—in your carry-on bag. (This list can change without notice—for details, see "What Can I Carry On?" on page 86.) These days I leave my Swiss Army knife at home, bring smaller bottles of toiletries, and carry on my bag as usual.

Be aware that many airlines have additional (and frequently changing) restrictions on the number, size, and weight of carry-on bags. Some European budget airlines, such as Ryanair and Air Berlin, use smaller carry-on dimensions than major airlines. (Restrictions can vary from airport to airport, even on the same airline.) Check your airline's website (or read the fine print on your airline e-ticket) for details.

If you check your bag, mark it inside and out with your name, address, and emergency phone

Pack light, since you won't have a mule to haul around your bags. (Or if you do, your spouse should complain.)

number. If you have a lock on your bag, you may be asked to remove it due to increased security checks, or it may be cut off so the bag can be inspected (to avoid this, consider a TSA-approved lock, described in the packing list later in this chapter). I've never locked my bag and never had a problem. Still, just in case, I wouldn't pack anything particularly valuable (such as cash or a camera) in my checked luggage.

As baggage fees increase, people who used to check their bags are now more likely to carry on their luggage. Reward yourself for packing light by arriving early for aircraft boarding—increasing the odds that you'll snare coveted storage space in the passenger cabin.

Remember, packing light isn't just about the trip over and back—it's about your traveling lifestyle. Too much luggage marks you as a typical tourist. It slams the back door shut. Serendipity suffers. Changing locations becomes a major operation. Con artists figure you're helpless. Porters are a problem only to those who need them. With only one bag, you're mobile and in control. Take this advice seriously.

Backpackademia—What to Bring?

How do you fit a whole trip's worth of luggage into a small backpack or suitcase? The answer is simple: Bring very little.

Spread out everything you think you might need on the living-room floor. Pick up each item one at a time and scrutinize it. Ask yourself, "Will I really use this snorkel and these fins enough to justify carrying them around all summer?" Not "Will I use them?" but "Will I use them enough to feel good about hauling them over the Swiss Alps?" Regardless of my budget, I would buy them in Greece and give them away before I would carry that extra weight over the Alps.

Don't pack for the worst-case scenario. Pack for the best-case scenario and simply buy yourself out of any jams. Risk shivering for a day rather than taking a heavy coat. Think in terms of what you can do without—not what will be handy on your trip. When in doubt, leave it out. I've seen people pack a whole summer's supply of deodorant or razors, thinking they can't get them there. The world is getting really small: You can buy Dial

When getting way off the beaten path—like this traveler, who's spending the night at a tiny guest house in Italy's Civita di Bagnoregio—you'll be glad you're packing light.

soap, Colgate toothpaste, Nivea cream, and Gillette razors in Sicily or Slovakia. Tourist shops in major international hotels are a sure bet whenever you have difficulty finding a personal item. If you can't find one of your essentials, ask yourself how more than 700 million Europeans can live without it.

Whether you're traveling for three weeks or three months, pack exactly the same. Rather than take a whole trip's supply of toiletries, take enough to get started and look forward to running out of toothpaste in Bulgaria. Then you have the perfect excuse to go into a Bulgarian department store, shop around, and pick up...something you think might be toothpaste.

Backpack or Rolling Bag?

A fundamental packing question is your choice of luggage. Of all the options, I consider only three: 1) a carry-on–size "convertible" bag with zip-away shoulder straps; 2) a carry-on–size "roll-aboard" bag; or 3) an internal-frame backpack.

Travelers who want the easy mobility of a backpack but with a more low-key appearance travel with bag #1: a convertible backpack/suitcase with zip-away shoulder straps (see photo on page 43). These bags give you the best of both worlds—a suitcase when in town, and a backpack when you want to be more mobile. I travel with this bag and keep it exclusively in the backpack mode. While these "soft" bags basically hang on your back and are not as comfortable for long hauls as an internal-frame backpack (#3, described later), they work fine for getting from the station to your hotel. And, at 9" × 22" × 14", they fit in the airplane's overhead lockers. I live out of this bag for three months each year— and I absolutely love it.

Carry-on–size "roll-aboard" bags (option #2, see photo) are well-designed and popular. Many of my staffers prefer this bag; its compact design makes it roomy while keeping it just small enough to fit in the plane's overhead locker. The advantage of bag #2 over bag #1: You can effortlessly wheel your gear around without getting sweaty. The downside: Bags with wheels cost $40–50 extra, weigh several pounds more, and delude people into think-

A 9" × 22" × 14" carry-on bag (with or without wheels) is the ideal size.

ing they don't need to pack so light. They are cumbersome on rough or uneven surfaces (crowded subways, hiking through a series of train cars, walking to your hotel in villages with stepped lanes and dirt paths, and so on)—but they're wonderful in airports (where check-in lines and distances to gates are longer than ever). A spin-off option is the hybrid bag, which has both wheels and backpack straps.

Most younger travelers "backpack" through Europe with an internal-frame backpack (option #3) purchased from an outdoor store. While these are the most comfortable bags to wear on your back, they can be expensive and are often built "taller" than carry-on size.

Base your decision on the strength of your back. The day will come when I'll be rolling my bag through Europe with the rest of the gang. But as long as I'm hardy enough to carry my gear on my back, I will. (Photos of Rick Steves bags can be found at the end of this book; convertible and roll-aboard bags are sold at www.ricksteves.com.)

Unless you plan to camp or sleep out a lot, a sleeping bag is a bulky security blanket. Even on a low budget, bedding is provided. (Hostels provide all bedding free or rent sheets for a small fee, and often don't allow sleeping bags.) Don't pack to camp unless you're going to camp.

Pack your bag only two-thirds full to leave room for picnic food and souvenirs. Sturdy stitching, front and side pouches, padded shoulder straps (for backpacks), and a low-profile color are virtues. I'm not wild about the bags with a zip-off day bag—I take my convertible backpack and supplement it with a separate day bag.

Entire books have been written on how to pack. It's really quite simple: Use packing cubes or mesh bags (one each for toiletries; underwear and socks; and miscellaneous stuff such as a first-aid kit, earplugs, clothesline, sewing kit, and gadgets). Roll clothes and store them in packing cubes to keep them compact—or, to reduce wrinkling, zip them up in airless baggies or a clothes compressor like the Flat Pack (described on page 53).

Clothing

The bulk of your luggage is clothing. Minimize by bringing less and washing more often. Every few nights you'll spend 10 minutes doing a little wash. This doesn't mean more washing; it just means doing it little by little as you go.

Be careful to choose dark clothes that dry quickly and either don't wrinkle or look good wrinkled. To see how wrinkled shirts will get, give everything a wet rehearsal by hand-washing and drying once at home. You should have no trouble drying clothing overnight in your hotel room (though it might take longer in humid or cold climates). I know this sounds barbaric, but my body dries out a damp pair of socks or a shirt in a jiffy. It's fun to buy clothes as you travel—another reason to start with less.

For winter travel, you can pack just about as light. Wear heavier, warmer, high-top, waterproof shoes. Add a warm coat, long johns (quick-drying Capilene polyester or super-light silk), scarf, gloves or mittens, hat, and an extra pair of socks and underwear since things dry more slowly. Pack with the help of a climate chart (see the appendix). Layer your clothing for warmth, and assume you'll be outside in the cold for hours at a time.

Many travelers are concerned about appropriate dress. During the tourist season (April–Sept), the concert halls go casual. I have never felt out of place at symphonies, operas, or plays wearing a decent pair of slacks and a good-looking sweater. Pack with color coordination in mind. Some cultural events require more formal attire, particularly outside of the tourist season, but the casual tourist rarely encounters these. Women travelers who prefer to wear pants and don't pack a dress or skirt will do just fine.

If you're trying to blend in, realize that shorts are uncommon in Europe. They're considered beachwear, exclusively for use in coastal or lakeside resort towns. While most Europeans won't be offended if you wear shorts, you might be on the receiving end of some second glances or puzzled stares. Shorts are especially uncommon on older women and in big cities, and the cutoff temperature for "hot enough for shorts" is much higher than in the US. Especially in southern Europe, no matter how hot it is, grown adults look goofy in shorts.

Shorts (and other skimpy summer attire) can also put a crimp in your sightseeing plans. Some churches, mostly in south-

In Britain, there's no bad weather...only inappropriate clothing.

ern Europe, have modest-dress requirements for men, women, and children: no shorts or bare shoulders. Except at the strict St. Peter's in Rome and St. Mark's in Venice, the dress code is often loosely enforced. If necessary, it's usually easy to improvise some modesty (buy a cheap souvenir T-shirt to cover your shoulders or a tablecloth for a skirt or kilt to cover your legs). At some heavily touristed churches in southern Europe,

One Carry-on Size Bag

Here's everything I traveled with for two months (photos taken naked in a Copenhagen hotel room): convertible 9" × 22" × 14" suitcase/backpack; lightweight nylon day bag; ripped-up sections of three guidebooks, notes, maps, journal, tiny pocket notepad; wristwatch; money belt (with debit card, credit card, driver's license, passport, plane e-ticket, railpass, cash, sheet of

phone numbers and addresses); second money belt clipped inside my bag for "semi-precious" documents (e.g., photocopies of the above); toiletries stuff bag (with squeeze bottle of shampoo, soap in a plastic container, shaver, toothbrush and paste, comb, nail clippers, squeeze bottle of liquid soap for clothes); bag with elec-

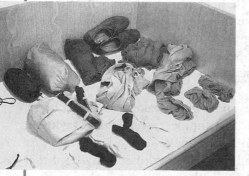

tronic gear (travel alarm clock, mobile phone and charger, MP3 player, cable for charging batteries, plug adapter); miscellaneous bag with family photos, tiny odds and ends; light rain jacket; long khaki cotton pants (button pockets), super-light long pants, shorts, five pairs of socks and underwear, long-sleeved shirt, two short-sleeved shirts, T-shirt; stuff bag with sweater, plastic laundry bag; light pair of shoes; and my camera (not pictured).

people hand out sheets of tissue paper you can wrap around yourself like a shawl or skirt.

But ultimately—so long as you don't wear something that's outrageous or offensive—it's important to dress in a way that makes you comfortable. No matter how carefully you dress, your clothes will probably mark you as an American. Frankly, so what? Europeans will know anyway. I fit in and am culturally sensitive by watching my manners, not the cut of my clothes.

Go casual, simple, and very light. Remember, in your travels you'll meet two kinds of tourists—those who pack light and those who wish they had. Say it once out loud: "PACK LIGHT."

What to Pack

*Indicates an item you can purchase online at www.ricksteves.com.

Shirts. Bring up to five short-sleeved or long-sleeved shirts in a cotton/polyester blend. Arrange mix according to season.

Sweater or lightweight fleece. Warm and dark is best—for layering and dressing up. Dark colors don't show wrinkles or stains.

Pants. Bring two pairs: one lightweight cotton and another super-lightweight for hot and muggy big cities and churches with modest dress codes. Jeans can be too hot for summer travel. Many like lightweight pants/shorts with zip-off legs. Button-down wallet pockets are safest (though still not as thief-proof as a money belt, described later).

Shorts. Take a pair with pockets; they double as a swimsuit for men.

Swimsuit. Especially for women.

Underwear and socks. Bring five sets (lighter dries quicker).

One pair of shoes. Take a broken-in, light, and cool pair, with Vibram-type soles and good traction (I like shoes by Ecco). Sturdy, low-profile tennis shoes with a good tread are fine, too. (Some people bring along an extra pair of sandals in case the shoes get wet.) For winter travel, bring heavy shoes (for warmth and to stay dry). See page 742 for top reader recommendations on footwear.

Jacket. Bring a light and water-resistant windbreaker that has a hood. Gore-Tex is good if you expect rain. For summer travel, I wing it without rain gear—but always pack for rain in Britain and Ireland.

Tie or scarf. For instant respectability, bring anything lightweight that can break the monotony and make you look snazzy.

***Money belt.** This hidden pouch—strapped around your waist and tucked under your clothes—is essential for the peace of mind it brings. You could lose everything except your money belt, and the trip could still go on. Lightweight and low-profile beige is best. For more information about money belts, see Chapter 24: Outsmarting Thieves.

Money. Bring your preferred mix of a credit card, a debit card, and an emergency stash of hard cash. I rely on a debit card for ATM withdrawals, a credit card, and a few hundred dollars in cash as a backup (in easy-to-exchange $20 bills). For details, see Chapter 13: Money.

Documents and photocopies. Bring your passport, printout of airline e-ticket, railpass or car-rental voucher, driver's license, student ID, hostel card, and so on. Photocopies and a couple of passport-type photos can help you get replacements more quickly if the originals are lost or stolen. Carry photocopies separately in your luggage and keep the originals in your money belt. In your luggage, you'll also want to pack a careful record of all reservations (print out your hotels' confirmation emails), along with a trip calendar page to keep things up-to-date as your trip evolves.

*Small daypack. This is great for carrying your sweater, camera, literature, and picnic goodies while you leave your large bag at the hotel or train station. Fanny packs (small bags with thief-friendly zippers on a belt) are a popular alternative, but are magnets for pickpockets and should never be used as money belts.

Camera. A digital camera and a high-capacity memory card mean no more bulky bags of film. A mini-tripod allows you to take crisp shots in low light with no flash. (For more camera details, see page 364.)

Water bottle. The plastic half-liter mineral water bottles sold throughout Europe are reusable and work great. If you bring one from home, make sure it's empty before you go through airport security (fill it at a fountain once you're through).

Wristwatch. A built-in alarm is handy. Otherwise, pack a small *travel alarm clock. At budget hotels, wake-up calls are particularly unreliable.

Earplugs. If night noises bother you, you'll love a good set of expandable foam plugs.

First-aid kit. See Chapter 23: Staying Healthy.

Medicine and vitamins. Keep medicine in original containers, if possible, with legible prescriptions.

Eyeglasses, contact lenses, and prescriptions. Contact solutions are widely available in Europe, but because of dust and smog, many travelers find their contacts aren't as comfortable in Europe. I wear my glasses, and I don't pack a spare pair, but I do bring a photocopy of my prescription just in case.

Sunscreen and sunglasses. Depending on the season and your destination.

*Toiletries kit. Sinks in cheap hotels come with meager countertop space and anonymous hairs. If you have a nylon toiletries kit that can hang on a hook or a towel bar, this is no problem. Put all squeeze bottles

With a hangable toiletries kit, you know the hairs on the toothbrush are yours.

in sealable plastic baggies, since pressure changes in flight can cause even good bottles to leak. (If you plan to carry on your bag, all liquids and gels must be in 3.4-ounce or smaller containers, and all of these items must fit within a single, quart-size sealable plastic baggie.) Consider a vacation from cosmetics. Bring a little toilet paper or tissue packets (sold at all newsstands in Europe). Fingernail clippers and tweezers are also handy.

Sealable plastic baggies. Bring a variety of sizes. In addition to holding your carry-on liquids, they're ideal for packing leftover picnic food, containing wetness, and bagging potential leaks before they happen. The two-gallon jumbo size is handy for packing clothing. Bring extras for the flight home, as they can be hard to find in Europe.

*Soap. Not all hotels provide soap. A plastic squeeze bottle of concentrated, multipurpose, biodegradable liquid soap is handy for laundry and more. In the interest of traveling friendlier to our environment, I never use the hotel bathroom "itsy-bitsies," preferring my own bar of soap or bottle of shampoo.

*Clothesline. Hang it up in your hotel room to dry your clothes. The handy twisted-rubber type needs no clothespins.

*Small towel. You'll find bath towels at all fancy and moderately priced hotels, and most cheap ones. Although $60-a-day travelers will often need to bring their own towel, $120-a-day folks won't. I bring a thin hand towel for the occasional need. Washcloths are rare in Europe. While I don't use them, many travelers recommend *quick-drying synthetic towels.

Sewing kit. Clothes age rapidly while traveling. Take along a few safety pins and extra buttons.

*Travel information. Rip out appropriate chapters from guidebooks and staple them together. When you're done, give them away.

*Map. Get a map best suited to your trip's overall needs, then pick up maps for specific local areas as you go.

Address list. To keep in touch, many travelers write blogs or send mass emails as they travel. But if you prefer to mail postcards, consider printing your mailing list onto a sheet of adhesive address labels before you leave. You'll know exactly who you've written to, and the labels will be perfectly legible.

Postcards from home and photos of your family. A small collection of show-and-tell pictures is always a great conversation piece with Europeans you meet.

*Small notepad and pen. A tiny notepad in your back pocket is a great organizer, reminder, and communication aid.

*Journal. An empty book to be filled with the experiences of your trip

will be your most treasured souvenir. Attach a photocopied calendar page
of your itinerary. Use a hardbound type designed to last a lifetime, rather
than a spiral notebook. My custom-designed Rick Steves Travel Journals
are rugged, simple blank books that come in two sizes. Another great
brand, with a nearly cult following among travel writers, is Moleskine
(www.moleskine.it).

Optional Bring-Alongs

*Indicates items you can purchase online at www.ricksteves.com.

Picnic supplies. Bring or buy a small tablecloth to give your meal some
extra class (and to wipe the knife on), salt and pepper, a cup, a *spoon, a
washcloth (to dampen and store in a baggie for cleaning up), and a Swiss
Army–type knife with a corkscrew and can opener (or buy the knife in
Europe if you want to carry your luggage on the plane). A plastic plate is
handy for picnic dinners in your hotel room.

*Packing cubes. These see-through, zip-up mesh containers keep your
clothes tightly packed and well-organized.

*Clothes compressor bag. This handy invention—I like the Flat Pack—
allows you to pack bulky clothes (such as sweaters and jackets) without
taking up too much space or creating wrinkles. Simply put the item in
the bag, roll it up to force the air out through the one-way nozzles, and
pack it away.

Shirt-folding board. Eagle Creek's Pack-It Folder (www.eaglecreek
.com) is a lightweight mesh container that comes with a thin board specially designed to fold and carry shirts with minimal wrinkling.

Small packet of tissue. Stick one of these—sold at newsstands and
pharmacies throughout Europe—in your daypack, in case you wind up
at a bathroom with no toilet paper.

Nightshirt. Especially for women.

Light warm-up suit. Use for pajamas, evening lounge outfit, instant
modest street wear, smuggling things, and going down the hall.

Spot remover. Bring Shout wipes or a dab of Goop grease remover in a
small plastic container.

Sandals or flip-flops.

Slippers. On winter trips, I bring comfy slippers with leather soles—
great for the flight and for getting cozy in my hotel room.

*Inflatable pillow (or "neck rest"). For snoozing in planes, trains, and
automobiles. Many travelers also swear by an ***eye mask** for blocking out
early-rising or late-setting sun.

Pillowcase. It's cleaner and possibly more comfortable to stuff your
own.

Hairdryer. People with long or thick hair appreciate a travel hairdryer in the off-season, when hair takes a long time to dry and it's cold outside (see "Electronics," later). These are generally provided in $100-plus hotel rooms.

Universal drain-stopper. Some hotel sinks and tubs have no stoppers. This flat, flexible disc—which works with any size drain—allows you to wash your clothes or take a bath. (A balled-up sock works in a pinch, too.)

*Hostel sheet. Bring one along (choose silk or cotton), or rent a sheet at hostels for about $4 per stay. It doubles as a beach or picnic blanket, comes in handy on overnight train rides, shields you from dirty blankets in mountain huts, and will save you money in other dorm-type accommodations.

*Tiny lock. Use it to lock your backpack zippers shut. Note that if you check your bag on a flight, the lock may be broken to allow the bag to be inspected. Improve the odds of your lock's survival by buying one approved by the TSA (Transportation Security Administration, the agency responsible for airport security). While you'll unlock the TSA-approved lock with a combination, security agents can open the lock without damaging it by using a special master key.

*Small flashlight. Handy for reading under the sheets after "lights out" in the hostel, late-night trips down the hall, exploring castle dungeons, and hypnotizing street thieves. Tiny-but-powerful LED flashlights—about the size of your little finger—are extremely bright, compact, and lightweight.

MP3/video player/radio. Partners can bring a Y-jack for two sets of earphones. Some travelers use digital recorders to capture pipe organs, tours, or journal entries. A small, portable radio adds a new dimension to your experience. For more details, see "Electronics," later.

*Adapters. Europe's electrical outlets are different from ours. For details, see "Electronics," later.

Office supplies. Bring paper, an envelope of envelopes, and some sticky notes (such as Post-Its) to keep your place in your guidebook.

Small roll of duct tape.

Mailing tube. Great for art lovers, this protects the posters and prints you buy along your trip. You can trim it to fit inside your backpack (though this obviously limits the dimensions of the posters you can carry).

A good paperback. There's plenty of empty time on a trip to either be bored or enjoy some good reading. If you're desperate, popular English-language paperbacks are often available in European airports and major train stations (usually for far more than their North American price).

Checklist of Essentials

- 5 shirts
- 1 sweater or lightweight fleece
- 2 pairs pants
- 1 pair shorts
- 1 swimsuit (women only)
- 5 pairs underwear and socks
- 1 pair shoes
- 1 rainproof jacket
- Tie or scarf
- Money belt
- Money—your mix of:
  - Debit card (for ATM withdrawals)
  - Credit card
  - Hard cash
  - Travelers checks (optional)
- Documents plus photocopies:
  - Passport
  - Printout of airline e-ticket
  - Driver's license
  - Student ID and hostel card
  - Railpass/car rental voucher
- Insurance details
- Daypack
- Sealable plastic baggies
- Camera and related gear
- Empty water bottle
- Wristwatch and alarm clock

- Earplugs
- First-aid kit
- Medicine
- Extra glasses/contacts and prescriptions
- Sunscreen and sunglasses
- Toiletries kit
- Soap
- Laundry soap
- Clothesline
- Small towel
- Sewing kit
- Travel information (guidebooks and maps)
- Address list (for sending postcards)
- Postcards and photos from home
- Notepad and pen
- Journal

Packing light: love it or leave it.

If you plan to carry on your luggage, note that all liquids must be in 3.4-ounce or smaller containers and fit within a single quart-size sealable baggie. For details, see www.tsa.gov/travelers.

Insect repellent. Especially for France and Italy.

*Collapsible umbrella. I like one that's small and compact, but still sturdy and well-constructed enough to withstand strong winds.

*Poncho. Hard-core vagabonds use a poncho—more versatile than a tarp—as protection in a rainstorm, a ground cloth for sleeping, or a beach or picnic blanket.

Gifts. Local hosts appreciate small souvenirs from your hometown (gourmet candy or crafts). Local kids love T-shirts and small toys.

Packing Tips for Women

Thanks to ETBD tour guides Joan Robinson, Ann Neel, and others for the following tips. At ETBD, Joan and Ann teach classes on "Packing Light and Right"; their suggested packing list for women is at www .ricksteves.com/womenpack.

If you're not going to wear it more than three times, don't pack it! Every piece of clothing you bring should complement every other item or have at least two uses (e.g., sandals double as slippers, a scarf as a shoulder wrap).

Shop Selectively: It's worth splurging a little to get just the right clothes for your trip. For durable, lightweight travel clothes, consider ExOfficio (www.exofficio.com, tel. 800-644-7303), TravelSmith (www .travelsmith.com, tel. 800-770-3387), Tilley Endurables (www.tilley.com, tel. 800-363-8737), Eddie Bauer (www.eddiebauer.com, tel. 800-426-8020), and REI (www.rei.com, tel. 800-426-4840). In general, neutrals (black, navy, khaki) dress up easily and can be extremely versatile.

Tops: Bring two or three T-shirts (or buy overseas), one or two short-sleeved blouses, and one or two long-sleeved shirts. Long-sleeved shirts with sleeves that roll up can double as short-sleeved shirts. Look for a wrinkle-camouflaging pattern or blended fabrics that show a minimum of wrinkles. Poly-blend fabric (such as Coolmax or microfiber) will often dry overnight.

Pants and Shorts: Dark-colored pants don't show dirt or wrinkles. Get a pair with a loose-fitting waistband that accommodates a money belt (and big Italian meals). Try the pants with the zip-off legs that convert to shorts. These are not especially stylish but are functional in Italy, allowing you to cover up inside churches and beat the heat outside.

If you bring shorts, one pair is probably enough, ideal for staying cool in a resort town or your hotel room. Europeans consider shorts to be beachwear. Women can blend in with the locals by wearing Capri pants instead.

Skirts: Some women bring one or two skirts because they're as cool and breathable as shorts, but dressier. And skirts make life easier than pants when you're faced with a squat toilet! A lightweight skirt made with a blended fabric will pack compactly. Make sure it has a comfy waistband or drawstring. Tilley (listed earlier) makes expensive but great skirts (and other items) from blended fabric that feels like cotton. Skirts go with everything and can easily be dressed up or down.

Shoes: Bring one pair of comfortable walking shoes. Mephisto, Ecco, and Rieker look dressier and more European than sneakers but are still comfortable. For a second pair, consider sandals or Tevas in summer, or dark leather flats in winter (can be worn with opaque hose and a skirt to dress up). Before you leave home, walk several miles in any footwear you'll be taking to be sure they're broken in.

Socks, Underwear, Pajamas, and Swimsuit: Cotton/nylon-blend socks dry faster than 100-percent cotton, which lose their softness when air-dried. Try silk, microfiber, or stretch lace underwear, which dry faster than all-cotton, but breathe more than nylon. Bring at least two bras (what if you leave one hanging over your shower rail by accident?). A sports bra can double as a hiking/sunning top. Shorts or lightweight pajama bottoms with a T-shirt will get you modestly to the bathroom down the hall. You don't need a bikini to try sunbathing topless on European beaches—local women with one-piece bathing suits just roll down the top.

Jacket: Neutral colors (black, khaki, navy) used to look more European than bright colors, but now everything from azure blue to pumpkin orange has made its way into European wardrobes. If your waterproof jacket doesn't have a hood, take a mini-umbrella or buy one in Europe. These are easy to find—umbrella vendors, like worms, appear with the rain.

Weather-specific Variations: In cold weather, silk long johns are great for layering, weigh next to nothing, and dry quickly. Bring gloves and some kind of warm hat for winter. If you're fair-skinned or prone to sunburn, bring a light, crushable, wide-brimmed hat for sunny days. Wear shoes that are water-resistant or waterproof.

Toiletries: All feminine products (even many of the same brands) are sold throughout Europe, but it's easier to figure out how many tampons, pads, or panty shields you'll need and bring them with you rather than having to buy a too-small or too-large box in Europe. If you bring birth control pills (or any timed-dosage prescription), take the time difference into account. If you usually take a pill with breakfast, take it with lunch or dinner in Europe. Remember to carry the pills onto the plane each way to take at your home-dosage time, too.

Accessorize, Accessorize: Scarves give your limited wardrobe just the color it needs. They dress up your outfit, are lightweight and easy to pack, and, if purchased in Europe, make a great souvenir. Some women bring a shawl-size scarf (often a fine cashmere wool version called a pashmina) to function as a sweater substitute, scarf, head wrap, or even a blanket on a train. Functional, cheap, but beautiful imitation pashminas can be found all over Europe if you forget yours. Sleeveless vests and button-up cardigans can be worn alone or mixed-and-matched with other clothes to give you several different looks as well as layers for cold weather. Most women feel safe wearing engagement/wedding rings while traveling, but leave other valuable or flashy jewelry at home. A few pairs of inexpensive earrings are fun to bring. Remember that your most important accessory is your hidden money belt.

Electronics

Electronic items, ranging from mundane adapters to fun phones and lightweight netbooks, are becoming an essential part of travel.

Adapters and Converters

Europe's electrical system is different from the United States' in two different ways: the voltage of the current and the shape of the plug.

First you'll need to consider the **voltage.** American appliances run on 110 volts, while European appliances are 220 volts. (These numbers can vary slightly—for example, 120 instead of 110 volts in the US.) Most newer travel accessories and electronic gadgets are "dual-voltage," which means they work on both American and European current. If you see a range of voltages printed on the item or its plug (such as "110–220"), you're OK in Europe. Some older appliances have a voltage switch marked 110 (US) and 220 (Europe)—switch it to 220 as you

In Europe, two kinds of adapters fit all outlets: Two little round prongs for the Continent, three big rectangular ones for Britain and Ireland.

pack. A few old, cheap American appliances aren't equipped to deal with the voltage difference at all, and they could be damaged or destroyed if plugged directly into a European wall outlet. In these cases, you'll need to buy a separate, bulky converter (about $30), which can be more expensive than simply buying a new dual-voltage appliance. With so many dual-voltage gadgets available, I haven't traveled with a separate converter in years. Still not sure? Ask the salesperson about voltage when you buy the appliance. Travel stores also offer useful advice on plugs and adapters (such as the "Electrical Connection Wizard" at www.magellans.com).

Once you've dealt with the voltage, you'll have to consider the **plug.** A small adapter allows American-style plugs (two flat prongs) to fit into British or Irish outlets (which take three rectangular prongs) or continental European outlets (which take two small, round prongs). I bring both continental and British adapters (handy for long layovers at Heathrow Airport). Secure your adapter to your appliance's plug with electrical or duct tape; otherwise it might stay in the outlet (and get left behind) when you pull out the plug. Many sockets in Europe are recessed into the wall; your adapter should be small enough so that the prongs seat properly in the socket. Also, newer outlets in Switzerland use a slightly modified "Type J" plug—similar to the rest of continental Europe, but with a hexagonal (rather than oval) shape. You might find that an older European adapter doesn't fit into a recessed Swiss outlet. If this happens to you, look for a special adapter or extension cord that allows you to use your European adapter.

Some budget hotel rooms have only one electrical outlet, occupied by the lamp. Hardware stores in Europe sell cheap three-way plug adapters that let you keep the lamp on and your camera battery and MP3 player charged.

Techie Take-Alongs

Here's a list of the gadgets and gizmos I bring to Europe. Remember that most travelers—going for vacation rather than work—won't need this much gear. Note that many of these things are high-ticket items; guard them carefully.

These days, mobile phones, MP3 players, and digital cameras are becoming integrated into a single smartphone—making everything that much more portable.

Digital camera. For details, see page 364.

Mobile phone. Your American mobile phone might work perfectly in Europe, or you can buy one to use while you're there. For details, see page 322.

Smartphone/handheld wireless device (such as a BlackBerry, iPhone, iPod Touch, iPad, or Palm Pre). You can access the Internet or send email, and most devices can be loaded with your addresses, calendar, games, music, and travel information. This is a handy compromise for travelers who need to stay plugged in, but don't want to lug along a heavy laptop. If your device is a phone, call your provider before you leave to activate international service, and carefully ask about extra charges for international roaming and data transfer—so you're not surprised by an astronomical bill when you get home. (In many cases, you can turn off the roaming feature and simply use your smartphone to access free or cheap Wi-Fi hotspots in Europe.) For details, see page 328.

When traveling with a smartphone, it's best to disable data roaming and use Wi-Fi to surf the Web.

Laptop computer or netbook. Most tourists want to pack light and will leave their computer at home. But if you love your laptop for emailing, organizing your photos, blogging, listening to music, watching movies, or just getting online to confirm tomorrow's sightseeing plan, increasingly easy Internet access in Europe makes bringing a laptop worth considering. And thanks to the rise of netbooks (tiny, super-portable laptops perfect for basic computing and Internet browsing), traveling with a computer is easier than ever. I also bring a charger and an extra battery for my laptop (I get three hours per battery; the second is only necessary for long flights or train trips). For tips on getting online with your laptop or netbook in Europe, see page 332.

Wireless hotspots allow you to get online from a park bench.

USB flash drive. If you're taking a laptop with you, a flash drive is a convenient and compact way to back up your files and photos in case anything happens to your computer. These miniature hard drives, about the size of a small pack of gum, plug directly into your computer's USB port (standard on virtually any computer worldwide). Even if you're not taking a laptop, a flash drive allows you to transport files you want to take with you to Europe. Some Internet cafés won't let you use flash drives because they're wary of transferring potentially infected files into their system. In this case, ask your hotelier if you can use the hotel computer.

Handheld GPS device (such as a Garmin, Magellan, or TomTom). If you'll be doing a lot of driving and have a portable GPS device at home, consider buying European map data so you can use it on vacation. For details, see page 151.

MP3/video player (such as an iPod). An MP3 player allows you to create a musical soundtrack for your trip, keep up with your favorite podcasts, or watch downloaded TV shows, movies, and vodcasts. You could bring a Y-jack for the headphones to share your music and videos with a travel partner or new friend. Consider packing a compact, portable external speaker.

E-book reader (such as a Kindle, Nook, Sony Reader, or iPad). If you enjoy e-books, bring an e-reader, though they work better for leisure reading than for guidebooks. For details, see "Digital Guidebooks" on page 13.

Chargers, adapters, and converters. Bring each device's charger—or look into getting a universal charger, with multiple plugs to fit each device (the octopus-shaped Chargepod is pricey but convenient, www .callpod.com). Remember to pack your plug adapter(s), and when you're traveling, be sure not to leave it in a hotel outlet. It's unlikely you'll need a voltage converter (described earlier, under "Adapters and Converters"), but if you do, bring it along, too.

PLANNING YOUR ITINERARY

6. When to Go

In travel-industry jargon, the year is divided into three seasons: peak season (roughly June through August), shoulder season (April through May and September through October), and off-season (November through March). Each has its pros and cons.

Peak-Season Strategies

Except for the crowds and high temperatures, summer is a great time to travel. The sunny weather, long days, and exuberant nightlife turn Europe into a powerful magnet. I haven't missed a peak season in 30

In peak season, sunbathers on the beach at Nice are packed like sardines. In shoulder season, it's wide open.

years. Here are a few tips to minimize the crowds and help keep your cool:

Arrange your trip with crowd control in mind. Consider, for instance, a six-week European trip beginning June 1, half with a Eurailpass to see the famous sights and half visiting relatives in Scotland. It would be wise to do the Eurail section first, enjoying those precious last three weeks of relatively uncrowded shoulder season, and then spend time with the family during the last half of your vacation, when Florence and Salzburg are teeming with tourists. Salzburg on June 10 and Salzburg on July 10 are two very different experiences.

St. Mark's Square in July—no wonder Venice is sinking...

Seek out places with no promotional budgets. Keep in mind that accessibility and promotional budgets determine a place's fame and popularity just as much as its worthiness as a tourist attraction. For example, Geneva is big and famous—with nothing special to offer the visitor. The beaches of Greece's Peloponnesian Peninsula enjoy the same weather and water as the highly promoted isles of Santorini and Ios but are out of the way, underpromoted, and wonderfully deserted. If you're traveling by car, take advantage of your mobility by leaving the well-worn tourist routes. The Europe away from the train tracks is less expensive and feels more peaceful and relaxed. Overlooked by the Eurail mobs, it's one step behind the modern parade.

Hit the back streets. Many people energetically jockey themselves into the most crowded square of the most crowded city in the most crowded month (St. Mark's Square, Venice, July)—and then complain about the crowds. You could be in Venice in July and walk six blocks behind St. Mark's Basilica, step into a café, and be greeted by Venetians who act as though they've never seen a tourist.

...but any time of the year, walk a few blocks away and it's just you and Venice.

Spend the night. Popular day-trip destinations near big cities and resorts such as Toledo (near Madrid), San Marino (near huge Italian beach resorts), and San Gimignano (near Florence) take on a more peaceful and enjoyable atmosphere at night, when the legions of day-trippers retreat to the predictable plumbing of their big-city hotels. Small towns normally lack hotels big enough for tour groups and are often inaccessible to large buses. So they will experience, at worst, midday crowds.

Be an early bird. In Germany, walk around Rothenburg's fortified wall at breakfast time, before the tour buses pull in and turn the town into a medieval theme park. Crack-of-dawn joggers and walkers enjoy a special look at wonderfully medieval cities as they yawn and stretch and prepare for the daily onslaught of the 21st century.

See how the locals live. Residential neighborhoods rarely see a tourist. Browse through a department store. Buy a copy of the local *Better Homes and Thatches* and use it to explore that particular culture. Get off the map. In Florence, for instance, most tourists stick to the small section of the city covered by the ubiquitous tourist maps. Wander beyond that, and you'll dance with the locals or play street soccer with the neighborhood gang.

Plan your museum sightseeing carefully. Avoid museums on their monthly free days, when they're most crowded. Because many Parisian museums are closed on Tuesday, nearby Versailles, which is open, is predictably crowded—very crowded. And it follows that Parisian museums are especially crowded on Monday and Wednesday. While crowds at the Louvre can't be avoided altogether, leaving home with a thoughtful itinerary can help. And for some top museums, you can reserve your visit in advance to avoid the lines entirely. (For more tips, see Chapter 25: Museum Strategies.)

THIS COULD BE YOU!

It's Tuesday at Versailles, and these people now have time to read their guidebooks, which warn: "On Tuesday, many of Paris' museums are closed, so Versailles has very long lines."

Arrive at the most popular sights early or late in the day to avoid tour groups. At 8:00 in the morning, Germany's fairy-tale Neuschwanstein Castle is cool and easy, with relaxed guides and no crowds. And very late in the day—when most tourists are long gone, exhausted in their rooms, or searching for dinner—I linger alone, taking artistic liberties with some of Europe's greatest art in empty galleries.

Prepare for intense heat. Europeans swear that it gets hotter every year. Even restaurants in cooler climates (like Munich or Amsterdam) now have ample al fresco seating to take advantage of the ever-longer outdoor-dining season. Throughout Europe in July and August, expect high temperatures—even sweltering heat—particularly in the south.

Be aware of the exceptions. Although Europe's tourist crowds can generally be plotted on a bell-shaped curve that peaks in July and August, there are odd glitches. For instance, Paris is relatively empty in July and August but packed full in June (conventions) and September (trade shows). Business-class hotels in Scandinavia are cheapest in the summer, when travel—up there, mostly business travel—is down.

In much of Europe (especially Italy and France), cities are partially shut down in July and August, when local urbanites take their beach breaks. You'll hear that these are terrible times to travel, but it's really no big deal. You can't get a dentist and many laundercttes are shut down, but tourists are basically unaffected by Europe's mass holidays. Just don't get caught on the wrong road on the first or 15th of the month (when vacations often start or finish), or try to compete with all of Europe for a piece of French Riviera beach in August.

Shoulder Season

For many, "shoulder season"—generally April, May, September, and October—combines the advantages of both peak-season and off-season travel. In shoulder season, you'll enjoy decent weather, long-enough daylight, fewer crowds, and a local tourist industry that is still eager to please and entertain.

Because fall and spring bring cooler temperatures in Mediterranean Europe, "shoulder season" in much of Italy, southern France, Spain, Croatia, and Greece can actually come with near-peak-season crowds and prices. For example, except for beach resorts, Italy's peak season is May, June, September, and October rather than July and August. Paris has its own surprising patterns (see above). Conversely, the Scandinavian countryside (such as the fjords of Norway) is a special case, with an extremely brief tourist season—basically from mid-June to late August. Avoid Scandinavia outside of this window.

If debating the merits of spring versus fall, consider your destination. Mediterranean Europe is generally green in spring, but parched in fall. For hikers, the Alps are better in early fall, because many good hiking trails are covered with snow through the spring.

On a budget note, keep in mind that round-trip airfares are determined by your departure date. Therefore, if you fly over during peak season and return late in the fall (shoulder season), you'll still pay peak-season round-trip fares.

Off-Season Europe

Each summer, Europe greets a stampede of sightseers and shoppers with eager cash registers. Before jumping into the peak-season pig pile, consider a trip during the off-season—generally November through March.

The advantages of off-season travel are many. Off-season airfares are often hundreds of dollars cheaper. With fewer crowds in Europe, you'll sleep cheaper. Many fine hotels drop their prices, and budget hotels will have plenty of vacancies. And while many of the cheap alternatives to hotels will be closed, those still open are usually empty and, therefore, more comfortable.

Off-season adventurers loiter all alone through Leonardo da Vinci's home, ponder in Rome's Forum undisturbed, kick up sand on virgin beaches, and chat with laid-back guards by log fires in French châteaux. In wintertime Venice, you can be alone atop St. Mark's bell tower, watching the clouds of your breath roll over the Byzantine domes of the church

Where are the tourists?

to a horizon of cut-glass Alps. Below, on St. Mark's Square, pigeons fidget and wonder, "Where are the tourists?"

Off-season adventurers enjoy step-right-up service at banks and tourist offices and experience a more European Europe. Although many popular tourist-oriented parks, shows, and tours will be closed, off-season is in-season for the high culture: the Vienna Boys' Choir, opera, and Lipizzaner stallions are in their crowd-pleasing glory.

But winter travel has its drawbacks. Because much of Europe is at Canadian latitudes, the days are short. It's dark by 5 p.m. The weather can be miserable—cold, windy, and drizzly—and then turn worse. But just as summer can be wet and gray, winter can be crisp and blue, and even into mid-November, hillsides blaze with colorful leaves.

Off-season hours are limited. Some sights close down entirely, and

Italy's Cinque Terre villages are empty in the winter...and the good restaurants close for a much-needed extended holiday.

most operate on shorter schedules (such as 10 a.m.–5 p.m. rather than 9 a.m.–7 p.m.), with darkness often determining the closing time. Winter sightseeing is fine in big cities, which bustle year-round, but it's more frustrating in small tourist towns, which often shut down entirely. In December, many beach resorts shut up as tight as canned hams. While Europe's wonderful outdoor evening ambience survives year-round in the south, wintertime streets are empty in the north after dark. English-language tours, common in the summer, are rare during the off-season, when most visitors are natives. Tourist information offices normally stay open year-round but have shorter hours in the winter. A final disadvantage of winter travel is loneliness. The solo traveler won't have as much of the built-in camaraderie of other travelers that she would find in peak season.

To thrive in the winter, you'll need to get the most out of your limited daylight hours. Start early and eat a quick lunch. Tourist offices close early and opening times are less predictable, so call ahead to double-check hours and confirm your plans. Pack for the cold and wet—layers, rainproof parka, gloves, wool hat, long johns, waterproof shoes, and an umbrella. Dress warmly. Cold weather is colder when you're outdoors trying to enjoy yourself all day long. And cheap hotels are not always adequately heated in the off-season. Use undershirts to limit the washing of slow-drying heavy shirts.

In the winter, most hotels are empty and charge less. To save some money, arrive late, notice how many open rooms they have (keys on the rack), let them know you're a hosteler (student, senior, artist, or whatever)

In the north, darkness falls early in the winter. This is Oslo at 3:30 p.m.

with a particular price limit, and bargain from there. The opposite is true of big-city business centers (especially in Berlin, Brussels, and the Scandinavian capitals), which are busiest and most expensive off-season.

Regardless of when you go, if your objective is to "meet the people," you'll find Europe filled with them 365 days a year.

7. Itinerary Skills

If you have any goals at all for your trip, make an itinerary. I never start a trip without having every day planned out. Your reaction to an itinerary may be, "Hey, won't my spontaneity and freedom suffer?" Not necessarily. Although I always begin a trip with a well-thought-out plan, I maintain my flexibility and make plenty of changes. An itinerary forces you to see the consequences of any spontaneous change you make while in Europe. For instance, if you spend two extra days in the sunny Alps, you'll see that you won't make it to the Greek Islands. With the help of an itinerary, you can lay out your goals, maximize their potential, avoid regrettable changes...and impress your friends.

For day-by-day descriptions of my favorite itineraries throughout Europe, see my "Sample Routes," starting on page 709 of the appendix.

Itinerary Considerations

If you deal thoughtfully with issues such as weather, culture shock, health maintenance, fatigue, and festivals, you'll travel happier.

Moderate the weather conditions you'll encounter. Match the coolest month of your trip with the warmest area, and vice versa. For a spring and early summer trip, enjoy comfortable temperatures throughout by starting in the southern countries and working your way north. If possible, avoid the midsummer Mediterranean heat and crowds of Italy and southern France. Spend those weeks in Scandinavia, Britain, Ireland, or the Alps (to increase your odds of sun in places prone to miserable weather). For more information, see the climate charts in the appendix.

Alternate intense big cities with villages and countryside. For example, break a tour of Venice, Florence, and Rome with an easygoing time in the hill towns or on the Italian Riviera. Judging Italy by Rome is like judging America by New York City.

Join the celebration. Hit as many festivals, national holidays, and arts seasons as you can. This takes some study. For a calendar of events, check with the national tourist office of each country you'll visit (websites and phone numbers listed in Chapter 3: Gathering Information). Also try www.whatsonwhen.com, www.ricksteves.com/festivals, and official festival websites (the bigger ones have their own). An effort to visit the right places at the right times will drape your trip with festive tinsel.

Save your energy for the biggies. Don't overestimate your powers of absorption. Rare is the tourist who doesn't become somewhat jaded after several weeks of travel. At the start of my trip, I'll seek out every great painting and cathedral I can. After two months, I find myself "seeing" cathedrals with a sweep of my head from the doorway, and I probably wouldn't cross the street for another Rembrandt. Don't burn out on mediocre castles, palaces, and museums. Sightsee selectively.

Establish a logical flight plan. It's been years since I flew in to and out of the same city. You can avoid needless travel time and expense by flying "open jaw"—into one airport and out of another. You usually pay just half the round-trip fare for each airport. Even if your "open jaw" flight plan is more expensive than the cheapest round-trip fare, it may save you lots of time and money when surface connections are figured in. For example, you could fly into London, travel east through whatever interests you in Europe, and fly home from Athens. This would eliminate the costly and time-consuming return to London. A good travel agent will know where flying "open jaw" is economical.

Take advantage of cheap flights within Europe. The recent proliferation of no-frills, low-budget airlines in Europe is changing the way people design their itineraries. A decade ago, you'd piece together a trip based on which towns could be connected by handy train trips (or, at most, overnight trains). But these days, it's relatively cheap and easy to combine, say, Portugal, Poland, and Palermo on a single itinerary. For more on cheap flights, see "Flying Within Europe" in Chapter 9: Flying.

See countries in order of cultural hairiness. If you plan to see Britain, the Alps, Greece, and Turkey, do it in that order so you'll grow steadily into the more intense and crazy travel. England, compared to any place but the United States, is pretty dull. Don't get me wrong—it's a great place to travel. But go there first, when cream teas and roundabouts will be exotic. And you're more likely to enjoy Turkey if you gradually work east.

Save your good health. Visit countries that may be hazardous to your health (North Africa or the Middle East) at the end of your trip, so you won't needlessly jeopardize your healthy enjoyment of the safer countries. If you're going to get sick, do it at the end of your trip so you can recover at home, missing more work—not vacation.

Minimize one-night stands. Even the speediest itinerary should be a series of two-night stands. I'd stretch every other day with long hours on the road or train and hurried sightseeing along the way in order to enjoy the sanity of two nights in the same bed. Minimizing hotel changes saves time and money and gives you the sensation of actually being comfortable in a town on the second night.

Leave some slack in your itinerary. Don't schedule yourself too tightly (a common tendency). Everyday chores, small business matters, transportation problems, constipation, and planning mistakes deserve about one day of slack per week in your itinerary.

Punctuate a long trip with rest periods. Constant sightseeing is grueling. Schedule a peaceful period every two weeks. If your trip is a long one, schedule a "vacation from your vacation" in the middle of it. Most people need several days in a place where they couldn't see a museum or take a tour even if they wanted to. A stop in the mountains or on an island, in a friendly rural town, or at the home of a relative is a great way to revitalize your tourist spirit.

Assume you will return. This "General MacArthur approach" is a key to touristic happiness. You can't really see Europe in one trip. Don't even try. Enjoy what you're seeing. Forget what you won't get to on this trip. If you worry about things that are just out of reach, you won't appreciate what's in your hand. I've taken dozens of European trips, and I still need more time. I'm happy about what I can't get to. It's a blessing that we can never see all of Europe.

Your Best Itinerary in Eight Steps

1. Read up on Europe and talk to travelers. Get a guidebook or two, take a class, contact the tourist offices. You must have some friends who'd love to show you their pictures. What you want to see is determined by what you know (or don't know). Identify your personal interests: WWII buffs study up on battle sites, wine-lovers brainstorm a wish list of wineries, and MacGregors locate their clan in Scotland. This is the time to grow a crop of ideas from which you'll harvest the dream trip.

2. Decide on the places you want to see. Start by listing everything you'd like to visit. Circle your destinations on a map. Have a reason for every stop. Don't visit Casablanca only because you liked the movie. And just because Apolo Ohno went to Torino, that doesn't mean you should, too.

Minimize redundancy. On a quick trip, focus on only one part of the Alps. England's two best-known university towns, Oxford and

Cambridge, are redundant. Choose one (I prefer Cambridge).

Example: Places I want to see—London, Alps, Bavaria, Florence, Amsterdam, Paris, the Rhine, Rome, Venice, Greece.

3. Establish a route and timeline. Figure out a logical geographical order and length for your trip. Pin down any places that you have to be on a certain date (and ask yourself if it's really worth stifling your flexibility). Once you've settled on a list, be satisfied with your efficient plan, and focus any more study and preparation only on places that fall along your proposed route.

4. Decide on the cities you'll fly in and out of. If your route is linear (like London to Athens), try flying "open jaw." If it's circular, fly round-trip. An "open jaw" plan is usually the most efficient and economical— especially if you take full advantage of it when establishing your starting and ending points.

5. Determine the mode of transportation. Do this not based solely on economical terms, but by analyzing what is best for the trip you envision.

Example: Since I'm traveling alone, going so many miles, and spending the majority of my time in big cities, I'd rather not mess with a car. I'll use a railpass.

6. Make a rough itinerary. Sketch out an itinerary, writing in the number of days you'd like to stay in each place (knowing you'll probably have to trim it later). Carefully consider travel time. Driving, except on expressways, is slower than in the United States. Check online to estimate how long various journeys will take, by rail (http://bahn.hafas.de/bin/query.exe/en) or by car (www.viamichelin.com). Consider night trains (NT) or overnight boats (NB) to save time and money.

Example: Logical order and desired number of days in each place:

3	*London*
5	*Paris*
3	*Alps*
2	*Florence*
3	*Rome (flight or NB)*
7	*Greece (flight or NB)*
1	*Bologna*
2	*Venice (NT)*
3	*Munich/Bavaria*
3	*Romantic Road/Rhine Cruise*

PLANNING YOUR ITINERARY

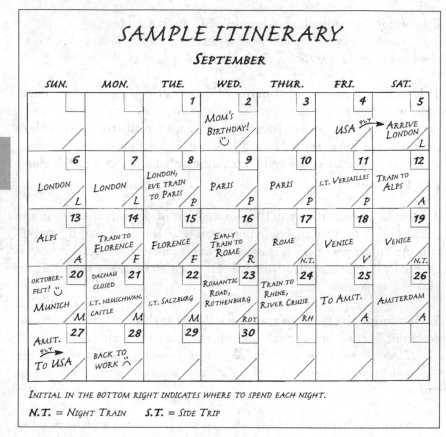

SAMPLE ITINERARY
SEPTEMBER

SUN.	MON.	TUE.	WED.	THUR.	FRI.	SAT.
		1	**2** MOM'S BIRTHDAY! ☺	**3**	**4** USA ᶠᴸʸ→	**5** ARRIVE LONDON / L
6 LONDON / L	**7** LONDON / L	**8** LONDON, EVE TRAIN TO PARIS / P	**9** PARIS / P	**10** PARIS / P	**11** S.T. VERSAILLES / P	**12** TRAIN TO ALPS / A
13 ALPS / A	**14** TRAIN TO FLORENCE / F	**15** FLORENCE / F	**16** EARLY TRAIN TO ROME / R	**17** ROME / N.T.	**18** VENICE / V	**19** VENICE / N.T.
20 OKTOBER-FEST! ☺ MUNICH / M	**21** DACHAU CLOSED S.T. NEUSCHWAN. CASTLE / M	**22** S.T. SALZBURG / M	**23** ROMANTIC ROAD, ROTHENBURG / ROT	**24** TRAIN TO RHINE, RIVER CRUISE / RH	**25** TO AMST. / A	**26** AMSTERDAM / A
27 AMST. ᶠᴸʸ TO USA	**28** BACK TO WORK ⌢̈	**29**	**30**			

INITIAL IN THE BOTTOM RIGHT INDICATES WHERE TO SPEND EACH NIGHT.

N.T. = NIGHT TRAIN   **S.T.** = SIDE TRIP

3   Berlin
4   Amsterdam
_____
39 TOTAL DAYS

Notes: I have 23 days for my vacation. Greece is time-consuming, even with an "open jaw" flight plan. If I eliminate Greece, I'll still need to cut nine days. Flying "open jaw" into London and out of Amsterdam is economical. Logical order may be affected by night-train possibilities.

Example: According to the guidebooks, I must keep these points in mind as I plan my trip. London: Theaters closed on Sunday, Speaker's Corner is Sunday only. Paris: Many museums are closed on Tuesday. Versailles and the Orsay Museum are closed on Monday. Florence: Museums are closed on Monday. Dachau: Closed on Monday. Note that I'm choosing to pay a little extra on my flight to let my trip stretch over the weekends and minimize lost work time. Yes, I may be a zombie on that first Monday back, but hey, what's more important?

7. Adjust by cutting, streamlining, or adding to fit your timeline or budget. Minimize travel time. When you must cut something, cut to save the most mileage. For instance, if Amsterdam and Berlin are equally important to you and you don't have time for both, cut the destination that saves the most miles (in this case, Berlin).

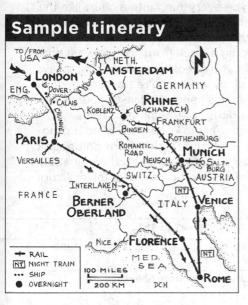

Minimize clutter. A so-so sight (Bologna) breaking a convenient night train (Rome–Venice) into two half-day journeys is clutter.

Trim time from each stop. Five days in Paris would be grand, but you can see the high points in three.

Consider economizing on car rental or a railpass. For instance, try to manage a 23-day trip on a 15-day train pass by seeing London, Paris, and Amsterdam before or after you use the pass.

Example: Itinerary and number of days adjusted to time limitations:

3	London
3	Paris
3	Alps
1	Florence
2	Rome (NT)
2	Venice (NT)
3	Munich/Bavaria
2	Romantic Road/Rhine Cruise
2	Amsterdam

23 TOTAL DAYS *(including 2 travel days)*

Notes: Get a 15-day Eurail Global Pass (valid from last day in Paris until first day in Amsterdam).

8. Fine-tune your itinerary. Study your guidebook. Maximize festival and market days. Be sure crucial sights are open the day you'll be in town.

Building Your Itinerary

Once my rough itinerary is set, I type everything into a chart like this one. This system keeps me organized, since I can collect all my reservations, train times, and other trip notes in one place. As I travel, I know at a glance where I'll be sleeping a week from now, or what time the train leaves on Saturday. Even if you're not a detail person, it pays to be disciplined about this, particularly when you're traveling in peak season or visiting popular spots. And it's handy to give to your family, friends, and co-workers who are curious about where you'll be.

Create an itinerary like this, then use it to keep track of your progress as you systematically set up your trip: Decide from guidebook listings or Web research where you want to stay in each destination. Make a template for an email room-reservation request letter. Work

Date	Travel
Fri, Sept 4	Fly to London after work (depart 18:45)
Sat, Sept 5	Arrive London at 11:45, check in at hotel, take orientation bus tour
Sun, Sept 6	Sightsee London (Tower of London, Shakespeare's Globe tour, Tate Modern)
Mon, Sept 7	See more London (Westminster Abbey, National Gallery, evening play)
Tue, Sept 8	Wrap up London (St. Paul's/The City, British Museum); take evening train to Paris (18:00–21:20)
Wed, Sept 9	Sightsee Paris (historic core incl. Notre-Dame, Sainte-Chapelle; also Louvre, Eiffel Tower at night)
Thu, Sept 10	Sightsee Paris (Champs-Elysées, Rodin Museum, Orsay)
Fri, Sept 11	Side-trip to Versailles
Sat, Sept 12	Take morning train to Swiss Alps (7:04–14:57 in Interlaken, transfer in Mannheim and Basel); maybe hike in late afternoon
Sun, Sept 13	Sightsee Alps (breakfast at the Schilthorn, Männlichen–Kleine Scheidegg hike)
Mon, Sept 14	Short morning hike and/or visit Trümmelbach Falls, afternoon train to Florence (from Interlaken 13:30–19:00)

and so on...

your way through your list and request rooms, slogging away until the entire trip is set up. Then...travel, enjoying a well-planned trip.

Notes and Reminders:

- Find out if my mobile phone works in Europe.
- Arrange for cat-sitter.
- Reserve Chunnel and overnight trains in advance.
- Make reservations for Eiffel Tower (Sept 7) and Florence's Uffizi Gallery (Sept 13).
- Find out about festivals—check online or call national tourist offices.
- Cancel newspaper, hold mail delivery, prepay bills.

Notes	Sleep
	Plane
Original London Sightseeing Bus Tour is discounted with guidebook	Luna Simone Hotel, **London** www.lunasimonehotel.com
Many theaters, churches & museums closed today; Speaker's Corner open today only	Luna Simone Hotel, **London**
Parliament open late; check for half-price play tickets at Leicester Square	Luna Simone Hotel, **London**
Confirm Paris hotel	Grand Hôtel Lévêque, **Paris** www.hotel-leveque.com
Museums crowded today; Louvre open late	Grand Hôtel Lévêque, **Paris**
Orsay open late	Grand Hôtel Lévêque, **Paris**
Reserve train for tomorrow?	Grand Hôtel Lévêque, **Paris**
Reserve Interlaken–Florence train for Monday?	Olle and Maria's B&B, **Gimmelwald** oeggimann@bluewin.ch
If rainy, visit Bern	Olle and Maria's B&B, **Gimmelwald**
If rainy, take morning train to Florence (from Interlaken 8:01–14:00); on arrival, do walking tour since most museums closed	Hotel Centrale, **Florence,** info@hotelcentralefirenze.it

PLANNING YOUR ITINERARY

My Favorite Home-Base Cities and Their Best Day Trips

Madrid: Toledo, Segovia, El Escorial, and even Sevilla, Córdoba, and Barcelona with the AVE bullet trains

Amsterdam: Alkmaar, Enkhuizen's Zuiderzee Museum, Arnhem's Folk Museum and Kröller-Müller Museum, Scheveningen, Delft/The Hague, Edam, and most of the Netherlands

Copenhagen: Frederiksborg Castle, Roskilde, Helsingør, Odense, and over the bridge to Malmö (Sweden)

Paris: Versailles, Chartres, Vaux-le-Vicomte, Fontainebleau, Chantilly, Giverny, Reims

London: Bath, Stonehenge, Stratford-upon-Avon, Cambridge, York, and many others; even Paris is less than three hours away by train

Arles: Pont du Gard, Nîmes, Avignon, and all of Provence

Florence: Siena, Pisa, San Gimignano, and many other hill towns

Venice: Padua, Vicenza, Verona, and Ravenna

Munich: Salzburg, "Mad" King Ludwig's castles (Neuschwanstein and Linderhof), Wieskirche, Oberammergau, and other small Bavarian towns

Sorrento: Naples, Pompeii, Herculaneum, Mount Vesuvius, Amalfi Coast, Paestum, and Capri

Remember that most cities close many of their major tourist attractions for one day during the week (usually Mon). It would be a shame to be in Madrid only on a Monday, when the Prado is *cerrado*. Paris closes the Louvre and many other sights on Tuesday. Write out a day-by-day itinerary. Note that when flying from the United States, you arrive in Europe the next day. When returning, you arrive home the same day (or so you hope).

The Home-Base Strategy

The home-base strategy is a clever way to make your trip itinerary smoother, simpler, and more efficient. Set yourself up in a central location and use that place as a base for day trips to nearby attractions.

The home-base approach minimizes set-up time (usually an hour). Searching for a good hotel can be exhausting, frustrating, and time-consuming. And hotels often give a better price, or at least more smiles, for longer stays. Many small B&Bs don't accept those staying only one night.

You are freed from your luggage. Being able to leave your luggage in the hotel lets you travel freely and with the peace of mind that you are set up for the night. Bags are less likely to be lost or stolen in your hotel than en route.

You feel "at home" in your home-base town. This comfortable feeling takes more than a day to get, and when you're changing locations every day or two, you may never enjoy this important sense of rootedness. Home-basing allows you to become attuned to the rhythm of daily life.

Day-trip to a village, enjoy the nightlife in a city. The home-base approach lets you spend the evening in a city, where there is more exciting nightlife. Most small countryside towns die after 9 p.m. If you're not dead by 9 p.m., you'll enjoy the action in a larger city.

Transportation is a snap. Europe's generally frequent and punctual train and bus systems (which often operate out of a hub anyway) make this home-base strategy practical. With a train pass, trips are "free"; otherwise, the transportation is reasonable, often with reductions offered for round-trip tickets (especially for "same-day return").

High-Speed Town-Hopping

When I tell people that I saw three or four towns in one day, many think, "Insane! Nobody can really see several towns in a day!" Of course, it's folly to go too fast, but many stop-worthy towns take only an hour or two to cover. Don't let feelings of guilt tell you to slow down and stay longer if you really are finished with a town. There's so much more to see in the rest of Europe. Going too slow is as bad as going too fast.

If you're efficient and use the high-speed town-hopping method, you'll amaze yourself with what you can see in a day. Let me explain with an example:

You wake up early in A-ville. Checking out of your hotel, you have one sight to cover before your 10 a.m. train. (You checked the train schedule the night before.) After the sightseeing and before getting to the station, you visit the open-air market and buy the ingredients for your brunch, and pick up a B-burg map and tourist brochure at A-ville's tourist office.

From 10 to 11 a.m. you travel by train to B-burg. During that hour you have a restful brunch, enjoy the passing scenery, and prepare for B-burg by reading your literature and deciding what you want to see. Just before your arrival, you put the items you need (camera, jacket, tourist information) into your small daypack. Then, upon arrival, check the rest of your luggage in a locker. (Most stations have storage lockers or a baggage-check desk—ask what time it closes when you drop off your bag.)

Before leaving B-burg's station, write down the departure times of the next few trains to C-town. Now you can sightsee as much or as little as you want and still know when to comfortably catch your train.

B-burg is great. After a snack in the park, you catch the train at 2:30 p.m. By 3 p.m. you're in C-town, where you repeat the same procedure you followed in B-burg. C-town just isn't what it was cracked up to be, so after a walk along the waterfront and a look at the church, you catch the first train out at 5 p.m.

You arrive in D-dorf, the last town on the day's agenda, by 5:30 p.m. A man in the station directs you to a good budget pension two blocks down the street. You're checked in and unpacked in no time, and, after a few horizontal moments, it's time to find a good restaurant and eat dinner. After a meal and an evening stroll, you're ready to call it a day. As you write in your journal, it occurs to you: This was a great sightseeing day. You spent it high-speed town-hopping.

8. Prioritizing Your Time

So much to see, so little time. How to choose? It depends on your interest and your tastes. One person's Barcelona is another person's Bucharest. But this highly opinionated chapter will give you suggestions based on my own lifetime of travel.

The Best and Worst of Europe—With No Apologies

Good travel writers should make hard choices and give the reader solid opinions. Just so nobody will accuse me of gutlessness, I've assembled a pile of spunky opinions. Chances are that you have too many stops on your trip wish list and not enough time. To make your planning a little easier, heed these warnings. These are just my personal feelings after more than 100 months of European travel. And if you disagree with any of them, you obviously haven't been there.

Let's start with the dullest corner of the British Isles, south Scotland. It's so boring the Romans decided to block it off with Hadrian's Wall. However, like Venice's St. Mark's Square at midnight and Napoleon's tomb in Paris, Hadrian's Wall covers history buffs with goose bumps.

London, York, Bath, and Edinburgh are the most interesting cities in

Britain. Belfast, Liverpool, and Glasgow are quirky enough to be called interesting. Oxford pales next to Cambridge, and Stratford-upon-Avon is little more than Shakespeare's house—and that's as dead as he is.

The west coast of Ireland (the Dingle Peninsula), Wales' Snowdonia

National Park, and England's Windermere Lakes District are the most beautiful natural regions of the British Isles. The North York Moors disappoint most creatures great and small.

Germany's Heidelberg, Ireland's Blarney Stone (slobbered on by countless tourists to get the "gift of gab"), Spain's Costa del Sol, and the French Riviera in July and August are among Europe's top tourist traps. The tackiest souvenirs are found next to Pisa's leaning tower and in Lourdes.

Kissing the Blarney Stone: Slathered with spit and lipstick, it's a standard stop for typical big-bus tours in Ireland.

Extra caution is merited in southwest England, a minefield of tourist traps. The British are masters at milking every conceivable tourist attraction for all it's worth. Here are some booby traps: the Devil's Toenail (a rock that looks just like...a toe-nail), Land's End (pay, pay, pay), and cloying Clovelly (a one-street town lined with knickknack shops selling the same goodies—like "clotted cream that you can mail home"). While Tintagel's castle, famous as the legendary birthplace of King Arthur, offers thrilling windswept and wave-beaten ruins, the town of Tintagel does everything in its little power to exploit the profitable Arthurian legend. There's even a pub in town called the Excali Bar.

England's Land's End...pay, pay, pay.

Sognefjord is Norway's most spectacular fjord. The Geirangerfjord, while famous as a cruise-ship stop, is a disappointment. The most boring countryside is Sweden's (I am Norwegian), although Scandinavia's best

Itinerary Priorities, Country by Country

Use this chart to get ideas on how speedy travelers can prioritize limited sightseeing time in various countries. Add places from left to right as you build plans for the best of that country in 3, 5, 7, 10, or 14 days. (These suggestions take geographical proximity into account. In some cases, the plan assumes you'll take a night train.) So, according to this chart, the best week in Britain would be spread between London, Bath, Cambridge, and the Cotswolds.

Country	3 days	5 days	7 days	10 days	14 days
Europe	Forget it	London, Paris	Amsterdam	Rhineland, Swiss Alps	Rome, Venice
Britain	London	Bath	Cambridge, Cotswolds	York	Edinburgh, N. Wales
Ireland	Dublin	Dingle Peninsula	Galway, Belfast	County Clare/ Burren	Antrim Coast, Aran Islands
France	Paris, Versailles	Normandy	Loire	Dordogne, Carcassonne	Provence, the Riviera
Germany	Munich, Bavarian castles	Rhine Valley, Rothenburg	More of Bavaria, Salzburg	Berlin	Baden-Baden, Black Forest, Dresden
Austria	Vienna	Salzburg	Hallstatt	Danube Valley, Tirol, Bavaria (Germany)	Innsbruck, Hall, Bratislava (Slovakia)

medieval castle is in the Swedish town of Kalmar.

Zürich and Geneva, two of Switzerland's largest and most sterile cities, share the "nice place to live but I wouldn't want to visit" award. Both are pleasantly situated on a lake—like Buffalo and Cleveland. And both are famous, but name familiarity is a rotten reason to go somewhere. If you want a Swiss city, see Bern or Luzern.

Geneva's newspaper objects to my "denigrating" its dull city on the Internet.

Country	3 days	5 days	7 days	10 days	14 days
Switzerland	Berner Oberland	Luzern	Bern, Lausanne	Zermatt, Appenzell, scenic rail trip	Lugano and Zürich
Italy	Florence, Venice	Rome	Cinque Terre	Civita, Siena	Sorrento, Naples, Pompeii, Amalfi Coast
Scandinavia	Copenhagen, side-trips	Stockholm	Oslo	"Norway in a Nutshell," Bergen	Helsinki, Tallinn
Spain	Madrid, Toledo	Sevilla, Granada	Barcelona	Andalucía	Costa del Sol, Morocco
Portugal	Lisbon, Sintra	The Algarve	Évora, Nazaré	Sights near Nazaré, Coimbra	Porto, Douro Valley
Eastern Europe	Prague	Budapest	Kraków and Auschwitz	Slovenia and Český Krumlov	Dalmatian Coast with Dubrovnik
Croatia & Slovenia	Dubrovnik	Mostar, Split	Korčula/ Hvar or Montenegro	Lake Bled, Plitvice Lakes	Ljubljana, Istria, more of Dalmatian Coast
Greece	Athens	Hydra	Delphi	Nafplio, Epidavros, Mycenae	Olympia, Monemvasia, Mani Peninsula

However, it's almost criminal to spend a sunny Swiss day in a city if you haven't yet been high in the Alps.

Bordeaux must mean "boredom" in some ancient language. If I were offered a free trip to that town, I'd stay home and clean the fridge. Connoisseurs visit for the wine, but Bordeaux wine country and Bordeaux city are as different as night and night soil. There's a wine-tourism information bureau in Bordeaux that, for a price, will bus you out of town into the more interesting wine country nearby.

Andorra, a small country in the Pyrenees between France and Spain, is as scenic as any other chunk of those mountains. People from all over Europe flock to Andorra to take advantage of its famous duty-free shopping. As far as Americans are concerned, Andorra is just a big

Spanish-speaking outlet mall. There are no bargains here that you can't get at home. Enjoy the Pyrenees with less traffic elsewhere. Among Europe's other "little countries," San Marino and Liechtenstein are also not worth the trouble.

Germany's famous Black Forest disappoints more people than it excites. If it were all Germany offered, it would be worth seeing. For Europeans, any large forest is understandably a popular attraction. But I'd say the average American visitor who's seen more than three trees in one place would prefer Germany's Romantic Road and Bavaria to the east, the Rhine and Mosel country to the north, the Swiss Alps to the south, and France's Alsace region to the west—all high points that cut the Black Forest down to stumps.

Norway's Stavanger, famous for nearby fjords and its status as an oil boomtown, is a large port that's about as exciting as...well, put it this way: Emigrants left it in droves to move to the wilds of Minnesota. Time in western Norway is better spent in and around Bergen.

Kraków (Poland) and Budapest (Hungary) are, after Prague, Eastern Europe's best cities. Conveniently located Bratislava—the capital of Slovakia, on the Danube between Vienna and Budapest—has not-quite-charming streets filled with dull cafés, forgettable museums, and tourists wishing they'd spent more time elsewhere. Likewise, Bucharest, Romania's capital, has little to offer. Its top-selling postcard is of the InterContinental Hotel. If you're heading from Eastern Europe to Greece, skip Thessaloniki, which deserves its place in the Bible but doesn't belong in travel guidebooks.

Europe's most scenic train ride is the Glacier Express, across southern Switzerland from Chur to Zermatt. The most scenic boat ride is from Stockholm to Helsinki—countless islands and blondes. Europe's most underrated sight is Rome's ancient seaport, Ostia Antica, and its most misunderstood wine is Portugal's *vinho verde* (green wine).

The best French château is Versailles, near Paris. The best look at Gothic is the Sainte-Chapelle church in Paris. The top two medieval castle interiors are Germany's Burg Eltz on the Mosel River and northern Italy's Reifenstein near the Brenner Pass. Lisbon, Oslo, Stockholm, Brussels, and Budapest are the most underrated big cities. For romance, Varenna on Italy's Lake Como murmurs "honeymoon."

The biggest mistakes that tourists make: packing too heavily, relying on outdated guidebooks, not wearing a money belt, and taking other people's opinions too seriously.

Happy travels!

TRANSPORTATION

If you're traveling independently, you can make your trip go more smoothly by learning the ins and outs of the many ways of getting from point A to point B—whether flying, riding the rails, driving, biking, hitching, or hiking.

9. Flying

Before you can enjoy Europe, you have to get there. Should you book your flight online, or use a travel agent? And once overseas, how can you use flights within Europe to your advantage? For starters, it helps to understand...

Our Travel Industry

Travel is a huge business—one of the planet's biggest industries. Most of what the travel industry promotes is decadence: Lie on the beach for two precious weeks of hedonism to make up for the other 50. That's where the money is, and that's where most of the interest is. Independent travelers fit the industry like a snowshoe in Mazatlán. Understand what shapes the information that shapes your travel dreams. Travel coverage in the mainstream media—whether online or in print—is made possible only with the support of advertisers. And those advertisers are more interested in filling cruise ships or tour buses than in turning people free to travel independently. Years ago, when I first started writing a weekly travel newspaper column, it was called "The Budget Traveler." Within a month of its appearance, that travel section's major advertisers met with the editor and explained they would no longer buy ads if he continued running a column with that name. Hastily, the editor and I found a new name. To save the column, we called it "The Practical Traveler"—the same subversive information, but with a more palatable title.

Many in the tourism industry don't understand travel "through the Back Door." The typical attitude I get when hobnobbing with bigwigs in Hilton hotel ballrooms is, "If you can't afford to go first class, save up and go next year." I'll never forget the bewilderment I caused when I turned down a free room in Bangkok's most elegant Western-style hotel in favor of a cheap room in a simple Thai-style hotel.

Of course, these comments are generalizations. There are many great travel agents in the industry who understand my frustration because they've also dealt with it. If you can find these kindred spirits, they'll work with your budget and your travel style to help you forge the trip of your dreams.

Travel can exploit impoverished local cultures. Or it can promote understanding, removing our hometown blinders and making our world more comfortable in its smallness. What the industry promotes is up to all of us—writers, editors, agents, and travelers.

Flying to Europe

Many of the same guidelines for flying to Europe apply whether you buy your ticket online or from a travel agent (both explained later in this chapter). The specific rules and regulations are confusing and always changing, but when you make the right choice, you get the right price. Plan on spending $700–1,200 for your basic round-trip ticket, plus another $300–500 in taxes, fuel surcharges, and other fees.

Dollars saved = discomfort + restrictions + inflexibility. Assuming you know your options, you get what you pay for. There's no such thing as a free lunch in the airline industry. (In fact, these days, there's usually no lunch at all.) Full fare is very expensive. You get the ultimate in flexibility, but I've never met anyone spending his or her own money who flew that way. Rather than grab the cheapest ticket to Europe, go with the best combination of reliability, economy, and flexibility for your travel needs. It generally makes sense to buy a less-expensive ticket and pay the penalty if you need to change.

Buy your tickets at the right time. Look for tickets as soon as you're ready to firmly commit to flight dates and ports. As you delay, dates sell out and prices generally go up. Special fares are limited to a few seats to jump-start departures. It's wise to look for tickets four to six months before you fly. Book your spring and summer travel in January, February, and March. In general, the sooner the better—but not all of the best fares are available in January, so keep an eye on the airfares (if booking on your own, check the airfare trend calendars at www.farecompare.com and www.bing.com/travel; if working with a travel agent, ask for advice on the best time to buy). Fall travel should probably be booked by May or June, because the trend for airfare prices and availability is known by then. If you're traveling in September—a very popular time to fly to Europe (particularly the first half of the month)—start looking even earlier. Travel during winter—November through March—can be purchased a month or so in advance (with the exception of winter breaks and holidays, which require earlier booking).

Airfares vary by season and by day. Find out when "peak season" begins and ends. At certain crucial times, moving your flight by one day (out of peak and into shoulder season) could save you hundreds of dollars. Likewise, fares are generally a bit cheaper for travel Monday through Thursday than for weekends.

Be aware of surcharges and taxes. Most airlines now levy a hefty "fuel surcharge," which varies depending on the airline and the price of fuel. Charges for checked bags are another headache; for the latest fees for major US and international carriers, check www.airlinealacarte.net or www.smartertravel.com (click on "Airline Fees: The Ultimate Guide"). Combined with airport taxes (which vary by city), these fees can add hundreds of dollars to your total ticket price. A "cheap" $300 round-trip off-season flight to London can more than double in price when all the fees are included...not quite such a bargain after all. It's always smart to figure out the complete price before you commit.

Consider flying "open jaw." I almost always fly "open jaw": into one city and out of another. In general, the fare is figured simply by taking half of the round-trip fare for each of those ports. I used to fly into Amsterdam, travel to Istanbul, and then (having rejected the "open jaw" plan because flying home from Istanbul costs $200 more than returning from Amsterdam) pay $200 to ride the train for two days

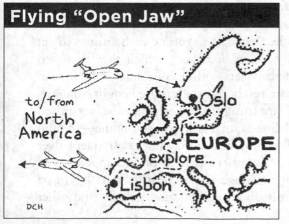

Flying "Open Jaw"

to/from North America

Oslo

EUROPE explore...

Lisbon

DCH

What Can I Carry On?

As of this writing (mid-2010), items prohibited in carry-on luggage on US flights include the following:

- **liquids** in containers larger than 3.4 ounces (and all of your liquid containers must fit into a single, quart-size sealable plastic baggie)
- **knives** and other sharp items (including box cutters, and scissors with blades four inches or longer in length)
- **blunt instruments** (such as ski poles, golf clubs, baseball bats, or martial arts weapons)
- **guns,** ammunition, and explosives
- **tools**—no hammers or saws at all; other tools (such as screwdrivers and wrenches) only if they are seven inches or shorter in length
- **lighters** and other flammable materials (though you're allowed to carry on one matchbook)
- **aerosol containers** are allowed only if they are toiletries that meet the liquids restrictions explained above; self-defense sprays (such as mace and pepper spray) are not permitted
- **"disabling chemicals"** such as bleach or chlorine

You can take an entire set of knives or a giant bottle of shampoo to Europe if you like—but you'll have to check your bag. (Certain items—such as matches or explosives—are not allowed in your checked luggage, either.)

back to Amsterdam to catch my "cheap" return flight. Now I see the real economy in spending more for "open jaw." "Open jaw" is cheapest when the same airline covers all segments of the round-trip journey.

Look into consolidator fares. These fares—which can be sold by travel agents or online—are often cheaper than buying direct from the airline. Consolidators are wholesalers who negotiate with airlines to get deeply discounted fares on a number of tickets, which they then sell cheaply (but with a mark-up) to travelers. While consolidator tickets can be a great deal, they can be more restrictive than those bought from airlines: They're "nonendorsable" (meaning that no other airline is required to honor that ticket if your airline is unable to get you home—though in practice this is rarely a problem), and you may not get frequent-flyer miles. And if the airline drops its prices (which often happens), you are stuck with what was, but no longer is, a cheap fare. If buying a consolidator ticket, ask carefully about cancellation policies and other restrictions.

Be warned that this list can change without notice—especially just after a terrorist threat. And be aware that restrictions can differ between the US and Europe, as well as between any two European countries. Don't assume you know what's allowed. Shortly before your flight, check the websites for your airline and any airports you're flying through. (This is an especially good idea if you're flying through London, which often enforces tighter restrictions than other European hubs.) For the latest rules on the American leg of your journey, check www.tsa.gov/travelers. For the United Kingdom, see www.dft.gov.uk/transportforyou/airtravel; for the European Union, see www.tsa.gov/approach/harmonization.shtm.

You might be tempted to pick up some duty-free booze on your way back home—but before you do, think carefully about your flight plan. You might see signs reassuring you that duty-free liquids—if purchased at the airport and sealed in a special bag—can be carried on board your flight. While this is true, it doesn't necessarily mean you can also carry them on a connecting flight. If you have a layover, you'll often have to pass through a new round of security checks, and duty-free liquids that were fine on your first leg may be seized when you change planes. If you have a US connection, duty-free liquids (even in the special sealed bags) will not be allowed through the security checkpoint.

TRANSPORTATION

Budget flights are restrictive. Most are nonchangeable and nonrefundable, but some offer changes on the return dates for a penalty of about $200. Even then, you typically need to make changes at least 24 hours before your departure to avoid losing the entire value of the ticket. If you need to change your return date in Europe, call your airline's European office. If that fails, I've found that airlines become more lenient if you go to their office in person with a good reason for your need to change the return date. If you absolutely must get home early, go to the airport. If you're standing at the airport two days before your ticket says you can go home, and seats are available, regardless of the rules, they may let you fly home early (at no extra cost). They win a happy customer and gain two more days to try to sell an empty seat. Besides, at that point, it's the easiest way to get rid of you.

Expect to get an electronic ticket. E-tickets are here to stay—most airlines no longer issue paper tickets. While travelers with an e-ticket can fly simply with a photo ID, it's always smart to bring the printed receipt with you in case there are complications at the airport. Be sure the receipt has your e-ticket number, not just the airline's reservation code.

Reserve a specific seat for maximum comfort. Most airlines let you choose your seat when you book. To avoid being squeezed in the middle of a row, pick one as early as possible. For pointers, see www.seat guru.com.

Review your ticket carefully when you book it. Double-check your dates, destinations, and exact spelling of your name. A simple second look as soon as you get your tickets can give you a chance to fix any mistakes...and save you enormous headaches later.

Check in online before heading to the airport. Most carriers' websites allow you to check in and print your boarding pass from home (or from your European hotel) 24 hours before departure time. This is a good way to confirm your flight schedule and seat assignment, and can save you from waiting in check-in lines at the airport.

Buying Plane Tickets Online

While booking your airfare through a travel agent (described in the next section) is still a good option, these days most people buy their own tickets online. Here are a few pointers for finding the best deal.

Surf the major Internet travel agencies. These websites compare several published fares on a particular route, then sort them by price. There are plenty of options, each with its own features. Travelocity.com and Expedia.com are built on conventional reservation systems used by travel agents. Airline consortiums founded the US-based Orbitz.com and the European-based Opodo.com. "Meta-search engines" such as Kayak .com and Mobissimo.com search dozens of other booking sites; Insidetrip .com ranks flights based on speed and comfort; and Tripadvisor.com sorts out all the variables, including fees, connections, and even the layout of the plane. Farecompare.com and Bing.com/travel track airfare trends and attempt to predict when specific journeys will be cheapest. These sites are a good place to start, but keep in mind that they don't include all airlines. Some travelers use these sites to determine which airline is cheapest, then go to that airline's own site to see if there's an even better deal. In a few cases, these sites can even beat the carrier's official site. They can sometimes also "mix and match" to connect the legs of a single trip by using multiple airlines, getting a great price (though these trips can be difficult to rebook in case of a delay or missed leg). Before booking, review the schedule carefully, watching out for very tight or very long (i.e., overnight) connections.

Check the airlines' official websites for deals. Even if the base fare is the same as on one of the comparison sites listed above, you can sometimes avoid third-party service fees by booking directly with the airline. Also, airline sites often offer special "Web-only" fares that are not published anywhere else. For example, SAS offers incredibly low prices for intercontinental flights each December. Their site (www.fly sas.com) becomes a Christmas calendar, and each day a new European destination is available—but only for one day. (You can sign up for email alerts that tell you the day's destination.)

If you're flexible, consider last-minute, take-what-you-can-get airfares from discount websites such as www.priceline.com, www.hot wire.com, and www.cheaptickets.com. Most of these rock-bottom discount sites have serious restrictions; for example, you can't always choose the time of day to fly, or what airline you prefer. But the savings could make it worthwhile if your travel dates are flexible.

Consider specialty sites. Some sites offer low fares at discounted rates for people who fit certain criteria, such as students, young people, and teachers. For example, www.statravel.com and www.student universe.com specialize in student travel.

Comparison-shop "air plus hotel" promotional deals. Some major Internet travel agencies and airlines offer "getaway" deals on their websites. For one low price, you get a round-trip flight to a European city, as well as a few nights' lodging at a hotel in that city. The hotels are generally soulless business hotels. But if the cost of the package is significantly less than buying the airfare and booking a hotel separately, go for it. Given Europe's high accommodations costs—especially in big cities—this can be an excellent value.

Sign up for email alerts. Most of the above sites can email you automated updates about low fares for specific routes—a handy way to find out about sales.

Be ready to buy. Once you have done your research and know what constitutes a good fare, don't hesitate to book if you find a deal. There can be up to 10 different pricing levels for each flight, fares fluctuate throughout the day, and cheap tickets are limited, so waiting to talk with your travel partner could cost you a good fare. Figure out in advance what you're looking for, then grab it when you find it.

Read the fine print. The advantage of using a travel agent is that you have an ally who understands the ins and outs of dealing with the airlines. When you book online, you're on your own. Whichever website you use, make sure it lists a phone number—you'll need to speak to a person if you have a problem. Understand the restrictions, policy on refunds or

---

Know Thy Travel Agent: A Quiz

One way to be sure your travel agent is enthusiastic about European travel and properly suited to helping you with your trip is to ask him or her a few questions. Here's a little quiz—complete with answers.

1. **What is "open jaw"?**
   a) A tourist in awe of the *Manneken-Pis*.
   b) A special-interest tour of Romania's dental clinics.
   c) An airline ticket that allows you to fly into one city and out of another.

2. **Which international boat rides are covered by the Eurailpass?**
   a) Poland to Switzerland.
   b) All of them.
   c) Italy to Greece, Germany to Denmark, and Sweden to Denmark.

3. **What's the age limit to sleep in a Hostelling International youth hostel?**
   a) Five.
   b) As high as 30 if you like hip-hop.
   c) There is none.

---

changes, and additional fees (such as a service charge or delivery fee that shows up only when you're in the final stage of booking).

Personally, I'd rather have my travel agent do the work.

Using a Travel Agent

While it may seem like an antiquated notion in today's Internet Age, a travel agent can be an invaluable tool for planning your trip. My travel agent is my vital ally—I've never gone to Europe without her help. Travel-agency recommendations from other travelers provide excellent leads, but the right agency doesn't guarantee the right agent. You need a particular person—someone whose definition of "good travel" matches yours. Ask for the agency's "independent Europe specialist." Once you find the right agent, nurture your alliance. Be loyal. Send her a postcard.

Travel agents can save you money. It takes a full-time and aggressive travel professional to keep up with the constantly changing airline industry. I don't have time to compare various Internet offers or sort through

4. **What is the most economical way to get from London's Heathrow Airport into London?**
   a) Walk.
   b) Ask the Queen for a lift.
   c) Don't. Spend your whole vacation at Heathrow.
   d) By subway ("Tube").

5. **What is an ISIC card?**
   a) A universal way to tell foreigners you're not feeling well.
   b) It beats three-of-a-kind.
   c) The International Student Identity Card, good for many discounts at sights and museums.

6. **Is there a problem getting a bed-and-breakfast in England's small towns without a reservation?**
   a) Not if you live there.
   b) Yes. Carry NoDoz in England.
   c) No.

7. **How much does a Hungarian visa cost?**
   a) $45.
   b) You can just charge it on your Visa card.
   c) More than a Greek urn.
   d) It's not required.

Answers: The last answer to each question is the correct one.

all the frustrating, generally too-good-to-be-true ads that appear in the Sunday travel sections. I rely instead on the experience of an agent who specializes in budget European travel.

Travel agent fees are a good investment. Now that airline commissions are a thing of the past, many agents charge a $35–100 fee per ticket. Travel agencies have also had to specialize, offering their customers something beyond just plane tickets—a friendly, knowledgeable human being you can call on in a travel-related emergency. In the long run, paying a modest fee is a worthwhile expense to ensure that you have the right—and cheapest—ticket for your trip. Think of it as a consulting cost for your travel agent's expertise.

You won't necessarily save money by booking directly with the airlines. Most airline representatives barely know what they're charging, much less their competitors' rates and schedules. (Plus, many airlines charge a fee to book with a live person by phone.) A good travel agent offers both regular airline fares and discounted consolidator fares (described earlier) that aren't available elsewhere and can save you money.

Use your agent only for arranging transportation. Although many agents can give you tips on Irish B&Bs and sporadic advice on biking in Holland, assume you'll do better if you use your travel agent only to get you to your destination. After that, rely on a good guidebook. Travel agents handle their clients with kid gloves. Don't let their caution clamp a ball and chain onto your travel dreams. I use an agent for my plane ticket, railpass or car rental, advice on visas, travel insurance, and health precautions...and nothing else.

Check student travel agencies—even if you're not a student. Any city with a university probably has a student travel agency. STA Travel (with 18 offices in the US, www.statravel.com, tel. 800-781-4040) offers budget fares even to non-students under age 26 and to teachers. Most big West Coast university campuses also have a more independent agency that is a member of University and Student Travel Nationwide. (Note that heavily discounted student tickets often don't count for frequent-flyer miles.)

Be loyal to your travel agent. Dumping your agent for a $30 savings on the Internet is a bad move. These days, many people milk good agents for all they're worth, and then buy tickets online. Because of this, it's tough to get good advice over the phone, and "browsers" usually get no respect. As a loyal customer, I enjoy the luxury of sitting down with my agent, explaining my travel plans, getting a briefing on my options, and choosing the best flight.

Frequent-Flyer Miles

While far from a sure thing, using your frequent-flyer miles to get to Europe can save you a bundle. What began as a way to reward customer loyalty has evolved into a profitable side-business for the airlines, who sell "award miles" to credit-card and other companies (who pass along those miles as incentives to their own customers). But as more people earn piles of miles, airlines are bumping up the number of miles (and additional fees) required to claim a seat. Here are some strategies for getting the most travel out of your miles. For more tips, check out www .flyertalk.com.

Book as far ahead as possible. Airlines reserve only a handful of "award seats" on each flight—and they go fast. While some additional seats might become available later, there's no way to know when (or if) they'll be released. The further ahead you book (ideally several months in advance), the more likely you'll get your choice of flights for the fewest

TRANSPORTATION

Flight vs. Train?

With the abundance of cheap flights within Europe, travelers can choose how to connect far-flung cities: hop a flight, or ride the rails?

Flying can save both time and money, especially on long journeys. A cheap flight can help a light sleeper avoid spending the night on a rattling train. In fact, the availability of inexpensive flights is changing the way travelers plan their itineraries. A decade ago, it would have been folly to squeeze Italy and Norway into a single two-week trip. Today that plan is easy and cheap.

But if you're focusing on a single country or region, and connecting destinations that are closer together, the train is still more practical. Europe's high-speed train network is getting faster and faster, covering even long distances in a snap. From London to Paris, the Eurostar Chunnel train can be faster than flying when you consider the train zips you directly from downtown to downtown. Train and car travel, unlike flights, keep you close to the scenery, to Europe, and to Europeans. Ground transportation is also less likely to be disrupted by bad weather, mechanical problems, or scheduling delays.

If you're environmentally minded, you already know that the greenest way to move your body around Europe is by train. Taking the train leaves a carbon footprint that's 70 to 90 percent smaller than if you'd flown. For that reason alone, some travelers choose to spend more time and money to ride the rails.

miles. Even if the "award seats" are booked up, you can sometimes use additional miles to get on the flight (for a first-class seat, or for a double-miles "rule-buster" seat—though these are being phased out).

Maximize the miles you earn. I'd never fly on a particular airline just to get the miles—for me, the price and convenience of a flight plan always trumps the potential for netting miles. But if you're flying anyway, you might as well get all the miles you can. For example, booking direct with the airline, rather than on a third-party booking site, might earn you bonus miles. Some credit cards allow you to accrue miles with each purchase (sometimes with an annual fee). But watch out if you buy your tickets on discount sites—depending on the seat code, some airlines may not credit the full amount of miles to your account.

Know about alliances. Most major airlines belong to one of three gigantic frequent-flyer collectives. For example, the Star Alliance includes North American airlines (United, US Airways, Air Canada) as well as

European carriers both big (Germany's Lufthansa, SAS Scandinavian, LOT Polish Airlines, Spanair) and small (TAP Air Portugal, Croatia Airlines, Slovenia's Adria Airways). Other alliances include SkyTeam (Delta, KLM, Air France, Alitalia, Czech Airlines) and OneWorld (American Airlines, British Airways, Air Iberia, Finnair, Malév Hungarian). If you have miles on any airline in the alliance, you can redeem them on any of the others. So, for example, if you're headed to Prague, try using your Delta miles first (allied with Czech Airlines); for Helsinki, see what you can get with your American Airlines miles (partnered with Finnair); and for Dubrovnik, check with United (allied with Croatia Airlines).

Use airline alliances to collect miles smartly. The same alliances work for collecting miles. You might not care about earning miles for an SAS or Air Portugal flight, but if you give them your United frequent-flyer number, the miles go into your United pot.

To redeem your miles, check online first, then call. Check if the flight you want is available on the airline's website. If not, don't give up. Call to speak with an airline agent. While this can come with a small additional fee, it's worth it to talk with a live person who has all your options at his or her fingertips—especially if you...

Do some research and know your options. There are a variety of ways to connect any two points. When you try to redeem miles, the agent might simply try the most straightforward route. If that route is sold out, ask him to check other ways. Better yet, do some homework before you call, and make a list (in order of preference) of the connections that would work for your trip. For example, if I'm going from Seattle to London, it's easiest to take a direct, nonstop flight. But if that's full, I'd be willing to settle for any one of the dozens of other possible connections through other cities.

If you're short on miles, you still have options. Look into buying miles from the airline, or paying a fee to transfer them from someone else (e.g., a spouse or relative). While it obviously wouldn't be cost-effective to do this for the entire value of a ticket, if you're 2,000 miles short on the 50,000-mile fare, buying or transferring miles can bring it within your reach for a relatively small cost. Many airlines also allow you to "pay" for one leg of the ticket with miles and the other in cash.

Watch the expiration date. For many airlines, miles expire at a certain point after you accrue them (usually one to two years). Know your miles' shelf-life, and use them before they're gone. Typically the miles must be used for a ticket before the expiration date, but the flight can occur anytime—even months later.

You're still responsible for taxes and fees. What were once "free" award seats can now cost as much as $300, depending on the airline and destination. But you're still flying for a fraction of the full fare.

Flying Within Europe

For most of my traveling life, I never would have considered flying point-to-point within Europe. It simply wasn't affordable. But today that kind of thinking seems *so* 20th century.

With the deregulation of airlines and the proliferation of extremely competitive discount carriers, suddenly Europe's vagabonds are jetsetters. More new no-frills airlines take off every year, and even some of the well-established carriers are following their lead. Before buying a long-distance train ticket, first visit a few budget airlines' websites to compare prices. You might be surprised.

Budget Airlines

Most of Europe's low-cost airlines operate user-friendly websites with interactive flight maps and straightforward online booking. To get the lowest fares, book long in advance. The cheapest seats sell out fast (aside from occasional surprise sales), leaving the pricier fares for latecomers.

Many budget airlines offer flights between major European cities for about $100, but you can find some remarkable deals if your timing is right. A tour guide on my staff recently booked an easyJet flight from London to Amsterdam for less than $50. Ryanair routinely flies from London to any one of dozens of European cities for about $20. And you might occasionally find it-must-be-a-typo promotional flights for less than €1. Even after adding taxes and airport fees, these flights are a great value.

While new budget airlines are continually being launched, a handful of them have been around long enough to be considered old-timers, including easyJet (www.easyjet.com) and Ryanair (www.ryanair.com). But there are dozens of other carriers (see sidebar).

To quickly narrow down your choices, use a website that specializes in searching for cheap flights on several budget airlines: www.skyscanner.net is the best, but you can also try www.wegolo.com and www.whichbudget.com. Be

Europe's no-frills, smaller airlines offer cut-rate fares and scaled-down services.

aware that these sites may ignore some budget carriers, and might not check with the major carriers (which can offer just-as-cheap promotional offers); to find the right connection, you may need to search several sites. You can also try searching on the big-name sites (such as Orbitz.com, Kayak.com, and Mobissimo.com), though these are less likely to catch all of the little, upstart budget airlines.

Many budget airlines have hubs; for instance, Ryanair has a hub in Dublin. It can make sense to check fares with an airline that uses either your starting point or your ending point as a hub. For example, for a trip from Dublin to Oslo, I'd look at Ryanair and also at Norwegian, which has a hub in Oslo. Several Britain-based "leisure airlines" specialize in connecting the British Isles to Spain, Portugal, and other popular holiday destinations in southern Europe. If this fits your itinerary, try Monarch (www.flymonarch.com) or Thomson (http://flights.thomson .co.uk).

Some budget airlines aren't as hub-focused, and even offer direct flights between cities they're not based in. For example, Air Berlin has extensive flight schedules in and out of more than a dozen different German cities—not just Berlin (www.airberlin.com).

Europe by Air is a good budget resource (www.europebyair.com, tel. 888-321-4737). They work with 13 European airlines, offering flights between more than a hundred cities throughout the Continent. Using their "flight pass" system, each coupon for a nonstop flight costs $99 plus tax (which can range from $50 to $90). Note that if you make a connection through one of Europe by Air's many hubs, you pay double—$99 for each flight to and from the hub.

Other budget-airline information sites—which have destination maps and recent airline news— include www.flycheapo.com and www.attitudetravel.com.

When exploring low-cost airlines, be creative. For example, let's say you need to get from Amsterdam to Rome. After a quick search, you may not find quite the flight you need, but you discover that a low-budget airline flies from Brussels to Rome for $130. It makes good travel sense to take a three-hour train ride from

Even if the name of your budget airline (such as Wizz Air) doesn't exactly inspire confidence, these carriers can get you to many destinations cheaper and a whole lot faster than the train.

Amsterdam to Brussels ($45 second-class) to catch the two-hour flight to Rome. The train from Amsterdam to Rome would have wasted 19 hours of your valuable vacation time and cost you $325. The train-plus-flight connection gets you there in half the time (including transfers) for nearly half the price.

All of these low-cost European airlines offer one-way flights without a cost increase or penalty. Consider linking cheap flights, either with the same or different airlines. But be very careful to leave plenty of time for the connection—since you're on your own if the delay of one flight causes you to miss another flight. This is especially risky if that "other flight" is your transatlantic flight back to the US. If you're using a budget carrier to connect to your US-bound flight, allow time to absorb delays—maybe even an overnight.

What's the Catch?

With cheaper airfares come new pitfalls. These budget tickets are usually nonrefundable and nonchangeable. Many airlines take only online bookings, so it can be hard to track down a person to talk to if problems arise. (Read all the fine print carefully, so you know what you're getting into.) Flights are often tightly scheduled to squeeze more flying time out of each plane, which can exaggerate the effects of delays. Deadlines are strictly enforced: If they tell you to arrive at the check-in desk an hour before the flight, and you show up 10 minutes late, you've just missed your flight—and have to buy a new ticket for the next flight. And, as these are relatively young companies, it's not uncommon for budget carriers to go out of business unexpectedly—leaving you scrambling to find an alternative.

Since budget airlines are not making much money on your ticket, they look for other ways to pad their profits—bombarding you with ads, selling you overpriced food and drinks on board (nothing's included), and gouging you with fees for everything, whether paying with a credit card, checking in at the airport, or carrying an infant on board. There are also expensive baggage restrictions. For instance, Ryanair charges a $50 fee for each checked bag (less if you pre-book online). If your checked bag weighs more than 15 kilograms (about 33 pounds), you'll also pay $30 per extra kilo. Don't assume your bag qualifies as carry-on—many budget airlines, such as Ryanair and Air Berlin, use smaller dimensions than other airlines. Virgin Atlantic has a 13-pound limit for carry-on bags. To avoid unpleasant surprises, read the baggage policy carefully before you book.

Another potential headache: Budget airlines sometimes use obscure

Budget Airlines Within Europe

These are just a few of the many budget airlines taking to the European skies. To discover more, check out www.skyscanner.net, or simply Google "cheap flights" plus the cities you're interested in. Note that new airlines appear—and old ones go out of business—all the time.

Airline and Contact Information	Hub(s)
Aer Lingus www.aerlingus.com US tel. 800-474-7424 Irish tel. 0818-365-000	Dublin (and other Irish airports)
Air Berlin www.airberlin.com US tel. 1-866-266-5588 German toll tel. 01805-737-800	Multiple German cities
bmi (and its subsidiary, **bmi baby**) www.flybmi.com and www.bmibaby.com US tel. 800-788-0555 British tel. 0800-788-0555	London (and other British airports)
Brussels Airlines www.brusselsairlines.com US tel. 516/740-5200 Belgian toll tel. 090-251-600	Brussels
Cimber Sterling www.cimber.com Danish tel. 70 10 12 18	Copenhagen (and two more Danish airports)
easyJet www.easyjet.com British toll tel. 0871-244-2366 From the US, dial 011-44-870-600-0000	Multiple cities, including London, Berlin, Paris, Liverpool, Geneva, Basel, Milan
Germanwings www.germanwings.com German toll tel. 0900-191-9100	Multiple German cities
Norwegian www.norwegian.no Norwegian tel. 81 52 18 15 From the US, dial 011-47-21 49 00 15	Oslo, Bergen, Copenhagen, and Stockholm

Airline and Contact Information	Hub(s)
Ryanair www.ryanair.com Irish toll tel. 0818-303-030 British toll tel. 0871-246-0000 From the US, dial 011-353-1248-0856	Multiple cities, including London, Liverpool, Glasgow, Dublin, Shannon, Brussels, Frankfurt, Milan, Pisa, Rome, Stockholm, Barcelona
SmartWings www.smartwings.net Czech toll tel. 900-166-565 From the US, dial 011-420-255-700-827	Prague and Budapest
Spanair www.spanair.com US tel. 888-545-5757 Spanish tel. 902-131-415	Madrid, Barcelona
Transavia www.transavia.com Dutch toll tel. 0900-0737 From the US, dial 011-352-2700-2728	Amsterdam
TUIfly www.tuifly.com German toll tel. 01805-757-510 From the US, dial 011-49-511-2200-4713	Multiple German cities
Vueling www.vueling.com Spanish toll tel. 807-001-717	Multiple Spanish cities, as well as Paris Orly
Wind Jet www.volawindjet.it Italian toll tel. 08-9965-6505	Catania, Sicily
Wizz Air www.wizzair.com Polish toll tel. 0703-503-010 Hungarian toll tel. 0690-181-181	Multiple Eastern European cities

For other options, consider www.airbaltic.com (Baltic capitals), www.fly airone.com (Rome, Milan, and Torino), www.flybaboo.com (Geneva), www .blue1.com (Helsinki and Stockholm), www.blueairweb.com (Bucharest), www.condor.com (Germany), www.estonian-air.com (Tallinn), www.flybe .com (southern England), www.helvetic.com (Zürich), www.flyniki.com (Vienna), www.meridiana.it (Torino, Verona), http://flights.thomson.co.uk (Britain), www.cityjet.com (London City Airport), www.wideroe.no (Oslo), and www.xl.com (Frankfurt and Paris).

TRANSPORTATION

airports. For example, one of Ryanair's English hubs is Stansted Airport, one of the farthest of London's airports from the city center. Ryanair's flights to Frankfurt actually take you to Hahn, 75 miles away. Sometimes you may wind up in a different (though nearby) country: For example, a flight advertised as going to Copenhagen, Denmark, might actually go to Malmö, Sweden, while a flight bound for Vienna, Austria, might land in Bratislava, Slovakia. These are still safe and legal airstrips, but it can take money and time to reach them by public transportation.

Budget Flights on Major Airlines

Faced with competition from budget airlines, some major European airlines (including British Airways, Lufthansa, Air France, Alitalia, SAS, KLM, LOT, and Croatia Airlines) have joined the discount-airfare game. In some cases, they simply sell a few seats on certain flights at a deep discount. In other cases, you must buy your transatlantic flight from the airline in order to take advantage of its intra-Europe budget fares. But it can be worth an extra $100 for an overseas flight in order to save on other flights within Europe. In some cases, you purchase an "air pass" (for $300–400)—a set of three or more flight coupons, each good for one nonstop flight. Be aware that with any air pass, a flight will "cost" two coupons if you need two connecting flights to reach your destination. Check with a travel agent for details.

The Fear of Flying

Like many people, I'm afraid to fly. I always think of the little rubber wheels splashing down on a rain-soaked runway and then hydroplaning out of control. Or the spindly landing gear crumbling. Or, if not that, then the plane tilting just a tad, catching a wing tip, and flipping over and bursting into flames.

Despite my fears, I still fly. The chances of being in an airplane crash are minuscule. I remind myself that every day 30,000 commercial planes take off and land safely in the United States alone. While airplanes do crash, entire years go by in which there are no passenger fatalities on any commercial American airline. The pilot and crew fly daily, and they don't seem to be terrified. Professional sports teams fly all over the place all the time. (If statistics allay your fears, see "Relative Risks: Fly or Drive?" on page 439.)

I guess it's a matter of aerodynamics. Air has mass, and the plane maneuvers itself through that mass. I can understand a boat coming into a dock—maneuvering through the water. That doesn't scare me. So I tell myself that a plane's a boat with an extra dimension to navigate, and its "water" is a lot thinner. Also, the pilot, who's still "flying" the plane after it lands, is as much in control on the ground as in the air. Only when he's good and ready does he allow gravity to take over.

Turbulence scares me, too. A United pilot once told me that he'd have bruises from his seat belt before turbulence really bothered him. Still, every time the plane comes in for a landing, I say a prayer, close my eyes, and take my pen out of my shirt pocket so it won't impale me if something goes wrong. And every time I stick my pen back in my shirt pocket, I feel thankful.

Wondering which airline to choose? For me, it doesn't matter; I have no favorite. If I arrive in Europe safely on the day I had hoped to, it was a great flight.

10. Train and Railpass Skills

The European train system makes life easy for the visitor. The great trains of Europe shrink what is already a small continent, making the budget whirlwind or far-reaching tour a reasonable and exciting possibility for anyone.

Generally, European trains go where you need them to go and are fast, frequent, and affordable. (They're faster and more frequent in the north and less expensive but slower in the south.) You can easily have dinner in Paris, sleep on the train, and have breakfast in Rome, Munich, or Madrid.

Most railpasses and many point-to-tickets—particularly for the fast trains—are not cheap. Digging the English Channel Tunnel, building a bridge between Denmark and Sweden, and adding bullet trains all over Europe cost money. It pays to know your options and choo-choose what's best for your trip.

You can buy a railpass (usually purchased before you go), point-to-point train tickets (generally bought in Europe but can be ordered in advance), or use a combination of both.

Railpasses

With a railpass, you can travel virtually anywhere, anytime, often without reservations. Just step on the right train, sit in an unreserved seat,

---

Free Guide to European Railpasses

Railpass details are confusing and tedious, but if you're planning to do Europe by rail on limited money, my annually updated *Guide to Eurailpasses* is very important. It's the only information source that compares rail deals available in the United States with rail deals available in Europe. My staff and I research and produce this guide annually. Our goal is to create smart consumers (as well as sell a few passes). It covers everything you need to know to order the best train pass for your trip, or to order nothing at all and save money by buying a pass or tickets in Europe. To view or download our free, up-to-date *Guide to Eurailpasses*, visit www.ricksteves.com/rail.

---

and, when the uniformed conductor comes, flash your pass. Fast, international, or overnight trains are more likely to require reservations, but despite that chore, a railpass is still a joy.

You get the most value out of a railpass when you use it for long travel days and in countries where train travel is more expensive. Use the map on page 110 to add up second-class ticket prices for your route. Compare the cost of the tickets to the price of the railpass that best suits your trip. If the costs are close, it makes sense to buy the pass (for the convenience of not having to buy tickets as you go).

Although the array of railpasses seems daunting, every pass has these features: it covers a specific geographical area (regional, country, or multiple countries); it has a fixed number of travel days; and it's either a consecutive-day pass or a flexipass (allowing you more flexibility to spread out your travel days). Some passes offer deals, such as Saverpasses (giving two or more companions a 15 percent savings) and some come in combination with car rental (rail-and-drive passes).

Comparing Railpasses

It's wise to compare and to think carefully about which type of pass will best fit your style of travel. For a multi-country trip, the options listed in

Eurailpass

"Saverpass" prices are per person for 2 or more traveling together. Youth passes are for travelers under 26 only, no discounts for companions. Kids 4-11 pay half of 1st class Individual or Saver fare; under 4 free. Prices listed are for 2010 and are subject to change.

EURAIL GLOBAL PASS CONTINUOUS

	1st Class Individual	1st Class Saver	2nd Class Youth
15 consec. days	$716	$607	$465
21 consec. days	927	787	602
1 month consec. days	1152	978	750
2 months consec. days	1626	1382	1058
3 months consec. days	2006	1711	1307

EURAIL GLOBAL PASS FLEXI

	1st Class Individual	1st Class Saver	2nd Class Youth
10 days in 2 months flexi	$844	$717	$551
15 days in 2 months flexi	1110	945	722

SELECTPASS INDIVIDUAL

1st Class	3 countries	4 countries	5 countries
5 days in 2 months	$453	$507	$559
6 days in 2 months	500	554	606
8 days in 2 months	593	647	700
10 days in 2 months	687	740	790
15 days in 2 months			1002

SELECTPASS SAVER

1st Class	3 countries	4 countries	5 countries
5 days in 2 months	$385	$429	$474
6 days in 2 months	427	473	515
8 days in 2 months	507	551	593
10 days in 2 months	582	627	670
15 days in 2 months			852

SELECTPASS YOUTH

2nd Class	3 countries	4 countries	5 countries
5 days in 2 months	$295	$329	$364
6 days in 2 months	328	360	393
8 days in 2 months	385	420	453
10 days in 2 months	445	479	512
15 days in 2 months			652

the **railpass price chart** on this page are a fine place to start.

Your most basic decision will be whether to buy a consecutive-day pass or flexipass. Which kind of traveler are you?

The intense, spontaneous, consecutive-day traveler. If you plan to travel nearly daily and cover a lot of ground, a consecutive-day pass is the right choice for you. You get unlimited train travel for the duration of the pass. If you have a 15-day pass, you can travel 15 consecutive days, taking trains many times each day. If you have a one-month pass, you can travel, for example, from April 26 through May 25. One-month passes last longer when started in a 31-day month. Eurail Global, BritRail, and Swiss passes offer this choice.

The relaxed, organized flexipass traveler. If you like to linger for a few days at various places, a flexipass is the better choice. Most passes are this type. You have a certain number of travel days to use within a longer window of time (for example, any 10 days within a two-month period). You can sprinkle these travel days throughout your trip or use them all in a row. You can take as many separate trips as you like within each travel day. A travel day runs from midnight to midnight, but luckily, an overnight train or boat ride uses only one travel day (the day you arrive).

Eurail Passes

Eurail Global Passes offer you unlimited first-class travel on all public railways in 21 European countries. These popular passes give you most of Europe

Eurail & Selectpass Coverage

*A **Eurail Global Pass** covers 21 countries, represented by the white bubbles. (BeNeLux is short for Belgium, Netherlands, and Luxembourg.) In contrast, the **Selectpass** offers more choices (all of the bubbles), but you select a smaller scope. You design your Selectpass by connecting a "chain" of any three, four, or five countries linked by direct lines in this diagram. Each bubble counts as one country, even though multiple countries may be included (such as Slovenia and Croatia).*

(except Britain and some of Eastern Europe) by the tail. Choose between the consecutive-day pass (ranging from 15 days to three months) or the cheaper flexipass (any 10 or 15 individual days in two months). Travel partners (2–5 people traveling together) save 15 percent with Saverpasses, available in consecutive-day and flexipass versions. Youths under 26 travel cheaper with second-class passes. Kids under 12 pay half the adult rate.

For the typical independent first-timer planning to see lots of Europe (from Norway to Portugal to Italy, for instance), the Eurail Global Pass is usually the best way to go. In a nutshell, you need to travel from Amsterdam to Rome to Madrid and back to Amsterdam to justify the purchase of a one-month Eurail Global Pass.

Eurail Selectpasses give you a selected number of "flexi" travel days in your choice of three, four, or five adjoining countries, whether connected by rail or ferry (for example, Denmark, Germany, and Finland; or Spain, France, Italy, and Greece). You can tailor this flexible pass to your trip instead of trying to make your trip fit a pass—for instance, purchase as few as five travel days to use in your selected countries over a period of two months. Discounts are available for children, youths, and

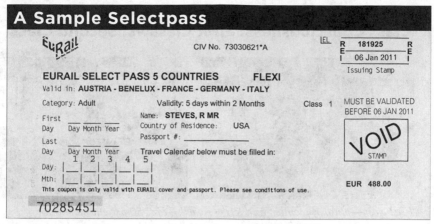

Don't write anything on your railpass before it's validated. When you're ready to use it, the ticket agent will fill in validity dates and your passport number, and stamp the validation box on the far right. Each day when you take your seat on the train, write down the date in ink (day first, then month) before the conductor comes around.

groups (of even just two people). Countries and number of days must be selected at the time of purchase and cannot be added in Europe. Note that available countries include one region not covered by the 21-country Eurail Global Pass (Bulgaria/Serbia/Montenegro)—but point-to-point tickets are relatively cheap in these countries if the extra zone doesn't "fit" on your pass. Travel in Britain, Slovakia, and Poland is not covered by Eurail Global Passes or Selectpasses, but those countries offer their own passes.

Be aware of **restrictions.** For instance, passes are good for use only in the countries listed or selected; so if your train goes through a country not on your pass, you must buy a separate ticket for that stretch in advance (or pay a fine for purchasing the ticket on board). So, if your pass doesn't cover Austria, but you take the Munich–Venice train route that cuts across Austria, it'll cost you about $40 in second class for the Austrian segment. To go from Berlin to Paris, you might pass through Belgium...and pay extra if your railpass covers only Germany and France. Railpasses do not cover any seat or sleeper reservations, though these extra costs may be required.

Also be aware of **bonuses.** Some boat, bus, and other non-rail rides are either free or discounted with any pass that covers the appropriate country (for international trips, the pass usually has to cover both countries to get full coverage). Free bonuses start a travel day of a flexipass, just as a train ride would. These include German Rhine boats, Swiss lake boats, and international ferry crossings (such as Ancona or Bari, Italy,

Class Consciousness: First Class vs. Second Class

First class—plusher, roomier, and less crowded—costs 50 percent more than second.

Normally, first class is configured with three plush seats per row (whether in a compartment or open-style seating), and second class has four skinnier, basic seats in the same space. Nearly every train has both first- and second-class cars, each going at precisely the same speed.

If you're on a tight budget, second class is plenty comfortable and makes lots of sense. Back Door travelers know that the nuns and soldiers are partying in second class. If you have the extra money, riding first class is less crowded and more comfortable (you'll sit with business travelers and railpass holders age 26 or older who had no choice). While individual first-class tickets cost 50 percent more

to Patra, Greece; and Sweden to Germany or Denmark). Discounted bonuses usually do not cost you a travel day, but travel must occur within the pass validity period. These discounts include the Ireland–France international ferry (30 percent off), the Brindisi–Patra international ferry (30–50 percent off), Germany's Romantic Road Bus (20 percent off), Switzerland's Jungfrau region private railway (25 percent off), and the Eurostar Chunnel train (special discounted fare varies).

Other Railpasses

Country passes focus on a single country or region. Virtually every European country has its own pass. These are especially important in Britain, which does not participate in the Eurail Global Pass or Eurail Selectpass. If you're limiting your travels to one country, a country pass is your best bet. Because short passes cost much more per day than long passes, a longer Eurail Selectpass is usually a better deal than patching

than second class, first-class railpasses generally bump your price up only 25–40 percent.

Still wrestling with the choice between first and second class? Sometimes the decision is made for you...

If you're considering a Eurail Global Pass or Selectpass: If you're age 26 or older, you must buy a first-class pass. Those under age 26 have the choice of buying either a second- or a first-class pass. For families traveling together, a first-class Saverpass for two costs the same as one first-class adult and one second-class youth, and keeps you together in first class.

If you're considering a non-Eurail pass: Most single-country, two-country, and regional passes are available in second-class versions for travelers of any age.

If you're under 26: Many passes are discounted for youths traveling second class. To be eligible, you must be under 26 (according to your passport) the day you validate the pass in Europe. Generally, children ages 4 to 11 get passes for half the cost of the adult first-class pass (kids under 4 travel free). Age limits vary a bit among different country passes.

Switching classes: Those with first-class passes may travel in second-class compartments (although the conductor may give you a puzzled look). Those with second-class passes can pay the 50 percent difference in ticket price to upgrade to first (not possible in Britain).

TRANSPORTATION

together several country passes. Several two-country passes are available for specific country pairs (e.g., France and Italy).

Rail-and-drive passes are popular varieties of many of these passes. Along with a railpass (Eurailpass, Eurail Selectpass, or individual country), you get vouchers for a few Hertz or Avis car-rental days. These allow travelers to do long trips by train and enjoy a car where they need the freedom to explore.

Money-Saving Railpass Tips

Consecutive-day and flexi railpasses offer a varying number of travel days. Once you've planned a route for your trip, fine-tuning your actual "moving days" will help you zero in on the best pass for your trip—and save you lots of money.

With careful juggling, a shorter pass can cover a longer trip. For example, you can take a one-month trip with a 21-day Eurailpass (about

$200 cheaper than a one-month pass) by starting and/or ending your trip in a city where you'd like to stay for several days or in a country not covered by your pass. On, say, a London–Rome trip, spend a few days in London, pay separately to take the Eurostar Chunnel train (not covered by any railpass) to Paris, sightsee in Paris for several days, then validate your consecutive-day pass when you leave Paris. Plan for your pass to expire in Rome, where you can easily spend a few days without the use of a railpass.

It can also make sense to buy a longer pass for a shorter trip. One long train ride (for example, $250 first class from Florence to Paris) at the end of a 25-day trip can justify jumping from a 21-day consecutive-day railpass to a one-month pass. Similarly, if you plan to travel for five to seven weeks, consider buying a two-month Eurail Global Pass for about $400 more than a one-month pass. Priced at just $22 per day, you can afford not to use a few days at the end.

Stretch a flexipass by paying out of pocket for shorter trips. Use your flexipass only for those travel days that involve long hauls or several trips. To determine whether a trip is a good use of a travel day, divide the cost of your pass by the number of travel days. For example, a 15-day, five-country Eurail Select Saverpass for about $900 costs about $60 per travel day. If a particular day trip costs significantly less than $60, pay out of pocket (and you'll have saved a flexi travel day for later in your trip).

Flexipasses are cheaper because they cover fewer days. Let's say you're planning a 21-day trip and choosing between a 21-consecutive-day Eurail Global Pass and a cheaper 10-days-in-two-months Eurail Global Flexipass. For about $75 more, the consecutive-day pass gives you the option to travel for 11 extra days, allowing you the freedom to take any train without wondering if a particular trip justifies the use of a travel day.

More travel days on a pass = cheaper cost per day. Compared to shorter passes, longer railpasses are cheaper per travel day. For example, for a 15-consecutive-day Eurail Global Pass at $675, you're paying $45 a day. With a three-month Eurailpass for $1,800, you're paying only $20 a day. Most one-hour train rides cost more than that.

One railpass can be better than two. To cover a multiple-country trip, it's usually cheaper to buy one Selectpass or Eurail Global Pass with lots of travel days than to buy several country passes with a few high-cost travel days per pass. If you decide to travel over a border (e.g., France to Germany) using separate France and Germany railpasses, you'll use up a day of each pass.

A Typical Ticket

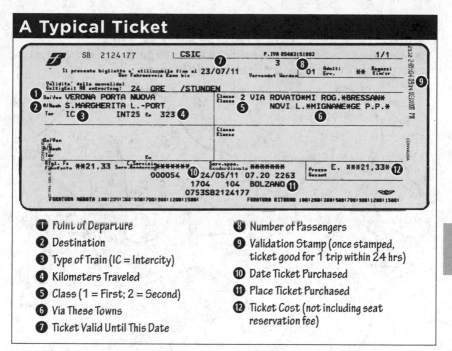

1. Point of Departure
2. Destination
3. Type of Train (IC = Intercity)
4. Kilometers Traveled
5. Class (1 = First; 2 = Second)
6. Via These Towns
7. Ticket Valid Until This Date
8. Number of Passengers
9. Validation Stamp (once stamped, ticket good for 1 trip within 24 hrs)
10. Date Ticket Purchased
11. Place Ticket Purchased
12. Ticket Cost (not including seat reservation fee)

This is a point-to-point ticket for travel in Italy, but train tickets across Europe have the same kind of information.

Point-to-Point Tickets

Point-to-point tickets can be a good budget option. Probably 10 percent of railpass travelers would have traveled more cheaply by buying tickets as they went. Point-to-point tickets are often your best bet in regions where rail travel is relatively cheap (such as Italy, Spain, and Eastern Europe) and for short travel distances anywhere.

Buying Tickets

You can buy train tickets either from home, or once you get to Europe. If your travel dates are set, and you don't want to risk a specific train journey selling out, it can be smart to get your tickets before your trip. If you want to be more flexible, or you're traveling at an off-peak time, you can keep your options open by buying tickets in Europe.

In the US: It's possible to purchase train tickets through your hometown travel agent, or at www.raileurope.com. But tickets purchased this way are usually more expensive than those bought in Europe. The websites for many European national rail companies allow customers to buy tickets online at the favorable European prices. Online tickets are sold for a specific date and time, and have strict refund restrictions, so don't lock

POINT-TO-POINT RAIL TICKETS: COST & TIME

This chart shows the cost of second-class train tickets. Connect the dots of your itinerary, add up the cost, compare it with a railpass, and see what is better for your trip.

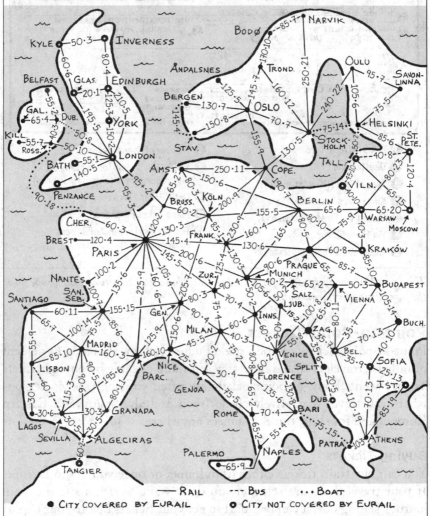

—— RAIL   --- BUS   ••• BOAT

● CITY COVERED BY EURAIL   ○ CITY NOT COVERED BY EURAIL

The **first number** between cities = **Approximate cost** in $US for a one-way, second-class ticket.

The **second number** = Number of **hours** the trip takes.

Important: These fares and times are for express trains where applicable and are based on European sources. Actual prices may vary due to currency fluctuations and local promotions. Local competition can cut the actual price of some boat crossings (from Italy to Greece, for example) by 50 percent or more. For approximate first-class rail prices, add 50 percent.

yourself into a schedule before you're ready to commit. Buying tickets on a European site can give you access to certain advance purchase discounts (explained under "Ticket Prices," later); if you wait until Europe to buy tickets, it could be too late to get these deals. However, each country's rail site has its own quirks—some are difficult (or impossible) for non-natives to use, and some don't accept American credit cards. For links to these national sites, see www.railfaneurope.net; for additional details on buying tickets on European sites, see www.ricksteves.com/rail.

In European Train Stations: You can buy tickets at the ticket windows, a travel office, or automated machines. Nearly every station has old-fashioned ticket windows staffed by human beings, usually marked by long lines of passengers waiting to buy tickets. Be sure you select the right line—larger stations have different windows for domestic, international, sleeper cars, immediate departures, and other types of tickets. Read signs carefully and, if you're not confident which line is right for you, ask locals or station attendants. (No matter which line you choose, it'll invariably be the slowest one.) When buying tickets, bridge any communication gap by writing out your plan: destination city, date (European-style: day/month/year), time (if you want to reserve a specific train), number of people, and first or second class.

If the station has a travel office (such as the *Reisezentrum* in major German stations) or travel agency, you might have to wait a bit longer to get your ticket (take a number as you enter)—but the staff is more likely to speak English, and can provide more patient guidance for a complicated itinerary.

Automated ticket machines usually have English instructions and are labeled with which types of payment they accept. Be aware that some machines won't take American credit cards (even if they claim to), or accept them only if you type in the PIN. If your card won't work, try inserting cash (if the machine accepts it), or buy your tickets at a window. In some places, you'll actually pay a surcharge for the privilege of buying your ticket from a person rather than a machine.

Europe is becoming automated. Given the high cost of labor, anyone insisting on talking to a real person at a ticket window will stand in long lines and pay a premium. Savvy travelers figure out the machines: Choose English, follow the step-by-step instructions, and get comfortable swiping your credit card and keying in your PIN.

It's often possible to buy tickets on board the train, but expect to pay an additional fee for the convenience. (If you're doing this, find the conductor to buy your tickets before he finds you; otherwise, your "fee" could turn into a much heftier "fine" for traveling without a valid ticket.)

If you want to buy your tickets in advance, you might be able to avoid trekking to the train station by visiting a neighborhood travel agency or a branch office for the national railroad. Sometimes this convenience comes with an extra fee, but it can save lots of time and hassle.

In some countries (such as France and Italy), point-to-point tickets must be validated by inserting them into a machine near the platform. If you have multiple parts to your ticket (for example, a ticket and a reservation), each one must be validated. Watch (or ask) locals and imitate.

Ticket Prices

European fares are based on the distance traveled. Each country has its own "euros per kilometer" formula. The speed of the train also affects the price (logically, a bullet train is pricier than a milk-run train). Increasingly, European rail companies are moving to a dynamic pricing system for their tickets (similar to airfares), where a fare can vary depending on demand and restrictions. A nonrefundable ticket purchased well in advance for a trip at an off-peak time can be substantially cheaper than a fully flexible ticket for the same journey during this morning's rush hour. Discounts can also help determine the price.

While each country has its own rules, here are a few factors that can affect fares:

• **Off-peak travel times** (such as mid-day or mid-week) can be cheaper than peak times.

• **Advance purchase** (at least a week or a month in advance) can save you money. On some trains (such as the Eurostar "Chunnel" train), there is not actually a "discount" for advance purchase, but the best rates sell out early.

• **Round-trip travel discounts** are available in many countries, sometimes in combination with advance purchase. In some places, a "day return" (round-trip in a single day) can be just a bit more expensive than a one-way ticket.

• **Children** ages 4–11 get ticket discounts in most of Europe (about 50 percent off, sometimes free with an adult), and kids under 4 always travel free on your lap.

• **Youths** ages 12–25 do not get many point-to-point savings, but a few discount cards exist.

• **Seniors** aged 60 and over can find a few more ticket deals, which may require a discount card purchased in Europe.

Note that, while many railpasses compel adult travelers to buy first class, travelers of any age can save 33 percent over first-class prices by purchasing second-class point-to-point tickets.

Unreserved, one-way tickets within a single country require your travel to be completed within a day, but allow stops and connections along the way. Unreserved international tickets (such as those commonly available in Germany, Austria, and Eastern Europe) allow two months to complete a journey with unlimited stopovers along the most direct route; if you want to reserve a seat or sleeper, you'll pay for it separately.

Seat Reservations

Making a seat reservation guarantees you a place to sit on the train. Reservations can be optional or required, depending on the route and train. Understanding the following guidelines can help you avoid an expensive mistake.

With Point-to-Point Tickets: You can purchase seat reservations when (and even after) you buy your ticket. Note that seat reservations are already included with many tickets, especially for the fastest trains (such as France's TGV, Eurostar Italia in Italy, Thalys through Belgium, or AVE in Spain), making it complicated for you to change your plans after you buy. Refund or exchange rules vary and are most restrictive if you buy the ticket at a discount.

With a Railpass: Railpasses cover 95 percent of all state-run trains in Europe, but they don't include seat reservation fees.

Required vs. Optional: Reservations are required for any train marked with an "R" in the schedule (e.g., high-speed trains such as France's TGV, Swiss scenic trains, and long rides in Spain, Italy, and Norway) and for *couchettes* and sleepers (see "How to Sleep on the Train," later). Internet schedules use the term "Reservation Compulsory" (while "Please Reserve" means it's optional). For many trains (local, regional, interregional, many EuroCity and InterCity trains, and Germany's speedy ICE), reservations are not necessary and not worth the trouble and expense unless you're traveling during a busy holiday period.

How Far to Reserve in Advance: Seat reservations, which cost from $5 to $35, can be made just a few hours in advance to up to two months or more (three months for TGV, Thalys, and other international routes from France; six months for Eurostar and Germany's City Night Line). Note that fast TGV trains in France and direct Paris–Italy day and night trains are popular routes that can sell out weeks ahead. All trains that require reservations also limit the number of seats available to pass-holders, saving the remaining places for full-fare ticket buyers.

It's wise to reserve at least several days ahead (or as soon as you're ready to commit to a date and time) for night trains, weekends, holidays, high season, routes with infrequent service, or any train you cannot afford to miss. It's also smart to reserve seats—even when they're not required—if you're traveling with a group (such as a family with children) that wants to sit together. Otherwise, you may end up scattered around the car wherever you can find free seats.

Where to Reserve: Whether you're buying point-to-point tickets or have a railpass, you can get seat reservations in Europe at train stations or travel agencies. Or, if you're ready to book well in advance, you can reserve through US travel agents who will deliver a printed reservation "ticket" to you. Reservations made in the US cost a little more. Most reservations are not changeable or refundable.

Europe's Train Stations

Train stations can be one of the independent traveler's best and most helpful friends. Take advantage of the assistance they can offer.

Train Information: Every station has a train information office eager (or at least able) to help you with your scheduling. I usually consult the timetables myself first and write down my plan, then confirm this with the information desk. Written communication is easiest and safest. Computer terminals offering all the train schedules are becoming more common. These are multilingual and can be real time-savers. Many even print out a schedule tailored to your trip.

Tickets: For tips on buying tickets, see page 109.

Tourist Information and Room-Finding Services: These are usually either in the station (in the case of major tourist centers) or nearby.

Whether old or new, bustling European train stations are temples of travel. Just pick a platform...and explore Europe.

City Name Variations

English Name	European Name
Athens (Gre.)	*Athina* in Greek, *Athenes* in German
Bolzano (Italy)	*Bozen* in German
Bratislava (Slovakia)	*Pressburg* in German, *Pozsony* in Hungarian
Bruges (Bel.)	*Brugge* in Flemish
Brussels (Bel.)	*Bruxelles* in French
Cologne (Ger.)	*Köln* (or *Koeln*)
Copenhagen (Den.)	*København*
Cracow (Pol.)	*Kraków*
Florence (Italy)	*Firenze*
Gdańsk (Pol.)	*Danzig* in German
Geneva (Switz.)	*Genève* in French, *Genf* in German
Genoa (Italy)	*Genova* (not Geneva)
Gothenburg (Sweden)	*Göteborg*
The Hague (Neth.)	*Den Haag*, *'S Gravenhage*
Helsinki (Fin.)	*Helsingfors* in Swedish
Lisbon (Port.)	*Lisboa*
London (Brit.)	*Londres* in French
Munich (Ger.)	*München* (or Muenchen) in German, *Monaco di Baviera* in Italian
Naples (Italy)	*Napoli*
Nuremberg (Ger.)	*Nürnberg* (or *Nuernberg*)
Padua (Italy)	*Padova*
Pamplona (Spain)	*Iruña* in Euskara (Basque)
Paris (Fr.)	*Parigi* in Italian
Prague (Czech.)	*Praha*
San Sebastián (Spain)	*Donostia* in Euskara (Basque)
Venice (Italy)	*Venezia*
Vienna (Aus.)	*Wien* in German, *Bécs* in Hungarian, *Dunaj* in Slovene, *Vídeň* in Czech, *Viedeň* in Slovak
Warsaw (Pol.)	*Warszawa* in Polish, *Warschau* in German

Pick up a map with sightseeing information and, if you need it, advice on where to find budget accommodations.

Getting Cash: Most stations have ATMs offering great rates 24 hours a day. Often the station's money-changing office is open long after others have closed (though the rates aren't as good). If you're in a jam, you can change money at some ticket windows as well.

Baggage Check: Most major stations have storage lockers and/or a luggage-checking service where, for about $2 to $5 a day, you can leave your bags. People traveling light can fit two rucksacks into one storage locker, cutting their storage costs in half. In some security-conscious train stations, lockers are no longer in use, and travelers must check their bags at a luggage-deposit desk—often after going through an airport-type security check. This service is expensive; you'll have to pay $5 to $10 to leave your bag. In extreme cases, they don't take laptop computers. (I recently spent a day in Marseille carrying around my laptop.) Allow plenty of time to retrieve your bag before boarding your train. Bag-check desks come with lines, can close for lunch in smaller stations, and usually aren't open all night. Ask about opening times, or look around to see if they're posted.

Waiting Rooms: Most stations have comfortable waiting rooms. Travelers with fancy tickets often enjoy fancy business or VIP lounges. The bigger stations are equipped with day hotels for those who want to shower, shave, rest, and so on. If, for one reason or another, I ever need a free, warm, and safe place to spend the night, a train station (or an airport) is my choice. Some stations boot everyone out from about midnight to 6 a.m. Ask before you bed down. Thieves work the stations in the wee hours. Be on guard.

Train stations often have good, long-hours grocery stores. This one in Vienna is open Monday–Sunday (i.e., every day), 5:30 a.m.–11 p.m.

Bus Connections: Train stations are also major bus stops, so connections from train to bus are generally no more difficult than crossing the street. Buses go from the stations to nearby towns that lack train service. If you have a bus to catch, be quick, since many are intended for commuters and are scheduled to connect with the train and leave promptly. If there's an air-

TRANSPORTATION

port nearby, you'll find bus or rail shuttle services (usually well-marked) at the train station.

Getting on the Right Track

Armed with a railpass, the independent traveler has Europe as a playground. Most will master the system simply by diving in and learning

from their mistakes. To learn more quickly—from someone else's mistakes—here are a few tips.

Many cities have more than one train station. Paris has six, Brussels has three, and even Switzerland's little Interlaken has two. Be sure you know whether your train is leaving from Interlaken Ost (East) or Interlaken West, even if that means asking what might seem like a stupid question. It's a safe bet that a city's stations are connected by train, subway, or bus. When arriving

Eurail freedom: My idea of good travel is being on this train platform. In five minutes, the train on track 7 is going to Berlin. In six minutes, a train will leave from track 8 for Copenhagen. And I've yet to decide which train I'll be on.

in a city (especially on a milk-run train), you may stop at several suburban stations with signs indicating your destination's name with the name of the neighborhood (e.g., Madrid Vallecas, Roma Ostiense, or Dresden Neustadt). Don't jump out until you've reached the central station (Madrid Chamartín, Roma Termini, or Dresden Hauptbahnhof)—ask fellow passengers or check your guidebook to find out which name to look for. You can also avoid arrival frustrations by confirming that your train stops at a city's main station rather than a suburban one. For instance, several trains to "Venice" leave you at Venice's suburban station (Venezia Mestre), where you'll be stranded without a glimpse of a gondola. (You'll have to catch another train to reach the main Venezia Santa Lucia station, on the Grand Canal.) On the other hand, it can be handy to hop out at a suburban station, if it's closer to your hotel than the main station. Many trains headed for Barcelona's big Sants station also stop at the Plaça de Catalunya subway station, which is near many recommended accommodations.

Some large stations have entirely separate sections for local trains and long-distance trains. It can take some time to find the part

TRANSPORTATION

TRANSPORTATION

"The Chunnel":
Speeding from Great Britain to France or Belgium

The fastest and most convenient way to get from Big Ben to the Eiffel Tower is by rail. Eurostar, a joint service of the Belgian, British, and French railways, is the speedy passenger train that zips you (and up to 800 others in 18 sleek cars) from downtown London to downtown Paris (at least 15/day, 2.5 hours) or Brussels (10/day, 2.25 hours) faster and easier than flying. The train goes 190 mph on either side of the Channel. The actual tunnel crossing is a 20-minute, black, silent, 100-mile-per-hour nonevent. Your ears won't even pop.

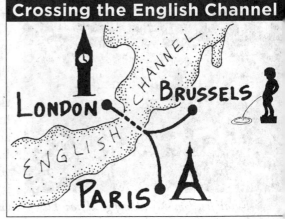

Crossing the English Channel

Eurostar fares (essentially the same between London and Paris or Brussels) are reasonable but complicated. Prices vary depending on how far ahead you reserve, whether you can live with restrictions,

of the station your train leaves from. For example, Madrid's Atocha station is divided between two parts: *cercanías* (local trains) and *AVE* (high-speed, long-distance trains). A Paris train station might have some tracks devoted to *Grandes Lignes* ("grand lines" to other cities), and others for *Transilien* (local milk-run trains to the surrounding Ile-de-France region). At Frankfurt Airport, regional trains depart from the *Regionalbahnhof*, while long-distance trains use the *Fernbahnhof*. Even more confusing, some large stations also have vast sections devoted to subway trains or regional buses.

Ask for help and pay attention. Managing in the stations and on the trains is largely a matter of asking questions, letting people help you, and assuming things are logical. I always ask someone on the platform if the train is going where I think it is. (Point to the train or track and ask, "Roma?") Uniformed train personnel can answer any question you can communicate. Speak slowly, clearly, and with caveman simplicity. Be observant. If the loudspeaker comes on while you're waiting for your

and whether you're eligible for any discounts (those who qualify include children, youths, seniors, railpass holders, and anyone making round-trips).

Fares can change without notice, but typically a one-way, full-fare ticket (with no restrictions on refundability) runs about $425 first class and $300 second class. Accepting more restrictions lowers the price substantially (figure $100–160 for second class, one-way), but these cheaper seats sell out quickly. And if you have a railpass, look into special discounted "passholder" tickets (about $80–160 for second class, one-way). For more details, visit www.ricksteves.com/eurostar.

Eurostar's monopoly expired at the beginning of 2010. Air France has already announced plans to run a competing high-speed rail service between London and Paris, but the economic downturn may put that on hold. Deutsche Bahn—Germany's state-run railway company—is negotiating with the Chunnel's owners about running direct, high-speed trains between London and Frankfurt or Köln.

Bus option: Crossing the Channel by bus and ferry takes more than twice as long as the Eurostar train at a fraction of the cost (London to Paris by Eurolines bus: about $30–65 one-way for economy fares booked at least three days in advance; 8 hours including ferry crossing, www.eurolines.com, British tel. 08705-143-219).

train at track 7, gauge by the reaction of those around you whether the announcement affects you. If, after the babble, everyone dashes over to track 15, assume your train is no longer arriving at track 7.

Scope out the train ahead of time. The configuration of many major trains is charted in little display cases on the platform next to where your train will arrive. As you wait, study the display to note where the first-class and sleeping cars are, whether there's a restaurant car, and which cars are going where. Some train schedules will say, in the fine print, "Munich-bound cars in the front, Vienna-bound cars in the rear." Knowing which cars you're eligible for can be especially handy if you'll be competing with a mob for a seat. When expecting a real scramble, I stand on a bench at the far end of the track and study each car as the train rolls by, noting where the empty places are. First-class cars are marked with a "1" on the outside, second-class cars with a "2." If there are several departures within an hour and the first train looks hopeless, I'll wait for the next.

The train on track 4 will stop at three Berlin stations. It was due to leave 10 minutes ago, but the sign notes it's 20 minutes später.

Never assume the whole train is going where you are. For long hauls, each car is labeled separately, because cars are usually added and dropped here and there along the journey. I'll never forget one hot afternoon in the middle of Spain. My train stopped in the middle of nowhere. There was some mechanical rattling. Then the train pulled away leaving me alone in my car...in La Mancha. Ten minutes later, another train came along, picked up my car, and I was on my way. To survive all of this juggling easily, be sure that the city on your car's nameplate is your destination. The nameplate lists the final stop and some (but not all) of the stops in between.

Every car has plenty of room for luggage. In more than 30 years of train travel, I've never checked a bag. Simply carry it on and heave it up onto the rack above the seat. I've seen Turkish families moving all their worldly goods from Germany back to Turkey without checking a thing. People complain about the porters in the European train stations. I think they're great—I've never used one. People with more luggage than they can carry deserve porters.

Luggage is never completely safe. There is a thief on every train

A handy diagram showing the configuration of your train (and at which settore, *or sector, each car will arrive) posted at the platform can help you decide where to stand while waiting for your train. Understanding this could make the difference between snagging a great seat...or having to hoof it to the other end of the train and scramble for what's left.*

This train started in Istanbul and will end in Wien Südbahnhof—Vienna's South Train Station.

(thieves' union regulations) planning to grab a bag (see Chapter 24: Outsmarting Thieves). Store your luggage within sight, rather than at the end of a train car. Before leaving my luggage in a compartment, I establish a relationship with everyone there. I'm safe leaving it among mutual guards. On longer trips, I clip and fasten my rucksack to the luggage rack. If one tug doesn't take the bag, a thief will usually leave it rather than ask, "*Scusi,* how is your luggage attached?"

Many train travelers are ripped off while they sleep. A $32 *couchette* (reserved berth in a sleeping compartment—described under "How to Sleep on the Train," later) is safer because an attendant monitors who comes and goes. Those sleeping for free in regular cars should exercise extreme caution. Keep your valuables in a money belt or at least securely attached to your body. You'll hear stories of entire train cars being gassed and robbed in Italy, Spain, and Eastern Europe. I think it's a myth— I wouldn't lose sleep over it.

Women need to be careful on all overnight rides. Women should use discretion when

Europe's trains are fast—pulling into the station with squashed birds on their windshields. You'd wait all your life to see a bird squashed onto the windshield of a train back home. I guess "DB" stands for "dead bird."

choosing a compartment. Sleeping in an empty compartment in southern Europe is an open invitation to your own private Casanova. Choose a room with a European granny or nun in it. That way you'll get a little peace, and Don Juan won't even try. A *couchette* (berth) is your best bet.

Breathe easy. While trains used to offer both smoking and non-smoking compartments, entirely smoke-free trains are now the standard in much of Europe. Smoking is not allowed on trains in Great Britain, Ireland, BeNeLux, France, Italy, Switzerland, Austria, Germany,

Norway, Sweden, and Poland. Smoking areas (clearly marked) are still offered on some trains in Spain (on trips 5 hours or longer), Denmark, Finland, and most of Eastern Europe. Smoking is also restricted inside stations.

Use train time wisely. Train travelers, especially Eurailers, spend a lot of time on the train. This time can be dull and unproductive, or it can be an opportunity to get organized and make plans for your next destination. It makes no sense to sit bored on the train and then, upon arrival, sit in the station for an hour reading your information and deciding where to go for hotels and what to do next.

Spend train time productively: studying, reading, writing postcards or journal entries, eating, or organizing. Talk to local people or other travelers. There is so much to be learned. Europeans are often less open and forward than Americans. You could sit across from a silent but fascinating and friendly European for an entire train ride, or you could break the ice by asking a question, quietly offering some candy, or showing your Hometown, USA, postcards. This can start the conversation flowing and the friendship growing.

Train Schedules: Breaking the Code

Learning to decipher train schedules makes life on Europe's rails easier. These list all trains that come to and go from a particular station each day, and are clearly posted in two separate listings: departures (the ones we're concerned with, usually in yellow) and arrivals (normally in white). Learn to use the 24-hour clock used in European timetables. After 12:00 noon, Europeans keep going—13:00, 14:00, and so on. To convert any time after noon, subtract 12 and add p.m. (16:00 is 4 p.m.).

In addition to posted schedules, most train stations have big schedule boards that flip up and list the next several departures. These often befuddle travelers who don't realize that all over the world, the same five easy-to-identify columns are listed: destination, major stops along the way, type of train, track number, and departure time. I don't care what language they're in; without much effort you can accurately guess which column is which.

In Munich's train station, departures and arrivals are clearly listed on easy-to-read electronic boards. Railroad staff is standing by to answer your questions.

Train-schedule computers (found across Europe) can save you many long waits in station information lines. Use them to understand all your options. Indicate your language, departure and arrival points, and rough time of departure, and all workable connections will flash on the screen.

17.26 ⊗3 X außer Sa 2.Kl	Schwabach 17.44 – **Roth 17.54**	2
17.28 ⊗2 2.Kl	N.-Frankenstadion 17.35 – Feucht 17.43 – Altdorf 18.00	3
17.29 ICE 1519/ ICE 1719 ♯	Augsburg 18.29 – M.-Pasing 18.57 – **München 19.09** ⊙	9
17.34 IC 2366 Sa, So*	Ingolstadt 18.39 – **München 19.37** ⊙ *auch 1.Nov	13
17.34 EC 24 ♯↑	*FRANZ LISZT* Würzburg 18.26 – Aschaffenburg 19.08 – Frankfurt (M) 19.41 – Frankfurt (Airport) 19.57 – Mainz 20.18 – Koblenz 21.10 – Bonn 21.40 – Köln 22.06 – Solingen-Ohligs 22.27 – Wuppertal 22.41 – Hagen 22.59 – **Dortmund 23.21** ⊙	7

Posted train schedules clearly mark the departure times, destinations, arrival times, and track numbers.

If you want to check schedules before you go to Europe, the Internet is your best resource (see "Online Train Schedules," later). Many railpasses come with a schedule booklet listing major connections. For a more comprehensive printed resource, consider *The Thomas Cook European Timetable*. Published several times a year (because schedules change with the season), it contains times for major stops on nearly every route in Europe, complete with maps (www.thomascooktimetables.com). Printed train schedules like these are a great help to the traveler if you can read them. In this chapter, you'll find a sample map and schedule to practice on. Understand it. You'll be glad you did.

Confirm your plans at the station. The person who knows for sure what's going on is the one at the train station information window. Let that person help you. He can fix mistakes and save you many hours. Just show your plan on a scrap of paper (e.g., Torino ⟶ Milano, 8:50–10:40; Milano ⟶ Verona, 13:05–14:27) and ask, "OK?" If your plan is good, he'll nod, direct you to your track, and you're on your way. If there's a problem, he'll solve it. Uniformed train employees on the platforms or on board the trains can also help.

Strikes can affect rail service anywhere in Europe (especially in Italy). They're usually announced long in advance in stations and the local news media. Most last just a

Know the local word for "strike": sciopero *(Italian),* grève *(French),* apergia *(Greek), and so on. They're a nuisance, but in many countries, a normal part of life.*

TRANSPORTATION

day. Anticipate strikes—ask your hotelier, talk to locals, look for signs—but don't feel bullied by them. In reality, sporadic trains lumber down main-line tracks during most strikes (preserving "essential service"), and the few remaining station personnel can tell you the expected schedule. While it's usually possible to get a refund for reservations affected by a strike, there are no refunds for partially used railpasses.

Online Train Schedules

More and more, travelers are ignoring printed or posted schedules in favor of user-friendly, extensive, and free online rail timetables. Each country's national rail company has its own website, but the one operated by German Rail (Deutsche Bahn) is ideal for virtually all of Europe: http://bahn.hafas.de/bin /query.exe/en. I use this site to plan my connections for almost every trip in Europe. While the site is designed for selling tickets, I've never bought one here—I just use it for the schedules.

Begin the search. Start with a station-to-station search. Enter just the city name, unless you know the name of the specific station you want (explained below). Remember to use European spellings. For example, Cologne is "Köln" in German, but you can spell it as "Koeln" to avoid having to figure out how to type ö. Likewise, instead

Deutsche Bahn's website provides a quick and convenient way to check train schedules in English for all of Europe. This schedule—from Paris to Venice—shows all the changes you'll have to make along the way, how long you'll have at each station, and the types of trains you'll be taking. You'll find this helpful tool at http://bahn.hafas.de/bin/query.exe/en.

of Munich or München, type "Muenchen." Prague is "Praha," Rome is "Roma," and Florence is "Firenze." (For more European names, see the "City Name Variations" sidebar earlier in this chapter; your guidebook should also explain this.) Also enter the date and time you'd like to travel, as close as you can guess. Schedules change seasonally, around June 10, September 10, and December 10 (though changes are often minor); this website posts updates as soon as they are available.

Refine the search. Many cities have several stations. After you click "Search," you may be asked to specify which station you want. For example, in Venice, you'll want the Santa Lucia station ("Venezia S. Lucia"), which is right on the Grand Canal—rather than the "Venezia Mestre" station on the industrial mainland. In Prague, you'll probably prefer the Main Station ("Praha hl.n."); in Vienna, you'll likely use the West Train Station ("Wien Westbahnhof"); and in Rome, most people want the Termini station ("Roma Termini"). Your choice of station will probably depend on the specific schedules or the location of your hotel—refer to your guidebook or ask your hotelier. To get the best use out of this site, figure out which station works best and request that station specifically in your search. If you don't specify, the computer may give you several options from different stations, or it may simply select its idea of the "most convenient station" (which may not be yours). For small towns, you might need to choose from several destinations with the same name. For example, there are many Rothenburgs in Germany, but the tourists' target is Rothenburg ob der Tauber. This can apply even to big cities. Frankfurt an der Oder—"Frankfurt (Oder)"—is a grim industrial town on the German–Polish border, while Frankfurt am Main—"Frankfurt (Main)"—is the bustling metropolis with the big airport. In Germany, your choice is likely to be followed by "Bahnhof" or "Bhf." (train station), or "Hauptbahnhof" or "Hbf." (main train station).

Review the schedule options. You'll be given a range of possibilities for your journey. Each one shows the start and end points (with stations specified), the times of departure and arrival, the duration, the number of changes, and the types of trains ("Products"). You can view other times for the connection, if available, by clicking "Earlier" or "Later" at the top and bottom of the "Time" column. Don't be surprised if no fare is listed in the "Standard fare" column—this site provides ticket prices only within Germany and for some international trips that originate in Germany.

Get more details. If you click the arrow next to the connection you're interested in, it'll show you a more detailed version, including the places where you'll have to change trains. If you click "Show intermediate stops," you can see each and every stop the train will make.

Check the fine print. "Compulsory reservation" means what it says, while "Please reserve" is recommended but optional. "International supplement" notes do not apply with railpasses.

No luck? This system shows the most direct and practical routes between two points. To design your own detour, add a "Via" (midpoint) city on the query screen. If, on the other hand, your destination is not covered at all (and if you spelled it correctly and used a current date), it likely doesn't have train service. For a comprehensive list of each country's railway sites, go to www.railfaneurope.net.

TRANSPORTATION

Scoping Out Schedules

Let's consider a typical train schedule in more detail. This one comes from the *Thomas Cook European Timetable,* but you'll see similar schedules everywhere. (For example, many major cities publish a free, complete timetable of all train departures from that station.)

First, find the trip you want to take on the appropriate train map. The number refers you to the proper timetable, which shows the schedule for trains along that route in both directions (a. = arrivals, d. = departures).

As an example, let's go from Turin to Venice (local spellings are always used:

Trains connect big cities, but also small towns—such as Manarola, in Italy's Cinque Terre.

Torino and Venezia). This is #350 on the map, so refer to table 350. Locate your starting point, Torino. Reading from left to right, you will see that trains leave Torino for Venezia at 7:08, 9:06, 15:08, 15:50, and 22:50. Those trains arrive in Venezia at 11:55, 13:59, 19:55, 21:25, and 5:08, respectively. Note that Venezia has two stations (Mestre and the more central Santa Lucia). As you can see, not all Torino departures go all the way to Venezia. For example, the 8:50 train only goes to Milan, arriving at 10:40. From there, the 10:50 train will get you to Venezia SL by 13:59. The 15:08 departure stops at Venezia Mestre, not actually in Venice. That's an inconvenience but not a big problem, since you can assume there are frequent connections from outlying stations to downtown. An overnight train is also shown: departing Torino at 22:50, arriving in Venezia by 5:08.

Train schedules are helpful in planning your stopovers. For instance, this table shows a train leaving Torino at 8:50 and arriving in Milan at 10:40. You could spend two hours touring Milan's cathedral, catch the 13:05 train for Verona (arrive at 14:27, see the Roman Arena and Juliet's balcony), and hop on the 19:10 train to arrive in Venezia by 20:35.

Each table has a schedule for each direction (only one is shown here) and a section explaining the many frustrating exceptions to the rules (not shown here). Symbols within the schedule also

Table 350 — TORINO - MILANO - VENEZIA

km		IC 645	IR 2007	IR 2009	IC 649	IR 2097	E 351	IC 651	EC 39	IC 657	IR 2107	EC 13	IR 2019	IR 2031	E 869
					⏳	⏳	✕		✕	⏳		✕			♦
0	Torino Porta Nuova 353 …d.	0708	0750	0850	0906	…	…	1108	…	1508	…	…	1550	2150	2250
6	Torino Porta Susa 353 …d.	0718	0800	0900	0915	…	…	1118	…	1518	…	…	1600	2200	2300
29	Chivasso 353 …d.	│	0816	0916	0933	…	…	…	…	…	…	…	1616	2216	2316
60	Santhia …d.	│	0834	0934	│	…	…	│	…	│	…	…	1634	2234	2334
79	Vercelli …d.	0802	0846	0946	1002	…	…	1202	…	1602	…	…	1646	2246	2346
101	Novara …d.	0818	0901	1001	1018	…	…	1218	…	1618	…	…	1701	2301	0001
153	Milano Centrale …a.	0850	0940	1040	1050	…	…	1250	…	1650	…	…	1740	2340	0040
		IC 647											IR 2109		
153	Milano Centrale …d.	0905	…	…	1105	1110	1210	…	1305	1705	1710	…	1810	…	0110
187	Treviglio …d.	│	…	…	│	1135	1235	…	│	…	1735	…	1835	…	0150
236	Brescia …d.	0952	…	…	1152	1206	1306	…	1352	1752	1806	…	1906	…	0239
263	Desenzano del Garda …d.	│	…	…	│	1224	1324	…	│	…	1824	…	1924	…	0257
278	Peschiera del Garda …d.	│	…	…	│	1235	1335	…	│	…	1835	…	1935	…	0309
300	Verona Porta Nuova …d.	1027	…	…	1227	1254	1354	…	1427	1827	1854	1910	1954	…	0331
325	San Bonifacio …d.	│	…	…	│	1311	1411	…	│	…	1911	…	2011	…	0347
351	Vicenza …d.	1100	…	…	1300	1332	1432	…	1500	1900	1932	1945	2032	…	0410
382	Padova …a.	1122	…	…	1323	1353	1453	…	1522	1922	1953	2004	2053	…	0433
411	Venezia Mestre …a.	1140	…	…	1346	1413	1513	…	1540	1940	2013	2024	2113	…	0454
411	Venezia Mestre …d.	1155	…	…	1349	1416	1516	…	1543	1955	2016	2026	2116	…	0459
420	Venezia Santa Lucia …a.	│	…	…	1359	1425	1525	…	1552	…	2025	2035	2125	…	0508
	Trieste Centrale 376 a	1345	…	…	…	…	…	…	…	2145	…	…	…	…	0910b

taken from Cook Timetable

indicate exceptions, such as which trains are first class or charge supplements. An X means you'll have to change trains; crossed hammers indicate the train goes only on workdays (daily except Sundays and holidays); a little bed means the train has sleeping compartments; an R in a box means reservations are required for that departure; and a cross means the train goes only on Sundays and holidays.

How to Sleep on the Train

The economy of night travel is tremendous. Sleeping while rolling down the tracks saves time and money, both of which, for most travelers, are limited resources. The first concern about night travel is usually, "Aren't you missing a lot of beautiful scenery? You just slept through half of Sweden!" The real question should be, "Did the missed scenery matter, since you gained an extra day for hiking the Alps, biking through tulips, or island-hopping in the Greek seas?" The answer: No. Maximize night trips.

Couchettes

To ensure a safer and uninterrupted night's sleep, you can usually reserve a sleeping berth known as a *couchette* (koo-SHET) at least a few days in advance from a travel agency, at the station ticket counter, or, if there are any available, from the conductor on the train. For about $32—a fraction of the cost of a cheap hotel bed—you'll get sheets, pillow, blankets, a fold-out bunk bed in a compartment with three to five other people, and, hopefully, a good night's sleep. On some popular routes, such as between Paris and Italy, reservations can sell out weeks in advance, making it worthwhile to commit before you even leave for Europe.

For $32, you can rent a couchette *(bunk bed) on your overnight train. Top bunks give you a bit more room and safety—but B.Y.O.B.& B. For much more on night trains in Europe, go to www.seat61.com.*

As you board, you'll give the attendant your *couchette* voucher and railpass or ticket. He deals with the conductors and keeps out the thieves so you can sleep uninterrupted. In case of a border check (rare in most of Europe these days), you'll either be woken up to show your passport, or your attendant will ask for your passport in advance and handle this task for you.

Some trains have more spacious four-berth *couchettes* (double rather than triple bunks for $50 apiece, may require first-class ticket on routes through France). Despite this exception, most *couchettes* are the same for both classes. When booking your *couchette*, you can request the top, middle, or bottom berth. While the top bunk gives you more privacy and luggage space, it can be hotter and stuffier than lower bunks and a

Car #126 from Copenhagen to Paris' North Station is second class (indicated by the large number 2), non-smoking (a crossed-out cigarette), and filled with couchettes *(the flat bed under the number 2).*

couple of inches shorter (a concern if you're six feet or taller). Compartments may be coed or single-gender, depending on the route. On the rare train that still permits smoking, you can request smoking or non-smoking.

Sleepers: Beds in two-bed or three-bed compartments range from about $40 to $150 per person. They are ideal though pricey for couples who want privacy. Single-sleeper costs range from $70 to $190.

Hotel Trains: If you're on a budget, avoid the fancy Spanish hotel trains. Running between Spain and France, Italy, and Switzerland, these overnight hotels-on-wheels are comfortable but expensive (even if discounted with a railpass: $105 per person in a quad, $160 per person in a double, and $245 or more for a single). Cheaper options (with a change at the Spanish border) exist on the Paris route.

Sleeping Free in Compartments

Shoestring travelers avoid a $32 *couchette* and just sack out for free, draping their tired bodies over as many unoccupied seats as possible. But trying to sleep overnight without a bed can be a waking nightmare. And even this level of "comfort" is not always free, since not all night trains offer standard seats—and many that do now require a $5 seat reservation. One night of endless head-bobbing, very swollen toes, a screaming tailbone, sitting up straight in a dark eternity of steel wheels crashing along rails, trying doggedly—yet hopelessly—to get comfortable, will teach you the importance of finding a spot to stretch out for the night. This is an art that vagabond night travelers cultivate. Those with the greatest skill at this game

They didn't rent a couchette.

sleep. Those not so talented will spend the night gnashing their teeth and squirming for relief.

A traditional train car has about 10 compartments, each with six or eight seats (three or four facing three or four). Some have seats that pull out and armrests that lift, turning your compartment into a bed on wheels. But this is possible only if you have more seats than people in your compartment. A compartment that seats six can sleep three. So if between 30 and 60 people choose your car, some will sleep and some will sit. Your fate depends on how good you are at encouraging people to sit elsewhere. There are many ways to play this game (which has few rules and encourages creativity). Here are my favorite techniques.

The Big Sleep: Arrive 30 minutes before your train leaves. Walk most of the length of the train but not to the last car. Choose a car that is going where you want to go and find an empty compartment. Pull two seats out to make a bed, close the curtains, turn out the lights, and pretend you are sound asleep. It's amazing. At 9 p.m. everyone on that train is snoring away! The first 30 people to get on that car have room to sleep. Number 31 will go into any car with the lights on and people sitting up. The most convincing "sleepers" will be the last to be "woken up."

The Hare Krishna Approach: I've heard of people trying this method—sitting cross-legged on the floor and chanting religious-sounding, exotically discordant harmonies, with a faraway look in their eyes. Most travelers who open the door to this scene will stare for a few seconds, then move on to another compartment. But be warned if you try this approach: You'll risk chanting the night away with five religious groupies who've joined you.

Using Reservation Cards to Your Advantage: Each compartment will have a reservation board outside the door. Never sit in a seat that is reserved because you'll be "bumped out" just before the train leaves. Few people realize that you can determine how far the people on a train will travel by reading their reservation tags. Each tag explains which segment of the journey that seat is reserved for. Find a compartment with three or four people traveling for just an hour or two, and for the rest of the night you will probably have that compartment to yourself. (However, some trains—such as the InterCity in Italy—no longer mark reserved seats.)

Remember that trains add and lose cars throughout the night. A train could be packed with tourists heading for Milan, and at 1 a.m. an empty Milan-bound car could be added. The difference between being packed like sardines and stretching out in your own fishbowl could be as little as one car away.

These tricks work not to take advantage of others, but to equal out

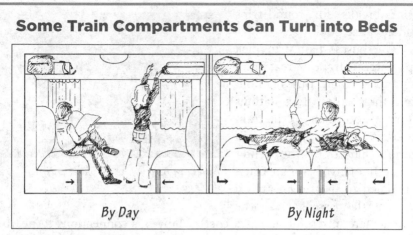

Some Train Compartments Can Turn into Beds

By Day   *By Night*

A Typical Train Compartment

For every night you spend on the train, you gain a day for sight-seeing and avoid the cost of a hotel. The more comfortably you sleep, the more you pay. But even free solutions can be manageable. Some traditional trains have seats that you can pull out to make a bed...assuming your compartment isn't too full.

the trainload. When all compartments are lightly loaded and people continue to load in, let the air out of your inflatable travel partner and make room for your new roommates. To minimize the misery on a full train, sit opposite your partner, pull out the seats, and share a single bed (and the smell of each other's feet).

Bus vs. Train

In most countries, trains are faster, more comfortable, and have more extensive schedules than buses. But in some countries—especially Greece, Turkey, and parts of Ireland, Croatia, the Czech Republic, Portugal, Spain, and Morocco—buses are often the better (or only) option. Bus trips are usually less expensive (especially in the British Isles) and are occasionally included on your railpass (where operated by the train companies, as many are in Germany, Switzerland, and Belgium).

Cheap, long-haul buses, such as Eurolines (www.eurolines.com), and hippie-type "magic buses," such as Busabout (www.busabout .com), can sometimes save you plenty over train fares. For example, Eurolines' priciest one-way bus fare from Amsterdam to Paris is $65, with advance tickets much cheaper (compared to $215 second class by train); from Barcelona to Madrid, it's $40 ($150 by train). You get price breaks for round-trips and advance booking.

Use buses mainly to pick up where Europe's great train system leaves off. Buses fan out from the smallest train stations to places too small for the train to cover. For towns with train stations far from the center (e.g., hill towns), buses are often scheduled to meet each arrival and shuttle passengers to the

Buses can help you reach places trains don't go.

main square (often for no extra cost). Many bus connections to nearby towns not served by train are timed to depart just after the train arrives.

Package bus excursions from big cities into the countryside, which are designed for sightseeing, can also serve as useful transportation. For ideas, see page 277.

Taxi Between Cities

While a budget traveler would generally never dream of hiring a taxi for a trip between cities, it can actually be a fairly good value. If you're headed somewhere that's a long train trip but a short drive away, a taxi can be an affordable splurge, especially if the cost is split between two or more people. Consider the time you'll save over public transportation (for example, one hour of sweat-free, hotel-door-to-hotel-door service versus several hours on public transit, including transfers to and from the train or bus station). Simply ask any cabbie what they'd charge (it could be an hourly rate, or even an off-meter flat rate—they know you have a cheap public-transit alternative and might be willing to deal if they want the work). Or ask at your hotel if they have a line on any taxi services that do the trip economically. See if you can find a driver who's accustomed to taking tourists on these trips. While not technically guides, these drivers often provide scant commentary on what you're seeing, and might even suggest some interesting stops along the way.

11. Driving in Europe

While most European travel dreams come with a clickety-clack sound-track, and most first trips are best by rail, you should at least consider the convenience of driving. Behind the wheel you're totally free, going where you want, when you want.

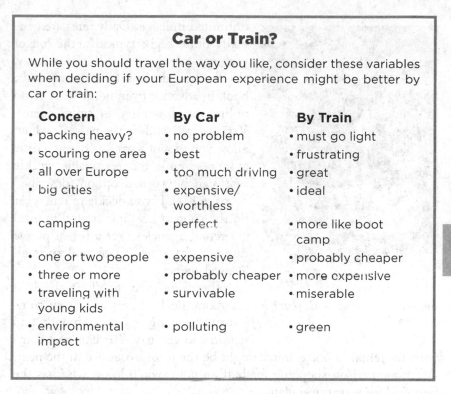

Car or Train?

While you should travel the way you like, consider these variables when deciding if your European experience might be better by car or train:

Concern	By Car	By Train
• packing heavy?	• no problem	• must go light
• scouring one area	• best	• frustrating
• all over Europe	• too much driving	• great
• big cities	• expensive/worthless	• ideal
• camping	• perfect	• more like boot camp
• one or two people	• expensive	• probably cheaper
• three or more	• probably cheaper	• more expensive
• traveling with young kids	• survivable	• miserable
• environmental impact	• polluting	• green

TRANSPORTATION

Driving runs circles around trains on countryside-focused trips. The super mobility of a car saves you time in locating budget accommodations in small towns and away from the train lines. This savings helps to rationalize the "splurge" of a car rental. You can also play it riskier in peak season, arriving in a town late with no reservation. If the hotels are full, you simply drive to the next town. And driving is a godsend for those who don't believe in packing light...you can even rent a trailer.

Every year, as train prices go up, car rental becomes a better option for budget travelers in Europe. While solo car travel is expensive, three or four people sharing a rented car will usually travel cheaper than the same group using railpasses.

Renting a Car

Renting a car in Europe tends to be more expensive and more complicated than in the US, thanks to byzantine insurance options and other additional fees (all explained in this section). But once you're free and easy behind the wheel of a European car, it's worth the hassle.

European cars are rented for a 24-hour day, usually with a 59-minute grace period. Cars are most economical when rented by the week with

Small car, big scenery...but shut the sun roof!

unlimited mileage. Daily rates are generally quite high; typically, the longer you rent for, the less it'll cost per day. For the best deal on long-term rentals, book in advance from home (easy to do online, or through your travel agent). Various rail-and-drive passes, which allow you to rent a car one day at a time at one-seventh the reasonable weekly rate, can be a good option (described on page 107). If you decide to rent a car on the spot, try calling around to local car-rental agencies (get a list of phone numbers from the TI), or book through a travel agency.

There's no way to chart the best car-rental deals. Rates vary from company to company, month to month, and country to country. The cheapest company for rental in one country might be the most expensive in the next. After comparison-shopping for half an hour, you'll know who has the best deal for your travel plans.

Most of the major US **rental agencies** (including Alamo/National, Avis, Budget, Dollar, Hertz, and Thrifty) have offices throughout Europe (each company's website and toll-free phone number is listed on page 140). You can request a quote from each company; or, to narrow it down more quickly, start by searching on a travel-booking site such as Expedia.com, Travelocity.com, or Kayak.com. Once you determine which companies seem to have the best rates for your trip, visit the companies' own websites to compare and book.

It can be cheaper to use a **consolidator,** such as Auto Europe (www .autoeurope.com) or Europe by Car (www.ebctravel.com). Consolidators compare rates among various companies (including many of the big-name firms), find the best deal, and—because they're wholesalers—pass the savings on to you. You pay the consolidator, and they issue you a voucher to pick up your car in Europe. However, there's a trade-off for the lower prices: If you use a consolidator, you're working with a middleman rather than directly with the vendor. This can make it more challenging to modify your reservation or register a complaint. Some of my readers have reported that consolidators are of little assistance in the event of a problem with the rental company. Don't count on the consolidator to intervene on your behalf.

Complicating your comparison-shopping are the many types of fees that can be tacked onto your base rental price (explained in "More Car-Rental Fees," later). You'll have to ask questions of the rental agency to determine your total cost.

Just as an "open-jaw" flight plan can save time and money, it can make sense to pick the car up in one city and drop it off in another. For maximum options, use a bigger company with offices in many cities. While dropping off in another country can incur an extra fee, there's typically no extra charge to do this within the same country—but always ask when you reserve, just in case.

When picking up your car, always check the entire vehicle for scratches, dings, and the gas level. If anything is not noted on the rental agreement, return to the counter to make adjustments. When you drop off the car, walk around the car again with the attendant to be sure there are no new problems. Otherwise, unexpected charges might show up on your credit-card statement. These are easier to dispute when the information is documented. On that same note, try to avoid dropping off your car after hours (at a drop box); it's best to finalize the rental and receive the paperwork in person.

Red Tape and Restrictions

Driver's Licenses and International Driving Permits: Your American or Canadian driver's license is all you need in most European countries, but some countries also require you to have an International Driving Permit (IDP), which provides a translation of your license—making it easier for the cop to write out the ticket. You can get an IDP at your local American Automobile Association or Canadian Automobile Association office ($15 plus the cost of two passport-type photos, www.aaa.com or www.caa.ca). The AAA is authorized by the US State Department to issue the permits; avoid scam artists peddling overpriced, fake international licenses.

Exactly where you need an IDP depends on who you talk to. People who sell them say you should have them almost everywhere. People who rent cars say you need them almost nowhere (though in some countries—such as Spain and Italy—it's possible you may be asked to show the permit to pick up your car). People who drive rental cars say the IDP is overrated, but can come in handy as a complement to your passport and driver's license. Those driving in Austria, Bosnia-Herzegovina, Greece, Hungary, Italy, Poland, Slovenia, and Spain are technically required to carry a permit, and could be fined if found without one. While that's the letter of the law, I've rented cars in dozens of countries without

Car Rental vs. Train: Comparing Rough Costs

When comparing the costs of renting a car, leasing a car, using a rail-pass, or buying point-to-point train tickets, consider these factors:
• the **duration** of your trip (this dramatically affects the cost of car rental, but is less important for train tickets or railpasses);
• the **miles** you cover (important for point-to-point train tickets, but irrelevant to railpasses and car leasing—except for gas costs; car rentals also usually come with unlimited mileage); and
• the **countries** you'll be visiting (very important for choosing a railpass, but less important for car rental or leasing—though you'll usually pay more to drop off in a different country than where you picked up).

Here are sample **per-person** prices for three different trips:

Means of Transport	2,000 miles in 3 wks*	4,000 miles in 5 wks**	6,000 miles 8 wks***
Railpass (first class)	$760	$1,000	$1,460
Train tickets (second class)	$900	$1,250	$2,800
Subcompact car rental (2 people)	$970	$1,430	$2,220
Subcompact car lease (2 people)	$780	$1,110	$1,510
Mid-sized car rental (4 people)	$590	$870	$1,330
Mid-sized car lease (4 people)	$560	$750	$990

Sample Itineraries
*2,000 miles in 3 weeks (see Best of Western Europe itinerary on page 720)
Amsterdam-Rhine Valley-Munich-Venice-Florence-Rome-Cinque Terre-Swiss Alps-Burgundy-Paris. The best railpass option for this route is a 10-day Eurail Global Flexipass.

an IDP—and have never been asked to show one. Even if you have an IDP, remember that you must carry your American or Canadian driver's license as well.

Age Limits: Minimum and maximum age limits for renting a car vary by country, type of car, and rental company. Younger and older renters can get stuck with extra costs, such as being required to buy extra insurance or pay a surcharge of $14–39/day (fortunately, there are usually maximum surcharge limits). Most companies will not rent a car to someone under 21, but those who are at least 25 years old should have no problem. Drivers over 70 may have trouble renting in the Czech Republic, Great Britain, Greece, Northern Ireland, Poland, Slovakia, Slovenia, and Turkey. If you're over 69, you'll pay extra to rent a car in the

Sample Itineraries (continued)
**4,000 miles in 5 weeks
Same as above, plus Barcelona, Madrid, Lisbon, Rothenburg, Provence, Tuscany. This trip is best with a 15-day Eurail Global Flexipass.
***6,000 miles in 8 weeks (see Whirlwind Tour on page 724)
Same as above, plus Scandinavia (Copenhagen, Bergen, Oslo, Stockholm), Berlin, Prague, Vienna, and more time along the route. The best railpass for this itinerary is a two-month (consecutive-day) Eurail Global Pass.

Fine Print
Rail: I've selected the most economical first-class railpass for each itinerary (since only travelers under 26 are eligible for second-class multi-country railpasses). These railpass prices can be higher or lower depending on the specifics of your trip (e.g., how many days of rail travel). Reservation fees (for overnight trains or seats on some high-speed trains) are not included. Assuming two or more people are traveling together, I've listed the "Saverpass" rates for railpasses; individual travelers will pay about 15 percent more.
Car Rental/Lease: To get these car-rental and lease rates, I've averaged rates from various consolidators and car-rental companies. Rates can vary dramatically—it pays to check around. These prices are for cars with manual transmission (automatic costs about $150 more per week). The prices in this chart include tax, the cost for dropping the car off in a different country ($100-300), and gas costs of about $5-7 per gallon at 35 mpg for smaller cars (30 mpg for mid-size cars). Rental-car rates in the chart also include CDW supplements (though not the "super CDW" to buy down the deductible) and fees for picking up at an airport (about 10 percent)—remember that leased cars do not come with these expenses. Costs for parking and tolls are not included (because they depend on the specific route and time spent in each place).

Republic of Ireland, where the official age limit is 75 (but people 75–79 can rent if they provide extensive proof of good health and safe driving). If you're considered too young or too old, look into leasing (explained later), which has less stringent age restrictions. (If you're traveling to Ireland, the closest leasing option is in London.) The student-oriented STA Travel is a good option for young renters (www.statravel.com, tel. 800-781-4040).

Crossing Borders: As Europe's internal borders fade, your car comes with the paperwork you need to drive wherever you like in Western and much of Eastern Europe. But if you're heading to a country in far-eastern or southeastern Europe that still has closed borders (such as Croatia, Bosnia-Herzegovina, or Montenegro), state your travel plans up front

In the mountainous northwest corner of Slovenia, you're just a few miles' drive from both Austria and Italy—and these days, you can cross those borders without stopping.

to the rental company when making your reservation. Some companies may have limits on eastward excursions (for example, you can only take cheaper cars, and you may have to pay extra insurance fees). When you cross these borders, you may be asked to show proof of insurance (called a "green card"). Ask your car-rental company if you need any other documentation for crossing the borders on your itinerary.

Some rental companies allow you to take a rental car from Britain to the Continent or to Ireland, but be prepared to pay high surcharges and extra drop-off fees (see "More Car-Rental Fees," later). If you want to drive in Britain, Ireland, and on the Continent, it's usually cheaper to rent three separate cars than one, thanks to the high cost of taking cars on ferries (between Ireland and Britain) and crossing under the English Channel via the pricey Eurotunnel (www.eurotunnel.com).

Car-Rental Expenses

To really compare car costs with train costs, figure your weekly unlimited-mileage rental rate, then add the following:

• **Tax,** clear and consistent within each country, is generally 18–25 percent (less in Spain, Ireland, and Luxembourg, and only 8 percent in Switzerland—but Swiss rental rates are that much higher). Tax can be higher for airport pickups.

• **CDW insurance supplement** (figure 20–40 percent extra, or about $15–35 a day—see page 142)

From sleek German autobahns to windy, cliffside Irish lanes, driving is a fun part of European travel.

Cost of Car Rental: About $750 a Week

Here's a very rough estimate for one week of car rental with unlimited mileage plus collision damage waiver (CDW) insurance. This is the average, ballpark weekly figure for the three-week, 2,000-mile trip listed on page 720.

Ford Fiesta (including tax): about $375/week
CDW: $15–35/day
Gas: $130/week ($5–7/gallon, 30 mpg, 100 miles/day)
Parking in big cities: $25–40/day
Freeway tolls: $4–9/hour (Mediterranean countries only)

• **Gas** ($130 a week, giving you about 700 miles; most rental agencies now rent "green" cars with still higher fuel efficiency—ask)
• **Tolls** for expressways in Italy, France, Spain, Portugal, Greece, and Croatia ($4–9 per hour); $13 to drive in downtown London; $40 for the toll sticker as you enter Switzerland, $10 each for toll stickers in Austria and the Czech Republic, $7 each for Slovakia and Hungary, and $20 for Slovenia.
• **Parking** ($25–40 a day in big cities, free otherwise)
• **Theft protection** (required in Italy, about $20/day)

More Car-Rental Fees

The fees noted above are just the beginning. Car-rental companies—including the biggies—have various quasi-legitimate ways to pad their profits, so it pays to be informed. Read this section carefully to know what you're getting into, and always read the fine print and ask a lot of questions when arranging your rental.

Insurance: Your biggest potential cost when renting a car is insurance—even if the rental price supposedly "includes" insurance. For all the details on this complex issue, see the following section.

Airport Fees: In some countries, you'll pay more to pick up a car at the airport or train station than in the town center (10–20 percent extra, or a flat fee of $30–150, depending on the destination and the company). When you're calling about prices, rental agents usually quote you this pricier airport pickup rate. Ask if they have a cheaper, downtown-pickup price. Some companies deliver the car to your hotel for free.

Refueling Fees: There can be additional charges for prepaying fuel costs. In Britain, Alamo/National requires renters to prepay for a full

Leading Car-Rental Companies

Consolidators work with major companies, comparing rates to find you the best deal. Or you can contact your favorite rental company directly.

Consolidators

Auto Europe	888-223-5555	www.autoeurope.com
Europe by Car	800-223-1516	www.ebctravel.com
Kemwel	877-820-0668	www.kemwel.com
Renault Eurodrive (leasing only)	888-532-1221	www.renaultusa.com

Major Car-Rental Companies

Alamo/National	877-222-9075	www.alamo.com
Avis	800-331-1212	www.avis.com
Budget	800-472-3325	www.budget.com
Dollar	800-800-3665	www.dollar.com
Hertz	800-654-3001	www.hertz.com
Thrifty	800-847-4389	www.thrifty.com

Before you commit, ask about whatever's applicable to your situation:

- weekly unlimited mileage rate
- age restrictions
- insurance costs
- CDW options (including "super CDW," or "zero-deductible" coverage)
- theft insurance (required in Italy)
- cost of adding another driver

tank of gas at the start of the rental, which means you can return the vehicle with an empty tank. In other countries (as in the US), this charge is usually optional. If you decide to pass on the prepaid option, and then forget to fill your tank before returning the car, you will be charged for a full tank of gas no matter how much is actually left in the tank. If you wait until you're actually at the rental office to look for a gas station, it can be stressful; since gas gauges are very forgiving, I start watching for a convenient fill-up point miles before I reach my final stop.

International Drop-Off Fees: It will generally cost an extra $100–300 to drop the car in a different country. You'll find exceptions, some happy (free) and some outrageous ($1,000+). The farther the distance

- drop-off fees within a country or in another country
- a list of offices in the countries you're visiting (consider the most efficient pick-up and drop-off points)
- whether it's cheaper to pick up the car at the airport or downtown

- if there is a covered trunk
- availability of extras, such as automatic transmission, child safety seats, or GPS
- restrictions on driving the car in all countries (particularly in far-eastern Europe)
- additional charges or local taxes, such as VAT (Value-Added Tax), an airport fee, or a mandatory refueling fee

Before you drive away, ask about:
- local laws you might not be aware of (for example, whether headlights are required to be on at all times)
- length of the grace period for drop-off (can be 30–59 minutes)
- how to use the wipers, alarm system, lights, radio, GPS, etc.
- what type of fuel the car takes (diesel vs. unleaded), the local term for that fuel type, and how to release the gas cap
- location of insurance "green card" and other paperwork
- making repairs and emergency roadside services
- changing a tire

between your start and end points, the higher the fee. While there's usually no fee to drop the car at a different location in the same country, it's always smart to double-check.

Automatic Transmission: Most rental cars in Europe have manual transmissions. Automatics can tack on an extra $100–200 per week—or, worse, may only be available if you upgrade to a bigger, more expensive car. Since supplies are limited, if you must have an automatic, you'll need to arrange it further in advance. Ideally, skip the automatic and brush up on your shifting skills. It's better to lurch through your hometown parking lot than grind your gears over the Alps.

TRANSPORTATION

Insurance Costs: The Collision Damage Waiver (CDW) Racket

When you rent a car, you are liable for a very high deductible, sometimes equal to the entire value of the car. There are various ways you can limit your financial risk in case of an accident.

Luckily, Bud paid extra for full insurance.

Car-Rental Company CDW: The simplest solution is to buy a collision damage waiver (CDW) supplement from the car-rental company. This technically isn't "insurance"; rather, it's a waiver: The car-rental company waives its right to collect a high deductible from you in the event the car is damaged. CDW covers everything except the undercarriage, roof, tires, and windshield. While each company has its own variation of CDW, it generally costs $15–35 a day (figure roughly 30 percent extra) and reduces the deductible, but does not eliminate it. Many rental companies have inclusive plans that come with both theft/loss insurance and a more reasonable CDW—ask. In general, it's cheaper to pay for this kind of coverage when you book than when you pick up the car.

A few years ago, CDW came with a low (or zero) out-of-pocket deductible and was a good value. But recently car-rental companies have dramatically increased these deductibles, with most now hovering at about $1,000–1,500 (or more, depending on the car type). So, when you pick up the car, the counter agent might try to sell you a second tier of coverage (called "super CDW" or "zero-deductible coverage") to buy down the deductible to zero or near zero. This is pricey—figure about an additional $10–30 per day—but it buys you peace of mind.

Since most of the major car-rental companies now come with these astronomical deductibles, the alternatives to CDW are worth considering carefully.

Credit-Card Coverage: Many credit-card companies offer their own type of zero-deductible collision coverage (comparable to CDW). By paying for your car rental with a credit card that offers this coverage, you can choose to decline the car-rental company's CDW coverage. Relying on credit-card coverage can be a hassle, but now that rental companies' CDW costs are stacking up, it can be worth it. Basically, if your car is damaged or stolen, your credit card will cover whatever cost you're liable for. Of course, restrictions apply and coverage varies between issuers. If you plan to use this coverage, carefully ask your credit-card company what kind of coverage they provide, the countries where the coverage is applicable, the maximum number of rental days they'll provide the coverage, and the types of vehicles they cover. Have them explain the worst-case scenario to you.

To use the coverage provided by your credit card, you'll have to decline the CDW offered by your car-rental company. Therefore, as far as some rental companies are concerned, you're technically liable for the full deductible (which can equal the cost of the car). Because of this, the car-rental company may put a hold on your credit card for the full value of the car. This is bad news if your credit limit is low—particularly if you plan on using that card for other purchases during your trip. (Consider bringing two credit cards—one for the rental car, the other for everything else.) If you don't have enough credit on your card to cover the car's value, the rental company may require you to purchase CDW insurance.

If you have an accident, the rental company will charge your credit card for the value of the damage (up to the deductible amount) or if the vehicle is stolen, the value of the deductible associated with theft. It's up to you to seek reimbursement for these charges from your credit-card company when you get home (you'll need to submit the police report and the car-rental company's accident report). Big, American-based rental companies are easier to work with if you have a problem.

Be warned that if you accept any coverage offered by the car-rental company, you automatically forego any coverage provided by your credit card. (In other words, if you buy CDW that comes with a reduced $1,000 deductible, don't expect your credit card to cover that deductible.) This may also be the case if you pre-book and prepay for a rental that already includes CDW and/or theft coverage.

Travel Guard CDW: Travel Guard sells renter's collision insurance at very affordable rates ($9/day plus a one-time $3 service fee covers you up to $35,000, $250 deductible, www.travelguard.com, tel. 800-826-4919). It's valid everywhere in Europe but the Republic of Ireland, and some Italian car-rental companies refuse to honor it. If your car-rental company doesn't honor this coverage, and you have to buy other coverage to replace it, Travel Guard will refund your money. Oddly, residents of Washington State and Texas aren't allowed to buy this coverage.

Remember that some comprehensive travel insurance policies include collision coverage if you rent your car through a travel agent. For details, see "Travel Insurance—To Insure or Not to Insure?" on page 38.

Leasing: Those needing a car for at least three weeks should look into leasing, which is tax-free and includes zero-deductible collision and theft insurance (see next section).

Exceptions: There are some exceptions to what I've described. If you rent a car in Italy, you're required to have theft insurance, and most car-rental companies' rates automatically include CDW coverage (which you sometimes can't decline). It's not unusual to decline CDW when you reserve your Italian car, only to find when you show up at the counter that you must buy it after all.

Car-rental companies in the Republic of Ireland are less amenable to letting renters waive CDW insurance in favor of credit-card coverage; some companies will only allow specific credit card brands to be used for that purpose. Check with your issuing bank to see if you are covered in Ireland, and bring written confirmation with you. Also unique to Ireland is that you sometimes have the option of buying down the deductible on your CDW at the time of booking (for about $15/day), rather than when you pick up the car.

Liability Insurance: It's unusual to purchase additional liability insurance when renting a car in Europe. With most European car-rental companies, any liability coverage you might need is already included in the price. But if you're concerned about this, ask for details when you rent.

The Final Say: Buying CDW—and the supplemental insurance to buy down the deductible, if you choose—is the easiest but priciest option. Using the coverage that comes with your credit card is cheaper, but can involve more hassle. If you're taking a short trip (but not in Italy or Ireland), the simplest solution is to buy Travel Guard's very affordable CDW. For longer trips, leasing is the best way to go.

Leasing and Buying

Leasing (technically, buying the car and selling it back) gets around many tax and insurance costs and is a great deal for people needing a car for three weeks or more. For trips eight weeks and longer, leasing can be more economical than buying a railpass. Leases are available for periods up to six months. Prices include all taxes, as well as zero-deductible theft and collision insurance (comparable to CDW), and you get to use a new car. Leased cars can most easily be picked up and returned in France, but for an additional fee you can also lease cars in the Netherlands, Belgium, Germany, Spain, Portugal, Italy, and Great Britain.

Europe by Car, which invented leasing more than 50 years ago, still offers good deals (for example, you can lease a Citroen C3 in France for as few as 17 days for $949, about $56 a day; www.ebctravel.com, tel. 800-223-1516). Renault Eurodrive offers similar deals (www.renaultusa.com). The longer you lease the car, the lower the price (a 60-day lease can be as inexpensive as $35 per day).

Although Americans rarely consider this budget option, Aussies and New Zealanders routinely buy used cars for their trips and sell them when they're done. The most common places to buy cars are Amsterdam, Frankfurt, London, and US military bases. In London, check Craigslist (london.craigslist.co.uk), the used-car market on Market Road (Tube: Caledonian Road), and look in London periodicals such as *Loot* (www.loot.com), which lists used cars as well as jobs, flats, cheap flights, and travel partners.

Campers: Consider the advantage of a van or motor home, which gives you the flexibility to drive late and just pull over and camp for free. Fairly cheap to run, these vehicles use diesel—about the same cost as gasoline, but with much better mileage (24–30 mpg average). For more tips on camping, see "Camping European Style" on page 229.

Behind the European Wheel

Horror stories about European traffic abound. They're fun to tell, but driving in Europe is really only a problem for those who make it one. Any good American driver can cope with European traffic.

Europe is a continent of frustrated race-car drivers. The most dangerous creature on the road is the timid American. Be assertive, observe, fit in, avoid big-city driving when you can, and wear your seat belt. For more tips, see www.ideamerge.com/motoeuropa.

Before you drive off, get to know your car. While you're still in the rental agency's parking lot, try out all the features and gadgets: turn on the radio, run the front and rear windshield wipers and sprayers, switch the headlights to high-beam, get comfortable with the gearshift, and so on. How do you change the GPS language to English? Do the headlights come on automatically with the engine? Does the car take unleaded or diesel—and how do you open the gas cap? Before leaving, get instructions for driving to your next stop (or at least to the expressway).

Drive European. After a few minutes on the autobahn, you'll learn that you don't cruise in the passing lane. Cruise in the right-hand lane on the Continent and the left-hand lane in Britain and Ireland.

And drive defensively. Be warned that some Europeans, particularly Italians, make up their own rules of the road. In Rome, my cabbie went through three red lights. White-knuckled, I asked, "*Scusi*, do you see red lights?" He said, "When I come to light, I look. If no cars come, red light *stupido*, I go through. If policeman sees no cars—*no problema*. He agree—red light *stupido*."

Learn the signs. All of Europe uses the same simple set of road symbols. Just take a few minutes to learn them. Many major rest stops have free local driving almanacs (or cheap maps) that explain such signs, roadside facilities, and exits.

You can drive in and out of strange towns fairly smoothly by following a few basic signs. Most European towns have signs directing you to the "old town" or the center (such as *centrum, centro, centar, centre-ville, Zentrum, Stadtmitte*). The tourist office, normally right downtown, will usually be clearly signposted (*i, turismo, VVV,* or various abbreviations that you'll learn in each country). The tallest spire often marks the center of the old town. Park in its shadow and look for the tourist information office. Avoid heavy traffic times. Big cities are great fun and nearly traffic-free for Sunday drives. Mediterranean resort areas are extremely congested on summer weekends.

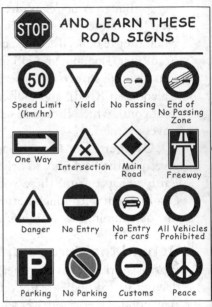

Use the Internet for route planning. Do some homework before getting behind the wheel. Various mapping websites suggest the fastest route between Point A and Point B, and offer fairly accurate estimates of how long the drive will take, barring traffic delays. Check www.via michelin.com, Google Maps (http://maps.google.com), www.theaa .com, or www.mappy.com. A GPS device (explained later) can also be helpful.

Navigate intelligently. Study the roads and major interchanges you'll be using before you set out. If you're headed for a small or mid-size town, know which big city is nearby to keep you headed in the right direction. In some countries, road numbers can help you find your way: For example, take road A-1 to London, then B-23 to Bristol, then C-456 to Bath. (But be warned that some roads can have more than one "number"—for example, the A-1 expressway can also be considered part of the B-23 highway.) In other countries, locals (and local signs) ignore the road numbers, so you'll navigate by town name. Signs can be color-coded: yellow for most roads, green or blue for expressways, and brown for sightseeing attractions. When leaving a city, look for "all directions" (*toutes directions, Alle Richtungen,* etc.) signs.

To save time, use the expressway. The shortest distance between any two European points is found on the *autobahn/strada/route/cesta*. Most international European expressways are designated with an "E" (similar to the "I" designation on American freeways), but they can also be named using national letters (for example, the main route between Paris and Lyon is known as both A6 and E15). Some prefer the more scenic and free national highway systems (*route nationale* in France). These small roads can be a breeze, or they can be dreadfully jammed up.

Better roads often come with tolls. It's free to drive on expressways in some countries, such most roads in Great Britain or Germany's famous autobahn. In other countries, you'll pay for the privilege. Sometimes you'll have to buy a toll sticker (usually called a "vignette") to display in your window. You'll pay about $40 for the highway permit decal as you enter Switzerland; about $10 apiece for Austria and the Czech Republic; $7 each for Hungary and Slovakia; and $20 for Slovenia. You can usually buy the toll sticker at border crossings, gas stations, and post offices (check to see if your rental car already has one that hasn't yet expired). If you don't have one, you'll soon meet your first local—in uniform. In most Mediterranean countries—including Italy, France, Spain, Portugal, Greece, and Croatia—you'll periodically encounter toll booths on major expressways ($4–9 per hour). Although tolls can add up (for example, figure about $90 to get from Paris to the French Riviera), the gas and time saved on European expressways justifies the expense. Note that in all these cases, if you're simply dipping into the country on secondary roads (such as around the town of Reutte, Austria, near Germany's Bavaria), you don't need to buy a toll sticker or otherwise pay for road use.

You'll pay to drive in some big cities. To drive in downtown London, you'll pay a $13 "congestion charge" (might increase in the near future). To drive in the "environmental zone" in the heart of Stockholm, Berlin, Frankfurt, or Köln, you'll pay a fee based on your car's emissions (this is also the case in London). Smaller, less-polluting models pay less or may be exempt. And you'll pay a toll to use the ring highways in Oslo and Bergen.

Big Brother is watching. In some countries, including Great Britain, traffic is monitored by automatic cameras that check your speed, click a photo, and send speeders tickets by mail. It's smart to know—and follow—the local speed limit. In Britain, these "camera cops" are clearly marked with a camera sign, but elsewhere you can get caught by surprise, particularly in Italy.

Car traffic is banned in many Italian city centers, including Rome,

Naples, Florence, Pisa, Lucca, Siena, San Gimignano, Orvieto, and Verona. Don't drive or park anywhere you see signs reading *Zona Traffico Limitato* (ZTL, often shown above a red circle). If you do, even briefly by accident, your license plate will be photographed (usually without your knowledge) and a hefty $150-plus ticket will be waiting for you at home. It can be an unpleasant ending to your trip. If your hotel is within a restricted area, ask your hotelier to register your car or direct you to legal parking.

Know the rules of the road. Many European countries require you to have your headlights on anytime the car is running, even in broad daylight. Nearly all countries forbid talking on a cell phone without a hands-free headset. Most countries require safety seats for children under age three, but a few—including Ireland and Germany—require boosters for kids under age 12 or under 4'11" (or under 4'5" in Sweden). In nearly all countries, children under 12 aren't allowed to ride in the front seat without a booster; a few ban kids from the front seat no matter what. Some laws are more obscure: Austria, Belgium, France, Italy, Norway, and Portugal require each driver to carry a reflective safety vest or kit with a reflecting triangle. Your car-rental company should be aware of these rules—just ask. Or you can research them on the US State Department website: go to www.travel.state.gov, click on "International Travel," then specify your country of choice and click "Traffic Safety and Road Conditions."

Get directions. When you call ahead to confirm your room, ask your hotelier for detailed directions on how to reach their place. If possible, figure out your arrival route on a map before you enter the city limits. (Many national or regional maps include basic city maps on the back.) While some cities helpfully post signs directing you to individual hotels, in many cases you're on your own.

Consider hiring cabbies. Even if you have a rental car, cabbies can be handy when you're driving lost in a big city. Many times I've hired a cab, showed him an elusive address, and followed him in my car to my hotel.

Go metric. Outside of Britain, you'll be dealing with kilometers.

To convert kilometers to miles, cut in half and add 10 percent (90 km/hr = 45 + 9 miles = 54 miles—not very fast in Europe). Do the math yourself: 140 km = 84 mph. Or 360 km = 216 miles. Some people prefer to multiply by 6 and drop the last digit (80 km/hr × 6 = 48 miles), though this can be challenging with large numbers (340 miles × 6 = ?). Choose whichever formula works for you.

Passing is essential. Americans are timid about passing. Be bold but careful. On winding, narrow roads, the slower car ahead of you may use turn-signal sign language to indicate when it's OK to pass. This is used inconsistently. Don't rely on it blindly.

Explore the roundabouts. In addition to intersections with stoplights, you'll encounter roundabouts, where traffic continually flows in

A roundabout: take a spin...or two.

a circle around a center island. While you'll see them sporadically throughout continental Europe (where vehicles move counterclockwise), roundabouts are everywhere in the British Isles (where traffic flows clockwise). These work wonderfully if you follow the golden rule: Traffic in roundabouts always has the right-of-way, while entering vehicles yield. For many, roundabouts are high-pressure circles that require a snap decision about something you don't completely understand: your exit. To replace the stress with giggles, make it standard operating procedure to take a 360-degree case-out-your-options exploratory circuit. Discuss the exits with your navigator, go around again if necessary, and then confidently wing off to the exit of your choice. When approaching an especially complex roundabout, you'll first pass a diagram showing the layout and the various exits. And in many cases, the pavement is painted with which lane to use if you're heading for a particular road or town.

Parking

Don't use a car for city sightseeing. Park it and use public transportation or taxis. City parking is a pain. Find a spot as close to the center as possible, grab it, and keep it. For overnight stops, it's crucial to choose a safe, well-traveled, and well-lit spot. A tourist's car parked overnight in a bad urban neighborhood will almost certainly be vandalized. In cities where traffic is worst, look for huge government-sponsored (cheap) park-and-rides on the outskirts, where a bus or subway will zip you easily into the center. It's often worth paying to park in a garage ($25–40 a day). Ask your hotelier for advice.

Gas

The cost of gas in Europe ($5–7 a gallon) sounds worse than it is. Distances are short, the petite cars get great mileage, and, when compared to costly train tickets (for the price of a two-hour train ride, you can fill your tank), expensive gas is less of a factor. You'll be impressed by how few miles you need to

Much of Europe uses cardboard or plastic "parking clocks" instead of parking meters. They often come with rental cars or can be bought cheap at gas stations, newsstands, or tobacco shops. Park, set the clock for the current time, and leave it on your dashboard. A street sign indicates how much time you have (according to this sign, parking is limited to 60 min, Mon–Fri, 8 a.m.–6 p.m.). The clock establishes when you arrived. In Germanic countries, where they're widely used, ask for a Parkscheibe.

travel to enjoy Europe's diversity. To minimize gas costs, consider renting a car that takes diesel, which usually costs about the same per liter but gets much better mileage.

Pumping gas in Europe is as easy as finding a gas station (the word "self-service" is universal), sticking the nozzle in, and pulling the big trigger. Gas prices are listed by the liter (about a quart, four to a gallon). As in the United States, most cars take unleaded, but diesel is still widely in use. In many countries, the pumps are color-coded to help you find the right kind of gas. When you pick up your rental car, be sure you know what kind of gas (and what color pumps) you need to use—this is often printed on or near the gas cap—and have them show you how to open the gas cap. Unleaded gas is called *petrol* or *benzine,* while diesel is known as *gasoil* or *gasol* (ask about the proper local term when you rent your car).

Freeway gas stations are more expensive than those in towns, but during siesta only freeway stations are open. Giant suburban supermarkets often offer the cheapest gas. Some pay-at-the-pump machines may not accept American credit cards (especially in the UK, France, and Scandinavia): Be prepared to pay inside.

GPS Devices

A GPS unit can be a helpful tool for navigating unfamiliar European roads...though I still prefer a good map and/or a trusted navigator. GPS devices (such as those by Garmin, Magellan, and TomTom) use satellite technology to track your precise location, and determine the best route for your journey using preloaded maps. A GPS unit leads you, turn-by-turn, from Point A to Point B with a small LCD map and (on better models) voice instructions.

You have three options for using GPS in Europe: You can sometimes get a GPS unit with your rental car or leased vehicle for an additional fee (around $15/day; be sure it's set to English and has all the maps you need before you drive off). If you have a portable GPS device at home, you can take it with you to Europe. Or, you can rent a GPS unit in the US to bring with you.

Many American GPS devices come loaded with only American maps. If you want to bring yours along, buy and upload European maps before your trip. (Check with your GPS device's manufacturer to find maps compatible with your unit, and for details on how to load them.) Note that some GPS mapping packages are designed for regional driving and might not have detailed street-by-street maps for a specific city; before you buy, be sure the maps will fit your travel needs.

Once on the road, don't trust your GPS blindly. Check the settings to see whether it's defaulting to the "most direct" or the "most scenic" route—a distinction that can translate to hours of extra driving. Some GPS units receive wireless traffic reports, then modify your route to help you avoid upcoming traffic jams; however, these automated detours onto back roads can wind up costing you even more time.

That's why, even if I'm using a GPS, I make it a point to also have a road map handy, and at least a vague sense of my route. One time, driving from St. Moritz to Lugano via Italy's Lake Como, I realized my GPS had just directed me right past the Lugano turnoff. Hitting the brakes and checking my map, I figured out it was aiming to send me on the freeway, then on a ferry across the lake. I stuck with the "slower" roads on the correct side of the lake...and got in an hour earlier. The lesson: GPS is most useful in conjunction with a good map and some common sense.

Joyriding

The British Isles are good for driving—reasonable rentals, no language barrier, exciting rural areas, and fine roads...and after one near head-on collision scares the bloody heck out of you, you'll have no trouble remembering which side of the road to drive on.

Other good driving areas are Scandinavia (hug the lip of a majestic fjord as you zip from village to village); Belgium and the Netherlands (yield to bikes—you're outnumbered); Spain and Portugal (explore out-of-the-way villages and hill towns); Germany (enjoy wonderfully engineered free-

ways much loved by wannabe race-car drivers); Switzerland and Austria (drive down sunny alpine valleys with yodeling on the stereo for auto ecstasy); and Slovenia (a tiny, picturesque country with many diverse sights hard to reach by public transit). The whirlwind, see-Europe-from-top-to-bottom type of trip is best by train.

12. Biking, Hitching, Walking, and Hiking

Biking

Biking is big in Europe. Riverside bike paths near Salzburg, Bruges, and along the Rhine have left me with top-notch memories. Some people travel almost exclusively by bike and wouldn't have it any other way. Rich Sorensen and Edwin McCain, who for years have gotten their travel thrills crisscrossing Europe by bike, helped me assemble the following tips on bicycle touring in Europe.

Wherever biking is fun, you'll find shops renting bikes and helmets.

Bicycle touring is cheap and rewarding. To see Europe on $50 a day, you don't need a time machine. What you need is a bike, farmers' markets, and campgrounds or hostels. Traveling this way, you'll not only save money and keep fit, but you'll experience a quieter side of Europe that travelers rarely see.

While bicycle touring is one of the cheapest ways to see Europe, most bikers choose to pedal for the sheer joy of it. Imagine low-gearing up a beautiful mountain road on a bike (smell the freshly mown hay), then picture an air-conditioned Mercedes with the windows closed and the stereo on (smell the upholstery). The driver might think, "Masochistic nut!"...but he also might notice the biker's smiling face—the face of a traveler who can see clearly from mountain to village and hear the birds singing, while anticipating a well-earned and glorious downhill run.

Determine if a bike is the best transportation for your trip. Define what part of Europe you want to experience, and then ask yourself some basic questions to see whether your bicycle will be your key to freedom or an albatross around your neck. Remember that it takes an entire day to travel the same distance by bicycle that you could cover in a single hour by train or car. Sixty miles per day is a high average. With bakery stops, Rich averages about 40. For example, if you have the entire summer free, you and your bike can cover a lot of ground through, say, France, Germany, BeNeLux, Switzerland, and Italy. But if you have a month or less, will you be content to focus on a single country or region? Given what you want to see in the time you have, is the slow pace of bicycling a worthwhile trade-off for the benefits? And finally, do you want to spend much more of your time in rural and small-town Europe than in cities?

Read a biking guidebook. Cicerone offers cycling guides to Britain (certain areas), France, France's Massif Central and Canal du Midi, the French Alps, the Loire Valley, Switzerland, the Danube, Spain, and the "Way of St. James" (Camino de Santiago). Consider *Cycle Europe: 20 Tours, 12 Countries,* by Jerry Soverinsky; John Powell's *Cycling the Rhine Route;* or Katherine Widing's *Bicycle Touring Holland with Excursions into Neighboring Belgium and Germany.* For Italy, try *Italy by Bike: 105 Tours from the Alps to Sicily,* by the Touring Club of Italy. For Britain, there's *John O'Groats to Lands End: The Official Cyclists Challenge Guide,* by Brian Smailes.

Adventure Cycling Association's *Cyclists' Yellow Pages* is a good resource directory (available annually in print or online), and their Cyclosource online store contains first-rate books, clothing, maps, and bike gear (www.adventurecycling.org, tel. 800-755-2453).

Take practice trips. Make sure you really enjoy taking long rides weighted down with loaded panniers. Try some 60-mile-a-day rides (5 hours at 12 mph) around home. If possible, take a weekend camping trip with everything you'll take to Europe. Know which tools to bring and learn basic repair work (like repairing flat tires, replacing broken spokes, and adjusting brakes and derailleurs). Ask about classes at your local bike shop.

Decide whether to go solo, with a partner, or with a tour. You can go it alone, with occasional pick-up pals on the way. As a loner, you'll go where, when, and as far and fast as you want. Traveling with a companion or two is more cost-effective and can be more fun, but make sure your partner's cycling pace and temperament are compatible with yours. Organized tours, which usually have sag wagons to carry gear, average an easy 30–40 miles a day. For information, check out Austin-Lehman Adventures (www.austinlehman.com, tel. 800-575-1540), Backroads (www.backroads.com, tel. 800-462-2848), Pack & Pedal Europe (www.tripsite.com, tel. 877-965-2064), or Randonnée Tours (self-guided tours only, www.randonneetours.com, tel. 800-242-1825). You can also check the ads in *Bicycling* magazine (www.bicycling.com) or *Adventure Cyclist* magazine (www.adventurecycling.org/mag).

Mountain biking is permitted on many trails.

When to go depends on where you go. Ideal biking temperatures are between 50 and 70 degrees Fahrenheit, so May is a good time to bike in the Mediterranean countries. Edwin started his five-week trip in Greece in May before it got too hot and then pedaled up through the Balkans to England. He had good temperatures all the way, but he also had headwinds (the prevailing westerlies). Rich and his wife, Risa, set out from Barcelona on a more leisurely spring-to-fall route that took them through France, England, Germany, Switzerland, Italy, and Greece, and they had not only ideal temperatures but also fewer headwinds.

Bring your bike from home. Although you can buy good touring bikes in Europe, they're no cheaper than here, and you're better off bringing a bike that you're sure is the right fit for you, your racks, and your panniers. Cyclists debate whether to tour on a thick-tired mountain bike or a touring bike with skinnier tires. Mountain-bike tires are much more forgiving on the occasional cobblestone street, but they are more durable than necessary for most European roads, and the chunky tread design will slow you down. In addition, straight mountain-bike handlebars will limit your hand positions, increasing fatigue on long riding days. If you already have a mountain bike, go ahead and take it, but add some bolt-on handlebar extensions.

Airlines have different bike-checking policies. Call your airline

A Traveler from the Past...or Riga

In Vienna, I met a man with a big gray beard, a toothy smile, and a battered bike. He looked like he had just dropped out of the 17th century. He seemed about my age (although a bit more weathered), spoke not a word of English, and radiated travel challenge, pride, and energy. To me, he was the embodiment of travel adventure in Europe. I tried to interview him, but he looked at me as if thawed out of some glacier. He just smiled and pointed to his flag. It was Latvian. He then pulled out a Magna Carta–like map with a red line tracing his route. His itinerary looked like the trip of a kid with ADD and a two-month Eurailpass—but he did

it all on a circa-1960 bike. I wanted to spend time with him. I wanted to talk with him. But I could only shake his hand and wish him (what I hope he under-stood was) well. While my "Europe through the gutter" days are long gone, he rekindled the inspiration I enjoy from those memories.

directly. More and more airlines are charging a fee for your bike and for the "bike box" they provide. If you carry on your bag, some airlines might let you treat your bike as your one allotted free piece of checked baggage. Most airlines require that bikes be partially disassembled and boxed. Get a box from your local bike shop, the airline, or from Amtrak (which sells cavernous bike boxes). Reinforce your box with extra cardboard, and be sure to put a plastic spacer between your front forks (any bike shop will give you one). Airlines require that pedals be taken off the bike; never leave them loose in the box. Attach them either to your rear rack or put them in one of your panniers. You can toss in your panniers, tent, and so on for extra padding, as long as you stay under the airline's weight limit. Bring the tools you'll need to get your bike back into riding form so you can ride straight out of the European airport.

Be prepared. Expect rain and bring good bikers' rain gear. A Gore-Tex raincoat can double as a cool-weather windbreaker. You'll also be exposed to the sun, so plan on using plenty of sunscreen. A bell is generally required by law in Europe, so you should have one on your bike—for giving a multilingual "Hi!" to other bikers as well as a "Look out, here I come!" Even if you never ride at night, you should at least bring a strobe-type taillight for the many long and unavoidable tunnels. Smaller Presta tire valves are standard in most of Europe, so if your bike has the automotive-type Shraeder valves, take along an adapter. To guard against unsightly road rash (and worse), always wear a helmet and biking gloves.

Obey Europe's traffic rules. Bikers generally follow the same rules as drivers. Some countries, such as the Netherlands, have rules and signs just for bikers: A bike in a blue circle indicates a bike route; a bike in a red circle indicates bikes are not allowed. Be alert; if you follow the blue bike signs, these required bike paths will get you through even some of the most complicated highway interchanges. Beware of the silent biker who might be right behind you, and use hand signals before stopping or turning. Stay off the freeways. Little roads are nicer for biking, anyway.

Use good maps. Michelin's Europe and individual country maps are fine for overall planning. In Europe, use local maps for day-to-day navigation. Michelin and Touring Club Italiano 1:200,000 maps reveal all the quiet back roads and even the steepness of hills. Don't be obsessed with following a preplanned route. Delightful and spontaneous side-trips are part of the spirit and joy of biking.

Taking your bike on a train greatly extends the reach of your trip. Every hour by rail saves a day that would have been spent in the saddle (and there's nothing so sweet as taking a train away from the rain and into a sunny place). To make sure you and your bike can travel on the same train, look for trains marked in timetables with little bicycle symbols, or ask at the station's information window. In some countries, trains that allow bikes require advance reservations.

Bike thieves abound in Europe. Use an improved Kryptonite-style bike lock to secure your bike to something sturdy. Never leave your pump, handlebar bag, panniers, water bottle, or laptop on your bike when you can't see it. Keep your bike inside whenever possible. At hostels, ask if there is a locked bike room, and, if not, ask or even plead for a place to put your bike inside overnight. Remember that hotels and many pensions don't really have rules against taking a bike up to your room. Just do it unobtrusively. You can even wheelie it into the elevator. Rich and Risa found campgrounds to be safe, but they always locked their bikes together.

Travel light...or camp. Unless you really love camping, staying in hostels or hotels makes more sense, since it frees you from lugging around a tent, sleeping bag, and cooking equipment. European campgrounds tend to be more crowded than American ones, so if you're willing to sacrifice privacy in order to mix with Europeans, camping can add a fun dimension to your trip.

Anyone can enjoy a gentle pedal through some of Europe's flat and inviting countryside.

A bike makes you more approachable. The most rewarding aspect of bicycling in Europe is meeting people. Europeans love bicycles, and they are often genuinely impressed when they encounter that rare American who rejects the view from the tour-bus window in favor of huffing and puffing through their country on two wheels. Your bike provides an instant conversation piece, the perfect bridge over a sea of cultural and language barriers.

Consider short-term rentals for bike-friendly cities or regions. Most of the tips here are for long-distance bike trips, but bikes can also be a fun change of pace if you're traveling by car or train. You can take the train from Paris to Amsterdam, then rent a bike for a few days to get around the city...and out into the tulip fields and windmills. In many countries (especially France, Germany, Austria, Belgium, and the Netherlands), train stations rent bikes and sometimes have easy "pick up here and drop off there" plans. For more on short-term bike rentals in Europe, see Chapter 19: Getting Around.

Hitchhiking: Rules of Thumb
Hitching, which Europeans call "auto-stop," is a popular and acceptable means of getting around in Europe. After picking up a Rhine riverboat

captain in my rental car and running him back to his home port, I realized that hitchhiking doesn't wear the same hippie hat in Europe that it does in the United States.

Without a doubt, hitching is the cheapest means of transportation. It's also a great way to meet people. Most people who pick you up are genuinely interested in getting to know an American.

The farther you get from our culture's determination to be self-sufficient, the more volunteerism you'll encounter. Bumming a ride is a perfect example. In much of rural Europe, anything with wheels and with room will let you in. You don't hitch; you just flag the vehicle down.

Hitching is risky. Although hitching in Europe is safer than hitching in the United States, there is an ever-present danger any time you get into a stranger's car. That, coupled with the overabundance of lawyers in the United States, means I cannot recommend it. Personally, I don't hitchhike at home, and I wouldn't rely solely on my thumb to get me through Europe. But I never sit frustrated in a station for two hours because there isn't a bus or train to take me 15 miles down the road. Riding my thumb out of train and bus schedule problems, I can usually get to my destination in a friendly snap.

Hitching can be time-consuming. Some places have 20 or 30 people in a chorus line of thumbs, just waiting their turns. Once I said what I thought was good-bye forever to an Irishman after breakfast. He was heading north. We had dinner together that night, and I learned a lot about wasting a day on the side of a road. You'll find that Germany, Norway, Ireland, and Great Britain offer generally good hitchhiking, while southern countries are less reliable.

Learn the gestures. The hitchhiking gesture is not always the outstretched thumb. In some countries, you ring an imaginary bell. In others, you make a downward wave with your hand. Observe and learn.

Crank up your good judgment. Feel good about the situation before you commit yourself to it. Keep your luggage on your lap, or at least out of the trunk, so if things turn sour, you can excuse yourself quickly and easily. Women should not sit in the back seat of a two-door car. A fake wedding ring and modest attire are indications that you're interested only in transportation.

Consider your appearance. Look like the Cracker Jack boy or his sister—happy, wholesome, and a joy to have aboard. Establish eye contact. Charm the driver. Smile. Stand up. Don't walk and hitch. Pick a good spot on the road, giving the driver plenty of time to see you and a safe spot to pull over. Look respectable and a little gaunt. Arrange your luggage so it looks as small as possible. Those hitching with very little or no luggage enjoy a tremendous advantage.

A man and a woman make the perfect combination. A single woman will get picked up quickly, but takes risks. Two women travel more safely and nearly as fast. A single man with patience will do fine. Two guys go slowly, and three or more should split up and rendezvous later. Single men and women are better off traveling together; these alliances are easily made at hostels. A man and a woman traveling together have it easy. If the woman hitches and the guy steps out of view around the corner or into a shop, they should both have a ride in a matter of minutes. (Dirty trick, but it works.)

Create pity. When I'm doing some serious hitching, I walk away from town and find a very lonely stretch of road. It seems that the sparser the traffic, the quicker I get a ride. On a busy road, people will assume that I'll manage without their ride. If only one car passes in five minutes, the driver senses that he may be my only chance.

Go the distance. To get the long ride, take a local bus out of town to the open country on the road to your destination. Make a cardboard sign with your destination printed big and bold in the local language, followed by the local "please." At borders, you might decide to choose only a ride that will take you entirely through that country. Use decals and license plates to determine where a car is from (and therefore likely heading). Every car has to have a large decal with a letter or two indicating in which country the car is registered. And in some countries (such as Germany, Italy, and Croatia), hometowns are indicated by the first few letters on the license plate.

Try to meet the driver directly. Find a spot where cars stop, and you can encounter the driver face to thumb. A toll booth, border, gas station, or—best of all—a ferry ride gives you that chance to smile and convince him that he needs you in his car or truck. Although it's easy to zoom past a hitchhiker at 60 mph and not feel guilty, it's much more difficult to turn down an in-person request for a ride.

Share-a-ride organizations match rides and riders. Start with To Share (particularly active in Spain, France, Italy, and Germany, http: //compartir.org), which lists ride possibilities in over a dozen European countries. Look for Mitfahrzentralen in Germany (www.mitfahren.org), FreeWheelers (www.freewheelers.co.uk) and Car-Pooling.com (www.car-pooling.com) in Britain, and Taxistop in Belgium (also features deals on ferries, www.taxistop.be). You may pay a small amount to join, and you help with gas expenses, but it works well and is much cheaper than train travel. Also ask about rides at student tourist information centers.

Informal ride services are posted on college and hostel bulletin boards all over Europe.

Hitching can become the destination. With the "hitch when you can't get a bus or train" approach, you'll find yourself walking down lovely rural roads and getting rides from safe and friendly small-town folk. I can recall some "it's great to be alive and on the road" days riding my thumb from tiny town to waterfall to desolate Celtic graveyard to coastal village and remembering each ride as much as the destinations. Especially in Ireland, I've found so much fun in the front seat that I've driven right by my planned destination to carry on with the conversation. In rural Ireland, I'd stand on the most desolate road in Connemara and hitch whichever way the car was coming. As I hopped in the driver would ask, "Where ya goin'?" I'd say, "Ireland."

Walking (and Dodging)

You'll walk a lot in Europe. It's a great way to see cities, towns, and the countryside. Walking tours offer the most intimate look at a city or town. A walker compliments the place she walks through by her interest, and will be received warmly. Many areas, from the mountains to the beaches, are best seen on foot.

Thanks to well-maintained trails, walking in the Dolomites can be a walk in the park—with better scenery.

Travelers who make walking a focus of their trip will find several series of books just for them, published by Lonely Planet (on Britain, Ireland, Italy, Scotland, and Spain, www.lonelyplanet.com), Sunflower Books (detailed guides for destinations throughout Europe, www.sunflowerbooks.co.uk), Interlink Books (Independent Walker's guides to France, Britain, and Ireland, www.interlinkbooks.com), Cicerone Press (trekking guides for many European countries, www.cicerone.co.uk), and Pili Pala Press (*Walking in Portugal* and *Walking the Camino de Santiago*, www.pilipala press.com).

Be on your toes: Walking in cities can be dangerous. More than 300 pedestrians are run down on the streets of Paris each year. The drivers are crazy, and politeness has no place on the roads of Europe. Cross carefully, but if you wait for a break in the traffic, you may never get a chance to cross the street. Look for a pedestrian underpass or, when all else fails, find a heavyset local person and just follow him like a shadow—one busy lane at a time—across that seemingly impassable street.

Runners and joggers can enjoy a good early morning town or city tour in addition to the exercise they get. Hotel receptionists usually know a good running route. Remember to carry identification and your hotel card with you.

Hiking

Imagine hiking along a ridge high in the Swiss Alps. On one side of you, lakes stretch all the way to Germany. On the other stands the greatest mountain panorama in Europe—the Eiger, Mönch, and Jungfrau. And

up ahead you hear the long, legato tones of an alphorn, announcing that a helicopter-stocked mountain hut is open, it's just around the corner...and the coffee schnapps is on.

Hiking in Europe is a joy. Travelers explore entire regions on foot. Switzerland's Jungfrau is an exciting sight from a hotel's terrace café, but those who hike the region enjoy nature's very own striptease as the mountain reveals herself in an endless string of powerful poses.

Romantics commune with nature from Norway's fjords to the English lakes to the Alps to the Dalmatian Coast. Trails are generally well-kept and carefully marked. Very precise maps (1:25,000 scale) are readily available.

You could walk through the Alps for weeks, sleeping in mountain huts, and never come out of the mountains. You're never more than a day's hike from a mountain village, where you can replenish your food supply or enjoy a hotel bed and a restaurant meal. Most alpine trails are free of snow by July, and lifts take less rugged visitors to the top in a sweat-free flash.

Throughout the Alps, trail markings are both handy and humiliating. Handy, because they show hours to hike rather than miles to walk to various destinations. Humiliating, because these times are clocked by local senior citizens. You'll know what I mean after your first hike.

If you prefer organized walks, look for Volksmarches (www.ivv -web.org). These 10-kilometer-or-longer walks are particularly popular in Germanic countries, involve lots of locals, and end with refreshments and socializing. Ask your hotel or the local tourist office for details.

Alpine trail signs show where you are, the altitude in meters, and how long in hours and minutes it takes to hike to nearby points.

Do some research before you leave. Buy the most appropriate hiking guidebook. Ask for maps and advice from the National Tourist Offices (for a list of tourist offices, see Chapter 3: Gathering Information).

TRANSPORTATION

MONEY

13. Money

I cashed my last traveler's check years ago. And I haven't stepped into a European bank in ages. Now, I get my cash from ATMs.

Euros

Eighteen European countries—and more than 330 million people—use the same currency. Using euros, tourists and locals can easily compare prices of goods between countries. And we no longer lose money or time changing money at borders.

Not all European countries have switched to euros. As of now, major

€uroland

Use euros in €uroland: Austria, Belgium, Cyprus, Finland, France, Germany, Greece, Ireland, Italy, Luxembourg, Malta, the Netherlands, Portugal, Slovakia, Slovenia, and Spain. Even though Montenegro and Kosovo are not in the EU, they use the euro as their official currency. Other €astern €uropean additions (such as Bulgaria, the Czech Republic, Estonia, Hungary, Latvia, Lithuania, Poland, and Romania) hope to adopt the euro sometime in the next several years.

holdouts include the United Kingdom, Denmark, Norway, Sweden, Switzerland, and Croatia. Each of these countries has its reasons for choosing not to use euros (for example, the Swiss are protecting their lucrative secret-banking tradition, which would disappear with the transparency that adopting the euro would require). Meanwhile, several Eastern European countries that have joined the EU—including the Czech Republic, Poland, Hungary, and the Baltic States—are working hard to satisfy requirements that will allow them to adopt the euro in the future. For now, these countries still use their traditional currencies.

Even in some non-Euroland countries, the euro is commonly used. For example, some Swiss ATMs give euros, most prices are listed in both Swiss francs and euros, and travelers can get by in that country with euro cash. But if you pay in euros, you'll get a rotten exchange rate. Ideally, if you're in the country for more than a few hours, stow your euros and get some local cash instead.

How to Pay: Plastic or Cash?

How should you pay for your day-to-day expenses in Europe: with a credit or debit card, or with cash from ATMs? Even if you use plastic for every little purchase at home, you might prefer to finance most of your European trip with cash.

In Europe, I use my credit card to book hotel reservations by phone, make major purchases (such as car rentals, plane tickets, and long hotel stays), and pay for things near the end of my trip (to avoid another visit to the ATM). If you'll be shopping a lot or settling bills at pricey business-class hotels, you might use your credit card more than I do—but you'll still be better off using cash for smaller purchases.

Because merchants pay sky-high commissions to credit-card companies, small European businesses (hotels, gift shops, and more) often prefer you to pay in cash. (Cash payments also allow them to avoid reporting—and being taxed on—all of their income.) Vendors might offer you a discount for paying with cash, or they might not accept credit cards at all.

To guard against identity theft, it's safer to minimize debit- and credit-card use; the less you use your cards, the less likely your information will be stolen. And in countries where chip-and-PIN cards are common (explained later, under "Chip-and-PIN Cards"), paying with cash helps you avoid the possibility that your credit card won't be accepted.

A dependence on plastic reshapes the Europe you experience. Pedro's Pension, the friendly guide at the cathedral, and most merchants in the market don't take credit cards. Going through the Back Door requires hard local cash.

Cash

Bring along some US dollars. While you won't use it for day-to-day purchases, American cash in your money belt comes in handy for emergencies—such as when banks go on strike or your ATM card stops working. I carry several hundred US dollars as a backup (in denominations of easy-to-cash 20s). I've been in Greece and Ireland when every bank went on strike, shutting down without warning. But hard cash is hard cash. People always know roughly what a dollar is worth, and you can always sell it.

Leave the traveler's checks at home. They're a waste of time (long lines at slow banks) and money (fees to get them, fees to cash them). ATMs are the way to go.

Use local money. Many Americans exclaim gleefully, "Gee, they accept dollars! There's no need to change money." Without knowing it, they're changing money—at a lousy rate—every time they buy something with their dollars. Anyone on a budget can stretch it by using local cash.

Figure out the money. You can check the latest exchange rate with the Currency Converter at www.oanda.com. To "ugly Americans,"

For information about using traveler's checks...see the 1995 edition of this book.

foreign money is "funny money." They never figure it out, get no respect from the locals, and are constantly ripped off. Local currencies are all logical. Each system is decimalized just like ours. There are a hundred "little ones" (cents, pence, groszy, stotinki) in every "big one" (euro, pound, złoty, lev). Only the names have been changed—to confuse the tourist. Examine the coins in your pocket soon after you arrive, and in two minutes you'll be comfortable with the "nickels, dimes, and quarters" of each new currency.

You don't need to constantly consult a currency convertor. Very roughly figure out what the unit of currency (euros, kroner, Swiss francs, or whatever) is worth in American dollars. For example, let's say the exchange rate is €1 = $1.25. If a strudel costs €5, then it costs five times $1.25, or about $6.25. Ten euros is about $12.50, and €200 = $250 (200 × $1.25, or 200 plus one-fourth). Quiz yourself. Soon it'll be second nature. Survival on a budget is easier when you're comfortable with the local currency.

Assume you'll be shortchanged. In banks, restaurants, at ticket booths, everywhere—expect to be shortchanged if you don't do your own figuring. Some people who spend their lives sitting in booths for eight hours a day taking money from strangers have no problem stealing from dumb tourists who don't know the local currency. For 10 minutes I observed a man in the Rome subway shortchanging half of the tourists who went through his turnstile. Half of those shortchanged caught him and got their correct change with apologies. Overall, about 25 percent didn't notice and went home saying, *"Mamma mia,* Italy is really expensive."

Paper money of any country is good at banks anywhere. Dollars are not sacred. If you leave Norway with paper money, that 100-kroner note is just as convertible as dollars at any European bank or exchange office. These days, even Polish złoty and Croatian kuna can be converted throughout Europe. Many people change excess local money back to dollars before they leave a country, then change those dollars into the next country's currency (e.g., they change euros to dollars in France, then dollars to pounds in Britain). This double changing is unnecessary and expensive—just change directly from euros to pounds. For convenience, you can sometimes do this even before leaving the first country (e.g., change your leftover euros to pounds in the Paris train station before boarding the Chunnel train to London).

Coins can become worthless when you leave a country. Since big-value coins are common in Europe, exporting a pocketful of change can be an expensive mistake. Spend them (on postcards, a newspaper, a

Avid coin collectors have the joy of filling in coin books, as the eight denominations of euro coins from 16 different countries make for a fun frontier in coin collecting. Europhiles can buy these books in Europe and chart their travels by gradually completing the collection.

phone call home, or food or drink for the train ride), change them into bills, or give them away. Otherwise, you've just bought a bunch of souvenirs. Note, however, that while euro coins each have a national side (indicating where they were minted), they are perfectly good in any country that uses the euro currency.

Get back to dollars at the end of your trip. At your final European country, gather any leftover bills and change them into that last currency to help fund your trip. If you have any foreign cash left before you fly home, change it into dollars at the European airport or simply spend it at the airport. You might get a few more dollars from your hometown bank for that last smattering of foreign bills, but it's clean and convenient to simply fly home with nothing but dollars in your pocket.

Cash Machines (ATMs)

Throughout Europe, cash machines (ATMs) are the standard way for travelers to get local currency. European ATMs work like your hometown machine and always have English-language instructions. Using your debit card with an ATM takes dollars directly from your bank account at home and gives you that country's cash. You'll pay fees, but you'll still get a better rate than you would for exchanging traveler's checks.

Ideally, use your debit card to take money out of ATMs. You can use a credit card, but you'll typically pay more in fees. For an explanation of the different cards, see the "Types of Cards" sidebar (next page).

Before you go, confirm with your bank or credit-card company that your card will work in Europe and alert them that you'll be making withdrawals while traveling—otherwise, they might freeze your card if they detect unusual spending patterns. Some banks automatically block US debit card use in certain countries (including the United Kingdom) to protect against fraud.

ATM transactions using bank-issued debit cards come with various fees. Your bank may levy a flat $2–5 transaction fee each time you use

Types of Cards

In general, people use debit cards and ATM cards for withdrawing cash from ATMs, and use credit cards to make purchases. Remember, my best advice is to pay for most purchases in Europe by using cash you withdraw from ATMs with your debit card.

Here are the details on the types of cards:

A **debit card** (sometimes called a "check card") is issued by your bank and draws cash from your bank account. Because it has a credit-card logo such as Visa or MasterCard, it can also be used to make purchases (note, though, if you're concerned about identify theft, it's safer to make purchases with cash or a credit card, since a debit card directly accesses your account). In a pinch, debit cards with a Visa or MasterCard logo can be used for over-the-counter cash advances (with a fee) at banks that accept those credit cards. It's also possible to buy prepaid debit cards—which you load with funds before you leave, then use like any other debit card—but these come with high fees and aren't worth considering for most trips.

An **ATM card** is similar to a debit card (i.e., draws money from your bank account), but because it lacks a Visa or MasterCard logo, it can be used only at ATMs—not for purchases. ATM cards have a logo on the back for either Plus (affiliated with Visa) or Cirrus (affiliated with MasterCard). You'll have to look for an ATM with a corresponding logo to be sure it'll work.

A **credit card** does not draw money from an account; rather, you're billed at the end of each month for any purchases or withdrawals you've made with it. Most credit cards work in ATMs (provided you know the PIN code)—but you're technically getting a cash advance, which is expensive.

Some European countries have started using **chip-and-PIN** technology for their debit cards. For more on this, see "Chip-and-PIN Cards," later.

---

an ATM, and/or may charge a percentage for the currency conversion (1–3 percent); the ATM you use might charge its own fee, too. If your bank charges a flat fee, make fewer visits to the ATM and withdraw larger amounts. (Some major US banks partner with "corresponding" European bank chains, meaning that you can use those ATMs with no fees at all—ask your bank.) Other fees may apply; for all the details, see "The Sleaze of Fees (and How to Avoid Them)," later. These additional expenses can pile up. Quiz your bank to figure out exactly what you'll pay for each withdrawal (for a list of questions, see page 172).

If you use a credit card (rather than a debit card) for ATM transactions, it's technically a "cash advance" rather than a "withdrawal"—and subject to an additional cash-advance fee. The moment you pull cash out of the ATM with a credit card, you're immediately bumped into the high-interest category with your new credit-card debt. If you want to use your credit card for ATM transactions without incurring this interest expense, you may be able to prepay the account—check with your bank.

Since some European keypads have only numbers, you'll need to know your personal identification number (PIN) by number rather than by letter; to determine this, just take a close look at your hometown bank's keypad. A PIN with more than four digits may not be accepted. Plan on being able to withdraw money only from your checking account. You might be able to dip into your savings account or transfer funds between accounts, but don't count on it.

Bringing two different cards provides a backup if one is demagnetized or eaten by a machine. Make sure the validity period of your card won't expire before your trip ends. It can be helpful to set up online access to your bank accounts. Most banks have secure websites that allow you to check balances and transfer funds; if you check your account periodically while in Europe, you can also see the exact exchange rate you're getting, whether the bank is levying any extra, unexpected fees, and if any fraudulent activity has occurred. However, be cautious when accessing your accounts from a public computer, which can pose a security risk.

How to use a European cash machine: Insert card, pull out cash.

Ask your bank how much you can withdraw per 24 hours, but be aware that many foreign ATMs have their own limits. If the ATM won't let you withdraw your daily maximum, you'll have to make several smaller withdrawals (and incur extra fees) to get the amount you want. Request a big amount on the small chance you'll get it. If you're lucky and the machine complies, you'll save on fees. If you're denied, try again, requesting a smaller amount. Few ATM receipts list the exchange rate, and some machines don't dispense receipts at all.

In some countries (especially in Eastern Europe), an ATM may give you high-denomination bills, which can be difficult to break. My

---

Transaction Fees Add Up

It pays to shop around for the best rates, both for debit-card ATM withdrawals and credit-card transactions. Consider these examples and you'll see how these fees can really add up over the length of your trip.

$300 ATM withdrawal (with debit card)

	Bank A	Bank B
Flat fee	$3	$5
Currency conversion fee	2% ($6)	0% ($0)
ATM noncustomer fee	$2	$2
Total fees	*$11*	*$7*

$600 credit-card purchase

	Bank A	Bank B
Visa/MC intl. trans. fee	1% ($6)	1% ($6)
Bank currency conversion fee	2% ($12)	0% ($0)
Total fees	*$18*	*$6*

MONEY

strategy: Request an odd amount of money from the ATM (such as 2,800 Czech *koruna* instead of 3,000). If the machine insists on giving you big bills, go immediately to a bank to break them.

If you're looking for an ATM, ask for a *retrait* or *distributeur (de billets)* in France, a cashpoint in the UK, and a *Bankomat* just about everywhere else. Many European banks have their ATMs in a small entry lobby, which protects users from snoopers and bad weather. When the bank is closed, the door to this lobby may be locked. In this case, look for a credit-card–size slot next to the door. Simply insert or swipe your debit or credit card in this slot, and the door should automatically open.

Stay away from commercial ATMs that aren't run by banks. These companies, such as the Travelex Money Machine, like to stack their machines next to bank ATMs in the hope that travelers will be too confused to notice the difference. The commercial ATMs charge outrageous extra fees—often double the cost of a bank ATM.

Paying with Plastic

American credit cards work throughout Europe (at hotels, larger shops and restaurants, travel agencies, and so on), although some countries are switching to new technology that may cause your US card to be rejected in certain automated machines (see "Chip-and-PIN Cards," later). Also, more and more merchants are establishing a $30 minimum for credit-card purchases. Visa and MasterCard are the most widely accepted. American Express is less common (because it costs merchants more) but is popular with some travelers for its extra services. The Discover card is completely unknown in Europe.

Plastic fans gloat that you get a better exchange rate by using your card. This may be true, *if* you have a card with particularly low fees (most credit cards charge about 1–3 percent per transaction—see the next section). But regardless of fees, realize that when you use your credit card, you're buying from businesses that have enough slack in their prices to absorb the fees the credit-card company charges the merchant (2–5 percent). In other words, those who travel on their plastic may be getting a better rate, but on a worse price. As more consumers believe they are getting "free use of the bank's money," we all absorb the percentage the credit-card companies are making in higher purchase prices.

The Sleaze of Fees (and How to Avoid Them)

Travelers returning from Europe often open their mail to discover they paid more for their trip than they thought they had. Over the last decade, banks have dramatically increased the fees they charge for overseas transactions using credit and debit cards. While these fees are legal, they're basically a slimy way for credit-card companies to wring a few more dollars out of their customers. A few years ago, a class-action settlement forced many banks to refund some of these fees, and most have (slightly) reduced the fees they charge for international transactions.

Visa and MasterCard levy a 1 percent fee on international transactions, and some banks that issue those cards also tack on a currency conversion fee (additional 1–2 percent). As mentioned earlier, there are also fees associated with using your card for ATM withdrawals—such as a flat $2–5 transaction fee, a percentage-based currency conversion fee, or a charge for using the ATM.

So, how can a smart traveler avoid—or at least reduce—these fees? Here are a few suggestions.

Ask about fees. Banks are required to break out international transaction fees as line items on your statement, helping you to see exactly what you're paying. But by the time you get your statement, it's too late—so it's smart to make a call before your trip to get the whole story. Carefully quiz your bank or credit-card company about the specific fees that come with using their card overseas. Even if your card didn't ring up fees the last time you went to Europe, there's a good chance it will now. Call and ask, and be persistent (see sidebar on next page).

If you're getting a bad deal, get a new card. Some companies offer

Questions to Ask Your
Credit-Card Company and Bank

Before your trip, call your credit-card company and your bank (for debit cards) to let them know you'll be using the cards in Europe. This will ensure that they don't decline foreign transactions. While you have them on the phone, here's a list of questions to ask. If the person doesn't know the answers, ask to speak to someone who does.

The Basics:
- Will my card work in Europe?
- What do you charge for withdrawals or purchases in Europe? Is it a percentage or flat fee? How much?
- Are there other currency conversion or foreign transaction fees I should know about?

To Get More Specific About Fees, Ask:
- What will the total charge be on my card—including all fees— if I take out €100 at an ATM with my debit card? Or if I pay for a €100 purchase with my credit card?

Specific to Debit Cards:
- What is my daily limit for ATM withdrawals in Europe? (If you want to change the limit, ask if you can.)
- Do you have any "partner" or "corresponding" banks in Europe where I can use my debit card at an ATM without paying an extra fee?

Specific to Credit Cards:
- What is my credit card's PIN? (You might need to know your credit card's PIN for some purchases in Europe.)
- If I use my credit card at an ATM, will the transaction be charged as a cash advance? Can I prepay my account to avoid that charge?

Theft or Loss:
- If my credit/debit card is lost or stolen, what is my liability?

Online Access:
- How do I set up online banking? (You might want to be able to access your accounts in Europe.)

far lower international fees than others—and a handful don't charge any fees at all. Capital One has a particularly good reputation for no-fee international transactions on both its credit cards and its ATM-accessible money market accounts (www.capitalone.com). Most credit unions have low-to-no international transaction fees. If you're going on a long trip, do some research and consider taking out a card just for international purchases. Bankrate has a good comparison chart of major credit cards and their fees (www.bankrate.com).

Avoid dynamic currency conversion (DCC). Some European merchants—capitalizing on the fact that many Americans are intimidated by unusual currencies—cheerfully charge you for converting their prices to dollars. This may seem like a nice service, but you'll actually end up paying more by adding yet another middleman to your transaction. Usually the dollar price is based on a lousy exchange rate (which can be set wherever the merchant likes—generally about 3 percent worse than the prevailing interbank rate). To make matters worse, even though you're paying in "dollars," your credit-card issuer may still levy its 1–3 percent "foreign transaction fee." The result: You could pay up to a 6 percent premium for the "convenience" of immediately seeing your charges in dollars.

Some merchants may disagree, but according to DCC provider Planet Payment, you have the right to decline this service at the store and have your transaction go through using local currency. If you're handed a receipt with two totals—one in the local currency and the other in US dollars—circle the amount listed in the local currency before you sign. If your receipt shows the total in dollars only, ask that it to be rung up again in the local currency. Your transaction will then be converted by Visa or MasterCard at or near the more favorable interbank rate.

Online purchases can be subject to fees. If you're buying from an international website, you can still get hit with currency conversion fees, even if you make the transaction while in the US. You might be able to bypass the fee if the vendor has a US office (in which case, call the US phone number rather than buying online).

The bottom line: Here's the best formula for saving money as you travel. Pay for as much as possible with cash (use a bank that charges low rates for international ATM transactions, and withdraw large amounts at each transaction—keeping the cash safe in your money belt). When using a credit card, use a card with the lowest possible international fees, and make sure your transactions are charged in the local currency—not dollars. Then smile and enjoy your trip, feeling very clever for avoiding so much unnecessary expense.

Chip-and-PIN Cards

Some parts of Europe—especially the British Isles, Scandinavia, France, Switzerland, Belgium, and the Netherlands—are adopting a chip-and-PIN system for their credit and debit cards. These "smartcards" come with an embedded microchip. When making a purchase, cardholders

When Europeans buy something with their chip-and-PIN card, they insert the card in a machine like this one, then type in their PIN.

must enter a PIN (similar to using a debit card for a point-of-sale purchase in the US). The chip inside the card then authorizes the transaction.

While handy for Europeans, chip-and-PIN cards are causing a few headaches for American visitors: Some machines that are designed to accept chip-and-PIN cards simply don't accept US credit cards. This is especially common with automated machines, such as those at train and subway stations, toll roads, parking garages, luggage lockers, bike-rental kiosks, and self-serve pumps at gas stations.

For example, after a long flight into Charles de Gaulle Airport in France, you find you can't use your credit card in the ticket machine for the train into Paris. Or, while driving in rural Switzerland on a Sunday afternoon, you discover that the few gas stations that are open only accept chip-and-PIN cards.

In most of these situations, a cashier is nearby who can take your credit card, swipe it, and have you sign the receipt the old-fashioned way. Automated machines might take your US credit card if you also know the card's PIN number. Every card has one—ask your bank for the number before you leave. (While using your credit card's PIN can help get you out of a jam, be aware that punching it in during a live transaction could increase your risk of fraud.)

For now, most hotels, restaurants, and shops that serve Americans will gladly accept your US credit card. However, at smaller shops, the merchant prefers that you don't use your credit card (since they pay a much higher commission on credit-card transactions than on chip-and-PIN ones). They might accept your credit card, but then ask you to type in the PIN. If this happens, politely ask them to print out a receipt for you to sign instead. If they refuse, either use your PIN or pay with cash.

Most of Western Europe should be totally converted to chip and PIN in 2012, and Canada will complete its conversion in 2015. Eventually some of these countries could stop accepting magnetic-strip cards, although most banking authorities think this won't happen in the short term—the American tourist market is too lucrative.

How can Americans get in on this action? A few US banks have plans to offer chip-and-PIN cards (called "travelers' credit cards") to their customers, possibly beginning in 2010. While convenient, this service will come with additional fees; before signing up, you'll want to weigh the convenience versus the cost of having your own chip-and-PIN card. In the long term, prepaid credit cards with chip-and-PIN technology are also coming to the US.

The bottom line: Don't be surprised if your credit card occasionally isn't accepted. Be aware that if your card is rejected, there's usually an alternative—either paying with cash, typing in your credit card's PIN, or paying with your credit card at a staffed ticket window. But in a few cases, you might simply be out of luck; drivers in particular need to be aware of potential problems when filling up at an automated gas station, entering an unattended parking garage, or exiting a toll road...you might just have to move on to the next gas station, or use the "cash only" lane at the toll plaza.

Identity Theft

With just two tidbits of key information about you, a criminal can steal your personal information and use it to rack up all kinds of expenses. The most susceptible pieces of information are your Social Security number and birth date. Identity theft has become aggravatingly common, but with some knowhow, you can take steps to protect yourself—especially when overseas.

Protect your credit and debit cards. Take as few credit and debit cards with you as possible, and keep them safely in your money belt. (For more tips on money belts and foiling pickpockets, see Chapter 24: Outsmarting Thieves.) Don't carry identification that includes your Social Security number unless you absolutely must.

Safeguard your PIN code. Memorize your personal identification number; you'd be surprised how many people write it on their card (which is extremely risky). "Shoulder surfing"—a thief watching you as you type your PIN into a keypad—is a common problem. When entering your PIN, carefully block other people's view of the keypad, covering it with your free hand.

Use your credit card sparingly. Restaurant servers and shop clerks might try to steal your credit-card information, sometimes by swiping it in a special machine that reads the card (a technique called "skimming") or by surreptitiously snapping a photo of it with their cell phone. Pay with cash instead. When you do use your credit card for purchases, check your receipts. If your entire credit-card number is printed on the

---

Damage Control for Lost Cards

If you lose your credit, debit, or ATM card, you can stop people from using your card by reporting the loss immediately to the appropriate global customer-assistance center. Call these 24-hour US numbers collect: Visa (410/581-9994), MasterCard (636/722-7111), and American Express (623/492-8427).

Have, at a minimum, the following information ready: the name of the financial institution that issued you the card, along with the type of card (classic, platinum, or whatever). Providing the following information will allow for a quicker cancellation of your missing card: full card number, whether you are the primary or secondary cardholder, the cardholder's name exactly as printed on the card, billing address, home phone number, circumstances of the loss or theft, and identification verification (your birth date, your mother's maiden name, or your Social Security number—memorize this, don't carry a copy). If you are the secondary cardholder, you'll also need to provide the primary cardholder's identification-verification details. You can generally receive a temporary card within two or three business days in Europe.

If you promptly report your card lost or stolen, you typically won't be responsible for any unauthorized transactions on your account, although many banks charge a liability fee of $50.

---

receipt, tear it up before you toss it.

Use your debit card even more sparingly. Use your debit card to withdraw sizable amounts of local cash from ATMs (and then stow it in your money belt to protect against pickpockets) so you can pay with cash whenever possible. Use your debit card only for cash-machine withdrawals. To make purchases, pay with cash or your credit card. Because a debit card draws funds directly out of your bank account, charges incurred by a thief are scary—it's *your* money that's gone, not the credit-card company's. Once you establish that your card was used fraudulently, you'll likely be liable for only $50, but it's still worrisome. If you're concerned about this, talk to your bank about setting a daily withdrawal limit for your ATM or debit card; you'll have to weigh the convenience of withdrawing large amounts of euros from your accounts...against the risk of a crook doing the same. Note that this limit applies to cash-machine withdrawals, not purchases.

Make a photocopy of your passport. With a copy, it's easier to replace your passport if it's lost or stolen. However, it's important to guard this photocopy as carefully as you would the original. I hide mine in a second money belt clipped into the bottom of my luggage (don't tell anyone). Bring along the standard phone numbers of your bank and credit-card company—US toll-free numbers do not work from Europe (see the "Damage Control for Lost Cards" sidebar).

Be careful when emailing. Don't send sensitive information (such as your credit-card number or Social Security number) in an email message, even from your personal computer. It's better to call or fax. Some people send their credit-card number in two halves, via two separate email messages. (For extra security, a few banks, such as Citibank and Bank of America, allow their customers to create virtual account numbers, which are one-time or short-term numbers linked to your regular credit card.) Some Internet forms request your credit-card number, but only enter and submit it if you're confident of the website's authenticity and if you have a secure connection. (If the web address begins with *https:* rather than *http:*, it's secure.) Be aware of the risk involved with storing sensitive personal information in your Web-based email account, which can be hacked into.

Be suspicious, especially on the Internet. Trust a phone call or email only if you've initiated the communication. Any unsolicited request for account information you receive through emails, websites, or pop-up windows should be considered fraudulent. For example, if "your bank" sends you an email message claiming they need to confirm details of your account, don't reply, don't follow the Web link in the message, and don't call the phone number in the email. Instead, call your bank using the phone number on your bank statement or the back of your debit or credit card. The sender of the fraudulent message is likely "phishing" or "spoofing"—pretending to be legitimate by carefully imitating the look of an actual organization to trick you into divulging your personal information.

Monitor your accounts. Upon returning home, verify the balance and charges on your debit and credit cards (check this information online from a secure computer, or call to ask). Whether or not you've recently been traveling, it's always smart to periodically check all of your accounts. Get a credit report to be sure that your credit history is accurate. (You can get one free each year—see www.annualcreditreport.com.)

What to do if your identity is stolen: If your credit or debit card is stolen, call immediately to cancel it (see "Damage Control for Lost Cards" sidebar). Other types of identity theft may take a long time— even months—to surface. In the event of any type of identity theft, file a police report (and send copies to creditors). Contact any one of the three major credit-reporting agencies to report the fraud (TransUnion, www.transunion.com, tel. 800-680-7289; Experian, www.experian.com, tel. 888-397-3742; or Equifax, www.equifax.com, tel. 888-766-0008). Also consider filing a report with the Federal Trade Commission (www .ftc.gov/idtheft) and the Social Security Office of the Inspector General (www.ssa.gov/oig/guidelin.htm). Other good resources are the Identity Theft Resource Center (www.idtheftcenter.org) and the Privacy Rights Clearinghouse (www.privacyrights.org).

As with preventing other kinds of theft, the key here is to keep your wits about you to protect your personal information. With a few precautions, you can spend your time in Europe lingering over a gelato instead of stressing over identity theft.

14. Your Budget

Most of today's Europe is more expensive than the United States, and the sloppy traveler can blow a small fortune in a hurry. If you travel like a big shot, you'd better be loaded. You can live well in Europe on a budget, but it will take some artistry.

I'm cautious about sending people to Europe with too much confidence and not enough money. The tips in this book are tried and tested in the worst circumstances every year. And my feedback from readers makes it clear: Enjoying Europe through the Back Door can be done—by you.

Budget Breakdown

Airfare: Airfares vary wildly depending on where you're flying from and to, the time of year, and other factors (such as airport taxes, fuel surcharges, and baggage fees). But for a round-trip flight between the US and Europe, figure about $1,000–1,500 total. Understand all of your options (maybe with the help of a good travel agent), and make the best choice. (See Chapter 9: Flying.) Traveling outside of peak season will save you several hundred dollars.

Transportation Within Europe: Transportation in Europe is reasonable if you take advantage of a railpass or split a car rental among three or four people. And cheap flights—about $100 one-way between most major European cities—can save time and money on long journeys. Transportation expenses are generally fixed. People who spend $8,000 for their vacation spend about the same on transportation as do those whose trips cost half as much. Your budget should not dictate how freely you travel in Europe. If you want to go somewhere, do it, but take advantage of whatever money-saving options you can. You came to travel.

Trip Costs

In 2011, you can travel comfortably for a month for $5,600—not including your airfare ($1,000–1,500). If you have extra money, it's more fun to spend it in Europe.

Allow approximately (per person):

$1,000	for a 15-days-in-two-months Eurailpass or shared car rental
800	for sightseeing and entertainment
200	for shopping and miscellany
+3,600	for room and board ($120 a day)
$5,600	

Students or rock-bottom budget travelers can enjoy a month of Europe at least as much for about a third less—$3,120 plus airfare.

Allow approximately (per person):

$720	for a one-month youth Eurailpass
500	for sightseeing and entertainment
100	for shopping and miscellany
+1,800	for room and board ($60 a day)*
$3,120	

*$30 for a hostel dorm bed or a bed in a private home with breakfast, $10 for a picnic lunch, $20 for dinner.

MONEY

Sightseeing/Entertainment: Sightseeing costs have risen more quickly than anything else. Admissions to major attractions are roughly $8–20; smaller sights are $2–5. Concerts, plays, and bus tours cost about $30. Don't skimp here. This category directly powers most of the experiences all the other expenses are designed to make possible.

Shopping/Miscellany: Figure an average of $2–3 each for bus and subway rides. Shopping can vary in cost from nearly nothing to a small fortune. Good budget travelers find that this category has little to do with assembling a trip full of lifelong and wonderful memories.

Room and Board: The area that will make or break your budget—over which you have the most control—is your eating and sleeping expenses. In 2011, smart travelers can thrive on $120 a day for room and board: $75 per person in a $150 hotel double with breakfast, $15 apiece for lunch, and $25 for dinner. That leaves you $5 for cappuccino or gelato. Remember that these prices are averages—Scandinavia, Britain, and Italy are more expensive, while Spain, Portugal, Greece, and Eastern Europe

Comparing *Apfels* to *Pommes*: Relative Prices in Europe's Top Cities

	double room at budget hotel / B&B	double room at mid-range tour hotel	double room at upscale business-class hotel	cheapest sleepable hostel bunk	typical main dish at dinner for a mid-range eatery	cost of a Big Mac	one ride on subway or local bus	one-hour train ride to a nearby town	entrance fee at a top museum
Amsterdam	$110	$165	$280	$34	$22	$4.50	$2.25	$15	$17.50
Athens	$95	$125	$200	$30	$15	$4	$1.40	$5	$17
Budapest, Kraków, Dubrovnik	$90	$120	$225	$20	$15	$3.20	$1.50	$5	$8
Copenhagen, Oslo	$130	$180	$300	$30	$25	$6	$4.20	$21	$15
London	$110	$200	$320	$32	$20	$3.70	$6.40	$39	$28*
Madrid, Lisbon	$80	$130	$175	$31	$16	$3.50	$1.40	$14	$9
Munich	$105	$125	$180	$29	$21	$5	$3.25	$28	$10
Paris	$130	$195	$290	$33	$25	$4	$2.40	$19	$15
Prague	$130	$205	$260	$20	$12	$3.70	$1	$6	$12
Rome	$140	$210	$280	$28	$15	$4	$1.40	$13	$18
Vienna	$100	$150	$210	$23	$21	$4	$2.40	$21	$15
Zürich	$120	$180	$250	$35	$28	$6.50	$4	$25	$8
Seattle	$100	$150	$230	$29	$15	$3.50	$2.25	$14	$15

*Many top museums are free in London.

Budget alone should not determine where you go in Europe. People on a shoestring budget can have a blast in Europe's most expensive countries...if they travel smart. But knowing roughly what you'll pay in various destinations can help you craft a more wallet-friendly itinerary. The chart on the opposite page attempts to compare apples to apples by showing rough costs in US dollars for basic tourist expenses in several of Europe's major cities (and, by way of comparison, my hometown in the USA). Note that prices in small towns and the countryside are, as a rule, far lower than in the cities listed here.

Fine Print: All prices in the chart are approximate, based on the most recent editions of Rick Steves guidebooks (and assume the exchange rate €1 = $1.25). All hotel rates are for a double room with private bathroom in the main tourist area during peak season (typically June–Sept), and include breakfast and tax. Train prices are for one-way, second-class tickets on regional (non-express) trains, and do not include reservations. For simplicity, some similarly priced cities (such as Copenhagen and Oslo) have been combined.

MONEY

are cheaper. Also, as a general rule, you'll pay less in the countryside and more in big cities.

If $120 per day is too steep for your budget, never fear—you can take advantage of simpler hotels and eateries to get by for less. Make your trip match your budget (rather than vice versa). The key is finding budget alternatives to international-class hotels and restaurants, and consuming only what you want to consume. If you want real tablecloths and black-tie waiters, your tomato salad will cost 20 times what it costs in the market. If you want a suite with fancy room service and chocolate on your pillow, you'll pay in a day what many travelers pay in a week.

My idea of "cheap" is simple but not sleazy. My budget philosophy is never sacrifice safety, reasonable cleanliness, sleep, or nutrition to save money. I go to safe, central, friendly, local-style hotels, and I shun swimming pools, people in uniforms, and transplanted American niceties in favor of an opportunity to travel as a temporary European. Unfortunately, simple is subversive, and the system is bullying even cozy Scottish bed-and-breakfast places into more and more amenities, more and more debt, and higher and higher prices.

I traveled every summer for years on a part-time piano teacher's income (and, boy, was she upset). I ate and slept well by learning and following these guidelines.

The Fundamentals of Budget Travel

You can get eight good, safe hours of sleep and three square meals in Europe for $60 a day if your budget requires it. If your budget is tight, remember these rules of thumb.

Minimize the use of hotels and restaurants. Enjoying the sights and culture of Europe has nothing to do with how much you're spending to eat and sleep. Take advantage of each country's many alternatives to hotels and restaurants. If your budget dictated, you could have a great trip without hotels and restaurants—and probably learn, experience, and enjoy more than most tourists.

Budget for price variances. The priciest parts of Europe (Scandinavia, Britain, much of Italy) can be twice as expensive as Europe's cheapest corners (Spain, Portugal, Greece, and Eastern Europe). Exercise those budget alternatives where they'll save you the most money. A hostel may save you $10 in Crete but $50 in Finland. In Scandinavia I picnic, walk, and sleep on trains, but I live like a king in Portugal or Poland, where my splurge dollars go furthest. And if your trip will last only as long as your money does, travel fast in the expensive countries and hang out in the cheap ones.

Swallow pride and save money. This is a personal matter, depending largely on how much pride and money you have. Many people cringe every time I use the word "cheap"; others appreciate the directness. I'm not talking about begging and groveling around Europe. I'm talking about drinking tap water at restaurants ($5 saved) and choosing a hotel room with a shower down the hall ($30 saved).

Find out the complete price before ordering anything, and say "no thanks" if the price isn't right. Expect equal and fair treatment as a tourist. When appropriate,

Lunch for $10, no problema

fight the price, set a limit, and search on. Remember, even if the same thing would cost much more at home, the local rate should prevail. If you act like a rich fool, you're likely to be treated as one.

MONEY

Avoid the tourist centers. The best values are not in the places with glossy menus in six languages out front. Find places that earn a loyal local following. You'll get more for your money. If you do follow the tourists, follow the savvy Germans; never follow tour groups.

Patronize family-run places. Small family-run places have cheaper labor (Mom, Pop, and the kids) and care more about their customers. For these reasons, they generally offer the best values for eating and sleeping.

Adapt to European tastes. Most unhappy people I meet in my travels could find the source of their problems in their own stubborn desire to find the United States in Europe. If you accept and at least try doing things the European way, besides saving money you'll be happier and learn more on your trip. You cannot expect the local people to accept you warmly if you don't accept them. Things are different in Europe—that's why you go. European travel is a package deal. Accept the good with the "bad." If you always require the comforts of home, then that's where you'll be happiest.

Be a good guest. To Europeans, Americans occasionally act as though they "just got off the boat" (putting shoes on train seats, chilling grapes in the bidet, talking loudly in restaurants, taking flash photos during Mass, hanging wet clothes out the hotel window, and consuming energy like it's cheap and ours to waste). The Europeans you'll deal with can sour or sweeten your experience, depending on how they react to you. When you're in good favor with the receptionist (or whomever), you can make things happen that people who try to let their bucks do all the talking can't.

Each year as I update my books, I hear over and over that my readers are the most considerate and fun-to-have guests. Thank you for traveling as temporary locals who are sensitive to the culture. It's fun to follow you in my travels.

15. Shopping

Gift shopping is getting very expensive. I remember buying a cuckoo clock 30 years ago for $5. Now a Big Mac at the Munich McDonald's costs that much.

Souvenir Strategies

Shop in countries where your dollar stretches furthest. Shop in Turkey, Morocco, Portugal, Spain, Greece, and Eastern Europe. For the price of a miniature pewter Viking ship in Norway, you can buy a real boat in Turkey.

Shop at flea markets. The most colorful shopping in Europe is at its flea markets. Among the best are Amsterdam's Waterlooplein (daily except Sunday), London's Portobello Market (daily except Sunday, best on Saturday), Madrid's El Rastro (Sunday only), and Paris' Puces St. Ouen (Saturday through Monday). Flea markets anywhere have soft prices. Bargain like mad. Pickpockets love flea markets—wear your money belt and watch your day bag.

Boxloads of Davids await busloads of tourists.

Check out large department stores. These often have a souvenir section with standard local knickknacks and postcards at prices way below the cute little tourist shops. While these large stores may seem daunting, they generally work just like ours. In big cities, most department-store staff are accustomed to wide-eyed foreign shoppers and can speak some English. The store directory (usually near the elevators or escalators) often includes English.

Stay in control. Shopping is an important part of most people's trips. But all too often, slick marketing and romantic window displays can succeed in shifting the entire focus of your vacation toward things in the tourist shops. (It's a lucrative business. Many souvenir merchants in Italy work through the tourist season, then "retire" for the rest of the year.) This sort of tourist brainwashing can turn you into one of the many people who set out to see and experience Europe but find themselves wandering in a trancelike search for signs announcing *Duty-Free Shopping*. I've seen half the members of a guided tour of the British Halls of Parliament skip out to survey an enticing display of plastic "bobby" hats, Big Ben briefs, and Union Jack panties. Even if the sign says, "Keep Italy green—spend dollars," don't let your trip degenerate into a glorified shopping spree.

Ask yourself if your enthusiasm is merited. More often than not, you can pick up a very similar item of better quality for a cheaper price at home. Unless you're a real romantic, the thrill of where you bought something fades long before the item's usefulness does. My life has more room for a functional souvenir than for a useless symbol of a place I visited. Even thoughtful shoppers go overboard. I have several large boxes in my attic labeled "great souvenirs."

Try to restrict your shopping to a stipulated time. Most people have an idea of what they want to buy in each country. Set aside one day to shop in each country, and stick to it. This way you avoid drifting through your trip thinking only of souvenirs.

To pack light, shop at the end of your trip. Enjoy the luxury of not being a shopper for 80 percent of your trip, then go hog-wild in the last country you visit and fly home heavy. One summer I had a 16-pound backpack and nothing more until the last week of my trip, when, in Spain and Morocco, I managed to accumulate two medieval chairs, two sets of bongos, a camelhair coat, swords, a mace, and a lace tablecloth... most of which are now in boxes in my attic.

Good souvenirs: My favorites are books (a great value all over Europe, with many editions that are impossible to find in the US), local crafts (well explained in guidebooks, such as hand-knit sweaters in Portugal or Ireland, glass in Sweden, painted beehive panels in Slovenia, or lace in Belgium), strange stuffed animals (at flea markets), CDs of music I heard live, posters (one sturdy tube stores 8–10 posters safely), clothing (see next section), photographs I've taken, and memories whittled lovingly into my journal.

Clothes Shopping

Many travelers enjoy shopping for "wearable souvenirs" in Europe, where the fashions can be quite different from back home. Options range from

MONEY

Clothes Sizing Conversion

Most items are sized differently in the US, the UK, and continental Europe. Here are some conversion tables to use as general guidelines (but note that no conversion is perfect). I've also included shortcuts for figuring out sizes. When a range is given (e.g., shoe size 36–37), it means that the European size straddles the American one (half-sizes are rare on the Continent)—look for a 36 that runs large, or a 37 that runs small.

Window-shopping the extravagant April Fair dresses in Sevilla can be a sight-seeing treat.

Women's Sizes

Pants, Dresses & Suits

US	2	4	6	8	10	12	14	16	18	20
Europe	32	34	36	38	40	42	44	46	48	50
UK	6	8	10	12	14	16	18	20	22	24

Shortcut: From US to Europe—add 30; from US to UK—add 4.

Blouses & Sweaters

US	32(S)	34(S)	36(M)	38(M)	40(L)	42(L)
Europe	40	42	44	46	48	50
UK	34	36	38	40	42	44

Shortcut: From US to Europe—add 8; From US to UK—add 2.

Shoes

US	5½	6	6½	7	7½	8	8½	9	9½	10
Europe	35–36	36	37	37–38	38	38–39	39	40	41	42
UK	3	3½	4	4½	5	5½	6	6½	7	7½

Shortcut: From US to Europe—add about 31; from US to UK—subtract 2½.

MONEY

Men's Sizes

Suits & Jackets

US/UK	34	36	38	40	42	44	46	48	50	52
Europe	44	46	48	50	52	54	56	58	60	62

Shortcut: From US to Europe—add 10; US and UK use the same sizing.

Shirts

US/UK	14(S)	14½(S)	15(M)	15½(M)	16(L)	16½(L)	17(XL)
Europe	36	37	38	39	40	41	42

Shortcut: From US to Europe—multiply by 2 and add about 8; US and UK use the same sizing.

Shoes

US	7½	8	8½	9	9½	10	10½	11	11½	12
Europe	39	39–40	40	41	42	43	44	45	45–46	46
UK	7	7½	8	8½	9	9½	10	10½	11	11½

Shortcut: From US to Europe—add about 32-34; from US to UK—subtract about ½.

Children's Sizes

Clothing

US/UK	2	4	6	8	10	14/13	16/15
Europe	1	2	5	7	9	10	12

Shortcut: From US to Europe—subtract 1-2 for smaller children and subtract 4 for juniors; US and UK use the same sizing.

Girls' Shoes

US	9½	10	11	12	13	1	2	3	4
UK	8	8½	9½	10½	11½	12½	13½	1½	2½
Europe	26	26–27	27–28	28–29	30	31	32–33	33–34	35

Shortcut: From US to Europe—for sizes up to 13 add 16-17, and for sizes 1 and up add about 30; from US to UK—subtract about 1½, except sizes 1 and 2, to which you'll add 11½.

Boys' Shoes

US	11½	12	12½	13	1	2	3	4	5
UK	11	11½	12	12½	13½	1½	2½	3½	4½
Europe	29	29–30	30–31	31	33	34	35	36	37–38

Shortcut: From US to Europe—for sizes up to 13 add 17½-18, and for sizes 1 and up add about 32; from US to UK—subtract about ½, except size 1, to which you'll add about 12½.

hole-in-the-wall boutiques to grand department stores to colorful street markets.

Europe-wide H&M (www.hm.com) and C&A (www.c-and-a.com) department-store chains are popular for stylish but affordable clothes; each country also has its own chains. My shopaholic staffers appreciate Benetton (www.benetton.com), but since the fashions vary by store and by country, they recommend that if you see an item you like, grab it rather than wait to pick it up at a later stop...you might never see that same style or color again. Some women also like buying high-quality underwear and camisoles in Italy, browsing at Intimissimi (www.intimissimi.it) or any large department store.

Remember that prices at street markets are often soft—especially if it's near the end of the day, you're paying cash, and you're buying multiple items (such as three scarves). Don't be afraid to bargain (see "Successful Bargaining," at the end of this chapter).

No matter where you buy, be aware that the US, the UK, and continental Europe all use slightly different sizing conventions. For the specifics, see

European department stores (such as Paris' regal Galeries Lafayette) can be as interesting as what's on sale.

the sidebar on the previous spread. Also note that European clothes are generally cut to fit more tightly than American clothes. Be prepared to swallow your pride and go up a size or two. If you wear a size medium leather jacket back home, you might need a large or XL in Italy.

European Union Value-Added Tax (VAT) Refunds

Every year, tourists visiting Europe leave behind millions of dollars of refundable sales taxes. While for some, the headache of collecting the refund is not worth the few dollars at stake, if you do any serious shopping, it's hard cash—free and easy.

The process isn't difficult; you just have to get the necessary documents from the retailer, carry your purchase with you, and track down the right folks at the airport, port, or border when you leave. These days you've got to check in early at the airport; this will give you something to do while you're hanging around.

VAT Rates and Minimum Purchases Required to Qualify for Refunds

Country of Purchase	VAT Standard Rate*	Minimum in Local Currency	Approx. Min. in US Dollars
Austria	20%	€75.01	$94
Belgium	21%	€125.01	$156
Croatia	23%	501 HRK	$100
Czech Republic	20%	2,001 CZK	$112
Denmark	25%	300 DKK	$51
Estonia	20%	601 EEK	$55
Finland	23%	€40	$50
France	19.6%	€175.01	$219
Germany	19%	€25	$31
Great Britain	17.5%	£30	$48
Greece	23%	€120	$150
Hungary	25%	42,001 HUF	$210
Ireland	21%	No minimum	No minimum
Italy	20%	€155	$194
Latvia	21%	30.26 LVL	$60
Lithuania	21%	200 LTL	$82
Luxembourg	15%	€74	$93
Netherlands	19%	€50	$63
Norway	25%	315 NOK	$53
Poland	22%	200 PLN	$67
Portugal	20%	€60	$75
Romania	19%	250 RON	$85
Slovakia	19%	€175	$219
Slovenia	20%	€50	$63
Spain	18%	€90.15	$113
Sweden	25%	200 SEK	$28
Switzerland	7.6%	300 CHF	$300
Turkey	18%	118 TRY	$83

* The VAT Standard Rates listed above—while listed as exact amounts—are intended to give you an idea of the rates and minimums involved. But VAT rates fluctuate based on many factors, including what kind of item(s) you are buying. Your refund will likely be less than the above rate, especially if it's subject to processing fees.

MONEY

Ideally—if you're charming, lucky, and have your passport handy—you can talk a merchant into taking the tax off the price right there at the store. But even so, you'll still need to get the proper documents stamped when you depart Europe.

The standard European Union Value-Added Tax ranges from 15 to 25 percent per country, averaging about 20 percent overall. Rates change, so you'll want to check with merchants when you're there.

Unlike business travelers, tourists aren't entitled to refunds on the tax they spend on hotels and meals. Still, you can get back most of the tax you paid on merchandise such as clothes, cuckoos, and crystal.

Almost all European countries require a minimum purchase for a refund, ranging from about $30 to several hundred dollars (Ireland has no minimum). You typically have to ring up the minimum at one retailer—you can't add up your purchases from various shops to reach the required amount—so you benefit from finding one spot where you can buy big. If you'll be on the road for a long time, shop near the end of your trip. You need to collect your refund within three months of your purchase.

Assuming you meet these criteria and you're still game, here's the drill. The details vary per country, but you follow the same basic steps.

Shop at stores that know the ropes. Retailers choose whether to participate in the VAT-refund scheme. Most tourist-oriented stores do; often you'll see a sign in the window or by the cash register (if not, ask). It'd be a shame to spend big bucks at a place and not have a chance of getting a refund. You'll also want to know whether the merchant handles refunds directly (which means a potentially bigger refund for you, but more hassle) or uses a service (quicker and easier, but the provider of this service takes a cut).

Get the documents. When you make your purchase, have the merchant fill out the necessary refund document, called a "cheque." You'll need to present your passport. Make sure the paperwork is done before you leave the store so there's nothing important missing. If they leave any blanks for you to fill out, be sure you understand what goes where. Attach your receipt to the form and stash it in a safe place.

What if the store ships your purchase to your home? You can still collect a refund, but the process varies by country. In Italy, the shipper gets your customs stamp for you and sends you the documents. In Germany, you take the documents home and then get a stamp at a German consulate or embassy once you receive the goods. Ask at the shop where you make your purchase how it works in their country.

MONEY

Know where to get your refund. If you buy merchandise in a European Union country and you're bringing the goods home with you, process your documents at your last stop in the EU, regardless of where you made your purchases. So if you buy sweaters in Denmark, pants in France, and shoes in Italy, and you're flying home from Greece, get your documents stamped in Athens. Be aware that if the currencies are different in the country where you made your purchase and where you process your refund—say, pounds and euros—you may have to pay an extra conversion fee. And don't forget—Switzerland, Norway, Croatia, and Turkey are not in the EU, so if you buy in one of those countries, get your documents stamped before you leave that particular country.

Bring your goods—unused—to the airport or border crossing. You're not supposed to use your purchased goods before you present them at customs. Some retailers, particularly those in Scandinavia, will staple and seal the shopping bag to keep people from cheating. If you show up at customs wearing your new shoes, officials might look the other way—or deny you a refund.

Arrive early. You'll have to wait in a special line at customs and then, if you're collecting your refund right away, at the refund office. In smaller airports, ports, and less-trafficked border crossings, finding the right customs agent can be tough. If you run out of time and have to leave without the stamp, you're probably out of luck. A few countries allow you to try to recover the refund through the embassy in your home country. Regardless, it's a lot of trouble.

Get your documents stamped. The customs export officer will stamp your documents after you present your purchased goods to verify that you are, indeed, exporting your purchase (try to keep the goods in your carry-on). Some officials will stamp your documents even if you haven't got your purchase with you, but others are stricter. If you bought something potentially dangerous (such as a set of knives in Spain) that you probably wouldn't even be allowed to carry on a plane, chase down a customs official to have a look before you check your bag.

Collect the cash—sooner or later. Once you get your form stamped by customs, you'll need to return it to the retailer or its representative at the airport, port, or border crossing. Many merchants work with a service such as Global Refund or Premier Tax Free, which have offices where you present your stamped document. They'll extract about 4 percent for their services, but it can be worth it—often they'll give you your refund in your currency of choice, right then and there. Otherwise, they'll credit the refund to your credit card (within one or two billing cycles). If the retailer handles VAT refunds directly, it's up to you to contact the merchant for your refund. You can mail the documents from home, or quicker, from your point of departure (using a stamped, addressed envelope you've prepared or one that's been provided by the merchant)—and then wait. It could take months. If the refund check comes in a foreign currency, you may have to pay $30 or so to get your bank to cash it.

Don't count on it. My readers have reported that, even when following all of the instructions carefully, sometimes the VAT refund just doesn't pan out. (For example, they have all of the paperwork ready when they get to the airport—but can't find the customs official to process it.) These problems seem most prevalent in Italy. Your best odds are for buying from a merchant who knows how to deal with the red tape for you—but even that is not infallible.

Only you can decide whether VAT refunds are worth the trouble. As for me, my favorite trip souvenirs are my photos, journal, and memories. These are priceless—and exempt from taxes and red tape.

Customs for American Shoppers

You are allowed to take home $800 worth of items per person duty-free, once every 30 days. The next $1,000 is taxed at a flat 3 percent. After that, you pay the individual item's duty rate. You can also bring in duty-free a liter of alcohol (slightly more than a standard-size bottle of wine; you must be at least 21), 200 cigarettes, and up to 100 non-Cuban cigars.

Because food items can carry devastating diseases or pests, they are strictly regulated. You may take home vacuum-packed cheeses; dried herbs, spices, or mushrooms; and canned fruits or vegetables, including jams and vegetable spreads. Baked goods, candy, chocolate, oil, vinegar, mustard, and honey are OK. Fresh fruits and vegetables (even that banana from your airplane breakfast) are not permitted. Meats are generally not allowed, though canned pâtés from some countries are usually permitted if made from geese, duck, or pork. Just because a duty-free shop in an airport sells a food product, it doesn't mean it will automatically pass US customs. Be prepared to lose your investment.

Note that you'll need to carefully pack any bottles of wine, jam, honey, oil, and other liquid-containing items in your checked luggage, due to limits on liquids in carry-ons. For tips on bringing duty-free liquids onto the plane, see "What Can I Carry On?" on page 86.

To check US customs rules and duty rates, visit www.cbp.gov, click on "Travel," and then "Know Before You Go." For details about mailing items from Europe to yourself or somebody else, see "Snail Mail," page 334.

Successful Bargaining

In much of the Mediterranean world, the price tag is only an excuse to argue. Bargaining is the accepted and expected method of finding a compromise between the wishful thinking of the merchant and the tourist. In Europe, bargaining is common only in the south, but you can fight prices at flea markets and with street vendors anywhere.

While bargaining is good for your budget, it can also become an enjoyable game. Many travelers are addicted hagglers who would gladly skip a tour of a Portuguese palace to get the price down on the black-clad lady's handmade tablecloth.

The Ten Commandments of the Successful Haggler

1. Determine if bargaining is appropriate. It's bad shopping etiquette to "make an offer" for a tweed hat in a London department store. It's foolish not to at a Greek outdoor market. To learn if a price is fixed, show some interest in an item but say, "It's just too much money." You've put the merchant in a position to make the first offer. If he comes down even 2 percent, there's nothing sacred about the price tag. Haggle away.

You can troll for quirky souvenirs at flea markets.

2. Shop around and find out what locals pay. Prices can vary drastically among vendors at the same flea market, and even at the same stall. If prices aren't posted, assume there's a double price standard: one for locals and one for you. If only tourists buy the item you're pricing, see what an Arab, Spanish, or Italian tourist would be charged. I remember thinking I did well in Istanbul's Grand Bazaar, until I learned my Spanish friend bought the same shirt for 30 percent less. Merchants assume American tourists are rich, and they know what we pay for things at home.

3. Determine what the item is worth to you. Price tags can be meaningless and serve to distort your idea of an item's true worth. The merchant is playing a psychological game. Many tourists think that if they can cut the price by 50 percent they are doing great. So the merchant quadruples his prices and the tourist happily pays double the fair value. The best way to deal with crazy price tags is to ignore them. Before you even see the price tag, determine the item's value to you, considering the hassles involved in packing it or shipping it home.

4. Determine the merchant's lowest price. Many merchants will settle for a nickel profit rather than lose the sale entirely. Promise yourself that no matter how exciting the price becomes, you won't buy. Then work the cost down to rock bottom. When it seems to have fallen to a record low, walk away. That last price  he hollers out as you turn the corner is often the best price you'll get. If the price is right, go back and buy. Prices often drop at the end of the day, when merchants are considering packing up.

5. Look indifferent. As soon as the merchant perceives the "I gotta have that!" in you, you'll never get the best price. He assumes Americans have the money to buy what they really want.

6. Employ a third person. Use your friend who is worried about the ever-dwindling budget or who doesn't like the price or who is bored and wants to return to the hotel. This trick can work to bring the price down faster.

7. Impress the merchant with your knowledge—real or otherwise. He'll respect you, and you'll be more likely to get good quality. Istanbul has very good leather coats for a fraction of the US cost. Before my trip I talked to some leather-coat sellers and was much better prepared to confidently pick out a good coat in Istanbul.

8. Obey the rules. Don't hurry. Bargaining is rarely rushed. Get to know the shopkeeper. Accept his offer for tea, and talk with him. He'll know you are serious. Dealing with the owner (no salesman's commission) can lower the price. Bid carefully. If a merchant accepts your price (or vice versa), you must buy the item.

9. Show the merchant your money. Physically hold out your money and offer him "all you have" to pay for whatever you are bickering over. He'll be tempted to just grab your money and say, "Oh, OK."

10. If the price is too much, leave. Never worry about having taken too much of the merchant's time and tea. They are experts at making the tourist feel guilty for not buying. It's all part of the game. Most merchants, by local standards, are financially well-off.

Remember, you can generally find the same souvenirs in large department stores at fair and firm prices. Department-store shopping is quicker, easier, and often cheaper—but not nearly as much fun.

SLEEPING AND EATING

16. Sleeping

Europe offers a wide range of accommodations: cheap hostels, cozy B&Bs, characteristic guest houses, various hotels (from small to large and simple to swanky), rental apartments, and campgrounds. There's certain to be a perfect home-away-from-home for you. First we'll cover the basics of finding, choosing, and reserving hotels. Then we'll take a spin through other types of accommodations.

Choose Hotels That Suit Your Budget

The majority of Americans traveling in Europe sleep in moderately priced hotels. Most of the accommodations I recommend in my guidebooks fall

into this category.

People often ask me how I choose which hotels to list. There's no secret trick to it: Just walk through the most inviting neighborhood in town, snoop around in each hotel, grab a price list, and jot down some notes... and by the end of the day, the best-value hotels stand out. I can spend a day in Amsterdam, scaling the stairs and checking out the rooms of 40 different hotels, all offering double rooms for \$100–230 a night. What's striking to me is how little correlation there is between what you pay and what you get. You are just as likely to spend \$150 for a big, impersonal place on a noisy highway as you are to spend \$100 for a charming, family-run guest house on a bikes-only stretch of canal.

I look for places that are clean, small, central, quiet at night, comfortable (firm beds), traditional, inexpensive, friendly, and not listed in other guidebooks. Obviously, a place meeting every criterion is rare, and many hotels fall short of perfection—sometimes miserably. But if I can find a place with, say, six out of those nine criteria...it's a keeper.

It pays to choose your accommodations thoughtfully. Expensive hotels can rip through a tight budget like a grenade through a dollhouse. I hear people complaining about that "\$300 double in Frankfurt" or the "\$500-a-night room in London." They come back from their vacations with bruised and battered pocketbooks, telling stories that scare their friends out of international travel and back to Florida or Hawaii one more time. True, you can spend \$500 for a double, but I never have. That's three days' accommodations for me.

My favorite type of European hotel: well-located, small, friendly, charming, and moderately priced

As far as I'm concerned, spending more for your hotel just builds a bigger wall between you and what you traveled so far to see. If you spend enough, you won't know where you are. Think about it. "In-ter-con-ti-nen-tal." That means the same everywhere—designed for people who deep down inside wish they weren't traveling, people spending someone else's money, people who need a strap over the toilet telling them no one's sat there yet. It's uniform sterility, a lobby full of Stay-Press Americans, English menus, and lamps bolted to the tables.

Europe's small, mid-range hotels may not have room service, but their staffs are more interested in seeing pictures of your children and helping you have a great time than in thinning out your wallet.

Here are a few factors to weigh when searching for a hotel that suits your budget:

Think small. Larger hotels are usually pricier than small hotels or

B&Bs, partly because of taxes (for example, in Britain, once a B&B exceeds a certain revenue level, it's required to pay an extra 15 percent VAT in addition to its other taxes). Hoteliers who pay high taxes pass their costs on to you.

Consider a cheap chain hotel. More and more hotel chains—offering cheap or moderately priced rooms—are springing up throughout Europe. The hotels that allow up to four people in a room are great for families. You won't find character at chain hotels, but you'll get predictable, Motel 6–type comfort. The huge Accor chain offers a range of options, from the cheap Formule 1 Hotels (mostly in France, www.hotelformule1.com) to the mid-range Ibis Hotels (sterile, throughout Europe, www.ibishotel.com) to the pricier, cushier Mercure and Novotel Hotels (for all Accor Hotels, see www.accorhotels.com, US tel. 800-515-5679). Britain has Travelodge

Europe's cheap, no-character hotels cater to local business travelers interested in going home with some of their per diem still in their pockets.

(www.travelodge.co.uk), Premier Inn (www.premierinn.com), and Jurys Inn (www.jurysinn.com, also found throughout Ireland). The easyHotel chain—based on the pay-as-you-go business model of their sister airline, easyJet—rents cheap and very basic rooms in major European cities, including London, Berlin, Zürich, and Budapest (www.easyhotel.com).

Know the exceptions. Hotels in northern Europe are pricier than those in the south, but you can find exceptions. In Scandinavia, Brussels, and Berlin, fancy "business hotels" are desperate for customers in the summer and year-round on weekends, when their business customers stay away. They offer some amazing deals through the local tourist offices. The later your arrival, the better the discount.

Be a smart consumer—don't stray above your needs. Know the government ratings. A three-star hotel is not necessarily a bad value, but if I stay in a three-star hotel, I've spent $70 extra for things I don't need. You can get air-conditioning, elevators, private showers, room service, a 24-hour reception desk, and people in uniforms to carry your bags. But each of those services adds $10 to your room cost, and, before you know it, the simple $80 room is up to $150. Additional charges can pile on top of this already-inflated room rate. For example, most moderately priced hotels offer Wi-Fi free to their guests, while the expensive places are more likely to charge for it.

Check the prices on the room list to find the best value. Room prices can vary tremendously within a hotel according to facilities provided. On their websites and near their reception desks, most hotels post a room summary that lists each room, its bed configuration, facilities, and maximum price (for one and for two people), sometimes broken down by season (low, middle, high). Also read the breakfast, tax, and extra-bed policies. By studying this information, you'll see that, in many places, a shower is cheaper than a bath, and a double bed is cheaper than twins. In other words, an inattentive couple who prefer a shower and a double bed can pay $20 more for a bath and twins. In some cases, if you want any room for two and you say "double," they'll think you'll only take a double bed. To keep all my options open (twin and double), I ask for "a room for two people." If you want a cheap room, say it. Many hoteliers have a few unrenovated rooms without a private bathroom; they usually don't even mention these, figuring they'd be unacceptable to Americans.

Put more people in a room. Family rooms are common, and putting four in a quad is much cheaper than two doubles. Many doubles come with a small double bed and a sliver of a single, so a third person pays very little. A family with two small children can ask for a triple and bring a sleeping bag for the stowaway.

Try to wrangle a discount for a longer stay, payment in cash, or booking direct. If you plan to stay three or more nights at a place, or if you pay in cash rather than by credit card (saving the hotelier the credit-card company's cut), it's worth asking if a discount is available. Also keep in mind that if you book direct—rather than going through a middleman, such as a hotel-booking website or TI room-finding service—you're saving the hotel from paying that intermediary their cut. This might make the hotelier more open to giving you a deal. Do some research. If the hotel rents rooms at a discount through a hotel-booking website, you can guess they'd take an offer of that same rate from you if you book direct—even if it's lower than the rates posted at the hotel.

If it's off-season, bargain. Prices usually rise with demand during festivals and in July and August. Off-season, try haggling. If the place is too expensive, tell them your limit; they might meet it.

Avoid doing outside business through your hotel. Go to the bullring and get the ticket yourself. You'll learn more and save money, and you won't sit with other tourists who drown your Spanish fire with Yankee-pankee. So often, tourists are herded together—by a conspiracy of hotel managers and tour organizers—at gimmicky folk evenings featuring a medley of cheesy cultural clichés kept alive only for the tourists. You can't relive your precious Madrid nights. Do them right—on your own.

Avoid hotels that require you to buy meals. Many national governments regulate hotel prices according to class or rating. In order to overcome this price ceiling (especially at resorts in peak season, when demand exceeds supply), hotels might require that you buy dinner in their dining room. Breakfast is normally included in the room rate, but in some countries it's an expensive, semi-optional tack-on. Sometimes an additional meal is required (this is called "half board," "half pension," or *demi-pension*); occasionally, a hotel will demand that you eat all three meals in their restaurant (known as "full board" or "full pension")—this option is rarely economical. I prefer the freedom to explore and sample the atmosphere of restaurants in other neighborhoods.

Europe's Budget Hotels: What's a Cheap Room?

Europe has many traditional old hotels—dingy, a bit run-down, central, friendly, safe, and government-regulated, offering good-enough-for-the-European-good-enough-for-me beds. In a typical budget European hotel, a double room costs an average of $100 a night. You'll pay about $80 at a pension in Madrid, $90 at a simple guesthouse in rural Germany or a B&B on the Croatian coast, and $130 for a two-star hotel in Paris or a private room in a Bergen pension. This is hardcore Europe: fun, cheap, and easy to find, particularly in Italy, France, Spain, Portugal, and Greece.

A typical budget hotel room: tidy, small, affordable

A typical room in an old-fashioned, low-end hotel has a simple bed (occasionally a springy cot, so always test it out before accepting the room); a rickety, old, wooden (or new, plastic) chair and table; a freestanding closet; a small window; old wallpaper; a good sink under a fluorescent light; a mysterious bidet; a view of another similar room across a tall, thin courtyard; peeling plaster; and a tiled or wood floor. The light fixtures are very simple, often with a weak and sometimes even bare and dangling ceiling light bulb. Naked neon is common in the south. While non-smoking places are catching on (and, in many countries, legally mandated), a lot of cheap rooms still come with ashtrays. You might have a TV, but likely not a telephone. While more and more European hotels are squeezing boat-type prefab showers and toilets into their rooms, the cheapest rooms still offer only a toilet and shower or tub down the hall, which you share with a half-dozen other rooms.

Rooms often come with a continental breakfast (usually served from about 7:30 to 10:00 a.m. in the breakfast room near the front desk): coffee, tea, or hot chocolate, and a roll that's firmer than your mattress. Breakfasts in northern and eastern Europe can be a bit heartier, with fruit, yogurt, cereal, and more. For details, see "Breakfast" on page 238.

In the lobby, there's nearly always a lounge with a TV, a phone, and a person at the desk who's a good information source. You'll climb lots of stairs, as a hotel's lack of an elevator is often the only reason it can't raise its prices. You'll be given a front-door key because the desk is not staffed all night.

Cheap hotels usually have clean-enough but depressing shower rooms, with hot water

1977: It slowly dawns on Rick that cheap beds aren't always good beds.

normally free and constant (but, in very rare cases, available only through a coin-op meter or at certain hours). The WC has toilet paper, but might have a missing, cracked, or broken lid. At a few hotels, you might be charged $3–5 for a towel and a key to the shower room. The cheapest hotels are run by and filled with people from the Two-Thirds World.

I want to stress that there are places I find unacceptable. I don't mind dingy wallpaper, climbing stairs, and "going down the hall," but I won't compromise when it comes to safety and friendliness.

The hotel I'm describing may be appalling to many Americans; to others, it's charming, colorful, or funky. To me, "funky" means spirited and full of character(s): a caged bird in the TV room, grandchildren in the backyard, a dog sleeping in the hall, no uniforms, singing maids, a night-shift man tearing breakfast napkins in two so they'll go farther, a handwritten neighborhood history lesson on the wall, different furniture in each room, and a willingness to buck the system when the tourist board starts requiring shoeshine machines in the hallways. An extra $40–50 per night will buy you into cheerier wallpaper and less funkiness.

Unfortunately, cheap hotels are becoming an endangered species. As Europe becomes more and more affluent, a powerful force is pushing hotels up in price and comfort. Land in big cities is so expensive that cheap hotels can't survive and are bought out, gutted, and turned into modern hotels. More and more Europeans are expecting what were once considered "American" standards of plumbing and comfort. A great value is often a hardworking family-run place that structurally can't fit showers in every room or an elevator up its spiral staircase. Prices are regulated and, regardless of how comfy and charming it is, with no elevator and a lousy shower-to-room ratio, it is—and will remain—a cheap hotel.

How to Find the Right Hotel

Whether you're booking your entire trip months in advance, or rolling into town after dark and finding a room on the fly, these tips will help you choose what's best for you and your budget.

Using Guidebooks

A trusted guidebook remains the best place to start your search for a great hotel. Find and use a guidebook whose travel philosophy matches yours. (For a rundown of various guidebooks, see page 11.) Get the most current edition possible—but even with the newest editions, don't be surprised if rates have increased slightly since the book was published.

Researching Hotels Online

The Internet is another excellent tool. You can use it in conjunction with your guidebook to learn more about recommended hotels, search for discounts, read fellow travelers' reviews, and fill in gaps when traveling beyond destinations covered by your guidebook.

If a guidebook's write-up of a particular hotel appeals to you, visit that hotel's website to glean additional information, check prices, and view photos of the rooms. Many hotels have a booking form right on their website (explained later, under "Making Reservations"). And some hotels (especially chain or business hotels) offer discounts only if you book on their website.

You can choose and book all of your hotels online without ever consulting a guidebook. Get a sense of the types of hotels available and the range of prices on websites such as Travelocity.com, Expedia.com, and Orbitz.com. Sites such as Mobissimo.com and Hotelscombined .com compile prices from travel agencies, consolidators, and hotel websites. Tripadvisor.com is one of the best sources for independent traveler reviews; the Graffiti Wall at www.ricksteves.com/graffiti is another source. If your travel dates are flexible, consider the deep discounts available on sites such as Priceline.com and EuroCheapo.com. Also consider the "air plus hotel" packages described on page 89.

What you won't easily find on these sites are links to individual hotels' actual websites—that's because the big guys want you to book through them (or their partners) for a fee. Once you've identified a promising option, do a Google search for the hotel's name to find its own website. You'll get more complete information, and you are more likely to save money by booking direct.

Bed-Finding as You Travel

While most travelers prefer to nail down room reservations long in advance (explained later), you can blow like the wind freely through Europe if you want, finding beds on the fly. These tricks work for me.

Travel with a good list of hotels. Even if you're footloose and fancy-free, you don't have to totally wing it. Bring along a good guidebook so you at least have a sense of your options (and the general price range in town) when you begin your search.

The early bird gets the room. If you anticipate crowds, go to great lengths to arrive in the morning when the most (and best) rooms are available. If the rooms aren't ready until noon, take one anyway. Leave your luggage behind the desk; they'll move you in later and you're set up—free to relax and enjoy the city. I would leave Florence at 7 a.m. to arrive in popular, crowded Venice early enough to get a decent choice of rooms. Consider the advantage of overnight train rides—you'll arrive, if not bright, at least early.

Your approach to room-finding will be determined by whether it's a "buyer's market" or a "seller's market"—based on the current demand. These trends can be obvious (a beach resort will be crowded in summer, empty in winter); in other cases, a guidebook or local TI can tip you off. Sometimes you can arrive late, be selective, and even talk down the price. Other times you'll happily accept anything with a pillow and a blanket.

Use the telephone. When you're ready to book, telephone the places in your guidebook that sound best. Not only will it save the time and money involved in chasing down these places with the risk of finding them full, but you're beating all the other tourists—with the same guidebook—who may be hoofing it as you dial. It's rewarding to arrive at a hotel when people are being turned away and see your name on the reservation list because you called first. If the room or price isn't what you were led to believe it would be, you have every right to say, "No, thank you." In peak times, a guidebook's top hotel listings are likely to be full. Don't hesitate to jump way down the list, where available rooms may abound.

Shop around. When going door-to-door, the first place you check is rarely the best. It's worth 20 minutes of shopping around to find the going rate before you accept a room. You'll be surprised how prices vary as you walk farther from the station or down a street strewn with B&Bs. Never judge a hotel by its exterior or lobby. Lavish interiors with shabby exteriors (blame the landlord who's stuck with rent control, not the hotel) are a cultural trait of Europe. (If you're traveling with a companion, one of you can watch the bags over a cup of coffee while the other runs around.)

Ask to see the room before accepting. Then the receptionist knows the room must pass your inspection. He'll have to earn your business. Notice the bellhop is given two keys. You asked for only one room. He's instructed to show the hard-to-sell room first. It's only natural for the hotel receptionist to try to unload the most difficult-to-sell room on the easiest-to-please traveler. Somebody has to sleep in it. If you ask to see both rooms, you'll get the better one. When you check out a room, point out anything that deserves displeasure. The price will come down, or they'll show you a better room. Think about heat and noise. Some towns never quiet down. I'll climb a few stairs to reach cheaper rooms higher off the noisy road. A room in back may lack a view, but it will also lack nighttime noise.

Consider hotel runners. As you step off the bus or train, you'll sometimes be met by hotel runners wielding pictures of their rooms for rent. My gut reaction is to steer clear, but these people are usually just hardworking entrepreneurs who lack the location or write-up in a popular guidebook that can make life easy for a small hotel or B&B owner. If you like the guy and what he promises, and his rooms aren't too far away, follow him to take a look. You are obliged only to inspect the room. If it's good, take it. If it's not, leave. You're probably near other budget accommodations anyway. Establish the location very clearly, as some of these people have good places located miserably far out of town. Especially in Eastern

"Welcome! I have rooms."

Europe, these room hawkers might not be affiliated with a hotel at all, but simply rent out vacant rooms in their own homes. If nothing else, taking the room for a night is an easy way to buy more time to seek out an even better option for the remainder of your stay. For details, see "Bed-and-Breakfast Places and Pensions," later in this chapter.

Use room-finding services only if necessary. Popular tourist cities usually have a room-finding service at the train station or tourist information office. They have a listing of that town's "acceptable" available accommodations. For a fee of a few dollars, they'll get you a room in the price range and neighborhood of your choice. Especially in a big city, their service can be worth the price when you consider the time and money saved by avoiding the search on foot.

I avoid room-finding services unless I have no listings or information of my own. Their hotel lists normally make no judgments about quality, so what you get is potluck. The stakes are too high for this to be acceptable (especially when you consider how readily available good hotel listings are in guidebooks). Remember the exception: In certain northern European cities—such as Brussels and the Scandinavian capitals—room-booking services can sometimes land you a deeply discounted room in an upscale business-class hotel.

Also, since many room-finding services profit from taking a "deposit" that they pocket, many managers of the best budget places tell the room-finding service they're full when they aren't. They know they'll fill up with travelers coming direct, allowing the hotelier to keep 100 percent of the room cost.

Recently, many tourist information offices have lost their government funding and are now privately owned. This creates the absurdity of a profit-seeking tourist information "service." Their previously reliable advice is now colored with a need to make a kickback. Some room-finding services work for a group of supporting hotels. Only if you insist will you get information on cheap sleeping options—dormitories, hostels, and sleep-ins. And beware: Many offices labeled "tourist information" are just travel agencies and room-booking services in disguise.

Follow taxi tips. A great way to find a place in a tough situation is to let a cabbie take you to his favorite hotel. They are experts.

Let hotel managers help. Have your current hotelier call ahead to make a reservation at your next destination (offer to pay for the call). If you're in a town and having trouble finding a room, remember that nobody knows the hotel scene better than hotel managers do. If one hotel is full, ask the hotelier for help. Often the manager has a list of neighborhood accommodations or will even telephone a friend's place that

Ask your friend who runs today's hotel to call tomorrow's hotel to make you a reservation in the native language.

rarely fills up and is just around the corner. If the hotel is too expensive, there's nothing wrong with asking where you could find a "not-so-good place." The most expensive hotels have the best city maps (free, often with other hotels listed) and an English-speaking staff that can give advice to the polite traveler in search of a cheap room. I find hotel receptionists to be understanding and helpful.

Leave the trouble zone. If the room situation is impossible, don't struggle—just leave. An hour by car, train, or bus from the most miserable hotel situation anywhere in Europe is a town—Dullsdorf or Nothingston—with the Dullsdorf Gasthaus or the Nothingston Inn just across the street from the station or right on the main square. It's not full—never has been, never will be. There's a guy sleeping behind the reception desk. Drop in at 11 p.m., ask for 14 beds, and he'll say, "Take the second and third floors—the keys are in the doors." It always works. Oktoberfest, Cannes Film Festival, St-Tropez Running of the Girls, Easter at Lourdes—your bed awaits you in nearby Dullsdorf. If you anticipate trouble, consider staying at the last train stop before the crowded city.

Be homeless for a night. In more than a thousand unreserved nights in Europe, I've been shut out three times. That's a 99.7 percent bedding average earned in peak season and very often in crowded, touristy, or festive places. What's so traumatic about a night without a bed, anyway? The cost of a wonderfully reservation-free trip is the remote chance you'll end up spending the night on a bench in the train-station waiting room. My survey shows that those who have the opportunity to be a refugee for a night have their perspectives broadened and actually enjoy the experience—in retrospect.

To Reserve or Not to Reserve?

I used to travel with absolutely no reservations. A daily chore was checking out several hotels or pensions and choosing one. Europe was ramshackle, things were cheap, and hotel listings were unreliable and unnecessary. Now, like hobos in a Jetsons world, budget travelers need to think one step ahead. Every Europe-bound traveler has to make a

Family-run hotels offer the warmest welcome and the best value.

decision: Am I willing to sacrifice spontaneity for the peace of mind of knowing exactly where I'll sleep each night?

For maximum spontaneity, find rooms as you travel. There's nothing more liberating than choosing which town to visit only when you step onto the rail platform, or heading to a new destination just to get away from the clouds or crowds. But doing this also makes it less likely you'll find a room that matches your budget and priorities. And even those who generally skip reservations like to at least reserve their arrival night in Europe (as jet-lagged room-finding can be stressful). Several tips for this strategy are explained in the previous section, "Bed-Finding as You Travel."

For a mix of predictability and flexibility, call ahead as you travel. If you don't want to book everything far in advance, but also don't want to simply show up without a room, calling a day or two ahead while on the road can be a good compromise. This works best when there's relatively little demand for rooms (in shoulder season or in less crowded places). In these situations, my standard room-finding tactic is to telephone in the morning to reserve my room for that night. I travel relaxed, knowing a good place is holding a room for me until late afternoon.

For maximum choice and peace of mind, book far in advance. Most travelers find that, to get into the most popular, best-value hotels, it's worth booking ahead. In fact, lately I've been getting aced out by my own readers at my favorite accommodations. So when I want to be certain to get my first choice, I reserve several weeks (or even months) in advance. For peak-season travel and when visiting big, popular cities (such as London, Paris, Madrid, Venice, and so on), I make my reservations as soon as I can pin down a date.

Making Reservations

If you decide to reserve rooms in advance, here are the basics.

Reserve by email, fax, or phone. These days, virtually every European hotel and B&B uses the Internet. An email in simple English communicates clearly, minimizes the language barrier, gives your hotel a quick and easy way to respond, and is free for both parties. While most accommodations still have fax machines, the hassle and expense of faxing are making it obsolete. For the rare, traditional place that lacks email, faxing (which is cheaper and comes with a smaller language barrier) is still preferable to calling. If you don't get a response to your fax, it usually means the hotel is already fully booked. Using the phone is ideal only if you want an immediate response.

Include all the key information in your reservation request. Whether you're emailing or faxing, the hotelier wants to know these key pieces of information (also included in the sample request form on the next page and at www.ricksteves.com/reservation):

- number and type of rooms (e.g., "1 double room")
- date and estimated time of arrival
- date of departure
- number of nights
- special needs (e.g., bathroom in the room or down the hall, twin beds vs. one big bed, air-conditioning, quiet, view, ground floor/no stairs, etc.)

To avoid confusion, use the European order for writing dates: day/month/year. For example, a couple reserving a two night stay would write the following: "Please reserve 1 double room for 2 nights, arriving 16 July 2011, departing 18 July 2011." Consider in advance how long you'll stay; don't just assume you can extend your reservation for extra days once you arrive.

In France, each hotel has a plaque next to its door telling you its category.

Wait to hear back, then confirm. Once they've offered you a room, that isn't a confirmation. You still must accept the reservation. Request a confirmation with the price quoted. It's smart to carry a printed copy of your confirmation—both to keep track of where you're staying, and as recourse in the rare situation that the hotel loses your reservation.

It can save time to book online. Many hotels have a reservation request form built into their websites. Type in your preferred dates, and the website automatically displays a list of available rooms and prices. To reserve, enter your contact information and credit-card number;

Hotel Reservation

To: _____   _____
         hotel   *email or fax*

From: _____   _____
          name   *email or fax*

Today's date: _____ / _____ / _____
                        day   *month*   *year*

Dear Hotel _____ ,

Please make this reservation for me:

Name: _____

Total # of people: _____   # of rooms: _____   # of nights: _____

Arriving: _____ / _____ / _____   My time of arrival (24-hr clock): _____
              day   *month* *year*   (I will telephone if I will be late)

Departing: _____ / _____ / _____
                day *month* *year*

Room(s): Single ____   Double ____   Twin ____   Triple ____   Quad ____

With: Toilet _____   Shower _____   Bath _____   Sink only _____

Special needs: View ____   Quiet ____   Cheapest ____   Ground Floor ____

Please email or fax confirmation of my reservation, along with the type of room reserved and the price. Please also inform me of your cancellation policy. After I hear from you, I will quickly send my credit-card information as a deposit to hold the room. Thank you.

_____
Name

_____
Address

_____
City   *State*   *Zip Code*   *Country*

Before hoteliers can make your reservation, they want to know the information listed above. You can use this form as the basis for your email, or you can photocopy this page, fill in the information, and send it as a fax (also available online at www.ricksteves.com/reservation).

the hotel will send you a confirmation via email. Two notes of caution: Before entering your credit-card number, make sure the site is secure (check for the *https:* in your browser's address bar). And don't mistake a booking agency site for the hotel's own booking form. While booking agencies can provide good deals, it's better to reserve directly with the hotel (eliminating the middleman and saving both you and the hotelier money).

Give a deposit. When you book your reservation, the hotelier will usually request your credit-card number as a deposit. I usually send my credit-card number in an email, but this does pose a security risk. To keep your number more secure, you could call or fax the hotel to give them the information. You can be billed if you don't show up (if your plans are iffy, ask about their cancellation policy—see below).

Small B&Bs, which don't accept credit cards, typically don't require a deposit; however, in places where no-shows are epidemic, some B&B owners request that you mail them a check (relatively straightforward) or wire them money (expensive and complicated) to hold a room for you.

Especially during slow times, many accommodations will hold a room without a deposit if you promise to arrive early in the day. The earlier you promise, the better your chances of being trusted. If you'll be a little late, call again to assure them you're coming.

If you must cancel, cancel far in advance. If you're staying at a small B&B, the owner loses money if you don't show up. It's polite to cancel as far ahead as possible, to give them time to fill that room. (Don't let these people down—I promised them you'd call if you can't make it.) Larger hotels tend to have stricter cancellation policies than US hotels. If you don't cancel far enough ahead—usually a day or two, but can be up to several weeks—you're obligated to pay for one night of your booking (charged on the credit card you gave them for the deposit). Especially if you think you might have to cancel, carefully confirm the hotel's cancellation policy when you book. It's also important to get a written record (via email) of your cancellation. (You might have to request this more than once, but it's worth it.) It's not unusual for hotels to lose track of your cancellation, then charge you when you don't show up.

Call ahead to reconfirm. Always reconfirm your room reservation a day or two in advance from the road. (This gives you time to improvise in the unlikely event that something goes wrong with your reservation.) Especially at a small B&B—where the owner might need to leave home to run errands—it's also courteous to mention your approximate arrival time.

Don't panic. If, after several tries, it seems that every hotel in town

Chill Out

As Europe gets hotter, more hotels are offering rooms with air-conditioning. (But be aware that regulations may prohibit turning on the air-conditioning between October and May.) Most A/C units come with a remote control, similar to one for a TV. The various remotes have basically the same features:

An A/C remote lets you cool off the room without even getting out of bed.

- Fan icon (click to toggle through the wind power, from light to gale)
- Louver icon (click to choose steady air flow or waves)
- Snowflake and sunshine icons (heat or cold; generally just one or the other is possible: cool in summer, heat in winter)
- Two clock settings (to determine how many hours the air-conditioning will stay on before turning off, or stay off before turning on)
- Temperature control (20 or 21 degrees Celsius is a comfortable temperature)

is full, don't worry. Hotels take only so many long-distance advance reservations. They never know how long guests will stay and like to keep a few beds for their regulars. Call between 8 and 10 a.m. the day you plan to arrive. This is when the receptionist knows exactly who's leaving and which rooms she needs to fill. She'll be eager to get a name for every available room. Those who are there in person are more likely to land a room. Many simple hotels don't bother with reservations more than a couple of weeks in advance, and some very cheap hotels take no reservations at all. Just show up and sleep with your money belt on.

Check-In Tips

Establish the complete and final price of a room up front. Know what's included and what taxes and other charges (e.g., breakfast, extra fee for air-conditioning) will be added. More than once I've been given a bill that was double what I expected. Dinners were required, and I was billed whether I ate them or not; so I was told—in very clear Italian.

When checking in, pick up the hotel's business card. In the most confusing cities, the cards come with a little map. Even the best path-finders get lost in a big city, and not knowing where your hotel is can be scary. With the card, you can hop into a cab and be home in minutes. Many larger hotels give out free city maps.

When you pay is up to the hotel and you. Normally I pay upon departure. If they want prepayment, that's fine, but unless I'm absolutely certain I'll be staying on, I pay one night at a time. Don't assume your room is yours once you're in. Make it clear when you check in how long you intend to stay, or you may get the boot.

Hotel Help and Hassles

Your hotelier can be a great help and source of advice. Hotels are in the business of accommodating people. If you need another blanket or an electrical adapter, just ask. Hoteliers can point you to the nearest Internet café, launderette, grocery store, restaurant, or show. They'll call a taxi for you, make restaurant reservations, telephone your next hotel, or give you driving instructions for your departure.

Many hoteliers can book bus tours for you (though they usually get a commission, so they might be biased in their recommendation). In Florence, hoteliers can make museum reservations for the Uffizi Gallery and for Michelangelo's *David*; ask when you book your room. If you arrive in town early or need to leave a town late, your hotel will usually store your bag for you while you sightsee.

But even at the best hotel, things can go awry. You may be on your dream trip, but you're still in the real world. Take a deep breath, and remember that things go wrong at home, too. If you state your concern to your hotelier kindly, you'll more likely be dealt with kindly.

When you enter a hotel room for the first time, survey it for prob-lems. Is the bathroom dirty and moldy? Is the window latch broken and unsafe? Are you next to a noisy elevator? Is the room too small? If the room you're shown doesn't meet your standards, ask to see a different one. It's easier to change rooms before you've moved in.

It can be disappointing to arrive at a hotel and find that your room is in a less desirable annex or in a partner hotel. If you feel the hotel has misrepresented its offer, it can help (though it's not essential) to show them a copy of their confirmation email. You don't need to stay.

Just like at your own house, hotels experience mechanical break-downs from time to time. The air-conditioning dies when you need it most. Sinks leak, hot water turns cold, toilets gurgle and smell. The Wi-Fi doesn't work. The elevator refuses to budge. Report your concerns calmly at the front desk. For more complicated problems, don't expect instant results.

Be prepared for regional differences in bedding. In France, some hotel beds have irregular pillows (shaped like a wedge or a log). To get an American-style pillow, look in the closet or ask at the desk. In alpine countries and in northern Europe, many hotels use covered duvets instead of a top sheet; don't be confused if your top sheet is "missing." At many hotels—especially in northern and Eastern Europe—a "double bed" is often two twin

French hotels sometimes come with Lincoln Log pillows.

beds pushed together, sometimes sheeted as one big bed. Don't count on getting a true double or queen-size bed, but it can help to specify "one big bed for two people." Or use the local lingo: *französische Leige* in German, *un lit de cent-soixante* in French, *matrimoniale* in Italian, *matrimonial* in Spanish, and so on.

Occasionally travelers encounter bedbugs—tiny blood-sucking insects that live in bedding and come out at night. Bedbugs may be visible in the seams of the mattress, but often the first signs of trouble are mysterious, itchy welts (similar to mosquito bites) on your legs and arms. These critters are a nuisance, but they don't spread disease. Bedbugs can show up even at fine hotels, brought in by the last guest. Don't automatically assume that the hotel is overrun with them. Report the problem, and see how it's dealt with. If it's a nice hotel, changing rooms should be enough.

Mosquitoes can also be pests. In warm climates, make sure there's a window screen; if there isn't, think twice about leaving your window open all day for ventilation. Insect repellant can help.

Europe seems to excel in thin-walled rooms, narrow streets that amplify traffic noise, and people who party until the wee hours in formerly romantic piazzas. I always consider these problems before settling into a room. If you suspect night noise will be a problem, ask for a room in the back or on an upper floor. Some travelers customarily ask for a quiet room when they book or reconfirm their reservation; if you wait to ask until you arrive, the quietest rooms might already be occupied. On the other hand, if you'd happily put up with some street noise to look out onto a square, be sure to ask for a view (which might cost extra).

"Too many stairs!" is a common complaint. In general, European hotels have more stairs and fewer elevators than we're used to. Think of it as exercise, and pack light. On the bright side, higher floors generally have better views and less street noise than lower ones. If you must have an elevator or ground-floor room, confirm they're available when you book. And be aware that European hotel elevators can be miniscule.

Americans are sometimes disappointed in the size of the breakfasts, especially in southern Europe (France, Italy, Spain, and Portugal), where a continental breakfast typically consists of just a roll or pastry and a cup of coffee. (You pick up a mid-morning snack at a market or bakery.)

If you're trying to dial out from your room but the phone won't work, try calling (or visiting) the reception desk. They might have to open up an outside line for you on the switchboard, or they can tell you if you have to dial an access number first. If the hotel has Wi-Fi, ask whether you need to pay to use it, and request the network name and password.

If something is stolen from your room, talk to the hotelier. To guard against theft, keep your valuables out of sight in your room. Some rooms come with a safe, and other hotels have safes at the front desk. Use them if you are concerned.

If you're in southern Europe and you're having trouble getting a problem solved at your hotel, ask to see the complaint book, which the hotelier is legally required to show you on request. Sometimes even just asking to see the complaint book will inspire the hotelier to see that your problem is fixed. If you've had a good experience, jot a friendly note in the hotel's guest book; conscientious hoteliers love to show these off to arriving guests.

Unfriendly staff can taint your stay, but don't let them ruin your trip. If you have difficulties to bring up, keep checking to see if a sympathetic staff member comes on shift, or just be persistent (kind but firm) with whomever you have to deal with. Generally the hotel staff doesn't like to have complainers overheard by other customers, so it can be effective to state your problems clearly and reasonably with witnesses around. The staff may accommodate you just to shut you up.

Checkout can pose problems if surprise charges pop up on your bill. Ask the hotelier to explain each item you're not sure about. Some charges are legitimate; for example, in some touristy areas, hotels charge a per-day tax that everyone has to pay. To avoid preventable charges, don't use the hotel-room phone to make international calls unless you have an

The 🔑 to Keys

Tourists spend hours fumbling with old skeleton keys in rickety hotel doors. The haphazard, nothing-square construction of old hotels means the keys need babying. Don't push them in all the way. Lift the door in or up. Try a little in, quarter turn, and farther in for full turn. Always turn the top of the key away from the door frame to open it. Some locks take two key revolutions to open. Leave the key at the desk before leaving for the day. I've never had my room

broken into in Europe. Confirm closing time. Some hotels lock up after their restaurant closes, after midnight, or during their weekly "quiet day" and expect you to keep the key to the outside door with you to get in after hours.

Plastic key cards (the size of a credit card) are becoming standard at many European hotels. If there's no slot to insert the card into, try simply touching the card to your door's keypad. Once inside the room, you may have to insert your card into a slot near the door to turn on the lights. This green measure is intended to prevent potentially energy-wasting guests from leaving the lights on when they're not in the room.

international calling card (and even then, ask first to be sure the hotel won't charge you to dial that "toll-free" access number). Some hoteliers have credit-card readers that mysteriously break when you want to check out, requiring you to pay in cash. Or you might be charged extra if you want to pay with your credit card. If you settle up your bill the night before you leave, you'll have time to discuss and address any points of contention.

Above all, keep a positive attitude. After all, you're on vacation. If your hotel is a disappointment, spend more time out enjoying the city you came to see.

Alternatives to Hotels

Consider these potentially money-saving alternatives to traditional hotels.

Bed-and-Breakfast Places and Pensions

Between hotels and hostels in price and style is a special class of accommodations: bed-and-breakfasts (B&Bs). These are small, warm, and family-run, and offer a personal touch at a budget price. They are the next best thing to staying with a family, and even if hotels weren't more expensive, I'd still choose this budget alternative.

Each country has these friendly accommodations in varying degrees of abundance, facilities, and service. Some include breakfast, some don't. They have different names from country to country, but all have one thing in common: They satisfy the need for a place to stay that gives you the

Bed-and-breakfasts offer double the cultural experience for half the price of a hotel.

privacy of a hotel and the comforts of home at a price you can afford.

While information on some of the more established places is available in many budget-travel guidebooks, the best information is often found locally, through tourist information offices, room-finding services, or even from the man waiting for his bus or selling apples. Especially in the British Isles, each B&B host has a network of favorites and can happily set you up in a good B&B at your next stop.

Many times, the information is brought to you. I'll never forget struggling off the plane on my arrival in Santorini. Fifteen women were begging me to spend the night. Thrilled, I made a snap decision and followed the most attractive offer to a very nice budget accommodation.

The "part of the family" element of a B&B stay is determined entirely by you. Chatty friendliness is not forced on guests. Depending on my mood and workload, I am often very businesslike and private during my stay. On other occasions, I join the children in the barn for

A special bonus when enjoying Britain's great B&Bs: You get your own temporary mother.

Terms for Private Rooms to Rent

Private rooms throughout Europe cost $40–60 per person and come with breakfast in Great Britain, Ireland, Germany, and Austria.

In...	Look for...
Great Britain & Ireland	Bed-and-Breakfast
Norway/Sweden	*Rom* or *Rum*
Denmark	*Værelser*
Germany/Austria	*Zimmer*
France	*Chambre (d'hôte)*
Italy	*(Affitta) Camere*
Spain	*Casa Particulare*
Portugal	*Quarto*
Greece	*Dhomatia*
Croatia/Slovenia	*Sobe*
Poland	*Pokoje*
Eastern Europe	*Zimmer* or "Rooms"

the sheep-shearing festivities.

Don't confuse European bed-and-breakfasts with their rich cousins in America. B&Bs in the United States are usually frilly, fancy places, very cozy and colorful but as expensive as hotels. In a European B&B, rather than seven pillows and a basket of jams, you get a warm welcome and a good price.

The British Isles: Britain's B&Bs are the best of all. As the name indicates, a breakfast comes with the bed, and (except in London) this is no ordinary breakfast. Most B&B owners take pride in their breakfasts. Their guests sit down to an elegant and very British table setting and feast on cereal, juice, bacon, sausage, eggs, broiled tomatoes, mushrooms, toast, marmalade, and coffee or tea. While you are finishing your coffee, the landlady (who by this time is probably on very friendly terms with you) may present

In most British towns, B&Bs line up along the same street—find one, and you've found a dozen.

you with her guest book, inviting you to make an entry and pointing out others from your state who have stayed in her house. Your hostess will sometimes cook you a simple dinner for a good price, and, if you have time to chat, you may get in on an evening social hour. When you bid her farewell and thank her for the good sleep and full stomach, it's often difficult to get away. Determined to fill you with as much information as food, she wants you to have the best day of sightseeing possible.

If you're going to the normal tourist stops, your guidebook will list some good B&Bs. If you're venturing off the beaten British path, you don't need (or want) a listing. The small towns and countryside are littered with places

Never judge a B&B by its name. Like most in Britain, this one is non-smoking and comes with numerous pleasant extras.

Shower Strategies

To go local, take quick showers. Americans are notorious (and embarrassing) energy gluttons—wasting hot water and leaving lights on as if electricity were cheap. Who besides us sings in the shower? European energy costs are shocking, and some hostels and budget hotels actually have coin-operated showers. It's a good idea to have an extra token handy to avoid that lathered look. A "navy shower," using the water only to soap up and rinse off, is a wonderfully conservative method, and those who follow you will more likely enjoy some warm *Wasser* (although starting and stopping the water doesn't start and stop the meter).

European showers: Each one has its own personality.

"C" can mean "hot." Most of the cold showers Americans take in Europe are cold only because they don't know how to turn the hot water on. Study the particular system, and, before you shiver, ask the receptionist for help. There are some very peculiar tricks. In Italy and Spain, "C" is for *caldo/caliente*—hot. In many British places, there's a "hot" switch at the base of the shower or even in the hallway. In Croatia, look for the switch with an icon of a hot-water tank (usually next to the room's light switch). You'll find showers and baths of all kinds. The red knob is hot and the blue one is cold—or vice versa. Unusual showers often have clear instructions posted.

Try a sponge bath. Nearly every hotel room in Europe comes with a sink, and some have a bidet. Sponge baths are fast, easy, and European. A bidet is that mysterious porcelain thing that looks like an oversized bedpan. Tourists use them as anything from a launderette to a vomitorium to a watermelon rind receptacle to a urinal. They are used by locals to clean the parts of the body that rub together when they walk, in lieu of a shower. Give it the old four S's—straddle, squat, soap up, and swish off.

Bring soap. Many dorm-style accommodations don't provide towels or soap. B.Y.O.S. Towels, like breakfast and people, get smaller as you go south. In simple places, you won't get a washcloth, and bath towels are not replaced every day. Increasingly, environmentally-minded hotels—even fancy ones—post a sign explaining that they'll replace towels left on the floor, but not those that are hanging to dry. In my experience, pricey hotels rarely stay true to this promise; your towels will probably be replaced no matter where you leave them.

Use the hall shower. The cheapest hotels rarely provide a shower or toilet in your room. Each floor shares a toilet and a shower "down the hall." To such a bathoholic people, this sounds terrible. Imagine the congestion in the morning when the entire floor tries to pile into that bathtub! Remember, only Americans "need" a shower every morning. Few Americans stay in these basic hotels; therefore, you've got what amounts to a private bath—down the hall. I spend 100 nights a year in Europe—probably shower 80 times—and I typically

have to wait four or five times each year. That's the price I pay to take advantage of Europe's simple hotels.

In the last decade, even the simplest places have added lots of private showers. For example, a hotel originally designed with 20 simple rooms sharing two showers will now be retrofitted with private showers in 14 of its rooms. That leaves a more reasonable six rooms rather than 20 to share the two public showers. Those willing to go down the hall for a shower enjoy the same substantial savings with much less inconvenience.

Throughout southern Europe, even the cheapest hotel rooms come with a bidet. Europeans use them to stay clean without a daily shower.

If you have your own shower, prepare to be cramped. Many European hotels have tiny bathrooms that have been squeezed into the corner of an already modest-size room. Showers can be surprisingly tight, especially if you're a larger person. Be careful bending over to pick up a dropped bar of soap—you might just hit your head on the toilet or sink.

Try other places to shower. If you are vagabonding or sleeping several nights in transit, you can buy a shower in "day hotels" at major train stations and airports, at many freeway rest stops, and in public baths or swimming pools. Most Mediterranean beaches have free, freshwater showers all the time.

I have a theory that after four days without a shower, you don't get any worse, but that's another book.

whose quality varies only in degrees of wonderful. I try not to take a B&B until I have checked out three. Styles and atmosphere vary from house to house, and besides, I enjoy looking through European homes.

Britain rates its B&Bs using a diamond system (1–5) that considers cleanliness, furnishings, and decor. But diamond definitions are pretty squishy. Few B&Bs make a big deal of the ratings, and fewer tourists even know the system exists.

Ireland has essentially the same system of B&Bs. They are less expensive than England's and, if anything, even more "homely" (i.e., cozy). You can expect a big breakfast and comfortable room, often in the town center.

Germany, Switzerland, and Austria: Look for *Zimmer Frei* or *Privatzimmer*. These are very common in areas popular with travelers (such as Austria's Salzkammergut Lake District and Germany's Rhine, Romantic Road, and southern Bavaria). Signs will clearly indicate whether they have available rooms (green) or not (orange). Especially in Austria, one-night stays are discouraged. Most *Privatzimmer* cost about $40 per person and include a hearty continental breakfast. *Pensions* and *Gasthauses* are similarly priced small, family-run hotels. Don't confuse *Privatzimmer* with *Ferienwohnung*, which is a

Bed-and-breakfast travelers scramble at the breakfast table.

self-catering apartment rented out by the week or fortnight.

France: The French have a growing network of *chambres d'hôte* (CH) where residents, mainly in the countryside and in small towns, rent double rooms for about the price of a cheap hotel ($75–120), but with breakfast included. Some CHs post *chambre* signs in their windows, but most are listed only through tourist offices. While your hosts likely won't speak English, they will almost always be enthusiastic and happy to share their home.

Italy: Check out Italy's good alternatives to its expensive hotels: *albergo, locanda,* and *pensione*. (While these are technically all bunched together now in a hotel system with star ratings, you'll still find these traditional names synonymous with simple, budget beds.) Private rooms, signposted as *camere libere* or *affitta camere,* are fairly common in Italy's small towns. Small-town bars are plugged into the B&B grapevine.

While breakfasts are rarely included, you'll sometimes get a kitchenette in the room. Drivers can try *agriturismi*, rooms in farmhouses in the countryside. Weeklong stays are preferred in July and August, but shorter stays are possible off-season. For a sampling, visit www.agriturismo italy.it.

Scandinavia: These usually luxurious B&Bs—called *rom, hus rum,* or, in Denmark, *værelser*—cost about $40–60 per person. By Scandinavian standards, these are incredibly cheap (well, not so incredibly, when you figure it's a common way for the most heavily taxed people in Europe to make a little money under the table). Unfortunately, many Scandinavian B&Bs are advertised only through the tourist offices, which very often keep them a secret until all the hotels are full. In my *Rick Steves' Scandinavia* guidebook, I list plenty of wonderful money-savers. An evening with a Scandinavian family offers a fascinating look at contemporary Nordic life. If they're serving breakfast, eat it. Even at $15, it's a deal by local standards and can serve as your best big meal of the day.

Spain and Portugal: Travelers get an intimate peek into their small-town, whitewashed worlds by renting *camas* and *casas particulares* in Spain and *quartos* in Portugal. In rural Iberia, wherever there's tourism, you'll find these budget accommodations. Breakfast is rarely included.

Greece: You'll find many $60-per-bed *dhomatia*. Especially in touristy coastal and island towns, hardworking entrepreneurs will meet planes, ferries, and buses as they come into town at any hour. In Greek villages with no hotels, ask for *dhomatia* at the town taverna. Forget breakfast.

Croatia and Slovenia: In these countries—where mass tourism and overpriced resort hotels reign—private rooms are often the best deal in town (no breakfast). You'll see signs advertising *sobe* (rooms) everywhere you look, or book one through a travel agency (10–30 percent extra). You'll generally pay extra if you stay less than three nights. Along the Dalmatian Coast, *sobe* skimmers meet every arriving ferry, targeting backpackers and eager to whisk you away to see

Guidebook listings will lead you to friendly Croatian sobe *hosts eager to invite you into their homes.*

their room. In the Slovenian countryside, look for tourist farms *(turistične kmetije)*, where you can sleep in a family's farmhouse for remarkably low prices (see www.slovenia.info/touristfarms). Croatia's Istria region has similar *agroturizam*s.

Apartment Rentals

Renting an apartment, house, or villa can be a fun and cost-effective way to delve into Europe. The per-night cost of a rental apartment is usually comparable to, or even cheaper than, a hotel room of similar standards... and it comes with more space and amenities. (Think of it as buying your accommodations "in bulk.") And since apartments come with kitchens, you can cook your own meals to save on restaurant expenses. While renting an apartment might seem like a splurge, groups of backpackers find that splitting the price of a cheap apartment can cost less than paying for several bunks at a youth hostel.

Apartments typically rent for a week or more, but many also accept shorter stays (sometimes with a surcharge). Staying for a full week gives the renter an opportunity to really get to know the town, and take advantage of day-trip possibilities. (Good home-base cities are also ideal apartment-rental cities—see the list on page 76.)

The options differ from country to country. For example, France has a popular network of rentable country homes called *gites* ($400–1,300/ week for 4–6 people, www.gites-de-france.fr). In Croatia, you'll spot a blue *apartman* sign by every other doorway, and shorter stays (3–4 days) are common. If rentals are a particularly good value in a specific country, your guidebook will explain the basics.

There are various ways to find rental apartments. In most cases, you'll deal directly with the owner; in other cases, you might work with an agency that maintains a network of rentals. (Sometimes the agency actually owns the apartments, and other times they act as a go-between.)

Using a rental agency is convenient, as the apartments have been screened, and the agency provides a sense of professionalism and predictability. However, you'll pay a bit more going through an agency than if you deal directly with a landlord.

Booking direct takes a little more effort, but cutting out the middleman also cuts cost and bureaucracy. Some guidebooks recommend specific apartments, and many local and national tourist offices (see list on page 33) can provide lists of rentals. But the Internet is the best tool for finding your perfect apartment—simply search for "vacation rental" or "holiday rental" and the town you're interested in, then browse your options. Craigslist (www.craigslist.org) works for finding apartment rentals in many European cities. Or use a clearinghouse website that specializes in helping renters find apartments, such as www.vrbo.com, www.vacationrentals.com, www.greatrentals.com, www.holiday-rentals .co.uk, www.rentavilla.com (more upscale), and www.interhome.us. You'll usually find photos of the rental (inside and out), as well as loads of other information (number of bedrooms and bathrooms, amenities, sometimes even a floor plan) to help you make your decision.

Once you've found a place that interests you, contact the owner for more information. From some clearinghouse sites, you'll click a link that says "send email" to fill out a form, and the site will send an email to the owner on your behalf.

Before you commit, be clear on the details. Get the street address and chart it on a map (such as www.google.com/maps) so you're clear on how convenient—or inconvenient—the location is. Request a written rental agreement and cancellation policy. When you make a reservation, you'll probably have to pay a deposit for your rental (can range from 10 to 50 percent). Ideally the owner will take your credit-card number for this, but you might have to mail a check or wire money. You'll pay the balance on arrival; most apartment owners prefer to be paid in cash, but some accept credit cards.

Arrange a time and place to meet and pick up the keys. Once you check in, you're on your own. While the apartment owner or manager might offer some basic assistance, don't expect them to provide all the services of a hotel reception desk. Your apartment likely won't be cleaned during a one-week stay unless you pay extra, but you'll have access to your own cleaning supplies (ask about this when you check in). Remember that the lack of these services is what keeps apartment rentals affordable.

Europe's Hostels

Europe's cheapest beds are in hostels. Several thousand hostels provide beds throughout Europe for $20–40 per night. The buildings are usually in good, easily accessible locations.

As Europe has grown more affluent, hostels have been remodeled to provide more plumbing and smaller rooms. Still, hostels are not hotels—not by a long shot. Many people hate hostels. Others love them and will be hostelers all their lives, regardless of their budgets. Hosteling is a philosophy. A hosteler trades service and privacy for a chance to live simply and communally with people from around the world.

SLEEPING AND EATING

Official Hostels vs. Independent Hostels

There are two different types of hostels: "official" hostels and "independent" hostels. While official hostels used to be the norm, more and more good independent alternatives are available.

Official hostels all belong to the same parent organization (Hostelling International, also known as International Youth Hostel Federation, or IYHF; www.hihostels.com). These hostels are required to adhere to various rules and guidelines. This is both good (you know exactly what you're going to get) and bad (they're more likely to be unimaginative, drab, and institutional).

You technically need to be a member of Hostelling International to stay at an HI hostel, but in practice anyone can stay at one for an extra fee. If you plan to spend at least six nights at official HI hostels, buy a membership card before you go ($28/year, free if you're under 18, $18 if you're over 54; available at your local student-travel office, any HI hostel office, or Hostelling International; www.hiusa.org, tel. 301/495-1240). However, if you think you may not spend six nights at HI hostels—or if you're not certain, and you think you might prefer independent hostels—don't buy the card in advance. Non-members who want to stay at HI hostels can get an "international guest card" at your first hostel. You'll pay about $5 extra per night for a "welcome stamp" to stick to this card, and once you buy six welcome stamps, you become a member. As independent hostels become a more popular option, this "pay-as-you-go" system for official hostels—rather than buying your membership up front—makes sense for many travelers.

If you're focusing on HI hostels, check their website, which lists HI hostels by country, with information on the number of beds, distance from the train station, directions, address, phone number, and day or season (if any) the hostel is closed (www.hihostels.com/web/guide .en.htm).

Independent hostels tend to be more easygoing and colorful, run by people who prefer to avoid the occasionally heavy-handed bureaucracy of HI. These non-HI hostels are looser and more casual, but not as predictably clean or organized as official hostels. Independent hostels don't require a membership card or charge extra for non-members, and generally have fewer rules. Many popular European destinations have wild and cheap student-run hostels that are popular with wild and cheap student travelers, but some independent hostels are tame and mature. Various organizations promote independent hostels, including www.hostelworld .com, www.hostelz.com, www.hostelseurope.com, and www.hostels.com. Independent Holiday Hostels of Ireland (www.hostels-ireland.com) is a network of more than 100 independent hostels, requiring no membership and welcoming all ages. All IHH hostels are approved by the Irish Tourist Board.

If you're staying at a mix of both official and independent hostels—as most hostelers do—Let's Go guidebooks offer the best all-around listings (www.letsgo.com).

Hosteling Tips

Unless noted, these tips apply to both official and independent hostels.

A youth hostel is not limited to young people. You may assume hostels aren't for you because, by every standard, you're older than young. Well, many countries have dropped the word "youth" from their hostels, and for years Hostelling International has given "youths" over the age of 54 a discount on the membership card. Even the last holdout, the German state of Bavaria, finally dropped its youths-only restriction. If you're alive, you're young enough to hostel anywhere in Europe (with the rare exception of some independent hostels that have age cutoffs of around 40). The average hosteler is 18–26, but every year there are more seniors and families hosteling.

Hostels provide "no frills" accommodations in clean dormitories. Hostels were originally for hikers and bikers, but that isn't the case these days—some newer hos-

Cooking in the hostel members' kitchen, this traveler lives in Europe on $20 a day for his bed, plus the price of groceries.

tels are downright plush. Still, expect humble conditions. At official hostels, the sexes are segregated, with 4–20 people packed in a room full of bunk beds. Many independent hostels have both segregated and mixed dorms. Hostels often have a few doubles for group leaders and couples, and rooms for families are increasingly common (and affordable). Strong, hot showers (often with coin-op meters) are the norm, but some very rustic, off-the-beaten-path hostels (or mountain huts) might have no showers at all.

Bedding can cost extra. Pillows and blankets are provided. Sometimes sheets are included in the cost, but often you have to pay extra to rent them (about $5). Another option is to bring your own sleep sack—a sleeping bag–type sack made of lightweight sheet material. You can make your own (fold over a queen-size sheet and sew it up), pur-chase one before your trip, or buy one at your first hostel in Europe. Concerned about bedbugs, some hostels now require you to rent sheets, even if you have your own. Because of this, and because a sleep sack takes up space in your luggage, I wouldn't bring one unless I knew I'd be staying at several hostels.

Hostels: Meet, drink, and be merry.

Many hostels offer meals and meeting places. Hearty, super-cheap meals are served, often in family-style settings. A typical dinner is fish sticks and mashed pota-toes seasoned by conversation with new friends from Norway to New Zealand. The self-service kitchen, complete with utensils, pots, and pans, is a great budget aid that comes with most hostels. Larger hostels even have a small grocery store. International friendships rise with the bread in hostel kitchens.

The hostel's recreation and living rooms are my favorite. People gather, play games, tell stories, share information, read, write, and team up for future travels. Solo travelers find a family in every hostel, and can always find a new travel partner; while those with partners do well to occasionally stay in a hostel to meet some new companions.

One of Europe's hostels—$25 a night, your own kitchen, a million-dollar view of the Swiss Alps, and lots of friends. Note the worldwide triangular hostel symbol.

Get to know your host. The people who live in and run hostels (sometimes called "wardens" in Britain) do their best to strictly enforce rules, quiet hours, and other regulations. Some are loose and laid-back, others are like Marine drill sergeants, but they all work toward the noble goal of enabling travelers to better appreci-ate and enjoy that town or region. While they are often overworked and harried, most hostel employees are great people who enjoy a quiet cup of coffee with an American and are happy to give you some travel tips or recommend a special nearby hostel. Be sensitive to the many demands on their time, and never treat them like hotel servants.

Hostels have drawbacks. Many hostels—especially official ones—have strict rules. Some lock up during the day (usually from 10 a.m. to 5 p.m.), and a few may have a curfew at night, when the doors are locked. Keep in mind that a curfew can be a big advantage—hostels that don't have curfews, especially in big cities, are more likely to have hostelers (often drunk and rowdy) returning at ungodly hours. The sounds you'll hear just after everyone's turned in remind me of summer camp—giggles, burps, jokes, and strange noises in many languages. Snoring is permitted and practiced openly.

Hostel rooms can be large and packed. Many school groups (especially German) turn hostels upside down (typically weekends during the school year and weekdays in the summer). Try to be understanding (many groups are disadvantaged kids); we were all noisy kids at one time. Get to know the teacher and make it a "cultural experience."

Theft can be a problem in hostels, but try this simple safeguard:

Stockholm's floating youth hostel, the af Chapman

Wear your money belt (even while sleeping) and don't leave valuables lying around (but no one's going to steal your tennis shoes or journal). Use the storage lockers that are available in most hostels.

Hostel selectively. Hostels come in all shapes and sizes, and some are sightseeing ends in themselves. There are castles (Bacharach, Germany), cutter ships (Stockholm), alpine chalets (Gimmelwald, Switzerland), huge modern buildings (Frankfurt), lakefront villas (Lugano), former prisons (Stockholm and Ljubljana, Slovenia), medieval manor houses (Wilderhope Manor, England), former choirboys' dorms (St. Paul's, London), country estates (Loch Lomond, Scotland), and former royal residences (Holland Park, London). Survey other hostelers and hostel employees for suggestions.

I've hosteled most in northern Europe, where hostels are more comfortable and the savings over hotels more exciting. (This is particularly

INFORMATION	
YOUNG £3.50	SHEET 80 p
JUNIOR £4.40	SHOWERS FREE
SENIOR £5.50	
DINNER £3.00	
BREAKFAST £2 30	
LUNCH PACK £1.60	
DOORS OPENED 7.30 AM	
RISING BELL & OFFICE OPEN 8.00	
BREAKFAST 8.30	
HOSTEL CLOSES 10.00	
HOSTEL REOPENS 5.00 PM	
DINNER 7.00	
HOSTEL CLOSES 11.00	
LIGHTS OUT 11.30	
WARDENS	
KEITH & JOAN BENNETT	
ASSISTANT WARDEN JAN VAN KAAM	
WE HOPE YOU ENJOY YOUR STAY AT	
STOW – ON – THE – OLD	

true in Scandinavia, where you find lots of Volvos in hostel parking lots; locals know that hostels provide the best—and usually only—$30 beds in town.) I rarely hostel in the south, where hostels are less common and two or three people can sleep just as cheaply in a budget hotel.

Big-city hostels are the most overrun by young backpackers. Rural hostels, far from train lines and famous sights, are usually quiet and frequented by a more mature crowd. If you have a car, use that mobility to visit places without train service and enjoy some of Europe's overlooked hostels.

Getting a hostel bed in peak tourist season can be tricky. The most popular hostels fill up every day. Most hostels will take telephone or email reservations. I always call or email ahead to try to reserve and at least check on the availability of beds. But don't rely solely on advance reservations, because many hostels hold some beds for drop-ins. Try to arrive early. If the hostel has a lockout period during the day, show up before the office closes in the morning; otherwise, line up with the scruffy gang for the 5 p.m. reopening, when any remaining beds are doled out.

Some hostels have a reservation system where, for a small fee, you can reserve and pay for your next hostel bed before you leave the last one. You can also book HI locations online (www.hi hostels.com, $3 nonrefundable booking fee plus 5 percent nonrefundable deposit per location booked, balance due at hostel on arrival, $3 refund for HI members at hostel) or by phone (US tel. 301/495-1240, 10 percent nonrefundable deposit per location booked, balance due to hostel on arrival). They accept Visa

In most hostels, there are dorm rooms for boys... and dorm rooms for girls.

and MasterCard and also sell hostel membership cards. Book at least a day in advance.

Hostel bed availability is unpredictable. Some obscure hostels are booked out on certain days six months in advance. But I stumbled into Oberammergau one night during the jam-packed Passion Play festival and found beds for a group of eight.

Camping European Style

Relatively few Americans take advantage of Europe's 10,000-plus campgrounds. Camping is the cheapest way to see Europe and is the middleclass European family way to travel. Campers give it rave reviews.

"Camping" is the international word for campground. Every town has a camping with enough ground to pitch a tent or park a caravan (trailer), good showers and washing facilities, and often a grocery store and restaurant, all for just a few dollars per person per night. In America, we think of campgrounds as being picturesque, rustic cul-de-sacs near a lake or forest. European campgrounds can range from functional (like park-and-rides) to vacation extravaganzas, with restaurants, mini-water parks, and discos. Campings forbid open fires, and you usually won't find a riverfront lot with a stove, table, and privacy. In general, European campgrounds are less private and secluded than the American version—basically a field with a smattering of trees, and lots of campers in close proximity. But they rarely fill up, and, if they do, the "Full" sign usually refers to trailers (most Europeans are trailer campers). A small tent can almost always be squeezed in somewhere.

Europe's campgrounds mix well with just about any mode of transportation. And light, modern camp gear makes camping without a car easier than ever. Tent and train can be a winning combination, though it can be challenging to find convenient transportation between the train station and the campground. On arrival at the station, stop by the TI and pick up a map that has campgrounds marked, camping leaflets, and bus directions. In some cases, buses shuttle campers from station to campground with ease. Stations generally have lockers in which those with limited energy can leave unneeded baggage.

Hitchhikers find camping just right for their tender budgets. Many campgrounds are located near the major road out of town, where long rides are best snared. Any hitching camper with average social skills can find a friend driving his way with an empty seat. A note on the camp bulletin board can be very effective.

Tents and bikes also mix well. Bikers enjoy the same we-can-squeeze-one-more-in status as hikers and are very rarely turned away.

Camping by car is my favorite combination. A car carries all your camp gear and gets you to any campground quickly and easily. Good road maps always pinpoint campings, and, when you're within a few blocks, the road signs take over. In big cities, the money you save on parking alone will pay for your camping. I usually take the bus downtown, leaving my camper van at the campground.

Learn about Campgrounds: Each country's national tourist office in the United States can send you information on camping in its country. The 2010 edition of *Europe by Van and Motorhome* contains all the details on renting, buying, and shipping an RV, and includes a free, personal consultation (David Shore and Patty Campbell, 268 pages, $16.95, free shipping for ETBD readers, Odyssey Press, www.roadtrip europe.com, tel. 800-659-5222, shorecam@aol.com). Consider getting *Camping Europe* by Carol Mickelsen (available on www.amazon.com) and *RV and Car Camping Vacations in Europe* by Mike and Terri Church (available through www.amazon.com or www.rollinghomes.com). The AA—Britain's AAA-type automobile club—publishes an annual guide called *Caravan & Camping Europe*. This excellent resource includes detailed listings for thousands of campgrounds in Western Europe, along with color maps for locating each one. Separate editions focus on France and Britain/Ireland. The Let's Go guides give good instructions on getting to and from campgrounds. Eurocampings has online information—including user reviews—on more than 8,000 campgrounds (www.eurocampings.co.uk).

Many campgrounds offer bungalows with kitchenettes and four to six beds. Comfortable and cheaper than hotels, these are particularly popular in Scandinavia.

Finding the Perfect Campground: Campings are well-posted, and local tourist information offices have guides and maps listing nearby campgrounds. Every country has good and bad campgrounds; most of them mirror their surroundings. If the region is overcrowded, dusty, dirty, unkempt, and generally chaotic, you're unlikely to find an oasis behind the campground's gates. A sleepy Austrian valley will probably offer a sleepy Austrian campground. "Weekend campings" are rented out on a yearly basis to local urbanites. Too often, weekend sites are full or don't allow what they call "stop-and-go" campers (you). Camping guidebooks indicate which places are the "weekend" types.

Prices: Prices vary according to facilities and style—sometimes it's by the tent, sometimes by the person. Expect to spend $7–10 per night per person.

Registration and Regulations: Camp registration is easy. As with most hotels, you show your passport, fill out a short form, and learn the rules. Checkout time is usually noon. English is the second language of campings throughout Europe, and most managers will understand the monoglot American.

European campgrounds generally require you to leave your passport with the office until you pay your bill. But many campgrounds will accept instead an International Camping Card ($30, also called a Camping Carnet). These cards may get you discounts at some campgrounds. The organization Family Campers and RVers sells the card to members ($30 per family for annual membership plus $30 for the carnet, www.fcrv.org, tel. 800-245 9755).

Silence usually reigns in European campgrounds beginning at 10 or 11 p.m. Noisemakers are strictly dealt with. Many places close the gates to cars after 11 p.m. If you do arrive after the office closes, set up quietly and register in the morning.

Campground Services: European campgrounds have great, if sometimes crowded, showers and washing facilities. Hot water, as in many

For a "room" with a view on a tight budget, pitch your tent in a secluded mountain valley.

hostels, is often metered, and you'll learn to carry coins and scrub quickly. At larger campgrounds, tenters appreciate the in-camp grocery store and café. The store, while high-priced, stays open longer than most, offering latecomers a chance to picnic. The café is a likely camp hangout, and Americans enjoy mixing in this easygoing European social scene. I've scuttled many nights on the town so I wouldn't miss the fun with new friends right in the camp. Camping, like hosteling, is a great way to meet Europeans. If the campground doesn't have a place to eat, you'll find one nearby.

Camping with Kids: A family sleeps in a tent a lot cheaper than in a hotel. Camping offers plenty to occupy children's attention, including playgrounds that come fully equipped with European kids. And as your kids make European friends, your campground social circle widens.

Safety: Campgrounds, unlike hostels, are remarkably theft free. Campings are full of basically honest, middle-class European families, and someone's at the gate all day. Most people just leave their gear zipped inside their tents.

Camping Equipment: Your camping trip deserves first-class equipment. Spend some time and money outfitting yourself before your trip. Plenty of stores carry exciting new gear—expert salespeople can get you up-to-date in a hurry.

For Europe, campers prefer a very lightweight "three-season" sleeping bag (consult the climate chart in the appendix for your probable bedroom temperature) and a closed-cell sleeping pad to insulate and soften the ground.

If you bring a stove from home, it should be the butane Gaz variety (but you can't take a Gaz cartridge on the plane—buy it there or you'll lose it here). I keep meals simple, picnicking and enjoying food and fun in the campground café. I'd suggest starting without a stove. If you find out you want one, buy it there. In Europe, it's much easier to find fuel for a European camp stove than for its Yankee counterpart.

Stoves and all other camping gear are cheaper at large superstores (found in Britain, France, Germany, and Spain) than at European backpacking stores. In the US, the cheap chains (Wal-Mart, Target, and Costco) sell cheap equipment. For pricier, fancier gear, consider REI (www.rei.com, tel. 800-426-4840), Campmor (www.campmor.com, tel. 888-226-7667), or L. L. Bean (www.llbean.com, tel. 800-441-5713).

Commit yourself to a camping trip or to a no-camping trip and pack accordingly. Don't carry a sleeping bag and a tent just in case.

Renting an RV or Van: Campanje, a Dutch company, specializes in long-term rentals of small-size, fully loaded camper vans and RVs (4–7 people) for camping through Europe. Rates run from $780 per week for a four-person camper van up to $1,280 per week for a seven-person RV (minimum 3 weeks), including tax and insurance. Ask about discounts for early booking and off-season (www.campanje.nl, Dutch tel. 030/244-7070, info@campanje.nl).

Free Camping: Informal camping, or "camping wild," is legal in most of Europe. Low-profile, pitch-the-tent-after-dark-and-move-on-first-thing-in-the-morning free camping is usually allowed even in countries where it is technically illegal. Use common sense, and don't pitch your tent informally in carefully controlled areas such as cities and resorts.

It's a good idea to ask permission when possible. In the countryside, a landowner will rarely refuse a polite request to borrow a patch of land for the night. Formal camping is safer than free camping. Never leave your gear and tent unattended without the gates of a formal campground to discourage thieves.

Hut-Hopping

Hundreds of alpine huts exist to provide food and shelter for hikers. I know a family who hiked from France to Slovenia, spending every night

along the way in a mountain hut. The huts are generally spaced four to six hours apart. Most serve hot meals and provide bunk-style lodging. Many alpine huts (like independent hostels) require no linen and wash their blankets annually. I'll never forget getting cozy in my top bunk while a German in the bottom bunk said, "You're climbing into zee germs of centuries." Hut-hoppers hike with their own sheets.

In the Alps, look for the word *Lager*, which means they have a coed loft full of $25-a-night mattresses. Good books on hut-hopping include the aging but still helpful *Switzerland's Mountain Inns* (Marcia and Philip Lieberman, Countryman Press) and *100 Hut Walks in the Alps* (Kev Reynolds, Cicerone Press). Both are available through www .amazon.com. The Swiss Alpine Club runs more than 150 hiker huts (www.sac-cas.ch).

Sleeping Free

There are still people traveling in Europe on $40 a day. The one thing they have in common (apart from B.O.) is that they sleep free. If even cheap pensions and hostels are too expensive for your budget, you too can sleep free. I once went 29 out of 30 nights without paying for a bed. It's not difficult, but it's not always comfortable, convenient, safe, or legal, either. This is not a vagabonding guide, but any traveler may have an occasional free night. Faking it until the sun returns can become, at least in the long run, a good memory.

Europe has plenty of places to roll out your sleeping bag. Some large cities, such as Amsterdam and Athens, are flooded with tourists

A bench with a view

during peak season, and many spend their nights dangerously in city parks. Some cities enforce their "no sleeping in the parks" laws only selectively. Big, crowded cities such as London, Paris, Munich, Venice, and Copenhagen run safe, legal, and nearly free sleep-ins (tents or huge dorms) during peak season. Away from the cities, in forests or on beaches, you can pretty well sleep where you like. I have found that summer nights in the Mediterranean part of Europe are mild enough that I am comfortable with just my jeans, sweater, and hostel sheet. I no longer lug a sleeping bag around, but if you'll be vagabonding a lot, bring a light bag.

Imaginative vagabonds see Europe as one big free hotel (barns, churches, buildings under construction, ruins, college dorms, etc.). Just keep your passport with you, attach your belongings to you so they don't get stolen, and use good judgment in your choice of a free bed.

Sleeping in Train Stations: When you have no place to go for the night in a city, you can always retreat to the station (assuming it stays open all night). It's free, warm, safe, and uncomfortable. Most popular tourist cities in Europe have stations whose concrete floors are painted nightly with a long rainbow of sleepy vagabonds. This is allowed, but everyone is cleared out at dawn before the normal rush of travelers converges on the station. In some cases, you'll be asked to show a ticket. Any ticket or train pass entitles you to a free night in a station's waiting room: You are simply waiting for your early train. Whenever possible, avoid the second-class lounges; sleep with a better breed of hobo in first-class lounges. For safety, lock your pack in a station locker or check it at the baggage counter.

Sleeping on Trains: Success hinges on getting enough room to stretch out, and that can be quite a trick (see Chapter 10: Train and Railpass Skills). It's tempting but quite risky to sleep in a train car that seems to be parked for the night in a station. No awakening is ruder than having your bedroom jolt into motion and roll toward God-knows-where. If you do find a parked train car to sleep in, check to see when it's scheduled to leave. Some Eurailers get a free if disjointed night by riding a train out for four hours and catching one back in for another four hours. Scandinavia, with Europe's most expensive hotels, offers *couchettes* for a reasonable $30–50.

Sleeping in Airports: An airport is a large, posh version of a train station, offering a great opportunity to sleep free. After a late landing, I crash on a comfortable sofa rather than waste sleeping time looking for a place that will sell me a bed for the remainder of the night. Many cut-rate inter-European flights leave or arrive at ungodly hours. Frankfurt airport is served conveniently by the train and is great for sleeping free—even if you aren't flying anywhere. Early the next morning you can book into a hotel and only pay for the following night. If your room is still occupied, leave your bag with the receptionist and get out to see the town.

A few large airports have sterile, womblike "rest cabins" that rent for eight hours at the price of a cheap hotel room (for example, see www.yotel.com for information on Heathrow and Gatwick locations).

Friends and Relatives

There is no better way to enjoy a new country than as the guest of a family. And, of course, a night with a friend or relative stretches your budget (usually along with your belly). I've had nothing but good experiences (and good sleep) at my "addresses" in Europe. There are two kinds of addresses: European addresses brought from home and those you pick up while traveling.

Before you leave, do some research. Dig up some European relatives. No matter how far out on the family tree they are, unless you're a real jerk, they're tickled to have an American visitor in their nest. I send my relatives an email or postcard announcing my visit to their

The Europeans you visit don't need to be next-of-kin. This Tirolean is the father of my sister's ski teacher. That's close enough.

town and telling them when I'll arrive. They answer with "Please come visit us" or "Have a good trip." It is obvious from their response (or lack of one) if I'm invited to stop by.

Follow the same procedure with indirect contacts. I have dear "parents away from home" in Austria and London. My Austrian "parents" are really the parents of my sister's ski instructor. In London, they are friends of my uncle. Neither relationship was terribly close—until I visited. Now we are friends for life.

This is not cultural freeloading. Both parties benefit from such a visit. Never forget that a Greek family is just as curious and interested in you as you are in them (and the same old nightly family meals are probably pretty boring). Equipped with hometown postcards, pictures of my family, and a bag of goodies for the children, I make a point of giving as much from my culture as I am taking from the culture of my host. I insist on no special treatment, telling my host that I am most comfortable when treated simply as part of the family. I try to help with the chores, I don't wear out my welcome, and I follow up each visit with postcards or emails to share the rest of my trip with my friends. I pay or reimburse my hosts for their hospitality only with a thank-you letter from home, possibly with photos of all of us together.

The other kind of address is one you pick up during your travels. Exchanging addresses is almost as common as a handshake in Europe. If you have a business or personal card, bring a pile. Some travelers even print up a batch of personal cards for their trip. When people meet, they invite each other to visit. I warn my friend that I may very well show up some day at his house, whether it's in Osaka, Auckland, Santa Fe, or Dublin. When I have, it's been a good experience.

Servas

Servas is a worldwide organization that connects travelers with host families with the noble goal of building world peace through international understanding. International travelers pay $85 to join, plus a refundable $25 deposit for up to five sets of country or regional host lists (additional $25 for 6–10 lists, refunded if you return the lists and complete a travel report when you return). They can stay for two nights (more only if invited) in homes of other members around the world. You'll correspond with your host to make arrangements, and no money changes hands (except to reimburse hosts for telephone calls). This is not a crash-pad exchange. It's cultural sightseeing through a real live-in experience. Plan to hang around to talk and share and learn. Offer to cook a meal or help out around the house. Many travelers swear by Servas as the only way to really travel and build a truly global list of friends. Opening your own home to visitors is not required, but encouraged. For more information, contact Servas (www.usservas.org, tel. 707/825-1714).

CouchSurfing, AirBnB, and Cultural Exchanges

CouchSurfing is a vagabond's alternative to Servas. Nearly a half million members in 225 countries host fellow "surfers" in their homes for free. The average age is 26, but all ages are welcome. If you don't feel comfortable staying with or hosting strangers, you can still participate by meeting for a drink and sharing travel stories (www.couch surfing.com).

AirBnB, generally a step up in class, similarly connects travelers with locals offering a place to stay, but for a fee (usually falling between the cost of a hotel and hostel). Beds range from air-mattress-in-living-room basic to plush-B&B-suite posh. The site's listings have plenty of pictures, easy ways to sort your options according to your preferences, and feedback from previous travelers. All arrangements, including payment, are handled via their website, giving you a safety net if things go wrong (www.airbnb.com).

Friendship Force International offers cultural exchange tours for the purpose of promoting global goodwill (www.thefriendshipforce.org, 404/522-9490). The London-based Globetrotters Club runs a network of hosts and travelers (annual membership approximately $30, www.globe trotters.co.uk).

House-Swapping

Many families enjoy a great budget option year after year. They trade houses (sometimes cars, too—but draw the line at pets) with someone at the destination of their choice. Veteran house-swappers offer these tips: Be triple-sure about where to find the key and how to open the door, find out beforehand how to get to the nearest food store, make sure your host family leaves instructions for operating the appliances, make arrangements in advance to handle telephone charges, and ask about any peculiarities with the car you'll be driving.

For information, contact HomeLink (www.homelink-usa.com, tel. 800-638-3841), HomeExchange.com (www.homeexchange.com, tel. 800-877-8723), or Intervac Home Exchange (www.intervacus.com, tel. 800-756-4663).

SLEEPING AND EATING

17. Eating

Many vacations revolve around great restaurant meals, and for good reason. Europe serves some of the world's top cuisine at some of the world's top prices. I'm no gourmet, so most of my experience lies in eating well cheaply. Galloping gluttons thrive on $25 a day—by picnicking. Those with a more refined palate and a little more money can mix picnics with atmospheric and enjoyable restaurant meals and eat well for $45 a day.

A fun neighborhood restaurant: no English menus, no credit cards, but good food, good prices, and a friendly staff

This $45-a-day budget includes a $15 lunch (cheaper if you picnic or eat fast food), a $25 good and filling restaurant dinner (more with wine or dessert), and $5 for your chocolate, cappuccino, and gelato needs. (This assumes that breakfast is included with your hotel room; if you have to buy breakfast, have a picnic lunch... or eat less gelato.) If your budget requires, you can find a satisfying dinner for $20 anywhere in Europe. If you have more money, of course, it's delightful to spend it dining well. And if you're a full-blown foodie, consider taking a cooking class while you're in Europe (for starters, see http://cookforfun.shawguides.com).

Breakfast

The farther north you go in Europe, the heartier the breakfasts. Heaviest are the traditional British fry and Scandinavian buffet breakfasts. Throughout the Netherlands, Belgium, Germany, Austria, Switzerland, and Eastern Europe, expect a more modest buffet—but still plenty of options (rolls, bread, jam, cold cuts, cheeses, fruit, yogurt, and cereal). In these countries,

The continental breakfast: bread, jam, cheese, and coffee

there's a good chance of finding hard-boiled eggs, but scrambled or fried eggs are relatively rare. As you move south and west (France, Italy, Spain, and Portugal), skimpier "continental" breakfasts are the norm. You'll get a roll with marmalade or jam, occasionally a slice of ham or cheese, and coffee or tea.

If your breakfast is sparse, supplement it with a piece of fruit and a wrapped chunk of cheese from your rucksack stash. Orange-juice fans pick up liter boxes in the grocery store and start the day with a glass in their hotel room. If you're a coffee drinker, remember that breakfast is the only cheap time to caffeinate yourself. Some hotels will serve you a bottomless cup of a rich brew only with breakfast. After that, the cups acquire bottoms. Juice is generally available at breakfast, but in Mediterranean countries, you have to ask...and you'll probably be charged.

Breakfast, normally "included" in your hotel bill, can sometimes be skipped and deducted from the price of your room. Ask what the breakfast includes and costs. In southern Europe, you can usually save money and gain atmosphere by buying coffee and a roll or croissant at the café down the street or by brunching picnic-style in the park. I'm a big-breakfast person at home. But when I feel the urge for a typical American breakfast in Europe, I beat it to death with a hard roll. You can find bacon, fried eggs, and orange juice, but it's nearly always overpriced and disappointing.

You can save $30 by forgoing the hotel breakfast, visiting the corner bakery, and picnicking on the steps of the church.

Few hotel breakfasts are worth waiting around for. If you need to get an early start, skip breakfast.

SLEEPING AND EATING

Picnics—Spend Like a Pauper, Eat Like a Prince

There is only one way left to feast for $10–15 anywhere in Europe: picnic. You'll eat better, while spending half as much as those who eat exclusively in restaurants.

I am a picnic connoisseur. While I'm the first to admit that restaurant meals are an important aspect of any culture, I picnic almost daily. This is not solely for budgetary reasons. It's fun to dive into a marketplace and

SLEEPING AND EATING

actually get a chance to do business. Europe's colorful markets overflow with varied cheeses, meats, fresh fruits, vegetables, and still-warm-out-of-the-bakery-oven bread. Many of my favorite foods made their debut in a European picnic.

To busy sightseers, restaurants can be time-consuming and frustrating. After waiting to be served, tangling with a menu, and consuming a budget-threatening meal, you walk away feeling unsatisfied, knowing your money could have done much more for your stomach if you had invested it in a picnic. Nutritionally, a picnic is unbeatable. Consider this example: cheese, thinly-sliced ham, fresh bread, peaches, carrots, a cucumber, half a liter of milk, and fruit yogurt or a freshly baked pastry for dessert.

To bolster your budget, I recommend picnic dinners every few nights. At home, we save time and money by raiding the refrigerator to assemble a pick-up dinner. In Europe, the equivalent is the corner deli or grocery store. There are plenty of tasty alternatives to sandwiches. Bakeries often sell little pizzas and meat pies. Supermarkets, many of which hide out in the basements of big-city department stores, are getting very yuppie—offering salads, quiche, fried chicken, and fish, all "to go." When staying several nights, I cozy up a hotel room by borrowing plates, glasses, and silverware from the breakfast room and stocking the closet with my favorite groceries (juice, fruits and vegetables, cheese, and other munchies).

Picnic Shopping

Nearly every town, large or small, has at least one colorful outdoor or indoor marketplace. Assemble your picnic here. Make an effort to communicate with the merchants. Most markets are not self-service: You point to what you want and let the merchant bag it and weigh it for you. Know what you are buying and what you are spending. Whether you understand the prices or not, act like you do (observing the

A quick dashboard picnic halfway through a busy day of sightseeing

weighing process closely), and you're more likely to be treated fairly.

Learn the measurements. The unit of measure throughout the Continent is a kilo, or 2.2 pounds. A kilo has 1,000 grams. One hundred grams (a common unit of sale) of cheese or meat tucked into a chunk of French bread gives you about a quarter-pounder.

Food can be priced in different ways. Watch the scale when your food is being weighed. It'll likely show grams and kilos. If dried apples

are priced at €2 per kilo, that's $2.50 for 2.2 pounds, or about $1.10 per pound. If the scale says 400 grams, that means 40 percent of €2 (or 80 euro cents), which is $1.

Not everything is strictly priced by the kilogram. Read the little chalkboard price information board carefully: Particularly in the case of specialty items, you might see things priced by the ½ kg, ¼ kg, 100 g, 500 g, and so on. Or it could be priced by the piece (*Stück* in German, *la piéce* in French, *pezzo* in Italian), the bunch, the container, and so on. If the pâté seems too cheap to be true, look at the sign closely. The posted price is probably followed by "100 gr."

If no prices are posted, be wary. Travelers are routinely ripped off by market merchants in tourist centers. Find places that print the prices. Assume any market with no printed prices has a double price standard: one for locals and a more expensive one for tourists.

I'll never forget a friend of mine who bought two bananas for our London picnic. He grabbed the fruit, held out a handful of change, and said, "How much?" The merchant took the equivalent of about $4. My friend turned to me and

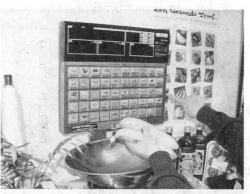

Put your banana in the bin, push the banana button, rip off the price sticker, and stick it on your banana.

said, "Wow, London really is expensive." Anytime you hold out a handful of money to a banana salesman, you're just asking for trouble.

Point, but don't touch. At produce stands and outdoor markets, it's considered rude for a customer to touch the goods. Tell the vendor (or point to) what you want.

If you want only a small amount... You'll likely want only one or two pieces of fruit, and many merchants refuse to deal in such small quantities. The way to get what you want and no more is to estimate what it would cost if the merchant were to weigh it and then just hold out a coin worth about that much in one hand and point to the apple, or whatever, with the other. Have a Forrest Gump look on your face that says, "If you take this coin, I'll go away." Rarely will he refuse the deal.

In supermarkets, it's a cinch to buy a tiny amount of fruit or vegetables. Many have an easy push-button pricing system: Put the banana on the scale, push the picture of a banana (or enter the banana bin number), and a sticky price tag prints out. You could weigh and sticker a single grape.

Europe's grocery stores have some surprisingly addictive snacks.

Picnic Drinks

There are plenty of cheap ways to wash down a picnic. Milk is always cheap and available in quarter, half, or whole liters. Be sure it's normal drinking milk. Strange white liquid dairy products in look-alike milk cartons abound, ruining the milk-and-cookie dreams of careless tourists. Look for local words for "whole" or "light," such as *voll* or *lett*.

Nutritionally, half a liter provides about 25 percent of your daily protein needs. Get refrigerated, fresh milk. Or look on the (unrefrigerated) shelves for the common-in-Europe but rare-in-America "long life" milk. This milk—which requires no refrigeration until it's opened—will never go bad...or taste good.

European yogurt is delicious and can usually be drunk right out of its container. Fruit juice comes in handy

This happy gang is living simply and well on the cheap: enjoying a picnic in Assisi, the hometown of St. Francis.

liter boxes (look for "100% juice" or "no sugar" to avoid Kool-Aid clones). Buy cheap by the liter, and use a reusable half-liter plastic mineral-water bottle (usually found next to the soft drinks) to store what you can't comfortably drink in one sitting. Liter bottles of Coke are cheap, as is wine in most countries. Local wine gives your picnic a

Picnic on the train—quick, hearty, scenic

nice touch. Any place that serves coffee has free boiling water. Those who have more nerve than pride get their plastic water bottle (a sturdy plastic bottle will not melt) filled with free boiling water at a café, then add their own instant coffee or tea bag later. Many hotels or cafés will fill a thermos with coffee for about the price of two cups.

Picnic Atmosphere

There is nothing second-class about a picnic. A few special touches will even make your budget meal a first-class affair. Proper site selection can make the difference between just another meal and *le pique-nique extraordinaire*. Since you've decided to skip the restaurant, it's up to you to create the atmosphere.

Try to incorporate a picnic brunch, lunch, or dinner into the day's sightseeing plans. For example, I start the day by scouring the thriving market with my senses and my camera. Then I fill up my shopping bag and have breakfast on a riverbank. After sightseeing, I combine lunch and a siesta in a cool park to fill my stomach, rest my body, and escape the early afternoon heat. It's fun to eat dinner on a castle wall enjoying a commanding view and the setting sun. Some of my all-time best picnics have been lazy dinners accompanied by medieval fantasies in the quiet of after-hours Europe.

Throughout France, signs direct you to the most scenic places to "pique-nique."

SLEEPING AND EATING

Mountain hikes are punctuated nicely by picnics. Food tastes even better on top of a mountain. Europeans are great picnickers. Many picnics become potlucks, resulting in new friends as well as full stomachs.

Table Scraps and Tips

Bring picnic supplies. Pack resealable plastic baggies (large and small, can be hard to find in Europe). Buy a good knife with a can opener and corkscrew in Europe (or bring it

Kick back and munch a picnic dinner in your hotel room.

from home, if you plan to check your luggage on the plane). In addition to being a handy plate, fan, and lousy Frisbee, a plastic coffee-can lid makes an easy-to-clean cutting board with a juice-containing lip. A dishtowel doubles as a small tablecloth, and a washcloth helps with clean-up. A disposable hotel shower cap contains messy food nicely on your picnic cloth. Bring a plastic, airline-type coffee cup and spoon for cereal, and a fork for take-out salad and chicken. Some travelers get immersion heaters (buy in Europe for a compatible plug) to make hot drinks to go with munchies in their hotel room.

Stretch your money. Bread has always been cheap in Europe. (Leaders have learned from history that when stomachs rumble, so do the mobs in the streets.) Cheese is a specialty nearly everywhere and is, along with milk, one of the Continent's cheapest sources of protein. The standard low-risk option anywhere in Europe is Emmentaler cheese (the kind with holes, which we

For restaurant food at halfway-to-picnic prices, visit the neighborhood rosticceria *or take-out deli.*

call "Swiss"). In season, tomatoes, cucumbers, and watermelons are good deals in Italy. Wine is a great buy in France and Spain. Anything American is usually expensive and rarely satisfying. Cultural chameleons eat and drink better and cheaper.

Make your big meal of the day a picnic lunch or dinner. Only a glutton can spend more than $10 for a picnic feast. In a park in Paris, on a Norwegian ferry, high in the Alps, on your dashboard at an autobahn rest stop, on your convent rooftop, or in your hotel room, picnicking is the budget traveler's key to cheap and good eating.

Eating Cheap

There are plenty of strategies for stretching your food budget on the road. While not necessarily high cuisine, they're undeniably cheap.

Cafeteria leftovers: even cheaper than picnics...

Cafeterias: "Self-service" is an international word. You'll find self-service restaurants in big cities everywhere, offering low-price, low-risk, low-stress, what-you-see-is-what-you-get meals. A sure value for your euro is a department-store cafeteria. These places are designed for the shopping housewife who has a sharp eye for a good value. At a salad bar, grab the small (cheap) plate and stack it like the locals do—high.

Institution-Affiliated Eateries: If your wallet is as empty as your stomach, find a cheap, humble cafeteria that's associated with (and subsidized by) a local institution—such as a university, city hall, church, hospital, charity, senior center, fire station, union of gondoliers, retired fishermen's club, and so on. (These are sometimes called "mensas.") Profits take a back seat to providing good food at a good price—and many of these eateries welcome the public to pull up a chair. Options range from a semi-swanky City Hall cafeteria in Oslo, to student canteens in university towns (such as Salzburg, Austria), to Poland's dreary-looking but cheap-and-tasty "milk bars." Don't be afraid to take advantage of these opportunities to fill yourself with a plate of dull but nourishing food for an unbeatable price in the company of locals. University cafeterias (generally closed during summer holidays) also offer a surefire way to meet educated, English-speaking young people with open and stimulating minds. They're often eager to practice their politics and economics, as

SLEEPING AND EATING

SLEEPING AND EATING

well as their English, on a foreign friend. This is especially handy as you travel beyond Europe.

Street Food: Every country has its own equivalent of the hot-dog stand, where you can grab a filling bite on the go: French *crêperies,* Greek souvlaki stands, Danish *pølse* (sausage) vendors, Italian *pizza rustica* take-out shops, Dutch herring carts, and Turkish-style *döner kebab* and falafel kiosks in Germany (and just about everywhere else).

For a good-value lunch in England (or most anywhere), follow the local business crowd to find the best sandwiches.

Falafel (fried chickpea croquettes wrapped in pita bread) is a good vegetarian option that's also popular with meat-eaters. If there's a long line at a particular stand, you can bet that customers appreciate the value that vendor provides. Bakeries are a good place to pick up basic sandwiches, tiny pizzas, or something equally cheap and fast but with more of a regional flavor (such as savory pasties in England or a *croque-monsieur* sandwich in France). The business lunch crowd invariably knows the best place for an affordable fill-the-tank bite.

Ethnic Restaurants: Throughout wealthy Northern Europe, immigrant communities labor at subsistence wages. Rather than eat bland and pricey local food, they (along with savvy residents and travelers) go cheap and spicy at simple diners and take-away stands serving Turkish, Middle-Eastern, Pakistani, and Asian food. These places usually offer the cheapest hot meals in town.

Eat where the immigrants do, and you'll save plenty.

McEurope: Fast-food restaurants are everywhere. Yes, the hamburgerization of the world is a shame, but face it—the busiest and biggest McDonald's in the world are in Tokyo, Rome, and Moscow. The burger has become a global thing. You'll find Big Macs in every language—it isn't exciting (and costs more than at home), but at least at McDonald's you know exactly what you're getting, and it's fast. A hamburger, fries, and shake can be fun halfway through your trip.

American fast-food joints are kid-friendly and satisfy the need for a cheap salad bar and a tall orange juice. They've grabbed prime bits of real estate in every big European city. Since there's no cover charge, this is an opportunity to savor a low-class paper cup of coffee while enjoying some high-class people-watching.

Each country has its equivalent of the hamburger stand (I saw a "McCheaper" in Switzerland). Whatever their origin, they're a hit with youths and a handy place for a quick, cheap bite to eat.

Cafés and Bars

From top to bottom, Europe is into café-sitting, coffee-sipping, and people-watching. Tourists are often stung by not understanding the rules of the game: In many countries, you'll pay less to stand and more to sit. In general, if you simply want to slam down a cup of coffee, order and drink it at the bar. If you want to sit a while and absorb that last museum while checking out the two-legged art, grab a table with a view and a waiter will take your order. This will cost you about double what it would at the bar. (Sometimes an outdoor table is more expensive than an indoor one.) If you're on a budget, always confirm the price for a sit-down drink. While it's never high profile, there's always a price list posted somewhere inside with the two- or three-tiered price system clearly labeled (e.g., cheap at the bar, more at a table, still more at an outside table). If you pay for a seat in a café with an expensive drink, that seat's yours for the entire afternoon if you like. Lingering with your bar-priced drink on a nearby public bench or across the street on the beach is usually OK—just ask first.

In European cafés, menus are two-tiered: cheaper at the bar, more expensive at a table.

In some coffee bars (especially in Italy), you pay for your drink at the cash register, then take your receipt to the bar, where you'll be served.

Restaurants

Restaurants are the most expensive way to eat. They can pillage and plunder a tight budget, but it would be criminal to pass through

Europe without sampling the specialties served in good restaurants. A country's high cuisine is just as culturally important as its museums. Experience it.

European restaurants are no more expensive than American restaurants. The cost of eating is determined not by the local standard, but by your personal standard. Many Americans can't find an edible meal for less than $30 in their hometown, but their next-door neighbors enjoy eating out for half that. If you can enjoy a $15 meal in Boston, Detroit, or Seattle, you'll eat well in London, Rome, or Helsinki for the same price. Last year I ate 100 dinners in Europe. My budget target was $15 for a simple, fill-the-tank meal; $25 for a good restaurant dinner; and $50 for a splurge feast. Forget the scare stories. People who spend $60 on dinner in Dublin and then complain either enjoy complaining or are fools. Let me fill you in on filling up in Europe.

Average tourists are attracted—like moths to a light bulb—to the biggest neon sign that boasts, *We speak English and accept credit cards*. Wrong! I look for a handwritten menu in the native language only, with a small selection. This means they're cooking what was fresh in the market this morning for loyal, return customers (and not targeting tourists).

Restaurants listed in your guidebook are usually fine, but too often when a place becomes famous this way, it goes downhill. You don't need those listings to find your own good restaurant. Ask your hotel receptionist, or even someone on the street, for a good place—not a good place for tourists, but a place they'd take a friend. Or leave the tourist center and stroll around until you find a restaurant with a happy crowd of locals. Be snoopy; look at what people are eating. After a few days in Europe, you'll have no trouble telling a genuine hangout from a tourist trap.

When entering a restaurant, feel free to seat yourself at any table that isn't marked "reserved." I try to catch a server's eye and signal to be sure it's OK for me to sit there. It also lets him know I'm ready to look at a menu. If the place is full, you're likely to simply be turned away: There's no "hostess" standing by to add your name to a carefully managed waiting list. Since European diners take their time with a meal, it's impossible to predict how quickly

These days, the Germans are splitting their bratwurst and kraut, too.

the tables will turn over. You might see people milling around outside a popular place hoping for a table to free up, but it's basically a chaotic, self-managing system—not monitored by any restaurant staff.

While portions may be expensive, they're often huge and splittable. A key challenge of budget eating is ordering just enough to fill you, while leaving nothing on your plate. If a single main dish is enough for 1.5 people (as many are), split it between you and your travel partner, and supplement it with a bowl of soup or something small. Splitting a dessert saves money and calories. The prices are high for Europeans, too. Waiters are generally understanding and accommodating.

Share fine things. Restaurateurs are happy to bring one dessert and as many spoons as needed.

Many European cities have a bustling, colorful "restaurant row," a street or square lined with characteristic eateries—such as Rue des Bouchers in Brussels, Rue Mouffetard in Paris, Rua das Portas de Santo Antão in Lisbon, Leidsedwarsstraat in Amsterdam, Campo de' Fiori in Rome, Adrianou street in Athens, and Prijeko street in Dubrovnik. The restaurants usually have straightforward menus of tourist-pleasing dishes, superficial elegance, and gregarious hawkers out front trying desperate sales pitches to lure in diners. Some of the restaurants are tourist traps with overpriced food and rotten service; others are frequented by natives and can offer great ambience and decent value. A good guidebook or a tip from a trusted local can help you figure out which is which.

Brussels' "restaurant row," Rue des Bouchers, is fun for a walk. And, if you understand the prices thoroughly, it's not a bad place to dine.

Eat with the season. In the summer, French onion soup and cheese fondue are only for tourists. White asparagus and porcini mushrooms are a treat for your palate in season...but come out of the freezer the rest of the year.

Techie travelers report they're generally pleased with the restaurant advice they've found on Twitter and Tripadvisor.com. And many cities have websites where residents post their own restaurant reviews (similar to Yelp.com in the US; ask locals for recommended sites).

Deciphering the Menu

European restaurants post their menus outside. Check the price and selection before entering. If the menu's not posted, ask to see one.

But be aware the word *menu* can mean a fixed-price meal (particularly in France and Italy, explained below). In Europe, what we call the "menu" usually goes by some variation on the word "card"—*la carte* in French, *Speisekarte* in German, *la carta* in Spanish, and so on.

Finding the right restaurant is only half the battle. Once seated, you need to order a good meal. Ordering in a foreign lan-

A small, handwritten menu in the local language is a good sign.

guage can be fun, or it can be an ordeal. Ask for an English menu—if nothing else, you might get the waiter who speaks the *goodest* English. Most waiters can give at least a very basic translation—"cheekin, bunny, zuppa, green salat," and so on. A phrase book or menu reader is very helpful for those who want to avoid ordering sheep stomach when all they want is a lamb chop.

Young taste buds having their horizons gently stretched

If you don't know what to order, go with the waiter's recommendation or look for your dream meal on another table and order by pointing. People are

Picking green peppers off their pizzas, my kids discover that in Italy, peperoni *doesn't mean spicy sausage.*

usually helpful and understanding to the poor and hungry monoglot tourist. If they aren't, you probably picked a place that sees too many of them. Europeans with the most patience with tourists are the ones who rarely deal with them.

People who agonize over each word on the menu season the whole experience with stress. If you're in a good place, the food's good. Get a basic idea of what's cooking, have some fun with the waiter, be loose and adventurous, and just order something.

To max out culturally, my partner and I order two different meals: one high-risk and one low-risk. We share, sampling twice as many dishes. At worst, we learn what we don't like and split the chicken and fries. My tour groups cut every dish into bits, and our table becomes a lazy Susan. If anything, the waiters are impressed by our interest in their food, and very often they'll run over with a special treat for all of us to sample—like squid eggs. With a gang of 10 travelers, I once ordered all 10 pizzas on the menu to come one after the other, each cut into 10 slices. We took our time, the waiters had fun, we savored a great variety, and everything was hot...it was the cheapest 10-course meal in Rome.

The "tourist *menu*" (*menù turistico* in Italy, *menu touristique* in France), popular in restaurants throughout Europe's tourist

MENU € 19,00
TURISTICO

ANTIPASTO di MARE

PRIMI PIATTI
RISOTTO alla PESCATORA
SPAGHETTI alla MARINARA
SPAGHETTI allo SCOGLIO
TRENETTE al PESTO

SECONDI PIATTI
PESCE ai FERRI
FRITTO MISTO
GRIGLIATA di CARNE

CONTORNI
PATATE FRITTE o INSALATA

This Italian menu turistico includes a seafood starter plate (antipasto di mare), then you get to choose a first course (primi piatti), a second course (secondi piatti), and a side dish (contorni, either French fries or salad)...all for €19.

For a good dining value, I look for a chalkboard daily special (menu del día).

zones, offers confused visitors a no-stress, three-course meal for a painless price that usually includes service, bread, and a drink. You normally get a choice of several options for each course. Locals rarely order this, but if the options intrigue you, the tourist *menu* can be a convenient way to sample some regional flavors for a reasonable, predictable price.

Another great value is the local "blue plate special": Small eateries in most countries offer this fresh, economical "*menu* of the day" to those looking for a good deal. Recognize the native word (*dagens rett* in Sweden, *menu del día* in Spain, *plat du jour* in France, *menù del giorno* in Italy). These are often limited to early seatings (with the time—usually before 7:30 p.m.—posted on the door and in the menu).

The best values in entrées are usually chicken, fish, and veal. Lately my travel partner and I, rather than getting entrées, have shared a memorable little buffet of appetizers—they're plenty filling, less expensive, and more typically local than entrées. Drinks (except for wine in southern Europe) and desserts can be the worst value. Skipping those, you can enjoy some surprisingly good $15 meals.

Restaurant Drinks

In restaurants, Europeans generally drink bottled water (for taste, not health). You can normally get free tap water, but you may need to be polite, patient, inventive, and know the correct phrase. There's nothing wrong with ordering tap water, and waiters are accustomed to this request. Availability of (and willingness to serve) tap water varies from country to country. It's sometimes considered a special favor, and while your glass or carafe of tap water is normally served politely, occasionally it just isn't worth the trouble, and it's best to put up with the bottle of Perrier or order a drink from the menu.

Bottled water is served crisp and cold, either with or without carbonation, usually by happier waiters. Most Americans don't like the bubbly stuff, but I do. Learn the phrase *con/avec/mit/con/*with gas or *senza/sans/ohne/sin/*without gas (in Italian, French, German, and Spanish, respectively), and you will get the message across. Acquire a taste for *acqua*

Tap Water in Five Languages

Italian: *acqua del rubinetto*
French: *une carafe d'eau*
German: *Leitungswasser*
Spanish: *agua del grifo*
Portuguese: *água da torneira*

In all other languages, just do the international charade: Hold an imaginary glass in one hand, turn on the tap with the other, and make the sound of a faucet. Stop it with a click of your tongue and drink it with a smile.

con gas. It's a lot more fun (and read on the label what it'll do for your rheumatism).

If your budget is tight and you want to save $5–10 a day, never buy a restaurant drink. Scoff if you have the money, but drinks can sink a tight budget. While water is jokingly called the "American champagne" by the waiters of Europe, with the cost of living going up for residents lately, these days it's not only tourists going with tap water. Last year in an Oslo restaurant, I counted 16 of 20 diners drinking tap water. (They were charged $1 a glass, but it was still a substantial savings over a $6 Coke.)

Drink like a European. Cold milk, ice cubes, and coffee with (rather than after) your meal are American habits. Insisting on any of these in Europe will get you nothing but strange looks and a reputation as the ugly—if not downright crazy—American. Order local drinks, not just to save money but to experience the culture and to get the best quality and service. The timid can always order the "American waters" (Coke, Fanta, and 7-Up), sold everywhere.

German pubs don't serve minors beer—but many locals do.

Buying local alcohol is cheaper than your favorite import. A shot of the local hard drink in Portugal will cost a dollar, while an American drink would cost more than the American price. Drink the local stuff with local people in local bars; it's a better experience than having a Manhattan in your hotel with a guy from Los Angeles. Drink wine in wine countries and beer in beer countries. Sample the regional specialties. Let a local person order you her favorite. You may hate it, but you'll never forget it.

Getting the Bill

In Europe, the meal is routinely the event of the evening. At good restaurants, service will seem slow. Meals won't always come simultaneously—it's fine to start eating when served. Europeans will spend at least two hours enjoying a good dinner, and, for the full experience, so should you. Fast service is rude service. If you need to eat and run, make your time limits very clear as you order.

To get the bill, you'll have to ask for it (catch the waiter's eye and, with raised hands, scribble with an imaginary pencil on your palm). Before it comes, make a mental tally of roughly how much your meal should cost. The bill should vaguely resemble the figure you expected. (It should at least have the same number of digits.) If the total is a surprise, ask to have it itemized and explained. Some waiters make the same "innocent" mistakes repeatedly, knowing most tourists are so befuddled by the money and menu that they'll pay whatever number lies at the bottom of the bill.

Tipping

Restaurant tips are more modest in Europe than in America. In most places, 10 percent is a big tip. If your bucks talk at home, muzzle them on your travels. As a matter of principle, if not economy, the local price should prevail. Please believe me—tipping 15 or 20 percent in Europe is unnecessary, if not culturally insensitive.

Tipping is an issue only at restaurants that have waiters and waitresses. If you order your food at a counter (in a pub, for example), don't tip.

At table-service restaurants, the tipping etiquette and procedure varies slightly from country to country. But in general, European servers are well-paid, and tips are considered a small "bonus"—to reward great service, or for simplicity in rounding the total bill to a convenient number. In many countries, 5 percent is adequate and 10 verges on excessive.

In Mediterranean countries, the "service charge" (*servizio* in Italian, *service* in French, *servicio* in Spanish)—usually figured at 10 or 15 percent of your total bill—can be handled in different ways. Sometimes the menu

Interpreting the Bill

Examine this sample Italian restaurant bill to get used to the charges you'll see in Europe.

Check each line item. Be sure you understand what each charge was for. You don't have to speak fluent Italian to recognize *minestrone* or *spaghetti carbonara*. Even *insalata mista* isn't a stretch, if you remember that you ate a mixed salad. But if it says *"4 birre"* and you don't remember drinking four beers, ask for an explanation (or an apology).

Pane e coperto ("bread and cover" charge) is a mandatory amount charged per customer just to sit down. Common in Italy, this is relatively rare in other countries—though (sadly) it's beginning to catch on at touristy restaurants in popular destinations (such as Prague)

A legitimate **servizio** (service) charge of 10 percent has been added. You don't need to leave a big tip (but if you were pleased with the service, you'd round the amount up to €60—an extra tip of about 3 percent). In many cases, rather than adding the 10 percent at the end of the bill, the prices already include the service charge (in which case, the menu might say *"servizio incluso."*)

Also notice that Europeans use a comma as a decimal point—so €58,30 is the same as €58.30.

Now hand over your cash and wait for the change...and don't leave until you get the correct amount back. When you collect your change, you can leave the tip on the table, or better, give the tip directly to your server.

Or you can pay with exact change, including the tip, and indicate you don't need any back. For this meal, I'd hand the server €60, smile, say *grazie,* and wave my hand to suggest he should keep the change.

```
VIA GARIBALDI 37, ROMA
Ristorante Colosseo
DI RICARDO STEFANO
                              IMPORTO
pan e coperto (x2)...4,00
insalata caprese..... 6,00
ins. mista.......... 4,00
spaghetti carbonara... 6,00
minestrone ........ 8,00
frutta .......... 4,00
tiramisú ......... 5,00
vino rosso (bottiglia)... 12,00
acqua min. (litro)..... 4,00
totale ........... 53,00
servizio 10%....... 5,30
totale ........ €58,30
documento
    RICEVUTA FISCALE
  COPIA PER IL CLIENTE
```

will note that the service is included (e.g., *servizio incluso*), meaning that the prices listed in the menu already have this charge built in. In other cases, the service might show up as a separate line item at the end of your bill. (In this case, in Italy, the menu might say *servizio non incluso*—meaning the individual prices don't include service.) Fixed-price tourist deals (a.k.a. *menu*) include service.

In northern and Eastern Europe, the menu or bill is less likely to address the "service charge," but you can usually assume that it's included in the prices.

Virtually anywhere in Europe, you can do as the Europeans do and (if you're pleased with the service) round up a euro or two. This can vary a bit. For example, a 10 percent tip is expected in Hungary. And in very touristy areas, some servers have noticed the American obsession with overtipping—and might hope for a Yankee-size tip. But the good news is that European servers and diners are far more laid-back about all this than we are. Any tip is appreciated, the stakes are low, and it's no big deal if you choose the "wrong" amount.

Typically, it's better to hand the tip to the waiter when you're paying your bill than to leave it on the table, particularly in busy places where the wrong party might pocket the change. In Germanic countries, rather than physically leaving a tip on the table, it's considered discreet and classy to say the total number of euros you'd like the waiter to keep (including his tip) when paying. So, if the bill is €42, hand him €50 while saying, "45." You'll get €5 back and feel pretty European. In most of Europe, servers prefer to be tipped in cash even if you pay with your credit card. (Otherwise the tip may never reach your server.)

Vegetarians

Vegetarians find life a little frustrating in Europe. Very often, Europeans think "vegetarian" means "no red meat" or "not much meat." If you are a strict vegetarian, you'll have to make things very clear. Write the appropriate phrase (see sidebar), keep it handy, and show it to each waiter before ordering your meal.

Vegetarians have no problem with continental breakfasts, which are normally meatless anyway. Meat-free picnic lunches are delicious, since

Salad bars are abundant and great for vegetarians.

> # Key Vegetarian Phrases
>
> **We are (I am) vegetarian. We (I) do not eat meat, fish, or chicken. Eggs and cheese are OK.**
>
> **German:** *Wir sind (Ich bin) Vegetarier. Wir essen (Ich esse) kein Fleisch, Fisch, oder Geflügel. Eier und Käse OK.*
>
> **French:** *Nous sommes (Je suis) végétarien. Nous ne mangeons (Je ne mange) pas de viande, poisson, ou poulet. Oeufs et fromage OK.*
>
> **Italian:** *Siamo vegetariani (Sono vegetariano/a). Non mangiamo (mangio) nè carne, nè pesce, nè polli. Uova e formaggio OK.*

bread, cheese, and yogurt are wonderful throughout Europe. Have some healthy snacks (such as nuts or fresh produce) on hand, in case you can't find a suitable meal.

A big plate of veggies makes for an energizing lunch...even if you're not a vegetarian.

It's in restaurants that your patience may be minced. Big-city tourist office brochures list restaurants by category. In any language, look under "V." For a good meal, vegetarians basically have two options: You could seek out a specifically vegetarian restaurant (most big cities have several). Or you could browse the menus at some fine-dining restaurants, many of which pride themselves on offering at least one good vegetarian option.

Cafeterias (such as the bright, cheery, fresh, affordable ones you'll find on the top floor of major department stores) are a good spot for vegetarians, since you can see exactly what you're getting and select an assortment of foods that suit your diet.

Each country has its own quirks: Italy seems to sprinkle a little meat in just about everything. German cooking normally keeps the meat separate from the vegetables. Hearty German salads, with beets, cheese, and eggs, are a vegetarian's delight. Vegetarians enjoy *antipasti* buffets, salad bars, and ethnic restaurants throughout Europe.

Some vegetarians have told me that they become more flexible while abroad. One of them explained, "I'm a strict vegetarian who believes it's

SLEEPING AND EATING

both morally wrong and environmentally harmful to eat meat. However, when I travel I recognize that food is an important part of a culture. I owe it to myself and the country I'm visiting to sample the specialties... even if some contain meat. If veggie travelers plan to do this, however, it helps to order meat that doesn't remind them of animals. Dishes without bones, faces, or feet are easier for the vegetarian traveler to eat." While this "flexitarian" attitude wouldn't be palatable to everyone, some travelers might find it liberating.

Local Specialties, One Country at a Time

Eating in Europe is sightseeing for your taste buds. Every country has specialties that are good, memorable, or both. At least once, seek out and eat or drink the notorious "gross" specialties: ouzo, horse meat, snails, raw herring, blood sausage, fried fish sperm, haggis, tripe stew, octopus, and so on. All your life you'll hear references to them, and you'll have actually experienced what everyone's talking about. Here are some tips to help you eat, drink, and be merry in Europe. For more on the delicious and diverse tastes of Europe—especially France and Italy—see Chapter 69: The Flavors of Europe.

Belgium

Belgians boast that they eat as heartily as the Germans and as well as the French. This tiny country is into big steaks and designer chocolates. While Godiva chocolate is considered the finest, most locals enjoy double the dose for the same investment by getting their fix at a perfectly good but less glitzy place.

According to Belgians, the best part of the crab is the guts.

Seafood—fish, eel, oysters, and shrimp—is especially well-prepared in Belgium. Mussels are served everywhere. You get a big-enough-for-two bucket and a pile of fries. Go local by using one empty shell to tweeze out the rest of the *moules*.

Belgian fries (*Vlaamse frites,* or "Flemish fries") taste so good because they're deep-fried twice—once to cook, and once to brown. The natives dunk them in mayonnaise... especially delicious if the mayo is flavored with garlic.

Belgium has more varieties and brands of beer than any other country—and the locals take their beers as seriously as the French do their wines. My favorite budget meal in Belgium is in an atmospheric old pub enjoying their finest beer (I love Chimay), some simple pub grub...and a gaggle of "beer pilgrims" who've flocked here from around the world to appreciate some of Europe's best brew.

Britain and Ireland

The British Isles' reputation for miserable food is now dated, and today's cuisine scene is lively, trendy, and surprisingly good. (Unfortunately, it can also be expensive.)

While you can seek out fine cuisine in Britain and Ireland, it's cheaper and easier to enjoy decent cuisine in great atmosphere. That means pub grub. For $15–20, you'll get a basic, budget, hot lunch or dinner in friendly surroundings.

British pubs generally serve traditional dishes, like fish-and-chips, roast beef, and meat pies. "Crisps" are potato chips. Irish pubs often serve Irish stew (mutton), chowders, pork dishes, and lots of potatoes.

Pub meals are usually served from noon to 2 p.m. and from 6 p.m. to 8 p.m., not throughout the day. Because pubs make far more money selling beer, they're quick to shut down their kitchen and fill the place with drinkers, rather than eaters, later in the evening. There's usually no table service. Order at the bar, then take a seat and they'll bring the food when it's ready (or sometimes you pick it up at the bar). Pay at the bar. Don't tip unless it's a place with full table service. Pubs that advertise their food and are crowded with regulars are less likely to be the kind that serve only lousy microwaved snacks.

Of course, in any town you'll find alternatives to pub grub. At classier restaurants, look for early-bird specials, allowing you to eat well and affordably, but early (at about 5:30–7 p.m., last order by 7 p.m.). A top-end restaurant often serves the same quality two-course lunch deals for a third the price of dinner. Picnickers and serious sightseers can grab gourmet sandwiches and sides from chains such as Pret A Manger, Tesco, Sainsbury's, and Marks & Spencer (or follow businesspeople on their lunch break to the best hole-in-the-wall sandwich shops).

Ethnic restaurants from all over the world add spice to England's cuisine scene. Eating Indian or Chinese is cheap (even cheaper if you take it out). Middle Eastern stands sell gyro sandwiches and *shwarmas* (lamb in pita bread).

The British take great pride in their beer. Many Brits think that drinking beer cold and carbonated, as Americans do, ruins the taste.

At pubs, long-handled pulls are used to pull the traditional, rich-flavored "real ales" up from the cellar. Short-hand pulls at the bar mean colder, fizzier, mass-produced, and less interesting keg beers. Try the draft cider (sweet or dry)...carefully.

When you say "a beer, please" in an Irish pub, you'll get a pint of Guinness (the black beauty with a blonde head). If you want a small beer, ask for a glass or a half pint. Never rush your bartender when he's pouring a Guinness.

If you're in Scotland and want a nonalcoholic drink, try Irn-Bru (pronounced "Iron Brew"). This bright-orange beverage tastes not like orange soda, but like bubblegum with a slightly bitter aftertaste. Be cautious sipping it—as the label understates, "If spilt, this product may stain."

For a distinctive local flavor in Britain, sample Marmite—a brown yeasty-salty spread that's every young Brit's peanut butter. But beware...a little Marmite goes a long way. In Scotland, try the famous haggis, a rich assortment of oats and sheep organs stuffed into a chunk of sheep intestine, liberally seasoned and boiled. Usually served with "neeps and tatties" (turnips and potatoes), it's tastier than it sounds and worth trying...once.

Eastern Europe

Eastern Europe offers good food for relatively little money—especially if you venture off the main tourist trail. The cuisine here is generally heavy, hearty, and tasty. Expect lots of meat, potatoes, and cabbage. Still, there's more variety in the East than you might expect.

Czech food is heavy on pork and kraut, but more modern eateries are serving up pasta and salads. Czechs are among the world's most enthusiastic beer *(pivo)* drinkers. The pub is a place to have fun, complain, discuss art and politics, talk hockey, and chat with locals and visitors alike.

In Poland, try the hearty soups (such as the red-beet borscht, or *barszcz*), tasty sauerkraut stew, and pierogi (ravioli-like dumplings with various fillings). Take advantage of Poland's amazingly cheap, government-subsidized milk bars *(bar mleczny)*, which usually offer tasty traditional specialties. And be sure to sample the national drink, *wódka*. Locals cut it with apple juice to make a cocktail they call *szarlotka* ("apple cake").

The quintessential ingredient in Hungarian cuisine is spicy paprika, which appears in red shakers alongside salt and pepper on tables. Meat of all kinds (especially goose liver) is popular. Seek out the sweet, creamy cold fruit soup *(hideg gyümölcs leves)*.

Slovenia and Croatia offer more variety. Choosing between strudel and baklava on the same menu, you're constantly reminded that this is a land where the Germanic world meets the Eastern Mediterranean. Slovenia has hearty, German-style food, with lots of sausage and buckwheat. In Croatia, the seafood is succulent and plentiful. Both countries have been influenced by Italian cuisine, with good pastas, pizzas, and gelato.

France

France is famous for its cuisine—and rightly so. Dining in France can be surprisingly easy on a budget, especially in the countryside. Small restaurants throughout the country love their regional cuisine and take great pride in serving it.

The *plat du jour* (daily special), salad plate, and *menu* (fixed-price, three- to six-course meal) are often good deals. To get a complete list of what's cooking, ask for *la carte* (not the *menu*). The cheese boards that come with multi-course meals

Cheers!

offer the average American a new adventure in eating. When it comes, ask for "a little of each, please" *(un peu de chaque, s'il vous plaît)*. Wine is the cheapest drink, and every region has its own wine and cheese. Order the house wine *(vin du pays)*. Classy restaurants are easiest to afford at lunchtime, when meal prices are usually reduced. France is known for particularly slow (as in polite) service. If you need to eat and run, make it clear from the start. Bars serve reasonably priced omelets, salads, and the *croque-monsieur*—your standard grilled cheese and ham sandwich.

French food, while delicious, at times stretches your culinary horizons. A few words to look out for: *cervelle* (brains), *ris de veau* (calf pancreas), *viande de cheval* (horse meat), *andouillette* (intestines), *langue* (tongue)...and, of course, *escargot* (snails) and *cuisses de grenouilles* (frog's legs).

Degustation gratuite is not a laxative, but an invitation to a free wine-tasting. You'll find *D/G* signs throughout France's wine-growing regions.

When buying cheese, be sure to ask for samples of the specialties. Croissants are served warm with breakfast, and baguettes (long, skinny loaves of French bread) are great for budget munching.

For a royal tour of French delicacies—regardless of your budget— assemble a gourmet picnic. Make a point of visiting the small specialty shops and picking up the finest (most expensive) pâtés, cheeses, and hors d'oeuvres. As you spread out your tablecloth, passersby will wish you a cheery *"Bon appétit!"*

Germany

Germany is ideal for the "meat-and-potatoes" person. With straight-forward, no-nonsense food at budget prices, Deutschland feeds me very well. Small-town restaurants serve up wonderful plates of hearty specialties for $12–20.

Germany's *Wurst* is the best anywhere, and *Kraut* is not as *sauer* as the stuff you hate at home. Only a tourist puts the sausage in a bun like a hot dog. Munch alternately between the meat and the bread ("that's why you have two hands"), and you'll look like a local. Generally, the darker the weenie, the spicier it is.

Potatoes are the standard vegetable, but *Spargel* (giant white asparagus) is a must in-season (early summer). The bread and pretzels in the basket on your table often cost extra.

When I need a break from pork, I order the *Salatteller* (big, varied dinner-size salad). For budget (and palate) relief in big-city Germany, find a Greek,

Ein *Beer*, ein *Pretzel*, und *Thou*

Turkish, or Italian restaurant. Fast-food stands are called *Schnell Imbiss*.

German wine (85 percent white) is particularly good from the Mosel and Rhine River Valleys. The Germans enjoy a tremendous variety and quantity of great beer. The average German drinks 30 gallons of beer a year.

Browse through supermarkets and see what Germany eats when there's no more beer and pretzels. Gummi bears, the bear-shaped jelly bean with a cult following, go by the name brand Goldbären here in their native land. Another sweet staple is Nutella, a sensuous chocolate-hazelnut spread (originally from Italy) that turns anything into a first-class dessert.

A few unusual German flavors are worth sampling. *Handkäse* is an especially pungent cheese, sometimes pickled in vinegar. Tourists flock to Rothenburg to buy, sample, and immediately throw away the notorious *Schneeballs*—made of balled-up strips of dough. *Schmalz*, a popular spread, is pure lard...literally. And at Bavarian beer halls, you're likely to see people munching on *Steckerlfisch*—an entire mackerel fish on a stick, roasted over a fire.

Greece

Greek food is simple...and simply delicious. The four Greek food groups are olives (and olive oil), salty feta cheese, tasty tomatoes, and crispy phyllo dough. Virtually every dish is built on a foundation of these four building-blocks.

The best snack deal in Europe—a Greek souvlaki

Menus are usually written in both Greek and Latin alphabets, but you're welcome to go into the kitchen and point to the dish you'd like. This is a good way to make some friends, sample from each kettle, get what you want (or at least know what you're getting), and have a truly memorable meal. (The same is true in Turkey.) Be brave.

Every meal seems to start with a classic Greek salad: Ripe tomatoes chopped up just so, rich feta cheese (sometimes in a long, thick slab that you break apart with your fork), olives, and onions, all drenched with olive oil. The best strategy at most tavernas is to split a salad and a few *mezedes* (appetizers) to taste several different flavors. If you're still hungry, split a main dish or two. Dunk bread into *tzatziki*, a refreshing cucumber and yogurt dip.

My favorite on-the-go Greek snack is a tasty shish kebab wrapped in flat bread called a souvlaki pita. Souvlaki stands, offering $3 take-out sandwiches, are all over Greece.

Savory, flaky phyllo-dough pastries called "pies" (*pita*, not to be confused with pita bread) are another budget staple of Greek cuisine; the most common are *spanakopita* (spinach), *tiropita* (cheese), *kreatopita* (lamb), and *meletzanitopita* (eggplant).

For dessert, don't miss the creamy yogurt with honey. The Greeks throw together honey, nuts, and phyllo dough to create delectable desserts—from baklava to *kataifi* (similar to shredded wheat, doused in honey).

Retsina is a pine-resin-flavored wine that is a dangerous taste to acquire. Ouzo is a powerful, love-it-or-hate-it, licorice-flavored apéritif. For American-style coffee, order "Nescafé"...but try the potent, grainy Greek coffee for a real kick. Eat when the locals do—late.

Italy

Italians eat huge meals consisting of a first course of pasta and a second plate of meat, plus a salad, fruit, and wine. The pasta course alone is usually enough to fill the average tourist. You'll save money by ordering pasta as your main course. Some fancier restaurants won't serve just pasta; find one that will, and you'll enjoy a reasonably priced meal of lasagna or minestrone and a salad.

Veggie lovers enjoy the restaurants that have self-serve *antipasti* buffets. These offer a variety of cooked appetizers spread out like a salad bar (pay per plate, not weight). A single plate of *antipasti* combined with a pasta dish makes a healthy, affordable, interesting meal for two. Note that anytime you eat or drink at a table, you'll be charged a cover *(coperto)* of a couple dollars. That, plus service *(servizio)*, makes even a cheap, one-course restaurant meal cost at least $15.

For inexpensive Italian eateries, look for the term *osteria, tavola calda, rosticceria, trattoria, pizzeria,* or "self-service." A meal-size pizza (sold everywhere for less than $12) and a cold beer is my idea of a good, fast, cheap Italian dinner. For a stand-up super-bargain meal, look for a Pizza Rustica shop, which sells pizza by weight. Just point to the best-looking pizza and tell them how much you want (200 grams is a filling meal). They weigh, you pay. They heat it, you eat it. *Panini* (sandwiches)—*calda* (toasted) if you ask—are cheap and widely available.

For the best budget gourmet meal in Italy, I find an *enoteca* (wine bar). Buy the best glass of fine wine you can afford, and nibble the snacks that come with it and are designed to complement the wine. This ingredient-driven light meal is similar in price to a full meal at a mid-range restaurant.

Three important phrases to know are *menù del giorno* (fixed-price meal of the day, usually a good deal), *pane e coperto* (charge for bread and cover), and *servizio incluso* (service included). But the most important words in your Italian vocabulary are *corposo* (full-bodied—as in wine)

Two fine reasons to savor Italy: gelato and the Riviera

and gelato—probably the best ice cream you'll ever taste. A big cone or cup containing a variety of flavors costs $3–5.

Cappuccino, rich coffee with a frothy head of steamed milk, is very popular, and it should be. Tiny coffee shops are tucked away on just about every street. All have a price list, and most require you to pay the cashier first and then take the receipt to the man who makes the drinks.

Experiment. Try coffee or tea *freddo* (cold) or *frappé* (blended with ice). Discover a new specialty each day. Bars sell large bottles of cold mineral water, with or without gas, for about $2.

Bar-hopping is fun. A carafe of house wine serves four or five people for about $10. Many bars have delicious *cicchetti* (cheh-KET-tee), local toothpick munchies. A *cicchetteria* is a great place for an entire meal of these pint-size taste treats. In big cities, many bars offer these munchies free during happy hour.

The Netherlands

Traditional Dutch food is basic and hearty, with lots of bread, cheese, soup, and fish. Dutch treats include pancakes, "syrup waffles," and cheese. An experience you owe your tongue in Holland: slurping down raw herring at an outdoor herring stand.

My favorite Dutch food

is Indonesian. Indonesia, a former colony of the Netherlands, gained its independence but left behind plenty of great restaurants. The cheapest meals, as well as some of the best splurges, are found in these "Indisch" or "Chinese-Indisch" restaurants. The famous rijsttafel ("rice table") is the ultimate Indonesian meal, with as many as 36 delightfully exotic courses, all eaten with rice. One meal is plenty for two, so order carefully. In a small-town restaurant, a rijsttafel can be a great bargain—two can split 12 exotic courses with rice for $30–40. *Bami* or *nasi goreng* are smaller and cheaper but still filling versions of a rijsttafel.

Order a beer, and you'll get a *pils,* a light lager. *Jenever* is Dutch gin flavored with juniper berries (and often other botanicals). While cheese gets harder and sharper with age, *jenever* grows smooth and soft. Old *jenever* is best.

Portugal

Portugal has some of the most enjoyable and cheapest eating I've found in Europe. Find a sailors' hangout and fill up on fresh seafood, especially clams, cockles, and the fish soup. The young *vinho verde* ("green wine") is an addictive specialty and a favorite of visiting wine buffs. In fishing towns, you'll find boiled *percebes* (barnacles) sold on the street; these are the Portuguese answer to beer nuts. Let a local show you how to strip and eat one. A fun excuse to visit the fine bakeries is to go on a quest for the best *pastel de nata.* These delightful mini–cream pies are sold everywhere, but  they originated near Lisbon in Belém, where you can visit the famous Casa Pasties de Belém and try the original.

Be warned that in restaurants, pricey little appetizers might be placed at your table as if they're free. These are fun and tasty, but if you nibble even one you'll be charged for the entire lot. To clear out the temptation, ask to have them taken away.

Scandinavia

Most Scandinavians avoid their highly taxed and very expensive restaurants. The cost of alcohol alone is sobering. The key to budget eating in Nordic Europe is to take advantage of the *smörgåsbord.* For about $20 (cheap in Scandinavia), breakfast *smörgåsbords* will fill you with plenty of hearty food. Since both meals are, by definition, all-you-can-eat, I opt

Smörgåsbord: *enough food to sink a Viking ship*

for the budget breakfast meal over the fancier, more expensive ($30) *middag*, or midday, *smörgåsbords*. Many train stations and ferries serve *smörgåsbords*.

For a budget lunch in Denmark, find a *smörrebröd* (open-face sandwich) shop. These places make artistic and delicious sandwich picnics to go. Or munch on a *pølse*, the Danish version of a hot dog.

All over Scandinavia, keep your eyes peeled for daily lunch specials called *dagens rett*. You can normally have all the vegetables (usually potatoes) you want when you order a restaurant's entrée. Just ask for seconds. Many Scandinavian pizzerias offer all-you-can-eat deals and hearty salad bars. (Your bill will double if you order a beer.) The cheapest cafeterias often close at about 5 or 6 p.m.

Fresh produce, colorful markets, and efficient supermarkets abound in Europe's most expensive corner. Liver paste is curiously cheap but tastes powerfully nutritious. The rock-bottom, bilge-of-a-Viking-ship-cheap meal is a package of cracker bread and a tube of sandwich spread. Handy tubes of cheese, shrimp, and even caviar spread are popular. To save money and enjoy the great Nordic outdoors, have a picnic of Scandinavian goodies or take-out food from one of the many ethnic eateries.

Licorice is a popular Scandinavian snack. Finland's distinctive *salmiakki* is a salty licorice, popularized after World War II when sugar was carefully rationed.

Spain

Spaniards eat to live, not vice versa. The Spanish diet—heavy on ham, deep-fried foods, more ham, weird seafood, and ham again—can be brutal on Americans more accustomed to salads, fruit, and grains. But it's relatively cheap—you can eat well in restaurants for $20.

The Spanish eating schedule—lunch from 1 p.m. to 4 p.m.,

At a traditional Spanish small-town bar, €2 buys you a glass of wine—and includes a tapa.

Tapas Tips

You can eat well any time of day in Spain's tapas bars. Tapas are small portions, like appetizers, of seafood, salads, meat-filled pastries, deep-fried tasties, and on and on—normally displayed under glass at the bar.

Tapas typically cost about €2, up to €10 for seafood. Most bars push larger portions called *raciones* (dinner-plate-sized) rather than smaller tapas (saucer-sized). Ask for the smaller tapas portions or a *media-ración* (listed as ½ *ración* on a menu), though many bars simply don't serve anything smaller than a *ración.*

Eating and drinking at a bar is usually cheapest if you stand at the counter *(barra).* You may pay a little more to eat sitting at a table *(mesa)* and still more for an outdoor table *(terraza).* Locate the price list (often posted in fine type on a wall somewhere) to know the menu options and price tiers. In the right place, a quiet snack and drink on a terrace on the town square is well worth the extra charge. But the cheapest seats sometimes get the best show. Sit at the bar and study your bartender—he's an artist.

Be assertive or you'll never be served. *Por favor* (please) grabs the guy's attention. Don't worry about paying until you're ready to

dinner after 9 p.m.—frustrates many visitors. Most Spaniards eat one major meal of the day: lunch *(almuerzo)* at 2 p.m., when stores close, schools let out, and people gather with their friends and family for the so-called "siesta." Because most Spaniards work until 7:30 p.m., a light supper *(cena)* is usually served at about 9 p.m. or 10 p.m.

To get by in Spain, either adapt yourself to the Spanish schedule and diet, or do the tapa tango. Bars and coffee spots serve tapas (hors d'oeuvres), sandwiches, and *tortillas* (omelets, great for a hearty breakfast). On my last trip, I ate at least one easy, quick, and very cheap tapas meal a day (see sidebar).

Two famous Spanish dishes are gazpacho (chilled tomato soup) and paella (saffron-flavored rice with seafood, chicken, and sausage). *Platos*

leave (he's keeping track of your tab). To get the bill ask: *"¿La cuenta?"* (I have fun with my pet alternative, *"¿La dolorosa?"* Literally meaning "the sadness"—roughly, "What's the damage?"—it's a colloquial way to ask for the bill.)

Chasing down a particular bar for tapas nearly defeats the purpose and spirit of tapas—they are impromptu. Just drop in at any lively place. I look for the noisy spots with piles of napkins and food debris on the floor (go local and toss your trash, too), lots of locals, and the TV blaring. Popular television-viewing includes bullfights and soccer games, American sitcoms, and Spanish interpretations of soaps and silly game shows (you'll see Vanna Blanco). While tapas are served all day, the real action begins late—9 p.m. at the earliest. But for beginners, an earlier start is easier and comes with less commotion.

Get a fun, inexpensive sampler plate. Ask for *una tabla de canapés variados* to get a plate of various little open-face sandwiches. Or ask for a *surtido de* (an assortment of...) *charcutería* (a mixed plate of meat) or *queso* (cheese). *Un surtido de jamón y queso* means a plate of different hams and cheeses. Order bread and two glasses of red wine on the right square—and you've got a romantic (and €10) dinner for two.

combinados (combination plates of three or more items) are a reasonable way to sample Spanish cuisine. For a more unusual Spanish taste, seek out *pulpo* (octopus)—especially popular in the northwest region of Galicia.

Spain is one of the world's leading producers of grapes, and that means lots of excellent wine. Sherry is the fortified wine from the Jerez region, and *cava* (from Catalunya) is Spain's answer to champagne. Rioja is a full-bodied wine from the north of Spain. Sangria (red wine mixed with fruit juice) is popular and refreshing.

Switzerland

Here at a crossroads of Europe, the food has a wonderful diversity:

heavy *Wurst-und-Kraut* Germanic fare; delicate, subtle French cuisine; and pasta dishes *all' Italiana*. But Swiss restaurant prices can ruin your appetite and send you running to a grocery store. Even locals find their restaurants expensive. The Migros and Co-op grocery stores sell gro-ceries for about the same prices you find in American stores—reasonable by Swiss standards.

Aside from clocks, banks, and knives, Switzerland is known for its cheeses: strong-flavored Gruyère, mild Emmentaler, and pungent Appenzeller, with a smell that verges on nauseat-ing...until you taste it.

Two of Switzerland's best-known specialties are cheese-based: fon-due and raclette. You eat fondue with a long fork, dipping cubes of bread into a pot of melted cheese and wine. Raclette is melted cheese over potatoes, pickled onions, and gherkins.

Another must-try dish, most typical in the mountains of the German-speaking areas, is *Rösti:* traditional hash browns with alpine cheese, sometimes served with an egg cracked over the top...yum.

And, of course, there's chocolate. The Swiss changed the world in 1875 with their invention of milk chocolate. Stroll the chocolate aisle of a grocery store and take your pick.

Turkey

Bring an appetite and order high on the menu in nice restaurants. Eating's cheap in Turkey. The typical eatery is a user-friendly cafeteria with giant bins of lots of delicacies you always thought were Greek. Kebabs are

a standard meaty snack. *Pide,* fresh out of the oven, is Turkish pizza. *Sütlaç* (rice pudding) and bak-lava will satisfy your sweet tooth. Munch pistachios by the pocketful. Tea in tiny hourglass-shaped glasses is served constantly every-where. A refreshing, milky yogurt drink called *ayran,* cheap boxes of cherry juice, and fresh-squeezed orange juice make it fun to quench your Turkish thirst. Or try the *rakı* (Turkish ouzo). Let a local show you how to carefully create a two-layered *rakı* drink by slowly dribbling in the water. For breakfast, get ready for cucumbers, olives, tomatoes, and lots of goat cheese and bread.

TRAVEL SAVVY

Once you're in Europe, how do you travel like a pro? The next several chapters focus on giving you pointers for enjoying your day-to-day European existence.

Most of these tips are geared for big cities—which, for many travelers, are the most intimidating part of a European trip. Struggling with the Chicagos, New Yorks, and L.A.s of Europe is easier if you take advantage of the local tourist information office, catch some kind of orientation tour, and learn the public-transportation system. You can't just wing it in Europe's large cities. Plan ahead. Have a guidebook for wherever you're traveling. As you approach by train or plane, spend the last hour reading and planning. Know what you want to see. To save time and energy, plan your sightseeing strategy to cover the city systematically and efficiently, one neighborhood at a time.

18. Getting Oriented

Tourist Information Offices

No matter how well I know a town, my first stop is always the tourist information office (abbreviated **TI** in my guidebooks). Any place with a tourist industry has an information service for visitors on the main square, in the City Hall, or at the train station, airport, or freeway entrance. You don't need the address—just follow the signs. A busy but normally friendly and multilingual staff gives out sightseeing information, reserves hotel rooms, sells concert or theater tickets, and answers questions.

Prepare a list of questions ahead of time. Write up a proposed sight-seeing schedule. Find out if it's workable or if you've left out any important

sights. Confirm closed days and free-admission days.

Ask for a city map, public-transit information, and a list of sights with current hours. Find out about special events and pick up any local entertainment guides. See if walking tours or self-guided walking-tour brochures or audioguides are available.

Your first stop in a new town: the tourist information office

Check on any miscellaneous concerns (such as safety, laundry, Internet access, bike rental, parking, camping, transportation tips for your departure, maps of nearby towns, or help with booking a room for your next destination). If the first person you talk to is rushed or uninterested, browse around for a few minutes and talk to someone else.

Europe is amazingly well organized. For instance, tourist offices in some major cities (particularly Scandinavian capitals) sell a "tourist card" for about $40–50, which includes 24 hours of free entrance to all the sights; free use of all the subways, buses, and boats; a booklet explaining everything; and a map. Do the arithmetic, based on what you want to see, to figure out whether this will save you money over paying for individual admissions and tickets.

At the Oslo tourist office, you can pick up a monthly entertainment guide, list of sights, 24-hour bus pass, telephone card, and city map.

If necessary, get ideas on where to eat and sleep. But remember, most tourist information offices aren't services—they're businesses that sell things and work on fees and commissions. They don't volunteer information on cheap alternatives to hotels, and they pocket any "deposits" collected on big "front door" places they recommend.

If you'll be arriving late, call ahead before the tourist office closes.

Good information (in English) is worth a long-distance phone call. Guidebooks and websites list the phone numbers.

Cruising the Internet as You Travel

With Europe's abundant Internet cafés and easy hotel Internet connections, I frequently go online as I travel—to check my email and sports scores back home, but also to travel efficiently. You can go online to check hours and temporary exhibit information for museums; research bus, train, or boat connections; confirm event schedules; get directions to your next hotel; compare walking-tour companies; and check the weather—all without picking up a phone. These days, you can even use the Internet to reserve a no-wait entry time at some of Europe's most crowded museums.

The Internet can also help you find a good restaurant or hotel. Sites such as Tripadvisor.com offer user reviews from other travelers. Many European cities and countries have their own similar sites (such as Yelp.com in the US) that feature restaurant reviews from locals, not travelers. While these sites are useful, be aware that anyone can post reviews—even the business itself (or its competitors). Take the advice with a grain of salt. Generally the more individual reviews a place has, the more reliable the information.

For more on getting online in Europe, see Chapter 22: Phones, Email, and Snail Mail.

More Information Sources

Big-hotel information desks, hostel employees, other travelers, and guidebooks are helpful. To find guidebooks in English, check newsstands and English sections in large bookstores. All big cities have English bookstores, and most general bookstores have guidebooks in English (especially of that city or region). If you find yourself in a town with no information and the tourist office is closed, a glance through a postcard rack will quickly show you the most famous sights.

Youth Centers: Many cities, especially in the north, have industrious youth travel-aid offices. Oslo has a great youth center called Use It (www.use-it.no), Tallinn has the Travelers' Tent (in front of the official TI), and several cities publish very practical youth-oriented budget-travel magazines (available at tourist offices).

Entertainment Guides: Big European cities bubble with entertainment, festivities, and nightlife. But these events won't come to you. New in town and unable to speak the native language, travelers can be oblivious to a once-in-a-lifetime event erupting just across the bridge.

A periodical entertainment guide is the ticket. Every big city has one, either in English (such as *What's On in Oslo*) or in the local language but easy to decipher (such as the *Pariscope* weekly). Sometimes the tourist office hands these out for free; other times, you'll have to buy one at a newsstand. In Florence and Rome, entertainment guides are published monthly by the big, fancy hotels and are available for free at their desks (look like a hotel guest and help yourself). Ask at your hotel about entertainment. Events are posted on city walls everywhere. Read posters. They are in a foreign language, but that really doesn't matter when it reads: *Weinfest, Música Folklórica, 9 Juni, 21:00, Piazza Majore, Entre Libre,* and so on. Figure out the signs—or miss the party.

Maps

The best and cheapest map is often the public-transit map. Try to get one that shows bus and tram lines, subway stops, and major sights. Many tourist offices and big-city hotels give out free city maps, as do some fast-food chains. Study the map to understand the city's layout. Relate the location of landmarks—your hotel, major sights, the river, main streets, and the train station—to each other. Use any viewpoint—such as a church spire, tower, hilltop, or top story of a skyscraper—to understand the lay of the land, retrace where you've been, and see where you're going next. Back on the ground, you won't be in such constant need of your map. For more on maps, see page 24.

Walking Tours and Local Guides

Walking tours are my favorite introduction to a city. Since they focus on just a small part of a larger whole (generally the old town center), they are thorough. The tours are usually conducted in English by well-trained guides who are sharing their town for the noble purpose of giving you an appreciation of its history, people, and culture—not to make a lot of money. Walking tours are personal, inexpensive, and a valuable education. I can't recall a bad one.

On your travels, you might run across start-up companies advertising free walking tours in major European cities, such as Munich, Berlin, Paris, and Florence. While the tours are

Guides bring museums and castles to life.

indeed free, tipping is expected; in fact, the guides don't earn money unless you tip. Personally, I avoid these tours. They're light on history, and the guides spend your valuable time heavily promoting their company's other tours (which are not free). I'd rather support tours offered by established companies, and pay upfront for hardworking guides whose goal is to make the city's history come alive.

Many tourist offices rent audioguides you can take for a walk, or provide do-it-yourself walking-tour leaflets. The avid walker should consider purchasing one of the many "turn right at the fountain"–type guidebooks that are carefully written collections of self-guided walks through major cities. My city guidebooks include these types of walking tours.

For the price of three seats on a forgettable quadrilingual tape-recorded city bus tour, you

Audioguides...for all the hair-raising details on Europe's historic sights

can often hire your own private guide for a personalized city tour (most cost-effective if you're traveling with a group). Every city has a long list of English-speaking professional guides who earn their living giving tours any way they can. They hire out by the day or half-day and generally follow a national guide service fee schedule (about $200 per half-day, which can mean two to four hours—ask when you book). In my research, I've grown accustomed to relying heavily upon these experts and generally find them well worth the investment. You can find and book guides by calling the local tourist information office (or visiting its website) in advance, or even by dropping by and arranging a guide upon arrival in a town. Although you get the contact information from the tourist office, you typically book the guide

Try a guided walk to learn about a town that's probably a thousand years older than your hometown.

by calling or emailing the person directly. When I meet particularly good independent guides, I include their contact information in my guidebooks.

Hiring a private guide is an especially good value in Eastern Europe and Russia, where guides tend to be young, intelligent, and enthusiastic... and charge half as much. The best guides are often those whose tours you can pick up at a specific sight. They usually really know their museum, castle, cathedral, or town.

Bus Orientation Tours

Many cities have fast-orientation bus tours like London's famous tours that take you around the city on a double-decker bus. You'll get a feel

A minibus tour of Bruges—name your language

for the urban lay of the land as you drive past the major sights and hear a live or recorded narration. The innovative "hop-on, hop-off" bus tours give tourists an all-day pass to hop on and off buses making a circular route through the city's top sights. These buses come by several times an hour and generally include live or tape-recorded narration. Since guide quality varies, if I find myself enjoying a particularly good guide, I'll stay on that bus for the entire route. They cost about $30–40, and, if you've got the money and not much time, they provide a good orientation. If I had only one day in a big city, I might spend half of it on one of these tours. Along with London, you'll find bus tours in Bath, York, Edinburgh, Oxford, Cambridge, Glasgow, Dublin, Copenhagen, Helsinki, Paris, Berlin, Munich, Vienna, Budapest, Prague, Madrid, Barcelona, Sevilla, Milan, Rome, Athens, Istanbul, and more.

As a popular trend, many cities now offer a public bus (e.g., Berlin's bus #100) or boat route (e.g., Amsterdam's museum boat) that connects many of the city's major sightseeing attractions. Tourists buy the one-day pass and make the circuit at their leisure. (See "Bus Basics" on page 283.)

Bus and Minibus Excursions

Bus tours out of the city can be worthwhile solely for the ride. Some sights are awkward to reach by public transportation, such as the

TRAVEL SAVVY

châteaux of France's Loire, King Ludwig's castles in Bavaria, the *Sound of Music* sights outside Salzburg, the D-Day beaches of Normandy, the rural meadows of Cornwall, and the pilgrimage site of Međugorje, near Dubrovnik. An organized tour not only whisks you effortlessly from one hard-to-reach-without-a-car sight to the next, but gives you lots of information as you go.

Sometimes you have a choice between a big, 50-seat bus (or "coach") and a smaller minibus. Typically the big-bus tours are a bit more professional and comfortable. Some are great. Others are boring and impersonal—with a multilingual recorded commentary that's so dry you might find the Chinese soundtrack more interesting than the English one. The minibus tours tend to have more personality and can

Minibus tours—such as this one, to the Irish countryside—can be an ideal way for non-drivers to reach far-flung sights.

get to places the big buses can't. Because it's a smaller group, you're likely to have a more engaging, entertaining guide and more camaraderie as you roll.

If you're about to spend $75 anyway for a train ticket—let's say, from London to Bath—why not spend $110 for a one-day bus tour from London that visits Salisbury, Stonehenge, and Bath? Bring your luggage and leave the tour in Bath before it returns to London, having enjoyed a day of transportation and information for not much more than a 90-minute train ticket. (But be aware that bus tour itineraries can change; your tour might arrive in Bath first, before visiting Stonehenge on the way back to London. Confirm the route before you book.)

These tours can also be of value to the budget-minded do-it-yourselfer: Pick up the brochure for a well-thought-out tour itinerary and do it on your own. Take buses at your own pace and tour every sight for a fraction of the cost.

19. Getting Around

Public Transportation

Shrink and tame big cities by mastering their subway and bus systems. Europe's public-transit systems are so good that many Europeans go through life never learning to drive. Their wheels are trains, subways, trams, and buses.

Save time, money, and energy. Too many timid tourists avoid buses or subways and waste time walking or money on taxis. Subways are speedy and comfortable, never slowed by traffic jams. And with the proper attitude, a subway ride can be an aesthetic experience, plunging you into the people- and advertisement-filled river of workaday life.

Get a transit map. With a map, anyone can decipher the code to cheap and easy urban transportation. Paris and London have the most extensive— and the most needed—subway systems.

Public transit—the European treat

Both cities come with plenty of subway maps and expert subway tutors. Understand the difference between the urban subway and suburban commuter trains—the latter can sometimes get you across town faster, but may require a different ticket.

Know your ticket options. In many cities, the same tickets are good on the subway, trams, and buses, including transfers between the systems; in other places, you'll need to buy a new ticket each time you transfer. Some cities offer deals, such as tourist passes allowing unlimited travel on all public transport for a day or several days. These "go as you please" passes may seem expensive, but, if you do any amount of running around, they can be a convenient money-saver. They can also save time—with a transit pass, you go directly to the train or bus, avoiding long ticket lines.

Buying individual tickets is usually the worst deal. Instead, look for money-saving options, such as Paris' 10-ticket *carnet* or London's prepaid Oyster

If you take advantage of public transportation, you can zip quickly, effortlessly, and inexpensively around Europe's most congested cities.

card. In the subway, you can buy tickets at windows and/or at vending machines; for buses, you can often buy them on board (usually exact change only). In a few cities (such as Munich), a valid railpass gets you free passage on some subway trains.

European subways and buses often use the honor system, but ticket-checkers do pass by sporadically. If you're caught without a valid ticket, you'll probably have to pay a hefty fine.

Ask for help. Europe's buses and subways are filled with local people who are happy to help lost tourists locate themselves. Confirm with a local that you're at the right platform or bus stop. If a ticket seems expensive, ask what it covers—$4 may seem like a lot until you learn

it's good for a round-trip, two hours, or several transfers. And if you tell them where you're going, passengers sitting around you will gladly tell you where to get off.

Be cautious. While public transportation feels safe, be constantly on guard. Per capita, there are more pick-pockets on Europe's subway trains and buses than just about anywhere else. Thieves—often dressed as successful professionals or as tourists—

tend to congregate wherever there are bottlenecks: on escalators, at turnstiles, at subway doors, and so on. Try to avoid traveling by subway with a lot of luggage, as not only does it make you a target, it's a hassle to navigate through the crowds. Buses that are particularly popular with tourists are equally popular with pickpockets. Be on the lookout, wear your money belt, and you'll do fine. (For more tips, see Chapter 24: Outsmarting Thieves.)

Subway Basics

Most of Europe's big cities are blessed with an excellent subway system, often linked effortlessly with suburban trains. Wise travelers know that learning a city's network of underground trains is a key to efficient sight-

As you'll constantly be reminded on London's Tube... mind the gap.

From Hotel to Museum: A Sample Subway Trip

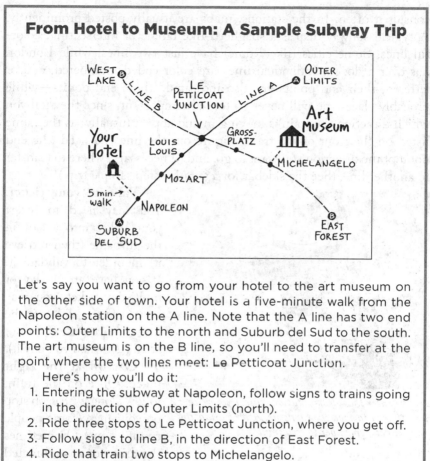

Let's say you want to go from your hotel to the art museum on the other side of town. Your hotel is a five-minute walk from the Napoleon station on the A line. Note that the A line has two end points: Outer Limits to the north and Suburb del Sud to the south. The art museum is on the B line, so you'll need to transfer at the point where the two lines meet: Le Petticoat Junction.

Here's how you'll do it:

1. Entering the subway at Napoleon, follow signs to trains going in the direction of Outer Limits (north).
2. Ride three stops to Le Petticoat Junction, where you get off.
3. Follow signs to line B, in the direction of East Forest.
4. Ride that train two stops to Michelangelo.
5. Use the neighborhood map in the station to locate the exit closest to the museum.

Congratulations—you've survived your first European subway trip!

seeing. European subways go by many names: "Metro" is the most common term on the Continent, except in German-speaking lands, where it's the "U-Bahn" or "S-Bahn." It's the "T-bane" in Oslo, the "T-bana" in Stockholm, and the "S-tog" in Copenhagen. Londoners (for whom "subway" means "pedestrian underpass") call it the "Tube" or "Underground." Here are a few tips for smooth sailing on Europe's subways.

Plan your route. Figure out your route before you enter the station so you can march confidently to the correct train. Get a good subway map (often included on free city maps, or ask for one at the station) and consult it often. In the stations, maps are usually posted prominently. A typical subway map is a spaghetti-like tangle of intersecting, colorful lines. Some cities (like Rome) have just two lines, while London has over a dozen. Individual lines are color-coded, numbered, and/or lettered; their end points are also indicated. These end points—while probably places you will never go to—are important, since they tell you which direction the train is moving in and appear (usually) as the name listed on the front of the train. Figure out the line you need, the end point of the direction you want to go, and (if necessary) where to transfer to another line. (See the sidebar for a step-by-step sample trip.)

As you enter the subway station, insert your ticket into the slot to open the turnstile. After validating your ticket, remember to reclaim it.

Validate your ticket. You may need to insert your ticket into a slot in the turnstile (then retrieve it) in order to validate it. If you have an all-day or multi-day ticket, you may only need to validate it the first time you use it, or not at all (ask when you buy it).

Get off at the right place. Once on the train, follow along with each stop on your map (some people count stops). Sometimes the driver or an automated voice announces the upcoming stop—but don't count on this cue, as a foreign name spoken by a native speaker over a crackly loudspeaker can be difficult to understand. If the train is crowded, move toward the doors one stop before you want to exit. As you pull into each station, its name will be posted prominently on the platform or along the wall. When the train stops, the doors may open automatically, or you may need to open them yourself by pushing a button or pulling a lever. Observe how people do it and imitate.

Transfer. Changing from one subway line to another can be as easy as walking a few steps away to an adjacent platform—or a bewildering wander via a labyrinth of stairs and long passageways. Fortunately, most subway systems are clearly signed—just follow along (or ask a local for help).

Exit the station. When you arrive at your destination station, follow exit signs up to the main ticketing area, where you'll usually find a posted map of the surrounding neighborhood to help you get your bearings. Individual exits are signposted by street name or nearby landmarks. Bigger stations have multiple exits. Choosing the right exit will help you avoid extra walking and crossing busy streets.

Bus Basics

Getting around town on the city bus system may seem daunting, but buses have some advantages over subways. Buses are often a better bet for shorter distances. Some buses go where the subway

Before exiting major subway systems like the Paris Métro, take a moment to familiarize yourself with the neighborhood map (plan du quartier), posted by the exits. Choose your exit smartly to surface near your destination.

can't (such as the top of Castle Hill in Budapest). Since you're not underground, it's easier to stay oriented and get the lay of the land. In fact, some public bus routes are downright scenic—Paris' bus #69 gives you a great sightseeing introduction to the city for around $2. The obvious disadvantage of buses is that they're affected by traffic—so it's often smart to avoid them during rush hour. If you take the bus, here are some tips.

Posted bus schedules tell you when the next bus is coming... and where it's going.

Plan your route. Tourist maps often indicate bus lines and stops. If yours doesn't, ask for a specific bus map at the TI. Many bus stops have timetables and route maps posted.

Validate your ticket. Tickets are checked on European buses in a variety of ways. Usually you enter at the front of the bus and show your ticket to the driver, or validate it by sticking it in an automated box. Sometimes you buy your ticket directly from the driver.

Transit Tips and Etiquette

For the Subway

- When waiting at the platform, stand out of the way of those exiting the train. Board the train only after everyone who wants to leave is off.
- In a crowded train, try not to block the exit (unless your stop is next). If you're blocking the door when the train stops, step out of the car and to the side, let others off, then get back on. Avoid using the hinged seats near the doors of some trains when the car is jammed; they take up valuable standing space or may be reserved for those with special needs.
- It's classy and polite to offer your seat to someone who needs it more (such as an elderly person or a mother with a small child).
- Talk softly in the cars. Listen to how quietly Europeans communicate and follow their lead.
- If there's a hubbub at the exit (the door won't open, or someone is loudly blocking it), assume that it's a distraction for pickpockets—put a hand on your valuables and refuse to get flustered.
- On escalators, stand on the right, pass on the left.
- Don't throw your subway tickets away too soon—you might need your current ticket to exit the system. Once you exit, throw away or tear used tickets to avoid confusing them with fresh ones.
- Street entertainers often use subway cars to perform for a captive audience. After they play, they'll solicit everyone for a few coins. Whether you choose to give or not is up to you.
- Subways generally operate from 6 a.m. until midnight—check locally. Subways rarely follow a specific schedule; instead, the trains just pass by at frequent but irregular intervals. Newer systems have electronic signs noting the amount of time until the next train arrives.

TRAVEL SAVVY

Stops are marked, but not always well. Bus stops, like subway stops, are named (usually for a cross-street or nearby landmark). Usually the stop is marked with this name, but it's often small or difficult to see from a moving bus. That means it can be tricky to...

Get off at the right stop. Have a sense of how long a ride is going to take. If it's only a few stops, try to sit near the

For the Bus

- If traveling on a crowded bus with luggage, avoid taking up two seats. Try standing next to your backpack or suitcase in the open space near the center door.
- Avoid rush-hour bus trips. When it's crowded, try to exit the bus quickly, before the masses flood on.
- City buses run frequently, especially during peak hours. Night buses run less frequently and follow limited routes, but are useful for night owls who don't want to spring for a taxi.
- Many cities have "round-the-town" tourist buses that give you an overview of the city. Some of these are hop-on, hop-off (such as Barcelona's Bus Turistic), while others require you to make the whole circuit. Some are part of the city bus system, but others require a special ticket. For more information, see "Bus Orientation Tours," page 277.
- In bike-friendly cities such as Amsterdam or Copenhagen, buses often let you off directly into busy bicycle lanes. Look to your right as you exit to avoid a collision.

TRAVEL SAVVY

door, so you can hop out easily. But for a longer cross-town trip, you'll have time to climb to the upper level of a double-decker and enjoy the sights. Sometimes knowing when to disembark is pretty obvious—such as if you're getting off at a prominent monument like the Eiffel Tower. But other times, it can be stressful. Follow the route on your map, looking for landmarks along the way: monuments, bridges, major streets, and so on. Befriend the driver or another passenger, and ask them to help you find the right stop. Smile and say, "Vaticano?"—then wait for them to signal to you when the bus reaches the Vatican.

You may have to signal for your stop. Some buses pull over at every stop, while others only stop by request—you'll push a button or pull a cord to let the driver know you want off. This means you can't necessarily navigate by counting stops. It helps to know the name of the stop *before* the one you want—after you pull away from that stop, signal that you want to get off at the next one.

Taxis

Taxis are underrated, scenic time-savers that zip you effortlessly from one sight to the next. Especially for couples and small groups who value their time, a taxi ride can be a good investment.

If your destination is obvious—such as Florence's Duomo—choosing the right stop is easy; otherwise, ask fellow passengers for help.

Taxis are especially cheap in Mediterranean countries and Eastern Europe. While cabs are expensive for the lone budget traveler, a group of three or four people can often travel cheaper by taxi than by buying three or four bus tickets. (You can go anywhere in downtown Lisbon, Prague, or Athens for about $15.)

Let's be honest: If you're going to get ripped off in Europe, it'll probably be by a cabbie con man. While crooked cabbies live everywhere, they seem most prevalent in southern and Eastern Europe.

Be extra careful at airports and train stations. Dishonest cabbies often lurk at these transit points, ready to take advantage of travelers who are jetlagged and travel-weary...just when they're most susceptible to getting ripped off.

To avoid this stress, and save money, you can hop on public transportation instead. Recently, I took a speedy train from Rome's airport to the train station downtown, then caught a bus to my hotel. It took me less than an hour to get from the airport to my hotel and cost €27 for the train fare and a handy week-long transit pass. A taxi alone would have cost €45.

If you want to catch a taxi from an airport, go to the official taxi stand, and join the queue rather than flag one down.

Always choose a well-marked cab. It should have a big, prominent taxi-company logo and telephone number. Avoid using unmarked beaters with makeshift taxi lights on top.

It's usually best for you to insist on the meter, though for certain standard trips (such as to or from the airport), it can be normal for the cabbie to use a set price. This works if you know the going rate. Ask your hotelier in advance how much a taxi ride should cost, or check www .worldtaximeter.com for estimated taxi fares in larger cities.

Sometimes tourists wrongly accuse their cabbies of taking the long way around or adding unfair extras, but there are lots of legitimate supplements (nights, weekends, baggage, extra person, airport ride, and so on).

In London, Paris, and Barcelona, meters are tamper-proof. That said, even cabbies with honest meters have ways of overcharging tourists. One common trick is for the cabbie to select the pricier "night and weekend" rate on his meter during a weekday. An explanation of the different meter rates should be posted somewhere in the cab, often in English; if you're confused about the tariff, ask your cabbie to explain. If you suspect foul play, following the route on your map or conspicuously writing down the cabbie's license information can shame them into being honest.

When you need a ride from a hotel or restaurant, you can have the staff call a taxi for you. This can dramatically decrease your odds of getting ripped off, but note that the meter will be under way by the time you get in (the meter starts ticking from the time the call is received).

In Western Europe, it's generally easy to flag down a cab, or ask a local to direct you to the nearest taxi stand. Taxi stands are often listed as prominently as subway stations on city maps; look for the little *T*s.

I enjoy cab rides. Many of my favorite insider tips and most interesting conversations have come from chatting up taxi drivers. But don't trust their advice blindly; cabbies can get kickbacks for recommending (and delivering you to) a particular restaurant or attraction.

These Sorrento cabbies hire by the hour and would love to show you around.

When you pay, it's best to use small bills. If you use a large bill, state the denomination out loud as you hand it to the cabbie. They can be experts at dropping a €50 note and picking up a twenty. Count your change. If, for whatever reason, I'm charged a ridiculous price for a ride, I put a reasonable sum on the seat and say good-bye.

To tip a good cabbie, round up. For a typical ride, round up to the next euro on the fare (to pay a €13 fare, give €14); for a long ride, to the nearest 10 (for a €76 fare, give €80). If the cabbie hauls your bags and zips you to the airport to help you catch your flight, you might want to toss in a little more. But if you feel like you're being driven in circles or otherwise ripped off, skip the tip.

While most travelers only use taxis for getting around within one city, I've also found them useful and efficient for going *between* cities. For more on this option, see page 132.

Bikes

Europe's cities are striving to become more pedestrian- and bike-friendly. The progress is gradual. Some cities (such as London, Rome, and Athens) are not yet set up well for bikers, but quite a few cities (including Stockholm, Amsterdam, Copenhagen, Berlin, Salzburg, Munich, and Bruges) are a delight on two wheels, offering an extensive network of well-marked bike lanes.

These lovers are enjoying their tandem bike ride...even though it's not a bicycle built for two.

In these cities, rather than relying on walking or public transportation, consider making a bike your mode of urban transport. Bikes cut transportation times in half compared to walking, giving you more time to spend at the sights. Rental bikes are bargains at $12–15 per day (the best deals are for multiple days).

Rental bikes generally come with strong locks. Always lock the frame (not the wheel) to the permanent rack. Bike thieves can be bold and brazen.

Many cities (including Copenhagen, Stockholm, Vienna, and Paris) have creative programs where hundreds of free or very cheap loaner bikes are locked to racks around town. While

Use your bike lock correctly. I learned this lesson the hard way...and suffered the embarrassment of returning just one wheel to my bike-rental place.

Bike tours are a fun, informative, and healthy way to see great cities with an entertaining guide.

this sounds handy, the system is designed mostly for residents to grab a bike for a quick errand, and can pose a challenge for tourists. Also, these bikes are very basic, sometimes in disrepair, and often plastered with ads—if you're serious about biking, pay to rent a good one.

For a quick but meaningful spin around town, consider a tour. Guided bike tours—which cater to the international backpacker crowd—are popular in cities throughout Europe (including Amsterdam, Bruges, Paris, Munich, Berlin, and Budapest), as well as many bike-friendly countryside areas. You'll get a young, entertaining, often foul-mouthed, sometimes informative guide who will show you the back streets and treats of the city or countryside. The various companies (generally started by disgruntled employees of other bike-tour companies) are highly competitive, and come and go all the time. Tours are typically fun, reasonable (about $25–30), good exercise, and an easy way to meet other travelers as well as get a fresh angle on an old city.

Biking in the countryside (using a small town as a springboard) is extremely popular in Europe. Thanks to the law of supply and demand, you can generally count on finding bike-rental shops wherever there are good bike-tripping options: along the Danube, the Rhine, and other idyllic river valleys; around Ireland's Dingle Peninsula; on Greek islands; and in the Alps for mountain biking on service roads.

For tips on long-distance bike trips in Europe, see Chapter 12.

Pedal your way to even better views.

TRAVEL SAVVY

20. Practicalities

Tipping

Tipping in Europe isn't as automatic and generous as it is in the United States, but in many countries, tips are appreciated, if not expected. As in the US, the proper amount depends on your resources, tipping philosophy, and the circumstances. That said, there are big tippers and there are misers the world over.

Tipping varies widely by country, but some general guidelines apply.

At restaurants, check the menu to see if service is included; if it isn't, a tip of 5–10 percent is normal (for details, see page 254). For taxis, round up the fare (see page 286). At hotels with porters, pay the porter a euro for each bag he carries; it's nice (but not required) to leave about a euro per overnight for the housekeeping staff when you depart.

Tipping for special service is optional. It's thoughtful to tip a couple of euros to someone who shows you a special sight and who is paid in no other way (such as the man who shows you an Etruscan tomb in his backyard). Guides who give talks at public sights or on bus or boat tours often hold out their hands for tips after they give their spiel. If I've already paid for the tour or admission to the sight, I don't tip extra (but if you feel you must tip, a euro or two is enough for a job well done). In general, if someone in the service industry does a super job for you, a tip of a couple of euros is appropriate...but not required.

When in doubt, ask. The French and British generally tip hairdressers, the Dutch and Swedish usually don't. If you're not sure whether (or how much) to tip for a service, ask your hotelier or the TI; they'll fill you in on how it's done on their turf.

Traveler's Toilet Trauma

Every traveler has one or two great toilet stories. Foreign toilets can be traumatic, but they are one of those little things that can make travel so much more interesting than staying at home. If you plan to venture away from the international-style hotels in your Mediterranean travels and become a temporary resident, "going local" may take on a very real meaning.

The vast majority of European toilets are similar to our own. But in a few out-of-the-way places, you might find one that consists simply of porcelain footprints and a squat-and-aim hole. If faced with one, remember: Those of us who need a throne to sit on are in the minority. Throughout the world, most humans sit on their haunches and nothing more.

One of Europe's many unforgettable experiences is the rare squat-and-aim toilet.

Toilet paper (like a spoon or a fork) is another Western "essential" that most people on our planet do not use. What they use varies. I won't get too graphic here, but remember that a billion civilized people on this planet never eat with their left hand. Some countries, such as Turkey, have very frail plumbing, and toilet paper will jam up the WCs. If the bathroom's wastebaskets are full of soiled toilet paper, leave yours there, too.

The WC scene has improved markedly in Europe, but it still makes sense to carry pocket-size tissue packs (easy to buy in Europe) for WCs *sans* TP.

Finding a Toilet

Finding a decent public toilet can be frustrating. I once dropped a tour group off in a town for a potty stop, and when I picked them up 20 minutes later, none had found relief. Most countries have few public rest rooms. But with a few tips, you can sniff out a biffy in a jiffy.

Restaurants: Any place that serves food or drinks has a restroom. No restaurateur would label his WC so those on the street can see, but you can walk into nearly any restaurant or café, politely and confidently, and find a bathroom. Assume it's somewhere in the back, either upstairs or downstairs. It's easiest in large places that have outdoor seating, because waiters will think you're a customer just making a quick trip inside. Some call it rude—I call it survival. If you feel like it, ask permission. Just smile, "Toilet?" I'm rarely turned down. American-type fast-food places are very common these days and usually have a decent and fairly "public" restroom. Timid people buy a drink they don't want in order to use

Going local

the bathroom, but that's generally unnecessary (although sometimes the secret bathroom door code is printed only on your receipt).

Public Buildings: When nature beckons and there's no restaurant or bar handy, look in train stations, government buildings, and upper floors of department stores. Parks often have restrooms, sometimes of the gag-a-maggot variety. Never leave a museum without taking advantage of its restrooms—free, clean, and decorated with artistic graffiti. Large, classy, old hotel lobbies are as impressive as many palaces you'll pay to see. You can always find a royal retreat here, and plenty of soft TP.

Coin-op Toilets on the Street: Some large cities, such as Paris, London, and Amsterdam, are dotted with coin-operated, telephone-booth-type WCs on street corners. Insert a coin, the door opens, and you have 15 minutes of toilet use accompanied by Sinatra Muzak. When you leave, it even disinfects itself. Some cities have free, low-tech public urinals (called *pissoirs*—no joke) that offer just enough privacy for men to find relief... sometimes with a view.

This high-tech public toilet offers a free, private place to do your business.

Trains: Use the free toilets on the train rather than those in the station to save time and money. Toilets on first-class cars are a cut above second-class toilets. I "go" first class even with a second-class ticket. Train toilets are located on the ends of cars, where it's most jiggly. A trip to the train's john always reminds me of the rodeo. Some toilets empty directly on the tracks. Never use a train's WC while stopped in a station (unless you didn't like that particular town). A train's WC cleanliness deteriorates as the journey progresses.

The Flush: After you've found and used a toilet, you're down to your last challenge—flushing it. Rarely will you encounter a familiar handle. Find some protuberance and push, pull, twist, squeeze, stomp, or pray to it until the water starts. Automatic urinals, sinks, and hand dryers are increasingly common.

The Tip: Paying to use a public WC is a European custom that irks many Americans. But isn't it really worth a few coins, considering the cost of water, maintenance, and cleanliness? And you're probably in no state to argue, anyway. Sometimes the toilet is free, but the woman in the corner sells sheets of toilet paper. Most common is the tip dish by the entry—the local equivalent of about 25 cents is plenty. Caution: Many attendant ladies leave only bills and too-big coins in the tray to bewilder the full-bladdered tourist. The keepers of Europe's public toilets have earned a reputation for crabbiness. You'd be crabby, too, if you lived under the street in a room full of public toilets. Humor them, understand them, and carry some change so you can leave them a coin or two.

Women in the Men's Room: The women who seem to inhabit Europe's WCs are a popular topic of conversation among Yankee males. Sooner or later you'll be minding your own business at the urinal and the lady will bring you your change or sweep under your feet. Yes, it is distracting, but you'll just have to get used to it—she has.

Getting comfortable in foreign restrooms takes a little adjusting, but that's travel. When in Rome, do as the Romans do—and before you know it...Euro-peein'.

Travel Laundry

I met a woman in Italy who wore her T-shirt frontward, backward, inside-out frontward, and inside-out backward, all to delay the laundry day. A guy in Germany showed me his take-it-into-the-tub-with-you-and-make-waves method of washing his troublesome jeans. And some travelers just ignore their laundry needs...and stink.

Whistler's laundry

Pack a self-service laundry kit. Bring a stretchable "travel clothesline." The cord is double stranded and twisted, so clothespins are unnecessary. Stretch it over your bathtub or across the back of your car, and you're on the road to dry clothes. Pack a concentrated liquid detergent in a small, sturdy, plastic squeeze bottle wrapped in a sealable baggie to contain leakage. A large plastic or mesh bag with a drawstring is handy for dirty laundry.

Wash clothes in the sink in your room. One of my domestic chores while on the road is washing my laundry in the hotel room sink. I bring a quick-dry travel wardrobe that either looks OK wrinkled or doesn't

TRAVEL SAVVY

wrinkle. (I test-wash my shirts in the sink at home before I let them come to Europe with me. Some shirts dry fine; others prune up.)

Every real hotel room in Europe has a sink, often equipped with a multilingual "no washing clothes in the room" sign. This (after "eat your peas") may be the most ignored rule on earth. Interpret this as "I have lots of good furniture and a fine carpet in this room, and I don't want your drippy laundry ruining things." You can wash clothes in your room carefully, wring them nearly dry, and hang them in a low-profile, nondestructive way. (Don't hang your clothes out the window.) The maid hardly notices my laundry. It's hanging quietly in the bathroom or shuffled among my dry clothes in the closet. Sometimes a hotel will remove the sink and tub stoppers in an attempt to discourage washing. Bring a universal drain-stopper from home, try using a wadded-up sock or a pill-bottle lid, or line the sink with your plastic laundry bag and wash in it. Some create their own washing machine with a large, two-gallon sealable baggie: soak in suds for an hour, agitate, drain, rinse.

Go ahead and ask! There's a good chance you can share the clothesline in the B&B's backyard or on the hotel's roof.

Wring wet laundry as dry as possible. Rolling it in a towel and twisting or stomping on it can be helpful (but many accommodations don't provide new towels every day). Always separate the back and front of hanging clothes to speed drying. Some travelers pack an inflatable hanger. Laid-back hotels will let your laundry join theirs on the lines out back or on the rooftop.

Smooth out your wet clothes, button shirts, set collars, and "hand iron" to encourage wrinkle-free drying. If your shirt or dress dries wrinkled, hang it in a steamy bathroom. A piece of tape is a good ad hoc lint brush. In very hot climates, I wash my shirt several times a day, wring it, and put it on damp. It's clean and refreshing, and (sadly) in 15 minutes it's dry.

Use a launderette occasionally. For a thorough washing, ask your hotel to direct you to the nearest launderette. In Western Europe, nearly every neighborhood has one. It takes about $10–15 and an hour if there's no line. (Many hostels have coin-op washers and dryers or heated drying rooms.)

Better launderettes have coin-op soap dispensers, change machines, English instructions, and helpful attendants. Others can be very frustrating; quite a few are completely automated, with no attendants and barely a word of English. Look around for a sign listing the "last wash" time, and stick to it. When it's closing time, an attendant might come by to evict you, or the machines might simply stop working.

Many of Europe's launderettes are completely unstaffed—it's just you, sparse English instructions, and dirty clothes.

While the exact procedure varies, it usually includes the same steps. First you'll select your machine, put in your clothes, and close the door (often locking it like a hatch). Then you'll add soap, normally in a small reservoir in the top of the washer. If you don't have soap, you can typically buy some there (look for an automated dispenser). The soap compartments on most washers have three reservoirs: for pre-wash, the main wash cycle, and softener. (Don't put your main wash soap into the pre-wash compartment, or it'll be washed away before its time.)

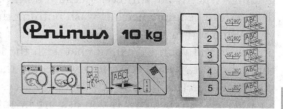

This laundry machine hurdles the language barrier with completely pictographic instructions: Insert your laundry, close the door, select the program, add the soap, and insert coins to start. The five buttons on the right let you select the washing program: The first water temperature (in Celsius) is for the pre-wash cycle, and the second is for the wash cycle. The pictures tell you where to put the soap and softener for each program (notice that the last two skip the pre-wash—no soap needed in compartment A).

While you might be able to pay at the washer itself, you'll more likely pay at a central unit. Note the number of your machine, then type that number into the central unit and insert coins (use exact change if possible—some machines don't give change). Sometimes you'll buy a token at a central unit, then insert it in the machine.

Select your cycle, either at the machine itself or at the central unit.

Here are some examples of the cycles you might see:

45° / 90° / 55 m	whites
45° / 60° / 50 m	colors
45° / 45° / 40 m	permanent press
— / 30° / 30 m	nylon
— / 20° / 25 m	delicates

The first number is the temperature in Celsius for the first cycle (pre-wash), the second is the temperature for the second cycle (main wash), and the third is how long the whole thing lasts. (For Celsius conversions, see page 312.)

While it's running, your machine will either have a dial displaying the cycle (on older machines) or a countdown timer (on newer machines) to let you know how much time is left.

Some washing machines have a built-in spin cycle; however, others leave clothes totally soaked. In this case, put your wet clothes in a special spin-dry machine (usually called a "centrifuge" or something similar) to wring out some excess water before moving your clothes to the dryer.

You'll generally buy drying time in smaller units (5- or 10-minute increments) rather than a full cycle. Most machines let you choose the drying temperature: low (cool and slow); medium (warmer but still slow); and high (speedy but shrinky). Because both washers and dryers at launderettes can be unpredictable, wash nothing that you value dearly.

While waiting for your clothes, use the time to picnic, catch up on postcards and your journal, or chat with the local crowd—launderettes throughout the world seem to give people the gift of gab. These days, many launderettes have handy Internet access or Wi-Fi (or ask about an Internet café nearby). If you ask attendants sweetly, they might be willing to transfer your clothes to the dryer, allowing you to slip out for some bonus sightseeing. (In these cases, it's appropriate to thank them by offering a small tip.)

Truly full-service places, which fold and sometimes even iron your laundry, are easier—just drop it off and come back in the afternoon—but much more expensive. Also pricey, but handiest of all: You can hire your hotel to do your laundry.

Regardless of the cost, every time I slip into a fresh pair of pants, I figure it was worth the hassle and expense.

21. Hurdling the Language Barrier

Confessions of a Monoglot

For English-speakers, that notorious language barrier is about two feet tall. It keeps many people out of Europe, but with a few communica-

New signs in Amsterdam's airport don't even bother with Dutch.

tion tricks and a polite approach, the English-only traveler can step right over it.

I've been saying this for more than 30 years, and during that time an entire generation of Europeans has grown up speaking more English than ever. English really has arrived as Europe's second language. According to recent studies, half of all Europeans now speak English. Historically, many European signs and menus were printed in four languages: German, French, English, and—depending on where you were—Italian, Spanish, or Russian. In the last few years, there's been a shift. In the interest of free trade and efficiency, the European Union has established English as Europe's standard language of commerce. Now most signs are printed in just two languages: the native language for locals and English for everyone else. In some airports, signs are now in English only.

While it's nothing to brag about, I speak only English. Of course, if I spoke more languages, I could enjoy a much deeper understanding of the people and cultures I visit. But even with English only, I have no

problems getting transportation and rooms, eating, and seeing the sights. While you can manage fine with the blunt weapon of English, you'll get along with Europe better if you learn and use a few basic phrases and polite words.

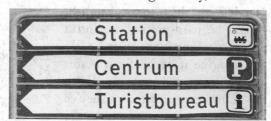

You don't have to speak Danish to understand this sign.

Having an interest in the local language wins the respect of those you'll meet. Get a good phrase book and start your practical vocabulary growing right off the bat. You're surrounded by expert, native-speaking tutors in every country. Let them teach you. Spend bus and train rides learning. Start learning the language when you arrive. Psychologically, it's hard to start later because you'll be leaving so soon. I try to learn five new words a day. You'd be surprised how handy a working vocabulary of 50 words is. A phrase book with a dictionary is ideal. Pocket-size two-language dictionaries are cheap and sold throughout Europe.

While Americans are notorious monoglots, Europeans are very good with languages. Make communication easier by choosing a multilingual person to speak with. Businesspeople, urbanites, well-dressed young people, students, and anyone in the tourist trade are most likely to speak English. Many Swiss grow up trilingual. Many young Scandinavians and Eastern Europeans speak several languages. People speaking minor languages (Dutch, Belgians, Norwegians, Czechs, Hungarians, Slovenes) have more reason to learn English, German, or French since their linguistic world is so small. All Croatians begin learning English in elementary school, and—since their TV programming is subtitled—they listen to Americans talk for hours each day. Scandinavian students of our language actually decide between English and "American." My Norwegian cousin speaks with a touch of Texas and knows more slang than I do.

Dutch is close enough to English that most any tourist can decipher this sign: It tells the opening hours (10 a.m. to 12 p.m., then 2 p.m. to 5 p.m.) on Maandag (Monday), Woensdag (Wednesday), Vrydag (Friday), and Zaterdag (Saturday).

We English-speakers are the one linguistic group that can afford to be lazy. English is the world's linguistic common denominator. When a Greek meets a Norwegian, they speak English. (You'd be hard-pressed to find a Greek speaking Norwegian.)

Imagine if each of our states spoke its own language. That's the European situation. They've done a great job of minimizing the communication problems you'd expect to find on a small continent with such a Babel of tongues. Most information a traveler must understand (such as road signs, menus, telephone instructions, and safety warnings) is printed either in English or in universal symbols. Europe's uniform road-sign system (see page 146) enables drivers to roll right over the language barrier. And rest assured that any place trying to separate tourists from their money will explain how to spend it in whatever languages are necessary. English always makes it.

Dominant as English may be, it's just good style to start every conversation by politely asking, "Do you speak English?," *"Parlez-vous anglais?," "Sprechen Sie Englisch?,"* or whatever. If they say "No," then I do the best I can in their language. Normally, after a few sentences they'll say, "Actually, I do speak some English." One thing Americans do well linguistically is put others at ease with their linguistic shortcomings. Your European friend is doing you a favor by speaking your language. The least we can do is make our English simple and clear.

Using Simple English

English may be Europe's lingua franca, but communicating does require some skill. If you have a trip coming up and don't speak French yet, forget it. It's hopeless. Rather than learning a few more French verbs, the best way to increase your ability to communicate is to master what the Voice of America calls "Special English."

Speak slowly, clearly, and with carefully chosen words. Assume you're dealing with someone who learned English out of a book—reading British words, not hearing American ones. They are reading your lips,

Hurdle the language barrier by thinking of things as multiple-choice questions and making educated guesses. This is a sign on a shop in Germany. It lists times. The top word can only mean "open times" or "closed times." I'd guess it lists hours open from (vom = from, if it rhymes, I go for it) the Fourth of July. Those six words on the left, most of which end in tag, must be days of the week. Things are open from 9:00–11:00 und from 16:00–18:00 (24-hour clock). On Mittwoch (midweek) afternoon... something different happens. Since it can only be open or closed, and everything else is open, you can guess that on Wednesdays, nach Mittag, this shop is geschlossen!

Europeans: Babel of Tongues

Europe's many languages can be arranged into a family tree. Most of them have the same grandparents and resemble each other more or less like you resemble your siblings and cousins. (Occasionally, an oddball uncle sneaks in whom no one can explain.) An understanding of how these languages relate to one another can help boost you over the language barrier.

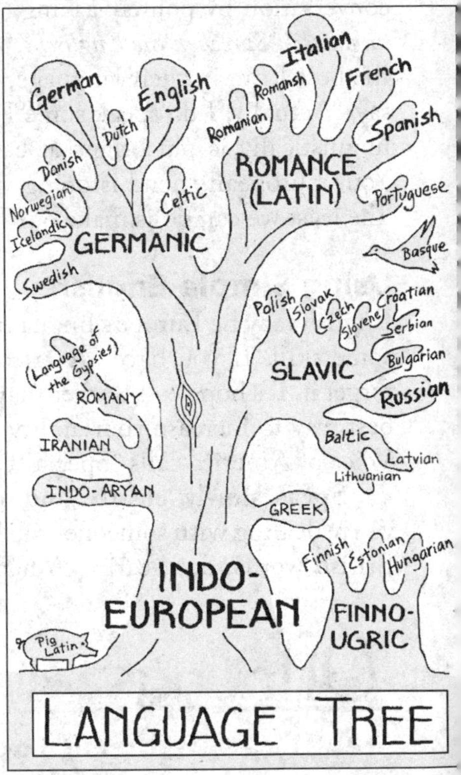

Romance Countries: Italy, France, Spain, and Portugal

The Romance family evolved out of Latin, the language of the Roman Empire ("Romance" comes from "Roman"). Few of us know Latin, but knowing any of the modern Romance languages helps with the others. For example, your high school Spanish will help you learn some Italian. Way off to the east, Romania has its own Latin derivative (Romanian).

LANGUAGE TREE

Tree labels: Italian, Romansh, French, German, English, Romanian, Spanish, Dutch, ROMANCE (LATIN), Danish, Celtic, Portuguese, Norwegian, Icelandic, GERMANIC, Basque, Swedish, Polish, Slovak, Czech, Croatian, Slovene, Serbian, Bulgarian, (Language of the Gypsies) ROMANY, SLAVIC, Russian, IRANIAN, Baltic, Latvian, Lithuanian, INDO-ARYAN, GREEK, Finnish, Estonian, Hungarian, INDO-EUROPEAN, FINNO-UGRIC, Pig Latin

Germanic Countries: The British Isles, Germany, the Netherlands, and Scandinavia

The Germanic languages, though influenced by Latin, are a product of the tribes of northern Europe (including the Angles and Saxons)—people the ancient Romans called "barbarians" because they didn't speak Latin. German is spoken by all Germans and Austrians, and by most Swiss. The people of Holland and northern Belgium speak Dutch (called Flemish in Belgium), which is very closely related to German. While Dutch is not *Deutsch*, a Hamburger or Frankfurter can almost read an Amsterdam newspaper. The Norwegians, Danes, and Swedes can read each other's magazines and enjoy their neighbors' TV shows.

Slavic Countries: The Czech Republic, Poland, Slovakia, Slovenia, Croatia, and More

Most Eastern European countries (except Hungary, Romania, and the Baltics) speak Slavic languages. While these languages are more or less mutually intelligible, spellings change as you cross borders; for example, Czech *hrad*, or castle, becomes Croatian *grad*. Farther east—in Serbia, Russia, Ukraine, Bulgaria, and elsewhere—the language sounds similar, but is written with the Cyrillic alphabet. The Baltic languages (Latvian and Lithuanian) are distantly related to Slavic tongues.

Finno-Ugric Countries: Hungary, Finland, and Estonia

Hungarian, Finnish, and Estonian are more closely related to Asian languages than to European ones—likely hinting that the Hungarians, Finns, and Estonians all share ancestors from Central Asia.

Multilingual Countries and Regions

Switzerland has four official languages: German, French, Italian, and Romansh (an obscure Romance tongue); most Swiss are at least bilingual. Alsace, on the French-German border, has been dragged through the mud during several French-German tugs-of-war; most residents speak both languages. Belgium waffles (linguistically), with the southern half (the Walloons) speaking French and the rest speaking Flemish.

Europe's Underdog Languages

Every year on this planet, a dozen or so languages go extinct. But thanks to Europe's recent determination to celebrate diversity, Europe's underdog languages—once endangered—are thriving once more.

The Basques, who live where Spain, France, and the Atlantic all touch, speak Euskara—mysteriously unrelated to any other European language.

England is surrounded by a "Celtic Crescent." In Scotland, Ireland, Wales, Cornwall, and Brittany (northwestern France), the old Celtic language survives. Seek out these die-hard remnants in proud gift shops and bookstores, Gaelic pubs, and the Gaeltachts (districts, mostly in Western Ireland, where the old culture is preserved by the government).

TRAVEL SAVVY

wishing it were written down, hoping to see every letter as it tumbles out of your mouth. Choose easy words and clearly pronounce each letter. (Crispy po-ta-to chips.) Use no contractions. When they aren't understood, many Americans speak louder and toss in a few extra words. Listen to other tourists, and you'll hear your own shortcomings. If you want to be understood, talk like a Dick and Jane primer. For several months out of every year, I speak with simple words, pronouncing every letter. When I return home, my friends say (very deliberately), "Rick, you can relax now, we speak English fluently."

Can the slang. Our American dialect has become a super-deluxe slang pizza not found on any European menu. The sentence "Can the slang," for example, would baffle the average European. If you learned English in a classroom for two years, how would you respond to the American who exclaims, "What a day!" or asks, "Howzit goin'?"

Keep your messages grunt-simple. Make single nouns work as entire sentences. When asking for something, a one-word question ("Photo?") is more effective than an attempt at something more grammatically correct ("May I take your picture, sir?"). Be a Neanderthal. Strip your message naked and drag it by the hair into the other person's mind. But even Neandertourists will find things go easier if they begin each request with the local "please" (e.g., "*Bitte*, toilet?").

Use internationally understood words. Some spend an entire trip telling people they're on *vacation*, draw only blank stares, and slowly find themselves in a soundproof, culture-resistant cell. The sensitive communicator notices that Europeans understand the word *holiday*, probably because that's what the English say. Then she plugs that word into her simple English vocabulary, makes herself understood, and enjoys a much closer contact with Europe. If you say *restroom* or *bathroom*, you'll get no relief. *Toilet* is direct, simple, and understood. If my car is broken in Portugal, I don't say, "Excuse me, my car is broken." I point to the vehicle and say, "Auto kaput."

Tips on Creative Communication

Even if you have no real language in common, you can have some fun communicating. Consider this profound conversation I had with a cobbler in Sicily:

"Spaghetti," I said, with a very saucy Italian accent.

"Marilyn Monroe," was the old man's reply.

"*Mamma mia!*" I said, tossing my hands and head into the air.

"Yes, no, one, two, tree," he returned, slowly and proudly.

By now we'd grown fond of each other, and I whispered, secretively,

International Words

As our world shrinks, more and more words leap their linguistic boundaries and become international. Sensitive travelers develop a knack for choosing words most likely to be universally understood ("auto" instead of "car"; "kaput" rather than "broken"; "photo," not "picture"). They also internationalize their pronunciation. "University," if you play around with its sound (oo-nee-vehr-see-tay), can be understood anywhere. The average American really flunks out in this area. Be creative.

Communication by analogy is effective. Anywhere in Europe (except in Hungary), "Attila" means "crude bully." When a bulky Italian crowds in front of you, say, "*Scusi,* Ah-tee-la" and retake your place. If you like your haircut and want to compliment your Venetian barber, put your hand sensually on your hair and say "Casanova." Nickname the hairstylist "Michelangelo" or "Rambo."

Here are a few internationally understood words. Remember, cut out the Yankee accent and give each word a pan-European sound.

Stop	Kaput	Vino
Restaurant	Ciao	Bank
Hotel	Bye bye	Rock 'n' roll
Post	Camping	OK
Auto	Picnic	Amigo
Autobus (booos)	Nuclear	Taxi
Yankee, Americano	Tourist	Mamma mia
Michelangelo (artistic)	Beer	Oo la la
Casanova (romantic)	Coffee	Moment
Disneyland (wonderland)	Tea	Hercules (strong)
Coke, Coca-Cola	No problem	Sex/Sexy
Attila (mean, crude)	Europa	Self-service
Toilet	Police	Super
English (Engleesh)	Telephone	Photo
Photocopy	Central	Information
Mañana	University	Passport
Chocolate	Pardon	Fascist
Rambo	Communist	Hello
Elephant (a big clod)	No	Bon voyage
Bill Gates	McDonald's	Obama
Disco	Computer	Sport
Internet	Holiday (vacation)	Gratis (free)
America's favorite four-letter words		

"*Molto buono,* ravioli."

He spat, "Be sexy, drink Pepsi!"

Waving good-bye, I hollered, "*No problema.*"

"*Ciao,*" he said, smiling.

Risk looking goofy. Even with no common language, rudimentary communication is easy. Butcher the language if you must, but communicate. I'll never forget the clerk in the French post office who flapped her arms and asked, "Tweet, tweet, tweet?" I understood immediately, answered with a nod, and she gave me the airmail stamps I needed. At the risk of getting birdseed, I communicated successfully. If you're hungry, clutch your stomach and growl. If you want milk, "moo" and pull two imaginary udders. If the liquor was too strong, simulate an atomic explosion starting from your stomach and mushrooming to your head. If you're attracted to someone, pant.

Be melodramatic. Exaggerate the native accent. In France, you'll communicate more effectively (and have more fun) by sounding like Maurice Chevalier or Inspector Clouseau. The locals won't be insulted; they'll be impressed. Use whatever French you know. But even English spoken with a sexy French accent makes more sense to the French ear.

In Italy, be melodic and exuberant, and wave those hands. Go ahead, try it: *Mamma mia!* No. Do it again. *MAMMA MIA!* You've got to be uninhibited. Self-consciousness kills communication.

Figure things out. Most major European languages are related, coming from (or at least being influenced by) Latin. Knowing that, words become meaningful. The French word for Monday (our "day of the moon") is *lundi* (lunar day). The Germans say the same thing—*Montag. Sonne* is sun, so *Sonntag* is Sunday. If *buon giorno* means good day, *zuppa del giorno* is soup of the day. If *Tiergarten* is zoo (literally "animal garden") in German, then *Stinktier* is skunk and *Kindergarten* is children's garden. Think of *Vater, Mutter, trink, gross, gut, rapide, grand, económico, delicioso,* and you can *comprender mucho.*

Make an educated guess and go for it. Can you read the Norwegian: "Central Sick House"? Too many Americans would bleed to death on the street corner looking for the word "hospital."

Tongue-Twisters (or "Tongue-Breakers")

These are a great way to practice a language—and break the ice with the Europeans you meet. Here are some that are sure to challenge you and amuse your new friends.

German	**Fischer's Fritze fischt frische Fische, frische Fische fischt Fischer's Fritze.**	Fritz Fischer catches fresh fish, fresh fish Fritz Fischer catches.
	Ich komme über Oberammergau, oder komme ich über Unterammergau?	I am coming via Oberammergau, or am I coming via Unterammergau?
Italian	**Sopra la panca la capra canta, sotto la panca la capra crepa.**	On the bench the goat sings, under the bench the goat dies.
	Chi fù quel barbaro barbiere che barberò così barbar-amente a Piazza Barberini quel povero barbaro di Barbarossa?	Who was that barbarian barber in Barberini Square who shaved that poor barbarian Barbarossa?
French	**Si ces saucissons-ci sont six sous, ces six saucissons-ci sont trop chers.**	If these sausages are six cents, these six sausages are too expensive.
	Ce sont seize cents jacinthes sèches dans seize cent sachets secs.	There are 1,600 dry hyacinths in 1,600 dry sachets.
Spanish	**Un tigre, dos tigres, tres tigres comían trigo en un trigal. Un tigre, dos tigres, tres tigres.**	One tiger, two tigers, three tigers ate wheat in a wheatfield. One tiger, two tigers, three tigers.
	Pablito clavó un clavito. ¿Qué clavito clavó Pablito?	Paul stuck in a stick. What stick did Paul stick in?
Portuguese	**O rato roeu a roupa do rei de Roma.**	The mouse nibbled the clothes of the king of Rome.
	Se cá nevasse fazia-se cá ski, mas como cá não neva não se faz cá ski.	If the snow would fall, we'd ski, but since it doesn't, we don't.

Excerpted from Rick Steves' Phrase Books—*full of practical phrases, spiked with humor, and designed for budget travelers who like to connect with locals.*

TRAVEL SAVVY

Happy Talk

English	French	Italian	German	Spanish
Good day.	Bonjour.	Buon giorno.	Guten tag.	Buenos dias.
How are you?	Comment allez-vous?	Come sta?	Wie geht's?	¿Cómo está?
Very good.	Très bien.	Molto bene.	Sehr gut.	Muy bien.
Thank you.	Merci.	Grazie.	Danke.	Gracias.
Please.	S'il vous plaît.	Per favore.	Bitte.	Por favor.
Do you speak English?	Parlez vous anglais?	Parla inglese?	Sprechen Sie Englisch?	¿Habla usted inglés?
Yes./No.	Oui./Non.	Si./No.	Ja./Nein.	Sí./No.
My name is...	Je m'appelle...	Mi chiamo...	Ich heisse...	Me llamo...
What's your name?	Quel est votre nom?	Come si chiama?	Wie heissen Sie?	¿Cómo se llama?
See you later.	Á bientôt.	A più tardi.	Bis später.	Hasta luego.
Goodbye.	Au revoir.	Arrivederci.	Auf Wiedersehen.	Adiós.
Good luck!	Bonne chance!	Buona fortuna!	Viel Glück!	¡Buena suerte!
Have a good trip!	Bon voyage!	Buon viaggio!	Gute Reise!	¡Buen viaje!
OK.	D'accord.	Va bene.	OK.	De acuerdo.
No problem.	Pas de problème.	Non c'è problema.	Kein Problem.	No hay problema.
Everything was great.	C'était super.	Tutto magnifico.	Alles war gut.	Todo estuvo muy bien.
Enjoy your meal!	Bon appétit!	Buon appetito!	Guten Appetit!	¡Qué aproveche!
Delicious!	Délicieux!	Delizioso!	Lecker!	¡Delicioso!
Magnificent!	Magnifique!	Magnifico!	Wunderbar!	¡Magnifico!
Bless you! (after sneeze)	À vos souhaits!	Salute!	Gesundheit!	¡Salud!
You are very kind.	Vous êtes très gentil.	Lei è molto gentile.	Sie sind sehr freundlich.	Usted es muy amable.
Cheers!	Santé!	Salute!	Prost!	¡Salud!
I love you.	Je t'aime.	Ti amo.	Ich liebe dich.	Te quiero.

Many letters travel predictable courses (determined by the physical way a sound is made) as related languages drift apart over the centuries. For instance, *p* often becomes *v* or *b* in the neighboring country's language. Italian menus always have a charge for *coperto*—a "cover" charge.

Practice your understanding. Read time schedules, posters, multilingual signs (and graffiti) in bathrooms and newspaper headlines.

Develop your ear for foreign languages by tuning in to the other languages on a multilingual tour. It's a puzzle. The more you play, the better you get.

A notepad can work wonders. Words and numbers are much easier to understand when they're written rather than spoken—and mispronounced. (My back-pocket notepad is my constant travel buddy.) To repeatedly com-

This is Danish for "tour bus." These days most come with air-conditioning.

municate something difficult and important (such as medical instructions, "I'm a strict vegetarian," "boiled water," "well-done meat," "your finest ice cream," or "I am rich and single"), have it written in the local language on your notepad.

Assume you understand and go with your educated guess. My master key to communication is to see most communication problems as multiple-choice questions, make an educated guess at the meaning of a message (verbal or written), and proceed confidently as if I understood it correctly. At the breakfast table the waitress asks me a question. I don't understand a word she says, but I tell her my room number. Faking it like this applies to rudimentary things like instructions on customs forms, museum hours, and menus. With this approach I find that 80 percent of the time I'm correct. Half the time I'm wrong I never know it, so it doesn't really matter. So 10 percent of the time I really blow it. My trip becomes easier—and occasionally much more interesting.

European Gestures

In Europe, gestures can contribute to the language barrier. Here are a few common gestures, their meanings, and where you're likely to see them.

Fingertips Kiss: Gently bring the fingers and thumb of your right hand together, raise to your lips, kiss lightly, and joyfully toss your fingers and thumb into the air. This gesture is used commonly in France, Spain, Greece, and Germany as a form of praise. It can mean sexy, delicious, divine, or wonderful. Be careful—tourists look silly when they overemphasize this subtle action.

Hand Purse: Straighten the fingers and thumb of one hand, bringing them all together and making an upward point about a foot in front of your face. Your hand can be held still or moved a little up and down at the wrist. This is a common and very Italian gesture for a query. It is used to say "What do you want?" or "What are you doing?" or "What is it?" or "What's new?" It can also be used as an insult to say "You fool." The hand

Very delicious!

purse can also mean "fear" (France), "a lot" (Spain), and "good" (Greece and Turkey).

Cheek Screw: Make a fist, stick out your index finger, and (without piercing the skin) screw it into your cheek. The cheek screw is used widely and almost exclusively in Italy to mean good, lovely, beautiful. Many Italians also use it to mean clever. But be careful: In southern Spain, the cheek screw is used to call a man effeminate.

Eyelid Pull: Place your extended forefinger below the center of your eye and pull the skin downward. In France and Greece this means "I am alert. I'm looking. You can't fool me." In Italy and Spain, it's a friendlier warning, meaning "Be alert, that guy is clever."

Forearm Jerk: Clench your right fist and jerk your forearm up as you slap your right bicep with your left palm. This is a rude phallic gesture that men throughout southern Europe often use the way many Americans "give someone the finger." This jumbo version of "flipping the bird" says "I'm superior" (it's an action some monkeys actually do with their penises to insult their peers). This "get lost" or "up yours" gesture is occasionally used by rude men in Britain and Germany as more of an "I want you" gesture about (but never to) a sexy woman.

Chin Flick: Tilt your head back slightly and flick the back of your fingers forward in an arc from under your chin. In Italy and France, this means "I'm not interested, you bore me," or "You bother me." In southern Italy it can mean "No."

"Thumbs Up," "V for Victory," and More: The "thumbs up" sign popular in the United States is used widely in France and Germany

to say "OK." (Note that it also represents the number one when counting throughout Europe.) The "V for victory" sign is used in most of Europe as in the United States. (Beware—the V with your palm toward you is the rudest of gestures in Britain.) "Expensive" is often shown by shaking your hand and sucking in like you just burned yourself. In Greece and Turkey, you signal "no" by jerking your eyebrows and head upward.

The "V for victory" sign is international.

In Bulgaria and Albania, "OK" is indicated by happily shaking your head left and right—as if you were signaling "no" in the US.

To beckon someone, remember that in northern Europe you bring your palm up, and in the south you wave it down. While most people greet each other by waving with their palm out, you'll find many Italians wave "at themselves" as infants do, with their palm towards their face. *Ciao-ciao.*

European Numbers and Stumblers
Europeans do many things differently from the way we do. Simple as these things are, they can be frustrating barriers and cause needless, occasionally serious problems.

Numbers: A European's handwritten numbers look different from ours. The number 1 has an upswing (γ). The number 4 often looks like a short lightning bolt ($\mathcal{4}$). If you don't cross your 7 ($\mathcal{7}$), it may be mistaken as a sloppy 1, and you could miss your train (and be mad at the French for "refusing to speak English"). Avoid using "#" for "number"—it's not common in Europe.

Counting: When counting with your fingers, start with your thumb. If you hold up your first finger, you'll probably get two; and making a "peace" sign to indicate the number two may get you three—or a punch in the nose in parts of Britain, where it's an obscene gesture.

Dates and Decimals: In Europe, dates appear as day/month/year, so Christmas is 25/12/11 instead of 12/25/11, as we would write it. And on the Continent, commas are decimal points and decimals commas, so

A Yankee–English Phrase Book

Oscar Wilde said, "The English have really everything in common with the Americans—except, of course, language." On your first trip to Britain, you'll find plenty of linguistic surprises. I'll never forget checking into a small-town bed-and-breakfast as a teenager on my first solo European adventure. The landlady cheerily asked me, "And what time would you like to be knocked up in the morning?" I looked over at her husband, who winked, "Would a fry at half-eight be suit-

Hmm... Where's the "exit"?

able?" The next morning I got a rap on the door at 8:00 and a huge British breakfast a half hour later.

Traveling through Britain is an adventure in accents and idioms. Every day you'll see babies in prams and pushchairs, sucking dummies as mothers change wet nappies. Soon the kids can trade in their nappies for smalls and spend a penny on their own. "Spend a penny" is British for a visit to the loo (bathroom). Older British kids enjoy candy floss (cotton candy), naughts and crosses (tic tac toe), big dippers (roller coasters), and iced lollies (popsicles), and are constantly in need of an Elastoplast or sticking plaster (Band-Aid).

It's fun to browse through an ironmonger's (hardware store) or chemist's shop (pharmacy), noticing the many familiar items with unfamiliar names. The school-supplies section includes sticky tape or Sellotape (adhesive tape), rubbers (erasers), and scribbling blocks (scratch pads). Those with green fingers (a green thumb) might pick up some courgette (zucchini), swede (rutabaga), or aubergine (eggplant) seeds.

In Britain, fries are chips and potato chips are crisps. A beefburger, made with mince (hamburger meat), comes on a toasted bap (bun). For pudding (dessert), have some gateau or sponge (cake).

The British have a great way with names. You'll find towns with names like Upper and Lower Piddle, Once Brewed, and Itching Field. This cute coziness comes through in their language as well. Your car is built with a bonnet and a boot rather than a hood and trunk. You drive on motorways, and when the freeway divides, it becomes a dual carriageway. And never go anticlockwise (counterclockwise) in a roundabout. Gas is petrol, a truck is a lorry, and when you hit a tailback (traffic jam), don't get your knickers in a twist (make a fuss), just queue up (line up) and study your Yankee–English phrase book.

A two-week vacation in Britain is unheard of, but many locals holiday for a fortnight in a homely (homey) rural cottage, possibly on the Continent (continental Europe). They might pack a face flannel (washcloth), torch (flashlight), and hair grips (bobby pins) in their bum bag (never a fanny pack!) before leaving their flat (apartment). On a cold evening it's best to wear the warmest

Don't take British road signs personally.

mackintosh (raincoat) you can find or an anorak (parka) with press studs (snaps). You can post letters in the pillar box and give your girlfriend a trunk (long distance) call. If you reverse the charges (call collect), she'll say you're tight as a fish's bum. If she witters on (gabs and gabs), tell her you're knackered (exhausted) and it's been donkey's years (ages) since you've slept. After washing up (doing the dishes) and hoovering (vacuuming), you can go up to the first floor (second floor) with a neat (straight) whisky and a plate of biscuits (cookies)

Somehow, "Broken TV" just doesn't have the same ring to it.

and get goose pimples (goose bumps) just enjoying the view. Too much of that whisky will get you sloshed, paralytic, bevvied, wellied, popped up, ratted, or even pissed as a newt.

All across the British Isles, you'll find new words, crazy humor, and colorful accents. Pubs are colloquial treasure chests. Church services, sporting events, the Houses of Parliament, live plays featuring local comedy, the streets of Liverpool, the docks of London, and children in parks are playgrounds for the American ear. One of the beauties of touring Great Britain is the illusion of hearing a foreign language and actually understanding it—most of the time.

a euro and a half is €1,50 and there are 5.280 feet in a mile. (Britain and Ireland use commas and decimal points like North America.)

Time: The 24-hour clock is used in any official timetable. This includes bus, train, and tour schedules. Learn to use it quickly and easily. Everything is the same until 12:00 noon. Then, instead of starting over again at 1:00 p.m., the Europeans keep on going—13:00, 14:00, and so on. For any time after noon, subtract 12 and add p.m. (18:00 is 6:00 p.m.). Remember that European time is six/nine hours ahead of the East/West Coasts of the US. (British, Irish, and Portuguese time is five/eight hours ahead.) Europe observes Daylight Saving Time (called "Summer Time" in the UK), but on a slightly different schedule than the US: Europe "springs forward" on the last Sunday in March (three weeks after most of North America) and "falls back" the last Sunday in October (one week before North America). For a handy online time converter, try www.timeanddate.com/worldclock.

Metric: European countries (except the UK) use kilometers instead of miles. A kilometer is six-tenths of a mile. To quickly translate kilometers to miles, cut the kilometer figure in half and add 10 percent of the original figure (e.g., 420 km = 210 + 42 = 252 miles). Some people prefer to drop the last digit and multiply by six: Quick, what's 150 km? (15 × 6 = 90 miles.) "36-26-36" means nothing to a European (or metric) girl-watcher. But a "90-60-90" is a real pistachio.

This birth-announcement sign doubles as a lesson in European measurements: Little Martin weighed 4,370 grams (1,000 grams = 1 kilo = 2.2 pounds, so he weighed about 4.3 times 2.2, or around 9.5 pounds) and was 53 centimeters long (100 cm = 1 meter = 39 inches, so 53 cm is just over 20 inches). He was born on 14.7.95 (July 14, 1995) at 21:09 (9:09 p.m.). Despite the reckless stork, mother and baby are doing fine.

Here are some easy ways to guesstimate metric measurements: Since a meter is 39 inches, just consider meters roughly equivalent to yards. A hectare equals about 2.5 acres. A liter is about a quart (1.056 quarts, to be exact)—four to a gallon. A centimeter (cm) is about half the distance across a penny, while a millimeter (mm) is about the thickness of a penny.

Temperatures: Europeans measure temperatures in degrees Celsius. Zero degrees C = 32 degrees Fahrenheit. You can use a formula to precisely convert temperatures in Celsius to Fahrenheit (divide C by 5, multiply by 9, and add 32 to get F). If that's too scary, it's easier and nearly as accurate to double the Celsius temperature and add 30. So if it's 27° C, double to 54 and add 30 to get 84° F (it's actually 81° F, but that's close enough for me). Chilly 10° C comes out to 50° F either way, and comfy 20° C is about 70° F (actually 68° F). To convert Fahrenheit to Celsius, subtract 32, divide by 9, then multiply by 5; or take the easy route—just subtract 30 and divide by 2. A memory aid: 28° C = 82° F—balmy summer weather. And a rhyme: 30 is hot, 20 is nice, 10 is cold, 0 is ice.

Addresses: House numbers often have no correlation to what's across the street. While odd is normally on one side and even is on the other, #27 may be directly across from #2.

Floors: Floors of buildings are numbered differently. The bottom floor is called the ground floor. What we would call the second floor is a European's first floor. So if your room is on the second floor (European), bad news—you're on the third floor (American). On the elevator, push whatever's below "1" to get to the ground floor.

22. Phones, Email, and Snail Mail

Communication for travelers in Europe has never been easier. Not only are more and more people speaking English, but telephoning is a cinch, whether you're making local, long-distance, or international calls. Email communication is so standard (and preferred) that many hotels are retiring their fax machines. Internet cafés and Wi-Fi hotspots are everywhere. And, of course, each country still has a postal system.

Smart Travelers Use the Telephone

Travel goes most smoothly for those who use the telephone. Call tourist offices to check sightseeing plans, train stations to confirm timetables, museums to see if an English tour is scheduled, restaurants to see if they're open, hotels to confirm reservations, and so on.

I get earnest emails from readers asking me to drop a hotel from my listings because they made a reservation, got a written confirmation, and still arrived to find no room available. Hotels make mistakes. Call a day or two in advance to double-check reservations. I even call again on the day of arrival to tell them what time I expect to get there (especially for a small hotel or B&B that may not have a 24-hour reception desk).

As we were filming my public television show in Ireland, I took a minute to call Avis in England to reconfirm our car pickup the next day at the ferry dock in North Wales. The man at Avis said, "Right-tee-o, Mr. Steves, we will have your car waiting for you, noon tomorrow, at Heathrow Airport." No, at North Wales! "Oh, sorry, Mr. Steves. It's good you called ahead." I didn't think, "Boy, Avis sure screwed up." I thought, "You can't travel smart without double-checking things by phone." The more I travel, the more I use the telephone.

Each country's phone system is different, but each one works—logically. The key to figuring out a foreign phone is to approach it without comparing it to yours back home. It works for the residents, and it can work for you.

Each country has phone booths with multilingual instructions. If you follow these step by step, the phone will work—usually. Operators generally speak some English and are helpful. International codes, instructions, and international assistance numbers are usually on the wall (printed in several languages) or in the front of the phone book. If I can't manage in a strange phone booth, I ask a local person for help.

Most European phone booths take phone cards rather than coins.

Types of Phones

Here are the different kinds of phones you'll encounter in Europe. Note that while European phones have keypads, you can't count on being able to access your stateside voice mail from Europe (particularly in Italy).

Card Phones: Most public phones in Europe work with insertable phone cards that you buy locally. While some card phones also accept coins, most don't. Great Britain doesn't have insertable phone cards, but their pay phones accept coins (see below) or major credit cards. For more on using an insertable phone card, see the next section, "Making Calls."

Coin-operated Phones: Coin-op phones are being phased out in most European countries (except Britain), but you'll still encounter a few. Have enough small coins to complete your call. Only entirely unused coins will be returned—so don't plug in large coins until it's clear that you'll be having a long conversation. The digital countdown meter warns you when you're about to be cut off. Many phones allow follow-on calls, so you won't lose your big-coin credit—look for this button and push it (rather than hanging up), then dial the next number.

Metered Phones: Calling shops and some post offices have metered phone booths. The clerk assigns you a booth and can help you with your long-distance prefixes. You sit in your private sweatbox, make the call, and pay the bill when you're done. Sometimes (especially at post offices), calls cost the same as from a public phone, but many of the calling shops specialize in long-distance calls and can have cheaper rates. Because these shops mostly cater to immigrants who want to phone home, you'll often find them in immigrant neighborhoods. Before using any metered phone service, be completely clear on the rates. For example, the listed price may be per *unit*, rather than per minute—if there are 10 "units" in a minute, your call costs 10 times what you expected. To avoid these unpleasant surprises, ask for the approximate price per minute before you call.

Hotel Phones: Using your hotel phone for limited local calls or calls using cheap international phone cards (described in the next section) works well, but otherwise it's an almost-criminal rip-off. I do this only when I'm feeling flush and lazy, for a quick "Call me in Stockholm at this number" message. Many hotels charge a fee for local and "toll-free" as well as long-distance or international calls—always ask for the rates before you dial.

You'll never be charged for receiving calls, so having someone from the US call you in your room can be a cheap way to stay in touch. First, get a long-distance plan or a prepaid card that offers good rates on calls from the US to Europe. (If you'll be making lots of calls to Europe, look into a prepaid provider such as www.onesuite.com, which is often cheaper than the big long-distance companies.) Give your family a list of your hotels' phone numbers before you leave. While you're on the road, you can set up calling times by email, quick pay-phone calls, or mobile phone text messages. Then relax in your room and wait for the ring.

Mobile Phones: For the ins and outs of mobile phones in Europe, see page 322.

Making Calls

There are a number of ways to pay for your phone calls. The best deals are available only in Europe. For each country I enter, I buy a low-denomination phone card for domestic calls (from phone booths) and an international calling card for calling home (from phone booths or my hotel room). It can also be handy to use a mobile phone for local calls (see "Mobile Phones," page 322). If you're bringing a laptop or netbook, keep in touch with people back home by talking for free over the Internet (see "Calling Over the Internet," page 329).

Insertable Phone Cards: Insertable phone cards, which can only be used in phone booths, are common throughout Europe (except Britain).

They are easy to use and sold conveniently at post offices, newsstands, street kiosks, tobacco shops, and train stations. Simply take the phone off the hook, insert the card, wait for a dial tone, and dial away. The price of the call (local or international) is automatically deducted while you talk. Domestic rates are cheap, and international rates, including to the US, are reasonable (rarely exceeding $1 per minute). Each European country has its own phone card—so your German card won't work in an Austrian phone. The only drawback is that the cheapest cards can cost $5—more phone time than you may need in that country. If you're as frugal as I am, you'll lie awake at night wondering how to productively use it up before you cross the next border. You can always blow through the remaining telephone time by calling home, or pass your card along to another traveler.

International Phone Cards: Calling from Europe to the United States can cost as little as a nickel a minute with handy international phone cards available in most of Europe. You can use international phone cards to make inexpensive calls from nearly any phone, including the one in your hotel room (ask at the front desk about hidden fees for toll-free calls, and in your room, check to make sure that your phone is set on tone instead of pulse).

International cards all work the same way and are simple to use. These prepaid cards come with a toll-free number and a PIN code (similar to cheap calling cards widely available in the US). The back of the card often contains basic instructions in English on how to make calls.

Scratch off the back to reveal your PIN, then dial the toll-free number to reach an automated operator. When prompted, dial in your PIN code. Then dial the number you want to call. A voice tells you how much is left in your account and connects you. The prompts are nearly always in English, but if they aren't, experiment: Dial your code, followed by the pound sign (#), then the phone number, then pound again, and so on, until it works.

If you're making lots of calls, you can avoid redialing the access number and PIN code by pressing whatever key (usually the pound sign) allows you to launch directly into your next call—just follow the instructions on the card.

Calls to the US generally cost 5–10 cents per minute, and you can also use the card to call within the same country or to another European country. Cards are generally marked as national or international. All cards work for both domestic or international calls, but you get better rates if you use the card for the purpose it was intended—so if you plan to use your card mostly for calls home, get an international card.

You can buy international phone cards at many kiosks, newsstands, long-distance phone shops, youth hostels, and Internet cafés, but the best selection is usually at hole-in-the wall shops catering to immigrants, who are the leading experts on calling home cheaply. Because there are so many brand names, simply ask for an international phone card and tell the vendor where you'll be making most calls ("to America"), and he'll select the brand with the best deal. Some international phone cards work in multiple countries—if traveling to Norway, Denmark, and Sweden, look for a card that you can use in all three places. Buy a lower-denomination card in case the card is a dud. Some shops also sell cardless codes, printed right on the receipt.

There's one catch: International phone cards are such a good deal that the national telecom companies in certain countries (including Germany and Great Britain) have cracked down. In these places, using one of these cards at a pay phone comes with a hefty surcharge that effectively negates the savings. However, even in these countries, international phone cards are still a good deal if you call from a fixed line (such as in a hotel room).

Remember that you don't need the actual card to use a card account, so it's shareable. You can write down the access number and PIN code in your notebook and share it with friends. Give the number of a still lively card to another traveler if you're leaving the country.

Be warned that you can only buy these cards in Europe—the big-name American calling cards that you buy in the US are usually a poor value (explained below).

Collect Calls: Calling collect is more complicated and always more expensive. It's cheaper and easier if you have your friend call you back, dialing direct from the States. Call cheap and fast from a phone booth and ask your friend to call you back at your hotel.

Student and Hostel Phone Cards: Many travel cards—such as the ISIC student identity card (see page 37) or the HI hostel membership card (see page 224)—also double as prepaid calling cards. Ask for details when you buy your card.

US Calling Cards: Calling-card services offered by American companies such as Sprint, AT&T, and Verizon are a rotten value (figure

TRAVEL SAVVY

about \$2–3/min from Europe to the US). These companies also offer pre-paid calling cards that you can buy in the US before leaving on your trip. But the rates to call home (about 20 cents a minute) are generally about double what you'll pay if you use international phone cards purchased in Europe.

How to Dial

Many Americans are intimidated by dialing European phone numbers. You needn't be. It's simple, once you break the code.

Making Calls within a European Country: About half of all European countries use area codes (like we do); the other half use a direct-dial system without area codes.

To make calls within a country that uses a direct-dial system (Belgium, the Czech Republic, Denmark, France, Greece, Italy, Norway, Poland, Portugal, Spain, and Switzerland), dial the same number whether you're calling across the country or across the street.

In countries that use area codes (such as Austria, Croatia, Britain, Finland, Germany, Hungary, Ireland, the Netherlands, Slovakia, Slovenia, Sweden, and Turkey), dial the local number when calling within a city, and add the area code if calling long-distance within the country. Example: To call a Munich hotel (tel. 089/264-349) within Munich, dial 264-349; to call it from Frankfurt, dial 089/264-349.

Note that some countries, particularly those with area codes, can have phone numbers of varying lengths. For instance, a hotel might have a seven-digit phone number and an eight-digit fax number.

Making International Calls: Always start with the international access code: 011 if you're calling from the US or Canada, 00 from any-where in Europe. (If you see a phone number that begins with +, you have to replace the + with the international access code.) Then dial the country code of the country you're calling (see chart on page 320).

What you dial next depends on the phone system of the country you're calling. If the country uses area codes, drop the initial zero of the area code, then dial the rest of the number. Example: To call the Munich hotel (tel. 089/264-349) from Italy, dial 00, then 49 (Germany's country code), then 89/264-349.

Countries that use direct-dial systems vary in how they're accessed internationally by phone. For instance, if you're making an interna-tional call to Denmark, the Czech Republic, Italy, Norway, Portugal, or Spain, simply dial the international access code, country code, and phone number. Example: To call a Madrid hotel (tel. 915-212-900) from Germany, dial 00, 34 (Spain's country code), then 915-212-900. But if

Desperate Telephone Communication

Let me illustrate with a hypothetical telephone conversation. I'm calling a hotel in Barcelona from a phone booth in the train station. I just arrived, read my guidebook's list of budget accommodations, and I like Pedro's Hotel. Here's what happens:

Pedro answers, "Hotel Pedro, grabdaboodogalaysk."

I ask, "Hotel Pedro?" (Question marks are created melodically.)

He affirms, already a bit impatient, "*Sí*, Hotel Pedro."

I ask, "*Habla* Eng-leesh?"

He says, "No, dees ees Ehspain." (Actually, he probably would speak a little English or would say "*momento*" and get someone who did. But we'll make this particularly challenging. Not only does he not speak English, he doesn't want to...for patriotic reasons.)

Remember not to overcommunicate. You don't need to tell him you're a tourist looking for a bed. Who else calls a hotel speaking in a foreign language? Also, you can assume he's got a room available. If he's full, he's very busy and he'd say "complete" or "no hotel" and hang up. If he's still talking to you, he wants your business. Now you must communicate just a few things, like how many beds you need and who you are.

I say, "OK." (OK is international for, "Roger, prepare for the next transmission.") "Two people"—he doesn't understand. I get fancy, "*Dos* people"—he still doesn't get it. Internationalize, "*Dos* pehr-son"—*no comprende*. "*Dos hombre*"—nope. Digging deep into my bag of international linguistic tricks, I say, "*Dos* Yankees."

"OK!" He understands that you want beds for two Americans. He says, "*Sí*," and I say, "Very good" or "*Muy bien.*"

Now I need to tell him who I am. If I say, "My name is Mr. Steves, and I'll be over promptly," I'll lose him. I say, "My name Ricardo (ree-KAR-do)." In Italy I say, "My name Luigi." Your name really doesn't matter; you're communicating just a password so you can identify yourself when you walk through the door. Say anything to be understood.

He says, "OK."

You repeat slowly, "Hotel, *dos* Yankees, Ricardo, coming *pronto*, OK?"

He says, "OK."

You say, "*Gracias, adiós!*"

Twenty minutes later you walk up to the reception desk, and Pedro greets you with a robust, "Eh, Ricardo!"

European Calling Chart

Just smile and dial, using this key:
AC = Area Code, LN = Local Number.

European Country	Calling long distance within ...	Calling from the US or Canada to ...	Calling from a European country to ...
Austria	AC + LN	011 + 43 + AC (without the initial zero) + LN	00 + 43 + AC (without the initial zero) + LN
Belgium	LN	011 + 32 + LN (without initial zero)	00 + 32 + LN (without initial zero)
Bosnia-Herzegovina	AC + LN	011 + 387 + AC (without initial zero) + LN	00 + 387 + AC (without initial zero) + LN
Britain	AC + LN	011 + 44 + AC (without initial zero) + LN	00 + 44 + AC (without initial zero) + LN
Croatia	AC + LN	011 + 385 + AC (without initial zero) + LN	00 + 385 + AC (without initial zero) + LN
Czech Republic	LN	011 + 420 + LN	00 + 420 + LN
Denmark	LN	011 + 45 + LN	00 + 45 + LN
Estonia	LN	011 + 372 + LN	00 + 372 + LN
Finland	AC + LN	011 + 358 + AC (without initial zero) + LN	999 + 358 + AC (without initial zero) + LN
France	LN	011 + 33 + LN (without initial zero)	00 + 33 + LN (without initial zero)
Germany	AC + LN	011 + 49 + AC (without initial zero) + LN	00 + 49 + AC (without initial zero) + LN
Gibraltar	LN	011 + 350 + LN	00 + 350 + LN
Greece	LN	011 + 30 + LN	00 + 30 + LN
Hungary	06 + AC + LN	011 + 36 + AC + LN	00 + 36 + AC + LN
Ireland	AC + LN	011 + 353 + AC (without initial zero) + LN	00 + 353 + AC (without initial zero) + LN
Italy	LN	011 + 39 + LN	00 + 39 + LN

European Country	Calling long distance within ...	Calling from the US or Canada to ...	Calling from a European country to ...
Montenegro	AC + LN	011 + 382 + AC (without initial zero) + LN	00 + 382 + AC (without initial zero) + LN
Morocco	LN	011 + 212 + LN (without initial zero)	00 + 212 + LN (without initial zero)
Netherlands	AC + LN	011 + 31 + AC (without initial zero) + LN	00 + 31 + AC (without initial zero) + LN
Norway	LN	011 + 47 + LN	00 + 47 + LN
Poland	LN	011 + 48 + LN (without initial zero)	00 + 48 + LN (without initial zero)
Portugal	LN	011 + 351 + LN	00 + 351 + LN
Slovakia	AC + LN	011 + 421 + AC (without initial zero) + LN	00 + 421 + AC (without initial zero) + LN
Slovenia	AC + LN	011 + 386 + AC (without initial zero) + LN	00 + 386 + AC (without initial zero) + LN
Spain	LN	011 + 34 + LN	00 + 34 + LN
Sweden	AC + LN	011 + 46 + AC (without initial zero) + LN	00 + 46 + AC (without initial zero) + LN
Switzerland	LN	011 + 41 + LN (without initial zero)	00 + 41 + LN (without initial zero)
Turkey	AC (if no initial zero is included, add one) + LN	011 + 90 + AC (without initial zero) + LN	00 + 90 + AC (without initial zero) + LN

- The instructions above apply whether you're calling a land line or mobile phone.
- The international access code (the first numbers you dial when making an international call) is 011 if you're calling from the US or Canada. It's 00 if you're calling from virtually anywhere in Europe (except Finland, where it's 999).
- To call the US or Canada from Europe, dial 00, then 1 (the country code for the US and Canada), then the area code and number. In short, 00 + 1 + AC + LN = Hi, Mom!

you're calling Belgium, France, Poland, or Switzerland, drop the initial zero of the phone number. Example: To call a Paris hotel (tel. 01 47 05 49 15) from London, dial 00, then 33 (France's country code), then 1 47 05 49 15 (phone number without initial zero).

Whether you're calling from the US or from within Europe, calls to a European mobile phone are substantially more expensive than calls to a fixed line.

Calling Home: To dial the US direct, first enter the international access code (00 from Europe), then the country code of the US (1), then the area code and the seven-digit number. To call me from France, dial 00-1-425/771-8303. Every country has its quirks. Try pausing between codes if you're having trouble. Off-hour calls are cheaper. Remember, from most of Europe, it's six hours earlier in New York and nine hours earlier in California.

Websites: For online instructions on calling between any two countries, see www.countrycallingcodes.com and www.howtocallabroad .com.

Communication Tips: Once you've made the connection, the real challenge begins. With no visual aids, getting the message across in a language you don't speak requires some artistry. Speak slowly and clearly, pronouncing every letter. Keep it very simple—don't clutter your message with anything more than what's essential. Don't overcommunicate—many things are already understood and don't need to be said (those last six words didn't need to be written). Use international or carefully chosen English words. When all else fails, let a local person on your end (such as a hotel receptionist) do the talking after you explain to him, with visual help, the message.

Mobile Phones

A mobile phone can come in handy while traveling. Imagine the efficiency of getting driving instructions from your hotel as you approach; or letting your friend know that your train is late but you're on your way; or being reachable day or night by loved ones back home (or a lost travel partner).

Mobile phones aren't for everybody. They're often not worth the cost or hassle. If your trip is brief, if you'll be visiting several countries in a relatively short period of time, or if you just really want to be on vacation, you can easily get by with phone cards you buy in Europe (described earlier). But if you're willing to pay more for the convenience of calling from wherever you are, a mobile phone may be a reasonable choice.

You have two basic mobile-phone options: Take your American

phone (if it works in Europe), or buy a phone in Europe. Either way, start by reading the "Mobile Phones 101" sidebar on the next page.

American Phones

First, figure out whether your phone works in Europe. Many T-Mobile or AT&T phones work fine abroad, while only specialized phones from Verizon or Sprint do—check your operating manual (look for "tri-band" or "quad-band").

Your mobile-phone service provider likely has an international plan, which allows you to roam throughout Europe using your home phone number. Most US providers charge $1.29 per minute

Mobile phones give B&B owners the freedom to run errands and their business at the same time.

to make or receive calls in Western Europe, and 20 to 50 cents to send or receive text messages, with no additional fees. (Rates for roaming in Eastern Europe vary, but are generally higher.)

Before you leave, call your mobile-phone service provider to ask whether your phone will work in Europe, what the rates are, whether there are any other fees (such as for data roaming), and whether you need to activate international calling on your plan. (This is usually free, though some companies also have the option of paying a monthly fee to lower the per-minute charges—but remember to deactivate this service when you return.)

A few caveats: Note that you'll be charged for incoming calls, even if you don't answer them (and, in some cases, even if your phone is turned off)—so tell your friends and co-workers not to call except in emergencies. And smartphones (such as the iPhone or BlackBerry) can incur hefty fees for data roaming (explained later).

If the rates are high or you plan on making a lot of calls, ask your mobile-phone provider for the code to "unlock" your phone. (You can also pay a third-party company for an unlock code, but it's less reliable.) Once your phone is unlocked, you can buy and change SIM cards as you travel. Rather than using your American number, you'll have a European number...and pay cheaper European rates. (The details on buying SIM cards are explained on page 325.)

TRAVEL SAVVY

Mobile Phones 101

The standard mobile-phone network in Europe, and much of the world, is called **GSM.** Some American mobile-phone companies—most notably T-Mobile and AT&T—use the same GSM technology as in Europe. Others (including Sprint and Verizon) use a different system called CDMA that is incompatible with European networks.

Within the GSM network, different regions operate on different **bands.** The United States uses two bands, and most of Europe uses two other bands. A GSM phone that's **tri-band** or **quad-band** operates on both US bands, plus one or both European bands—so it works well at home and abroad.

The "identity" of a GSM mobile phone—your phone number and account information—is stored on a removable fingernail-sized chip, called a **SIM card,** which fits into the back of the phone. The phone won't work without a SIM card.

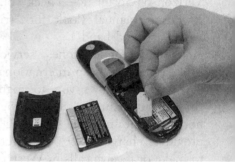

Some phones are electronically **"locked"** so that you can't switch SIM cards—therefore, you must stay loyal to your original service provider. But you can usu-

Your phone's SIM card is hiding behind the battery.

European Phones

It can be surprisingly affordable to **buy** a basic "pay as you go" mobile phone in Europe. Shop around at the ubiquitous corner phone marts or at mobile-phone counters in big department stores. No contracts are necessary—most phones come loaded with prepaid calling time—and additional minutes are usually easy to buy.

Your basic choice is between a phone that's "locked" to work with a single provider (starting around $20 for the most basic models), or a more versatile "unlocked" phone that allows you to switch out SIM cards to access multiple networks (starting around $60). To save even more, look for special promotions or shops that sell used phones. (You can also buy European phones online from the US, but it's generally cheaper and easier to get one in Europe.)

These days, car-rental companies, mobile-phone companies, and even some hotels offer the option to **rent** a mobile phone with a European number. While this seems convenient, hidden fees (such as high per-minute charges or expensive shipping costs) can really add up,

ally get this lock removed—or **"unlocked"**—allowing you to replace the original SIM card with one from a different company. This is especially useful if you want to use the phone in multiple countries, as you can buy a different SIM card in each one. While switching SIM cards may sound intimidating, it's actually quite simple: Just pop out the phone's battery, pull out the chip, and put in the new one.

If you venture outside your mobile phone's home area, you're **roaming.** Making calls when you're roaming in a foreign country can be expensive. To avoid high roaming fees, some Europeans switch SIM cards as they cross borders. (The EU regulates roaming fees within their territory—but if you're roaming with a non-EU SIM card, it could be pricey.)

Europeans have been **texting** for years. Also known to Europeans as an **"SMS"** (short message service), a text message is a short bit of text that's sent from one mobile phone to another. Europeans like texting because it's much cheaper than calling—usually 5-10 cents to send and nothing to receive (potentially more if you're roaming outside your SIM card's home country).

Europeans might not understand the American term "cell phone." Try **"mobile"** (pronounce it the way Brits do—rhymes with "smile") or **"Handy"** (most common in Germany).

making it a bad value.

Be aware that if you're having people call you on your European mobile phone number, it's typically much more expensive (even double) for them than calling a fixed line. Your loved ones back home might save money phoning you at your hotel, rather than calling your mobile phone.

Buying SIM Cards

If you have an unlocked phone—whether brought from the US or purchased in Europe—you can buy a SIM card to make it work in Europe. Remember that a SIM card is a small, fingernail-size chip that stores your phone number and other information. If your phone is unlocked, getting your own European phone number is surprisingly easy and cheap.

Each country has various service providers, all of whom sell their own SIM cards. Since these companies are very competitive, they're pretty much the same—just look for a good deal. SIM cards, which generally cost around $5–15, come with a European phone number and starter credit. These days, mobile-phone companies are working hard to attract customers; I've bought a few SIM cards that came with more calling credit than the cost of the card (for example, a €5 card that includes €7 of credit)—making the SIM card effectively free.

While you can buy European SIM cards online from the US, they're usually overpriced—just buy one when you arrive in Europe. You can buy a SIM card at a mobile-phone shop, as well as (in many countries) at a newsstand. However, a newsstand vendor will give you virtually no help in using the card.

Instead, for first-timers, it's worth the extra time to go to a mobile phone shop, where an English-speaking clerk can help you explore your options, get your SIM card inserted and set up, and show you how to use it. Note that some mobile phone shops sell SIM cards for only one provider, while others offer a wide range. Unless you're certain you want a particular company, look for a place that gives you several options, then ask the clerk which one is best for the types of calls you're going to make. (Mostly domestic or international calls? Are you using it only in that country, or planning to "roam" with it across a border?) The mobile phone desk in a big department store is another good place to check.

When you buy the SIM card, ask for a list of calling rates: for making phone calls and sending text messages—both domestic and international—and for roaming (if you'll be leaving the country). If you're calling from the SIM card's home country, you'll generally pay around 10–20 cents per minute for domestic calls to fixed lines, and nothing to receive calls. Calls to the US can cost $1 per minute or more—but using an international phone card (described earlier) with your mobile phone can bring that cost down to pennies.

A SIM card works most affordably in the country where you buy it. If you roam with the SIM card in another country, call prices go up, and you pay to receive incoming calls. If your SIM card is from an EU country, fees are regulated when roaming within the EU: You'll pay no more than about 60 cents per minute to make calls, or 25 cents per minute to receive calls. If your SIM card is from a non-EU country—or if you're traveling in one—roaming fees can be much higher. If you'll be making a lot of calls, it can be cheaper to buy a new SIM card for that country.

When you first insert a new SIM card, you might be prompted to enter the "SIM PIN" (a code number that came with your SIM card). In some cases, you'll be asked for this every time you turn on the phone—which can be a hassle. Fortunately, this feature can usually be disabled; look through your phone's menu and security features, or ask the shop clerk for help.

Text messages and other instructions from the service provider are generally in another language. It's often possible to switch this to English—again, get help from the shop clerk.

Be sure you know how to check your remaining credit balance. This is different for each phone company, but generally you'll enter a three-digit number, then #, then hit "send." The remaining amount should pop up on your screen. You can buy additional prepaid credit as you go: Buy a printed voucher from that provider at a mobile-phone shop or newsstand, then punch in the numbers from the voucher to add the time to your phone.

Before leaving the shop, go through the entire process, from turning on the phone, to checking your credit balance, to actually making a call—to the store, or, for fun, to the shop clerk's personal phone.

In some places, getting a local SIM card is as simple as buying a pack of gum. In Greece, I walked up to a newsstand and bought a SIM card for about $5; in the Brussels train station, I bought one from a vending machine. But other countries are regulating SIM cards more carefully, so you might have to fill out some paperwork and show your passport before buying the card.

Finally, be aware that most European SIM cards expire after a certain period of inactivity (typically 3–12 months)—including any credit you have left on the card. So saving your Italian SIM card for next year's trip isn't a sure thing.

Traveling with a Mobile Phone in Europe

No matter what kind of phone you use, as you cross each border, you'll usually receive a text message welcoming you to the new country's network, and explaining how to use their services. If traveling within the EU, the message will indicate how much it costs to make and receive calls while in that country.

Remember to store your phone numbers in the phone itself, rather than on the SIM card—or you'll lose access to them when you switch SIMs. When storing phone numbers, include the plus (+) sign and the country code so your calls will go through, regardless of where you're calling from.

The Bottom Line on Mobile Phones

For the majority of travelers, phone booths are still the best way to make calls in Europe. But if you travel frequently, a mobile phone is a great convenience. Here's a wrap-up of my advice for those who want to go mobile:

If your American mobile phone will work in Europe... Take it and use it if you have a reasonable calling plan. But if you will be making lots of calls, first get it "unlocked" so you can switch out the SIM card in Europe (and get better rates).

If your American phone won't work in Europe... Skip the rentals. It's cheaper and relatively painless to buy a new phone there. If you're planning to visit multiple countries, make sure it's an "unlocked" phone so you can change SIM cards as you cross borders.

I've roamed with my American phone in two dozen different countries. No more noisy, urine-perfumed phone booths for me...I travel Europe with a mobile phone.

The iPhone and Data-Roaming Fees

Smartphones, such as the iPhone, Blackberry, and those running Google's Android operating system, often work in Europe—but at a cost. Upon returning home, some users have been surprised with huge data-roaming bills for browsing the Internet or even simply for receiving emails. With the iPhone, you pay nearly 2 cents per kilobyte downloaded in Europe. This means you'll pay about $40 to watch a three-minute video clip from YouTube or email a large digital image (either of which is around 2 megabytes). While downloading a few emails (figure around 20 cents to send or receive a basic message) and doing some casual Internet browsing doesn't involve such large kilobyte loads, these charges can add up fast. (The EU is imposing stricter regulation of data-roaming fees, which will reduce the cost in the future.)

If you have an iPhone, you can pay extra for an international data-roaming plan; however, it's still quite expensive (e.g., $25 per month to download up to 20 megabytes in 90 countries, including many in Europe). Better yet, simply turn off the data-roaming feature in the iPhone's menu. You can still access the Internet and download emails by getting online at public Wi-Fi hotspots (sometimes free, sometimes for a fee). It's also wise to turn off the "fetch new data" feature, which automatically synchs your device with your email account and calendar. You can still synch these items manually when you find Wi-Fi. My fool-proof solution is to simply remove the SIM card from my iPhone. I can still get online with Wi-Fi, but my iPhone completely loses its phone capabilities...it basically becomes an iPod Touch.

The technology is evolving quickly, and more affordable solutions are popping up all the time. For example, Skype and other calling applications allow your Wi-Fi-connected iPhone to make cheap or free calls over the Internet (described next). Tech-savvy travelers should do some homework before their trip to fully understand these and other options.

Calling over the Internet

Some things that sound too good to be true...actually are true. If you have access to a fast Internet connection, you can talk to people around the world (such as from Europe to the US, or vice versa) over the Internet—for free. This technology, called Voice over Internet Protocol (VoIP; sometimes also known as Internet telephony or broadband phone), can save you a lot of money on calls home from Europe.

VoIP technology makes it easy to keep in touch via your computer for free.

Skype (www.skype.com) is the dominant provider of VoIP, but other companies (including Google Talk, www.google.com /talk) work in much the same way. To get started, you visit the website to download the free application and to register. Once you're signed up, you can talk online via your computer to a buddy with a computer running the same program. If both of you have webcams, you can see each other while you chat. All of this is free.

Skype (the name is a shortened form of "sky peer to peer") also works for making calls from your computer to telephones worldwide. In this case it's not free, but the rates are very reasonable (generally less than you'd pay with a long-distance telephone plan). I can sit at my computer at home, using Skype to call phone numbers all over Europe to reserve hotels for my whole trip, quickly and affordably. And when I'm in Europe, if I'm traveling with my Skype-enabled laptop, I can get online and make calls to phone numbers in the US—or call ahead to confirm tomorrow's hotel in Europe—for pennies a minute.

With Skype, you can also buy a phone number in your home country that links to your computer wherever you are traveling. Your grandma makes a "local phone call" in Omaha, and you "pick up" on your laptop in Barcelona. While this all has to be set up online, it's fairly user-friendly and can save you a bundle on a long trip.

Again, computer-to-computer calls are always free—no matter where in the world you are—and the sound quality is generally at least as good

TRAVEL SAVVY

as a standard phone connection (although the video can be choppy). The program uses your computer's built-in speakers, webcam, and microphone, if it has them. If your computer lacks a microphone, or if you want to improve the voice and sound quality, you can buy an operator-type headset for around $20. A cheap webcam also costs about $20.

You can use VoIP even if you're traveling without a laptop or netbook. Many European Internet cafés already have Skype, as well as microphones and webcams, built into their machines—you just need to log on and chat away. But remember that the service works well only if both parties have a high-speed Internet connection.

What about those of us who carry a mobile phone to Europe instead of a computer? Increasingly, you can even use VoIP from certain Internet-enabled smartphones (such as the iPhone), bypassing the expensive rates mobile-phone companies charge for international calls. A Skype app is available for some smartphones, or you can use a third-party service such as Fring (www.fring.com), which works as a kind of Skype-to-mobile-phone gateway. Even the iPod Touch—which isn't designed as a phone—can be used to make Skype calls to computers or phones, if you have an external microphone and a Wi-Fi connection. Tech-savvy travelers can look into the latest options.

Other companies, such as Vonage (www.vonage.com), allow you to place calls over the Internet using an actual fixed-line phone, with cheaper rates to Europe than those offered by most old-fashioned long-distance companies. And services such as www.rebtel.com allow for super-cheap international phone calls over the Internet, but work only if you're always calling the same number (such as a relative who's living abroad).

Even if you're not using VoIP, it's worth knowing about because of its increasing popularity in Europe. It's only a matter of time before a new European friend who wants to keep in touch asks you, "Do you use Skype?"

Internet Access in Europe

To get online in Europe, you basically have two choices: Use public Internet terminals (such as an Internet café, library, or your hotel), or access Wi-Fi hotspots with your own laptop or netbook.

Internet Terminals

Finding public Internet terminals in Europe is a breeze. These days, many hotels and hostels have a few computers in the lobby for their guests to use (sometimes free, sometimes for a fee). Otherwise, head for an Internet café (also called a cybercafé). While these places don't

Where It's @

Europeans have different names for, and different ways to type, the @ symbol; below are a few. Remember that the Alt Gr (Alternate Graphics) key is to the right of the space bar.

Language and Name	Pronounced	How It's Typed
French		
signe arobase	seen ah-roh-bahs	Alt Gr + 0
German		
At-zeichen; also		
Klammeraffe ("monkey hug") or		
A-Affenschwanz		
("A with a monkey tail")	"at"-tsei-khehn	Alt Gr + Q
Italian		
chiocciola ("snail")	kee-OH-choh-lah	Alt Gr + @
Spanish and Portuguese		
arroba	ah-ROH-bah	Alt Gr + 2

always serve food or drinks—sometimes they're just one big, functional, sweaty room filled with computers—they are an easy and affordable way to get online. Large European chains offer inexpensive access in big cities.

Even if a small town lacks an Internet café, there's always some way to get online—at libraries, bookstores, post offices, copy shops, video stores, and so on. Ask the TI, your hotelier, any young person, or another traveler for the nearest place to access the Internet.

You'll want an email account that you can access from anywhere through the Internet. Consider one of the major Web-based email providers that offer free accounts, such as Google's Gmail (www.gmail.com), Hotmail (www.hotmail.com), Yahoo! Mail (mail.yahoo.com), or AOL (www.aol.com).

European computers typically use non-American keyboards. Most letters are the same as back home, but a few are switched around, and many of the command keys are labeled in a foreign language. It takes time to find the right keys. Many European keyboards have an "Alt Gr" key (for "Alternate Graphics") to the right of the space bar; press this to insert the extra symbol that appears on some keys. If you can't locate a special character (such as the @ symbol), simply copy it from a Web page and paste into your email message.

On many computers, you can look for a box in the lower-right-hand corner of the screen where you can click and select which type of keyboard you prefer. Or ask the clerk for help. Often a simple keystroke or click of the mouse can make the foreign keyboard work like an American one.

In Italy, because of an anti-terrorism law, you may be asked to show your passport (carry it in your money belt) when using a public Internet terminal. The proprietor will likely make a copy.

Europe's Internet cafés, often open long hours, allow travelers to get online.

Be aware that using a public Internet terminal can come with security risks. Some computers are loaded with damaging "malware," such as "key logger" programs that keep track of what you're typing—including passwords. You can ask the Internet café or hotel what sort of security software their machines are running. If you're not convinced it's secure, don't access any sites (such as online banking) that could be sensitive to fraud. Avoid storing personal information (such as passport and credit-card numbers) online. If you need important documents, email or phone home and have them sent by fax. For more on these precautions, see the information on identity theft on page 175.

Getting Online with Your Laptop or Netbook

With the abundance of cheap Internet cafés in Europe, you don't need to bring your own computer. But as laptops shrink, Internet access becomes widespread, and blogging becomes more popular, many travelers are taking their computers with them to Europe. There are several ways to get online from your laptop or netbook:

Wi-Fi (wireless Internet access, sometimes called "WLAN" in Europe) is increasingly common. If your laptop is Wi-Fi capable, you'll be able to get online at many hotels and cafés. Sometimes it's free; other times, you'll have to buy a drink or pay a fee to get the password. (Strangely, while many budget and midrange hotels offer free Wi-Fi to their guests, the pricier places usually charge a hefty fee.) When I check into a hotel, I ask them for the network name (in case several are in range) and password so I can log on right away. Some towns even have

Wi-Fi "hotspots" scattered around highly trafficked areas. Occasionally this is free, but you'll usually have to pay to get the password (at the TI or an Internet café). Just find whichever idyllic spot you like best—a bench overlooking a sandy beach, on a floodlit piazza, or along a bustling people-watching boulevard—then log on and surf away. You can look up public hotspots—free or paid—at www.jiwire.com (look for "Wi-Fi Finder" on the home page); try to track down potential spots before you arrive at your next destination. While accessing Wi-Fi is safer than logging on to a shared or public computer, it can pose a security risk. Make sure that your laptop's firewall is up-to-date and activated, and access only legitimate hotspots (for example, the one named for your hotel).

Many hotel rooms, and some Internet cafés, have **high-speed Internet jacks** that you can plug into with an Ethernet cable (with an RJ45 plug; looks like an oversized phone cord)—no special software or password required. I travel with a small length of Ethernet cable just in case, but most hotels will loan you one if you ask. Again, while this is usually free, some hotels charge a fee for access.

For those who want constant access in one country, **cellular modems** (also known as wireless modems or mobile broadband) may be the way to go. A mobile phone company routes your Internet connection over its 3G network. Usually you buy a "dongle"—it looks like a USB flash drive—that you insert into your laptop's USB slot. If you need more consistent Internet access than scattered Wi-Fi hotspots will provide, this could be a good option. In the UK, Vodafone offers a pay-as-you-go package with 90 hours of browsing for about $40 (www.vodafone.co.uk/broadband). T-Mobile has similar plans in the UK and Germany (www.t-mobile .co.uk).

The old-fashioned way of getting online is to access a **dial-up** Internet service provider from your hotel room. This can be useful if you can't find a Wi-Fi signal, but it's impractical for casual travelers since you have to arrange it in advance with a service provider.

Blogging

Instead of sending postcards or lengthy bulk emails to family and jealous co-workers back home, more and more travelers are writing blogs. Short for "Web log," a blog is an online journal where you can write about your experiences and post photos and short video clips. Set your blog up before you leave and access it on the road wherever you have Internet access. If you don't have your own website, plenty of free services are ready to host a blog for you. Many have email notification systems that tell your friends when your blog is updated and allow readers to post comments (expect a ribbing for those crooked Eiffel Tower photos).

Blogger (www.blogger.com), Wordpress (www.wordpress.com), and Typepad (www.typepad.com) are good general blog hosts. People who use social-networking sites such as Facebook (www.facebook.com) and Twitter (www.twitter.com) simply blog through their pages there. Travelpod (www.travelpod.com), MyTripJournal (www.mytripjournal .com), and Realtravel (www.realtravel.com) are specialized for travelers and provide custom maps with "pins" for the places you've visited. Also check out Travelblog (www.travelblog.org) and Travellers Point (www .travellerspoint.com). When choosing a website to host your blog, check the fine print to see how long your blog will be stored, whether you can later download your photos and text and in what format, and if there's a fee for premium services, such as uploading high-resolution photos. Also consider whether to make your blog "public" (anyone can see it) or "private" (viewable only by invited guests).

If you'd like to follow along on my travels via my blog, check out www.ricksteves.com/blog.

Snail Mail

Sending Packages Home: Shoppers lighten their load by sending packages home by surface mail. Postage is expensive. A box the size

If you accumulate a shoebox's worth of dead weight, mail it home and keep on packing light.

of a small fruit crate costs about $40 by slow boat. Books are much cheaper if they are sent separately. Post offices in some countries have limits on how big or heavy your packages can be. In Germany and Great Britain, any surface-mail package for overseas delivery is limited to 2 kilograms (about 4.5 pounds)— for more than that, you must use airmail. France ships surface packages up to 30 kilograms (about 66 pounds).

Customs regulations amount to 10 or 15 frustrating minutes of filling out forms with the normally unhelpful postal clerk's semi-assistance. Be realistic in your service expectations. Remember, European postal clerks are every bit as friendly, speedy, and multilingual as American postal clerks.

You can mail one package per day to yourself worth up to $200 duty-free from Europe to the US (mark it "personal purchases"). (If you mail an item home valued at $250, you pay duty on the full $250, not $50.) When you fill out the customs form, keep it simple and include the item's value (contents: clothing, books, souvenirs, poster, value $50). For alcohol, perfume containing alcohol, and tobacco valued at more than $5, you will pay a duty. You can also mail home all the "American Goods Returned" you like (e.g., clothes you packed but no longer need) with no customs concerns—but note that these goods really must be American (not Bohemian crystal or a German cuckoo clock), or you'll be charged a duty. If it's a gift for someone else, they are liable to pay customs if it's worth more than $100 (mark it "unsolicited gift"). For details, visit www .cbp.gov and search for "Know Before You Go."

Post offices usually sell boxes and string or tape for about $5. Service is best north of the Alps. (The fastest way to get a package home from Italy is to use the Vatican post office...or take it home in your suitcase.) Small-town post offices can be less crowded and more user-friendly. Every box I've ever mailed has arrived—bruised and battered but all there—within six weeks. To send precious things home fast, I use DHL (e.g., to send the tapes shot for my TV series, it cost me $100 for 2-day service). DHL has offices in any big city, listed in local phone books and online at www.dhl.com.

Receiving Mail: Now that telephoning and emailing are so cheap and easy, I see little need to receive mail in Europe. But if you still want to get snail mail on the road, minimize mail pickups to maximize your flexibility. Arrange your mail stops before you leave. Every city has a general delivery service. Pick a small town with only one post office and no crowds. Have letters sent to you in care of "Poste Restante." Tell your friends to print your last name in capitals, underline it, and omit your middle name. If possible, avoid the Italian male...I mean, mail.

Friends or relatives in Europe are fine for mail stops. Or, to avoid mail pickup commitments on a long trip, have mail sent to a friend or relative at home. When you know where you'll be, you can telephone them from Europe with instructions on where to mail your letters. Second-day US–Europe services are reliable and reasonable, but allow up to four days for a delivery to a small town.

23. Staying Healthy

Get a Checkup
Just as you'd give your car a good checkup before a long journey, it's smart to meet with your doctor before your trip. Get a general checkup and ask for advice on maintaining your health on the road. Obtain recommended immunizations and discuss proper care for any pre-existing medical conditions while traveling. Bring along a letter from your doctor describing any special health problems and a copy of any pertinent prescriptions. If you have any heart concerns, pack a copy of a recent EKG.

Travel-medicine Specialists: While I consider Europe as safe as the US, those traveling to more exotic destinations should consult a travel-medicine physician. Only these specialists keep entirely up-to-date on health conditions for travelers around the world. Tell the doctor about every possible destination on your vacation itinerary, confirmed or not. Then you can have the flexibility to take that impulsive swing through Turkey or Morocco knowing that you're prepared medically and have the required shots. Ask the doctor about Havrix (a vaccine that protects against hepatitis A—see www.havrix.com), Twinrix (protects against both hepatitis A and B—see www.twinrix.com), antidiarrheal medicines, and any extra precautions. The Centers for Disease Control offers updated information on every country (www.cdc.gov).

Dental Checkup: Get a dental checkup well before your trip. (You don't want that crown you got right before you left to fall out on the plane, do you?) Emergency dental care during your trip is time- and money-consuming, and can be hazardous and painful. I once had a tooth crowned by a German dentist who knew only one word in English, which he used in question form—"Pain?"

Jet Lag, Your Flight, and the First Day of Your Trip
Anyone who flies through multiple time zones has to grapple with the biorhythmic confusion known as jet lag. When you switch your wristwatch six to nine hours forward, your body says, "Hey, what's going on?" Body clocks don't reset so easily. All your life you've done things on a 24-hour cycle. Now, after crossing the Atlantic, your body wants to eat when you tell it to sleep and sleep when you tell it to enjoy a museum.

Too many people assume their first day will be made worthless by jet lag. Don't prematurely condemn yourself to zombiedom. Most people I've traveled with, of all ages, have enjoyed productive—even hyper— first days. You can't avoid jet lag, but with a few tips you can minimize the symptoms.

Leave home well-rested. Flying halfway around the world is stress-ful. If you leave frazzled after a hectic last night and a wild bon-voyage

party, there's a good chance you won't be healthy for the first part of your trip. An early-trip cold used to be a regular part of my vacation until I learned this very important trick: Plan from the start as if you're leaving two days before you really are. Keep that last 48-hour period sacred (apart from your normal work schedule), even if it means being hectic before your false depar-ture date. Then you have two

Jet lag hits even the very young.

orderly, peaceful days after you've packed so that you are physically ready to fly. Mentally, you'll be comfortable about leaving home and starting this adventure. You'll fly away well-rested and 100 percent capable of enjoying the bombardment of your senses that will follow.

On the flight, drink plenty of liquids, eat lightly, and rest. Long flights are dehydrating. I ask for "two orange juices with no ice" every chance I get. Eat lightly, stay hydrated, and have no coffee and only minimal sugar until the flight's almost over. Alcohol and sedatives will stress your body and aggravate jet lag. Avoid the slight chance of getting a blood clot in your leg during long flights by taking short walks hourly. While seated, flex your ankles and don't cross your legs. Some people are more prone to clots (factors include obesity, age, use of oral contracep-tives or hormone replacement therapy, pregnancy, smoking, and genet-ics). The in-flight movies are good for one thing—nap time. With two or three hours' sleep during the transatlantic flight, you'll be functional the day you land.

Reset your mind to local time. When the pilot announces the European time, reset your mind along with your wristwatch. Don't prolong jet lag by reminding yourself what time it is back home. Be in Europe.

On arrival, stay awake until an early local bedtime. If you doze off at 4 p.m. and wake up at midnight, you've accomplished nothing. Plan a good walk until early evening. Jet lag hates fresh air, daylight, and exercise. Your body may beg for sleep, but stand firm: Refuse. Force your body's transition to the local time. You'll probably awaken very early on your first morning. Trying to sleep later is normally futile. Get out and enjoy a "pinch me, I'm in Europe" walk, as merchants set up in the marketplace and the town slowly comes to life. This will probably be the only sunrise you'll see in Europe.

Consider jet-lag cures. The last thing I want to do is promote a pharmaceutical, but I must admit that the sleep aid Ambien (generic name Zolpidem) has become my friend in fighting jet lag. Like all prescription medications, Ambien can have side effects—read and follow the directions, and carefully discuss using it with your doctor. The stuff is powerful (almost comically so). I use it very sparingly. Generally I fall asleep without a problem on my first night in Europe, but wake up wired after only four hours. So I keep a half-tablet of Ambien on my bedside table and pop it when I awaken to enjoy about three more solid hours of sleep. Managing a good seven hours of sleep on night one in Europe (or after flying home) hastens my transition to local time. That way, I'm not disabled by sleepiness that first afternoon and can stay awake until a decent bedtime. (I also use a half-tablet of Ambien to get some sleep in a noisy place, or if I'm coming down with a cold and want to sleep it off.) Other travelers rave about melatonin, a hormone that supposedly helps recalibrate your internal clock (available over-the-counter in the US, but illegal in some European countries).

The best prescription is this: Leave home unfrazzled, minimize jet lag's symptoms, force yourself into European time, and give yourself a chance to enjoy your trip from the moment you step off the plane.

Traveling Healthy

Europe is generally safe. All the talk of treating water with purification tablets is applicable only south and east of Europe. Using discretion and common sense, I eat and drink whatever I like in Europe. As our world becomes more chemical, reasons for concern and caution will increase on both sides of the Atlantic.

I was able to stay healthy throughout a six-week trip traveling from Europe to India. By following these basic guidelines, I never once suffered from Tehran Tummy or Delhi Belly.

Eat nutritiously. The longer your trip, the more you'll be affected by an inadequate diet. Budget travelers often eat more carbohydrates and less protein to stretch their travel dollars. This is the root of many nutritional problems. Protein helps you resist infection and rebuilds muscles. Get the most nutritional mileage from your protein by eating it with the day's largest meal (in the presence of all those essential amino acids). Supplemental super-vitamins, taken regularly, help me to at least feel healthy. If you have a serious dietary restriction, have a multilingual

Europe Goes Smoke-Free

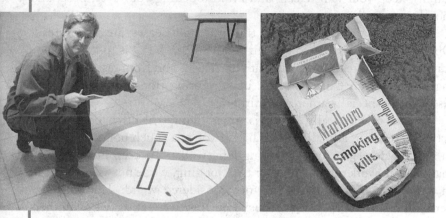

Good news for your health: Europe is getting enthusiastic about not smoking. Cigarette packages make it really clear: "Smoking kills"; and Berlin's subway—like much of Europe—is now smoke-free.

One out of every three Europeans smokes, but new legislation across Europe is trying to change things. The following countries prohibit smoking in any enclosed public space—Cyprus, Denmark, Estonia, Finland, France, the Republic of Ireland, Italy, Latvia, Lithuania, the Netherlands, Norway, Portugal, Slovenia, Spain, and the United Kingdom—although some countries allow for sealed-off and well-ventilated smoking rooms in restaurants and bars. Countries that have some sort of smoking ban (generally covering workplaces, hospitals, schools, theaters, public transportation, and sometimes restaurants) are Austria, Belgium, Croatia, the Czech Republic, Germany, Greece, Montenegro, Poland, Slovakia, Sweden, Switzerland, and Turkey. These countries are considering smoking bans: Hungary and Serbia. It seems that it's only a matter of time before all of Europe—and its visitors—will breathe easier.

TRAVEL SAVVY

friend write it in the native language on the back of a business card and use it to order in restaurants.

Use good judgment. Avoid unhealthy-looking restaurants. Meat should be well cooked and, in some places, avoided altogether. Have "well done" written on a piece of paper in the pertinent language and use it when ordering. Pre-prepared foods gather germs (a common cause of diarrhea). Outside of Europe, be especially cautious. When in serious doubt, eat only thick-skinned fruit...peeled.

Keep clean. Wash your hands often (or use a hand sanitizer, such as Purell), keep your nails clean, and avoid touching your eyes, nose, and mouth.

Practice safe sex. Sexually transmitted diseases are widespread. Obviously, the best way to prevent acquiring an STD is to avoid exposure. Condoms (readily available at pharmacies and from restroom vending machines) are fairly effective in preventing transmission. AIDS is also a risk, especially among prostitutes.

Exercise. Physically, travel is great living—healthy food, lots of activity, fresh air, and all those stairs! If you're a couch potato, try to get in shape before your trip by taking long walks. To keep in shape, you may want to work out during your trip. Jogging, while not as widespread in Europe as it is in the US, is not considered weird. Traveling joggers can enjoy Europe from a special perspective—at dawn. Swimmers will find that Europe has plenty of good, inexpensive public swimming pools. Whatever your racket, if you want to badly enough, you'll find ways to keep in practice as you travel. Most big-city private tennis and swim clubs welcome foreign guests for a small fee, which is a good way to make friends as well as stay fit.

Get enough sleep. Know how much sleep you need to stay healthy (generally 7–8 hours per night). If I go more than two nights with fewer than six hours' sleep, I make it a priority to catch up—no matter how busy I am. Otherwise, I'm virtually guaranteed to get the sniffles.

Give yourself psychological pep talks. Europe can do to certain travelers what southern France did to Vincent van Gogh. Romantics can get the sensory bends, patriots can get their flags burned, and anyone can suffer from culture shock.

Europe is crowded, can still be smoky, and is not particularly impressed by America or Americans. It will challenge givens that you always assumed were above the test of reason, and most of Europe on the street doesn't really care that much about what you, the historical and cultural pilgrim, have waited so long to see.

Take a break: a long, dark, air-conditioned trip back to California in a movie theater; a pleasant sit in an American embassy reading room surrounded by eagles, photos of presidents, *Time* magazines, and other Yankees; or a visit to the lobby of a world-class hotel, where any hint of the traditional culture has been lost under a big-business bucket of intercontinental whitewash. It can do wonders to refresh the struggling traveler's spirit.

European Water

I drink European tap water and any water served in restaurants. Read signs carefully, however: Some taps, including those on trains and airplanes, are not for drinking. If there's any hint of nonpotability—a decal showing a glass with a red "X" over it, or a skull and crossbones—don't drink it. Many fountains in German-speaking countries are for drinking, but others are just for show. Look for *Trinkwasser* ("drinking water") or *Kein Trinkwasser* ("not drinking water").

The water at many European public fountains is safe to drink...unless your travel partner has dirty hands.

The water (or, just as likely, the general stress of travel on your immune system) may, sooner or later, make you sick. It's not necessarily dirty. The bacteria in European water are different from those in American water. Our bodily systems—raised proudly on bread that rips in a straight line—are the most pampered on earth. We are capable of handling American bacteria with no problem at all, but some people can go to London and get sick. Some French people visit Boston and get sick. Some Americans travel around the world eating and drinking everything in sight and don't get sick, while others spend weeks on the toilet. It all depends on the person.

East of Bulgaria and south of the Mediterranean, do not drink untreated water. Water can be treated by boiling it for 10 minutes or by using purifying tablets or a filter. Bottled water, beer, wine, boiled coffee and tea, and bottled soft drinks are safe as long as you skip the ice cubes. Coca-Cola products are as safe in Syria as they are at home.

Traveler's First-Aid Kit

You can buy virtually anything you need in Europe. (You might not find Sudafed, but you can get the European equivalent.) But if you're accustomed to a very specific, name-brand medication, it's easier to bring it from home.

It's also handy to bring along the following:

- Band-Aids
- soap or alcohol preps (antiseptic Handi-Wipes or Purell-type hand sanitizer)

TRAVEL SAVVY

- antibiotic cream (in Europe, you may need a prescription to buy skin ointments with antibiotics)
- moleskin (to cover blisters)
- tweezers
- thermometer in a hard case
- non-aspirin pain reliever (your US brand of preference: Advil, Tylenol, etc.)
- medication for colds and diarrhea
- prescriptions and medications (in labeled, original containers)

Particularly if you'll be hiking in isolated areas, bring a first-aid booklet, Ace bandage, space blanket, and tape and bandages.

For Eye Care: Those with corrected vision should carry the lens prescription as well as extra glasses in a solid protective case. Contact lenses are used all over Europe, and the required solutions for their care are easy to find.

Basic First Aid

Travel is much more fun when you're healthy. Be proactive to stay well. If you do get sick, take action to regain your health.

Headaches and Other Aches: Tylenol (or any other non-aspirin pain reliever) soothes headaches, sore feet, sprains, bruises, Italian traffic, hangovers, and many other minor problems. If you're buying it overseas, Europeans may be more familiar with the term "paracetamol" (pare-ah-SEET-ah-mall).

Abrasions: Clean abrasions thoroughly with soap to prevent or control infection. Bandages help keep wounds clean but are not a substitute for cleaning. A piece of clean cloth can be sterilized by boiling for 10 minutes or by scorching with a match.

Blisters: Moleskin, bandages, tape, or two pairs of socks can prevent or retard problems with your feet. Cover any irritated area before it blisters. Many walkers swear by Body Glide, a solid anti-chafing stick sold in running shops and sporting-goods stores.

Motion Sickness: To be effective, medication for motion sickness (Bonine or Dramamine) should be taken one hour before you think you'll need it. This medication (or Tylenol PM) can also serve as a mild sleep aid.

Swelling: Often accompanying a physical injury, swelling is painful and delays healing. Ice and elevate any sprain periodically for 48 hours. A package of frozen veggies works as a cheap ice pack. If your foot or leg is swollen, buy or borrow a bucket and soak the affected area in cold water, or sit on the edge of a cool swimming pool. Take an anti-inflammatory drug like ibuprofen (Advil, Motrin). Use an Ace bandage to immobilize, reduce swelling, and provide support. It is not helpful to "work out" a sprain—instead, cut back on activities that could aggravate the injury.

Fever: A high fever merits medical attention. A normal temperature of 98.6° Fahrenheit equals 37° Celsius. If your thermometer reads 40°C, you're boiling at 104°F.

Colds: It's tempting to go, go, go while you're in Europe—but if you push yourself to the point of getting sick, you've accomplished nothing. Keep yourself healthy and hygienic. If you're feeling run-down, check into a good hotel, sleep well, and force fluids. (My trick during the hectic scramble of TV production is to suck on vitamin C tablets.) Stock each place you stay with boxes of juice upon arrival. Sudafed (pseudoephedrine) and other cold capsules are usually available, but may not come in as many varieties.

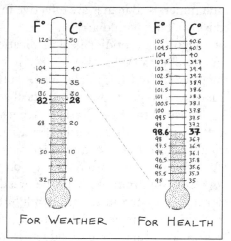

Europe takes its temperature using the Celsius scale, while we opt for Fahrenheit. For weather, remember that 28°C is 82°F—perfect. For health, 37°C is just right.

Diarrhea: Get used to the fact that you might have diarrhea for a day. (Practice that thought in front of the mirror tonight.) If you get the runs, take it in stride. It's simply not worth taking eight Pepto-Bismol tablets a day or brushing your teeth in Coca-Cola all summer long to avoid a day of the trots. I take my health seriously, and, for me, traveling in India or Mexico is a major health concern. But I find Europe no more threatening to my health than the US.

I've routinely taken groups of 24 Americans through Turkey for two weeks. With adequate discretion, we eat everything in sight. At the end of the trip, my loose-stool survey typically shows that five or six travelers coped with a day of the Big D and one person was stuck with an extended weeklong bout.

To avoid getting diarrhea, eat yogurt. Its helpful enzymes ease your system into the country's cuisine.

If you get diarrhea, it will run its course. Revise your diet, don't panic, and take it easy for 24 hours. Make your diet as bland and boring as possible for a day or so (bread, rice, applesauce, boiled potatoes, clear

TRAVEL SAVVY

soup, toast, weak tea). Keep telling yourself that tomorrow you'll feel much better. You will.

If loose stools persist, drink lots of water to replenish lost liquids and minerals. Bananas are effective in replacing potassium, which is lost during a bout with diarrhea.

Don't take antidiarrheal medications if you have blood in your stools or a fever greater than 101°F (38°C)—you need a doctor's exam and antibiotics. A child (especially an infant) who suffers a prolonged case of diarrhea also needs prompt medical attention.

I visited the Red Cross in Athens after a miserable three-week tour of the toilets of Syria, Jordan, and Israel. My intestinal commotion was finally stilled by a recommended strict diet of boiled rice and plain tea. As a matter of fact, after five days on that dull diet, I was constipated.

Constipation: With all the bread you'll be eating, constipation, the other side of the intestinal pendulum, is (according to my surveys) as prevalent as diarrhea. Get exercise, eat lots of roughage (raw fruits, leafy vegetables, prunes, or bran tablets from home), and everything will come out all right in the end.

Pharmacies and Doctors

If you're sick on your trip, don't be a hero. Get help to get on the road to recovery as soon as possible. Throughout Europe, people with a health problem go first to the pharmacy, not to their doctor. European pharmacists diagnose and prescribe remedies for most simple problems. They are usually friendly and speak English, and some medications that are by prescription only in the US are available over the counter (surprisingly cheaply) in Europe. If necessary, the pharmacist will send you to a doctor or the health clinic.

*Regardless of the local word for "pharmacy" (*farmacia *in Spanish,* Apotheke *in German,* pharmacie *in French), you can always look for the green cross.*

A visit to a clinic (or the emergency drop-in section of a hospital), while time-consuming, is actually an interesting travel experience. You'll sign in with the receptionist and answer a few questions, take a seat, and eventually meet your nurse or doctor. Every year I end up in a European clinic for one reason or another, and every time I'm impressed by the efficiency, effectiveness, and price. (Visits to the doctor at the neighborhood clinic are generally free—even for a traveler.)

If you're sick in your hotel and would rather not go out, the hotel receptionist can generally call a doctor who will make a house call. In this case, you'll be diagnosed, billed, and required to pay on the spot. Prescription in hand, you'll trudge off to a 24-hour pharmacy, pick up the necessary medicine, and be on the mend pronto.

For traveling beyond Europe, getting an English-speaking and Western-trained doctor is a reasonable concern. In that case, consider joining **IAMAT,** the International Association for Medical Assistance to Travelers. You'll get a list of English-speaking doctors in member countries who charge affordable, standardized fees for medical visits (membership is free but a donation is requested, www.iamat.org, tel. 716/754-4883). Those needing IAMAT-type services, but who don't have a membership, can get referrals for medical help from other agencies that deal with Americans on the road (such as embassies, consulates, tourist offices, large hotels, and American Express offices).

For information on medical insurance for a European trip, see page 41.

Women's Health Issues

For specific advice on women's health, I turned to Europe Through the Back Door researcher Risa Laib, who wrote the following section based on her experiences traveling solo (and pregnant) through Europe.

You can find whatever medications you need in Europe, but you already know what works for you in the United States. It's easiest to B.Y.O. pills, whether for cramps, yeast infections, or birth control. Some health-insurance companies issue only a month's supply of birth control pills at a time; ask for a larger supply for a longer trip. Tampons and pads, widely available in Europe, are sold—for more than the US price—at supermarkets, pharmacies, and convenience stores. You'll rarely see the range of brands and sizes typical in American supermarkets, so if you're used to a particular brand, it's simpler and cheaper to bring what you'll need from home.

Women prone to yeast infections should bring their own over-the-counter medicine (or know the name and its key ingredient to show a pharmacist in Europe). Some women get a prescription for Diflucan, a powerful pill that cures yeast infections quicker and tidier than creams and suppositories. If you get a yeast infection in Europe and lack medication, go to a pharmacy. If you encounter the rare pharmacist who doesn't speak English, find an English-speaking local woman to write out "yeast infection" for you in the country's language to avoid the embarrassing charade.

You can treat minor urinary tract infections with unsweetened cranberry juice (available in northern Europe) or with cranberry pills (made from cranberry juice concentrate) sold at health food stores. If you often get urinary tract infections, bring antibiotics and a prescription from your doctor.

Traveling When Pregnant: Some couples want to time conception to occur in Europe so they can name their child Paris, Siena, or wherever. (Be thoughtful about this, or little Zagreb may harbor a lifelong grudge against you.) Consider bringing a pregnancy test from home to help you find out when you can celebrate.

If you'll be traveling during your first pregnancy, rip out a few chapters from a book on pregnancy to bring along. It's hard to find basic information on pregnancy in English in much of Europe. If you want certain tests done (such as amniocentesis), ask your doctor when you need to be home.

In the first trimester, climbing all the stairs can be exhausting—packing light is more essential than ever. You might find it easier to travel in the second trimester, when your body's used to being pregnant and you're not yet too big to be uncomfortable. Note that no airline wants you on board when you're eight months pregnant.

Wear comfortable shoes that have arch supports. If you'll be traveling a long time, bring loose clothing (with elastic waistbands) and shoes a half size larger to accommodate your changing body. Keep your valuables (cash, passport, etc.) in a neck pouch rather than a constricting money belt.

Pace yourself and allow plenty of time for rest. Contact an English-speaking doctor if you become ill; medical care in most European countries is reassuringly good.

Seek out nutritious food (though some of it may make you nauseated, just as in America). Picnics, with drinkable yogurt, are often healthier than restaurant meals. Pack baggies for carrying snacks. Bring prenatal vitamins from home, plus a calcium supplement if you're not a milk drinker.

It's actually pleasant to be pregnant in Europe. People are particularly kind. And when your child is old enough to understand, she'll enjoy knowing she's already been to Europe—especially if you promise to take her again.

24. Outsmarting Thieves

Europe is safe when it comes to violent crime. But it's a very "dangerous" place from a petty purse-snatching, pickpocketing point of view. Thieves target Americans—not because they're mean, but because they're smart. Loaded down with valuables in a strange new environment, we stick out like jeweled thumbs. If I were a European street thief, I'd specialize in Americans. My card would say "Yanks Я Us." Americans are known as the ones with all the good stuff in their bags and wallets. Recently I met an American woman whose purse was stolen, and in her purse was her money belt. That juicy little anecdote was featured in every street-thief newsletter.

If you're not constantly on guard, you'll have something stolen. One summer, four out of five of my traveling companions lost cameras in one way or another. (Don't look at me.) In more than 30 summers of travel, I've been mugged once (in a part of London where only fools and thieves tread), had my car broken into six times (broken locks and shattered windows, lots of nonessential stuff taken), and had my car hot-wired once (it was abandoned a few blocks away after the thief found nothing to take). But I've never had my room rifled and never had any money belt–worthy valuables stolen.

Remember, nearly all crimes suffered by tourists are nonviolent and avoidable. Be aware of the pitfalls of traveling, but relax and have fun.

Tourists are often the targets of thieves at major sights in Italy, especially around Rome's Forum and the Florence train station. Some will pose as beggars—using babies or newspapers to distract you while they rip you off.

TRAVEL SAVVY

Limit your vulnerability rather than your travels. Leave precious valuables at home and wear your money belt on the road. Most people in every country are on your side. If you exercise adequate discretion, aren't overly trusting, and don't put yourself into risky situations, your travels should be about as dangerous as hometown grocery shopping. Don't travel fearfully—travel carefully.

Money Belts

Money belts are your key to peace of mind. I never travel without one. A money belt is a small, zippered fabric pouch that fastens around the waist under your pants or skirt. You wear it completely hidden from sight, tucked in like a shirttail—over your shirt and under your pants. (If you find it uncomfortable to wear a money belt in front—as many women do—slide it around and wear it in the small of your back.)

If you need to access your money belt, just reach casually into your pants and (ignoring the curious glances of onlookers) pull it out.

With a money belt, all your essential documents are on you as securely and thoughtlessly as your underpants. Have you ever thought about that? Every morning you put on your underpants. You don't even think about them all day long. And every night when you undress, sure enough, there they are, exactly where you put them. When I travel, my valuables are just as securely out of sight and out of mind, around my waist in a money belt. It's luxurious peace of mind. I'm uncomfortable only when I'm not wearing it.

Operate with a day's spending money in your pocket. You don't need to get at your money belt for every euro. Your money belt is your deep storage—for select deposits and withdrawals. Lately, I haven't even carried a wallet. A few bills in my shirt pocket—no keys, no wallet—and I'm on vacation!

Precautions: Never leave a money belt "hidden" on the beach while you swim. It's safer left in your hotel room. In hostel or dorm situations where your money belt shouldn't be left alone in your room, you can shower with it (hang it—maybe in a plastic bag—from the nozzle). Keep your money-belt contents dry (sweat-free) with a plastic sheath or baggie.

Tour of a Money Belt

Packing light applies to your money belt as well as your luggage. Here's what to pack in your money belt:

Passport. You're legally supposed to have it with you at all times.

Railpass. This is as valuable as cash.

Driver's license. This works just about anywhere in Europe and is necessary if you want to rent a car on the spur of the moment.

Credit card. It's required for car rental and handy to have if your cash runs low.

Debit card. A Visa debit card is the most versatile for ATM withdrawals. (I no longer use traveler's checks.)

Cash. Keep only major bills in your money belt.

Plastic sheath. Money belts easily get sweaty and slimy. Damp plane tickets and railpasses can be disgusting and sometimes worthless. Even a plain old plastic baggie helps keep things dry.

Contact list. Print small, and include every phone number or email address of importance in your life.

Trip calendar page. Include your hotel list and all necessary details from your itinerary (see sample itinerary, page 72).

TRAVEL SAVVY

Purses and wallets are handy for odds and ends and a day's spending money, but plan on losing them. A button-down flap or a Velcro strip sewn into your front or back pocket slows down fast fingers. Those with nothing worth stealing (cars, video cameras, jewelry, and so on) except what's in their money belt are virtually invulnerable.

Tips on Avoiding Theft

Thieves thrive on confusion, crowds, and tourist traps. Here's some advice given to me by a thief who won the lotto.

Keep a Low Profile: Never leave your camera lying around where hotel workers and others can see it and be tempted. Keep it either around your neck or zipped safely out of sight. Luxurious luggage lures thieves. The thief chooses the most impressive suitcase in the pile—never mine. Things are much safer in your room than with you in a day bag on the streets. Hotels are a relative haven from thieves and a good resource for advice on personal safety.

On Trains and at the Station: On the train, be alert at stops, when thieves can dash on and off—with your bag. When sleeping on a train (or at an airport, or anywhere in public), clip or fasten your pack or suitcase to the seat, luggage rack, or yourself. Even the slight inconvenience of undoing a clip deters most thieves. Women shouldn't sleep in an empty train compartment. You're safer sharing a compartment with a friendly family. Be on guard in train stations, especially upon arrival, when you may be overburdened by luggage and overwhelmed by a new location. If you check your luggage, keep the claim ticket or key in your money belt—thieves know just where to go if they snare one of these.

Public Transit and Flea Markets: Crowding through big-city subway turnstiles is a popular way to rip off the unsuspecting tourist. Imaginative artful-dodger thief teams create a fight or commotion to distract their victims. Crowded flea markets and city buses that cover the tourist sights (such as Rome's notorious #64) are also happy hunting grounds. Thief teams will often block a bus or subway entry, causing the person behind you to "bump" into you. While I don't lock my zippers, most zippers are lockable, and even a twist-tie or key ring is helpful to keep your bag zipped up tight. Don't use a waist (or "fanny") pack as a money belt. Thieves assume this is where you keep your goodies.

Your Rental Car: Thieves target tourists' cars—especially at night. Don't leave anything even hinting of value in view in your parked car. Put anything worth stealing in the trunk (or, better yet, in your hotel room). Leave your glove compartment open so the thief can look in without breaking in. Choose your parking place carefully. Your hotel receptionist knows what's safe and what precautions are necessary.

Make your car look as local as possible. Leave no tourist information lying around. Put a local newspaper under the rear window. More than half of the work that European automobile glass shops do is repairing windows broken by thieves. Before I choose where to park my car, I check to see if the parking lot's asphalt glitters. If you have a hatchback, leave the trunk covered during the day. At night take the cover off the trunk and lay it on the back seat

You can judge the safety of a European parking lot by how it glitters.

so the thief knows you're savvy and can see there's nothing stored in the back of your car. Many police advise leaving your car unlocked at night. Worthless but irreplaceable things (journal, spent film, etc.) are stolen only if left in a bag. It's better to keep these things with you, or if need be, lay them loose in the trunk. In major cities in Spain, crude thieves reach into windows or even smash the windows of occupied cars at stoplights to grab a purse or camera. In Rome, my favorite pension is next to a large police station—a safe place to park, if you're legal.

Scams

Many of the most successful scams require a naive and trusting tourist. The sneakiest pickpockets look like well-dressed businesspeople, generally with something official-looking in their hand. Lately, many are posing as tourists with fanny packs, cameras, and even guidebooks. Be wary of any unusual contact or commotion in crowded public (especially touristy) places. If you're alert and aren't overly trusting, you should have no problem. Here are some clever ways European thieves bolster their cash flow. (For more examples, look in the appendix for excerpts from my Graffiti Wall message board.)

Thieving moms with their babies are hard at work. Be careful. The wrap—not her left arm—is holding the baby...freeing that hand to pick your pocket.

TRAVEL SAVVY

Don't confuse the €2 coin (left, value $2.50) with the old 500-lira coin (right, value $0).

Slow Count: Cashiers who deal with lots of tourists thrive on the "slow count." Even in banks, they'll count your change back with odd pauses in hopes the rushed tourist will gather up the money early and say *"Grazie."* Also be careful when you pay with too large a bill. Waiters seem to be arithmetically challenged. If giving a large bill for a small payment, clearly state the value of the bill as you hand it over. Some cabbies or waiters will pretend to drop a large bill and pick up a hidden small one in order to shortchange a tourist. In Italy, the now-worthless 500-lira coin looks like a €2 coin—be alert when accepting change. Other coins (such as Turkey's one-lira coin, worth 55 cents; and Thailand's 10-baht coin, worth 25 cents) also resemble a €2 coin.

Oops! You're jostled in a crowd as someone spills ketchup or fake pigeon poop on your shirt. The thief offers profuse apologies while dabbing it up—and pawing your pockets. There are variations: Someone drops something, you kindly pick it up, and you lose your wallet. Or, even worse, someone throws a baby into your arms as your pockets are picked. Assume beggars are pickpockets. Treat any commotion (a scuffle breaking out, a beggar in your face) as fake—designed to distract unknowing victims. If an elderly woman falls down an escalator, stand back and guard your valuables, then...carefully...move in to help.

The "Helpful" Local: Thieves posing as concerned locals will warn you to store your wallet safely—and then steal it after they see where you stash it. If someone wants to help you use an ATM, politely refuse (they're just after your PIN code). If a bank machine eats your ATM card, see if there's a thin plastic insert with a tongue hanging out that crooks use to extract it. (A similar scam is to put something sticky in the slot.) Some thieves put out tacks and ambush drivers

In Berlin, the police teach the public the latest shell-game scam. On the streets of Europe, anything that seems too good to be true...is.

with their "assistance" in changing the tire. Others hang out at subway ticket machines eager to "help" you, the bewildered tourist, buy tickets with a pile of your quickly disappearing foreign cash. If using a station locker, beware of the "hood Samaritan" who may have his own key to a locker he'd like you to use. And skip the helping hand from official-looking railroad attendants at the Rome train station. They'll help you find your seat...then demand a "tip."

The Attractive Flirt: A single male traveler is approached by a gorgeous woman on the street. After chatting for a while, she seductively invites him for a drink at a nearby nightclub. But when the bill arrives, it's several hundred dollars more than he expected. Only then does he notice the burly bouncers guarding the exits. There are several variations on this scam. Sometimes, the scam artist is disguised as a lost tourist; in other cases, it's simply a gregarious local person who (seemingly) just wants to show you his city. Either way, be suspicious when invited for a drink by someone you just met; if you want to go out together, suggest a bar of your choosing instead.

Fake Police: Two thieves in uniform—posing as "Tourist Police"— stop you on the street, flash their bogus badges, and ask to check your wallet for counterfeit bills or "drug money." You won't even notice some bills are missing until after they leave. Never give your wallet to anyone.

Groups of teenagers, using newspapers to distract their prey, pickpocket tourists strolling the beach promenade in Nice. Not nice.

Young Thief Gangs: These are common all over urban southern Europe, especially in the touristy areas of Milan, Florence, and Rome. Groups of boys or girls with big eyes, troubled expressions, and colorful raggedy clothes play a game where they politely mob the unsuspecting tourist, beggar-style. As their pleading eyes grab yours and they hold up their pathetic message scrawled on cardboard, you're fooled into thinking that they're beggars. All the while, your purse, fanny pack, or backpack is being expertly rifled. If you're wearing a money belt and you understand what's going on here, there's nothing to fear. In fact,

TRAVEL SAVVY

In your wallet, you've got a little cash, a phone card...and this funny note to the thief. Cut it out and take it along.

DEAR THIEF...

ENGLISH: Sorry this contains so little money.
Consider changing your profession.

ITALIANO: Mi dispiace per te che ci siano così pochi soldi.
Sara' meglio che cambi lavoro.

FRANCAIS: Je suis désolé d'avoir si peu d'argent.
Considérez un changement de carrière.

DEUTSCH: Tut mir leid dass meine Geldbörse so wenig Geld enthält. Vielleicht sollten Sie sich einen neuen Beruf auswählen.

ESPAÑOL: Lamento que encuentre tan poco dinero.
Vaya pensando en cambiar de trabajo.

having a street thief's hand slip slowly into your pocket becomes just one more interesting cultural experience.

The Found Ring: An innocent-looking person picks up a ring on the ground in front of you and asks if you dropped it. When you say no, the person examines the ring more closely, then shows you a mark "proving" that it's pure gold. He offers to sell it to you for a good price—which is several times more than he paid for it before dropping it on the sidewalk.

The "Friendship" Bracelet: A vendor approaches you and aggressively asks if you'll help him with a "demonstration." He proceeds to make a friendship bracelet right on your arm. When finished, he asks you to pay a premium for the bracelet he created just for you. And, since you can't easily take it off on the spot, you feel obliged to pay up. (These sorts of distractions by "salesmen" can also function as a smokescreen for theft—an accomplice is picking your pocket as you try to wriggle away from the pushy vendor.)

Leather Jacket Salesman in Distress: A well-spoken, well-dressed gentleman approaches you and explains that he's a leather jacket salesman, and he needs directions to drive to a nearby landmark. He chats you up ("Oh, really? My wife is from Omaha!") and gives you the feeling that you're now friends. When finished, he reaches in his car and pulls out a "designer leather jacket" he claims is worth hundreds of dollars, which he gives to you as a gift for your helpfulness. Oh, and by the way, his credit card isn't working, and could you please give him some cash to buy gas? He takes off with the cash, and you later realize that you've paid way too much for your new 100 percent vinyl jacket.

Room "Inspectors": There's a knock at your door and two men claim to be the hotel's room inspectors. One waits outside while the other comes in to take a look around. While you're distracted, the first

thief slips in and takes valuables left on a dresser. Don't let people into your room if you weren't expecting them. Call down to the hotel desk if "inspectors" suddenly turn up.

The Stripper: You see a good-looking woman arguing with a street vendor. The vendor accuses her of shoplifting, which she vehemently denies. To prove her innocence, she starts taking off her clothes—very slowly. Once she's down to her underwear, the vendor apologizes and she leaves. Suddenly all the men in the crowd find out that their wallets have "left," too, thanks to a team of pickpockets working during the show.

The Broken Camera: Everyone is taking pictures of a famous sight, and someone comes up with a camera or cell phone and asks that you take his picture. But the camera or cell phone doesn't seem to work. When you hand it back, the "tourist" fumbles and drops it on the ground, where it breaks into pieces. He will either ask you to pay for repairs or lift your wallet while you are bending over to pick up the broken object.

Talkative Cashiers: The shop's cashier seems to be speaking on her phone when you hand her your credit card. But listen closely and you may hear the sound of the phone's camera shutter, as she takes a picture of your card.

Crooked Cabbies: The scam you'll most likely encounter in Europe is being overcharged by a taxi driver. For tips on avoiding this problem, see page 286.

If You Are Ripped Off...

Even the most careful traveler can get ripped off. If it happens, don't let it ruin your trip. Many trips start with a major rip-off, recover, and with the right attitude and very light bags, finish wonderfully.

Immediately after a theft, get a police report if you intend to make an insurance claim. If you lose your credit, debit, or ATM card, follow the damage control tips on page 176 (also printed in all my city and country guidebooks). For tips on what to do in case of identity theft, see page 175.

Before you leave on your trip, make two sets of photocopies of your valuable documents and tickets. Pack a copy and leave a copy at home. It's easier to replace a lost or stolen passport, railpass, car-rental voucher, or plane e-ticket if you have a photocopy proving that you really owned what you lost. A couple of passport-type pictures you've brought from home can expedite the replacement process.

American embassies or consulates are located in major European cities. They're there to help American citizens in trouble, but don't fancy themselves as travelers' aid offices. They will inform those at home that you need help, assist in replacing lost or stolen passports, and arrange for emergency funds to be sent from home (or, in rare cases, loan it to you directly).

25. Museum Strategies

Culture Beyond the Petri Dish

Europe is a treasure chest of great art. You'll see many of the world's greatest museums. These tips will help you make the most of your visit.

Study your guidebook. Some museums now require reservations, such as the Alhambra (in Granada, Spain), the church that houses Leonardo da Vinci's *Last Supper* (Milan), Giotto's Scrovegni Chapel (Padua), and the Borghese Gallery (Rome). If you don't reserve in advance, you'll likely miss out.

At many great galleries, such as the Uffizi in Florence, you can wait in line for two hours...or call ahead for an appointment and walk right in. Remember: Lines like this are not for the entry turnstile, but for the ticket booth.

At Florence's famous galleries—the Accademia (Michelangelo's *David*) and the Uffizi (the showcase for Italian Renaissance art)—it's smart to book ahead. You can also reserve a time to visit the Vatican Museum in Rome. While hundreds of tourists are sweating in the long lines, you can just show up at your reserved entry time and spend your time in the museums instead of the lines.

Know the closed days. Most museums are closed one day during the week (usually Monday, sometimes Tuesday; Jewish sights are typically closed Saturday). If

In Europe, there are two kinds of travelers: smart ones...and those who wait in lines. Good guidebooks offer crowd-beating tips. For Rome's Colosseum, buy your ticket 200 yards away at the Palatine Hill—which never has a line—and skip directly past the not-so-smart travelers pictured here.

you've got only one day for the Sistine Chapel, avoid Sunday. It's either closed, or—on the last Sunday of the month—free and terribly crowded, when it feels more like the Sardine Chapel. It can be worth paying the entrance fee to avoid the rampaging hordes on a museum's free day.

Arrive early (or late) at popular sights. If you show up by 8:00 in the morning at Neuschwanstein, Bavaria's famous fairy-tale castle, you'll get a ticket. Come an hour later and you'll either wait a long time or find that tickets are sold out—or worse, both.

Some museums are open late one or two nights a week. For instance, London's Tate Modern stays open Friday and Saturday evenings—when the crowds disappear and you're glad you came.

A victim of the Louvre

Museum passes (such as the Paris Museum Pass) and combo-tickets allow you to bypass the long admission lines and walk right in. More and more, Europe's most popular sights are being paired in combo-tickets with sights few people pay to see. The bad news: You have to pay for both to visit one. The good news: You can avoid the line at the congested sight by buying your ticket at the less-popular sister sight. You can wait up to an hour to get into Rome's Colosseum or Venice's Doge's Palace—or buy a combo-ticket (at another participating yet less-crowded site) and just scoot inside.

Note that many museums stop selling tickets and start shutting down rooms 30 to 60 minutes before closing. My favorite time in museums is the cool, lazy, last hour. But I'm careful to get to the far end early, see the rooms that are first to shut down, and work my way back toward the entry.

These tricks aren't secrets. They're in any good, up-to-date guidebook. Just read ahead.

Learn about art. If the art's not fun, you don't know enough about it. I remember touring the National Archaeological Museum in Athens as an obligation. My mom said it would be a crime to miss it. It was boring. I was convinced that the people who looked like they were enjoying it were actually just faking it—trying to look sophisticated. Two years later, after a class in classical art history, that same museum was a fascinating trip into the world of Pericles and Socrates, all because

With a good guidebook, you stand a chance of finding Michelangelo's Slaves *in the Louvre.*

of some background knowledge. Some pre-trip study makes the art more fun. When you understand the context in which it was made, art becomes the closest thing to a time-machine that Europe offers.

Be selective. A common misconception is that a great museum has only great art. A museum such as the Louvre in Paris is so big (the building itself was at one time the largest in Europe), you can't possibly cover everything—so don't try. Only a fraction of a museum's pieces are really masterpieces.

With the help of a tour guide or guidebook, focus on just the museum's top two hours. Some of Europe's great museums provide brief pamphlets recommending the best basic visit. With this selective strategy, you'll appreciate the highlights when you're fresh. If you have any energy left afterward, you can explore other areas of specific interest to you. For me, museum-going is the hardest work I do in Europe, and I'm rarely good for more than two or three hours at a time. If you're determined to cover a large museum thoroughly, try to tackle one section a day for several days.

Try to get a tour. Phone ahead. Some museums offer regularly scheduled tours in English. If the tour is in the native language only, politely let the guide know at the beginning that there are several English-speaking people in the group who'd love some information.

Audioguide tours are getting more and more popular at museums (sometimes included in the entry cost, sometimes a few dollars extra). These portable devices allow you to dial up generally worthwhile information in English on particular pieces of art. If you bring

Stroll with a chatty curator through Europe's greatest art galleries, thanks to digital audioguides.

along a Y-jack and an extra pair of headphones, two people can save half by sharing the same audioguide. (Unfortunately, this isn't possible with wand-style audioguides.) If you're traveling in Paris, London, or Italy with an MP3 player (such as an iPod), consider taking along one of my audio tours (described on page 31).

Eavesdrop. If you are especially interested in one piece of art, spend half an hour studying it and listening to each passing tour guide tell his or her story about *David* or the *Mona Lisa* or whatever. They each do their own research and come up with different information to share. Much of it is true. There's nothing wrong with this sort of tour free-loading. Just don't stand in the front and ask a lot of questions.

Watch the video. Many sights have videos or films about the attraction (included in the entry price). These are generally well worth your time. I make it standard operating procedure to ask when I arrive at a sight if there is a video in English.

Make sure you don't miss your favorites. On arrival, look through the museum's guidebook index or the gift shop's postcards to make sure you won't miss anything of importance to you. For instance, I love Salvador Dalí's work. One time I thought I was finished with a museum, but as I browsed through the postcards... Hello, Dalí. A museum guide was happy to show me where this Dalí painting was hiding. I saved myself the disappointment of discovering too late that I'd missed it.

At the Louvre, it's worth fighting through crowds of amateur paparazzi to see the Venus de Milo...who's ready for her close-up.

More and more museums offer a greatest-hits plan or brochure. Some (such as London's National Gallery) even have a computer study room where you can input your interests and print out a tailored museum tour.

Miscellaneous Tips: Particularly at huge museums, ask if your ticket allows in-and-out privileges. Check the museum map or brochure at the entrance for the location of particular kinds of art, the café, and bathrooms (usually free and clean). Also, note any special tours or events or early closings of rooms or wings. Get comfortable: Check your bag and coat—in some places, bag check is required. (If you want to try to

Some of Europe's Best Open-Air Folk Museums

The Netherlands and Belgium

- **Zaanse Schans,** near Zaandijk, 30 miles north of Amsterdam. Windmills, wooden shoes, etc. (www.zaanseschans.nl).
- **Dutch Open-Air Folk Museum,** in Arnhem, Netherlands. Holland's first and biggest (www.openairmuseum.nl).
- **Zuiderzee Open-Air Museum,** in Enkhuizen, Netherlands. Lively setting, lots of craftspeople (www.zuiderzeemuseum.nl).
- **Bokrijk Open-Air Museum,** between Hasselt and Genk, in Belgium. Old Flemish buildings and culture in a natural setting (www.bokrijk.be).

Denmark

- **Funen Village (Den Fynske Landsby),** just south of Odense. Life in the 18th century (museum.odense.dk).
- **The Old Town (Den Gamle By),** Århus. Sixty houses and shops show Danish town life from 1580–1850 (www.dengamleby.dk).

Finland

- **Seurasaari Island,** near Helsinki. Reconstructed buildings from all over Finland (www.nba.fi/en/seurasaari_openair museum).
- **Luostarinmäki Handicraft Museum,** Turku. The life and work of 19th-century crafts-people (www.turku.fi/maakuntamuseo).

Germany

- **Vogtsbauernhof Black Forest Open-Air Museum,** in Gutach. A collection of farms filled with exhibits on the traditional dress and lifestyles (www.vogtsbauernhof.org).

Great Britain

- **Blists Hill Victorian Town,** Ironbridge Gorge. Shows life from the early days of the Industrial Revolution (www.ironbridge.org.uk).
- **Beamish Open-Air Museum,** northwest of Durham. Life in northeast England in 1900 (www.beamish.org.uk).
- **St. Fagans National History Museum,** near Cardiff. Old

keep your bag with you, carry it low and under your arms like a purse, not on your back.) Cameras are usually allowed if you don't use a flash or tripod; look for signs or ask. If your camera has an automatic flash, know how to turn it off.

Open-Air Folk Museums

Many people travel in search of the old life and traditional culture in action. While we book a round-trip ticket into the romantic past, those we photograph with the Old World balanced on their heads are struggling to dump that load and climb into the modern world. In Europe, most are succeeding.

buildings and craftspeople illustrate traditional Welsh ways (www.museumwales.ac.uk/en /stfagans).

Hungary

- **Skanzen,** in Szentendre, near Budapest. Traditional architecture from around Hungary (www.skanzen.hu).
- **Hollókő,** near Budapest. An old-fashioned village where people still live (www.holloko.hu).

Ireland

- **Bunratty Folk Park,** near Limerick. Buildings from the Shannon area and artisans at work (www.shannonheritage .com).
- **Ulster Folk and Transport Museum,** at Cultra, near Belfast. Traditional Irish lifestyles and buildings from all over Ireland (www.uftm.org.uk).
- **Glencolumbcille Folk Museum,** Donegal. Thatched cottages show life from 1700–1900. A Gaelic-speaking cooperative runs the folk village and a traditional-crafts industry (www.glenfolkvillage.com).

Norway

- **Norwegian Folk Museum,** at Bygdøy, near Oslo. Norway's first, with 150 old buildings from all over Norway and a 12th-century stave church (www.norskfolke.museum.no).
- **Maihaugen Folk Museum,** at Lillehammer. Folk culture of the Gudbrandsdal Valley. Norway's best (www.maihaugen.no).

Sweden

- **Skansen,** Stockholm. One of the best museums, with more than 100 buildings from all over Sweden, craftspeople at work, live entertainment, and a Lapp camp with reindeer (www .skansen.se).
- **Kulturen,** Lund. Features southern Sweden and Viking exhibits (www.kulturen.com)

Switzerland

- **Ballenberg Swiss Open-Air Museum,** just northeast of Lake Brienz, near Interlaken. A fine collection of old Swiss buildings with furnished interiors (www.ballenberg.ch).

The easiest way, and more than ever the only way, to see the "real local culture" is by exploring open-air folk museums. True, it's culture on a lazy Susan, but the future is becoming the past faster and faster, and in many places it's

Traditional culture is kept alive in Europe's open-air folk museums.

TRAVEL SAVVY

the only "Old World" you're going to find.

An open-air folk museum is a collection of traditional buildings from every corner of a country or region, carefully reassembled in a park, usually near the capital or a major city. These sprawling museums are the best bet for the hurried (or tired) tourist craving a magic-carpet ride through that country's past. Log cabins, thatched cottages, mills, old schoolhouses, shops, and farms come complete with original furnishings and usually a local person dressed in the traditional costume who's happy to answer any of your questions about life then and there.

To get the most out of your visit, start by picking up a list of that day's special exhibits, events, and activities at the information center, and take advantage of any walking tours. In the summer, folk museums buzz with colorful folk dances, live music performances, and young craftspeople specializing in old crafts. Many traditional arts and crafts are dying, and these artisans do what they can to keep the cuckoo clock from going the way of the dodo bird. Some of my favorite souvenirs are those I watched being dyed, woven, or carved by folk-museum artists.

Popularized in Scandinavia, these sightseeing centers of the future are now found all over the world. The best folk museums are still in the Nordic capitals. Oslo's, with 150 historic buildings and a 12th-century

At Stockholm's open-air folk museum, you may be entertained by this rare band of left-handed fiddlers.

stave church, is just a boat ride across the harbor from the City Hall. Skansen, in Stockholm, gets my first-place ribbon for its guided tours, feisty folk entertainment, and Arctic camp complete with reindeer and Lapp dancing.

Switzerland's Ballenberg Open-Air Museum, near Interlaken, is a good alternative when the Alps hide behind clouds.

There is no shortage of folk museums in the British Isles. For an unrivaled look at the Industrial Revolution, spend a day at Blists Hill Victorian Town in Ironbridge Gorge, northwest of Stratford-upon-Avon. You can cross the world's first iron bridge to see the factories that lit the fuse of our modern age.

Folk museums teach traditional lifestyles better than any other kind of museum. As our world hurtles past 100 billion McDonald's hamburgers served, these museums will become even more important. Of course, they're as realistic as Santa's Village, but how else will you see the elves?

26. Travel Photography

Every year I ask myself whether it's worth the worry and expense of mixing photography with my travels. After I return home and relive my trip through those pictures, the answer is always "Yes!" Here are some tips and lessons that I've learned from the photographic school of hard knocks.

Good shots are made by the photographer, not the camera. For most people, a very expensive camera is a bad idea. Your camera is more likely to be lost, broken, or stolen than anything else you'll travel with. An expensive model may not be worth the risks and headaches that accompany it.

When buying a camera, get one that will do what you want and a little bit more. You are buying one not only for the trip, but also for use later.

Don't buy a camera a day or two before you fly. Not every camera works perfectly right out of the box. Practice shooting indoors and outdoors before you leave, and study the results. Check your pictures

The Vatican Museum staircase: Have fun with composition and find creative new angles.

for good exposure and sharp focus. If they're not right, take it back. Do the same checks with the replacement camera. Do your learning on hometown Main Street—before you're standing at the base of the Eiffel Tower, wondering how to zoom out.

Digital Cameras

Digital cameras are the standard—I haven't picked up a film camera in nearly a decade. Most of the photos in this book were taken with a digital camera.

Digital cameras have opened up a world of possibilities for photographers. You can view and delete photos immediately, allowing you to take several shots of a subject, then keep only the best one. You're free to experiment with artsy angles, tricky lighting, and nighttime shots without wasting film. Digital photos are also easier to share: Post your favorites on your trip blog or social networking site,

A good eye is more important than an extra lens.

email them directly to your family and friends, or print them to create an old-fashioned scrapbook. Printing digital images is reasonably priced (most photo labs charge about 12–20 cents per print)—and, since you can choose only the very best pictures to print, you know they'll all be keepers.

Buying a Digital Camera

There's a wide range of digital cameras available. How to choose? Narrow down your options based on the criteria here. Ask your friends what they recommend and why. Flip through sales fliers to see which models are hot right now. Then read reviews and compare specs on your likely choices. You'll find extremely detailed technical information, in-depth professional reviews, and informal consumer reviews at www.cnet.com, www.steves-digicams.com, and www.dpreview.com (more user reviews are at www.epinions.com).

Once you've gotten an overview, head to a store to test-drive the likely candidates. Most stores that sell digital cameras have floor models that you can try out. While you can buy your camera from any big chain store, I prefer the personal attention I get from a smaller outfit (such as www.glazerscamera.com). Purchasing a camera at your local camera shop buys you a wealth of advice when you want it. Be aware that some camera specialty shops work on commission (which may color their advice).

These factors will help you zoom in on your ideal camera:

Resolution: Digital cameras are classified by resolution—that is, by how many megapixels make up each image. (A pixel is a tiny building-block of an image, and one megapixel equals one million pixels.) Any camera that's three megapixels or more will produce crisp images and suitable 4" × 6" prints. The more megapixels, the sharper the image—and the better it'll look when printed (especially for larger prints). As camera prices drop, and high-quality 14-megapixel cameras become affordable, it's hard to justify buying a 9-megapixel model just to save a few bucks.

Brand-name: Digital cameras are available from most traditional camera makers (such as Nikon, Olympus, and Canon), as well as from electronics or computer companies (such as Sony and Hewlett-Packard). Many avid photographers already have a favorite brand, but anyone who wants decent images should pay a little extra for a big-name-brand, rather than the no-name cheapos you'll see advertised.

Size and Type (Compact vs. SLR): If you travel a lot, you might prefer a camera that's as lightweight as possible. Several models—often called "compact" or "ultracompact"—are almost as small as a deck of cards but still take high-resolution pictures. There are trade-offs—smaller cameras have smaller lenses, and the image quality can suffer slightly. But many people find that since they can slip the camera into a pocket, they're more likely to

Cameras come in many different shapes and sizes, from slip-in-your-pocket compact to high-quality SLR to sneaky periscope-style.

take it everywhere...and use it more. Serious photographers can consider more elaborate SLR digital cameras (with interchangeable lenses and a satisfying, old-fashioned shutter click). These cameras are bulky, but produce beautiful, professional-looking images.

Ease of Use: Some cameras are made for first-time users, with only a few bells and whistles to negotiate. Other types appeal to semi-pro photographers, and require you to sit down with a manual to figure out how to use the flash. If you're buying a new camera, ask lots of questions in the store and get a good demo on everything you'll need to do (zoom in, delete bad photos, transfer pictures to a computer's hard drive, turn the flash or LCD screen on and off to save battery power, and so on). See how long the camera takes to "boot up" once you turn it on and between photos. Some high-megapixel cameras take a while to go from shot to shot, which can cost you spontaneity as you try to capture a fleeting moment.

Camera Gadgets and Accessories

A mini-tripod is light and easy to carry, and allows you to take remarkably clear low-light shots—like this serene twilight image of Moscow's Red Square.

Like many hobbies, photography allows you to spend endless amounts of money on accessories. The following are particularly useful to the traveling photographer. But be careful not to take so much gear on your trip that you become a slave to your gadgets.

Mini-tripod: About five inches high, this great little gadget screws into most cameras, sprouts three legs, and holds everything perfectly still for slow shutter speeds, timed exposures, and automatic shutter-release shots. (It looks like a small lunar-landing module; some are flexible enough to wrap around posts.) Because the flash on my camera gives a harsh image, I prefer to use existing light—which often requires a tripod. A conventional tripod is too large to lug around Europe. Those without a mini-tripod use a tiny beanbag (or sock filled with rice) or get good at balancing their camera on anything solid and adjusting the tilt with the lens cap or strap. If you're planning to use a mini-tripod, you might consider bringing a shutter release cable (if your camera accepts one).

Gadget Bag: The most functional and economical way to carry your camera gear is in a small nylon stuff bag made for hikers. A formal camera bag is unnecessary and attracts thieves. Most camera stores now sell a line of camera backpacks that have padded compartments to protect your gear (and don't say "steal me" like a camera bag).

Tissue, Cleaner, and Lens Cap: A lens-cleaning tissue and a small bottle of cleaning solution are wise additions to any gadget bag (use cleaning solution sparingly and only for greasy spots—too much cleaner can damage your lens). Leave your protective camera case at home and protect your lens with a cap that dangles on its string when you're shooting. Most non-SLR cameras automatically retract and cover the lens when not in use.

SLR Lenses and Filters: Whether you're shooting film or digital, an SLR camera gives you more options for add-ons. No-frills photographers will stick with the mid-range lens that comes with the camera; serious shutterbugs can look into zoom, wide-angle, or image stabilization lenses. If you invest in a zoom lens, get one that covers both ends of the visual range—close-ups to long shots. A 24–105mm lens gives you a great medium-wide angle that zooms to a medium-telephoto. Make sure all your lenses have a haze or UV filter. It's better to bang and smudge up your filter than your lens.

SLR cameras give you the maximum in adaptability, including interchangeable lenses.

The only other filter you might use is a polarizer, which eliminates reflections and enhances color separation, but you can lose up to two stops of light with it. Don't use more than one filter at a time, and don't go cheap. You're placing another layer of glass in front of your shooting lens. If the filter is poor, your images will not be as sharp as they should be. Some photographers suggest using a lens shade in daylight; it keeps stray light off the front of the camera to prevent "lens flare" and enhances the color saturation of your images.

Memory: Digital cameras store photos on a memory card. You can choose the resolution of your images; the higher the resolution, the more storage space each image takes up. Memory cards come in different types (including CompactFlash, Secure Digital, and Sony's Memory Stick, depending on your camera) and different sizes (from 4 to 16 gigabytes). I travel with a six-megapixel camera and a two-gigabyte memory card.

Taking photos at high resolution, I can fit about 500 photos onto my memory card. For more tips on storing your images—especially on a long trip—see "Storing Digital Images," below.

Batteries: Some digital cameras come with a battery that can be recharged; others take AA batteries (which the camera will burn through amazingly quickly). Rechargeable or lithium AA batteries last much longer than disposable alkalines, and are significantly cheaper in the long run—you can buy a good set of rechargeable nickel–metal hydride (NiMH) batteries and a charger for

There are several different types of memory cards. Figure out which one your camera uses, get the highest-capacity one you can afford, and consider buying an extra one for additional storage.

about $20. Before you buy, make sure the charger will work in Europe (look for the voltage numbers "110V" and "220V"), and take an adapter to plug it in (for details, see "Electronics," page 58). Be aware that you cannot pack loose lithium batteries in your checked luggage—but you can carry spare rechargeable batteries in your carry-on as long as they're sealed inside a plastic zip-lock bag or in their original packaging.

TV Adapter Cable: Many cameras come with a cable that allows you to plug directly into a TV set. If you're staying at a hotel in Europe with a modern TV, you can enjoy a big-screen digital slideshow while you're still on the road.

Storing Digital Images

The biggest disadvantage of a digital camera is the dilemma of how to store all of your photos when you're on a lengthy trip. The easiest solution is to edit your images ruthlessly and often, keeping only the very best shots. (The people who wind up watching your slideshow will thank you for it.) But even the most selective shutterbug will eventually run out of room. Here are some options.

Upload to a laptop. Since I usually travel with a laptop, I can simply upload my photos to my computer every so often. (Then, for added safety, I can burn them to a CD or DVD, or back them up on a high-capacity USB flash drive.) This is ideal...unless you're leaving the laptop at home.

Don't skimp on memory. Buy the biggest memory card you can. These days, memory is so cheap that there's no reason not to travel with enough to cover your entire trip. Consider getting a second memory card to increase your capacity, or as a backup if your first card is lost or damaged (memory cards are available in Europe, but they're more expensive).

In a pinch, empty your memory card as you go. Many European photo stores and Internet cafés can burn your images to a DVD or CD for about $7–10. (Be mindful of how much memory you need; there's no point burning three CDs when one DVD would do the job.) Burning a photo disc also provides peace of mind; if anything happens to your camera, your images are safely backed up.

Consider lower resolution. If you plan to use your photos only for emailing or posting to a website, and if you're certain you won't want to print any of your photos, you can get by with taking photos at a lower resolution. In order to get double the shots on my memory card, I sometimes shoot at the grainier "basic" level rather than the memory-gobbling fine resolution level. But I've sometimes regretted taking lower-resolution images—such as when I've captured a really great shot, but the resolution is too low to make a satisfactory print.

Back up for safety. Even if you have plenty of memory room, it's wise to occasionally back up your photos one way or another in case your camera is stolen. The more you value your photos, the more you should treat them as a precious souvenir to be protected.

Tricks for a Good Shot

Most people are limited by their photographic skills, not by their camera. Understand your camera. Devour the manual. Take experimental shots, make notes, and see what happens. If you don't understand f-stops or depth of field, find a photography class or book and learn (for tips on taking pictures, visit www.photosecrets.com and www.betterphoto.com). Camera stores sell good books on photography in general and travel photography in particular. I shutter to think how many people are underexposed and lacking depth in this field.

A sharp eye connected to a wild imagination will be your most valuable piece of equipment. Develop a knack for what will look good and

Find a creative angle.

be interesting after the trip. The skilled photographer's eye sees striking light, shade, form, lines, patterns, texture, and colors.

Look for a new slant to an old sight. Postcard-type shots are boring. Everyone knows what the Eiffel Tower looks like. Find a unique or different approach to sights that everyone has seen. Shoot the bell tower through the horse's legs or lay your camera on the floor to shoot the Gothic ceiling.

Vary your perspective—add extra depth with a foreground.

Capture the personal and intimate details of your trip. Show how you lived, who you met, and what made each day an adventure (a close-up of a picnic, your leech bite, laundry day, or a schoolboy playing games with his nose).

Vary your perspective. You can shoot close, far, low, high, during the day, and at night. Don't fall into the rut of always centering a shot. Use foregrounds to add color, depth, and interest to landscapes.

Be bold and break rules. For instance, we are told never to shoot into the sun. But some into-the-sun shots bring surprising results. Try to use bad weather to your advantage. Experiment with strange or difficult light situations. Buy a handbook on shooting photos in existing light.

Maximize good lighting. Real photographers get single-minded at the "magic hours"—early morning and late afternoon—when the sun is very low, the light is rich and diffused, and the colors glow. Plan for these times. Grab bright colors. Develop an eye for great lighting; any time of day, you may luck into a perfectly lit scene. Some of my best photos are the result of great lighting, not great subjects.

Get close. Notice details. Get closer...real close. Eliminate distractions. Get so close that you show only one thing. Don't try to show it all in one shot. For any potentially great

Fill the lens with your subject.

The best people shots are up close and well lit, with a soft background.

shot, I try several different variations—then delete the ones that don't pan out.

People are the most interesting subjects. It takes nerve to walk up to people and take their picture. It can be difficult, but if you want some great shots, be nervy. Ask for permission. (In any language, point at your camera and ask, "Photo?") Your subject will probably be delighted. Try to show action. A candid is better than a posed shot. Even a "posed candid" shot is better than a posed one. Give your subject something to do. Challenge the kid in the market to juggle oranges. Many photographers take a second shot immediately after the first portrait to capture a looser, warmer subject. The famous war photographer Robert Capa once said, "If your pictures aren't good enough, you're not close enough." My best portraits are so close that the entire head can't fit into the frame.

Buildings, in general, are not interesting. It does not matter if Karl Marx or Beethoven was born there—a house is as dead as its former resident. As travel photographers gain experience, they take more people shots and fewer buildings or general landscapes.

Expose for your subject. Even if your camera is automatic, your subject can turn out to be a silhouette. Get those faces in the sun or (even better) lit from the side.

When shooting a portrait, the sun should be behind you. Have the sunlight hit the subject's face at an angle by making sure it's coming over your right or left shoulder. This creates dramatic highlights and shadows on the subject's face. Avoid

Capture the magic with just the right light.

TRAVEL SAVVY

shooting outdoor portraits during the lighting "dead zone," between 11 a.m. and 2 p.m. If you have to shoot then, use your camera's flash to fill the shadows that form in the eye sockets, under the nose, and under the chin. High-end cameras have an adjustable power setting on the flash. Use it to get the right ratio of sunlight to fill light.

Don't be afraid to handhold a slow shot. At most major museums, you're not allowed to use a flash (which ages paintings) or a tripod. Tripods enable you to take professional (profitable) shots that could compete with those at the museum gift shop. (Nearly every important museum has a good selection of top-quality slides, cards, and prints at reasonable prices.)

Despite these restrictions, you can take good shots by holding your camera as still as possible. If you can lean against a wall, for instance, you become a tripod instead of a bipod. Placing your elbows on a flat surface also helps. Wait until you breathe out to take the picture (when you hold your breath, your body shakes more). Use a self-timer or a shutter release cable, which clicks the shutter more smoothly than your finger can. With these tricks, I get good pictures inside a museum at 1/30 of a second. Many new digital cameras use "image stabilization" to help in these situations.

Bracket shots when the lighting is tricky. The best way to get good shots in difficult lighting situations is to "bracket" your shots (take several different pictures of the same scene, slightly varying the exposure settings for each one). With a digital camera, you can simply delete the unsuccessful attempts, but this approach is even

Back lighting "puts an edge" on ice-cream lickers.

worthwhile with a film camera (one great shot is worth several in the garbage can). Automatic cameras usually meter properly up to 8 or 10 seconds, which makes night shots easy, though bracketing may still be necessary.

Traveling with a Video Camera

With video cameras getting better, smaller, and more affordable, more and more Americans are compromising a potentially footloose and fancy-free trip to shoot their own vacation videos. To me, a still camera is trouble enough. But thousands of amateur videographers happily seeing Europe through their viewfinders can't all be wrong.

Stow that Camera

When not using your camera or camcorder, keep it in a small, padded case inside your day bag. Many go through their entire trip with a camera strapped around their neck. That's a tourist's badge that puts a psychological wall between you and Europe. To locals, it just screams, "Yodel."

Airport Scanners

If you are still shooting with film, never check it in your luggage—carry it on. Even then, it's safest not to let undeveloped film go through a scanner (which can produce lines, color changes, and spots in the emulsion). Instead, place it in a clear plastic bag and request to have it "hand checked." Security will do it if you insist. So insist, politely.

Those of us with digital cameras are not entirely off the hook. Scanners emit magnetic and/or X-ray energy that can scramble blank memory cards. If your blank memory cards go through the scanner, it's smart to format them afterwards in your camera.

Once Back Home...

Relive your trip by organizing, editing, improving, and sharing your digital images.

First, come up with a system to keep your photos organized on your computer. You can simply create folders and subfolders, or you can use a more advanced photo-organizing program, such as Google's free Picasa (http://picasa.google.com), which also includes editing and sharing features.

Now it's time to improve your pictures. While a basic photo-editing program probably came with your camera, serious shutterbugs use Adobe Photoshop Elements (a basic, easy-to-use program for novices) or Adobe Photoshop CS5 (for more advanced work). You can't imagine how much better your photos will look until you use this software. Full disclosure: Virtually every photo in this book was improved by using Photoshop.

When it comes time to share your images, you have many options. You can make prints of your favorite shots (upload them or bring a CD of them to a photo-developing shop or major pharmacy). You can make a scrapbook the old-fashioned way (print your favorites and paste them into a book), or you can create and print your own custom-bound, professional-looking scrapbook (try www.mypublisher.com). Or you can share them with family and friends by posting them to your blog or social-networking site, or uploading them to a photo-sharing site (such as www.flickr.com, www.photobucket.com, www.snapfish.com, or Google's Picasa).

If you'd like to do a slideshow (to be viewed with a digital projector or on a TV), Google's Picasa and other photo-organizing programs can help you. Microsoft PowerPoint works as well for vacation photos as it does for dry financial reports (though you might need to shrink the slideshow's resolution to help it load and advance more quickly). When putting your slideshow together, be mindful that no one wants to suffer through an endless parade of lackluster and look-alike shots. Set a limit and prune your show until it bleeds. Keep it tight. Keep it moving. Leave the audience crying for more...not for mercy.

SPECIAL CONCERNS

Embracing new experiences is a lot easier to do if you're well-prepared. This chapter addresses those of you who have special concerns—solo female travelers, people of color, gay people, families, seniors, travelers with disabilities, and even big-bus tour members who want their independence. With assistance from people who share these concerns, I've assembled advice to help you make the most of your trip.

27. The Woman Traveling Alone

In my classes, women often ask, "Is it safe for a woman to travel alone through Europe?" This is a question best answered by women. Europe Through the Back Door managing editor Risa Laib wrote this chapter based on her solo experience and tips contributed from other travelers: Gail Morse, Peggy Roberts, Suzanne Hogsett, Bharti Kirchner, Kendra Roth, Gretchen Strauch, Ann Neel, and Heidi Sewell. Collectively, these women have more than a decade of solo travel experience in dozens of countries.

Note that many of these tips are equally useful for anyone traveling solo—male or female.

Every year, thousands of women, young and old, travel to Europe on their own. You're part of a grand group of adventurers. Traveling alone, you'll have the chance to make your own discoveries and the freedom to do what you like. It becomes habit-forming.

As a solo woman, you're more approachable than a couple or a solo man. You'll make friends from all over the world, and you'll have experiences that others can only envy. When you travel with a partner, you need to compromise, your focus narrows, and doors close. When you're on your own, you're open to the moment.

Traveling alone immerses you in Europe.

Your friends and family may try to talk you out of solo travel, worrying for your safety and regaling you with horror stories. Remind them—and yourself—that millions of women have traveled alone, and will continue to do so time and time again.

Solo travel is fun, challenging, vivid, and exhilarating. It's a gift from you to you. Prepared with good information and a positive attitude, you'll thrive in Europe. And you'll come home stronger and more confident than ever before. Here's how to make it happen.

Getting Inspired

Read exciting books written by solo women travelers about their experiences (try Dervla Murphy's outrageous adventures). For practical advice, read "how-to" travel guidebooks written by and for women (such as those listed on page 382).

Seek out other women travelers. Invite them out for dinner and pepper them with questions. Visit online forums for your destination and send email to other women for advice.

Take classes. A foreign-language course is ideal. Consider a class in European history, art history, or travel skills.

Keep up on international news so you can discuss local politics. Study a map of Europe—get to know your neighbors.

Pretend you're traveling alone before you ever leave America. Practice reaching out. Strike up conversations with people in the grocery line. Consciously become more adaptable. If it rains, marvel at the miracle.

Think hard about what you want to see and do. Create the vacation of your dreams.

Facing the Challenges

These are probably your biggest fears: vulnerability to theft, harassment, and loneliness. Take heart. You can tackle each of these concerns head-on. If you've traveled alone in America, you're more than prepared for Europe. In America, theft and harassment are especially scary because of their connection with assault. In Europe, you'll rarely, if ever, hear of violence. Theft is past tense (as in, "Where did my wallet go?"). As for experiencing harassment, you're far more likely to think, "I'm going to ditch this guy ASAP" than, "This guy is going to hurt me."

Loneliness is often the most common fear. But, remember, if you get lonely, you can do something about it.

For tips on women's health concerns and traveling while pregnant, see "Women's Health Issues" in Chapter 23: Staying Healthy.

Traveling Alone Without Feeling Lonely

Here are some tips on meeting people, eating out, and enjoying your evenings.

Meeting People: Stay in hostels and you'll have a built-in family (hostels are open to all ages). Or choose small pensions and B&Bs, where

Stay in hostels to swap tales and advice with other adventurous women.

the owners have time to talk with you. At most tourist sites, you'll meet more people in an hour than you would at home in a day. If you're feeling shy, cameras are good icebreakers; offer to take someone's picture with their camera.

Take your laundry and a deck of cards to a launderette and turn solitaire into gin rummy. You'll end up with a stack of clean clothes and interesting conversations.

If traveling with an MP3 player (such as an iPod), bring along a Y-jack and a second set of headphones to share your music.

Take a walking tour of a city (ask at the tourist information office). You'll learn about the town and meet other travelers, too. If you're staying in a hostel, check their boards—some hostels will arrange group tours.

It's easy to meet people on buses and trains. You're always welcome at a church service; stay for the coffee hour. When you meet locals who speak English, find out what they think—about anything.

Play with kids. Learn how to say "pretty baby" in the native language. If you play peek-a-boo with a baby or fold an origami bird for a kid, you'll make friends with the parents as well as the children.

Try pairing up with another solo traveler. Stay for a while in a small town or return to a city you enjoyed. The locals will remember you, you'll know the neighborhood, and it'll feel like home.

Eating Out: Consider quick and cheap alternatives to formal dining. Try a self-service café, a local-style fast-food restaurant, or a small ethnic eatery. Visit a supermarket deli and get a picnic to eat in the square or a park (families often frequent parks). Get a slice of pizza from a take-out shop and munch it as you walk along, people-watching and window-shopping. Eat in the members' kitchen of a hostel; you'll always have companions. Make it a potluck.

A restaurant feels cheerier at noon than at night. If you like company, eat in places so crowded and popular that you have to share a table or ask other single travelers if they'd like to join you. Assume that many couples would enjoy a third party at their dinner table to stoke the conversation.

If you eat alone, be busy. Use the time to learn more of the language. Practice your verbal skills with the waiter or waitress (when I asked a French waiter if he had kids, he proudly showed me a picture of his twin girls). Read a guidebook, a novel, or the *International Herald Tribune*. Do trip-planning, draw in your journal, or scrawl a few postcards to the folks back home.

Phrase book + big smile = plenty of friends

An afternoon at a café is a great way to get some writing done; for the cost of a beverage and a snack, you'll be granted more peace and privacy than at a public fountain or other open space.

Most countries have a type of dish or restaurant that's fun to experience with a group. When you run into tourists during the day, make plans for dinner. Invite them to join you for, say, a rijsttafel dinner in the Netherlands, a *smörgåsbord* in Scandinavia, a fondue in Switzerland, a paella feast in Spain, or a spaghetti feed in an Italian trattoria.

At Night: Experience the magic of European cities at night. Go for a walk along well-lit streets. With gelato in hand, enjoy the parade of people, busy shops, and illuminated monuments. Night or day, you're invariably safe when lots of people are around. Take advantage of the wealth of evening entertainment: concerts, movies, puppet shows, and folk dancing. Some cities offer tours after dark. You can see Paris by night on a river cruise.

During the evening, visit an Internet café. Send travel news to your friends and family. You'll find friendly answers in your inbox the next time you have the opportunity to get online.

If you like to stay in at night, get a room with a balcony overlooking a square. You'll have a front-row seat to the best show in town. An MP3 player loaded with familiar tunes can also help cheer you. Call home, a friend, your family. With cheap international phone cards, it's actually inexpensive. Read novels set in the country you're visiting. Learn to treasure solitude. Go early to bed, be early to rise. Shop at a lively morning market for fresh rolls and join the locals for coffee.

Protecting Yourself from Theft

As a woman, you're often perceived as being more vulnerable to theft than a man. Here are some tips to help keep you safe.

Carry a daypack instead of a purse. Leave expensive-looking jewelry at home. Keep your valuables in your money belt and tuck your wallet (containing only a day's worth of cash) in your front pocket. Keep your camera zipped up in your daypack. In crowded places (buses, subways, street markets), carry your daypack over your chest or firmly under one arm. Ask at your hotel or the tourist office if there's a neighborhood you should avoid, and mark it on your map.

Avoid tempting people into theft. Make sure valuables in your hotel room are kept out of sight. Wear your money belt when you sleep in hostels. When you're sightseeing, never set down anything of value (such as a camera, wallet, or railpass). Either hold it in your hand or keep it zipped away. If you're sitting down to rest, eat, or check your email, loop a strap of your daypack around your arm, leg, or chair leg. Remember, you're unlikely ever to be hurt by thieves. They want to separate you from your valuables efficiently and painlessly, without alerting you.

Dealing with Men

In small European towns, men are often more likely to speak English than women. If you never talk to men, you could miss out on a chance to learn about the country. So, by all means, talk to men. Just choose the men and choose the setting.

SPECIAL CONCERNS

In northern Europe, you won't draw any more attention from men than you do in America. In southern Europe, particularly in Italy, you'll get more attention than you're used to, but it's usually in the form of the "long look"—nothing you can't handle.

Be aware of cultural differences. In the Mediterranean world, when you smile and look a man in the eyes, it's often considered an invitation. Wear dark sunglasses and you can stare all you want.

Dress modestly to minimize attention from men. Take your cue from what the local women wear. In Italy, slacks and skirts (even short ones) are considered more proper than shorts.

Wear a real or fake wedding ring and carry a picture of a real or fake husband. There's no need to tell men that you're traveling alone, or whether you're

In Italy, sometimes blondes have more trouble.

actually married or single. Lie unhesitatingly. You're traveling with your husband. He's waiting for you at the hotel. He's a professional wrestler who retired from the sport for psychological reasons.

If you'd like to date a guy, meet him at a public place. Tell him you're staying at a hostel—you have a 10 p.m. curfew and 29 roommates. Better yet, bring a couple of your roommates along to meet him. After the introductions, let everyone know where you're going and when you'll return.

Handling Harassment

The way you handle harassment at home works in Europe, too.

In southern Europe, men may think that if you're alone, you're available. Keep your stride confident and look away from men trying to attract your attention. If a man comes too close to you, say "no" firmly in the local language. That's usually all it takes. Tell a slow learner that you want to be alone. Then ignore him. (Some women pretend they don't understand English by shrugging and mumbling a phrase in another language.)

If he's obnoxious, solicit the help of others. Ask people at a café or on the beach if you can join them for a while.

If he's well-meaning but too persistent, talk openly to him. Turn him into an ally. If he's a northern Italian, ask him about southern Italian men. Get advice from him on how you can avoid harassment when you travel farther south. After you elicit his "help," he'll be more like a brother than a bother to you.

Usually men are just seeing if you're interested. Only a few are difficult. If a man makes a lewd gesture, look away and leave the scene. Harassers don't want public attention drawn to their behavior. I went out for a walk in Madrid one evening, and a man came up much too close to me, scaring me. I shouted, "Get!" And he was gone. I think I scared him as much as he scared me. Ask a local woman for just the right thing to say to embarrass jerks. Learn how to say it, loudly. (The Rick Steves' Phrase Books have a whole section on phrases handy for women.)

If you feel like you're being followed, trust your instincts. Don't worry about overreacting or seeming foolish. Forget ladylike behavior— start screaming and acting crazy if the situation warrants it. Or head to the nearest hotel and chat up the person behind the desk until your would-be admirer moves on. Ask the hotelier to call you a cab to take you to your own hotel, hostel, or B&B.

If you feel the need to carry mace, take a self-defense class instead. Mace will be confiscated at the airport, but knowledge and confidence are yours to keep. And, remember, the best self-defense is common sense.

Traveling Smart

Create conditions that are likely to turn out in your favor. By following these tips, you'll have a safer, smoother, more enjoyable trip.

Be self-reliant so that you don't need to depend on anybody unless you want to. Always carry cash, food, water, a map, a guidebook, and a phrase book. When you need help, ask another woman or a family.

When you use cash machines, withdraw cash during the day on a busy street, not at night when it's dark with too few people around.

Walk purposefully with your head up. Look like you know where you're going. Use landmarks (such as church steeples) to navigate. If you get lost in an unfriendly neighborhood, go into a restaurant or store to ask for directions or to study your map.

Learn enough of the language to get by. With a few hours' work you'll know more than most tourists and be better prepared to deal with whatever situation arises. At a bus station in Turkey, I witnessed a female tourist repeatedly asking in English, louder and louder, "When does the bus leave?" The frustrated ticket clerk kept answering her in Turkish, "Now, now, now!" If you know even just a little of the language, you'll

SPECIAL CONCERNS

Resources for the Woman Traveling Alone

Travel books for women fall into three camps: practical advice, tales from the road, and stories to inspire you. While there are hundreds of books to choose from, here are some classics and best sellers to get you started.

Thalia Zepatos' *A Journey of One's Own: Uncommon Advice for the Independent Woman Traveler* delivers recommendations on everything from how to trek in Nepal to how to handle sexual harassment. *Safety and Security for Women Who Travel*, by Sheila Swan and Peter Laufer, offers tips on self-protection. *Traveling Solo: Advice and Ideas for More than 250 Great Vacations*, by Eleanor Berman, has advice on specific destinations for solo travelers.

If reading travelogues will inspire you to make your solo trip a reality, consider *A Woman's World: True Life Stories of World Travel; Gutsy Women: Travel Tips and Wisdom for the Road;* and *A Woman's Europe: True Stories,* all edited by Marybeth Bond. *Expat: Women's True Tales of Life Abroad* gives readers a glimpse of what it means to head to a new country for more than just a vacation. *A Woman Alone: Travel Tales from Around the Globe* has essays on travel in exotic locations. For humorous tales about traveling as a woman, try *The Unsavvy Traveler: Women's Comic Tales of Catastrophe; Sand in My Bra and Other Misadventures: Funny Women Write from the Road;* and its sequels: *More Sand in My Bra, Whose Panties Are These?,* and *The Thong Also Rises.*

There's an entire cottage industry of travel memoirs by women describing a journey that changed their lives forever. These titles, unlike the collections of essays above, follow one person's story throughout the length of the book. The most famous of these is prob-

make it much easier on yourself and those around you.

Before you leave a city, consider visiting the train or bus station you're going to leave from, so you'll know where it is, how long it takes to reach it, and what services it has. Note if the station seems clean, well-lit, and safe. Reconfirm your departure time.

Skip hitchhiking. But if you absolutely have to hitch, choose people to ask, instead of being chosen. Try your luck at a gas station, restaurant, on a ferry, or in the parking lot of a tourist attraction. Ideally, pair up with another traveler.

When taking the train, avoid staying in empty compartments, especially at night. Rent a *couchette* for overnight trains. For about $32, you'll stay with like-minded roommates in a compartment you can lock, in a

ably Frances Mayes' *Under the Tuscan Sun,* which is so popular that she wrote a sequel, *Bella Tuscany: The Sweet Life in Italy.* Mayes writes about other European destinations in *A Year in the World: Journeys of a Passionate Traveller.* Other reader favorites include *Eat, Pray, Love: One Woman's Search for Everything Across Italy, India, and Indonesia* (Elizabeth Gilbert); *Long Ago in France: The Years in Dijon* (M. F. K. Fisher); *Tales of a Female Nomad: Living at Large in the World* (Rita Golden Gelman); *Almost French: Love and a New Life in Paris* (Sarah Turnbull); *Without Reservations: The Travels of an Independent Woman* and *Educating Alice: Adventures of a Curious Woman* (both by Alice Steinbach); and *A Thousand Days in Venice* and *A Thousand Days in Tuscany* (both by Marlena De Blasi). For a change of pace from books, seek out the 2000 Italian film *Bread and Tulips* (Pane e Tulipani), an inspiring story of a woman who heads to Venice—solo—and finds her destiny.

As for online resources, check out *Journeywoman,* a site where women share travel tips (www.journeywoman.com), and take a look at my Graffiti Wall to see what other women travelers say (www.ricksteves.com/graffiti).

car monitored by an attendant. You'll wake reasonably rested with your belongings intact.

It's possible to ask for a female roommate on overnight trains. (You'll have better luck if the train isn't crowded.) Some countries, such as Spain, are better about accommodating these requests than others. In France, a one-bed compartment closest to the conductor is set aside for women, but it's the most expensive type of accommodation. In general, ask what the options are, make the request to bunk with other women, and hope for the best—but don't count on it.

If you're departing late at night and the bus or train station is sketchy, ask your B&B owner if you can hang out in their breakfast room—generally untouched in the evening—until you need to leave for the station.

Cafés, including busy Internet cafés with long hours, can also be a better spot to kill time than the train station waiting room.

If you're not fluent in the language, accept the fact that you won't always know what's going on. There's a reason why the Greek bus driver drops you off in the middle of nowhere. It's a transfer point, and another bus will come along in a few minutes. You'll often discover that the locals are looking out for you.

The same good judgment you use at home applies to Europe. Start out cautious and figure out as you travel what feels safe to you.

Treat yourself right—get enough rest, healthy food, and exercise. Walking is a great way to combine exercise and sightseeing. I've jogged alone in cities and parks throughout Europe without any problems. If a neighborhood looks seedy, head off in another direction.

Relax. There are other trains, other buses, other cities, other people. If one thing doesn't work out, something else will. Thrive on optimism.

Have a grand adventure!

28. People of Color

People who are not of European descent might be concerned about how they'll be treated abroad. In short, does it matter that you look different from most Europeans? I've collected the following advice from a wide range of people of color who have lived or traveled extensively in Europe.

First, it's helpful to keep in mind the huge historical and cultural differences between the US and Europe—especially relating to race relations. One-third of the US population is non-white, compared to less than 5 percent of people living in Europe.

Despite this racial homogeneity, some parts of Europe do have a long history of ethnic minorities. Colonial powers such as Great Britain and the Netherlands have seen a steady influx of transplants from their overseas holdings for many centuries. But in the decades since World War II—as Europe has built a new prosperity, and immigrants have arrived seeking a better life—Europe has become much more ethnically diverse.

As immigrants—both new and old, and from every corner of the world (mostly Africa, the Middle East, the Caribbean, and South America)—have come to Europe, white Europeans have often struggled to adapt. Progress can be slow. Some white Europeans are frustrated by large numbers of immigrants—and now their descendants—who, they claim, stick together in tight communities, cling to the culture of their homeland, and are slow to adopt European culture. The immigrants would likely counter that they've found few opportunities to integrate with their European neighbors. Just as in the US, immigrants are sometimes perceived as challenging lifelong residents for jobs, or as taking advantage of the welfare system. Another thorny issue is the friction between European Christianity and the Islamic faith of many immigrants. But the minority group subject to the most overt racism in Europe isn't made up of new immigrants at all: It's the Roma (or Gypsies). For centuries, white Europeans have regarded this population—which likely shares ancestors with the people of today's India—with suspicion and fear. This is especially pervasive in Eastern Europe and in Italy, which have large numbers of Roma.

It's possible for Americans of color to be mistaken for an immigrant or a Roma—particularly in areas where minorities are more common

(such as French cities with large African communities). But many Europeans can spot Americans a mile away, regardless of their skin color. And, because American culture is pervasive worldwide, any stereotypes Europeans might have about your race are likely formed by our own popular culture—for example, by actors, musicians, athletes, and characters on popular TV shows. African American travelers report that the overseas popularity of President Obama has only improved their experience in Europe.

Travelers of color and mixed-race couples tell me that their most common source of discomfort in Europe is being stared at. While this might seem to indicate disapproval (as it could in some parts of the US), consider the more likely possibility that it's just a combination of curiosity and impoliteness. Put simply, for many Europeans, you're just not who they're used to seeing. Their response to a person of color likely isn't hostility...but naiveté. (One traveler explained that this isn't racism, but "rarism"—Europeans reacting not to one's race, but to one's rarity.)

Because the US has grappled more directly with its race issues, many Americans at least pay lip service to a "political correctness" that helps insulate minorities from overtly hateful speech. Europeans tend to be more opinionated and blunt, and aren't shy about voicing sweeping

SPECIAL CONCERNS

generalizations about any topic—including race. Many travelers find this jarring and hurtful, while some consider it weirdly refreshing ("at least it's out in the open").

Travelers of color report being frustrated by racial profiling, particularly at border crossings or airport security. (One traveler speculated that this might come from the desire to prevent immigrants from entering the country and competing with natives for jobs.) It's possible you'll be more closely scrutinized than other travelers, before being allowed to continue on your way.

These trends obviously vary greatly by country and by region, but in most places, you'll probably be treated no worse than you would be in the US. Very traditional small towns are less diverse, and may be less welcoming, than big, cosmopolitan cities.

It can also help to consider the country's politics and history. Remember, former colonial powers—such as the Netherlands, Portugal, and Great Britain—are no strangers to immigrants from their African, Middle Eastern, Asian, Caribbean, and South American former colonies. This can be both good (because locals accustomed to this diversity might be more accepting of people who look different)...and bad (some locals may have formed negative stereotypes about certain groups). In some countries, such as Austria and France, immigration issues are a hot-button political topic—dividing the populace and making the person on the street more tuned in to race issues.

The situation is reversed in areas that have a very limited experience with people of color, such as the former communist countries in Eastern Europe. In these places, you might find more ignorance and insensitivity, but fewer hard-and-fast negative stereotypes.

If you're concerned about how you'll be treated in a specific destination, ask fellow travelers of color what their experiences were there. An excellent resource for African Americans, including destination-specific reports from several travelers, is www.blacktravels.com. Or check out the "Minority Travelers' Forum" section on my online Graffiti Wall (www.ricksteves.com/graffiti).

Will you encounter unfriendliness in your travels? Definitely. Everyone does. But be careful not to over-attribute grumpiness to racism—again, keep in mind the vast difference in cultural context. In the words of one traveler of color: "I think we're more likely to interpret bad behavior from non-Americans as being racist because of our history with white Americans. Often their impatience is just because we're American and we're clueless about other people's cultures and practices."

No matter your race, the best advice for any traveler is to have a positive attitude. Focus on all the nice Europeans you'll meet, rather than the few unenlightened exceptions. If you feel uncomfortable or mistreated, head somewhere else. And remember that most Europeans are as interested in learning about you as you are in learning about them.

29. Gay Travelers

First-time travel can be intimidating—and maybe even more so as a gay man, lesbian, or same-sex couple. Will you be harassed, denied a room at a hotel, or made to feel uncomfortable and unsafe?

Fortunately, Europe is in many ways *more* supportive than the US when it comes to gay rights. The European Union specifically includes gay and lesbian citizens in its antidiscrimination laws, and European countries generally don't prohibit gay personnel from serving in the military on the basis of their sexuality.

The Netherlands—and Amsterdam in particular—has offered equal rights to gay men and lesbians for decades. The world's first legal marriage for a gay couple occurred in Amsterdam in 2001.

The Netherlands is the strongest example of an overall rule of thumb: Attitudes about homosexuality are more accepting in northern Europe, and less so in the south, east, and/or in countries with strong conservative religious traditions. You'll find more tolerance in the cities than in rural areas.

In progressive Amsterdam, this "Homomonument"—shaped like a giant pink triangle—honors all gay men and lesbians who have been persecuted for their homosexuality.

Another useful guideline: Countries with the most legal rights for gays and lesbians are also most likely to be welcoming. If a country has laws explicitly covering gay rights and allowing for gay unions, you can expect to feel more comfortable and relaxed during your visit, in everything from dealing with hoteliers to being recognized as partners by doctors in the emergency room. Take the time to do a little bit of online research into various destinations so you'll know what to expect. For a handy country-by-country checklist, go to www.wikipedia.org and search for "LGBT rights in Europe."

In general, the best countries for gay rights—and for gay travelers—are the Netherlands, Belgium, Scandinavia (especially Denmark), and Great Britain (particularly London), as well as Germany, Switzerland, and cities in Spain and Portugal.

In other countries, the record is mixed, with fewer legal rights. Austria has a vibrant gay scene in its cities, while in Ireland—a conservative Catholic country through most of the 20th century—readers report a generally welcoming environment even in country B&Bs. Paris has a gay mayor and a gay neighborhood (the Marais), but many rural French communities adhere to an unspoken "don't ask, don't tell" ideology of not flaunting your sexuality. Italy is a similar story of general acceptance but raised eyebrows—and possibly denied rooms—in rural areas and in the south. Some of Greece's islands are well-known gay destinations. Slovenia and Croatia have both legalized civil unions between same-sex couples, and Eastern European capitals such as Prague and Budapest have liberal attitudes on par with what you'll find in big Western European cities.

But the farther east you venture in the former Soviet Bloc, the less progressive things become. Particularly in rural areas of Eastern Europe, responses range from reasonably accepting to outright hostile. For example, Poland's recently deceased president called homosexuality "unnatural," and Serbia has banned gay unions. Even farther east, in places such as Romania, laws outlawing homosexuality were lifted in recent decades, but acceptance lags behind. Proceed with caution.

For every traveler, straight or gay, respect brings respect. Say "please" and "thank you" in the native language when talking with your B&B owner, and you may find that what initially seemed like surliness has faded—and had nothing to do with your request for a two-person bed. Some readers prefer to be up front when they're making a booking, specifying that they are a gay or lesbian couple, while others prefer to keep it private and hope for the best.

Bring a good guidebook. You can supplement your resources with gay-themed materials and research. Many publishers produce guidebooks specifically written for gay travelers, including Frommer's and Damron. Other books routinely cover gay nightlife even if they're not gay-themed, especially city guides like the *Time Out* series. For recommendations online, try websites such as www.outtraveler.com and www.purpleroofs.com. Lesbian couples can review this book's Chapter 27: The Woman Traveling Alone, since much of the same advice applies.

But what will your experience *really* be like as you travel? Before you go, ask other gay or lesbian friends about their European experiences. If you'll be traveling as a couple, sit down one night over dinner to discuss the kind of trip you want to have. Are you comfortable holding hands and being affectionate in public? When making reservations or introductions, will you identify each other as a "partner," "spouse," or "friend"? (Having a ready response is better than stumbling out your reply on the spot.) Will you stay in mostly gay neighborhoods and establishments? Just working through these things ahead of time can allay a lot of your concerns.

Consider your own comfort level as you plan your trip. Once in Europe, stay aware of your surroundings, and do what feels safe. If you run into trouble, the simplest solution is often just to move on. For example, if you get "attitude" from a waiter—whether you're alone or with your partner—it's often just a good idea to pack up and try another restaurant. Life is too short to hassle with those who treat you badly, whatever the circumstance, especially on your vacation.

When you get home, share your experiences with other gay and lesbian travelers. Go to my Graffiti Wall, where you can post your tips and stories online (www.ricksteves.com/graffiti).

Don't let your worries limit what you're there to see. Trust your instincts, but most of all—travel. The world is waiting for you.

30. Family Travel

Taking Your Children to Europe

European families, like their American counterparts, enjoy traveling. You'll find more and more kids' menus, hotel playrooms, and kids-go-crazy zones at freeway rest stops all over Europe. Your child will be your ticket to countless conversations. Traveling with an infant or toddler can be challenging, but parents with a babe-in-arms will generally be offered a seat on crowded buses, and sometimes be allowed to go to the front of the line at museums.

Grade-school kids are often the easiest travelers, provided you schedule some kid-friendly activities every day. They're happiest staying

Connecting with European families can be a highlight of a family vacation abroad.

in rural places with swimming pools and grassy fields to run around in.

High-schoolers feel that summer break is a vacation they've earned. If this European trip is not *their* trip, you become the enemy. They crave the bright lights and action of the big city. Ask for their help. Kids can get excited about a vacation if they're involved in the planning stages. Consider your child's suggestions and make real concessions. "Europe's greatest collection of white-knuckle rides" in Blackpool might be more fun than another ruined abbey.

My kids are young adults now, but I remember what it was like taking them to Europe at various ages. In this chapter, I've included the lessons I've learned from parenting in Europe, along with tips collected from readers on my website's Graffiti Wall (www.ricksteves.com/graffiti).

International adventure is a great foundation for a mountain of memories. The key to a successful family trip is making everyone happy, including the parents.

Planning

You'll need the proper documents. Even babies need passports. If you're traveling with a child who isn't yours (say, a niece or grandson), bring

along a signed, notarized document from the parent(s) to prove to authorities that you have permission to take the child on a trip.

It's a good idea to take extra passport photos with you. Since infants and toddlers change so quickly, carry photos that were taken for the passport, as well as ones taken close to your departure date. For children at any age, take an official copy of his or her birth certificate, along with a photocopy of the child's passport. Keep these separate from your passports—these documents will allow

Resources for Traveling with Kids in Europe

Common sense and lessons learned from day trips at home are your best sources of information. *Take Your Kids to Europe* is full of practical, concrete lessons from firsthand family-travel experience, and the only good book I've seen for those traveling with kids ages 6–16 (by Cynthia Harriman, Globe Pequot Press, 8th edition, 2007). The best book I've found on traveling with infants is Lonely Planet's *Travel with Children* (5th edition, 2009), which covers travel worldwide, including Europe. For families interested in hiking, biking, and sailing abroad, pick up *Adventuring with Children: An Inspirational Guide to World Travel and the Outdoors* (by Nan Jeffrey, Avalon House, 1995). Cadogan offers many worthwhile books in its Take the Kids series, including books on London, Paris, Ireland, and more. Also consider Fodor's *Around London with Kids, Around Paris with Kids, Around Rome with Kids,* and *Family Adventures.* For solo parents, there's Brenda Elwell's *Single Parent Travel Handbook* (Globalbrenda Publishing, 2002).

What's more fun: A museum or Disneyland Paris?

you to get a replacement passport for your child quickly and easily.

Most parents hold onto their kids' passports, but if you have older children that will be out on their own, you might get them a money belt or neck pouch for carrying their cash and ID.

You'll find that because you are in a foreign country, your kids are more likely to stick close to you. But if you're worried about your younger children getting lost, consider ordering dog tags with contact information (see www.dogtagsonline.com). Give each child a business card from your hotel so they have local contact information. Another option is an ID Inside wristband, with a hidden pocket that holds a disposable waterproof ID card (www.id-inside.com). You can easily switch out the ID card, updating your hotel name and contact information as you travel. Or try the Lost & Found Temporary Tattoo, a washable tattoo with a space for you to write a contact phone number (www.tattooswithapurpose.com).

At home, encourage your kids to learn about the countries, cities, sights, and people they'll be visiting. Even simple Wikipedia articles can provide enough background to pique a child's curiosity. Read books such as *The Diary of Anne Frank* for Amsterdam or *The Thief Lord* for Venice. Watch movies together, such as *The Sound of Music* for Salzburg, *The Red Balloon* for Paris, or *The Secret of Roan Inish* for Ireland. Your hometown library can be a great resource for age-appropriate books and movies.

Get a jump on foreign phrases, learning the top 20 or so before you leave home. Capitalize on whatever hobbies your kids have or games they play that may relate to the history of the places you're visiting, especially if your family has some sort of connection to the "old country." Give them the chance to try out foreign specialties in advance by eating at ethnic restaurants, or get a cookbook and make meals together at home. Many US cities host celebrations of different cultures—look for Greek, French, Italian, Hungarian, or other European festivals in your town for your family to enjoy.

What to Bring

The amount of gear you need depends on the age of your child. Since a baby on the road requires a lot of equipment, the key to happiness is a rental car or a long stay in one place. If you're visiting friends or family, give them ample notice, and they may be able to borrow a car seat, stroller, and travel crib so you won't have to pack it. If you have older kids, let them know they will be pulling their own roll-aboard luggage through airports and down cobblestone streets. Pack as light as you can, but if you figure you'll need it (based on your experience taking trips near home), trust your judgment.

For young kids, it's helpful to have a **stroller** and a baby **backpack.** The light umbrella strollers can easily navigate cobblestones—just make sure you spend a little extra on a solidly built one that can take the bumps, such as Peg Pérego (www.pegperego.com) or Maclaren (www.maclaren baby.com). Backpacks are great if you need to keep your hands free, and when you're traveling on subways and buses. Prepare to tote more than a tot. A combo purse/diaper bag with shoulder straps is ideal. You

SPECIAL CONCERNS

can always stow it in your stroller's basket if you tire of carrying it yourself. Be on guard: Purse snatchers target parents (especially while busy and off-guard, as when changing diapers).

Some parents bring a **travel bed,** although hotels can usually supply a crib (ask in advance when you reserve the room). One travel model—PeaPod Plus—is a pop-up tent with an air mattress, sleeping bag, and hand pump (www.kidco.com). Other parents use a portable playpen as a bed for their child. Bringing a travel bed means your child never has to sleep in a "strange" bed—avoiding possible sleeping problems. However, carting around a travel bed or playpen makes more sense if you'll be traveling by car.

Drivers should bring a **car seat,** buy one in Europe, or see if the car-rental company can provide one (usually the most expensive option). Pack along a car-seat clip in case you need to secure the car seat to the shoulder-strap seat belt. In addition to being required safety equipment while driving, a car seat can be a stress-saver when traveling by plane, train, or bus. Although it may seem like a bulky carry-on, a car seat is more comfortable for your child to sit in than a seat designed for an adult, and is a familiar place for a nap. Kids are used to car seats and know how to behave in them.

If your child uses **formula,** consider bringing your own supply—the formula offerings in most of Europe are very different from those at home. Before you fly away, be sure you've packed acetaminophen, diaper rash cream, a thermometer, and any special medications your baby may need (keeping in mind the air travel rules about liquids—see "What Can I Carry On?" on page 86).

For older kids, today's technology can make the difference between a dream trip and a nightmare. Splurge for a portable **DVD player** or **iPod.** Load it with movies and TV shows, and get a splitter so two kids can watch at the same time. There's nothing like a favorite show to help calm your kids before bedtime. A **Nintendo DS** or other handheld game system can fill hours traveling between destinations. Consider giving each of your kids his or her own **digital camera** or cheap **video camera.** They can take pictures and make movies from their own perspective. Along with their journals, it will help them remember more about the trip. Bring the family **laptop** or **netbook;** you'll find that your teens will use it (more than you) to stay in touch with friends back home.

You can easily buy toys and sports equipment in Europe. For the athletic child, a Whiffle ball and bat guarantee hours of amusement with newfound friends. A rubber ball lets kids play soccer on foreign turf. When you're in France or Italy, consider purchasing a set of *boules* or *pétanque* balls (called *bocce* in Italy); this popular form of outdoor bowling is played on public squares. (The balls are heavy, though, so only get them if you're staying in one place or traveling by car.)

For quiet time in the hotel room, buy a set of Legos once you're in Europe—the popular building blocks are excitingly different from those found in the US. A small indoor Frisbee is fun.

But don't overdo it. One family of four reported taking three suitcases, two backpacks, and a stroller to Spain. European taxis are much smaller than American ones, so every time they traveled between cities, they had to use two taxis to transfer to the airport or train station. Even with kids, you can pack light. Make the older ones carry their own bags. Do laundry more often. If there's a sudden cold snap, buy an extra sweater in Europe rather than bringing one along.

In the Air

Your cute gurgling baby might become an airborne Antichrist as soon as the seat-belt light goes off. You'll pay 10 percent of the ticket cost to take a child under the age of two on your lap for an international flight. The child doesn't get a seat, but many airlines have baby perks for moms and dads who request them in advance—roomier bulkhead seats, hang-from-the-ceiling bassinets, and baby meals. (Note, however, that many child-safety experts advise against holding a baby in your lap on the plane, and suggest that you buy a ticket and strap your child into his or her car seat instead.)

After age two, a child's ticket typically costs 60–80 percent of the adult fare—a major financial ouchie (some sale fares do not allow any discounts for kids). From age 12 on, kids pay full fare.

For long flights, choose a red-eye when possible so your child (and hopefully you) can sleep while you travel. Pick flights with few connections; nonstop works best. Decide if you want to sit near the aisle or window. A window seat gives your active child only one escape route, plus the added entertainment of the window. However, a toddler who needs frequent diaper changes and sits quietly may be more comfortable by the aisle.

Watching the in-flight movie (if kid-appropriate) can help pass a few hours in the air.

Tire out your tykes before boarding the plane. If you fly at night, consider having your child skip that afternoon's nap. While you're waiting to board, get your kids up and moving as much as possible. Finally, when you're on the plane and it's time for sleep, follow normal bedtime routines. Change your child into pajamas, tuck her in with a blanket, and read a story or two.

Be prepared. The batteries might go out on your DVD player or iPod. For younger kids, make sure to have lots of toys and surprises, such as a Mini Slinky or stickers. Bring snacks (such as raisins and granola bars), activity supplies (washable markers, paper, various activity books—mazes, connect-the-dots, Mad Libs), books for reading, and small stuffed toys.

Be warned—jet lag can be kiddie purgatory. If you can tolerate some—OK, maybe a lot of—crankiness on the first day, keep young children awake until a reasonable bedtime. After junior passes out from exhaustion, hopefully the whole family will sleep through the night and wake up when the locals do. Take it easy at the beginning (maybe even starting with a rural destination), allowing a couple of low-impact days to get over jet lag.

Lodging

Some kids do better staying in an **apartment or house** than in a hotel. Self-catering flats rented by the week or two-week period, such as *gîtes* in France and villas in Italy, give a family a home on the road. To cut costs, try home-sharing services that let you swap houses with a European family (see page 237; for apartment rentals, see page 222). Many families prefer settling down this way and side-tripping from a home base. Not only is it cheaper, but you get to spend time together cooking, watching movies, and just hanging out. It's a cultural experience just to see European TV together. But be aware that European standards on televised sex and nudity are much more relaxed than in the US; you might stumble on some uncensored movies, or even soft-core porn, next to the Nickelodeon channel.

If you're traveling with older kids, consider **hostels.** Families can hostel very cheaply, especially in high-priced Scandinavia. Family membership cards are inexpensive, and there's no age limit. Many hostels

In very tight European hotel rooms, you might have to stow your kids in the closet...

have "members' kitchens" where the family can cook and eat for the price of groceries. Some hostels also offer family rooms.

If your kids love camping, rent a **camper van or small RV.** Kids and campgrounds—with swings, slides, and plenty of friends—mix wonderfully. Suddenly your family and the French kids over at the next tent are best buddies (see page 232).

Most **hotels,** especially those catering to business travelers, have large family rooms. London's big, budget chain hotels allow two kids to sleep for free in their already reasonably priced rooms. A swimming pool is a bonus at these chain hotels.

In some countries, you may need to know the necessary phrases to communicate your needs. If you have a family of four and your children are young, request a triple room plus a small extra child's bed. Traveling with teenagers, you may need two rooms: a double (one big bed) and a twin (a room with two single beds). In much of Europe, a "double" bed is actually two twins put together. These can easily be separated.

Be careful about staying in small hotels or B&Bs with a baby. If your child wakes up in the middle of the night, you're going to wake up everybody else. Some B&Bs won't take even children, or impose an age limit (such as no kids under 8); ask before booking.

...or, better yet, ask for an extra bed.

Choosing lodging close to your daytime activities is smart in case your little traveler needs to return for a nap or supplies. Request quiet rooms away from the street and bar downstairs. If your child is used to sleeping in his or her own space, look for rooms with a partition, large closet, or other area in which you can separate your child when it's bedtime (baby can even sleep in the bathroom).

If you have young children, childproof the room immediately on arrival. A roll of masking tape makes quick work of electrical outlets. Place anything breakable up out of reach. Proprietors are generally helpful to considerate and undemanding parents.

With a toddler, budget extra to get a bath in your room—a practical need and a fun diversion. Some showers have a 6-inch-tall "drain extension" and a high lip to create a kid-friendly bathing puddle.

Food

Keep children fed. Even with a big breakfast, don't expect them to "power through" to a late lunch. A short snack break will help in the long run.

Find the most scenic perch for your picnic.

Make sure to pack along or stop to buy high-quality food as often as possible—a real sandwich, pasta, or yogurt.

Buying bread, cheese, fruit, and drinks in the morning means you can picnic anytime, anywhere. Kids find that foreign grocery stores are an adventure, so bring them along and let them help shop. Get take-away food from one of the many (usually cheap) food stands in big cities— French fries, bratwurst or *Currywurst*, crêpes, or a sandwich.

Eat gelato, croissants, or chocolate every day (gelato should be twice a day)—whatever is a "specialty" treat of the country you are in. It's a cultural experience and a great way to get off your feet and take a break.

At home, you may try to avoid bribes, but the promise of a treat can make a huge difference to everyone's cooperation when you're out and about—and don't have space for a "time out."

An occasional Big Mac or Whopper between all the bratwurst and kraut helps keep the family happy. You'll get your food relatively quickly, and the kids will almost always eat hamburgers, fries, or chicken nuggets. As much as adults love eating at European restaurants, kids get restless. The pacing is slow, and it can be stressful. Plan ahead and bring something for your child to do while waiting for dinner (or the check) to arrive.

Eat dinner early (around 6–7 p.m.) to miss the romantic crowd. Skip the famous places. Look instead for relaxed cafés or pubs (kids are welcome, though sometimes restricted to the restaurant section or courtyard area). Don't expect high chairs to be available; use your stroller in a pinch.

In restaurants (or anywhere), if your infant is making a disruptive fuss, apologetically say the local word for "teeth" (*dientes* in Spanish, *dents* in French, *denti* in Italian, *Zähne* in German), and annoyed people will become sympathetic.

At fancier hotels, you can get babysitters, usually from professional agencies. The service is expensive but worth the splurge when you crave a leisurely, peaceful evening out.

Since many restaurants don't have high chairs, you might have to do a little juggling at mealtime.

Activities

Review the day's plan at breakfast with the entire family. It should always include a kid-friendly activity. Hands-on tours, from cheesemaking to chocolate factories, keep kids engaged. Go to sports or cultural events, but don't insist on staying for the entire event.

Kids need plenty of exercise. Allow time for a few extra runs on the luge. Small towns often have great public swimming pools, and big cities have recreation centers or water parks (check out Paris' Aquaboulevard). Mountain bikes are easily rentable (with helmets), suddenly making the Alps cool. Local TIs can help you dig up these treats.

Let your kids make decisions: choosing lunch spots, deciding which stores to visit. (The cheapest toy selection is usually in the large department stores.) Turn your kid into your personal tour guide and navigator. If you use my guidebooks, have your child lead you on

Hands-on activities, such as this candlemaking demonstration, bring museums to life for kids.

my self-guided walks and museum tours.

Europe is full of kiddie discounts, but you have to ask. Many activities—most importantly train rides—are free for infants and toddlers. School-age children often fall into the reduced fare category, but sometimes they ride free, too. Some museums are free for kids under a certain age. When adults have to pay to eat breakfast at hotels, their kids sometimes eat free—worth a whole lot of money, especially when you're in Scandinavia.

Since a trip is a splurge for the parents, the kids should enjoy a larger allowance, too. Provide ample money and ask your kids to buy their own treats, *gelati*, postcards, and trinkets within that daily budget. In exchange for the extra allowance, require them to keep a daily journal or scrapbook. Expect older kids to carry and use the currency. If you don't want your younger child to carry cash, Mom or Dad can be the "banker" and keep a tally of expenses.

Help your kids collect and process their observations. If you buy the actual journal at your first stop, it becomes a fun souvenir in itself. Kids like cool books—pay for a nice one. The journal is important, and it should feel that way. Encourage the kids to record more than just a trip log...collect feelings, smells, tastes, reactions to cultural differences, and so on. Grade-school kids enjoy pasting in ticket stubs or drawing pictures of things they've seen.

Young kids will do better in museums if you let them buy postcards in the gift shop first and then have a scavenger hunt to find the artwork on their postcards. "I spy"

Journaling trip experiences is fun for kids—and lets them create a personalized souvenir.

games are also a fun way to get the kids to pay attention when they start to get bored. Have the younger ones count how many babies they can find in all the paintings in the room—or dogs, or crowns. Follow my crowd-beating tips on easy entry to major sights—kids despise long lines even more than you do (see page 356).

Older kids enjoy audioguides available at the museum or my free podcasts (www.ricksteves.com/audiotours). Audioguides let your kids feel independent in their sightseeing. They also allow you a few moments to learn about the artwork, too.

SPECIAL CONCERNS

The Steves Kids Vote on Britain's Best and Worst

Imagine being a teenager forced to spend a big part of your summer vacation with robo-tourist Rick Steves (alias Dad). Jackie and Andy did that a while ago. What were the highlights? Here are the results of the post-trip interview:

Best City: Blackpool—England's white-knuckle ride capital! The Pepsi Max Big One (one of the world's fastest and highest roller coasters) is still the best. A tip: Avoid the old wooden-framed rides. They're too jerky for parents.

Best Nature Experience: Horseback riding through the Cotswolds with a guide who'll teach you to trot (www.cotswoldsriding.co.uk). Wear long pants. One hour is plenty.

Types of Tours: Open-deck bus tours are good for picnic lunches with a moving view. At museums, audioguide tours are nice because you can pick and choose what you want to learn about.

Worst Food: The "black pudding" that so many B&B people want you to try for breakfast...it's a gooey sausage made of curdled blood.

Best New Food: Chocolate-covered digestive biscuits and vinegar on chips (that's British for "French fries").

Most Boring Tour: The Beatles tour in Liverpool: Most kids couldn't care less about where Paul McCartney went to grade school or a place called Strawberry Fields.

Try a guided walking tour. Some parents are leery of group tours because they're afraid their kids will be the most disruptive members. But your kids will listen to a guide more than they will listen to you. Being in a group of adults can tone down even the wildest child.

Audioguides can keep kids engaged and entertained at museums and on bus tours.

Funniest Activity: The Bizarre Bath walking tour is two hours of jokes and not a bit of history. It's irreverent and dirty—but in a way that parents think is OK for kids.

Best Activities: Leisure (LEZH-ur) Centres in almost every town have good swimming pools. Some B&Bs have DVD and/ or video players and movie libraries. Other B&Bs have a rental place nearby that rents to their guests. Checking email and surfing the Web at Internet cafés is fun.

Best Theater: Shakespeare's Globe in London. First tour the theater to learn about how and why it was built like the original from 1600. Then buy cheap "groundling" tickets to see the actual play right up front, with your elbows on the stage. The actors involve the audience...especially the groundlings.

Most Interesting Demonstrations: The precision slate-splitting demonstration at the slate mines in North Wales. The medieval knight at the Tower of London who explained his armor and then demonstrated medieval sword fighting tactics—nearly killing his squire.

Consider visiting an amusement park as an end-of-trip reward—the promise of Legoland in Denmark, Blackpool in England, or Disneyland Paris can keep your kids motoring through the more mundane attractions. In parks, look for puppet shows, pony rides, merry-go-rounds, small zoos, or playgrounds. Paris's Luxembourg Gardens is renowned for its toy sailboat rentals at the main pond (and they'll even let your kids play on the grass—usually a no-no at French parks).

At least every other day, take an extended break. Return to your hotel or apartment after lunch for two hours for napping, reading, or listening to the iPod. What you lose in sightseeing time you will gain in energy levels.

It can be hard for kids to hang around grown-ups all day, so help your kids connect with other children. In hot climates, kids hang out on the squares (in cities and villages alike) when the temperature begins to cool in the late afternoon, often staying until late in the evening. Take your children to the European nightspots to observe—if not actually make—the scene (such as the rollerbladers at the Trocadéro in Paris or the crowd at Rome's Trevi Fountain).

Just a few phrases spoken by your kids will open many doors. Made a point of teaching them "thank you," "hello," and "good-bye" in the country's language. You'll find nearly everyone speaks English, but small phrases out of the mouths of babes will melt the cool of surly museum guards or harried shop clerks.

European amusement parks—such as Denmark's Legoland—are fun for kids of all ages.

Internet cafés allow kids to keep in touch with friends at home and European pals they meet on their trip. These days, blogging is popular and accessible even for kids (see page 333). Or, for a few euros, kids can purchase an international phone card and chat cheaply with friends back home. If you're traveling with a mobile phone, your kids can use it to text or send photos back to their friends in the US.

Getting somewhere can be more fun than touring a sight. Your son might not care about the Crown Jewels, but he may go nuts riding the double-decker bus getting there. Kids love subway maps, train schedules, and plotting routes. The Paris Métro is especially fun, as many stations have boards that light up the route when you press the button for your destination. Even the automated ticket kiosks are entertaining. Allow time for all of this, rather than just rushing onto a subway train or bus. After a teaching run, let your child actually lead the family on subway journeys—kids love the challenge.

In a crowded situation, having a unique family noise (a whistle or call, such as a "woo-woop" sound) enables you to easily get each other's attention. Consider buying cheap walkie-talkies in Europe to help you relax when the kids roam (don't bring walkie-talkies from home, as ours use a different bandwidth and are illegal in Europe). Or consider buying a cheap "pay as you go" mobile phone for them in Europe (explained on page 324); this can also be helpful in case of emergencies.

When using public transportation, have a backup plan for what to do in case you get separated in the crowd or if one of you gets off the Metro before the other (for example, plan to meet at the next stop—or, if all else fails, plan to reconvene at the hotel—make sure everyone has a hotel business card).

Public WCs can be hard to find. Try department stores, museums, and restaurants, particularly fast-food places.

This is not the United States of Litigation. Europeans love children, but their sense of child-proofing public spaces is vastly different from ours. You may find a footbridge across a raging river has child-sized gaps between the railings. Windows in fourth floor hotel rooms may be easy to open and unscreened. The hot water may scald you in about 30 seconds. Don't judge. But do pay attention.

Leave the Kids at Home?

When parents tell me they're going to Europe and ask me where to take their kids, I'm tempted to answer, "to Grandma and Grandpa's on your way to the airport." It's easy to make the case against taking the kids. Traveling with kids is expensive. (Starting at age 12, they fly for full fare. Out of exhaustion and frustration, you may opt for pricey conveniences like taxis and the first restaurant you find with a kid-friendly menu.) And two adults with kids spend twice as much to experience about half the magic of Europe per day that they might without. Also, older kids would very often rather stay home to enjoy their school break with friends.

If you and your partner have 20 days for a family vacation, are on a budget, and are dreaming of an adult time in Europe, consider this plan: Go for 10 days without the kids and really enjoy Europe as adults rather than parents—the savings from leaving them at home will easily cover top-notch child care. Then fly home and spend the other 10 days with your kids—camping, at a water park, or just playing with them at home. (If your kids have a "cool" but responsible young-adult relative somewhere else in the US who they'd enjoy getting to know better, offer to pay to fly them there and watch your kids while you're gone.)

Some parents won't bring their kids until they are old enough to

enjoy the trip. They should be able to stand a day of walking and be ready to eat what is in front of them—and sleep where you stay. They should be able to carry their own daypacks with some clothes, journal, and a couple of toys. It's about the same age as when a child is ready for a long day at Disneyland.

You'll find your European trips will definitely change with children, but many parents wouldn't dream of leaving their kids behind. Your vacation will be much more about playgrounds and petting zoos than about museums and churches. Some of your best memories may be of your son playing in a sandbox with the girls who live next to your rental cottage, or your daughter going on a zip line at the local playground. Traveling with kids, you'll live more like a European and less like a tourist. And, if done well, you'll take home happy memories that you'll share for a lifetime.

31. Savvy Seniors

More people than ever are hocking their rockers and buying plane tickets. Many senior adventurers are proclaiming, "Age matters only if you're a cheese." Travel is their fountain of youth.

These days, many "seniors" are more energetic than their backpacker grandkids. But even for these folks, the topics covered below can be of particular interest. I'm not a senior—yet—so I put an appeal on the Graffiti Wall of my website (www .ricksteves.com/graffiti) asking seniors to share their advice. Thanks to the many who responded, here's a summary of top tips from seniors who believe it's never too late to have a happy childhood. (For more suggestions, see page 745.)

Their fountain of youth is Europe!

When to Go: Since most seniors are retired and can travel whenever they want, it's smart to aim for shoulder season (April, May, Sept, Oct). This allows you to avoid the most exhausting things about European travel: crowds and the heat of summer.

Planning: The Internet is an invaluable resource for booking flights, checking train schedules, researching and reserving hotels, and lots

SPECIAL CONCERNS

Resources for Seniors

Ed Perkins writes an excellent "Seniors on the Go" column at www.smartertravel.com/senior-travel. AARP's website has a good section on travel (www.aarp.org/travel). Senior-travel books include *Unbelievably Good Deals and Great Adventures That You Absolutely Can't Get Unless You're Over 50*, by Joan Rattner Heilman (McGraw-Hill); *Travel Unlimited: Uncommon Adventures for the Mature Traveler*, by Alison Gardner (Avalon); and *The Grown-Up's Guide to Running Away from Home: Making a New Life Abroad* by Rosanne Knorr (Ten Speed Press).

more. If you're not already an Internet whiz, enlist someone to help you. Hometown travel classes (often offered by travel stores or libraries) are a good way to inspire you and help kick-start your planning.

Travel Insurance: Seniors pay more for travel insurance—but are also more likely to need it. Find out exactly whether and how your medical insurance works overseas. (Medicare is not valid outside the US; check your supplemental insurance coverage for exclusions.) Preexisting conditions are a problem, especially if you are over 70, but there are plans that will waive those exclusions. When considering additional travel insurance, pay close attention to evacuation insurance, which covers the substantial expense of getting you to adequate medical care in case of an emergency—especially if you are too ill to fly commercially. For more on your complicated travel-insurance options, see page 38.

Packing: Hauling a big bag is a major concern for seniors. Instead, bring a roll-aboard suit-case. Figure out ways to smoothly carry your luggage, so you're not wrestling with several bulky items. For example, if you bring a second bag, make it a small one that stacks neatly (or even attaches) on top of your wheeled bag. Packing light is even more important for seniors—when you pack light,

Seniors can travel as footloose and fancy-free as their teenaged grandkids.

you're younger. To lighten your load, take fewer clothing items and do laundry more often. Bring along a magnifying glass to help you read detailed maps and small-print schedules, and a small notebook to jot down facts and reminders.

Medications and Health: Be certain to take a full supply of any medications with you. It can be difficult and time-consuming to fill a prescription in Europe, and even nonprescription medications (such as vitamins or supplements) may not be available abroad in the same form you're used to. Pharmacists overseas are often unfamiliar with American brand names, so you may have to use the generic name instead (for example, atorvastatin instead of Lipitor). Before you leave, ask your doctor for a list of the precise generic names of your medications, and the names of equivalent medications in case of unavailability. If you wear hearing aids, be sure to bring spare batteries—it can be difficult to find a specific size in Europe. For more health tips, see Chapter 23: Staying Healthy. If your mobility is limited, you'll find more tips and resources in Chapter 32: Travelers with Disabilities Take on the World.

Flying: If you're not flying direct, check your bag—because if you have to transfer to a connecting flight at a huge, busy airport, your carry-on bag will become a lug-around drag. If you're a slow walker, ask the airline or flight attendant to arrange transportation so you can easily make your next flight. Since cramped leg room can be a concern for seniors, book early to reserve aisle seats (or splurge on roomier "economy plus" or first class). Be careful to stay hydrated during long flights, and take short walks hourly to avoid the slight chance of getting a blood clot.

Accommodations: If stairs are a problem, request a ground-floor room. Think about the pros and cons of where you sleep: If you stay near the train station at the edge of town, you'll minimize carrying your bag on arrival; on the other hand, staying in the city center gives you a con-

venue place to take a break between sights (and you can take a taxi on arrival to reduce lugging your bags). To save money, try hostels, which offer the bonus of ready-made friends (and you'll really impress all the young-sters you're bunking with). No matter where you stay, ask about your accommodations' accessibility quirks—

whether it's at the top of a steep hill, has an elevator or stairs to upper floors, and so on—before you book.

Getting Around: Subways involve a lot of walking and stairs (and are a pain with luggage). Consider using city buses or taxis instead. With lots of luggage, definitely take a taxi (better yet, pack light). If you're renting a car, be warned that some countries and some car-rental companies have an upper age limit—to avoid unpleasant surprises, mention your age when you reserve (for details, see Chapter 11: Driving in Europe).

Senior Discounts: Just showing your gray hair or passport can snag you a discount on many sights, and even some events such as concerts. (The British call senior discounts "concessions" or "pensioner's rates.") Always ask about discounts, even if you don't see posted information about one—you may be surprised. But note that at some sights, US citizens aren't eligible for the senior discount (because the US is notorious for not reciprocating).

Seniors can get deals on point-to-point rail tickets in Scandinavia,

Pilgrims of all ages hike from France to Santiago de Compostela in northwest Spain.

France, Belgium, and more (including the Eurostar Chunnel crossing between Britain and France). To get rail discounts in some countries—such as Austria, Britain, and Spain—you can purchase a senior card at a local train station (valid for a year, but worthwhile even on a short trip if you take several train rides during your stay). Railpasses for Britain and France give seniors a discount in first class. It's rare, but a few airlines do offer discounts to seniors. Always ask.

Sightseeing: Many museums have elevators, and even if these are freight elevators not open to the public, the staff might bend the rules for older travelers. Take advantage of the benches in museums; sit down frequently to enjoy the art and rest your feet. Go late in the day for fewer crowds and cooler temperatures. Many museums offer loaner wheelchairs. Take bus tours (usually two hours long) for a painless overview of the highlights. Boat tours—of the harbor, river, lake, or fjord—are a pleasure. Hire an English-speaking cabbie to take you on a tour of a city or region (if it's hot, spring for an air-conditioned taxi). Or participate in the life of local seniors, such as joining a tea dance at a senior center. If you're traveling with others but need a rest break, set up a rendezvous point. Many seniors find that one day of active sightseeing needs to be followed by a quiet day to recharge the batteries. For easy sightseeing, grab a table at a sidewalk café for a drink and people-watching.

Educational and Volunteer Opportunities: For a more meaningful cross-cultural experience, consider going on an educational tour such as those run by Exploritas (formerly Elderhostel), which offers study programs around the world designed those over 55 (one to four weeks, call or check online for a free catalog, www.exploritas.org, tel. 800-454-5768). For ideas on volunteer programs, see "Resources for Socially Responsible European Travel" on page 427.

Long-term Trips: Becoming a temporary part of the community can be particularly rewarding. Settle down and stay a while, doing side-trips if you choose. You can rent a house or apartment, or go a more affordable route, and "swap" houses for a few weeks with someone in an area you're interested in (for more on this home-exchange option, see page 237). Various websites (including www.transitionsabroad.com and www.escapeartist.com), books (such as the Living Abroad In... series, www.livingabroadin.com), and magazines (such as *International Living,* www.internationalliving.com) offer tips about retiring to a foreign land, either long-term or short-term.

32. Travelers with Disabilities Take On the World

Thanks to Susan Sygall and the staff from Mobility International USA for this section.

More and more people with disabilities are heading to Europe, and more of us are looking for the Back Door routes. We, like so many of our nondisabled peers, want to get off the tourist track and experience the real France, Italy, or Portugal. Yes, that includes those of us who use wheelchairs. I've been traveling the "Rick Steves way" since about 1973—and here are some of my best tips.

Susan Sygall, in Italy's Cinque Terre

I use a lightweight manual wheelchair with pop-off tires. I take a backpack that fits on the back of my chair and store my daypack underneath my chair in a net bag. Since I usually travel alone, if I can't carry it myself, I don't take it. I keep a bungee cord with me for the times I can't get my chair into a car and need to strap it in the trunk or when I need to secure it on a train. I always insist on keeping *my own* wheelchair up to the airline gate, where I then check it at the gate. When I have a connecting flight, I again insist that I use my own chair.

Bathrooms are often a hassle, so I have learned to use creative ways to transfer into narrow spaces. To be blatantly honest, when there are no accessible bathrooms in sight, I have found ways to pee discreetly just about anywhere (outside the Eiffel Tower or on a glacier in a national park). You gotta do what you gotta do, and hopefully one day the access will improve, but in the meantime there is a world out there to be discovered. Bring along an extra pair of pants and a great sense of humor.

I always try to learn some of the language of the country I'm in, because it cuts through the barriers when people stare at you (and they will) and also comes in handy when you need assistance in going up a curb or a flight of steps. Don't accept other people's notions of what is possible—I have climbed Masada in Israel and made it to the top of the Acropolis in Greece.

If a museum lacks elevators for visitors, be sure to ask about freight elevators. Almost all have them somewhere, and that can be your ticket to seeing a world-class treasure.

I always get information about disability groups where I am going. See the resources listed in the next section for a number of organizations to try. They will have the best access information, and many times they will become your new traveling partners and friends. They can show you the best spots. Remember that you are part of a global family of people with disabilities.

It can be helpful to contact tourism offices and local transit providers before you travel. Some even include information about accessibility for people with disabilities on their websites.

Each person with a disability has unique needs and interests. Many of my friends use power wheelchairs, are blind or deaf, or have other disabilities—they all have their own travel tips. People who have difficulty walking long distances might want to think of taking a lightweight wheelchair or borrowing one when needed—many places in Europe have mobility scooter rentals, and bike shops are excellent for tire repairs if you get a flat. Whether you travel alone, with friends, or with an assistant, you're in for a great adventure.

SPECIAL CONCERNS

Don't confuse being flexible and having a positive attitude with settling for less than your rights. I expect equal access and constantly let people know about the possibility of providing access through ramps or other modifications. When I believe my rights have been violated, I do whatever is necessary to remedy the situation so that the next traveler, or disabled people in that country, won't have the same frustrations.

Know your rights as a traveler with a disability. If, under the Americans with Disabilities Act, you feel you have been discriminated against (such as not being allowed on a US tour company's tour of Europe because of your disability), call the US Department of Justice ADA Information Line at 800-514-0301 or 800-541-0383 TTY, or visit www.ada.gov. The US Department of Transportation's Aviation Consumer Protection Division (ACPD) handles complaints regarding the Air Carrier Access Act, and has a toll-free Disability Hotline (tel. 800-778-4838 or 800-455-9880 TTY, http://airconsumer.ost.dot.gov). Many countries have disability rights laws and/or have passed the UN Convention on the Rights of Persons with Disabilities (www.un.org /disabilities), and should be aware of any legal obligations. Do your part to explain why you think accessibility is a human right.

Keep in mind that accessibility can mean different things in different countries. In some countries, people rely more on human-support systems than on physical or technological solutions. People may tell you their building is accessible because they're willing to lift you and your wheelchair over the steps at the entryway. Be open to trying new ways of doing things, but also ask questions to make sure you are comfortable with the access provided.

Many of Europe's newer trains are fully accessible to people who use wheelchairs.

If you are interested in studying, teaching, or volunteering abroad, contact the National Clearinghouse on Disability and Exchange (NCDE) at Mobility International USA for free information and referrals (see listing on next page). Whether you're considering traveling abroad to learn a new language, or looking for a way to make your experience more meaningful by volunteering, the NCDE has resources to answer many of your questions. You can also get online and do your own investigating. Search for "travel" and "disability."

Hopefully more books will include accessibility information—which will allow everyone to see Europe "through the Back Door." Let's work toward making that door accessible so we can all be there together.

Additional Resources

Mobility International USA (MIUSA) is a nonprofit organization whose mission is to empower people with disabilities around the world to achieve their human rights through international exchange and international development. MIUSA periodically sponsors international exchange programs for people with disabilities. They also sell useful resources, such as the book *Survival Strategies for Going Abroad: A Guide for People with Disabilities,* in which more than 20 experienced travelers with disabilities share stories, tips, and resources related to participating in international programs. This easy-to-use guide addresses the disability-related aspects of participating in international exchange programs, including choosing a program, applying, preparing to travel, adjusting to life in a new country, and returning home (www.miusa.org, tel. 541/343-1284, info@miusa.org).

The **National Clearinghouse on Disability and Exchange (NCDE)** provides free information about work, study, teaching, volunteer, and research opportunities abroad for people with disabilities. The NCDE offers many resources, including an online database with information about exchanges and disability organizations worldwide; the free publication *Preparing for an International Career: Pathways for People with Disabilities;* Web resources addressing many travel issues faced by people with disabilities; and the free online journal *A World Awaits You,* with tips and stories about a wide range of exchange opportunities. NCDE is a project sponsored by the Bureau of Educational and Cultural Affairs of the US State Department and administered by MIUSA (www.miusa .org/ncde).

Access-Able Travel Source sponsors a useful website (www.access -able.com) that has access information and resources for travelers with disabilities, and offers a free email newsletter. They have information about guidebooks, accessible transportation, wheelchair travel, scooter rental, disabled-travel forums, accessible transportation, and more (tel. 303/232-2979, fax 303/239-8486, information@access-able.com, Bill Randall).

The **Society for Accessible Travel and Hospitality (SATH),** an educational nonprofit membership organization, publishes an online travel magazine and offers travel advice ($49 membership, $29 for

SPECIAL CONCERNS

students and seniors, www.sath.org, tel. 212/447-7284, fax 212/447-1928, sathtravel@aol.com).

Several organizations specialize in **health** issues: The **International Association for Medical Assistance to Travelers (IAMAT)** provides a directory of English-speaking doctors around the world (described on page 345, www.iamat.org, tel. 716/754-4883, info@iamat.org). The **Centers for Disease Control and Prevention (CDC)** maintains health-related information online, including travel preparation and health tips for travel worldwide (www.cdc.gov/travel). **Shoreland's Travel Health Online** offers health advice, a planning guide, and country information (www.tripprep.com).

Traveling with a **service animal** adds another layer of planning to your trip. Allow plenty of time to obtain the necessary documents—guide dogs must meet health standards to avoid quarantines. The National Clearinghouse on Disability and Exchange offers a helpful tip sheet, *Frequently Asked Questions about Traveling with Guide Dogs and Other Types of Service Animals* (www.miusa.org/ncde/tipsheets/service dogs). **Assistance Dogs Europe** (www.assistancedogseurope.org) and the **International Association of Assistance Dog Partners** (www.iaadp.org) can provide overseas contacts.

Even More Websites: In addition to the organizations listed above, you can find helpful resources and links on the websites for **Emerging Horizons** (www.emerginghorizons.com), **Flying with Disability** (www.flying-with-disability.org), **Gimp on the Go** (www.gimponthego.com), **Rolling Rains Report** (http://rollingrains.com), **Disabled Peoples' International** (www.dpi.org), and **MossRehab ResourceNet** (www.mossresourcenet.org/travel.htm). **AARP**'s website features articles written for seniors and slow walkers (www.aarp.org/destinations). Deaf individuals in need of American Sign Language interpreting may find options at **Overseas Interpreting Company** (http://overseas interpreting.com). **Access Abroad** is a good resource for students with disabilities planning to study abroad (www.umabroad.umn.edu/access). The **International Transport Forum** provides a country-by-country guide for using your US-issued disabled parking placard in Europe (www.internationaltransportforum.org/europe/ecmt/accessibility /parking.html). For travel tips and inspirational feedback from my readers, check out the "Accessible Europe" topic at www.ricksteves.com /graffiti.

Tours: If you'd rather not go it alone, several groups run accessible tours to Europe, including **Accessible Journeys** (wheelchair trips to Britain, France, and Holland, www.disabilitytravel.com, tel. 800-846-

4537), **Flying Wheels Travel** (escorted tours to Great Britain and France, plus custom itineraries, www.flyingwheelstravel.com, tel. 877-451-5006), and **Nautilus Tours and Cruises** (tours to France, Belgium, and the Netherlands, plus cruises to other destinations, www.nautilustours.com, tel. outside California 800-797-6004, tel. in California 818/591-3159). **Accessible Europe** is a collection of European travel agents and tour operators who specialize in disabled travel (www.accessibleurope.com).

33. Bus Tour Self-Defense

Many American tourists see Europe on an organized bus tour and don't even consider using a guidebook. Rather than wander around without direction, they pay a company to organize their trip and provide a professional guide. For some people, having someone else do the driving, arrange the hotels, and make the decisions takes the stress and work out of travel. In this case, tours can be a great option. The key is finding the right one.

When considering tours, remember that some of the best sellers are those that promise more sightseeing than is reasonable in a given amount of time. No tour can give you more than 24 hours in a day or seven days in a week. What the "blitz" tour can do is give you more hours on the bus. Choose carefully among the itineraries available. Do you really want a series of one-night stands? Bus drivers call tours with ridiculous itineraries "pajama tours." You're in the bus from 8 a.m. until after dark, so why even get dressed?

Many who take an organized bus tour could have managed fine on their own.

A typical big-bus tour has a professional, multilingual European guide and 40–50 people sharing 50 seats. The tour company is probably very big, booking rooms by the thousand and often even owning the hotels it uses. Typically, the bus is luxurious and fairly new, with a high, quiet ride, comfy seats, air-conditioning, and a toilet on board.

Tour hotels fit American standards—large, not too personal, and offering mass-produced comfort, good plumbing, and double rooms. Your hotel's location is important. It can make the difference between a

---

Cheap Trick Bus Tours

The cheapest bus tours are impossibly cheap. There's literally no profit in their retail price. They can give you bus transportation and hotels for about what the tourist-off-the-street would pay for just the hotels alone. An independent (but lazy) traveler on a tight budget can think of the tour as a tailored bus pass with hotels tossed in, and it can actually be a cheap trick. Skip out of the shopping, don't buy any of the optional tours, and every day you can do your own sightseeing. Simply apply the skills of independent travel to the efficient, economical trip shell an organized coach tour provides.

---

fair trip and a great trip. Beware: Some tour companies save money by parking you in the middle of nowhere. If the tour brochure says you'll be sleeping in the "Florence area," that could be halfway to Bologna (and you'll spend half your sightseeing time on transportation to and from the city center). Centrally located hotels maximize your sightseeing efficiency. Get explicit locations in writing before your trip.

Big, cheap bus-tour meals can be a lowlight. Included meals can often be forgettable buffets that hotel restaurants require large groups to take. The prices are driven to almost inedible lows by the tour company. A common complaint among tourists is that hotel meals don't match the country's cuisine. While this generally isn't true at smaller, family-run hotels and pensions, meals can be a big disappointment in the larger, impersonal tourist hotels.

Remember, when 50 tourists drop into a "cozy" pub, coziness sneaks out the back door. A good stop for a guide is one with great freeway accessibility and bus parking; where guides and drivers are buttered up with free coffee and cakes (or even free meals); where they speak English and accept credit cards; and where 50 people can go to the bathroom at the same time. *Arrivederci, Roma.*

Your Tour Guide

Guides generally prefer to spoon-feed Europe to you—from their menu. Sights may be chosen for their convenience rather than merit. Many tours seem to make a big deal out of a statue in Luzern called the *Lion Monument.* When the guide declares this mediocre sight is great, obedient tourists ooh and awe in unison. What makes it "great" for the guide is that Luzern (which has a hotel owned by the tour company, but not a lot of interesting sights) was given too much time in the itinerary, and

Comparing Tours

When you're selecting a tour, the cost you're quoted isn't the only factor to consider. Investigate how many people you'll be traveling with as well as what extras you'll be expected to cover. Most tour companies include customer feedback on their websites— look around and see what previous tour members have to say.

Here is a summary of information we gathered from the websites of eight popular European tour companies (Abercrombie & Kent, Cosmos, Globus, Insight, Maupintour, Perillo, Tauck, and Trafalgar). All are advertised as fully guided. Prices per day do not include airfare.

	Higher-end Tours	Rick Steves' Tours	Lower-end Tours
Price per day	$350–915	$192–299	$120–285
Maximum Group Size	20–40	24–28	40–50
Meals Included	50–75%	50%	35–50%
Sightseeing Included	All included	All included	Most costs extra
Tips Included	All except guide	All included	None included

the *Lion Monument* has easy tour-bus parking. However, Leonardo da Vinci's *Last Supper* in Milan may be passed over, because it's expensive to visit and its mandatory reservation system is inconvenient.

Empathize with your guide. Leading a tour is a demanding job with lots of responsibility, paperwork, babysitting, and miserable hours. Very often, guides are tired. They're away from home and family, often for months on end, and are surrounded by foreigners having an extended party that they're probably not in the mood for. Most guides treasure their time alone and, except for romantic adventures, keep their distance from the group socially. Each tourist has personal demands, and a big group can amount to one big pain in the bus for the guide.

To most guides, the best

The standard European guide does the leading...and you do the following.

Questions to Ask Tour Companies

When calling tour companies, here are questions to ask:

Nail down the price.
- What does the price actually include? (How many nights and days? How many meals? Admission to sights? Exactly what kind of transportation?)
- If the dollar drops, will the tour price stay the same or will a supplement be charged?
- If the tour doesn't fill up, will the price increase? Are prices lower for off-season tours?
- Do you take credit cards? (If you're dealing with a tour company that's not well established, pay by credit card. A credit-card company can be a strong ally in resolving disputes.)
- Do singles pay a supplement? Can singles save money by sharing rooms?
- Are optional excursions offered? Daily? Average cost?
- Is trip interruption/cancellation insurance included?
- Will the guide and driver expect to be tipped? How much? How often?
- Are there any other costs?
- Do customers receive any freebies for signing up?

Find out how much the guide guides.
- Is the guide also the driver?
- Does the guide give talks on the cities, history, and art?
- What are the guide's qualifications (education, experience, fluency in languages)?

group is one that lets them do the thinking and is happy to be herded around. As long as people on board don't think too much or try to deviate from the plan, things go smoothly and reliably, and you really will see (but not necessarily experience) a lot.

Tour companies often put guides in a difficult position. Many companies pay their guides little (or even no) wage. The guides then earn their living from: 1) commissions on the optional daily sightseeing excursions they sell; 2) kickbacks on the souvenirs their group buys from retailers the tour patronizes; and 3) trip-end tips. An experienced and aggressive guide can make $300–500 a day. A guide who's also good can make tour members happy.

Run a reality check on your dream trip.
- How many tour members will be on the tour?
- Roughly what is the average age and singles-to-couples ratio?
- Are children allowed? What is the minimum age?
- How many seats on the bus? Is there a bathroom on the bus? How much time is spent on the bus each day?
- Is smoking allowed?
- Roughly how many hours a day are spent shopping and watching product demonstrations?
- How much free time is usually allotted at each sight, museum, and city?
- Are all the hotels located downtown, or are they on the outskirts?
- What's the average length of stay at hotels? One night? Two?
- Does each room have a private bathroom? Air-conditioning?
- What percentage of included meals are eaten at the hotel?

Let's get personal.
- How many years have you been in business?
- Roughly how many tours do you run a year?
- What is your policy if you have to cancel a tour?
- What are your refund policies before and during the tour?

Request:
- The detailed itinerary and location of hotels.
- The names and phone numbers of satisfied customers, though these aren't always given out.
- Written tour evaluations, if available (may be posted on their website).

This all sounds pretty pessimistic. But I'm not anti-tours. In fact, my company offers tours. I started my career leading those miserable big-bus tours for other companies, figured out what didn't work, and then designed my own tours. Three decades later, they're still going strong. Our tours sidestep the predictable pitfalls because we pay our guides well and forbid kickbacks (making their focus the tour members' experience, not padding their own paycheck); we keep our groups small (28 people maximum, with even fewer on most departures); we include plenty of free time and actively teach our tour members how to best use it; and we use friendly, local hotels and restaurants that other tours are too big to use. (For all the details, see http://tours.ricksteves.com.)

That said, my tours aren't right for everybody. Certain travelers prefer the 50-person bus tours...and those are the tours they should take. But no matter which tour you choose, you can make the most of it.

How to Enjoy a Bus Tour

Keep your guide happy. Independent-type tourists tend to threaten guides. Maintain your independence without alienating your guide. Don't insist on individual attention when the guide is hounded by countless others. Wait for a quiet moment to ask for advice or offer feedback. If a guide wants to, he can give his entire group a lot of extras—but when he pouts, everyone loses. Your objective, which requires some artistry, is to keep the guide on your side without letting him take advantage of you.

A well-chosen tour can be a fine value, giving you a great trip and a breakfast table filled with new friends.

Discriminate among optional excursions. While some activities may be included (such as the half-day city sightseeing tours), each day one or two special excursions or evening activities, called "options," are offered for $30–50 a day. Each person decides which options to take and pay for. To make sure you're not being ripped off on excursion prices, ask your hotelier the going rate for a gondola ride, Seine River cruise, or whatever.

Some options are great, but others are not worth the time or money. While illuminated night tours of Rome and Paris are marvelous, I'd skip most "nights on the town." On the worst kind of big-bus-tour evening, several bus tours come together for the "evening of local color." Three hundred Australian, Japanese, and American tourists drinking watered-down sangria and watching flamenco dancing on stage to the rhythm of their digital camera bleeps is big-bus tourism at its grotesque worst.

Your guide promotes excursions because she profits from them. Don't be pressured. Compare. Some options are cheaper through your tour than from the hotel concierge. Some meals are actually a better value with the group. Keep an open mind. While you are capable of doing plenty on your own, optional excursions can be a decent value—especially when you factor in the value of your time.

But don't let bus tour priorities keep you from what you've traveled all the way to Europe to see. In Amsterdam, some tour companies instruct their guides to spend time in the diamond-polishing place instead of the Van Gogh Museum (no kickbacks on Van Gogh). Skip out if you like. Your guide may warn you that you'll get lost and the bus won't wait. Keep your independence (and the hotel address in your money belt).

Be informed. Tour guides call the dreaded tourist with a guidebook an "informed passenger." But a guidebook is your key to travel freedom. Get maps and tourist information from your (or another) hotel desk or a tourist information office. Tour hotels are often located outside the city, where they cost the tour company less and where they figure you are more likely to book the options just to get into town. Ask the person behind the desk how to catch the bus downtown. Taxis are always a possibility, and, with three or four people sharing, they're affordable. Team up with others on your tour to explore on your own. No city is dead after the shops are closed. Go downtown and stroll.

If you shop...shop around. Many people make their European holiday one long shopping spree. This suits your guide and the local tourist industry just fine. Guides are quick to say, "If you haven't bought a Rolex, you haven't really been to Switzerland," or "You can't say you've experienced Florence if you haven't bargained for and bought a leather coat." Any tour guide in Europe knows that if she's got Americans on board, she's carting around a busload of stark raving shoppers. In Venice, as I orient my groups, merchants are tugging at my arm and whispering, "Bring your groups to our glassworks next time. We'll give you 15 percent back on whatever they spend—and a free glass 'orse!"

Don't necessarily reject your guide's shopping tips; just keep in mind that the prices you see often include a 10–20 percent kickback. Tour guides are clever at dominating your time, making it difficult for shoppers to get out and discover the going rate for big purchases. Don't let them rush you. Never swallow the line, "This is a special price available only to your tour, but you must buy now."

Remember, as your cruise ship docks in Turkey, that some cruise companies don't even hire a guide. They actually rent their groups out to the highest bidder. That "scholar" who meets you at the dock is actually a carpet salesman in disguise. He'll take you to the obligatory ancient sight and then to the carpet shop. The demonstrations (by carpet sellers, glass merchants, and so on) are usually interesting. Use your newfound knowledge from the demonstration to shop around; you may find an item of equal quality for less elsewhere. Bargain.

Spend time with locals who never deal with tourists. The only natives most tour groups encounter are hardened business people who know how to make money off tour groups. Going through Tuscany in a flock of 50 Americans following your tour guide's umbrella, you'll meet all the wrong Italians. Break away. One summer night in Regensburg, I skipped out. While my tour was still piling off the bus, I enjoyed a beer—while overlooking the Danube and under shooting stars—with the great-great-great-grandson of the astronomer Johannes Kepler.

PERSPECTIVES

34. Attitude Adjustment

The Ugly American

Some Americans' trips suffer because they are treated like ugly Americans. Those who are treated like ugly Americans are treated that way because they *are* ugly Americans. They aren't bad people, just ethnocentric.

Even if you believe American ways are better, your trip will go more smoothly if you don't compare. Enjoy doing things the European way during your trip, and you'll experience a more welcoming Europe.

Europe sees two kinds of travelers: Those who view their new surroundings through air-conditioned bus windows while socializing with their noisy American friends, and those who are taking a vacation from America, immersing themselves in different cultures, experiencing different people and lifestyles, and broadening their perspectives.

Europeans judge you as an individual, not by your nationality. I have never been treated like the ugly American. If anything, my American-ness has been an asset in Europe.

But you'll see plenty of ugly Americans slogging through a sour Europe, mired in a swamp of complaints. Ugly Americanism is a disease, but fortunately there is a cure: a change in attitude. The best over-the-counter medicine is a mirror. Here are the symptoms.

The ugly American:

- criticizes "strange" customs and cultural differences. She doesn't try to understand that only a Hindu knows the value of India's sacred cows, and only a devout Spanish Catholic appreciates the true worth of his town's patron saint.

- demands to find America in Europe. He throws a fit if the air-conditioning breaks down in a hotel. He insists on orange juice and eggs (sunny-side up) for breakfast, long beds, English menus, ice in drinks, punctuality in Italy, and cold beer in England. He measures Europe with an American yardstick.
- invades a country while making no effort to communicate with the "natives." Traveling in packs, he talks at and about Europeans in a condescending manner.

The Thoughtful American

The thoughtful American celebrates the similarities and differences in cultures. You:

- seek out European styles of living. You are genuinely interested in the people and cultures you visit.
- want to learn by trying things. You forget your discomfort if you're the only one in a group who feels it.
- accept and try to understand differences. Paying for your Italian coffee at one counter and then picking it up at another may seem inefficient, until you realize it's more sanitary: The person handling the food handles no money.
- are observant and sensitive. If 60 people are eating quietly with hushed conversation in a Belgian restaurant, you know it's not the place to yuk it up.
- maintain humility and don't flash signs of affluence, especially in poorer countries. You don't joke about the local money or overtip. Your bucks don't talk.
- are positive and optimistic in the extreme. You discipline yourself to focus on the good points of each country. You don't dwell on problems or compare things to "back home."
- make an effort to bridge that flimsy language barrier. Rudimentary communication in any language is fun and simple with a few basic words. On the train to Budapest, you might think that a debate with a Hungarian over the merits of a common European currency would be frustrating with a 20-word vocabulary, but you'll surprise yourself at how well you communicate by just breaking the ice and trying. Don't worry about making mistakes—communicate!

I've been accepted as an American friend throughout Europe, Russia, the Middle East, and North Africa. I've been hugged by Bulgarian workers on a Balkan mountaintop; discussed the Olympics over dinner in the

Thank You

Arabic	**shukran**	Hebrew	**todah**
Bulgarian	**blagodarya**	Hungarian	**köszönöm**
Croatian	**hvala**	Iraqi	**shukran**
Czech	**děkuji**	Italian	**grazie**
Danish	**tak**	Polish	**dziękuję**
Dutch	**dank u wel**	Portuguese	**obrigado**
English	**thank you**	Russian	**spasiba**
Estonian	**tänan**	Slovak	**d'akujem**
Finnish	**kiitos**	Slovene	**hvala**
French	**merci**	Spanish	**gracias**
German	**danke**	Turkish	**teşekkür**
Greek	**efharisto**		**ederim**

home of a Greek family; explained to a young, frustrated Irishman that California girls take their pants off one leg at a time, just like the rest of us; and hiked through the Alps with a Swiss schoolteacher, learning German and teaching English.

Go as a guest; act like one, and you'll be treated like one. In travel, as in the rest of life, you often reap what you sow.

Travel as a Political Act

Recently I've been devoting a lot of time and energy to thinking about travel in a new way: as an invaluable tool for broadening your perspective to fit more comfortably into our ever-smaller world. I think of this approach as "travel as a political act," which is also the title of a recent book I've written (for the details, see page 18).

I was raised thinking the world was a pyramid with the US on top and everyone else trying to get there. I believed our role in the world was to help other people get it right...American-style. If they didn't understand that, we'd get them a government that did.

But travel changed my perspective. I met intelligent people— nowhere near as rich, free, or blessed with opportunity as I was—who wouldn't trade passports. They were thankful to be Nepali, Estonian, Turkish, Nicaraguan, or whatever...and I was perplexed. I witnessed stirring struggles in lands that found other truths to be self-evident and God-given. I learned of Nathan Hales and Patrick Henrys from other nations who only wished they had more than one life to give for their

Broadening Your Perspective Through Travel

When you travel—whether to Europe or around the world—your best souvenir can be a global perspective. Here are some examples of ways my travels have shaped the way I see the world.

What a difference perspective makes. When I bragged about how many gold medals our American Olympians were winning, my Dutch friend replied, "Yes, you have many medals, but per capita, we Dutch are doing five times as well."

Scandinavians place their City Hall on the main square like a temple to good government. Oslo's is wallpapered with murals celebrating how a society can work together for the benefit of all.

country. I saw national pride that wasn't American.

My travels—whether in Egypt, Afghanistan, El Salvador, Turkey, or the Netherlands—teach me more about my country as well as the rest of our world. Travel has sharpened both my love of what America stands for and my connection with our world. And lessons I've learned far from home combined with my passion for America have heightened my drive to challenge my countrymen to higher ideals. Crass materialism and a global perspective don't mix. We can enjoy the fruits of our hard work

When I shudder at Switzerland's high taxes, my friend Olle asks, "What's it worth to live in a country with no hunger, no homelessness, and where everyone has access to good health care and a top-quality education?"

Europeans love their fuel-efficient "Smart Cars." Oil-friendly American politicians laugh at them.

These 13-year-old Salvadoran girls, whose parents eke out a living from scavenging off a garbage dump, have the same pride, dignity, and worth as my daughter.

and still be a loved and respected nation.

By connecting me with so many people, travel has heightened my concern for people issues: a well-educated electorate, a healthy environment, civil liberties, quality housing, nutrition, health care, and education. I've learned to treasure—rather than fear—the world's rich diversity. And I believe that America—with all its power, wisdom, and goodness—can do a better job of making our world a better place.

PERSPECTIVES

Responsible Travel

As we learn more about the problems that confront the earth and human-kind, more and more people are recognizing the need for the world's industries, such as tourism, to function as tools for peace. According to the World Travel and Tourism Council, tourism is a $7 trillion-a-year industry that employs more than 230 million people. As travelers become more sophisticated and gain a global perspective, the demand for socially, environmentally, and economically responsible means of travel will grow. Peace is more than the absence of war, and if we are to enjoy the good things of life—such as travel—the serious issues that confront humankind must be addressed now.

Although the most obvious problems relate specifically to travel in the developing world, European travel also offers some exciting socially responsible opportunities. In this chapter are a few sources of information for the budding "green" traveler.

Consume responsibly in your travels—do your part to conserve energy. If your hotel overstocks your room with towels, use just one. Carry your own bar of soap and bottle of shampoo rather than rip open all those little soaps and shampoo packets. Bring a lightweight plastic cup instead of using and tossing a plastic glass at every hotel. Turn the light off when you leave your room. Limit showers to five minutes. Return unused travel information (booklets, brochures) to the tourist information office or pass it on to another traveler rather than toss it into a European landfill. In little ways, we can make a difference.

Understand your power to shape the marketplace by what you decide to buy, whether in the grocery store or in your choice of hotels. In my travels (and in my writing), whenever possible, I patronize and support small, family-run businesses (hotels, restaurants, shops, tour guides). I choose people who invest their creativity and resources in giving me simple, friendly, sustainable, and honest travel experiences—people with ideals. Back Door places don't rely on slick advertising and marketing gimmicks, and they don't target the created needs of people whose values are shaped by capitalism gone wild. Consuming responsibly means buying as if your choice is a vote for the kind of world we could have.

Making the Most of Your Trip

Accept that today's Europe is changing. Among the palaces, quaint folk dancers, and museums, you'll find a living civilization grasping for its future while we romantic tourists grope for its past. This presents us with a sometimes painful dose of truth.

Today's Europe is a complex, mixed bag of tricks. It can rudely slap

Resources for Socially Responsible European Travel

Global Volunteers, a nonprofit organization, offers useful "travel with a purpose" trips throughout the world (www.global volunteers.org, tel. 800-487-1074, email@globalvolunteers.org). The work varies per country, but if Europe's your goal, you'll likely work with vulnerable children in Romania, help with a renovation project at the peace center in Ireland, assist at a home for disabled youth in Greece, or teach conversational English in Italy, Hungary, Poland, Ukraine, or Romania.

Volunteers for Peace, a nonprofit organization, runs international work camps to promote goodwill through friendship and community service. European options include historical preservation, festival event planning, conservation projects, AIDS awareness instruction, and social work with disabled or elderly people (www.vfp.org, tel. 802/259-2759, info@vfp.org).

SCI-International Voluntary Service runs work camps with projects involving children, the elderly, the environment, or local culture and history (www.sci-ivs.org, tel. 434/336-3545, sciivs .placement@gmail.com).

The **Center for Global Education** (at Augsburg College in Minneapolis) organizes powerfully educational tours to Central America and South Africa. The three trips of theirs in which I participated gave me the most vivid and perspective-stretching travel experiences I've ever enjoyed. (For trip journals of my CFGE experiences in El Salvador and Nicaragua—including my 2005 adventure—see www.ricksteves.com/centam.) For their latest "reality tour" schedule, visit www.augsburg.edu/global, or call 800-299-8889.

The book *Volunteer Vacations: Short-Term Adventures That Will Benefit You and Others* (10th edition), by Bill McMillon, Doug Cutchins, and Anne Geissinger, lists 500 options for one- to six-week domestic and foreign volunteer programs. Get a copy of this book if you'd like to restore medieval ruins, work in wildlife reserves, or care for refugee children in camps and orphanages (order from www.amazon.com or through the Independent Publishers Group, www.ipgbook.com, tel. 800-888-4741).

Other good books (all available through www.amazon.com) include the *International Directory of Voluntary Work* (10th edition), by Victoria Pybus (Vacation Work); *How to Live Your Dream of Volunteering Overseas,* by Joseph Collins, Stefano DeZerega, and Zahara Heckscher (Penguin USA); and *Green Volunteers: The World Guide to Voluntary Work in Nature Conservation* (7th edition), by Fabio Ausenda (Universe).

PERSPECTIVES

you in the face if you aren't prepared to accept it with open eyes and an open mind. Europe is getting crowded, tense, seedy, polluted, industrialized, hamburgerized, and far from the everything-in-its-place, fairy-tale land it may have once been.

If you're not mentally braced for some shocks, local trends can tinge your travels. Hans Christian Andersen's statue has four-letter words scrawled across its base. Amsterdam's sex shops and McDonald's share the same streetlamp. In Paris, armies of Sudanese salesmen bait tourists with ivory bracelets and crocodile purses. Many a Mediterranean hotel keeper would consider himself a disgrace to his sex if he didn't follow a single woman to her room. Drunk punks do their best to repulse you as you climb to St. Patrick's grave in Ireland, and Greek ferryboats dump mountains of trash into their dying Aegean Sea. A 12-year-old boy in Denmark smokes a cigarette like he was born with it in his mouth, and in a Munich beer hall, an old drunk spits *Sieg heil*s all over you. The Barcelona shoeshine man will triple-charge you, and people everywhere eat strange and wondrous things. They eat next to nothing for breakfast, mud for coffee, mussels in Brussels, and snails in Paris, and dinner's at 10 p.m. in Spain. Beer is room-temperature here and flat there, coffee isn't served with dinner, and ice cubes are only a dream. Roman cars stay in their lanes like rocks in an avalanche, and beer maids with huge pretzels pull mustard packets from their cleavage.

Contemporary Europe is alive and in motion. Today's problems will fill tomorrow's museums. Feel privileged to walk the vibrant streets of Europe as a sponge—not as a judge. Be open-minded. Absorb, accept, and learn.

Don't be a creative worrier. Some travelers tend to sit at home before their trip—all alone, just thinking of reasons to be stressed. Travel problems are always there; you just notice them when they're yours. Every year there are air-controller strikes, train wrecks, terrorist attacks, small problems turning into large problems, and old problems becoming new again.

Travel is exciting and rewarding because it requires you to ad-lib, to be imaginative and spontaneous while encountering and conquering surprise challenges. Make an art out of taking the unexpected in stride. Relax—you're on the other side of the world playing games in a continental backyard. Be a good sport, enjoy the uncertainty, and frolic in the pits.

Many of my readers' richest travel experiences were the result of seemingly terrible mishaps: the lost passport in Slovenia, having to find a doctor in Ireland, the blowout in Portugal, or the moped accident on Corfu.

Global Climate Change and European Travel

During a recent heat wave in Italy, I switched hotels because it was too hot to sleep without air-conditioning. It was the first time I had done that, and it was a kind of personal defeat—since I've always prided myself on not needing air-conditioning.

As they've sweltered through summer after summer, Europeans (and their visitors) have long embraced the "inconvenient truth" that things are heating up.

There's no doubt in Europe (and among Europeans) that things are warming up. Nearly everywhere in the Alps, summer skiing is just a memory, and—even in the winter—ski resorts are in desperate straits for lack of snow. Eating outdoors in formerly cool-climate Munich or Amsterdam now feels like an anachronistic thing to do. Dutch boys went a decade (1997–2007) without a frozen canal to skate on. Scandinavia is seeing a spike in summertime visitors from Mediterranean countries (seeking a break from the heat).

A day of reckoning is coming, when honest travelers will agree that flying to Europe pumps more carbon into the atmosphere than our earth can handle and still sustain the climate we all find comfortable. Europeans are starting to see "carbon taxes" that force consumers to pay for zeroing out the negative impact their purchases have on the environment. I have friends who, despite cheap airfares, ride the train to minimize the environmental cost of their intra-European travel. (For more on this choice, see page 101.)

As a business that promotes travel, my company (Europe Through the Back Door) has been exploring the ethics of our work and how we can honestly be carbon-neutral. As of 2010, we're purchasing enough renewable energy to offset the entire carbon footprint of the electricity consumption in our Edmonds, Washington, offices. We've also signed a pledge to reduce our energy consumption by 10 percent. Of course, there's plenty more that can be done to counterbalance the environmental costs of international travel. If you have ideas, please share them on the Graffiti Wall at www.ricksteves.com/graffiti.

PERSPECTIVES

Expect problems, tackle them creatively. You'll miss a museum or two and maybe blow your budget for the week. But you'll make some

When I see a bunch of cute guys on a bench, I ask 'em to scoot over...

friends and stack up some memories. And this is the essence of travel that you'll enjoy long after your journal is shelved and your trip is stored neatly in the photo album of your mind.

KISS: "Keep it simple, stupid!" Don't complicate your trip. Simplify! Travelers get stressed and cluttered over the silliest things, which, in their niggling ways, can suffocate a happy holiday: registering your camera with customs before leaving home, standing in a long line at the post office on a sunny day in the Alps, worrying about the correct answers to meaningless bureaucratic forms, making a long-distance hotel reservation in a strange language and then trying to settle on what's served for breakfast, having a picnic in pants that make you worry about grass stains, and sending away for Swedish hotel vouchers. Timeshares, frequent-flyer incentives, VAT refunds...concerns like these are outlawed in my travels.

People can complicate their trips with video cameras, special tickets for free entry to all the sights they won't see in England, inflatable hangers, immersion heaters, instant coffee, 65 Handi-Wipes, and a special calculator that figures the value of the euro to the third decimal. They ask for a toilet in 17 words or more, steal artificial sweeteners and plastic silverware off the plane, and take notes on facts that don't matter. Travel more like Gandhi—with simple clothes, open eyes, and an uncluttered mind.

Ask questions. If you are too proud to ask questions, your trip will be dignified but dull. Many tourists

...and 30 years later, I'm still one of the gang.

are actually too afraid or timid to ask questions. The meek may inherit the earth, but they make lousy travelers. Local sources are a wealth of information. People are happy to help a traveler. Hurdle the language barrier. Use a paper and pencil, charades, or whatever it takes to be understood. Don't be afraid to butcher the language.

Ask questions—or be lost. If you are lost, or just lonely and in need of human contact, take out a map and look lost. You'll get help. Perceive friendliness and you'll find it.

Be militantly humble—Attila had a lousy trip. All summer long I'm pushing for a bargain, often for groups. It's the hottest, toughest time of year. Tourists and locals clash. Many tourists leave soured.

When I catch a Spanish merchant shortchanging me, I correct the bill and smile, *"Adiós."* When a French hotel owner blows up at me for no legitimate reason, I wait, smile, and try again. I usually see the irate ranter come to his senses, forget the problem, and work things out.

"Turn the other cheek" applies perfectly to those riding Europe's magic carousel. If you fight the slaps, the ride is over. The militantly humble and hopelessly optimistic can spin forever.

Make yourself an extrovert, even if you're not. Be a catalyst for adventure and excitement. Meet people. Make things happen or often they won't. The American casual-and-friendly social style is charming to Europeans who are raised to respect social formalities. While our slap-on-the-back friendliness can be overplayed and obnoxious, it can also be a great asset for the American interested in meeting Europeans. Consider that cultural trait a plus. Enjoy it. Take advantage of it.

If people stare...sing cowboy songs.

I'm not naturally a wild-and-crazy kind of guy. But when I'm shy and quiet, things don't happen, and that's a bad rut to travel in. It's not easy, but this special awareness can really pay off. Let me describe the same evening twice—first with the mild-and-lazy me, and then with the wild-and-crazy me.

The traffic held me up, so by the time I got to that great historical building I've always wanted to see, it was six minutes before closing. No one was allowed to enter. Disappointed, I walked to a restaurant and couldn't make heads or tails out of the menu. I recognized "steak-frites" and settled for a meat patty and French fries. On the way home I looked into a colorful pub but it seemed kind of exclusive, so I walked on. A couple waved at me from their balcony, but I didn't know what to say, so I ignored them. I returned to my room and did some laundry.

That's not a night to be proud of. A better traveler's journal entry would read like this:

I got to the museum only six minutes before closing. The guard said no one could go in now, but I begged, joked, and pleaded with him. I had traveled all the way to see this place, and I would be leaving early in the morning. I assured him that I'd be out by six o'clock, and he gave me a glorious six minutes in that building. You can do a lot with a Botticelli in six minutes when that's all you've got. Across the street at a restaurant that the same guard recommended, I couldn't make heads or tails out of the menu. Inviting myself into the kitchen, I met the cooks and got a firsthand look at what was cookin'. Now I could order an exciting dish and know just what I was getting. Delizioso! *On the way home, I passed a pub, and, while it seemed dark and uninviting, I stepped in and was met by the only guy in the place who spoke any English. He proudly befriended me and told me, in very broken English, of his salty past and his six kids, while treating me to his favorite brew. As I headed home, a couple waved at me from their balcony, and I waved back, saying "Buon giorno!" I knew it didn't mean "Good evening," but they understood. They invited me up to their apartment. We joked around—not understanding a lot of what we were saying to each other—and they invited me to their summer cottage tomorrow. What a lucky break! There's no better way to learn about this country than to spend an afternoon with a family. And to think that I could've been back in my room doing the laundry!*

Pledge every morning to do something entirely different today. Meet people and create adventure—or bring home a boring journal.

Becoming a Temporary European

Most travelers tramp through Europe as if they're visiting the cultural zoo. "Ooo, that guy in lederhosen yodeled! Excuse me, could you do that again in the sunshine with my wife next to you so I can take a snapshot?" This is fun. It's a part of travel. But a camera bouncing on your belly tells locals you're hunting cultural peacocks. When I'm in Europe, I'm the best German or Spaniard or Italian I can be. While I drink coffee at home, after a long day of sightseeing in England, "a spot of tea" really does feel right. I drink wine in France and beer in Germany. In Italy, I eat small breakfasts. Find ways to really be there. For ideas on connecting, consider these (and also see the Graffiti Wall tips in the appendix):

Go to church. Many regular churchgoers never even consider a European worship service. But any church would welcome a traveling

American. And an hour in a small-town church provides an unbeatable peek into the community, especially if you join them for coffee and cookies afterwards. I'll never forget going to a small church on the south coast of Portugal one Easter. A tourist stood at the door video-taping the "colorful natives" (including me) shaking hands with the priest after

Mass with the sun's rays, daily in St. Peter's

the service. You can experience St. Peter's by taking photographs...or by taking a seat at Mass.

Root for your team. For many Europeans, the top religion is soccer. Getting caught up in a sporting event is going local. Whether enjoying soccer in small-town Italy or hurling in Ireland, you'll be surrounded by a stadium crammed with devout fans. Buying something to wear or wave with the hometown colors helps me remember whose side I'm on.

Play where the locals play. A city's popular fairgrounds and parks are filled with families, lovers, and old-timers enjoying a cheap afternoon or evening out. European communities provide their heavily taxed citizens with wonderful athletic facilities. Check out a public swimming pool, called a "leisure center" in Britain. While tourists outnumber locals five to one at the world-famous Tivoli Gardens, Copenhagen's other amusement park, Bakken, is enjoyed purely by Danes. Disneyland Paris is great, but Paris' Parc Astérix is more French.

Experiment. Some cafés in the Netherlands (those with plants in the windows or Rastafarian colors on the wall) have menus that look like the inventory of a drug bust back in the United States. Marijuana is less controversial in Holland than tobacco (which was recently banned in public spaces). For a casual toke of local life without the risk that comes with smoking in the United States, drop into one of these cafés and roll a joint. (See Chapter 50: Amsterdam's Counter-Culture.)

Take a stroll. Across southern Europe, communities have a *paseo*, or stroll, in the early evening. Stroll along. Join a *Volksmarch* in Bavaria to spend a day on the trails with people singing "I love to go a-wandering" in its original language. Remember, hostels are the American target, while mountain huts and "nature's friends huts" across Europe are filled mostly with local hikers. Most hiking centers have alpine clubs that welcome foreigners and offer organized hikes.

Get off the tourist track. Choose destinations busy with local holiday-goers but not on the international tourist map. Campgrounds are filled with Europeans in the mood to toss a Frisbee with a new American friend (bring a nylon "Whoosh" Frisbee). Be accessible. Accept invitations. Assume you're interesting and do Europeans a favor by finding ways to connect.

Challenge a local to the national pastime. In Greece or Turkey, drop into a teahouse or *taverna* and challenge anyone to a game of backgammon. You're instantly a part (even a star) of the café or bar scene. Normally the gang will gather around, and what starts out as a simple game becomes a fun duel of international significance.

Connect with people. Greeks and Turks love a game of backgammon.

Contact an equivalent version of your club. If you're a member of a service club, bridge club, professional association, or international organization, make a point to connect with your foreign mates.

Search out residential neighborhoods. Ride a city bus or subway into the suburbs. Wander through a neighborhood to see how the people live when they're not wearing lederhosen and yodeling. Visit a supermarket. Make friends at the launderette.

Drop by a school or university. Mill around a university and check out the announcement boards. Eat at the school cafeteria. Ask at the English-language department if there's a student learning English whom you could hire to be your private guide. Be alert and even a little bit snoopy. If you stumble onto a grade-school talent show—sit down and watch it.

Truly become a local. The ultimate way of becoming a temporary European is to actually become one—by moving to Europe. For ideas on how to do this, see the "Overseas Work and Study" sidebar.

Join in. When you visit the town market in the morning, you're just another hungry shopper, picking up your daily produce. You can snap photos of the pilgrims at Lourdes—or volunteer to help wheel the chairs of those who've come in hope of a cure. Traveling through the

Blend into Europe: Shop at the town market.

wine country of France during harvest time, you can be a tourist taking photos—or you can pitch in and become a grape-picker. Get more than a photo op. Get dirty. That night at the festival, it's just grape-pickers dancing—with you.

If you're hunting cultural peacocks, remember they spread their tails best for people...not cameras. When you take Europe out of your viewfinder, you're more likely to find it in your lap.

Foreign Study Opportunities

It's becoming standard for good universities to strongly encourage students to take a semester abroad. Interested students can get all of the details at their campus foreign study office (start by reading the "Overseas Work and Study" sidebar).

Here's my personal take on why spending a semester or two overseas is invaluable...from a parent's perspective. When my son, Andy, was a student at the University of Notre Dame, he enjoyed a fabulous semester abroad in Rome. The fundamental decision for students like Andy—along with whether they should miss fall football season or the fun of spring on campus—is choosing between Europe and the developing world. A semester in Africa or Latin America gives a real-life experience in the rough-and-tumble reality of poverty and powerfully humanizes the often-quoted statistic that "half of humanity is trying to live on $2 a day." Time spent in China or India (whose economies are growing at a much faster pace than their conventional Western European counterparts) introduces a student to emerging economic powerhouses that our country will compete with throughout that student's work life. But a semester in Europe offers (for many) an opportunity to connect with our roots; follow up on language, art, and history courses already taken; and enjoy that traditional "Grand Tour" of the Old World.

The real education of a semester abroad takes place outside of the classroom. It's hard for students to really focus on lectures and homework with so many cultural experiences so close (and parents so far). Each week the buzz is about who's going where on the weekend and how many classes they're skipping to do it. From his base in Rome, Andy

Overseas Work and Study

If you're adventurous and unattached, the most rewarding European experience can be to get a job or enroll at a school abroad. Expatriates enjoy the daily routine and built-in circle of co-workers or classmates (and potential friends). If you're interested in becoming a full-time European, consider these helpful resources:

Vacation Work publishes Susan Griffith's *Work Your Way Around the World* (14th edition) and *Summer Jobs Worldwide* (40th edition), edited by David Woodworth and Victoria Pybus. Also consider the *Directory of Jobs & Careers Abroad* (13th edition), edited by Deborah Penrith; *The Expert Expatriate: Your Guide to Successful Relocation Abroad,* by Melissa Brayer Hess and Patricia Linderman; and *GenXpat: The Young Professional's Guide to Making a Successful Life Abroad,* by Margaret Malewski.

Transitions Abroad (www.transitionsabroad.com) is a great resource for anyone considering working or studying abroad, with a huge compendium of online articles and listings for overseas opportunities. They publish several books, including *Work Abroad: The Complete Guide to Finding a Job Overseas* (4th edition) and *The Alternative Travel Directory*: *The Complete Guide to Traveling, Studying and Living Overseas* (7th edition).

If you're a student—whether at a university or a language-study program—your school can typically help you arrange accommodations (either a home-stay or an apartment shared with other students). You'll be eligible for student discounts and can take advantage of economical school-organized field trips. If you're already a student, ask about study-abroad programs at your campus office. Or contact the Council on International Educational Exchange, which offers for-credit programs in 12 European countries (www.ciee.org/isp, tel. 800-407-8839).

For information online, www.expatexchange.com offers postings from expats in virtually every European country.

would gather a small gang for each three-day weekend: skiing in the Swiss Alps, hiking in the Cinque Terre, biking the Amalfi Coast, or sharing an apartment in Cefalù, Sicily. He ended up traveling 13 out of his 17 weekends abroad. For a longer break, they combined their meager resources and chartered a yacht with a captain from Athens. Flights are often cheaper than hopping the train—Andy found a $32 ticket and flew to Dublin for St. Patrick's Day festivities.

Learning the language, making new friends from around the world, flirting with foreigners, getting comfortable with a bustling foreign city, and mastering the late-night scene while going through the motions in classes all add up to a life-changing and unforgettable semester. And it's a bonding experience with fellow students, who will be friends for life.

For more on these opportunities, see my son's website (www .andysteves.com) or Facebook page (Andy Steves' Weekend Student Adventures), designed to share his journal and pool experiences among students so that all can get the very most out of their foreign study experience in Europe.

35. Terrorism, Political Unrest, and Your Travel Dreams

Terrorism

In the wake of the terrorist attacks of September 11, 2001, our media was filled with reports of Americans feeling jittery about travel. But the travelers I talked to then (and now) are unfazed. While mindful that war is serious business, they continue to pursue their travel plans. Maybe it's just the kind of travelers we're dealing with, but for most of the last decade (9/11 notwithstanding), our guidebooks and tours have never sold better. The fact is that more than 12 million Americans go to Europe every year, and for the last several years, not a single one has been killed by terrorists.

Even though it's in the news, terrorism is nothing new. Today travelers worry about al-Qaeda. In the 1970s, we worried about Italy's Red Brigades, Basque separatists, and the Irish Republican Army. And a century ago, the Habsburgs worried about these same issues—back when terrorists were called "anarchists." Here are some thoughts on keeping the risk in perspective and traveling safely.

Don't plan your trip thinking you can slip over there and back while there's a lull in the action. It's in your interest, psychologically, to plan your trip assuming there will be a terrorist event somewhere in the world sometime between now and your departure date. It will be all over the news, and your loved ones will leap into action trying to get you to cancel your trip.

Your loved ones' hearts are in the right place, but your trip's too important for sensationalism and hysteria to get in the way. Numbers don't lie: The odds against being killed by terrorists are astronomical (see the "Relative Risks" sidebar). While our foreign policy in the first

Paris' see-through garbage cans give terrorists one less place to hide a bomb.

decade of the 2000s likely increased the risk of terrorist attacks on Americans, I believe that risk is no greater for an American in Milan or Paris than at home in Miami or Pittsburgh.

It's human nature to feel anxious about some things, even when our brains tell us it's unfounded. I know that about 30,000 commercial planes take off and land safely in the United States every day, and entire years go by without a single fatality in the US airline industry. Even so, I'm still edgy on take-off. But the twinges of anxiety haven't kept me, or most other folks, at home.

While many travelers may feel fine about their physical safety, many grumble about airport security headaches. Europe, the acknowledged world leader in quality security, has been on "orange alert" since the 1980s. Be grateful for and patient with security procedures. I also expect a 30-minute delay for extra security when I leave and enter the US (for which I am thankful). I use the extra

time to meditate on the thought, "How has America's place in our world changed...and why?"

If you want to worry about something, worry about this: Each year, more than 13,000 Americans are shot to death in the United States by handguns (compared to about 1,000 in Germany).

Whether because of fear of terrorism, or the uncertainty surrounding the global economic crisis, some Americans have put their travel dreams on hold and decided to stay home. That's OK. I'm still

Security on Europe's trains is tighter than ever these days. At this London train station, the police keep a close eye on who boards the Eurostar for Paris.

Relative Risks: Fly or Drive?

You may die this year from a number of causes. Here are a few of your odds:

Heart disease	1 in 375
Cancer	1 in 500
Car accident	1 in 21,000
Gunshot	1 in 23,000
Hit by a car while walking	1 in 48,000
Drowning	1 in 850,000
Lightning	1 in 6.3 million
Airline accident	1 in 8 million
Terrorist attack	1 in 9 million

Afraid of flying these days? Worldwide, more than a million people die each year in road accidents—about the same as if a fully loaded 747 crashed every four hours. According to some experts, the decrease in air travel (and increase in car travel) in the anxiety-filled months after 9/11 led to an estimated 1,000 more fatalities on the road than if people had just kept flying.

If a plane blows up tomorrow, America will likely freak out—but it has no effect on the fact that flying is by far the safest way to travel. Drive or fly? You make the call.

---

bringing home TV shows that they can watch from the safety of their living room sofas. But those of us who are able would rather enjoy the fun and wonders of Europe firsthand. Travel is a springboard for experiencing the beauty of our fascinating world. And there's never been a better time to dive in.

Political Unrest

Political turmoil is part of life these days, and security in Europe has never been tighter. Countries from Britain to Italy continue to deal with internal discord, from separatists to religious extremists. An awareness of current social and political problems is as important to smart travel as a listing of top sights. As some popular destinations are entertaining tourists with "sound and light" shows in the old town, they're quelling angry demonstrations in the new town.

Travel broadens our perspective, enabling us to rise above the 24-hour advertiser-driven infotainment we call news and see things as citizens of our world. By plugging directly into the present and getting the

PERSPECTIVES

European take on things, a traveler gets beyond traditional sightseeing and learns "today's history."

There are many peoples fighting the same thrilling battles for political rights we Americans won more than 200 years ago. And while your globe may paint Greece orange and Bulgaria green, racial, religious, and linguistic groups rarely color within the lines.

The only real difference for Americans exploring Europe since 9/11 is that you'll be interviewed by these guys before boarding your plane back into the US.

Understand a country's linguistic divisions. It's next to impossible to keep everyone happy in a multilingual country. Switzerland has four languages, but *Deutsch ist über alles.* In Belgium, there's tension between the Dutch- and French-speaking halves. And Hungarians living in Slovakia had to rely on European Court intervention to get road signs in their native language. Like many French-Canadians, Europe's linguistic underdogs will tell you their language receives equal treatment only on cereal boxes, and many are working toward change.

Look beyond the pretty pictures in your tourist brochures for background on how your destination's demographic makeup may be causing problems today or tomorrow. If you're planning a trip to Poland, for example, start clipping newspaper articles and surfing the Web a few months in advance to gather political news on what's happening (information you'll seldom find in guidebooks).

With this foundation and awareness, you can get the most out of the nearly unavoidable opportunities to talk with involved locals about complex current situations. At any pub on the Emerald Isle, you'll get an earful of someone's passionate feelings about "the Troubles." In Russia and Eastern Europe, whenever you want some political or economic gossip, sit alone in a café. After a few minutes and some eye contact, you'll have company and a fascinating chat. Young, well-dressed people are most likely to speak (and want to practice) English. Universities can be the perfect place to solve the world's problems with a liberal, open-minded foreigner over a cafeteria lunch.

As the global economic crisis wracks Europe, European governments and businesses are struggling to continue providing the generous

Practical Tips for Safe and Smooth Travel

All of us want to travel as safely as possible. Here are some tips.

Consider State Department travel advisories (http://travel .state.gov)**...but don't trust them blindly.** A threat against the embassy in Rome doesn't affect my sightseeing at the Pantheon. While I travel right through many advisories (which can seem politically motivated), other warnings (for example, about civil unrest in a country that's falling apart) are grounds to scrub my mission. Keep in mind that in recent years, Canada and many European countries have issued travel advisories to their citizens for a land they consider more dangerous than their own: the US. For other perspectives, check the British (www.fco.gov.uk) and Canadian (www.voyage.gc.ca) government travel warnings.

Be patient. Be thankful for security measures that may delay you. Call airports to confirm flight schedules before heading out. And allow plenty of time to catch your flight.

Pack lighter than ever to minimize airport frustrations. The current conditions at airports favor those with carry-on-size luggage. The basic limits have not changed (generally one 9" × 22" × 14" bag plus a day bag—but check with your airline). Those checking bags incur longer waits, fees, and less flexibility. Nimble ones with carry-on bags do better in the scramble to get through the flight-schedule shuffling that follows any major disaster or scare.

Avoid being a target by melting into Europe. Fancy luggage and jewelry impress only thieves and give you a needlessly high profile. Travel and look like a local. This is smart travel anytime. Likely targets include icons of American culture—towering American corporations, fancy high-profile American tour groups, military and diplomatic locations, and luxury hotels. Stay in local-style places. Terrorists don't bomb Pedro's Pension. That's where they sleep.

Two weeks after 9/11, I was in Padua, the town where Copernicus studied and Galileo taught. The square was filled with college students sharing drinks and discussing America's response to "our new reality." As we talked, I kept dipping little strips of bread into a puddle of olive oil on my plate, tiptoe-style. Watching me do this, my new friend said, "You make the *scarpette*...little shoes."

My Italian wasn't good enough to tell him my thoughts: Travel is a celebration of life and freedom. Terrorists will not take that away from me. My mission in life is to inspire Americans to travel, one by one—"making the little shoes"—to absorb and savor the wonders of Europe.

PERSPECTIVES

cradle-to-grave benefits that their citizens expect. As these items are trimmed from the budget, new waves of protests sweep across the already strike-happy Continent. While American tourists are at virtually zero risk from these demonstrations, it's smart to be aware of them so that

you can avoid being in the wrong place at the wrong time...and to better understand one more facet of the European experience.

Wherever you travel, be prepared for a challenge when the topic shifts to American foreign policy. Among deaf people, the international sign-language symbol for "American" is the "fat cat"—holding your arms around an imaginary big belly. Like it or not, people around the world look at America as the kingpin of a global and ruthless game of Monopoly. As a person who loves his country, I see travel as a patriotic exercise in promoting people-to-people diplomacy and global understanding.

36. Understanding the European Union

A desire for peace and prosperity is powering some sweeping changes that are taking place in today's Europe. Over the last generation, many European countries have gone from being bitter rivals to member states in one of the world's strongest economies: the European Union. Bringing together such a diverse collection of separate nations—with different languages, cultures, and soccer teams—is almost unprecedented.

EU Nations

The European Union: Austria, Belgium, Bulgaria, Cyprus, Czech Republic, Denmark, Estonia, Finland, France, Germany, Greece, Hungary, Ireland, Italy, Latvia, Lithuania, Luxembourg, Malta, Netherlands, Poland, Portugal, Romania, Slovakia, Slovenia, Spain, Sweden, and the United Kingdom

Today, the 27-nation European Union includes most of Western Europe (except Switzerland and Norway) and a large part of Eastern Europe. The EU is a free-trade zone with its own currency (the euro, used in about half the member countries). But it's much more than that: The EU is increasingly a political unit that looks, acts, and quacks like a single unified nation-state. While not a "United States of Europe," the EU has an elected Europe-wide Parliament that passes laws on economic policy and some social and foreign policy issues.

As you travel in Europe today, you can't avoid hearing about the EU. Everyone has an opinion. "Eurocrats" and other optimists see it as a bold and idealistic experiment in unity, mutual understanding, and shared priorities. On the other hand, "Euroskeptics" view it as a bloated, overly bureaucratic monster that's threatening to wring the diversity and charm out of the Old World. Here's a snapshot of the EU to help you navigate the many interesting conversations you'll have about it with your new European friends.

The History of the EU

World War II left 40 million dead and a continent in ruins, and it convinced Europeans that they must work together to maintain peace. Wedged between competing superpowers (the US and the USSR), they also needed to cooperate economically to survive in an increasingly global economy. Just after the war ended, visionary Eurocrats began convincing reluctant European nations to relinquish elements of their sovereignty and merge into a united body.

The transition towards unity happened very gradually, bit by bit. It started in 1948, when Belgium, the Netherlands, and Luxembourg—jointly called "BeNeLux"—established a free trade zone. Then, in 1951, the former archenemies Germany and France joined with Italy and the BeNeLux countries to form the European Coal and Steel Union. They relaxed trade barriers, shared resources, subsidized private business, and maximized profits. Based on their success, the same group of countries established the European Economic Community (the EEC, also called the "Common Market") in 1957, expanding economic cooperation to include all industries.

Progress came in fits and starts, but over the following 30 years the number of member states in the Common Market doubled. As trade between member countries increased in the 1970s and 1980s, they recognized the need for closer cooperation on currency and money. The result was the establishment of the European Currency Unit (the ECU, precursor to the euro). While the ECU was not a paper currency, it enabled member countries to trade and conduct financial transactions without worrying about currency fluctuations and exchange fees.

In 1992, with the Treaty of Maastricht, the 12 member countries of the Common Market made a leap of faith: They decided to try to create a "European Union" that would have free movement of capital, goods, services, and labor. The by-product would be a common currency, continued removal of trade barriers, introduction of EU passports, and elimination of border checks between member countries. In 2002, most EU members adopted a single currency (the euro), and for all practical purposes economic unity was a reality. Ten member states joined in 2004 and two more in 2007—creating the world's seventh largest "country" (1.7 million square miles), with the third largest population (491 million), and an economy that beats the US' as the world's biggest ($16 trillion GDP).

The EU Today

The European Union is governed from Brussels, the unofficial capital of Europe (though some EU institutions meet in Strasbourg, Frankfurt, Luxembourg, and other cities). The EU does not have checks and balances like America's executive/legislative/judicial branches of government. It does have a Parliament, but it is primarily governed by the European Commission (with Commissioners appointed by individual member governments and approved by the Parliament) and the Council of Ministers. Daily business is conducted by an army of bureaucrats and policy wonks.

While the recently passed Lisbon Treaty tries to stream-

The EU headquarters—a vast and shiny complex of skyscrapers in Brussels—welcomes visitors on guided tours to take a peek at Europe at work.

line EU responses to conflicts and issues, there's no unified foreign or economic policy among the member countries. The European response to the Balkan wars in the early 1990s, the Iraq War of the mid-2000s, and the Greek financial crisis of 2010 has demonstrated that Europe isn't always prepared to speak with a single voice. Likewise, the EU has

US vs. EU—By the Numbers

	US	EU
Population	307 million	491 million
Land area	3.7 million sq. miles	1.7 million sq. miles
Gross domestic product (GDP)	$14.3 trillion	$16 trillion
Life expectancy	78.1 years	78.7 years
Infant mortality rate	6.2 deaths/1,000	5.72 deaths/1,000
Internet users	231 million	247 million
Annual military budget	$667 billion*	$254 billion*

*2006 figures from the Center for Strategic and International Studies, Washington D.C.

Statistics from the CIA's World Factbook, *2010*

no single chief executive with powers similar to America's president—the much weaker president of the European Council is appointed for a two-and-a-half-year term. And unlike America's federation of 50 states, Europe's member states retain the right to opt out of some EU policies.

As Europe unites, downtrodden peoples are enjoying more autonomy. The Scottish Parliament originated around 1235, was dissolved by England in 1707, and returned in 1999. Its extravagant, and therefore controversial, Edinburgh digs opened in 2004.

Britain, for example, belongs to the EU but chose not to adopt the euro as its currency. The Lisbon Treaty tries to avoid total gridlock—a single county can no longer veto measures on climate change, energy security, or emergency aid—but consensus is still necessary in the areas of taxes, foreign policy, defense, and social programs. Having many different departments with overlapping responsibilities helps ensure that final decisions are acceptable to most member states.

PERSPECTIVES

The EU cannot levy taxes (that's still done through national governments, which then fund the EU), and it cannot deploy troops without each nation's approval. For practical purposes, the military and major foreign policy decisions are still largely the domain of individual countries. It's a delicate balance trying to develop laws and policies for all Europeans while respecting the rights of nations, regions, and individuals. An oft-quoted EU slogan is "promoting unity (economic and political) while preserving diversity (cultural)."

The scope of the EU grows with each year, as they try to establish standards for taxes, laws, environmental practices, goods, and services. They also coordinate local police and security forces.

The EU is currently financing an ambitious 21st-century infrastructure of roads, high-speed trains, high-tech industries, and communication networks. The goal is to create a competitive, sustainable, environmentally friendly economy that improves the quality of life for all Europeans. This involves government and private industry working hand in hand—a kind of "socialism" with a global perspective. Their success so far is making some elements of the more competitive American-style free-market capitalism seem outmoded and short-sighted.

New roads (such as this one in Ireland) are bringing the infrastructure in Europe up to speed. These EU-funded projects come with a billboard and EU flag reminding drivers where the funding came from.

Still, Europe has its problems, and many ordinary Europeans remain skeptical of the EU. As Europe struggles with the same economic crisis gripping the US, some of its generous social programs are going by the wayside. Some chafe at the overly regulated business environment and high taxes. They complain about the bureaucracy and worry that their unique national cultures will be swallowed up and Eurofied. Northern Europe is reluctant to bail out southern European countries—such as Greece—in order to prop up the euro, while the southerners resent the cuts demanded by the northerners.

The French and Germans still mix like wine and sauerkraut. Brits still tell insulting jokes about Italians, and vice versa. Nations still duke it out for world domination...on the soccer field. And while the euro remains relatively strong, high prices make the Continent's famed *dolce vita* more expensive than ever not only for ordinary Europeans but also for American travelers.

But despite the problems facing them, Europeans don't want to go back to the way it used to be; most recognize that a strong and unified Europe is necessary to compete in a global economy.

Once the economy has recovered, the next step for the EU is further expansion: Croatia, the Republic of Macedonia, Iceland, and Turkey are in line to become members. Most Eastern European members hope to someday adopt the euro. And the reforms of the Lisbon Treaty may buffer the damage from the recent financial storm, in the long run making Europe more unified and powerful than ever.

Europe is enthusiastic about civil rights. In Spain, Catalans celebrate a double dose of liberty with this statue at Cadaqués, the hometown of Salvador Dalí.

PART TWO
BACK DOORS

Europe is your playground...and it's time for recess.

CONTENTS

Europe's Back Doors

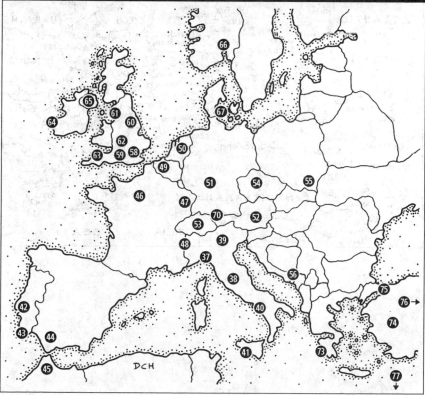

DCH

What Is a Back Door, and How Can
I Find One of My Own?

The travel skills covered in the first half of this book enable you to open doors most travelers don't even know exist. Now I'd like you to meet my "Back Doors." I'm the matchmaker, and you and the travel bug are about to get intimate. By traveling vicariously with me through these chapters, you'll get a peek at my favorite places. And, just as important, by internalizing this lifetime of magic travel moments, you'll develop a knack for finding your own.

Europe is a bubbling multicultural fondue. A Back Door is a steaming forkful. It could be an all-day walk on an alpine ridge, a sword-fern fantasy in a ruined castle, or a friendly swing with a bell-ringer in a church spire. You could jam your camera with Turkish delights or uncover the village warmth hiding in a cold metropolis. By learning where to jab your fork, you'll put together a travel feast that exceeds your wildest dreams.

Some of my Back Doors are undiscovered towns that have, for various reasons, missed the modern parade. With no promotional budgets to attract travelers, they're ignored as they quietly make their traditional way through just another century. Many of these places won't hit you with their cultural razzle-dazzle. Their charms are too subtle to be enjoyed by the tour-bus crowd. But, learning from the experiences described in this second half of the book, Back Door travelers make their own fun.

We'll also explore natural nooks and undeveloped crannies. These are rare opportunities to enjoy Europe's sun, beaches, mountains, and natural wonders, without the glitz. While Europeans love nature and are fanatic sun worshippers, they have an impressive knack for enjoying themselves in hellish crowds. Our goal is to experience Europe's quiet alternatives: lonesome stone circles, desolate castles, breezy bike rides, and snippets of the Riviera not snapped up by entrepreneurs.

With a Back Door angle on a big city, you can slip your fingers under its staged culture and actually find a pulse. Even London has a warm underbelly, where you'll rumble with a heart that's been beating for 2,000 years.

And finally, to squeeze the most travel experience out of every mile, minute, and dollar, look beyond Europe. Europe is exciting, but a dip into Turkey, Morocco, or Egypt is well worth the potential diarrhea.

The promotion of a tender place that has so far avoided the tourist industry reminds me of the whaler who screams, "Quick, harpoon it before it's extinct!" These places are this Europhile's cupids. Publicizing them gnaws at what makes them so great. But what kind of a travel writer can keep his favorite discoveries under wraps? Great finds are too hard to come by to just sit on. I keep no secrets.

With ever-more-sophisticated travelers armed with ever-better guidebooks, places I "discovered" 10 or 15 years ago are undeveloped and noncommercial only in a relative sense. And certain places that I really rave about suffer from Back Door congestion now. Every year or so, I revisit my poster-child village discoveries (Gimmelwald, Dingle, Ærø, Salema, and the Cinque Terre) and, while more crowded now, they are still great. At least from my experience, Back Door readers are pleasant people to share Europe with.

People recommended in this book tell me that Back Door readers are good guests who undo the "ugly" image created by the more demanding and ethnocentric American tourists. By traveling sensitively, you're doing a favor for yourself, as well as for the Europeans you'll meet, for the travelers who'll follow you...and for me. Thank you.

These Back Doors combine to give you a chorus line of travel thrills. I've written these chapters to give you the flavor of the places, not for you to navigate by. Better yet, my various country guidebooks provide you with all the details necessary to splice your chosen Back Doors into a smooth trip. Bon voyage!

ITALY

37. The Cinque Terre: Italy's Fiat-Free Riviera

"A sleepy, romantic, and inexpensive town on the Riviera without a tourist in sight." That's the mirage travelers chase around busy Nice and Cannes. Pssst! Although hardly free of tourists, the most dream-worthy stretch of the Riviera rests in Italy just across the border, between Genoa and Pisa. It's Italy's Cinque Terre.

Leaving the nearest big city, La Spezia, your train takes you into a mountain. Ten minutes later, you burst into the sunlight. Your train nips in and out of the hills, teasing you with a series of Mediterranean views. Each scene is grander than the last: azure blue tinseled in sunbeams, carbonated waves hitting desolate rocks, and the occasional topless sunbather camped out like a lone limpet.

The Cinque Terre (pronounced CHINK-weh TAY-reh), which means "five lands," is a quintet of villages clinging to this most inaccessible bit of Riviera coastline. Each is a variation on the same theme: a well-whittled pastel jumble of homes filling a gully like crusty sea creatures in a tide pool. Like a gangly clump of oysters, the houses grow on each other. Residents are the barnacles—hungry, but patient. And we travelers are like algae, coming in with the tide.

The rugged villages of the Cinque Terre, founded by Dark Age locals hiding out from marauding pirates, were long cut off from the modern world. Only with the coming of the train was access made easy. Today, the villages draw hordes of hikers, and the castles protect only glorious views. To preserve this land, the government has declared the Cinque Terre a national park. Visitors hiking between the towns now pay a small entrance fee (about $7 for a one-day pass), which stokes a fund designed to protect the flora and fauna and keep the trails clean and well-maintained.

The government, recognizing how wonderfully preserved these towns are, has long prohibited anyone from constructing any modern buildings. For that reason, today there are no big, comfortable hotels in the area—great news for Back Door travelers because it keeps away the most obnoxious slice of

The Cinque Terre's Five Towns

the traveling public: those who need big, comfortable hotels. But rugged travelers, content to rent a room in a private home or simple *pensione,* enjoy a land where the villagers go about their business as if the surrounding vineyards are the very edges of the earth.

Vernazza

Overseen by a ruined castle, with the closest thing to a natural harbor, Vernazza is my Cinque Terre home base. Only the occasional noisy slurping up of the train by the mountain reminds you there's a modern world out there somewhere.

From Vernazza's harbor, wander through the jumble of a tough community living off the sea...or living off travelers who love the sea. The church bells dictate a relaxed tempo. Yellow webs of fishing nets, tables bedecked with umbrellas, kids with plastic shovels, and a flotilla of gritty little boats tethered to buoys provide splashes of color. And accompanying the scene is the soundtrack of a dream...a celebrate-the-moment white noise of children, dogs, and waves.

Vernazza's one street connects the harbor with the train station before melting into the vineyards. Like veins on a grape leaf, paths and stairways reach from Main Street into this watercolor huddle of houses. All of life is summer reruns in this hive of lazy human activity. A rainbow of laundry flaps as if to keep the flies off the fat grandmothers who clog ancient doorways.

Vernazza, my home base in the Cinque Terre

Residents spend early evenings doing their *vasche* (laps), strolling between the station and the breakwater. Sit on a bench and study this slow-motion parade.

Sailors who suckle at salty taverns brag that while Portofino sold out, "Vernazza is locally owned." Years ago, fearing the change it would bring, they stopped the construction of a major road into the town and region.

Today, at the top end of town, Vernazza's cruel little road hits a post. No cars enter this village of 600 people. Like the breakwater keeps out the waves at the bottom of the town, the post keeps out the modern storm at the top. But Vernazza's ruined castle no longer says "stay away." And its breakwater—a broad, inviting sidewalk edged with seaside boulders—sticks into the sea like a finger beckoning the distant excursion boats.

The Five-Village Cinque Terre Hike

Follow the fragrant trail through sunny vistas from Riomaggiore to Monterosso al Mare. Since my mind goes on vacation with the rest of me when I'm here, I think of the towns by number for easy orientation. They go—east to west—from one (Riomaggiore) to five (Monterosso).

For a great day, catch the early train to Riomaggiore, hike from towns one through four, and catch

The Via dell'Amore path connects two Cinque Terre towns—Riomaggiore and Manarola—with grand views.

ITALY

Vernazza: View from a Vineyard

It's a sunny afternoon a thousand years ago in the Cinque Terre, long before it became the Italian Riviera. This string of humble villages, surrounded by terraced vineyards, is a two-day sail from Genoa.

A leathery old farmer, taking a break from tending his grape vines, picks a cactus fruit to quench his thirst. Suddenly, howls come from the crude, stony tower crowning a bluff that marks his village of Vernazza. Turkish pirates are attacking.

Avoiding powerhouse cities like nearby Genoa and Pisa, pirates delight in the villages. These Cinque Terre towns, famous since Roman times for their white wine, are like snack time for rampaging pirates. Villagers run for cover down corridors buried deep in the clutter of homes that clog Vernazza's ravine.

Nine centuries pass. Another leathery grape-picker is startled by the roar of a smoke-billowing train. Emerging from the newly built tunnel, it flies a red, white, and green flag. It's 1870, and the feudal and fragmented land of Italy is finally united. This first Italian train line, an engineering triumph of fledgling Italy, laces together Turin, Genoa, Rome...and, by chance, tiny Vernazza.

Decades later, in the 1930s, an Italian dictator teams up with a German tyrant. The war they started is going badly. In 1943, the German Führer calls on Vernazza's teenage boys to report for duty. The boys, who are told they'll only work in German farms and factories, know they'll end up as fodder on the front. Rather than dying for Hitler, they become resistance fighters. Running through the night, they climb the ancient terraces into the hills high above the village cemetery.

The 1970s bring on a different battle scene. Hippies exercise their right to lie naked on the Cinque Terre's remote Guvano beach. Outraged, an angry armada of villagers—fully clothed and accompanied by a raft of reporters—converges on the rat pack of sunburned urbanite hedonists.

the boat from Vernazza to the resort town of Monterosso for some beach time. From there, a five-minute train ride takes you home to Vernazza for the sunset and a seafood dinner.

The first town of the Cinque Terre, Riomaggiore (#1), has seduced famed artists into becoming residents. The biggest non-resort town of the five, Riomaggiore is a disappointment from the station. But the tunnel next to the train tracks takes you to a fascinating tangle of colorful homes leaning on each other as if someone stole their crutches. There's homemade gelato next door to Bar Centrale. And Riomaggiore's beach, an uncrowded cove, is a two-minute walk from town.

Next, the age of tourism arrives. In 1978, a college-aged American backpacker, stumbling onto the region, finds the traditions vivid, the wine cheap, and the welcome warm. Inspired by the Cinque Terre and similar places throughout the Continent, he declares the region

a "Back Door" and writes what will later become a top-selling guidebook on Europe.

By the 1990s, word of this paradise is out. More and more travelers visit, staying in apartments rather than in hotels. One day, at the crack of dawn, another invasion comes...this time by land. A platoon of Italian tax inspectors blitzes the sleepy town, rousting out the tourists and cornering locals renting unlicensed rooms. B&B income in Vernazza is suddenly no longer tax-free.

Today, gnarled old men still tend their grapevines. Now Vernazza's castle, named "Belforte" centuries ago for the screams of its watchmen, watches over tourists. And the screams ringing out are of delight from children playing on the beach below.

But the economy has changed. The poor village is now a rich village, living well in its rustic and government-protected shell. Tourism drives the economy as the less-calloused residents feed and house travelers. While the private rooms rented are basic, the cuisine—super-charged by a passion for pasta, pesto, and seafood—is some of Italy's best. The sunny scene is a happy collaboration between locals, travelers, a long past, a lazy present...and no thought of tomorrow.

From Riomaggiore, follow signs for *Via dell'Amore* ("Walkway of Love"). This photogenic 20-minute promenade leads to Manarola (#2) and is wide enough for baby strollers. While you'll find no beach in Manarola, stairways lead to remote rocks for sunbathing. Uppity little Manarola rules its ravine and drinks its wine while its sun-bleached walls slumber on. Buy a picnic before walking to the beaches of Corniglia.

Corniglia (#3)—the only Cinque Terre town not directly on the water—sits smugly on its hilltop, a proud and victorious king of the mountain. Most visitors—lured to Corniglia by its scrawny, stony beach and the Cinque Terre's best swimming—never tackle the 370 stairs that zigzag up to the actual town. Those who make the Corniglian climb are rewarded by the Cinque Terre's finest wine and most staggering view.

Corniglia has cooler temperatures, a windy belvedere, a few restaurants, and more than enough private rooms for rent.

Legend says that the village was originally settled by a Roman farmer who named it for his mother, Cornelia. Since ancient times, when Corniglian wine was so famous that vases found at Pompeii touted its virtues, wine has been this town's lifeblood. Follow the pungent smell of ripe grapes into an alley cellar and get a local to let you dip a straw into her keg.

Ten minutes out of Corniglia on the high trail to Vernazza, you'll see Guvano beach far below. This nude-for-now beach made headlines in Italy in the 1970s, as clothed residents in a makeshift armada of dinghies and fishing boats retook their town beach. But big-city nudists still work on all-around tans in this remote setting.

The crowd is Italian counterculture: pierced nipples, tattooed punks, hippie drummers in dreads, and nude exhibitionist men. The ratio of men to women is about three to two. About half the people on the pebbly beach keep their swimsuits on.

The 90-minute hike from Corniglia (#3) to Vernazza (#4) is the wildest and greenest of the coast. The trail is as rugged as the people who've worked the terraced vineyards that blanket the region. Flowers and an ever-changing view entertain you at every step. As you make your sweaty way high above the glistening beaches, you'll ponder paying for your trip with the photos you've shot. The trail descends scenically into Vernazza, from where you can take the train, the boat, or the scenic, up-and-down-a-lot hike to town #5. Trails are rough (some readers report

"very dangerous") and narrow, but easy to follow.

Monterosso al Mare (#5), happy to be appreciated, boasts the area's only sandy beach. This is a resort with cars, hotels, paddleboats, and crowds under rentable beach umbrellas. Adventurers in search of no-tan-line coves, refreshing waterfalls, and natural (and dangerous) high dives find them tucked away along the coast between towns #4 and #5.

Regardless of which town you call home, getting around is easy. While these towns are barely accessible by car, the nearly hourly milk-run train connects all five towns for about $2. A ferry provides a more relaxed and scenic town-hopping option.

Traditions ring through the Cinque Terre as persistently as the church bells—which remind residents of the days before tourism. The fishermen out at sea could hear the bells. The men in the vineyards high on the mountain could hear them, too. In one village, the hotel keepers tried to stop the bells for the tourists who couldn't sleep. But the people of the village nearly revolted, and the bells ring on.

You'll eat well in the Cinque Terre. This is the home of pesto. Basil—which loves the region's temperate climate—is mixed with cheese (half parmigiano cow cheese and half pecorino sheep cheese), garlic, olive oil, and pine nuts, then poured over pasta. If you become addicted, don't worry: Small jars of pesto are sold in the grocery stores.

And the *vino delle Cinque Terre*, famous throughout Italy, flows cheap and easy throughout the region. If you like sweet, sherrylike wine, try the Sciacchetrà wine—served with a cookie. While 10 kilos of grapes yield seven liters of wine, 10 kilos of grapes make only 1.5 liters of Sciacchetrà, which is made from near-raisins. If your room is up a lot of steps, be warned: Sciacchetrà comes with 50 percent more alcohol than regular wine.

In the cool, calm early evening, sit on the Vernazza breakwater nursing a glass of wine. Paint a dream in vineyard greens and Mediterranean blues. Nowhere else does the lure of the Mediterranean, Italy, and village life combine so potently to shipwreck a speedy itinerary.

*For good-value accommodations in **Vernazza,** try Trattoria Gianni (sea views, near castle, Piazza Marconi 5, tel. 0187-821-003, tel. 0187-812-228, www .giannifranzi.it) or Albergo Barbara (sea views, on harbor square, Piazza Marconi 30, tel. 0187-812-398, mobile 338-793-3261, www.albergobarbara .it). For all the travel specifics, see this year's edition of Rick Steves' Italy.*

38. Hill Towns of Central Italy

Too many people connect Venice, Florence, and Rome with straight lines. Break out of this syndrome, and you'll lick a little of the Italy that the splash of Venice, the finesse of Florence, and the grandeur of Rome were built upon.

The hill towns of central Italy hold their crumbling heads proudly above the noisy flood of the 21st century and offer a peaceful taste of what eludes so many tourists. Sitting on a timeless rampart high above the traffic and trains, hearing only children in the market as the rustling wind ages the weary red-tile patchwork that surrounds me, I find the essence of Italy.

There are a dozen great touristy towns and countless ignored communities casually doing time and drinking wine. See some of each.

The Big-Name Hill Towns

Siena, unlike its rival, Florence, is a city to be seen as a whole rather than as a collection of sights. While memories of Florence consist of dodging Vespas and pickpockets between museums, Siena has an easy-to-enjoy Gothic soul: Courtyards sport flower-decked wells, churches modestly hoard their art, and alleys dead-end into red-tiled rooftop panoramas. Climb to the dizzy top of the 100-yard-tall bell tower and reign over urban harmony at its best. At twilight, first-time poets savor that magic moment when the sky is a rich blue dome no brighter than the medieval towers that seem to hold it high.

Il Campo, Siena's great central piazza, with its gently tilted floor fanning out from the City Hall tower, is like a people-friendly stage set. It offers the perfect invitation to loiter.

Siena turns tourists into poets.

Think of it as a trip to the beach without sand or water. Wander among lovers stroking guitars and each others' hair. Il Campo immerses you in a troubadour's world where bellies become pillows. For a picnic dessert on the Campo, try *panforte*, Siena's claim to caloric fame. This rich, chewy concoction of nuts, honey, and candied fruits impresses even fruitcake-haters.

The *panforte* of medieval churches is Siena's cathedral. Its striped facade is piled with statues and ornamentation. And the chewy interior, decorated from top to bottom, comes with the heads of 172 popes peering down from the ceiling over the fine inlaid art on the floor. This is as Baroque as Gothic gets.

For those who dream of a city with a traffic-free core, Siena is it. Take time to savor the first European square to go pedestrian (1966), and

Hill Towns of Central Italy

then, just to be silly, wonder what would happen if they did it in your town.

Assisi, a worthy hometown for St. Francis, is battling a commercial cancer of tourist clutter. In summer, the town bursts with flash-in-the-pan St. Francis fans and monastic knickknacks. But those able to see past the tacky monk mementos can actually have a "travel on purpose" experience.

In the early 1200s, a simple friar from Assisi challenged the decadence of church government and society in general with a powerful message of simplicity, nonmaterialism, service to the community, and a "slow down and smell God's roses" lifestyle. Like Jesus, Francis taught by example. A huge monastic order grew out of his teachings, which were gradually embraced by the church. In 1939, Italy made Francis its patron saint.

The Basilica of St. Francis, built upon his grave, is one of the artistic highlights of medieval Europe. Open again, restored, and safe after being damaged by the earthquakes of 1997, it's covered with precious frescoes by Giotto, Cimabue, Simone Martini, and other leading artists of the day.

A perch of Franciscan splendor, overlooking Assisi

With a quiet hour in the awesome basilica, some reflective reading (there's a bookstore in the courtyard), and a meditative stroll through the back streets, you can dissolve the tour buses and melt into the magic of Assisi. Grab a picnic and hike to the ruined castle, surrounded by the same Tuscan views and serenaded by the same birdsong Francis enjoyed.

Most visitors are day-trippers. Assisi after dark is closer to a place Francis could call home.

San Gimignano bristles with towers and bustles with tourists. A thrilling silhouette from a distance, Italy's best-preserved medieval skyline gets better as you approach. With 14 towers still standing (out of an original 60 or so), it's a fun and easy stop. In the 13th century, back in the days of Romeo and Juliet, towns were run by feuding noble families who would periodically battle things out from the protective bases of their respective family towers. Sunset's the right time to conquer San Gimignano's castle. Climb high above the crowds, sit on the castle's summit, and imagine the battles Tuscany's porcupine has endured.

Orvieto, the tourist's token hill town, sits majestically on its throne of volcanic tuff, offering an impressive hill-capping profile to those on the train or *autostrada* to Rome. Its cathedral, with

So often photography—and a little wine—bring out the warmth in Italian women.

some fascinating Signorelli frescoes, is surrounded by an excellent tourist information office, a fine Etruscan collection at the archaeological museum, and a world-class gelato shop. With three popular gimmicks (ceramics, cathedral, and Classico wine), Orvieto is loaded with tourists by day and quiet by night. Drinking a shot of wine in a ceramic cup as you gaze up at the cathedral lets you experience the essence of Orvieto all at once. Buses run six days a week from Orvieto to Bagnoregio, near the queen of hill towns, Civita di Bagnoregio.

Civita di Bagnoregio

Of all the Italian hill towns, Civita di Bagnoregio is my favorite. Less well-known than the famous hill towns mentioned above, it deserves more description.

People who've been here say "Civita" (chee-VEE-tah) with warmth and love. This precious chip of Italy, a traffic-free community with a grow-it-in-the-valley economy, has so far escaped the ravages of modernity. Please approach it with the same respect and sensitivity you would a dying relative, because—in a sense—that's Civita.

Civita teeters atop a pinnacle in a vast canyon ruled by wind and erosion. But, while its population has dropped to a handful, the town survives (and even has a website: www.civitadibagnoregio.it).

The saddle that once connected Civita to its bigger and busier sister town, Bagnoregio, eroded away. Today a bridge connects the two towns. A man with a Vespa does the same work his father did with a donkey—ferrying the town's goods up and down the umbilical bridge that connects Civita with a small, distant parking lot and the rest of Italy. Rome,

The perfect hill town, Civita di Bagnoregio

Civita di Bagnoregio

ITALY

just 60 miles to the south, is a world away.

Entering the town through a cut in the rock made by Etruscans 2,500 years ago, and heading under a 12th-century Romanesque arch, you feel history in the huge, smooth cobblestones. This was once the main Etruscan road leading to the Tiber Valley and Rome.

Inside the gate, the charms of Civita are subtle. Those searching for arcade tourism wouldn't know where to look. There are no lists of attractions, orientation tours, or museum hours. It's just Italy. Civita is an artist's dream, a town in the nude. Each lane and footpath holds a surprise. The warm stone walls glow, and each stairway is dessert to a sketch pad or camera.

Sit in the piazza. Smile and nod at each passerby. It's a social jigsaw puzzle, and each person fits. The old woman hanging out in the window monitors gossip. A tiny hunchback lady is everyone's daughter. And cats, the fastest-growing segment of the population, scratch their itches on ancient pillars.

Civita's young people are gone, lured away by the dazzle of more modern places where they can take part in Italy's cosmopolitan parade. And as old people become frail, they move into apartments in nearby Bagnoregio.

Today, Civita's social pie has two slices: the aging, full-time residents; and rich, big-city Italians who are slowly buying up the place for their country escapes. Buoyed by my writing, exposure in German and French travel magazines, and its increasing popularity as a movie backdrop (e.g., for the made-for-TV movie, *Pinocchio*, in 2008), Civita can see up to 200 tourists a day on summer weekends. In summer, visit on a weekday.

Explore the village. The basic grid street plan of the ancient town survives—but its centerpiece, a holy place of worship, rotates with the cultures: first an Etruscan temple, then a Roman temple, and today a church. The pillars that stand like bar stools in the square once decorated the pre-Christian temple.

Step into the church. The heartbeat and pride of the village, this is where festivals and processions start, visitors are escorted, and the town's past is honored. Enjoy paintings by students of famous artists; relics of the hometown-boy Saint Bonaventure; a dried floral decoration spread across the floor; and a cool, quiet moment in a pew.

Just around the corner from the church, on the main street, is Bruschette con Prodotti Locali, Rossana and Antonio's cool and friendly wine cellar. Pull up a stump and let them or their daughters, Arianna and Antonella, serve you *panini* (sandwiches), *bruschetta* (garlic toast with tomato), wine, and a cake called *ciambella*. The white wine has a taste reminiscent of dirty socks. But it's made right here. After eating, ask to see the cellar with its traditional winemaking gear and provisions for rolling huge kegs up the stairs. Grab the stick and tap on the kegs to measure their fullness.

The ground below Civita is honeycombed with ancient cellars (for keeping wine at the same temperature all year) and cisterns (for collecting rainwater, since there was no well in town). Many of these date from Etruscan times.

Explore further through town, but remember nothing is abandoned. Everything is still privately owned. Vittoria, numb to her eye-boggling view of the valley, shows off the latest in a 2,000-year line of olive presses that have filled her ancient Etruscan cave. Buy a postcard in Italian.

On weekends, Vittoria's sons Sandro and Felice, and her grandsons Maurizio and Fabrizio, run Antico Frantoio Bruschetteria, the local equivalent of a lemonade stand, selling *bruschetta* to visitors. Bread toasted on an open fire, drizzled with the finest oil, rubbed with pungent garlic, and topped with chopped tomatoes—these edible souvenirs stay on your breath for hours and in your memory forever.

At the end of town, the main drag shrivels into a trail that leads past a chapel (once a jail) and down to a tunnel—now barred to entry—that was cut through the hill under the town since Etruscan times. It was widened in the 1930s so farmers could get between their scattered fields more easily.

Civita has only a few restaurants, which cluster near the piazza. At Trattoria Antico Forno ("Antique Oven"), you eat what's cooking. Owner Franco slices and dices happily through the day. Spaghetti, salad, and wine on the Antico Forno patio, cuddled by Civita—I wouldn't trade it for all-you-can-eat at Maxim's.

Spend the evening. After dinner, sit on the church steps with people who've been doing exactly this for 60 years. Children play on the piazza until midnight. As you walk back to your car—that scourge of the modern world that enabled you to get here—stop under a lamp on the donkey path, listen to the canyon...distant voices...*fortissimo* crickets.

Towering above its moat, Civita seems to be fortified against change. But the modern world is a persistent battering ram. Civita will be great for years, but never as great as today.

Virgin Hill Towns

Italy is spiked with similar hill towns. Gubbio, Todi, Volterra, and Arezzo are discovered but rarely visited. Cortona (with a hostel set in a remodeled 13th-century palace), Pienza (a Renaissance-planned town), and Montepulciano (with its dramatic setting) are touristy but also worth the hill-town lover's energy and time.

Any guidebook lists popular hill towns. But if you want to dance at noon with a toothless lady while your pizza cooks, press a good-luck coin into the moldy ceiling of an Etruscan wine cellar, or be introduced to a mediocre altarpiece as proudly as if it were a Michelangelo, then stow your guidebook, buy the best map you can find, and explore.

Many bigger hill towns have a train station nearby (with a shuttle bus beginning its winding climb to the old town center shortly after your train arrives). But to find your own gem, you'll need to leave the train lines. Take the bus, hitch, or rent a car for a few days. If you're using a rail-and-drive pass, all the better—this is car country.

Hill towns, like the Greek Islands, come in two basic varieties: discovered...and virgin. The difference, touristically speaking, is that "discovered" towns know what tourism is and have an appetite for the money that comes with it. "Virgin" towns are simply pleased you dropped in.

Sorano, Pitigliano, Poppi, Trevi, and Bagnaia (near Viterbo) have almost no tourism. Bevagna (near Assisi) features Roman ruins and twin dark Romanesque churches on its main square.

Perfect Back Door villages, like hidden pharaohs' tombs, are worth uncovering. Photographers delight in hill towns. Their pictorial collections (such as *Italian Hilltowns*, by Norman F. Carver) are a fine source of information. Study these, circling the most intriguing towns on your map. Talk to travelers who have studied or lived in Italy. Ask locals for their favorites. Scan the horizon for fortified towers. Drive down dead-end roads far from the nearest advertising budget.

Hill towns are a vital slice of the Italian pizza—crumbly crust with a thick, gooey culture. Don't just chase down my favorites or your guidebook's recommendations. Somewhere in the slumber of Umbria and the texture of Tuscany, the ultimate hill town awaits your discovery.

*For good-value accommodations in **Siena**, try Alma Domus (convent-run hotel, request view room, Via Camporegio 37, tel. 0577-44-177, www .hotelalmadomus.it, info@hotelalmadomus.it); in **Assisi**, Hotel Ideale (Piazza Matteotti 1, tel. 075-813-570, www.hotelideale.it, info@hotelideale.it); and in **Orvieto**, Hotel Corso (Corso Cavour 343, tel. 076-334-2020, www .hotelcorso.net, info@hotelcorso.net). In **Civita**, try Franco Sala's Civita B&B (rooms on town square, tel. 076-176-0016, mobile 347-611-5426, www .civitadibagnoregio.it, fsala@pelagus.it); or, in nearby **Bagnoregio**, Romantica Pucci B&B (Piazza Cavour 1, tel. 076-179-2121, www.hotelromanticapucci .it, hotelromanticapucci@libero.it). For all the travel specifics, see this year's edition of Rick Steves' Italy.*

39. North Italy Choices: Milan, Lakes, or Mountains

Italy, Europe's richest cultural brew, intensifies as you plunge deeper. If you like it as far south as Rome, go farther—it gets better. But if Italy's wearing you down, you'll enjoy a milder Italy in the north, complete with the same great cappuccino, gelato, and people-watching.

North Italy's charms come in three packages: urban Milan, romantic lakes, and alpine Dolomites. All are within three hours of Venice, Florence, and each other.

Milan

Milan is today's Italy. The rise of modern Italy can be blamed on cities like Milan. As the saying goes, for every church in Rome, there's a bank in Milan. Italy's second city has a hardworking, fashion-conscious population of more than 1.3 million. From publicists to pasta power lunches,

ITALY

Milan is Italy's industrial, banking, TV, publishing, and convention capital.

Much of Milan is ugly, with a recently bombed-out feeling (a legacy of World War II). Its huge financial buildings are as manicured as its parks are shaggy. As if to make up for its harsh concrete shell, its people and windows are works of art. Milan is an international fashion capital. Even the cheese is gift-wrapped.

Milan's cathedral dominates the main square.

Milan's cathedral, the city's centerpiece, is the fourth-largest church in Europe. At 480 feet long and 280 feet wide, forested with 52 sequoia-sized pillars and more than 2,000 statues, the place can seat 10,000 worshippers. Hike up to the rooftop—a fancy crown of spires—for great views of the city, the square, and, on clear days, the Swiss Alps.

The cathedral square, Piazza Duomo, is a classic European scene. Professionals scurry, label-conscious kids loiter, and young thieves peruse. Facing the square, the Galleria Vittorio Emanuele, Milan's great four-story-high, glass-domed arcade, invites you in to shop or just sip a slow latte. Some of Europe's hottest people-watching turns that pricey cup into a good value. Enjoy the parade. For good luck, locals step on the testicles of the Taurus in the floor's zodiac mosaic. Two girls explained that it's even better if you twirl.

The immense Sforza Castle, Milan's much-bombed and rebuilt brick fortress, is overwhelming at first sight. But its courtyard has a great lawn for picnics and siestas. Its museum features interesting medieval armor, furniture, Lombard art, and a Michelangelo statue with no crowds—his unfinished *Rondanini Pietà*. The Brera Art Gallery, Milan's top collection of paintings, is world-class (although you'll see better in Rome and Florence).

La Scala is possibly the world's most prestigious opera house. Opera buffs will love the museum's extensive collection of things that would mean absolutely nothing to the MTV crowd: Verdi's top hat, Rossini's eyeglasses, Toscanini's baton, Fettucini's pesto, and the original scores, busts, portraits, and death masks of great composers and musicians.

Leonardo's ill-fated *Last Supper* is flecking off the refectory wall of the church of Santa Maria delle Grazie. The fresco suffers from Leonardo's

Train Connections in North Italy

experimental use of oil. Decay began within six years of its completion. It's undergone more restoration work than Cher and is now viewable only with a reservation—spots are booked a few months in advance (best to call them directly, tel. 02-9280-0360 in Italy or from the US 011-39-02-9280-0360; possible to reserve online at www.cenacolovinciano.net, but problematic website often does not show available ticket dates). Most of the original paint is gone, but tourists still enjoy paying $12 to see what's left.

More of Leonardo's spirit survives in Italy's answer to the Smithsonian, the Leonardo da Vinci National Science and Technology Museum. While most tourists visit for the hall of Leonardo's designs illustrated in wooden models, the rest of this vast collection of industrial cleverness is just as fascinating. Plenty of push-button action displays the development of trains, radios, old musical instruments, computers, batteries, and telephones, alongside chunks of the first transatlantic cable.

Italy's Lakes

The Italian Lakes, at the base of Italy's Alps, are a romantic and popular destination for Italians and their European neighbors. The million-euro question is "Which lake?" For a complete dose of Italian-lakes wonder and aristocratic old-days romance, visit Lake Como.

Lined with elegant 19th-century villas, crowned by snow-capped mountains, buzzing with ferries, hydrofoils, and little passenger ships, this is a good place to take a break from the intensity and obligatory turnstile culture of central Italy. Handy, accessible, and offbeat, Lake Como is

On Lake Como, ferries hop from town to town.

Italy for beginners. It seems that half the travelers you'll meet on Lago di Como have tossed their itineraries overboard and are actually relaxing. The area's isolation and flat economy have left it pretty much the way the 19th-century romantic poets described it.

While you can circle the lake by car, the road is narrow, congested, and lined by privacy-seeking walls, hedges, and tall fences. This is train-and-boat country. Trains whisk you from intense Milan into the serenity of Lago di Como in an hour. Then, happy-go-lucky ferries sail scenically from port to port.

The town of Bellagio, "the Pearl of the Lake," is a classy combination of tidiness and Old World elegance. If you don't mind that tramp-in-a-palace feeling, it's a fine place to surround yourself with the more adventurous of the soft travelers and shop for umbrellas and ties. The heavy curtains between the arcades keep the tourists and their poodles from sweating. While Johnnie Walker and jewelry sell best at lake level, the residents shop up the hill.

Menaggio, directly across the lake from Bellagio and just eight miles from Lugano in Switzerland, feels more like a real town than its neighbors. Since the lake is too dirty for swimming, consider its fine public pool.

One hop from Menaggio or Bellagio by ferry, the town of Varenna offers the best of all lake worlds. On the quieter side of the lake, with a romantic promenade, a tiny harbor, narrow lanes, and its own villa, Varenna is the right place to munch a peach and ponder the place where Italy is welded to the Alps. Varenna's volume goes down with the sun.

After dark, the *passerella* (lakeside walk) is adorned with lovers pressing silently against each other in the shadows.

The Dolomites

The Dolomites, Italy's dramatic mountainous rooftop, serve alpine thrills with Italian sunshine. The famous valleys and towns of the well-developed region suffer from an après-ski fever, but the bold, snow-dusted mountains and green meadows offer great hikes. The cost for reliably good weather is a drained-reservoir feeling. Lovers of the Alps may miss the lushness that comes with the unpredictable weather farther north.

Don't forget Italy's Alps, the Dolomites.

A hard-fought history has left this part of Italy bicultural and bilingual, with *der* emphasis on the *Deutsch*. Residents speak German first. Many wish they were still Austrian. In the Middle Ages, the region faced north, part of the Holy Roman Empire. Later it was firmly in the Austrian Habsburg realm. After Austria lost World War I, its South Tirol (Südtirol) became Italy's Alto Adige. Mussolini did what he could to Italianize the region, including giving each town an Italian name. The government has wooed cranky German-speaking locals with economic breaks that make this one of Italy's richest areas (as prices attest). Today, signs and literature in the autonomous province of Südtirol/Alto Adige are in both languages.

In spite of all the glamorous ski resorts and busy construction cranes, local color survives in a blue-aproned, ruddy-faced, long-white-bearded way. There's yogurt and yodeling for breakfast. Culturally as much as geographically, the area feels Austrian. (The western part of Austria is named after Tirol, a village that is now actually in Italy.)

Lifts, good trails, outdoor activity–oriented tourist offices, and a decent bus system make the region especially accessible. But it's expensive. Most towns

Treating the Alps like a beach, in Italy's Dolomites

have no alternative to $120 doubles in hotels, or $75 doubles in private homes. Beds usually come with a hearty breakfast, a rarity in Italy.

The seasons are brutal. The best time to visit—when everything is open and booming, but also at full price and crowded—is from mid-July through September. After a dreary November, the snow hits, and it's busy with skiers until April. May and early June are dead (though the sedentary sort will enjoy the views and tranquility). The most exciting trails are still under snow, and the mountain lifts are shut down. Most mountain huts and budget accommodations are closed, as the locals are more concerned with preparing for another boom season than catering to the stray off-season tourist.

By car, circle north from Venice and drive the breathtaking Grande Strada delle Dolomiti, or Great Dolomite Road (65 miles: Cortina d'Ampezzo–Pordoi Pass–Sella Pass–Val di Fassa–Bolzano; toll possible). In the spring and early summer, passes labeled "Closed" are often bare, dry, and, as far as local drivers are concerned, wide open. Conveniently for Italian tour operators, no direct public-transportation route covers the Great Dolomite Road.

With limited time and no car, maximize mountain thrills and minimize transportation headaches by taking the train to Bolzano, then catching a public bus into the mountains.

If Bolzano (or "Bozen" to its German-speaking residents) weren't so sunny, you could be in Innsbruck. This arcaded old town of 100,000, with a great open-air market on Piazza Erbe, is worth a Tirolean stroll and a stop at its Dolomite information center. To chill out, see Bolzano's Ice Man, a 5,300-year-old body found frozen with his gear some years ago (described in Chapter 68: Offbeat Europe).

Tourist offices in any Dolomite town are a wealth of information.

I wouldn't steer you wrong: Hiking through Dolomite meadows is an udderly heifer-vescent experience.

Before choosing a hike, get their advice. Ideally, pick a hike with an overnight in a mountain hut and make a telephone reservation. Most huts, called *refugios*, offer reasonable doubles, cheaper dorm *(Lager)* beds, and good, inexpensive meals.

Many are tempted to wimp out on the Dolomites and admire the spires from a distance. They take the cable car into the hills above Bolzano, to the cute but very touristy village of Oberbozen. Don't. Bus into the

Dolomites instead.

Europe's largest high-alpine meadow, Alpe di Siusi, spreads high above Bolzano, separating two of the most famous Dolomite ski-resort valleys (Val di Fassa and Val Gardena). Measuring three miles by seven and a half miles, and soaring 6,500 feet high, Alpe di Siusi is dotted by farm huts and wildflowers and surrounded by dramatic (if distant) Dolomite peaks and cliffs.

The Sasso Lungo mountains at the head of the meadow provide a storybook Dolomite backdrop, while the bold, spooky Mount Schlern stands gazing into the haze of the Italian peninsula. Not surprisingly, the Schlern, looking like a devilish *Winged Victory*, gave ancient peoples enough willies to spawn legends of supernatural forces. Fear of the Schlern witch, today's tourist-brochure mascot, was the cause of many a broom-riding medieval townswoman's fiery death.

A nature preserve, the alpine meadow is virtually car-free. A gondola whisks visitors up to the park from the valley below. Within the park, buses take hikers to and from key points along the tiny road all the way to the foot of the postcard-dramatic Sasso peaks. Meadow walks are ideal for flower lovers and strollers, while chairlifts provide springboards for more dramatic and demanding hikes.

The Alpe di Siusi is my recommended one-stop look at the Dolomites

Castelrotto/Kastelruth: Your home base in the Dolomites

because of its easy accessibility to those with or without cars, the variety of walks and hikes, the quintessential Dolomite views, and the charm of neighboring Castelrotto as a home base.

The town of Castelrotto (population: 2,000; German name: Kastelruth) was built for farmers rather than skiers. It has good bus connections, fine and friendly hotels, and more village character than any town around. Pop into the church to hear the choir practice. And be on the town square at 2:45 p.m. as the bells peal and the moms bring home their preschoolers.

At Europe Through the Back Door, where I work, many consider Italy the greatest country in Europe. If all you have is 10 days, do Venice, Florence, Rome, the hill towns, and the Riviera. If you have more time and seek intensity, head south. But to round out your itinerary with all the best of Italy and none of the chaos, splice in a little of the Dolomites, the lakes, and Milan.

*For good-value accommodations in **Milan**, try Hotel Grand Duca di York (splurge, Via Moneta 1, tel. 02-874-863, www.ducadiyork.com); in **Varenna**, Hotel Olivedo (at ferry dock, tel. 0341-830-115, www.olivedo.it) or Albergo Milano (splurge, Via XX Settembre 35, tel. 0341-830-298, www.varenna .net); and in **Castelrotto/Kastelruth**, Alla Torre/Gasthof zum Turm (Kofelgasse 8, tel. 0471-706-349, www.zumturm.com). For all the travel specifics, see this year's edition of Rick Steves' Italy.*

40. Naples, the Amalfi Coast, and a Steamy Volcano

Naples Bay rounds out any trip to Italy with an *antipasto misto* of travel thrills. Serene Sorrento, an hour south of Naples' urban intensity, is a great home base and the gateway to the much-drooled-over Amalfi Coast. From the jet-setting island of Capri to the stunning Amalfi Coast towns, from ancient Pompeii to even more ancient Paestum, this is Italy's coast with the most. Naples is Italy intensified, from its best (birthplace of pizza and Sophia Loren) to its worst (home of the Camorra, Naples' "family" of organized crime).

On a quick trip, give the area three days. With Sorrento as your sunny springboard, spend a day exploring the Amalfi Coast, a day split between Pompeii and the town of Sorrento, and a day enjoying the street scene in Naples. Paestum, the crater of Vesuvius, Herculaneum, and the island of Capri are all good reasons to give the area a few more days.

For a blitz day trip from Rome, you could have breakfast on the early Rome–Naples express, do Naples and Pompeii in a day, and be back at your hotel in time for *Letterman*. That's exhausting but more interesting than a third day in Rome. (In the heat of the afternoon, Naples' street life slows and many sights close. Things pick up again in the early evening.)

Sorrento, wedged on a ledge between the mountains and the Mediterranean, is an attractive resort of 20,000 residents and—in the summer—as many tourists. It's as well-located for regional sightseeing as it is a pleasant place to stay and stroll. The Sorrentines have gone out of their way to create a completely safe and relaxed place for tourists to spend money. Everyone seems to speak fluent English and work for the Chamber of Commerce. Spritzed by lemon and olive groves, this

Naples and the Amalfi Coast

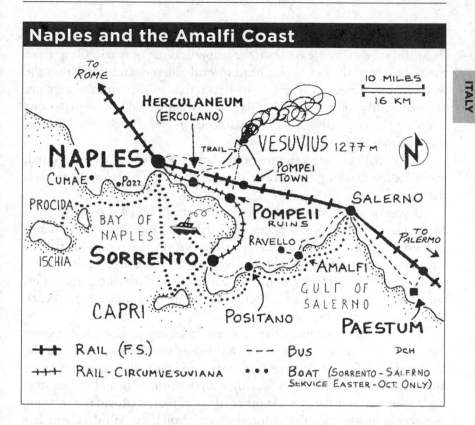

TO ROME

HERCULANEUM (ERCOLANO)

TRAIL

VESUVIUS 1277 M

POMPEI TOWN

NAPLES

CUMAE • POZZ

PROCIDA

BAY OF NAPLES

POMPEII RUINS

SALERNO

TO PALERMO

RAVELLO

ISCHIA

SORRENTO

AMALFI

GULF OF SALERNO

CAPRI

POSITANO

PAESTUM

10 MILES
16 KM

N

━┿━ RAIL (F.S.)

━╫━ RAIL - CIRCUMVESUVIANA

--- BUS

••• BOAT (SORRENTO - SALERNO SERVICE EASTER - OCT. ONLY)

DCH

gateway to the Amalfi Coast has an unspoiled old quarter, a lively main shopping street, a spectacular cliffside setting, and easy public transportation (Circumvesuviana trains run twice hourly to Naples, stopping at Pompeii and Herculaneum en route; and blue or green-and-white SITA buses depart nearly hourly from the Sorrento train station to the Amalfi Coast).

The **Amalfi Coast** offers one of the world's great bus rides: The coastal trip from Sorrento to Salerno will leave your mouth open and your camera smokin'. You'll gain respect for the Italian engineers who built the road—and even more respect

for the bus drivers who drive it. As you hyperventilate, notice how the Mediterranean, a sheer 500-foot drop below, twinkles.

Cantilevered garages, hotels, and villas cling to the vertical terrain. Beautiful sandy coves tease from far below and out of reach. Gasp from the right side of the bus as you head toward Salerno, and the left on the way back to Sorrento. Traffic is so heavy that in the summer cars are allowed to drive only every other day—even-numbered license plates one day, odd the next. (Buses and tourists foolish enough to drive here are exempt from this system.)

The Amalfi Coast towns are pretty but generally touristy, congested, overpriced, and a long hike above tiny beaches. The real Amalfi thrill is the scenic drive.

If you need a destination, consider Positano, an easy day trip from Sorrento. Specializing in scenery and sand, the town of Positano hangs halfway between Sorrento and Amalfi town on the most spectacular stretch of the coast. A three-star sight from a distance, Positano is a pleasant (if expensive) gathering of women's clothing stores and cafés, with a good but pebbly beach. There's little to do here but enjoy the beach and views, and window-shop.

Capri, made famous as the vacation hideaway of Roman emperors Augustus and Tiberius, is today a world-class tourist trap where gawky tourists search for the rich and famous but find only their prices. A quick boat ride from Sorrento, this four-mile-by-two-mile "Island of Dreams" is a zoo in July and August. At other times of year, it provides a relaxing and scenic break from the cultural gauntlet of Italy. While Capri has some Roman ruins and an interesting 14th-century Carthusian monastery, its chief attraction is its famous Blue Grotto and its best activity is a scenic hike.

Pompeii, stopped in its tracks by the eruption of Mount Vesuvius in A.D. 79, offers the best look anywhere at what life in Rome must have been like nearly 2,000 years ago. An entire city of well-preserved ruins is yours to explore. Once a thriving commercial port of 20,000, Pompeii grew from Greek and Etruscan roots to become an important Roman city. Then Pompeii was buried under 30 feet of hot mud and volcanic ash. For archaeologists, this was a shake 'n' bake windfall, teaching them volumes about daily Roman life.

When touring Pompeii, remember this was a booming trading

city. Most streets would have been lined with stalls and jammed with customers from sunup to sundown. Chariots vied for street space with shoppers, and many streets were off-limits to chariots during shopping hours (you'll still see street signs with pictures of men carrying vases—this meant pedestrians only). Pompeii's best art is in the Naples Archaeological Museum (see next page).

Herculaneum—smaller, less ruined, and less crowded than its famous sister, Pompeii—offers a closer look at ancient Roman life. Caked and baked by the same eruption in A.D. 79, Herculaneum is a small community of intact buildings with plenty of surviving detail.

Vesuvius, mainland Europe's only active volcano, has been sleeping restlessly since 1944. Complete your Pompeii or Herculaneum experience by scaling the volcano that made them famous. The 4,000-foot summit of Vesuvius is accessible by car, Vesuviana Mobilità shuttle bus (about $11 round-trip, leaves from the Herculaneum station), or taxi (about $125 round-trip from Naples). From the Vesuvius parking lot, pay about $10 and hike 30 minutes to the top for a sweeping Bay of Naples view, desolate lunar-like surroundings, and hot rocks. On the top, walk the entire crater lip for the most interesting views. The far end overlooks Pompeii. Be still and alone to hear the wind and tumbling rocks in the crater. Any steam? Vesuvius is closed when erupting.

Paestum is one of the best collections of Greek temples anywhere— and certainly the most accessible to Western Europe. Serenely situated, it's surrounded by fields and wildflowers and a modest commercial strip. Founded by the Greeks in the sixth century B.C., it was a key stop on an important trade route. It was conquered first by Romans in the third century B.C. and later by malaria-carrying mosquitoes that kept the site wonderfully desolate for almost a thousand years. Rediscovered in the 18th century, Paestum today offers the only well-preserved Greek ruins north of Sicily.

Naples, a thriving Greek commercial center 2,500 years ago, remains

southern Italy's leading city, offering a fascinating collection of museums, churches, eclectic architecture, and crazy traffic. The pulse of Italy throbs in this urban jungle. Like Cairo or Bombay, it's appalling and captivating at the same time, the closest thing to "reality travel" you'll find in Western Europe. But this tangled mess still somehow manages to breathe, laugh, and sing—with a captivating Italian accent.

Overcome your fear of being run down or ripped off long enough to talk with people: Enjoy a few smiles and jokes with the man running the neighborhood tripe shop or the woman taking her day-care class on a walk through the traffic.

For a quick visit, start with the Archaeological Museum, explore a few streets, and celebrate your survival with pizza.

Naples' Archaeological Museum offers the closest possible peek into the artistic jewelry boxes of Pompeii and Herculaneum. The actual archaeological sites, while impressive, are barren—the best frescoes and mosaics ended up here. The Secret Room (for which you need to reserve an entry time at the ticket desk) displays R-rated Roman "bedroom" art. A museum highlight is the Farnese Collection—a giant hall of huge, bright, and wonderfully restored statues excavated from Rome's Baths of Caracalla. You can almost hear the *Toro Farnese* snorting. This largest intact statue from antiquity (a third-century copy of a Hellenistic original) was carved out of one piece of marble and restored by Michelangelo.

Marble lovers chisel out time for the Cappella Sansevero, six blocks southeast of the Archaeological Museum. This small chapel is a Baroque explosion mourning the body of Christ,

Naples: an urban jungle with straight streets and friendly cops

lying on a soft pillow under an incredibly realistic veil—all carved out of marble (by Giuseppe "Howdeedoodat" Sammartino, 1750). Loving statues, each carved from a single piece of marble, adorn the altar. *Despair* (by Francesco Queirolo, 1759) struggles with a marble rope net, while *Modesty* poses coyly under her full-length marble veil (by Antonio Corradini, 1752). For your inner ghoul, descend into the crypt for a creepy look at two 200-year-old studies in varicose veins. Was one decapitated? Was one pregnant?

Take time to explore Naples. This living medieval city is its own best sight. Couples artfully make love on Vespas, while surrounded by more fights and smiles per cobblestone than anywhere else in Italy.

Paint a picture with these thoughts: Naples has the most intact ancient Roman street plan anywhere. Imagine life here in the days of

Caesar (retain these images as you visit Pompeii), with street-side shop fronts that close up to form private homes after dark. Today is just one more page in a 2,000-year-old story of city activity: all kinds of meetings, beatings, and cheatings; kisses, near misses, and little-boy pisses.

The only thing predictable about this Neapolitan mix is the friendliness of its shopkeepers and the boldness of its mopeds. Concerned residents will tug on their lower eyelid, warning you to be wary. Pop into a grocery shop and ask the man to make you his best ham-and-mozzarella sandwich.

For a peek behind the scenes in the shade of wet laundry, venture down a few narrow streets lined by tall apartment buildings. Black-and-

white death announcements add to the clutter on the walls. Widows sell cigarettes from plastic buckets. Buy two carrots as a gift for the woman on the fifth floor if she'll lower her bucket down to pick them up. One wave works wonders as six floors of balconies fill up, each with its own waving family. Walking around, craning my neck upward, I feel like a victorious politician among hordes of supporters. It's a *Laugh-In* wall with each window and balcony vying for a photo: Mothers hold up babies, sisters pose arm in arm, a wild pregnant woman stands on a fruit crate holding her bulging stomach, and an old, wrinkled woman fills her paint-starved window frame with a toothy grin. A contagious energy fills the air. It hurts to say *arrivederci*.

For good-value accommodations in **Sorrento,** *try Hotel Mignon Meublè (Via Sersale 9, tel. 081-807-3824, www.sorrentohotelmignon.com) or Hotel Minerva (cliff-hanging views, Via Capo 30-32, tel. 081-878-1011, www .minervasorrento.com). For all the travel specifics, see this year's edition of* Rick Steves' Italy.

41. Sassy, Spicy Sicily

Jabbing his pole like a one-pronged pitchfork into the slow red river of molten rock, the ashtray salesman pulled out a wad of lava. I scrambled back as he swung it by me and plopped it into a mold. His partner snipped it off with big iron clippers and rammed it into shape. The now

Auntie Pasta says, "It's ciao time!"

shapely mass was dropped into a bucket of water that steamed and hissed. Cooling on a crispy black ledge were a dozen more lava ashtrays, each with the words "Mount Etna, Sicily" molded into it.

As the red lava poured out of its horribly hot trap door, I unzipped the ski parka I'd rented for $1 at the lift. At 11,000 feet, even on a sunny day, it's cold on top of Mount Etna... unless you're three feet from a lava flow.

At the edge of the volcano, I surveyed the island that I had just explored on my scriptwriting mission for a TV show on Sicily. Old lava flows rumbled like buffalo toward teeming Catania. The island's sprawling second city butted up against a crescent beach that stretched all the way to Taormina, the Santorini of Sicily, popular with Italians who dress up to travel. And to my right was the hazy, high, and harsh interior. Two hours later, I had dropped my rental car at the Catania airport and was flying back to Rome, a rough script unfolding on my laptop screen.

Sicily sights are hard to grasp. Its historic and artistic big shots just don't ring a bell. The folkloric traditions, such as marionette theaters promoted by tourist brochures, seem to play out only for tour groups. And the place must lead Europe in litter. But there's a

The Greek theater at Sicily's Taormina: With a view like this, no play is a tragedy.

workaday charm here. If you like Italy for its people, tempo, and joy of living—rather than for its Botticellis, Guccis, and touristic icons—you'll dig Sicily.

Sicily, standing midway between Africa and Europe, really is a world unto itself. While part of Italy, it's not quite that simple. Even though (with government encouragement) the siesta is fading out of Italian life,

ITALY

Sicily

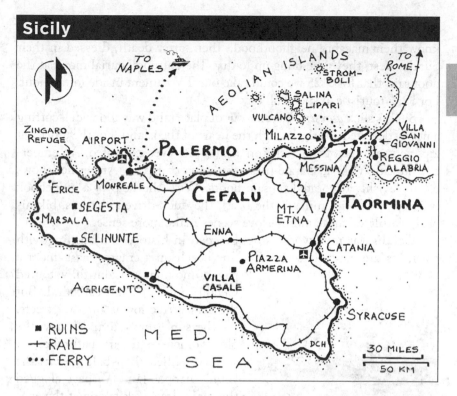

it thrives in Sicily. As European safety regulations take hold in the north, with laws requiring helmets on motorbikers, hair continues to fly in the Sicilian wind.

Palermo is the Rome of Sicily, with lavish art, boisterous markets, and holy cannoli. In the market, animals hang like anatomy lessons, sliced perfectly in half. *Fichi di India,* the fist-size cactus fruit that tastes like a cousin of the kiwi, are peeled and yours for less than a buck.

Palermo offers a great bone experience—skull and shoulders above anything else you'll find in Europe. Its Cappuccin crypt is a subterranean gallery filled with 8,000 "bodies without souls" howling silently at their mortality. For centuries, people would thoughtfully

Even in death, Italians know how to look cool.

choose their niche before they died, and even linger there, getting to know their macabre neighborhood. Then, after death, dressed in their Sunday best, they'd be hung up to dry. The entrepreneurial monk at the door said that for $125 we could take our TV camera inside for an hour. For $2, a tourist can spend all day.

Sicily's slick *autostrada* seems out of place (and way too wide), cutting a nearly deserted swath through the heart of the island. For the tourist, it zips you to some of the best Roman mosaics ever excavated. An emperor's hunting villa at Casale (near the town of Piazza Armerina) shows off 50 lavishly decorated mosaic floors. With the help of a guidebook (Giuseppe di Giovanni's is the best), the duck-driven chariots, bikini-clad triathletes, and amorous love scenes make more sense.

Cefalù was my favorite stop. Steeped in history and bustling with color, it's dramatically set with a fine beach on a craggy coast under a

pagan mountain. I dutifully toured Cefalù's museum and cathedral. But the real attraction is on the streets. As the sun grew red and heavy, the old women—still in bathrobes, it seemed—filled their balconies as the young people (and Vespas) clogged the main drag. Tsk-tsking at the age-old flirting scene, the women gossiped about the girls below.

My friend—ignoring the boy-toy girls—told me of the motorbike he lusted after. It was a classic Vespa from the '70s...with a body that's "round like a woman's." Just then, another guy galloped up on his very round, very blue, classic Vespa. He declared, "It's the only Vespa I've ever owned. I got it when I was 14. That was in 1969. The year man first walked on the moon—that was the year I first rode this Vespa." My friend and a few other guys gathered around almost worshipfully. The old women in the balconies and the mini-skirted flirts no longer existed. Cefalù and its teeming main drag were just Mediterranean wallpaper as that round, blue Vespa dripped in Sicilian testosterone.

Later, at a café overlooking the beach, I sipped my *latte di mandorla* (almond milk) with the locals who seemed to be posted there on duty to make sure that big, red sun goes down. Little wooden boats, painted brightly, sat plump on the beach. Above them, the fisherman's

Travel smart in Sicily: Pay your respects to the Big Cheese.

clubhouse filled what was a medieval entry through the town wall. I wandered in.

I was greeted warmly by the senior member, "Il Presidente." The men go by nicknames and often don't even know their friends' real names. Since 1944, Il Presidente has spent his nights fishing, gathering anchovies under the beam of his gas-powered *lampara*. When he took the pre-Coleman vintage lamp off its rusty wall hook, I saw tales of a lifetime at sea in his face. As he showed me the ropes he wove from straw and complained that the new ropes just aren't the same, I lashed him to my budding script.

*For the TV script, see www.ricksteves.com/tv. For good-value accommodations in **Palermo**, try Grande Albergo Sole (splurge, Corso Vittorio Emanuele 291, tel. 091-604-1111, www.angalahotels.it) or Hotel Moderno (budget, Via Roma 276, tel. 091-588-683, www.hotelmodernopa.com); in **Cefalù**, Hotel Riva del Sole (Via Lungomare 25, tel. 092-142-1230, www.rivadelsole.com); in Taormina, Hotel Continental (Via Dionisio 2a, tel. 094-223-805, www.continentaltaormina.com).*

PORTUGAL, SPAIN, AND MOROCCO

42. Lisbon's Gold Still Shines

Barely elegant outdoor cafés, glittering art, and the saltiest sailors' quarter in Europe make Lisbon an Iberian highlight. Portugal's capital is a wonderful mix of now and then. Old wooden trolleys shiver up its hills, bird-stained statues guard grand squares, and people sip coffee in Art Nouveau cafés.

Present-day Lisbon is explained by its past. Her glory days were the 15th and 16th centuries, when explorers such as Vasco da Gama opened new trade routes, making Lisbon the queen of Europe. Later, the riches of Brazil boosted Lisbon even higher. Then, in 1755, an earthquake leveled the city, killing nearly a quarter of its people.

A lazy viewpoint overlooking Lisbon's Alfama

Lisbon was rebuilt on a strict grid plan, symmetrically, with broad boulevards and square squares. The grandeur of pre-earthquake Lisbon survives in only three neighborhoods: Belém, the Alfama, and the Bairro Alto.

While the earthquake flattened a lot of buildings, and its colonial empire is long gone,

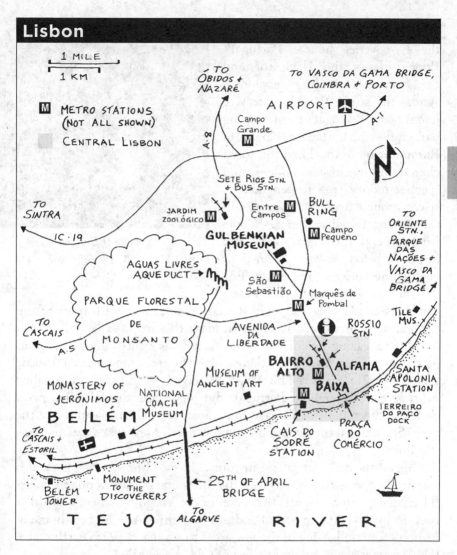

Lisbon

1 MILE
1 KM

Ⓜ METRO STATIONS (NOT ALL SHOWN)

CENTRAL LISBON

TO ÓBIDOS & NAZARÉ

TO VASCO DA GAMA BRIDGE, COIMBRA & PORTO

AIRPORT ✈

Campo Grande Ⓜ

A-1

A-8

TO SINTRA

IC-19

SETE RIOS STN. & BUS STN.

JARDIM ZOOLÓGICO

Entre Campos Ⓜ

BULL RING

Campo Pequeno Ⓜ

GULBENKIAN MUSEUM

TO ORIENTE STN., PARQUE DAS NAÇÕES & VASCO DA GAMA BRIDGE ↗

AGUAS LIVRES AQUEDUCT →

PARQUE FLORESTAL

DE MONSANTO

São Sebastião Ⓜ

Marquês de Pombal Ⓜ

TILE MUS.

TO CASCAIS

A-5

AVENIDA DA LIBERDADE

ℹ

ROSSIO STN.

SANTA APOLONIA STATION

MONASTERY OF JERÓNIMOS

NATIONAL COACH MUSEUM

MUSEUM OF ANCIENT ART

BAIRRO ALTO Ⓜ

ALFAMA

BAIXA Ⓜ

BELÉM

TERREIRO DO PAÇO DOCK

TO CASCAIS & ESTORIL

CAIS DO SODRÉ STATION

PRAÇA DO COMÉRCIO

BELÉM TOWER

MONUMENT TO THE DISCOVERERS

← 25TH OF APRIL BRIDGE

TO ALGARVE

T E J O

R I V E R

PORTUGAL

Lisbon's heritage survives. Follow me through a day in Lisbon.

After breakfast, grab a trolley or taxi to Torre de Belém (Belém Tower). The Belém District, four miles from downtown, is a pincushion of important sights from Portugal's Golden Age, when Vasco da Gama and company made her Europe's richest power.

The Belém Tower, built in Manueline style (ornate Portuguese late-Gothic), has guarded Lisbon's harbor since 1555. Today, it symbolizes the voyages that made her powerful. This was the last sight sailors saw as they left—and the first one they'd see when they returned, loaded down with gold, diamonds, and venereal diseases.

Nearby, the giant Monument to the Discoveries honors Portugal's Prince Henry the Navigator and the country's leading explorers. Across the street, the Monastery of Jerónimos is Portugal's most exciting building—with my favorite cloister in Europe. King Manuel had this giant church and its cloisters built—using "pepper money," a 5 percent tax on spices brought back from India—in thanks for the discoveries. Sailors would spend their last night here in prayer before embarking on their frightening voyages. The Manueline style of this giant church and cloister

Enjoying the peace of Europe's finest cloister at Lisbon's Monastery of Jerónimos

combines late Gothic and early Renaissance features with motifs from the sea, the source of the wealth that made this art possible.

Before leaving Belém, take your taste buds sightseeing at a famous pastry shop, Casa Pasteis de Belém (a block from the monastery at Rua de Belém 84–92). This is the birthplace of the wonderful cream tart called *pastel de nata* throughout Portugal. But in Lisbon, they're called *pastel de Belém*. Since 1837, locals have come here to get them warm out of the oven. Sprinkle on the cinnamon and powdered sugar, get a *café com leite*, and linger.

Spend the early afternoon in your choice of Lisbon's fine museums waiting for the setting sun to rekindle the action in the Alfama. A colorful sailors' quarter, this was the center of the Visigothic town, a rich district during the Arabic period and now the shiver-me-timbers home of Lisbon's fisherfolk. One of the few areas to survive the 1755 earthquake, the Alfama is a cobbled cornucopia of Old World color.

Wander deep. This urban jungle's roads are squeezed into tangled stairways and confused alleys. Bent houses comfort each other in their romantic shabbiness, and the air drips with laundry and the smell of clams and raw fish. Get lost. Poke aimlessly, sample the ample grapes, avoid rabid-looking dogs, peek through windows. Make a friend, pet a chicken. Taste the *branco seco*—the local dry wine.

Gradually zigzag your way up the castle-crowned hill until you reach a viewpoint, the little green square called Miradouro de Santa Luzia. Rest here and survey the cluttered Alfama rooftops below you.

A block away is Largo Rodrigues Freitas, a square with several scruffy, cheap, very characteristic eateries. Treat yourself to the special—a plate of boiled clams.

If you climb a few more blocks to the top of the hill, you'll find the ruins of Castelo de São Jorge. From this fortress, which has dominated the city for more than 1,000 years, enjoy the roaming peacocks and a commanding view of Portugal's capital city.

In the late afternoon, for a quintessential Lisbon drink, duck into one of the funky hole-in-the-wall shops throughout town and ask for a *ginginha* (zheen-zheen-yah). Sold for about a buck a shot, it's a sweet liquor made from the sour cherry–like ginja berry, sugar, and schnapps. The only choices are: with or without berries (*com* or *sem fruta*) and *gelada* if you want it from a chilled bottle out of the fridge—very nice. In Portugal, when someone is impressed by the taste of something, they say, *"Sabe melhor que nem ginjas"* (It tastes even better than ginja).

Spend the evening at a Portuguese bullfight. It's a brutal sport, but the bull lives through it and so will you. The fight starts with an equestrian duel—a fast bull against a graceful horse and rider. Then the fun starts. A colorfully clad eight-man team enters the ring strung out in a line as if to play leapfrog. The leader taunts *O Touro* noisily, and, with testosterone sloshing everywhere, the bull and the man charge each other. The speeding bull plows into the leader head-on. Then—thud, thud, thud—the raging bull skewers the entire charging crew. The horns are wrapped so no one gets gored—just mashed.

In a Portuguese bullfight, the matador is brutalized, too.

The crew wrestles the bull to a standstill, and one man grabs the bull's tail. Victory is complete when the team leaps off the bull and the man still hanging onto the tail "water-skis" behind the enraged animal. This thrilling display of insanity is repeated with six bulls. After each round, the bruised and battered leader limps a victory lap around the ring.

Portugal's top bullring is Lisbon's Campo Pequeno (fights generally on Thu and Sun, mid-June–Sept; other arenas offer fights most Sundays,

Easter–Oct). Half the fights are simply Spanish-type *corridas* without the killing. For the real slam-bam Portuguese-style fight, confirm that there will be *grupo de forcados*.

For a modern Lisbon experience, visit Parque das Nações, where Lisbon celebrated the 500th anniversary of Vasco da Gama's voyage to India by hosting Expo '98 (ride the Metro to the last stop on the red line—Oriente, walk to the water, turn right, and join the people strolling along the riverside). The Vasco da Gama mall has a top-floor beer garden with outside decks that let you drink in the Tejo River view. I ate dinner surrounded by chattering locals, while great platters of fish, meat, fries, salad, and lots of wine and beer paraded frantically in every direction. Despite the food chaos and fab views, somehow the lovers at the next table ignored everything but each other's eyes.

For good-value accommodations in **Lisbon,** *try Hotel Evidencia Lisboa Tejo (Condes de Monsanto 2, tel. 218-866-182, www.evidenciahoteis.com) or the cheaper Pensão Residencial Gerês (Calçada do Garcia 6, tel. 218-810-497, www.pensaogeres.com). For all the travel specifics, see the latest edition of* Rick Steves' Portugal.

43. Salema, on Portugal's Sunny South Coast

"Let's get the *cataplanas*," said my friend, urging me to try the fish stew at Ze's Carioca Restaurant in Salema.

Overhearing her, Ze came to our table and said, "I have developed a secret recipe for this specialty. If you don't like it, you don't pay."

"What if we don't like anything else we order?" I asked.

Salema: Catch the Algarve before it's gone.

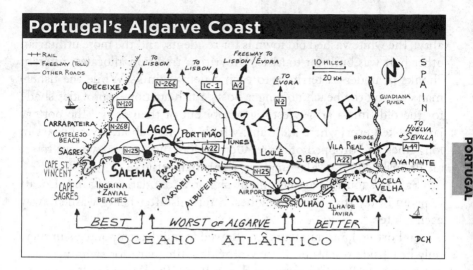

Portugal's Algarve Coast

"If you don't pay, I break your fingers," Ze said cheerfully.

We ordered the *cataplanas*. Savoring our meal, we savored one of the last true villages on the Algarve—Salema.

Any place famous as a "last undiscovered tourist frontier" no longer is. But the Algarve of your dreams survives—just barely. To catch it before it goes, find a fringe. It took me three tries. West of Lagos, I tried Luz and Burgau, both offering only a corpse of a fishing village, bikini-strangled and Nivea-creamed. Then, just as darkness turned couples into peaceful silhouettes, I found Salema.

Any Algarve town with a beach will have tourism, but few mix tourism and realism as well as little Salema. It's my kind of resort—three beachside streets, many restaurants, a few hotels, time-share condos up the road, a couple of bars, English and German menus, a classic beach with a paved promenade, and endless sun.

Tucked away where a dirt road hits the beach on Portugal's southwestern tip, Salema is an easy 15-mile bus ride or hitch from the closest train station in Lagos. Don't let the ladies hawking rooms in Lagos waylay you into staying in their city by telling you Salema is full.

With the horn-tooting arrival of the flatbed trucks, the parking lot that separates the jogging shorts from the black shawls becomes a morning market on weekdays. The *1812 Overture* horn of the fish truck wakes you at 8 a.m. Then the bakery trailer rolls in, steaming with fresh bread (about 8:30–11:00), followed by a fruit-and-vegetables truck, and a five-and-dime truck for clothing and odds and ends. And, most afternoons around 14:00, the red mobile post office stops by (unless the government cuts its funding).

Salema is still a fishing village—but just barely. It has a split personality: The whitewashed old town is for residents, and the more utilitarian other half was built for tourists. Unwritten tradition allocates different chunks of undersea territory to each Salema family. While the fisherman's hut on the beach no longer hosts a fish auction, it provides shade for the old-timers arm-wrestling octopi out of their traps. The pottery jars stacked everywhere are traps, which are tied about a yard apart in long lines and dropped offshore. Octopi, looking for a cozy place to set an ambush, climb inside—making their final mistake.

Salema's tourist-based economy sits on a foundation of sand. Locals hope and pray that their sandy beach returns after being washed away each winter.

In Portugal, restaurateurs are allowed to build a temporary, summer-only beachside restaurant if they provide a lifeguard for swimmers and run a green/yellow/red warning-flag system. The Atlântico Restaurant, which dominates Salema's beach, takes its responsibility seriously—providing lifeguards and flags through the summer...and fresh seafood by candlelight all year long.

Residents and tourists pursue a policy of peaceful coexistence at the beach. Tractors pull in and push out the fishing boats, two-year-olds toddle in the waves, topless women read German fashion mags, and old men really do mend the nets. British, German, and Back Door connoisseurs of lethargy laze in the sun, while locals grab the shade.

On the west end of the beach, look for the dinosaur footprints in a big, flat, yellowish raised rock 200 yards past the Atlântico restaurant (beside the rusty pipe sticking out of the cliff). From this beach at low tide, you may be able to climb over the rocks to secluded Figueira Beach, several miles away. While the days of black widows chasing topless Nordic women off the beach are gone, nudity is still risqué today. Over the rocks and beyond the view of prying eyes, Germans grin and bare it.

So often, tourism chases the sun and quaint folksiness. And the quaint folksiness survives only with the help of tourist dollars. Fishermen boost their income by renting spare bedrooms to the ever-growing stream of tan fans from the drizzly North. One year I arrived at 7 p.m. with a group of eight people and no reservations. I asked some locals, *"Quartos?"* Eyes perked, heads nodded, and I got nine beds in three homes at $20 per person. *Quartos* line Salema's main residential street, offering simple rooms with showers, springy beds, and glorious Atlantic views.

If you need to do some touring, drive 15 minutes to the best romantic, secluded beach in the region: Praia do Castelejo, complete with a good restaurant, just north of Cape Sagres.

But Salema's sleepy beauty kidnaps our momentum. Leaving Ze's restaurant with stomachs full and fingers intact, we take a glass of wine from the Atlântico's waterfront bar and sip it with the sunset in a beached paddleboat. Nearby, a dark, withered granny shells almonds with a railroad spike, dogs roam the beach like they own it, and a man catches short fish with a long pole. Beyond him is Cape Sagres—the edge of the world 500 years ago. As far as the gang sipping port and piling olive pits in the beachside bar is concerned, it still is.

*For good-value accommodations in **Salema**, try Pensión Maré (Praia de Salema, tel. 282-695-165, www.the-mare.com) or Casa Duarte (tel. 282-695-206 or 282-695-307). For all the travel specifics, see the latest edition of Rick Steves' Portugal.*

44. Andalucía's Arcos de la Frontera and the Route of the White Villages

When tourists head south from Madrid, it's generally for Granada, Córdoba, Sevilla, or the Costa del Sol. The big cities have their urban charms, but the Costa del Sol is a concrete nightmare, worthwhile only as a bad example. The most Spanish thing about the south coast is the sunshine—but that's everywhere. For something different and more authentic, try exploring the interior of Andalucía along the "Route of the White Villages." The Ruta de Pueblos Blancos, Andalucía's charm bracelet of cute towns, gives you wonderfully untouched Spanish culture.

Spend a night in the romantic queen of the white towns, Arcos de la Frontera. Towns with "de la Frontera" in their names were established on the front line of the Christians' centuries-long fight to recapture Spain

In Arcos, locals brag that only they see the backs of the birds as they fly.

Spain's White Villages

from the Moors, who were slowly pushed back into Africa. Today, these hill towns—no longer strategic or on any frontier—are just passing time peacefully.

Arcos smothers its hilltop, tumbling down all sides like the train of a wedding dress. While larger than most other Andalusian hill towns, it's equally atmospheric. The labyrinthine old center is a photographer's feast. Viewpoint-hop through town. Feel the wind funnel through the narrow streets as drivers pull in car mirrors to fit around tight corners.

Residents brag that only they see the backs of the birds as they fly. To see why, climb to the viewpoint at the main square high in the old town. Belly up to the railing—the town's suicide jumping-off point—and look down. Ponder the fancy cliffside hotel's erosion concerns, orderly orange groves, flower-filled greenhouses, and the fine views toward Morocco.

The thoughtful traveler's challenge is to find meaning in the generally overlooked tiny details of historic towns such as Arcos. On one visit, I discovered that a short walk from Arcos' church of Santa María to the church of San Pedro (St. Peter) is littered with fun glimpses into the town's past.

The church of Santa María faces the main square. After Arcos was reconquered from the Moors in the 13th century, this church was built—atop a mosque. In the pavement is a 15th-century magic circle: 12 red and 12 white stones—the white ones marked with various constellations. When a child came to the church to be baptized, the parents would stop here first for a good Christian exorcism. The exorcist would stand inside the protective circle and cleanse the baby of any evil spirits. This was also a holy place back in Muslim times. While residents no longer use it, Islamic Sufis still come here in pilgrimage every November.

In 1699, an earthquake cracked the church's foundation. Arches were added to prop it against neighboring buildings. Thanks to these, the church survived the bigger earthquake of 1755 (which destroyed much of Lisbon). All over town, arches support earthquake-damaged structures.

Lately the town rumbles only when the bulls run. Señor González Oca's tiny barbershop (behind the church) is plastered with posters of bulls running Pamplona-style through the streets of Arcos during Holy Week. An American from the nearby Navy base at Rota was killed here by a bull in 1994.

Small towns like Arcos come with lively markets. On my last visit, I was encouraged by the pickle woman to try a *banderilla*, named for the bangled spear that a matador sticks into the bull. As I gingerly slid an onion off the tiny skewer of pickled olives, onions, and carrots, she told me to eat it all at once. Explosive!

An important part of any Spanish market is the meat stall—the *salchichonería*. Since Roman times in Spain, December has been the season to slaughter pigs and cure (salt and dry) every possible bit of meat into various hams and sausages. By late spring, the now-salty meat is cured and able to withstand the heat.

Near the market is a convent. The spiky security grill over the window protects cloistered nuns. Tiny peepholes allow the sisters to look out unseen. I stepped into the lobby to find a one-way mirror and a blind, spinning, lazy Susan–type cupboard. I pushed the buzzer, and a sister spun out some boxes of freshly baked cookies for sale. When I spun back the cookies with a *"No, gracias,"* a Monty Python–esque voice countered, "We have cupcakes as well." I bought a bag of these *magdalenas*, both to support their church work and to give to kids on my walk. Feeling like a religious Peeping Tom, I actually saw—through the not-quite one-way mirror—the sister in her flowing robe and habit momentarily appear and disappear.

Walking on toward St. Peter's, I passed Roman columns plastered into street corners—protection from reckless donkey carts. The walls are scooped out on either side of the windows, a reminder of the days when women stayed inside but wanted the best possible view of any people-action in the streets.

Arcos' second church, St. Peter's, really is the second church. It lost an extended battle with Santa María for papal recognition as the leading church in Arcos. When the pope finally recognized Santa María, pouting parishioners from St. Peter's even changed their prayers. Rather than say "María, mother of God," they prayed "St. Peter, mother of God."

The tiny square in front of the church—about the only flat piece of pavement around—serves as the old-town soccer field for neighborhood kids. I joined the game and shared my cupcakes.

Until a few years ago, this church also had a resident bellman who lived in the spire. He was a basket-maker and a colorful character—famous for bringing in a donkey, which grew too big to get back out. Finally, there was no choice but to kill and eat the donkey.

Exploring on, I entered a cool, dark bar filled with very short, old guys. In Spain, any man in his late 80s spent his growth-spurt years trying to survive the brutal Civil War (1936–1939). Those who did, generally did so just barely. That generation was a head shorter than the people of the next.

In the bar, the gang—side-lit like a Rembrandt portrait—was fixed on the TV, watching the finale of a long series of bullfights. El Córdobes was fighting. His father, also called El Córdobes, was the Babe Ruth of bullfighting. El Córdobes uses his dad's name even though his dad sued him not to. Today, this generation's El Córdobes is the Ichiro of bullfighting.

Marveling at the bar's fun and cheap list of wines and hard drinks, I ordered a Cuba Libre for $2. The drink came tall and stiff, with a dish of peanuts. Suddenly everyone gasped—all eyes on the TV. El Córdobes had been hooked and did a cartwheel over the angry bull's head. The gang roared as El Córdobes buried his head in his arms and the bull trampled and tried to gore him. The TV repeated the scene many times.

El Córdobes survived and—no surprise—eventually killed the bull. But as he made his victory lap and picked up bouquets from adoring fans, the camera zoomed in on the rip exposing his hip and a 10-inch-long bloody wound. The short men around me would remember and talk about this moment for years.

That evening, I caught the sunset from the viewpoint, then took in dinner at Restaurante El Convento, surrounded by the plants and

SPAIN

Zahara reigns in Spain, rising mainly above the plain.

arches of another old convent—this one long replaced by the best restaurant in town. The walls are decorated with bronzed newspaper pages heralding many culinary awards. As church bells clanged, I poured a *vino tinto con mucho cuerpo* (full-bodied red wine) from the Rioja region, and ordered up the best-quality ham, *jamón ibérico*, from acorn-fed pigs with black feet.

From Arcos, the back road to Ronda is spiked with plenty of undiscovered and interesting hill towns. About half the towns I visited were memorable. Only Arcos (by bus) and Ronda (by train) are easily accessible by public transportation. Other towns are best seen by car. Good information on the area is rare but not necessary. Pick up the tourist brochure on the white towns at a nearby big-city tourist office, get a good map, and fire up your spirit of adventure.

Along with Arcos, here are my favorite white villages:

Zahara, a tiny town with a tingly setting under a Moorish castle, has a spectacular view. During Moorish times, Zahara was contained within the fortified castle walls above today's town. It was considered the gateway to Granada and a strategic stronghold for the Moors by the Spanish Christian forces of the *Reconquista.*

Today, the castle is little more than an evocative ruin with a commanding view (always open, free, and worth the climb). And Zahara is a fine overnight stop for those who want to hear only the sounds of birds, wind, and elderly footsteps on ancient cobbles.

Grazalema, another postcard-pretty hill town (located within huge and rugged Sierra de Grazalema Natural Park), offers a royal balcony for a memorable picnic, a square where you can watch old-timers playing cards, and plenty of quiet, whitewashed streets to explore. Plaza de Andalucía, the main square a block off the view terrace, is the hub for day-trippers. The town has several decent little bars and restaurants, and shops sell the town's famous handmade wool blankets and good-quality leather items. While the area is known as the rainiest place in Spain, the clouds seem to wring themselves out before they reach the town—I've only ever had blue skies.

Estepa, spilling over a hill crowned with a castle and convent, is a freshly washed, happy town that fits my dreams of southern Spain. It's situated halfway between Córdoba and Málaga, but it's light years away from either. Atop Estepa's hill is the convent of Santa Clara, worth three stars in any guidebook but found in none. Enjoy the territorial view from the summit, then step into the quiet, spiritual perfection of the church.

In any of these towns, evening is prime time. The promenade begins as everyone gravitates to the central square. The spotless streets are polished nightly by the feet of families licking ice cream. The whole town strolls—it's like "cruising" without cars. Buy an ice-cream sandwich and join the parade.

*For good-value accommodations in **Arcos**, try Hotel El Convento (Maldonado 2, tel. 956-702-333, www.hotelelconvento.es) or Hotel los Olivos (Paseo de los Boliches 30, tel. 956-700-811, www.hotel-losolivos.es). For all the travel specifics, see this year's edition of* Rick Steves' Spain.

45. Morocco: Plunge Deep

Walking through the various souks of the labyrinthine medina, I found sights you could only dream of in America. Dodging blind men and people with clubfeet, I was stoned by smells, sounds, sights, and feelings. People came in all colors, sizes, temperaments, and varieties of deformities. Milky eyes, charismatic beggars, stumps of limbs, sticks of children, tattooed women, walking mummies, grabbing salesmen, teasing craftsmen, seductive scents, half-bald dogs, and little boys on rooftops were reaching out from all directions.

Oooh! Morocco! Slices of Morocco make the *Star Wars* cantina scene look bland. And it's just a quick cruise from Spain. You can catch a boat to Tangier, Morocco, from Tarifa, Gibraltar, or Algeciras. As you step off the boat in Tangier, you realize that the crossing has taken you further culturally than did the trip from the US to Iberia.

Tantalizing Tangier

For decades, the coastal city of Tangier deserved its image as the "Tijuana of Morocco." But that has changed. Tangier was a neglected hell-hole for a generation. It was an international city—favored by the West and therefore disdained by the previous king of Morocco, who made it a point to divert national investment *away* from Morocco's fourth city.

The current king, Mohammed VI, who took the throne in 1999, believes Tangier should be a great city once again. To show his support, the first city he visited after his coronation was Tangier. Restorations are now taking place on a grand scale—the beach has been painstakingly cleaned, pedestrian promenades are popping up everywhere, and gardens bloom with lush, new greenery. The difference is breathtaking. The place is still exotic...but likeably exotic.

Tangier's newly pedestrianized Grand Socco—which used to be a perpetual traffic jam—sparkles with the pride of a new affluence.

I'm uplifted by the new Tangier because it is affluent and modern, without having abandoned its roots and embraced Western values. A visit here lets a Westerner marinated in anti-Muslim propaganda see what Islam aspires to be, and can be—and realize it is not a threat.

But the hotels—and their staffs—are still quirky. Recently when I checked into Hotel Continental, flamboyant Jimmy, who's always around and runs the shop adjacent to the lobby, greeted me. Test him—he knows every telephone area code in the US.

Hotel Continental had me wondering if I'd find the English Patient. Gramophones gathered dust on dressers under dingy lights, and day after day, a serene woman painted a figure-eight in the loose tiles with her mop. My guidebook listed the hotel's phone and email data more accurately than their own printed material—it was a 70-room hotel with not a sheet of paper in its office.

In the morning, roosters and the call to prayer worked together to wake me and the rest of that world. When the sun was high enough to send a rainbow plunging into the harbor amid ferries busily coming and going, I stood on my balcony and surveyed Tangier kicking into gear. Women in colorful flowing robes walked to sweat shops adjacent to the port—happy to earn $8 a day sewing for big-name European clothing lines.

It's a fascinating time for Morocco. The king is modernizing. His queen was a commoner. Moroccans say she's the first queen to be seen in public. They have never seen the king's mother. (They don't even know what she looks like.) Walking the streets, you see a modest new affluence, lots of vision and energy, and no compromise with being Arabic.

Moroccans don't seem to emulate or even care about the US. Al-Jazeera blares on teahouse TVs—with stirring images of American atrocities inflicted on fellow Muslims. But people seem numb to the propaganda. I felt not a hint of animosity to me as an American—something I had been concerned about. There was no political edge to any graffiti or posters. Ruled by Spain in the 19th century and France in the 20th, it's a rare place where signs are in three languages....and English doesn't make the cut (it's Arabic, French, and Spanish). In this Muslim city, you'll find a synagogue, Catholic and Anglican churches, and the town's largest mosque—all within close proximity of one another.

The market scene is a wonderland of everything—except pork. Mountains of brilliant olives, a full palette of spices, children with knives happy to perform for my camera. Each animal is slaughtered in accordance with Halal: in the name of Allah, with a sharp knife, its head pointed to Mecca, drained of its blood.

Tangier's markets are a barrage on all the senses...including the nose.

Ferries from Tarifa, Spain, sail to Tangier eight times daily ($90 round-trip). Even if you're visiting Morocco independently, I recommend hiring a guide to show you around Tangier. You can arrange one through the ferry company in Tarifa (www.frs.es) or at the TI in Tangier (in the new town at Boulevard Pasteur 29).

Taking a tour to Tangier is easier but less rewarding. A typical day-trip tour includes the round-trip ferry crossing and a guide who meets you at a prearranged point in Tangier. All offer essentially the same five-hour experience: a city bus tour, the famous ride-a-camel stop, a drive through the ritzy palace neighborhood, a walk through the medina, a look at a sales-starved carpet shop, and lunch. Tours generally cost about $90, roughly the same price as a ferry ticket alone—the tour company makes its money off commissions if you shop (www.frs.es or www.speed linestours.com).

During my stay, I met gracious Moroccans eager to talk and share. About the only time I saw other Western tourists was when I crossed paths with one of the day-tripping tour groups. Those on the tours walked in a tight single-file, clutching their purses and day bags nervously to their bellies like paranoid kangaroos, as they bundled past one last spanking line of street merchants to get safely back onto the ferry to

Package-tour visitors to Tangier feel like they're being held hostage by it. Independent travelers melt into it.

Europe. I was so comfortable, and they were so nervous and embattled. The pathetic scene reminded me of some kind of self-inflicted hostage crisis. Do yourself a favor—visit Tangier on your own.

The Best of Morocco

Rewarding as a visit to Tangier is, you can't fully experience Morocco in a day trip from the Costa del Sol. Plunge deep and your journal will read like a Dalí painting. While Morocco is not easy traveling, it gets rave reviews from those who plug this Islamic detour into their European vacation.

0	٠	SIFR
1	١	WAAHID
2	٢	ITNEEN
3	٣	TALAATA
4	٤	ARBA'A
5	٥	KHAMSA
6	٦	SITTA
7	٧	SAB'A
8	٨	TAMANYA
9	٩	TIS'A
10	١٠	'ASHRA

Rabat, Morocco's capital, is a good first stop. This comfortable, most-European city in Morocco lacks the high-pressure tourism of the towns on the north coast. Or, for a pleasant break on the beach and a relaxing way to break into Morocco, spend a day at Asilah, between Tangier and Larache.

Taxis are cheap and a real bargain when you consider the comfort, speed, and convenience they provide in these hot, dusty, and confusing cities. Eat and drink carefully in Morocco. Bottled water and bottled soft drinks are safe. The extra-cautious have "well-cooked" written in Arabic on a scrap of paper and flash it when they order meat. I found the couscous, *tajine*, and omelets uniformly good. The Arabs use different

Morocco

number symbols. Learn them. You can practice on license plates, which list the number twice (using their numbers and "ours"). Morocco was a French colony, so French is more widely understood than English. A French phrase book is handy. Travel very light in Morocco. You can leave most of your luggage at your last Spanish hotel for free if you plan to spend a night there on your return from Africa.

After Rabat, pass through Casablanca (great movie, dull city) and catch the Marrakech Express south. You'll hang your head out the window of that romantic old train and sing to the passing desert.

Marrakech is the epitome of exotic. Take a horse-drawn carriage from the station to downtown and find a hotel near the Djemaa el Fna, the central square of Marrakech, where the action is. Desert musicians, magicians, storytellers, acrobats, snake charmers, gamblers, and tricksters gather crowds of tribespeople who have come to Marrakech to do their market chores. As a tourist, you'll fit in like a clown at a funeral. Be very careful, don't gamble, and hang onto your wallet. You're in another world, and you're not clever here. Spend an entire day in the colorful medina wandering aimlessly from souk to souk. There's a souk for each trade, such as the dyers' souk, the leather souk, and the carpet souk.

In the medina, you'll be badgered—or "guided"—by small boys all claiming to be "a friend who wants to practice English." They are after money, nothing else. If you don't want their services, make two things crystal clear: You have no money for them, and you want no guide. Then completely ignore them. Remember that while you're with a guide, he'll get commissions for anything you buy. Throughout Morocco, you'll be pestered by these obnoxious hustler-guides.

Moroccan road signs: Beware of toboggans.

I often hire a young and responsive boy who speaks enough English to serve as my interpreter. It seems that if I'm "taken," the other guides leave me alone. And that in itself is worth the small price of a guide.

The market is a shopper's delight. Bargain hard, shop around, and you'll come home with some great souvenirs. Government emporiums usually have the same items you find in the market, but priced fairly. If you get sick of souks, shop there and you'll get the fair price, haggle-free.

From Marrakech, consider getting to Fès indirectly by taking an exciting seven-day loop to the south. While buses are reliable and efficient throughout Morocco, this tour is best by car, and it's easy to rent a car in Marrakech and drop it off in Fès.

Drive or catch the bus south over the rugged Atlas Mountains to Saharan Morocco. Explore the isolated oasis towns of Ouarzazate, Tinerhir, and Er-Rachidia. If time permits, the trip from Ouarzazate to Zagora is an exotic mud-brick pie. These towns each have a weekly "market day," when the tribespeople gather to do their shopping. This is your chance to stock up on honeydew melons

What century is it?

and goats' heads. Stay in Tinerhir and climb to the roof of your hotel for a great view of the busy marketplace.

Venture out of town into the lush fields, where you'll tumble into an almost biblical world. Sit on a rock and dissect the silence. A weary donkey, carrying a bearded old man in a white robe and turban, clip-clops slowly past you. Suddenly, six Botticelli maidens flit like watercolor confetti across your trail and giggle out of sight. Stay tuned. The show goes on.

Bus rides in this part of Morocco are intriguing. I could write pages about experiences I've had on Moroccan buses—good and bad—but I don't want to spoil the surprise. Just ride them with a spirit of adventure, cross your fingers, and keep your bag off the rooftop.

Saharan Adventure

Heading south from Er-Rachidia, a series of mud-brick villages bunny-hop down a lush river valley and into the Sahara. Finally the road melts into the sand, and the next stop is, literally, Timbuktu.

The strangeness of this Alice-in-a-sandy-Wonderland world, untempered, can be overwhelming—even frightening. The finest hotel in Erfoud, the region's major town, will provide a much-needed refuge, keeping out the sand, heat waves, and street kids, and providing safe-to-eat and tasty local food, reliable information, and a good and affordable bed.

Leave Europe and a warm Islamic welcome awaits.

But the hotel is only your canteen and springboard. Explore! If you plan to go deep into the desert, hire a guide. Choose one you can understand and tolerate, set a price for his services, and before dawn, head for the dunes.

You'll drive to the last town, Rissani, and then farther south over 15 miles of natural asphalt to the oasis village of Merzouga. There's plenty of tourist traffic at sunrise and in the early evening, so hitching is fairly easy. A couple of places in Merzouga rent spots on their terrace for those who spend the night.

Before you glows a chain of sand-dune mountains. Climb one. It's not easy. I seemed to slide farther backward with each step. Hike along a cool and crusty ridge. Observe bugs and their tracks. Watch small sand avalanches you started all by yourself. From the great virgin summit, savor the Sahara view orchestrated by a powerful silence. Your life sticks out like a lone star in a black sky. Try tumbling, rolling, and sloshing down your dune. Look back and see the temporary damage one person can inflict on a formerly perfect slope. Then get back in your car before the summer sun turns the sand into a steaming griddle and you into an omelet. Off-season, the midday desert sun is surprisingly mild.

On a student–exchange program, my daughter Jackie became part of her very own Moroccan village family.

Merzouga is full of very poor people. The village children hang out at the ruins of an old palace. A ragtag percussion group gave us an impromptu concert. The children gathered around us tighter and tighter, as the musicians picked up the tempo. We shared smiles, warmth, and sadness. A little Moroccan Judy Garland saw out of one eye, the other cloudy as rice pudding. One gleaming six-year-old carried a tiny sleeping brother slung on her back. His crusty little fly-covered face was too tired to flinch. We had a bag of candy to share and tried to get 40 kids into an orderly line to march past one by one. Impossible. The line degenerated into a free-for-all, and our bag became a piñata.

Only through the mercy of our guide did we find our way back to Rissani. Camels loitered nonchalantly, looking very lost and not caring. Cool lakes flirted, a distant mirage, and the black hardpan road stretched endlessly in all directions.

Then, with a sigh, we were back in Rissani, where the road starts up again. For us, it was breakfast time, and Rissani offered little more than some very thought-provoking irony. My friends and I could find no "acceptable" place to eat. Awkwardly, we drank germ-free Cokes with pursed lips, balanced bread on upturned bottle caps, and swatted laughing legions of flies. We were by far the wealthiest people in the valley—and the only ones unable to enjoy an abundant variety of good but strange food.

Observing the scene from our humble rusted table, we saw a busy girl rhythmically smashing date seeds; three stoic, robed elders with horseshoe beards; and a prophet wandering through with a message for all that he was telling to nobody.

Our Er-Rachidia hotel was Western-style—as dull and comforting as home. We listened to music and enjoyed the pool, resting and recharging before our next Saharan plunge.

Saharan Nightlife

Desert dwellers and smart tourists know the value of a siesta during the hottest part of the day. But a Saharan evening is the perfect time for a traveler to get out and experience the vibrancy of North African village life. We drove 10 miles north of Erfoud to a fortified mud-brick oasis village. There was no paint, no electricity, not a car in sight—only people, adobe walls, and palm trees. Absolutely nothing other than the nearby two-lane highway hinted of the modern world.

We entered like Lewis and Clark without Sacagawea, knowing instantly we were in for a rich experience. A wedding feast was erupting, and the whole town buzzed with excitement, all decked out in colorful robes and their best smiles. We felt very welcome.

The teeming street emptied through the medieval gate onto the field, where a band was playing squawky, oboe-like instruments and drums. A circle of 20 ornately dressed women made siren noises with tongues flapping like party favors. Rising dust diffused the lantern light, giving everything the grainy feel of an old photo. The darkness focused our attention on a relay of seductively beautiful, snake-thin dancers. A flirtatious atmosphere raged, cloaked safely in the impossibility of anything transpiring beyond coy smiles and teasing twists.

Then the village's leading family summoned us for dinner. Pillows, blankets, a lantern, and a large, round filigreed table turned a stone cave into a warm lounge. The men of this family had traveled to Europe and spoke some English. For more than two hours, the women prepared dinner and the men proudly entertained their New World guests. First was the ritualistic tea ceremony. Like a mad chemist, the tea specialist mixed it just right. With a thirsty gleam in his eye and a large spike in his hand, he hacked off a chunk of sugar from a coffee-can–size lump and watched it melt into Morocco's basic beverage. He sipped it, as if testing a fine wine, added more sugar, and offered me a taste. When no more sugar could be absorbed, we drank it with cookies and dates. Then, with the fanfare of a pack of Juicy Fruit, the men passed around a hashish pipe. Our shocked look was curious to them. Next, a tape deck brought a tiny clutter of music, from Arab and tribal Berber music to James Brown, reggae, and twangy Moroccan pop. The men danced splendidly.

Finally the meal came. Fourteen people sat on the floor, circling two round tables. Nearby, a child silently waved a palm-branch fan, keeping the flies away. A portable washbasin and towel were passed around to start and finish the meal. With our fingers and gravy-soaked slabs of bread, we grabbed spicy meat and vegetables. Everyone dipped eagerly into the delicious central bowl of couscous.

So far, the Moroccan men dominated. Young girls took turns peeking around the corner and dashing off—much like teenyboppers anywhere. Two older women in striking, black-jeweled outfits were squatting attentively in the corner, keeping their distance and a very low profile. Then one pointed to me and motioned in charades, indicating long hair, a backpack, and a smaller partner. I had been in this same village years earlier. I had longer hair and a backpack and was traveling with a short partner. She remembered my 20-minute stay so long ago! People in remote lands enjoy a visiting tourist and find the occasion at least as memorable as we do. So many more doors open to the traveler who knocks.

After a proud tour of their schoolhouse, we were escorted across the field back to our car, which had been guarded by a silent, white-robed man. We drove away, reeling with the feeling that the memories of this evening would be the prize souvenir of our trip.

*For good-value accommodations in **Tangier**, try Hotel Continental (Dar Baroud 36, tel. 0539-931-024, hcontinental@iam.net.ma) or the swankier Rif & Spa Hotel (Avenue Muhammad VI 152, tel. 0539-349-300, www .hotelsatlas.com). For more travel specifics, see this year's edition of* Rick Steves' Spain.

FRANCE

46. Paris: A Grand Boulevard and a Petite Lane

Paris is the epitome of elegance, a cultural touchstone for art, fashion, food, literature, and good living. Come ready to be charmed by that Parisian *je ne sais quoi*. For me, the true magic of Paris is in its sweeping boulevards and intimate lanes. Start at the Arc de Triomphe, saunter down the grand avenue des Champs-Elysées, then disappear down rue Cler.

The Grand Boulevard: Champs-Elysées

My cabbie plunges into the grand traffic circle where a dozen boulevards converge on the Arc de Triomphe. Like referees at gladiator camp, traffic cops are stationed at each entrance to this traffic circus and let in bursts of eager cars. As marble Lady Liberties scramble up Napoleon's arch, heroically thrusting their swords and shrieking at the traffic, all of Paris seems drawn into this whirlpool.

I say to the cabbie, "There must be an accident every few minutes here."

He responds, "In Paris, a good driver gets only scratches, not dents. But bad drivers...If there is an

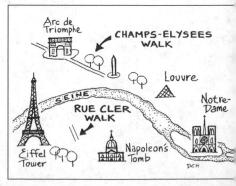

accident here, each driver is considered equally at fault. This is the only place in Paris where the accidents are not judged. No matter what the circumstances, insurance companies split the costs fifty-fifty."

It's a game of fender-bender chicken. This circle is the great equalizer. Tippy little Citroën 2CVs, their rooftops cranked open like sardine lids, bring lumbering buses to a sudden, cussing halt.

While we're momentarily stalled on the inside lane, I pay and hop out. The cabbie drives away, leaving me under Europe's grandest arch and at the top of its ultimate boulevard. My plan is to stroll the length of the Champs-Elysées (literally, "Elysian Fields"). But first, the flame of France's unknown soldier—flickering silently in the eye of this urban storm—seems to invite me to savor this grandiose monument to French nationalism.

The Arc de Triomphe affords a great Paris view, but only to those who earn it—there are 284 steps to the top. Begun in 1809, the arch was intended to honor Napoleon's soldiers, who, in spite of being vastly outnumbered by the Austrians, scored a remarkable victory at the Battle of Austerlitz. Napoleon died long before the arch was completed, but it was finished in time for his 1840 funeral procession to pass underneath, carrying his remains (19 years dead) home to Paris from exile in St. Helena.

The Arc de Triomphe is dedicated to the glory of all French armies. Like its Roman ancestors, this arch has served as a parade gateway for

triumphal armies (French or foe) and important ceremonies. From 1940 to 1944, a large swastika flew from here as Nazis goose-stepped daily down the Champs-Elysées. In August 1944, Charles de Gaulle led Allied troops under this arch as they celebrated liberation.

Standing under the arch, you're surrounded by names of French victories since the Revolution, the names of great French generals (underlined if they died in battle), and by France's Tomb of the Unknown Soldier. Every day at 6:30 p.m. since just after World War I, the flame is rekindled and new flowers set in place, but any time of day it's a place of patriotic reverence.

Once you've climbed to the top of the arch, look down along the huge axis that shoots like an arrow all the way from the Louvre, up

FRANCE

Champs-Elysées Walk

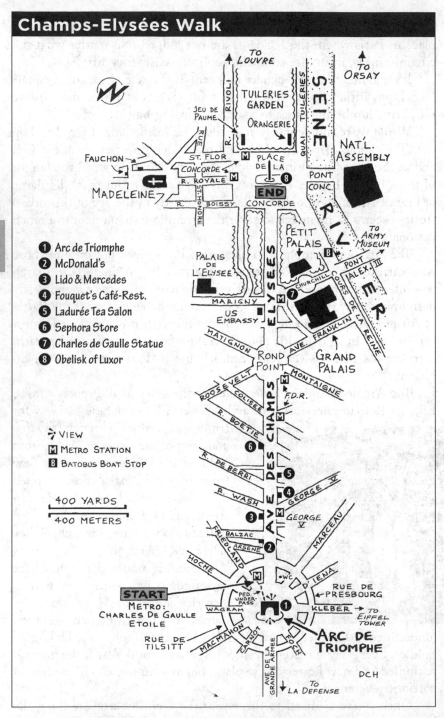

1 Arc de Triomphe
2 McDonald's
3 Lido & Mercedes
4 Fouquet's Café-Rest.
5 Ladurée Tea Salon
6 Sephora Store
7 Charles de Gaulle Statue
8 Obelisk of Luxor

↗ VIEW
M METRO STATION
B BATOBUS BOAT STOP

400 YARDS
400 METERS

TO LOUVRE
TO ORSAY
TULERIES GARDEN
JEU DE PAUME
ORANGERIE
SEINE RIVER
NAT'L. ASSEMBLY
FAUCHON
R. RIVOLI
RUE
ST. FLOR
CONCORDE
R. ROYALE
PLACE DE LA
MADELEINE
R. ST. HONORE
R. BOISSY
END CONCORDE
PONT CONC.
QUAI TULERIES
PETIT PALAIS
TO ARMY MUSEUM
B
PONT ALEX III
PALAIS DE L'ELYSEE
CHURCHILL
COURS DE LA REINE
MARIGNY
US EMBASSY
ELYSEES
GRAND PALAIS
MATIGNON
ROND POINT
AVE. FRANKLIN
ROOSEVELT
COLISEE
F.D.R.
MONTAIGNE
R. BOETIE
R. DE BERRI
AVE DES CHAMPS
R. WASH
GEORGE V
BALZAC
FRIEDLAND
ARSENE
HOCHE
START
METRO: CHARLES DE GAULLE ETOILE
PED. UNDER-PASS
WAGRAM
WC
D'IENA
RUE DE PRESBOURG
KLEBER
TO EIFFEL TOWER
ARC DE TRIOMPHE
MARCEAU
GEORGE V
MACMAHON
RUE DE TILSITT
AVE DE LA GRANDE ARMEE
TO LA DEFENSE
DCH

the Champs-Elysées, through the arch, then straight down the avenue de la Grande-Armée to a forest of distant skyscrapers around an even bigger modern arch in suburban La Défense. Notice the contrast between the skyscrapers in the suburbs and the more uniform heights of buildings closer to the arch. The beauty of Paris—basically a flat basin with a river running through it—is man-made. There's a harmonious relationship between the width of its grand boulevards and the standard height and design of the buildings. This elegant skyline is broken only by venerable historic domes and spires—and the lonely-looking Montparnasse Tower, which stands like the box the Eiffel Tower came in. The appearance of this tower served as a wake-up call in the early 1970s to preserve the historic skyline of downtown Paris.

In the mid-19th century, Baron Georges-Eugène Haussmann set out to make Paris the grandest city in Europe. The 12 boulevards that radiate from the Arc de Triomphe were part of his master plan: the creation of a series of major boulevards, intersecting at diagonals, with monuments (such as the Arc de Triomphe) as centerpieces of those intersections. Haussmann's plan did not anticipate the automobile—obvious when you watch the traffic scene below. But see how smoothly it really functions. Cars entering the circle have the right-of-way (the only roundabout in France with this rule); those in the circle must yield. Parisian drivers navigate the circle like a comet circling the sun—making a parabola. They quickly arc toward the smoothly flowing center. Then, a couple of avenues before their desired exit, they begin working their way back out.

A stroll down the Champs-Elysées will give you Paris at its most Parisian: monumental sidewalks, stylish shops, elegant cafés, and glimmering showrooms. Europe's characteristic love of strolling (a stately paced triathlon of walking, window shopping, and high-profile sipping) dates from the booming 19th century, when leisure time and cash were abundant for the upper classes.

So, don an aristocratic air. From the Arc de Triomphe, amble gently downhill to the immense and historic square called place de la Concorde. But before you stroll, you must master the name. Say it: shahn-zay-lee-zay.

Even small-town French kids who haven't traveled beyond a TV screen know that this is their country's ultimate parade ground, where major events all unfold: the Tour de France finale, Bastille Day parades, and New Year's festivities.

In 1667, Louis XIV opened the first section of the street as a short extension of the Tuileries Gardens. This year is considered the birth of Paris as a grand city. The Champs-Elysées soon became *the* place to

Making Scents of It All

Strolling the Champs-Elysées, you'll come to Sephora, the incredible flagship store (at #72) of the huge perfume and cosmetics chain. Take your nose sightseeing and glide down Sephora's ramp into a vast hall of cosmetics and perfumes. Grab a disposable white strip from a lovely clerk, spritz it with a sample, and sniff. The store is thoughtfully laid out: The entry hall is lined with new products.

In the main showroom, women's perfumes line the right wall and men's line the left—organized alphabetically by company, from Armani to Versace. The mesmerizing music, chosen just for Sephora, makes you crave cosmetics.

cruise in your carriage. (It still is today—traffic can be jammed up even at midnight.) One hundred years later, the café scene arrived.

The grand café scene survives today, amid pop clothing outlets and music megastores. Two cafés, Fouquet's and Ladurée (a block apart on the quiet side of the boulevard), are among the most venerable in Paris. Even elegant cafés like these often have humble roots. (Fouquet's started as a coachman's bistro.) Today, Parisians keep 12,000 cafés in business.

Fouquet's gained fame as the hangout of French biplane pilots during World War I (Paris was just a few nervous miles from the Western Front). It also served as James Joyce's dining room. Today, it's pretty stuffy—unless you're a film star. The golden plaques at the entrance honor winners of France's Oscar-like film awards, the Césars. While the hushed interior is at once classy and intimidating, the outdoor setting is great for people-watching—and you can pay $8 for the most expensive shot of espresso I found in Paris.

You're more likely to see me hanging out at Ladurée, munching on a *macaron*. This classic 19th-century tea salon/restaurant/*pâtisserie* has an interior right out of the 1860s. Non-patrons can discreetly wander in through the door farthest downhill and peek into the cozy rooms upstairs. The bakery makes cute little cakes and gift-wrapped finger sandwiches. The traditional *macarons* (which look like tiny hamburgers) come in a pastel palette of flavors from mint to raspberry to rose—these really are worth the journey. Get a frilly little gift box to go, or pay the *rançon* and sit down for a *très elegant* coffee and enjoy the Champs-Elysées show.

From the 1920s through the 1960s, this was a street of top-end hotels, cafés, and residences—pure elegance. Parisians actually dressed up to come here. Then, in 1963, the government pumped up the neighborhood's commercial metabolism by bringing in the RER (commuter train). Suburbanites had easy access, and *pfft*—there went the neighborhood.

The coming of McDonald's—a hundred yards farther down on the left at #140—was a shock to the boulevard. At first it was only allowed to have white arches painted on the window. Today, it legally spills out onto the sidewalk—provided it offers café-quality chairs and flower boxes.

As fast food and pop culture invaded and grand old buildings began to fall, Paris realized what it was losing. In 1985, a law prohibited the demolition of the elegant building fronts that once gave the boulevard a uniform grace. Today, many of the modern businesses hide behind preserved facades. As you stroll, imagine the boulevard pre-'63, with only the finest structures lining both sides all the way to the palace gardens.

The *nouvelle* Champs-Elysées, revitalized in 1994, has new benches and lamps, broader sidewalks, all-underground parking, and a fleet of green-suited workers who drive motorized street cleaners. Plane trees (a kind of sycamore that thrives despite big-city pollution) provide a leafy ambience.

As you stroll, you'll notice the French appetite for good living. The foyer of the famous Lido, Paris' largest cabaret, comes with leggy photos and a perky R-rated promo video. Movie-going on the Champs-Elysées is popular. Showings *(séances)* with a "v.o." *(version originale)* next to the time indicate the film will be in its original language.

Luxury-car dealerships show off their futuristic "concept cars" alongside their current and classic models. Buying a new Mercedes here is like a fashion makeover—you pick out a leather jacket and purse to match. That new-car smell is a far cry from the 19th century, when this block carried the aroma of horse stables (which evolved into upper-crust limousine garages en route to today's dealerships).

At the Rond-Point des Champs-Elysées, the shopping ends and the park begins. This round, leafy traffic circle is always colorful, lined with flowers or festive seasonal decorations (thousands of pumpkins at Halloween, hundreds of decorated trees at Christmas). Avenue Montaigne, cutting off to the right, is lined by the most exclusive shops in town—places where you need to make an appointment to buy a dress.

A long block past the Rond-Point, at avenue de Marigny, look to

FRANCE

Polite Paris

The "mean Parisian" problem is a holdover from Charles de Gaulle days. It's definitely fading, but France's lingering reputation of

Enjoy the French.

rudeness can create a self-fulfilling expectation. If you want to enjoy the French, you can. Make it your goal.

The French, as a culture, are pouting. They used to be the crème de la crème, *the* definition of high class. Their language was the lingua franca—everyone wanted to speak French. There was a time when the czar of Russia and his family actually spoke better French than Russian. A US passport even has French on it—a holdover from those French glory days.

Modern French culture is reeling—humiliated by two world wars, lashed by Levi's, and crushed by the Big Mac of American culture. And our two cultures aren't natural buddies. The French enjoy subtleties and sophistication. American culture sneers at these fine points. We're proud, brash, and like to think we're rugged individualists. We are a smiley-face culture whose bank tellers are fined if they forget to say, "Have a nice day." The French don't find slap-on-the-back niceness terribly sincere.

Typically, Americans evaluate the French by the Parisians they meet. Big cities anywhere are colder than small towns. And, remember, most of us see Paris at the height of the hot, busy summer, when those Parisians who can't escape on vacation see their hometown flooded with insensitive foreigners who butcher their language and put ketchup on their meat. That's tough to take smiling, and if you're looking for coldness, this is a good place to start.

To make the Parisians suddenly 40 percent friendlier, learn and liberally use these four phrases: *bonjour, s'il vous plaît, merci,* and *pardon.* And to really revel in French friendliness, visit an untouristy part of the countryside and use those four phrases. Oh, and *vive la différence*—celebrate the differences.

the other side of the Champs-Elysées to find a statue of General Charles de Gaulle. Ram-rod straight, he strides out toward the boulevard as he did on the day Paris was liberated in 1944 (6' 4" tall, walking proudly for the length of the Champs-Elysées, as others around him ducked during sporadic gunfire).

From here, it's a straight shot down the last stretch of the boulevard to the sprawling 21-acre square called the place de la Concorde. Its centerpiece is the 3,300-year-old Obelisk of Luxor. It was carted here from Egypt in the 1830s, a gift to the French king. The gold-leaf diagrams on the obelisk tell the story of its laborious journey.

During the French Revolution, this was the place de la Révolution. A guillotine stood where the obelisk now stands. A bronze plaque memorializes the place where Louis XVI, Marie-Antoinette, and about 1,200 others were made "a foot shorter on top." Invented as a humane alternative to the poorly aimed executioner's

Place de la Concorde, formerly "place de la Révolution"

axe, the guillotine's efficiency was breathtaking. It took a crew of three: one to manage the blade, one to hold the blood bucket, and one to catch the head and raise it high to the roaring crowd.

Standing in the shadow of that obelisk with your back to the Louvre while you look up the grandest boulevard in Europe, you can't help but think of the sweep of history...and those great *macarons*.

The Petite Lane: Rue Cler

After taking a turn along Paris' showcase of a boulevard, tune into the rhythm of real life—hop in a cab and say, *"Rue Cler, s'il vous plaît."*

The rue Cler, lined with little food shops, captures the art of Parisian living. Shopping for groceries is an integral part of daily life here for three good reasons: Refrigerators are small (tiny kitchens), produce must be fresh, and it's an important social event. Shopping is a chance to hear about the butcher's vacation plans, see photos of the florist's new grandchild, relax over *un café*, and kiss the cheeks of friends (the French standard is twice for regular acquaintances, three times for friends you haven't seen in a while).

Rue Cler—traffic-free since 1984—offers plenty of space for tiny stores and their patrons to spill into the street. It's an ideal environment for this ritual to survive in and for you to explore. The street is lined with the essential shops—wine, cheese, chocolate, bread—as well as a bank and a post office. And the shops of this community are run by people who've found their niche: boys who grew up on quiche, girls who know a good wine. The people you see in uniform are likely from the Ecole Militaire (military school, Napoleon's alma mater, two blocks away).

There's no better place to assemble the ultimate French picnic. Visit when the market is open and lively, in the morning or early evening (dead on Sunday evening and all day Monday). Remember that these shops are busy serving regular customers. Be polite (say *"Bonjour, Madame/Monsieur"* as you enter and *"Au revoir, Madame/Monsieur"* when

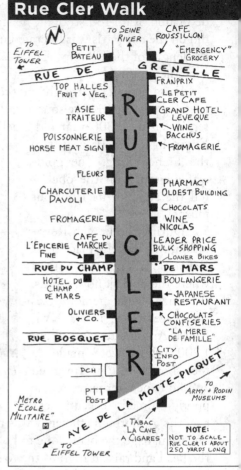

Rue Cler Walk

you leave), and be careful not to get in the way.

Have the cabbie drop you off at the intersection of rue Cler and rue de Grenelle, so you can start your walk where the pedestrian section of rue Cler does.

Café Roussillon is a neighborhood fixture. Drinks at the bar *(comptoir)* are about half the price of drinks at the tables *(salles)*. Notice the list of wines sold by the little (7 cl.) glass on the blackboard. Also displayed are various *cheque déjeuner* decals, advertising that this café accepts lunch "checks." In France, an employee lunch subsidy program is an expected perk. Employers issue these checks (worth about $12) for the number of days an employee works in a month. Sack lunches are rare, since a good lunch is sacred.

Each morning, Top Halles fruits and vegetables receives fresh produce that has been trucked in from farmers' fields to Paris' huge Rungis market—Europe's largest, near Orly Airport—then dispatched to merchants with FedEx-like speed and precision. Good luck finding a shopping bag—locals bring their own two-wheeled carts or reusable bags. Also, notice how the earth-friendly French resist unnecessary packaging.

Parisians—who know they eat best by being tuned into the seasons—shop with their noses. Try it. Smell the cheap foreign strawberries. One sniff of the torpedo-shaped French ones *(gariguettes)* in June, and you know which is better. Find the herbs in the back. Is today's delivery in? Look at the price of those melons. What's the country of origin? It must be posted. If they're out of season, they come from Guadeloupe. Many people buy only local products.

The Franprix across the street is a small Safeway-type store. Opposite Grand Hôtel Lévêque is Asic Traiteur. Fast Asian food is popular in

Paris. These shops—about as common as bakeries now—are making an impact on Parisian eating habits.

Just past the hotel is a wine shop. Shoppers often save this stop for last, after they have assembled their meal and are ready to pick the appropriate wine. The wine is classified by region. Most "Parisians" (born elsewhere) have an affinity for the wines of their home region. Check out the great prices. Wines of the month—in the center—sell for about $11. You can get a fine bottle for $17. The clerk is a counselor who works with your needs and budget.

Smell the *fromagerie* next door. A long, narrow, canopied cheese table brings the *fromagerie* into the street. Wedges, cylinders, balls, and miniature hockey pucks all powdered white, gray, and burnt marshmallow—it's a festival of mold. The street cart and front window feature both cow and goat cheeses. *Ooh la la* means you're impressed. If you really like cheese, show greater excitement with more *las*. *Ooh la la la la.* My local friend once held the stinkiest glob close to her nose, took an orgasmic breath, and exhaled, "Yes, it smells like zee feet of angels." Go ahead... inhale.

Step inside and browse through some of the 400 different types of French cheese. A cheese shop—lab-coat-serious but friendly, and

known as a "BOF" for *beurre, oeuf,*
and *fromage*—is where people
go for butter, eggs, and cheeses.
In the back room are *les meules,*
the big, 170-pound wheels of
cheese (made from 250 gallons of
milk). The "hard" cheeses are cut
from these. Don't eat the skin of
these big ones...they roll them on
the floor. But the skin on most
smaller cheeses—the Brie, the
Camembert—is part of the taste.

*The cheese shop—known as BOF
(beurre, oeuf, fromage)—sells butter,
eggs, and cheese.*

At dinner tonight, you can
take the cheese course just before
or as the dessert. On a good cheese
plate you have a hard cheese (like
Emmentaler, a.k.a. "Swiss cheese"), a flowery cheese (maybe Brie or
Camembert), a bleu cheese, and a goat cheese—ideally from different
regions. Because it's strongest, the goat cheese is usually eaten last.

Across the street is the fish shop *(poissonerie)*. Fresh fish is brought
into Paris daily from ports on the English Channel, 110 miles away. In
fact, fish here is likely fresher than in many towns closer to the sea,
because Paris is a commerce hub (from here, it's shipped to outlying
towns). Anything wriggling?

Next door, check out the storefront at the Crêperie Ulysée en Gaule.
The stones and glass set over the doorway advertise horse meat: *Boucherie
Chevaline*. While today this shop serves non-equine souvlaki and crêpes,
the classy storefront survives from a previous occupant. Created in the
1930s and signed by the artist, it's a work of art fit for a museum.

Wander on past the flower shop and pharmacy (in Europe, the first
diagnosis and prescription are made by the pharmacist; if it's out of his
league, he'll recommend a doctor). Notice the oldest and shortest building. It's from the early 1800s, when this street was part of a village near
Paris and lined with structures like this. Of course, over the years Paris
engulfed these surrounding villages—and now the street is a mishmash
of architectural styles.

Charcuterie Davoli sells mouthwatering deli food to go. Because
Parisian kitchens are so small, these gourmet delis are handy, even
for those who cook. A deli lets hosts concentrate on creating the main
course, and then buy beautifully prepared side dishes to complete a fine
dinner. Notice the system: Order, take your ticket to the cashier to pay,

and return with the receipt to pick up your food.

The Café du Marché, on the corner, is *the* place to sit and enjoy the rue Cler action. For a reasonable meal, grab a chair and check the chalk menu listing the *plat du jour* (blue plate special). Notice how the new no-smoking-indoors laws have made outdoor seating and propane heaters a huge hit.

The shiny, sterile Leader Price grocery store (across the street, on the corner) is a Parisian Costco, selling bulk items. Because storage space is so limited in most Parisian apartments, bulk purchases are unlikely to become a big deal here. The trend is to stock up on nonperishables by shopping online, pick up produce three times a week, and buy fresh bread daily.

A short side-trip west to 8 rue du Champ de Mars takes you to L'Epicerie Fine, where gentle Pascal and Joanna tempt visitors with fine gourmet treats. Their mission in life is to explain to travelers, in fluent English, what the French fuss over food is all about. Let them help you assemble a picnic as they educate you with generous tastes of caramel, balsamic vinegar, and French and Italian olive oil.

Back on the rue Cler, you'll come upon a *boulangerie,* diagonally across from Café du Marché. Residents debate the merits of *boulangeries.* It's said that a baker cannot be good at both bread and pastry. At cooking school, they major in one or the other. Here, the baker makes good bread, and another baker does the tasty little pastries for him.

Next door is a strangely out-of-place Japanese restaurant. Sushi is mysteriously for sale everywhere in Paris these days. Locals explain that the phenomenon is the same as when Chinese restaurants were spreading like gastronomic weeds. Real French restaurants found it hard to compete with these inexpensive places, and in some areas, authorities actually forbid business permits to Chinese restaurants.

A bit farther along, La Mère de Famille Gourmand Chocolats Confiseries has been in the neighborhood for 30 years. The wholesalers wanted the owner to take new products, but she kept the old traditional candies, too. "The old ladies, they want the same sweets that made them so happy 80 years ago," she says. Until a few years ago, chocolate was dipped and decorated right on the premises. As was the tradition in rue Cler shops, the merchants resided and produced in the back and sold in the front.

Across the street, you'll find Oliviers & Co. Olive Oils. Typical of a ritzy neighborhood like this, this shop sells fine gourmet goodies from the south of France and olive oil from around the Mediterranean. They are happy to give visitors a taste test. Try the tapenade. Use their tiny spoons to sample three distinct oils.

Walk on toward the end of rue Cler. An electronic signpost directs residents to websites for information—transportation changes, surveys, employment opportunities, community events, and so on. Across the busy street is a *tabac* (tobacco shop). In addition to tobacco, *tabacs* also serve their neighborhoods as a kind of government cash desk. All sell stamps and most sell public-transit tickets and parking cards.

Rue Cler ends at the post office. The Ecole Militaire Métro stop is just down the street. If you bought a picnic along this walk, head for the nearby benches and gardens: From the post office, avenue de la Motte-Picquet leads to two fine parks—turn left for the Army Museum or right for the Eiffel Tower.

Settle in and enjoy your Parisian feast. *Bon appétit!*

To sleep in Paris' **rue Cler neighborhood,** *consider the Grand Hôtel Lévêque (29 rue Cler, tel. 01 47 05 49 15, www.hotel-leveque.com) or Hôtel du Champ de Mars (7 rue du Champ de Mars, tel. 01 45 51 52 30, www.hotelduchamp demars.com). In the* **Marais neighborhood,** *try the Grand Hôtel Jeanne d'Arc (3 rue de Jarente, tel. 01 48 87 62 11, www.hoteljeannedarc.com, information @hoteljeannedarc.com) or Hôtel Castex (5 rue Castex, tel. 01 42 72 31 52, www.castexhotel.com). For all the particulars on Paris, see this year's edition of* Rick Steves' Paris.

47. Alsace and Colmar: Vintage France

The French province of Alsace stands like a flower-child referee between Germany and France. Bounded by the Rhine River on the east and the well-worn Vosges Mountains on the west, this is a green region of Hansel-and-Gretel villages, ambitious vineyards, and vibrant cities.

Alsace has changed hands several times between Germany and France because of its location, natural wealth, naked vulnerability, and the fact that Germany considered the mountains as the natural border while France saw the Rhine as the dividing line. Centuries as a political pawn between Germany and France have given Alsace a hybrid culture. On doorways of homes, you'll see names like Jacques Schmidt or Dietrich Le Beau. Natives who curse do so bilingually. Half-timbered restaurants serve sauerkraut and escargot.

Wine is the primary industry, topic of conversation, dominant mouthwash, and perfect excuse for countless festivals.

Alsace's wine road, the Route du Vin, is an asphalt ribbon tying 90 miles of vineyards, villages, and feudal fortresses into an understandably popular tourist package. The dry and sunny climate has produced good wine and happy tourists since Roman days.

During the October harvest season, all Alsace erupts into a carnival of colorful folk costumes, traditional good-time music, and Dionysian smiles. I felt as welcome as a grape picker, and my tight sightseeing plans became as hard to follow as a straight line.

If you can pick grapes, you might land a job in October. For a hard day in the vineyards, you'll get room and board, a modest wage, and an intimate Alsatian social experience lubricated liberally, logically, by plenty of wine.

Wine tasting is popular throughout the year. Roadside *dégustation* signs invite you into wine *caves*, where a producer will serve you

all seven Alsatian wines from dry to sweet, with educational commentary (probably in French) if requested. Try Crémant d'Alsace, the Alsatian sparkling wine. *Cave*-hopping is a great way to spend an afternoon on the Route du Vin. With free samples and fine $10 bottles, French wine-tasting can be an affordable sport.

The small *caves* are fun, but be sure to tour a larger wine co-op. Beer-drinking Germans completely flattened many Alsatian towns in 1944. The small family-run vineyards of these villages sprang back as large, modern, and efficient cooperatives. Among the best of these is the big and modern Wolfberger Wine Cooperative in Eguisheim (Cave Vinicole d'Eguisheim).

There's more to Alsace than meets the palate. Centuries of successful wine production built prosperous, colorful villages. Countless castles capped hilltops to defend the much-invaded plain, and wine wasn't the only art form loved and patronized by connoisseurs.

Alsatian towns are historic mosaics of gables, fountains, medieval bell towers and gateways, ancient ramparts, churches, and cheery old inns. More than anywhere in France, you'll find plenty of budget beds in private homes ($70–90 doubles, ask at village tourist offices or look for *chambre d'hôte* signs). While Colmar is the best home-base city, petite Eguisheim, with plenty of small hotels, a minimum of tour crowds, and maximum village charm, is the ideal small-town home. Nearby Riquewihr and Kaysersberg are two more crackerjack villages. A scenic

FRANCE

path—one of countless in the region—connects these two towns. Take a hike or rent a bike. Drop by a castle or two. Climb the tallest tower and survey Alsace, looking as it has for centuries—a valley of endless vineyards along the Route du Vin.

Colmar

Colmar, my favorite city in Alsace, sees few American tourists but is popular with Germans and the French. This well-pickled old town of 70,000 is a handy springboard for Alsatian explorations.

Historic beauty was usually a poor excuse to be spared the ravages of World War II, but it worked for Colmar. The American and British military were careful not to bomb the half-timbered old burghers' houses, characteristic red- and green-tiled roofs, and cobbled lanes of Alsace's most beautiful city.

Today, Colmar is alive with colorful buildings, impressive art treasures, and German tourists. Schoolgirls park their rickety horse carriages in front of City Hall and are ready to give visitors a clip-clop tour of the old town. Antique shops welcome browsers, and hoteliers hurry down the sleepy streets to pick up fresh croissants in time for breakfast.

Colmar offers heavyweight sights in a warm, small-town package. By the end of the Middle Ages, the walled town was a thriving trade center filled with rich old houses. The wonderfully restored tanners' quarters is a quiver of tall, narrow, half-timbered buildings. Its confused rooftops struggle erratically to get enough sun to dry their animal skins. Nearby you'll find "La Petite Venise," complete with canals and gondola rides.

Colmar combines its abundance of art with a knack for showing it off. The artistic geniuses Grünewald,

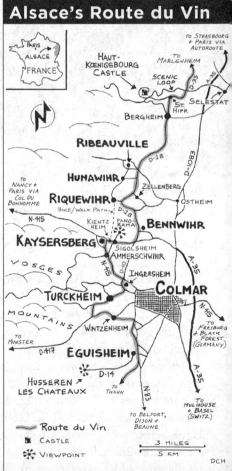

Alsace's Route du Vin

German or French? Colmar is both.

Schongauer, and Bartholdi all called Colmar home.

Frédéric-Auguste Bartholdi, who created our Statue of Liberty a century ago, adorned his hometown with many fine, if smaller, statues. Don't miss the little Bartholdi museum, offering a good look at the artist's life and some fun Statue of Liberty trivia.

Four hundred years earlier, Martin Schongauer was the leading local artist. His *Madonna in the Rose Garden* could give a drill sergeant goose bumps. Looking fresh and crisp, it's set magnificently in a Gothic Dominican church. I sat with a dozen people, silently, as if at a symphony, as Schongauer's *Madonna* performed solo on center stage. Lit by 14th-century stained glass, its richness and tenderness cradled me in a Gothic sweetness that no textbook could explain. Even if you become so jaded that you "never want to see another Madonna and Child," give this one a chance.

The Unterlinden Museum, one of my favorite small museums, is housed in a 750-year-old convent next to the tourist office. It has the best collection anywhere of Alsatian folk art and art exhibits ranging from Neolithic and Gallo-Roman archaeological collections to works by Monet, Renoir, Braque, and Picasso. It's a medieval and Renaissance home show. You can lose yourself in a 17th-century Alsatian wine cellar complete with presses, barrels, tools, and aromas.

The highlight of the museum (and for me, the city) is Matthias Grünewald's gripping Isenheim altarpiece. This is actually a series of paintings on hinges that pivot like shutters. Designed to help people in a hospital suffer through their horrible skin diseases (long before the age of painkillers), it's one of the most powerful paintings ever. Stand petrified in front of it and let the agony and suffering of the Crucifixion drag its fingers down your face. Just as you're

Grünewald's gripping Crucifixion

about to break down and sob with those in the painting, turn to the happy ending—a psychedelic explosion of Resurrection happiness. It's like jumping from the dentist's chair directly into a Jacuzzi. We know very little about Grünewald except that his work has played tetherball with human emotions for 500 years.

Colmar's tourist information office provides city maps, guides, and a room-finding service. They can also suggest side-trips around Alsace's wine road or into Germany's Black Forest and nearby Freiburg, or a tour of the Maginot Line.

For maximum fun, remember that Colmar goes crazy during its 10-day wine fest in August. You'll enjoy plenty of revelry—feasting, dancing, music, and wine—Alsatian-style.

*For good-value accommodations in **Colmar**, try Hôtel le Rapp (1 rue Weinemer, tel. 03 89 41 62 10, www.rapp-hotel.com) or the budget Maison Marin Jund (12 rue de l'Ange, tel. 03 89 41 58 72, www.martinjund.com). For all the travel specifics, see this year's edition of Rick Steves' France.*

48. From France to Italy over Mont Blanc

Europe's ultimate mountain lift towers high above the tourist-choked French resort town of Chamonix. Ride the Aiguille du Midi *téléphérique* (gondola) to the dizzy 12,600-foot-high tip of a rock needle. As you get in, remind yourself that this thing has been going back and forth now since 1954; surely it'll make it one more time. Chamonix shrinks as trees fly by, soon replaced by whizzing rocks, ice, and snow, until you reach the top. Up there, even sunshine is cold. The air is thin. People are giddy (those prone to altitude sickness are less

Dangle silently for 40 minutes as you glide over the glacier from France to Italy.

giddy). Fun things can happen if you're not too winded to join locals in the halfway-to-heaven tango.

The Alps spread out before you. In the distance is the bent little Matterhorn (called "Cervin" in French). You can almost reach out and pat the head of Mont Blanc, at 15,771 feet, the Alps' highest point.

Alpine Crossing from France to Italy

Next, for Europe's most exciting border crossing, get into the tiny red gondola and head south. Dangle silently for 40 minutes as you glide over glaciers and a forest of peaks to Italy. Hang your head out the window; explore every corner of your view. You're sailing a new sea.

Cross into Italy at Helbronner Point (11,371 feet) and descend into the remote Italian Valle d'Aosta. It's a whole different world.

Your starting point for this adventure is Chamonix, a convenient overnight train ride from Paris or Nice. Chamonix is a resort town—packed in August but surprisingly easy and affordable the rest of the year. Like Switzerland's Interlaken, it's a launchpad for mountain worshippers. The town has an efficient tourist information center and plenty of affordable accommodations.

From Chamonix, days of hikes and cable-car rides are within easy reach. The best hikes are opposite the most staggering peaks on the Gran Balcon Sud, a world of pristine lakes, great Mont Blanc range views, and hang gliders lunging off the cliff from the Brévent lift station. Watching these daredevils fill the valley like spaced-out butterflies is a thrilling spectator sport. Probably the best hike—two hours each way—is from the top of the Flégère lift to Lac Blanc. While demanding, the trail is well-signed and the views are breathtaking.

For the ultimate ride, take that *téléphérique* to the Aiguille du Midi. This lift is Europe's highest and most spectacular ($60 round-trip from Chamonix, daily 6 a.m.–4:30 p.m. in the summer, shorter hours off-season, smart to reserve up to 10 days in advance, www.compagniedu montblanc.com). If the weather is good, forget your budget. Afternoons are most likely clouded and crowded. In August, ride very early to avoid miserable delays. If you plan to dillydally, ride directly to your farthest point and linger on your return.

To both save a little money and enjoy a hike, buy a ticket to the top of the Aiguille du Midi, but only halfway back down. This gives you a chance to look down at the Alps and over at the summit of Mont Blanc from your lofty 12,600-foot lookout. Then you descend to the halfway point (Plan de l'Aiguille), where you're free to frolic in the glaciers and hike to Mer de Glace. Then you can catch a train at Montenvers back to Chamonix.

From the top of the Aiguille du Midi, you can continue (weather permitting) over the mountain to Italy. It's a long trip; the last departure is at about 2 p.m. The descent from Helbronner Point takes you into the remote Italian Valle d'Aosta, where a dash of France and a splash of Switzerland blend with the already rich Italian flavor and countless castles to give you an easy-to-like first taste of Italy.

The Alps from atop the Aiguille du Midi, 12,600 feet up

The town of Aosta, your best valley home base, is a two-hour bus ride from the base of the lift in La Palud (hourly departures, change in Courmayeur). If a fellow cable-car passenger has a car parked in La Palud, charm a ride to Aosta.

"The Rome of the Alps," as Aosta is called, has many Roman ruins and offers a great introduction to the fine points of Italian life: cappuccino, gelato, and an obligatory evening stroll. An evening here is a fine way to ease into *la dolce vita.*

Chamonix, the Aiguille du Midi, and the Valle d'Aosta—surely a high point in anyone's European vacation.

*For good-value accommodations in **Chamonix,** try Hôtel de l'Arve (60 impasse des Anémones, tel. 04 50 53 02 31, www.hotelarve-chamonix.com) or Hôtel Richemond (228 rue du Docteur Paccard, tel. 04 50 53 08 85, www .richemond.fr, richemond@wanadoo.fr). For all the travel specifics, see this year's edition of* Rick Steves' France.

BELGIUM AND THE NETHERLANDS

49. Bruges: Pickled in Gothic

With a smile, the shop owner handed me a pharaoh's head and two hedgehogs and said that her husband was busy downstairs finishing off another batch of chocolates. Happily sucking on a hedgehog, I walked out of the small chocolate shop with a $3, 100-gram assortment of Bruges' best pralines—filled-chocolate delights.

Bruggians are connoisseurs of chocolate. You'll be tempted by display windows all over town. Godiva is considered the best big factory brand, but for quality and service, drop by one of the many family-run shops. Pray for cool weather—they close down when it's hot.

With Renoir canals, pointy gilded architecture, vivid time-tunnel art, and stay-awhile cafés, Bruges is a joy. Where else can you bike along a canal, munch mussels and wash them down with the world's best beer, see a Michelangelo, and savor heavenly chocolate, all within 300 yards of a bell tower that jingles every 15 minutes? And do it all without worrying about a language barrier.

The town is Brugge (BROO-ghah) in Flemish, and Bruges (broozh) in French and English. Its name comes from the Viking word for "wharf." Right from the start, Bruges was a trading center. By the 14th century, Bruges had a population of 35,000 (similar to London) and the most important cloth market in northern Europe. But by the 16th century, the harbor had silted up and the economy had collapsed.

Like so many small-town wonders, Bruges is well-pickled because

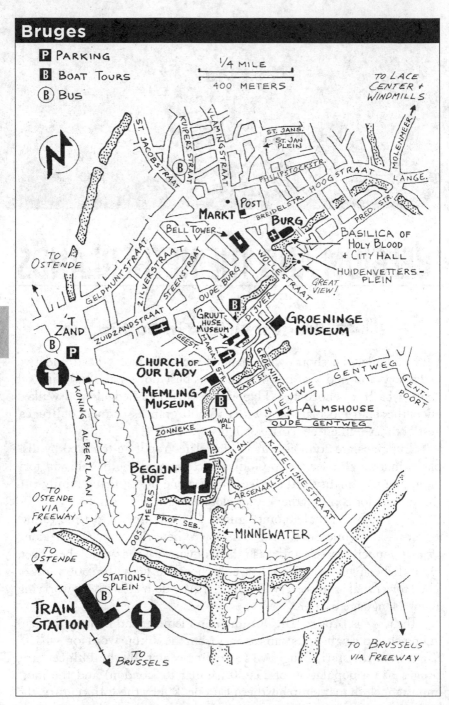

its economy went sour. But rediscovered by modern-day tourists, Bruges thrives. This uniquely well-preserved Gothic city is no secret, but even with crowds, it's the kind of city where you don't mind being a tourist.

Bruges makes a fine first night on the Continent for travelers arriving from England: It's just 15 minutes by train from Ostende, where boats dock from Dover, and an hour from Brussels, where the Eurostar train arrives from London.

Bruges' Market Square, ringed by great old gabled buildings and crowned by the belfry, is the colorful heart of the city. Under the belfry are two great Belgian french-fry stands, a small metal model of the tower, and a Braille description of the old town.

This bell tower has towered over Market Square since 1300. Climb 366 steps to survey the town. Just before the top, peek into the carillon room. On the quarter hour, the 47 bells are played mechanically with the giant barrel and

Bruges: canals, fine beer, a Michelangelo, and even a leaning tower

movable tabs. For concerts, a carillonist plays the manual keyboard with fists and feet rather than fingers. Be there on the quarter hour when things ring. It's *bellissimo* at the top of the hour.

Within a block or three, you'll find a day's worth of sights. The Basilica of the Holy Blood is famous for its relic of the blood of Christ, which, according to tradition, was brought to Bruges in 1150 after the Second Crusade. The City Hall has the oldest and most sumptuous Gothic hall in the Low Countries. The Gruuthuse Museum, a wealthy brewer's home, is filled with a sprawling smattering of everything from medieval bedpans to a guillotine. The church of Our Lady, standing as a memorial to the power and wealth of Bruges in its heyday, has a delicate *Madonna and Child* by Michelangelo, said to be the only statue of his to leave Italy in his lifetime. A medieval hospital, now the Memling Museum, contains much-loved paintings by the greatest of the Flemish Primitives, Hans Memling.

Yadda, yadda, yadda...Michelangelo, the blood of Christ, leaning bell towers, and guillotines. You'd expect any medieval powerhouse to show off trinkets from its glory days. But Bruges has fun experiences, too.

A Stop in Brussels

Bruges isn't the only highlight in Belgium. Consider a short stop in Brussels, one of Europe's underrated cities. If traveling by train, it's easy to do, whether you're transferring in Brussels for Bruges, or just passing through the country. Anyone taking the three-hour train ride from Paris to Amsterdam will stop in Brussels, but few even consider getting out. Each train on this route stops in Brussels, and there's always another train coming in an hour or so. Leave an hour early, arrive an hour late, and give yourself two hours in Brussels. Luckily for the rushed tourist, Brussels Central Station has easy baggage storage and puts you two blocks (just walk downhill) from the helpful tourist

Brussels' Grand Place is the place to kick back with a brew.

office, a colorful pedestrian-only city core, Europe's greatest city square (Grand Place), and its most overrated and tacky sight, the *Manneken-Pis* (a much-photographed statue of a little boy who thinks he's a fountain). Brussels has three stations: Nord, Midi, and Central. Ask if your train stops at Central (middle) Station. If you have to get off at Nord or Midi, don't worry—subway-like connecting trains run every few minutes. You'll have no trouble finding English-speaking help.

The Paris–Brussels–Amsterdam rail route is virtually monopolized by high-speed, reservations-required Thalys trains. Direct Thalys trains also make the whole Paris–Amsterdam trip, but if you plan a stop in Brussels, you can take a nonreserved train for the Brussels–Amsterdam leg. Note that only railpasses that include France are accepted by Thalys. If your pass doesn't also cover BeNeLux (Belgium, the Netherlands, and Luxembourg), you'll pay more for that portion of the trip. While first class includes a meal (reservations about $85 with railpass), go second class (reservations $50) if you're on a budget. Thalys limits the number of seats available to railpass travelers, particularly on popular morning and evening runs, so you may need to reserve your seat a few days in advance.

The De Halve Maan brewery tour is a handy way to pay your respects to perhaps the favorite local beer. The "Brugse Zot" is one of the only beers still brewed in Bruges, and the happy gang at this working family brewery gives entertaining and informative 45-minute tours in two languages. At De Halve Maan ("The Half Moon"), they remind their drinkers that "the components of the beer are vitally necessary and contribute to a well-balanced life pattern. Nerves, muscles, visual sentience, and a healthy skin are stimulated by these in a positive manner. For longevity and lifelong equilibrium, drink Brugse Zot in moderation!"

Belgians are Europe's beer connoisseurs, and this country boasts more than 120 varieties of beer and 580 different brands. Duvel ("Devil"), a potent brew, is, even to a Bud Light kind of guy, obviously great beer. Trappist is monk-made beer, and Dentergems is made with coriander and orange peel. Those who don't drink beer enjoy the cherry-flavored Kriek and strawberry-flavored Frambozen. Each beer is served in its own unique glass.

Walk off your beer buzz with a stroll through the *begijnhof* (buh-HINE-hof). For reasons of war and testosterone, there were more women than men in the medieval Low Countries. The order of Beguines offered women (often single or widowed) a dignified place to live and work. When the order died out, many *begijnhof*s were taken over by towns for subsidized housing, but some, like this one, became homes for nuns. You'll find *begijnhof*s all over Belgium and the Netherlands. Bruges' *begijnhof* almost makes you want to don a habit and fold your hands as you walk under its wispy trees and whisper past its frugal little homes.

For more peace, wander back in time to Bruges' four windmills, strung out along a pleasant, grassy canalside park. Joust with a windmill or just have a picnic.

Every once in a while as you travel, you stumble onto a town that somehow missed the 21st-century bus. Ironically, many of these wonderfully preserved towns are so full of Old World charm because, for various reasons, their economies failed. The towns became so poor that no one even bothered to tear them down to build more modern towns. England's Cotswolds lost their export market. Toledo was abandoned as Spain's capital. Stranded-in-the-past Dutch fishing towns were left high and dry as the sea around them was drained and the land reclaimed. And Bruges' harbor silted up.

Today, while some of these towns slumber on, many—like Bruges—enjoy a renewed prosperity by making "tourist dreams come true."

BELGIUM

*For good-value accommodations in **Bruges**, try Hotel Heritage (Niklaas Desparsstraat 11, tel. 050-444-444, www.hotel-heritage.com) or Koen and Annemie Dieltiens' B&B (Waalse Straat 40, tel. 050-334-294, www.bedandbreakfastbruges.be). For all the travel specifics, see the latest edition of* Rick Steves' Amsterdam, Bruges & Brussels.

50. Amsterdam's Counter-Culture

Amsterdam is a laboratory of progressive living, bottled inside Europe's most 17th-century city. Like Venice, this city is a patchwork quilt of canal-bordered islands, anchored upon millions of wooden pilings. But unlike its dwelling-in-the-past cousin, Amsterdam sees itself as a city of the future, built on good living, cozy cafés, great art, street-corner jazz... and a spirit of live-and-let-live.

During its Golden Age in the 1600s, Amsterdam was the world's richest city, an international sea-trading port, and the cradle of capitalism. Wealthy, democratic burghers built a planned city of tree-shaded canals lined with townhouses topped with fancy gables. Immigrants, Jews, outcasts, and political rebels were drawn here by its tolerant atmosphere, and painters like young Rembrandt captured that atmosphere on canvas.

Approach Amsterdam as an ethnologist observing a fascinating and unique culture. A stroll through any neighborhood is rewarded with things

Cruise by Amsterdam's stately 17th-century buildings.

that are commonplace here but rarely found elsewhere. Carillons chime quaintly in neighborhoods selling sex, as young professionals smoke pot with impunity next to old ladies in bonnets selling flowers. Observe the neighborhoods' quirky system of "social control," where an elderly man feels safe in his home knowing he's being watched over by the hookers next door.

Prostitution has been legal here since the 1980s. Most prostitutes opposed legalization, not wanting taxes and bureaucratic regulations. The women are often entrepreneurs, renting space and running their own businesses. Women usually rent their space for eight-hour shifts. A good spot costs $140 for a day shift and $210 for an evening. Popular pros-

THE NETHERLANDS

Amsterdam Overview

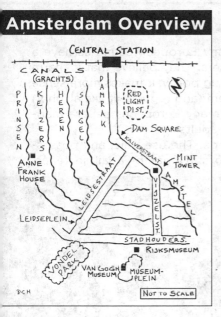

titutes charge $35–70 for a 20-minute visit and make about $700 a day. They fill out tax returns, and many belong to a loose union called the Red Thread.

Amsterdam's mayor recently engineered a deal to close about 50 of the city's prostitution windows; prices—what the women pay and what they charge their customers—may go up as a result.

The rooms look tiny from the street ("Do they have to do it standing up?"), but most are just display windows, opening onto a room behind or upstairs with a bed, a sink, and little else. Prostitutes are required to keep their premises hygienic, make sure their clients use condoms, and avoid minors.

The law, not pimps, protects prostitutes. If a prostitute is diagnosed with AIDS, she gets a subsidized apartment to encourage her to quit the business. Shocking as this may seem to some, it's a good example of a pragmatic Dutch solution—getting the most dangerous prostitutes off the streets to combat the spread of AIDS.

The Dutch people are unique. They may be the world's most handsome people—tall, healthy, and with good posture—and the most open, honest, and refreshingly blunt. They like to laugh. As connoisseurs of world culture, they appreciate Rembrandt paintings, Indonesian food, and the latest French films, but with an un-snooty, blue-jeans attitude.

Un-snooty, but not un-sooty—about a third of the Dutch people smoke tobacco. Holland has a long tradition as a smoking culture, being among the first to import the tobacco plant from the New World. Still, their version of the Surgeon General is finally waking up to the drug's many potential health problems. Warning stickers bigger than America's are required on cigarette packs, and some of them are almost comically blunt, such as: "Smoking will make you impotent...and then you die." (The warnings have prompted gag stickers like "Life can kill you.")

Since 2008, a Dutch law has outlawed smoking tobacco almost everywhere indoors: on trains, and in hotel rooms, restaurants, cafés, and bars. But smoking remains part of an overall diet and regimen that—no denying it—somehow makes the Dutch people among the healthiest in the world. Tanned, trim, firm, 60-something Dutch people sip their

Marijuana in Europe

Compared to the United States, many European countries have a liberal attitude toward marijuana users. They believe that if "harm reduction" is the aim of a nation's drug policy, it makes more sense to treat marijuana as a health problem (and regulate it like alcohol) than as a criminal one. Simply put, many Europeans believe marijuana can be enjoyed responsibly by adults.

Still, drugs are not legal in Europe. The use, sale, and possession of any illegal drug can lead to stiff fines or a jail sentence. While laws against the use of drugs such as cocaine, heroin, LSD, and Ecstasy are strictly enforced, marijuana is more often classified as a "soft drug" and its recreational use tolerated in private or in certain bars.

But even in the most liberal countries, the sale of marijuana is permitted only in certain places. In Amsterdam and other Dutch cities, "coffeeshops"—often sporting red, green, and yellow Rastafarian flags—

Coffeeshops in Amsterdam offer a wide array of bongs.

are allowed to sell small amounts for personal use to people over 18.

beers, take a drag, and ask me why Americans murder themselves with Big Macs.

If you can't avoid tobacco in Amsterdam, why not make it part of your sightseeing? At Rokin 92, the House of Hajenius is a temple of cigars—a "paradise for the connoisseur" showing "175 years of tradition and good taste." To enter this sumptuous Art Deco building with its painted leather ceilings is to step back into 1910. Visitors can sniff fine pipe tobacco from brown-capped canisters. The shop's "personal humidifiers" allow customers to call in an order and have their cigars waiting for them at just the right humidity.

Of course, smokers in Europe's counterculture mecca don't enjoy just tobacco. Throughout Amsterdam, you'll see "coffeeshops"—pubs selling marijuana—with menus that look like the inventory of a drug bust.

Most of downtown Amsterdam's coffeeshops feel grungy and fore-

Recently, Switzerland, Britain, and other countries have also been liberalizing their approach to marijuana.

Remember that you are subject to the laws of the country in which you travel when abroad, so be sensible and err on the side of caution. People who run coffeeshops warn that even a country that is "soft on soft drugs" needs to make a few marijuana arrests each year to maintain its favorable trade status with the United States (which wants European countries to maintain a harder stance on marijuana use).

Be warned that anywhere in Europe, especially in countries adjacent to countries famous for being easy on marijuana, border patrols can be particularly strict. And driving under the influence of any drug is a serious offense that can land you in jail, if not in a car crash.

Because I believe the US's current war on marijuana is as futile and counterproductive as our Prohibition against alcohol was in the 1930s, and because I believe that the responsible recreational use of marijuana among adults is a civil liberty, I am a proud board member of the National Organization for the Reform of Marijuana Laws (NORML). To learn more about my views on this issue, do a Google search for "Rick Steves marijuana." For an overview and country by country summary of European drug laws, see the NORML website (www.norml.org). Americans interested in "going local" with marijuana in Europe may be interested in the vast and rapidly growing discussion on the Graffiti Wall at www.ricksteves.com/graffiti.

boding to a typical middle-aged American traveler. The neighborhood places (and those in small towns around the countryside) are much more inviting to people without piercings and tattoos.

Paradox is the most *gezellig* (cozy) coffeeshop I found—a mellow, graceful place. The managers, Ludo and Wiljan, and their staff are patient with descriptions, and are happy to walk you through all your options. This is a rare coffeeshop that serves light meals. The juice is fresh, the music is easy, and the neighborhood is charming (two blocks from Anne Frank House at Eerste Bloemdwarsstraat 2, tel. 020/623-5639, www.paradoxamsterdam.demon.nl).

Ludo explained to me that the Dutch think the concept of a "victimless crime" is a contradiction in terms. Although hard drugs are illegal, marijuana causes about as much excitement as a bottle of beer. If a tipsy tourist calls an ambulance after smoking too much pot, medics just say,

"Drink something sweet and walk it off."

Amsterdam also has several "Smartshops"—bright, clean, fully professional retail outlets that sell a wide array of drugs, many of which are illegal in America. Their "natural" drugs include harmless nutrition boosters (royal jelly), harmful but familiar tobacco, organic versions of popular dance-club drugs (herbal Ecstasy), and joints made from an unpredictable mix of marijuana and other substances, sold under exotic names like "Herbal Love." The best-seller: marijuana seeds. Prices are clearly marked, with brief descriptions of the drugs, their ingredients, and effects.

The knowledgeable Smartshop salespeople enjoy talking about these "100-percent-natural products that play with the human senses." Still, my fellow Americans, *caveat emptor!* We've grown used to thinking, "If it's legal, it must be safe. If it's not, I'll sue." While legal in Amsterdam, some of these substances can cause powerful, often unpleasant reactions. If you've never taken drugs recreationally, don't start here.

The Dutch also like plants you can't smoke, as I learned strolling through one of the oldest botanical gardens in the world. The De Hortus Botanical Garden dates from 1638, when medicinal herbs were grown here. The collection expanded in the 17th and 18th centuries as a wealth of flora was brought from faraway places by the Dutch East India Company. Today, its 6,000 different varieties of plants are spread throughout several greenhouses and a tropical palm house. No mobile phones are allowed because "our collection of plants is a precious community—treat it with respect." The "residents" are described thoughtfully: "A Dutch merchant snuck a coffee plant out of Ethiopia, which ended up in this garden in 1706. This first coffee plant in Europe was the literal granddaddy of the coffee cultures of Brazil—long the world's biggest coffee producer."

Electric Ladyland's Nick Padalino glows with pride as he adds more color to Amsterdam's colorful Jordaan district.

Amsterdam's tolerant culture has attracted some colorful residents. Nick Padalino is one cool cat who—with the help of ultraviolet lights—has found his niche in life. Nick's flowery window display hides a fluorescent wonderland: Electric Ladyland, a tiny, unique museum featuring black-light art (Tweede Leliedwarsstraat 5-HS, tel. 020/420-3776, www.electric-lady-land.com). Nick lovingly demonstrates fluorescent minerals from all over the world and fluorescence in everyday objects (stamps, candy, and so on). He seems to get a bigger kick out of it than even his customers. Pulling out one of his prize artifacts, Nick says, "This is the historic first fluorescent crayon from San Francisco, from the 1950s. Wow. See the label? It says, 'Use with black light for church groups.' Wow."

Yes, Amsterdam is known for its tolerance of soft drugs—but the Dutch also think progressively about more mundane matters, like transportation. Amsterdam's 750,000 residents own nearly that many bikes. The Dutch average four bikes per family (many people own two: a long-distance racing bike and an in-city bike, often deliberately kept in poor maintenance so it's less enticing to the many bike thieves). The Dutch appreciate the efficiency of a self-propelled machine that travels five times faster than walking, without pollution, noise, parking problems, or high fuel costs. A speedy bicyclist can traverse the historic center in 10 minutes. Pedestrians also enjoy the quiet of a people-friendly town where bikes outnumber cars.

Another way to see the city is by boat: Amsterdam has more canals than Venice. Amsterdam's canals tamed the flow of the Amstel River, creating pockets of dry land to build on. The city's 100 canals are about 10 feet deep, crossed by some 1,200 bridges, fringed with 100,000 Dutch elm and lime trees, and bedecked with 2,000 houseboats. A system of locks near the central train station controls the flow outward to (eventually) the North Sea, and the flow inward of the tides. The locks are opened periodically to flush out polluted water. Some of the boats in the canals look pretty funky by day, but Amsterdam is an unpretentious, anti-status city. When the sun goes down and the lights come on, people cruise the sparkling canals with an on-board hibachi grill and a bottle of wine, and, as my Dutch friends report, "Even scows can become chick magnets."

Amsterdam, a bold experiment in freedom, may box your Puritan ears. Take it all in, then pause to watch the summer sunset—at 10 p.m.—and see the Dutch Golden Age reflected in a quiet canal.

*For good-value accommodations in **Amsterdam**, try The Toren (Keizersgracht 164, tel. 020/622-6352, www.thetoren.nl) or Hotel Keizershof (Keizersgracht 618, where Keizers canal crosses Nieuwe Spiegelstraat, tel. 020/622-2855, www.hotelkeizershof.nl). For all the travel specifics, see the latest edition of* Rick Steves' Amsterdam, Bruges & Brussels.

GERMANY, AUSTRIA, AND SWITZERLAND

51. Rothenburg and the Romantic Road

Thirty years ago, I fell in love with a Rothenburg in the rough. At that time, the town still fed a few farm animals within its medieval walls. Today its barns are hotels, its livestock are tourists, and Rothenburg is well on its way to becoming a medieval theme park.

But Rothenburg is still Germany's best-preserved walled town. Countless travelers have searched for the elusive "untouristy Rothenburg." There are many contenders (such as Michelstadt, Miltenberg, Bamberg, Bad Windsheim, and Dinkelsbühl), but none holds a candle to the king of medieval German cuteness. Even with crowds, overpriced souvenirs, a Japanese-speaking night watchman, and, yes, even with *Schneeballen*, Rothenburg is still the best. Save time and mileage and be satisfied with the winner.

In the Middle Ages, when Frankfurt and Munich were just wide spots in the road, Rothenburg was Germany's second-largest city, with a whopping population of 6,000. Today, it's the country's most exciting medieval town, enjoying tremendous popularity with tourists.

To avoid the hordes of day-trippers, spend the night. In the deserted moonlit streets, you might hear the sounds of the Thirty Years' War still echoing through turrets and clock towers.

A walking tour helps bring the ramparts alive. The tourist information office on the Market Square offers $8 tours in English led by a local historian—usually an intriguing character (April–Oct and Dec daily at

2 p.m., Jan–March Sat only at 11 a.m., no tours in Nov, plus the more colorful Night Watchman's tour Easter–Dec nightly at 8 p.m.). A thousand years of history is packed between the cobbles.

For the best view of the town and surrounding countryside, climb the Town Hall tower. For more views, walk the wall that surrounds the old town. This 1.5-mile walk atop the wall is at its most medieval before breakfast or at sunset.

Rothenburg's fascinating Medieval Crime and Punishment Museum, all unusually well-explained in English, is full of legal bits and diabolical pieces, instruments of punishment and torture, and even an iron cage—complete with a metal nag gag. Some react with horror, others wish for a gift shop.

St. Jakob's Church contains the one must-see art treasure in Rothenburg: a glorious 500-year-old altarpiece by Riemenschneider, the Michelangelo of German woodcarvers. Pick up the brochure that explains the church's art treasures and climb the stairs behind the organ for Germany's greatest piece of woodcarving.

To hear the birds and smell the cows, take a walk through the Tauber Valley. The trail leads downhill from Rothenburg's idyllic castle gardens to a cute, skinny, 600-year-old castle, the summer home of the town's mayor in the 15th century, Mayor Toppler. While called a castle, the floor plan is more like a four-story tree house. It's intimately furnished and well worth a look. On the top floor, notice the 1945 photo of a bombed-out Rothenburg. From here, walk past the covered bridge and trout-filled Tauber to the sleepy village of Detwang, which is actually older than Rothenburg and has a church with another impressive Riemenschneider altarpiece.

Warning: Rothenburg is one of Germany's best shopping towns. Do it here, mail it home, and be done with it. Lovely prints, carvings, wine glasses, Christmas-tree ornaments, and beer steins are popular.

The Käthe Wohlfahrt Christmas trinkets phenomenon is spreading across the half-timbered reaches of Europe. In Rothenburg, tourists flock to two Käthe Wohlfahrt Christmas Villages (just off Market Square). These Santa wonderlands are filled with enough twinkling lights to require a special electric hookup, instant Christmas mood music (best appreciated on a hot day in July), and American and Japanese tourists hungrily filling little woven shopping baskets with $7–12 goodies to hang on their trees. (OK, I admit it, my Christmas tree sports a few KW ornaments.) Prices have tour-guide kickbacks built into them. I prefer the friendlier Friese shop (on the northwest corner of Market Square), which offers cheaper prices, less glitter, and more variety.

At the English Conversation Club, held every Wednesday night at Mario's hotel, Altfränkische Weinstube am Klosterhof, locals enjoy a weekly excuse to get together, drink, and practice their fanciest English on each other and on visiting tourists. Anneliese, who runs the Friese shop (see above) and is a regular at the Conversation Club, invites me to join her, so I meander into the pub through candlelit clouds of smoke and squeeze a three-legged stool up to a table already crowded with her family.

Anneliese pours me a glass of wine, then pulls a *Schneeball* (a pow-dered-doughnut–like "snowball") from a bag. Raising a cloud of pow-

dered sugar as she pokes at the name on the now empty bag, she says, "Friedel is the bakery I explained you about. They make the best *Schneeball*. I like it better than your American doughnut. Everyday I eat one. But only at this bakery."

Shoving a big doughy ball my way, she says, "You like to eat this?"

I break off a little chunk, saying, "Only a teeny-weeny *bisschen*."

For years, Anneliese has play-fully tried to get me to write good things about *Schneeballen*. I put *Schneeballen* (which originated in a hungrier age as a way to get more mileage out of leftover dough) in that category of penitential foods—like lutefisk—whose only purpose is to help younger people remem-ber the suffering of their parents. Nowadays these historic pastries are pitched to the tourists in caramel, chocolate, and other flavors unknown in feudal times.

As Anneliese finishes the *Schneeball,* we share our favorite slang and tongue twisters. But medieval Rothenburg is waiting. I drain my glass of wine and bid a cheery, *"Tschüss!"*

In the night, I find myself alone with Rothenburg. The winds of history polish half-timbered gables. Following the grooves of centuries of horse carts, I head down to the castle garden. From a distance, the roars of laughter tumbling like waves out of *Biergarten*s and over the ramparts sound as medieval as they do modern.

Sitting in a mossy niche in the town wall, I finger the medieval stonework. Notching my imaginary crossbow, I aim an arrow into the dark forest that surrounds the city. Even now, it feels good to be within these protective walls.

On the ramparts after dark, I look over a choppy sea of red-tiled roofs to the murky and mysterious moat beyond the wall. The cannons are loaded. Torches illuminate the gory heads of bad guys on pikes that greet visitors at the city gates. With a dash of moonlight and a splash of wine, Rothenburg once again is a crossroads where modern-day travelers meet medieval wayfarers.

Romantic Road

The Romantic Road, which winds scenically from the Rhine to Bavaria through Germany's medieval heartland, is the best way to connect the dots between Frankfurt and Munich. Peppered with pretty towns today because it was such an important and prosperous trade route 600 years ago, this popular road is no secret. But even with the crowds, it's a must.

Along the Romantic Road (and especially just off it), many visitors find the Germany that they have come to see. On the side roads, flower boxes decorate the unseen sides of barns and no unfamiliar car passes unnoticed. Church-steeple masts sail seas of rich, rolling farmland, and fragrant villages invite you to slow down. Stop wherever the cows look friendly or a town fountain beckons. At each village, ignore the signposts and ask an old woman for directions to the next town—just to hear her voice and enjoy the energy in her eyes. Thousands of tourists pass through. Few stop to chat.

After Rothenburg, consider these top stops along the Romantic Road: Dinkelsbühl, Rothenburg's well-preserved medieval sister city, comes with old walls, towers, gateways, and the peaceful green waters of the moat defending its medieval architecture from the 21st century. Würzburg has a fine Baroque prince bishop's Residenz—the Versailles of

Germany's Romantic Road

50 MILES
100 KM

ROMANTIC ROAD BUS ROUTE
AUTOBAHN — OTHER ROADS
++ RAIL LINES ✈ AIRPORT

TO KÖLN

FRANKFURT

MAINZ

TO KOBLENZ

GERMANY

A-7

A-3

MAIN

WÜRZBURG

BAD MERGENTHEIM

WEIKERSHEIM

CREG.

ROTHENBURG

19

RHINE

STEINACH

NÜRNBERG

A-3

REGENS-BURG

A-6

A-81

TREUCH.

DINKELSBÜHL

NÖRDLINGEN

DONAU-WORTH

ANSBACH

A-5

STUTTGART

A-8

A-7

ULM

AUGS-BURG

INGOL-STADT

DACHAU

✈

MUNICH

DANUBE

LANDSBERG AM LECH

19

KAUFBEUREN

A-95

TO SALZ-BURG

A-8

KEMPTEN

WIES.

FÜSSEN

OBER.

GARMISCH

A-12

REUTTE

LECH

INNSBRÜCK

SWITZ.

AUSTRIA

N

NOT ALL ROADS & RAIL LINES ARE SHOWN

GERMANY

Franconia—and an oh-wow Baroque chapel. Another lovely carved altar-piece by Riemenschneider (and the unique thimble museum across the street) is just outside Rothenburg at Creglingen. To the south is the flamboyant church called the Wieskirche, near Oberammergau, and "Mad" King Ludwig's Disney-esque Neuschwanstein Castle, near Füssen.

The sections from Füssen to Landsberg and Rothenburg to Weikersheim are most characteristic. (If you're driving with limited time, drive these and then connect Rothenburg and Munich by autobahn.) Caution: The similarly promoted "Castle Road" (between Rothenburg and Mannheim) sounds intriguing but is much less interesting.

A car or bike gives you complete freedom—just follow the brown *Romantische Strasse* signs. This is the best way to connect the castles of the Rhine and the lederhosen charm of Bavaria. Those without wheels have a couple of options. The Deutsche Touring company runs buses daily between Frankfurt and Munich in each direction (early May–late Oct, tel. 069/790-3261, www.romanticroadcoach.de). Or you can take public transportation: The larger towns—including Rothenburg, Würzburg, and Füssen—are well-connected by train. Some of the more out-of-the-way places (such as Dinkelsbühl, Creglingen, and the Wieskirche) are still reachable, but require a more complicated public-bus connection.

For good-value accommodations in **Rothenburg,** *try Gästehaus Raidel (ramshackle, Wenggasse 3, tel. 09861/3115, www.romanticroad.com/raidel) or Hotel Gerberhaus (classy, Spitalgasse 25, tel. 09861/94900, www.gerber haus.rothenburg.de). For all the travel specifics, see this year's edition of* Rick Steves' Germany.

52. Hallstatt, in Austria's Commune-with-Nature Lake District

With one of the longest life spans and one of the shortest work weeks in Europe, Austrians spend their ample free time focusing on the fine points of life: music, a stroll, pastry, and a good cup of coffee. Austrians specialize in good living and *Gemütlichkeit*. A distinctly Austrian concept, and as difficult to translate as it is to pronounce, it means a warm, cozy, friendly, focus-on-the-moment feeling. Even tourists catch on in the Salzkammergut Lake District, where big-city Austrians go to relax.

Far from the urban rat race, though just two hours by train from Salzburg, this is the perfect place to commune with nature, Austrian-style. The Salzkammergut is a lushly forested playground dotted with

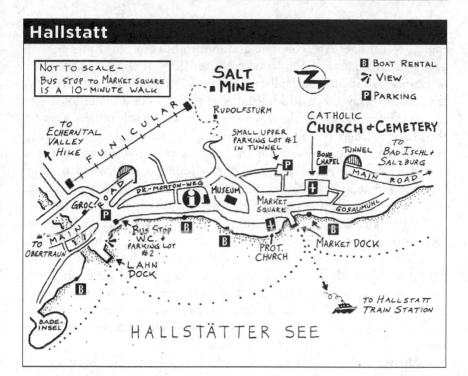

Hallstatt

NOT TO SCALE—
BUS STOP TO MARKET SQUARE
IS A 10-MINUTE WALK

SALT MINE

B BOAT RENTAL
🕮 VIEW
P PARKING

RUDOLFSTURM

TO ECHERNTAL VALLEY HIKE

FUNICULAR

SMALL UPPER PARKING LOT #1 IN TUNNEL

CATHOLIC CHURCH & CEMETERY

BONE CHAPEL

TUNNEL

TO BAD ISCHL & SALZBURG

GROC. ROAD

DR. MORTON-WEG

MUSEUM

MAIN ROAD

P

MARKET SQUARE

GOSAUMÜHL

TO MAIN OBERTRAUN

BUS STOP W.C. + PARKING LOT #2

R

B

PROT. CHURCH

MARKET DOCK

B

LAHN DOCK

B

TO HALLSTATT TRAIN STATION

BADE-INSEL

HALLSTÄTTER SEE

cottages. Trains, buses, and boats lead the traveler through gentle mountains and shy lakes, winding from relaxed village to relaxed village.

The Salzkammergut's pride and joy is the town of Hallstatt. The minute it popped into view, I knew Hallstatt was my alpine Oz. It's just the right size (900 people), wonderfully remote, and almost traffic-free. A tiny ferry takes you from the nearest train station, across the fjord-like lake, and drops you off on the town's storybook square.

Bullied onto its lakeside ledge by a selfish mountain, Hallstatt seems tinier than it is. Its pint-size square is surrounded by ivy-covered guest houses and cobbled lanes. It's a toy town. You can tour it on foot in about 10 minutes. Except in August, when tourist crowds trample most of Hallstatt's charm, there's no shortage of pleasant $35-per-person *Privatzimmer* (bed-and-breakfast places).

A boat shuttles travelers from the nearest train station to the Back Door town of Hallstatt in Austria.

Nearly three thousand years ago, this area was the salt-mining capital of Europe. An economic and cultural boom put it on the map back in Flintstone times. In fact, an entire 700-year chapter in the story of Europe is called "The Hallstatt Period." A humble museum next to the tourist office shows off Hallstatt's salty past. For a better look, you can tour what the locals claim is the world's oldest salt mine, located a thrilling funicular ride above downtown Hallstatt. You'll dress up in an old miner's outfit, ride trains into the mountain where the salt was mined, cruise subterranean lakes, scream down a long wooden chute (praying for no splinters), and read brief and dry English explanations while entertaining guides tell the fascinating story in German. You can return to Hallstatt by funicular, but the scenic 40-minute hike back into town is (with strong knees) a joy.

Hallstatt outgrew its little ledge, and many of its buildings climb the mountainside, with the street level on one side being three floors above the street level on the other. Land is limited—so limited that there's not enough room for the dead. Remains evicted from the cemetery are stacked neatly in an eerie chapel of decorated bones (see "Boning Up on Europe's Relics" in Chapter 68: Off-Beat Europe).

Passing time in and around Hallstatt is easy. The little tourist office will recommend a hike—the 9,845-foot Mount Dachstein looms overhead—or a peaceful cruise in a rented canoe. Most people go to Hallstatt simply to relax, eat, shop, and stroll.

The husband of a woman whose Hallstatt B&B I've recommended for years takes me and my TV crew out in his handmade, traditional Fuhr *boat.*

My challenge these days, along with finding untouristed destinations, is to find vivid cultural traditions that survive in places that are now well-discovered...like Hallstatt. On a recent visit, the sun rose late over the towering Alps as my friend, who runs a restaurant here, took me for a spin in his classic boat. It's a *Fuhr,* a centuries-old boat design, made wide and flat for shipping heavy bushels of locally mined salt across shallow waters. Lunging rhythmically on the single oar, he said, "An hour on the lake is for me like a day of vacation." I asked about the oarlock, which looked like a skinny dog-chew doughnut, and he told me, "It's made from the gut of a bull—not of a cow, but a bull."

Returning to the weathered timber boathouse, we passed a teenage boy systematically grabbing trout from the fishermen's pen and killing them one by one with a stern whack to the noggin. Another man carried them to the tiny fishery to be gutted by a guy who, 40 years ago, did the stern whacking. A cat waited outside the door, confident his breakfast would be a good one. And restaurateurs and homemakers alike—their dining rooms decorated with trophies of big ones that didn't get away—lined up to buy fresh trout to feed the hungry tourists, or a good fish to cook for a special friend.

Traditions are embattled everywhere by a bullying modern world. Yet they manage to survive. Despite tourism—and sometimes thanks to tourism—traditional Europe hangs in there. To cloak yourself in the *Gemütlichkeit*, flowers, and cobblestones of Austria's Salzkammergut Lake District, visit Hallstatt.

*For good-value accommodations in **Hallstatt**, try Gasthof Simony (Marktplatz 105, tel. 06134/8231, www.hallstatt.net/gasthof/simony) or Gasthof Zauner (Marktplatz 51, tel. 06134/8246, www.zauner.hallstatt.net). For all the travel specifics, see the current edition of Rick Steves' Vienna, Salzburg & Tirol.*

53. Gimmelwald: For the Swiss Alps in Your Lap

When told you're visiting Gimmelwald, Swiss people assume you mean the famous resort in the next valley, Grindelwald. When assured that Gimmelwald is your target, they lean forward, widen their eyes, and—

with their sing-songy Swiss German accent—they ask, "Und how do you know about Gimmelvald?"

The traffic-free village of Gimmelwald hangs nonchalantly on the edge of a cliff high above Lauterbrunnen Valley, 30 minutes south of Interlaken by car or train. This sleepy village has more cow troughs

"Downtown" Gimmelwald

Berner Oberland

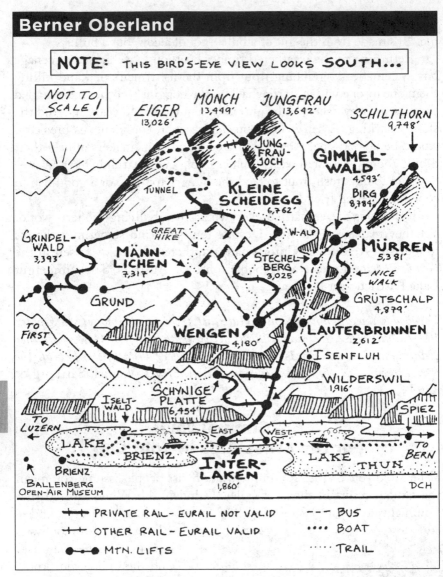

NOTE: THIS BIRD'S-EYE VIEW LOOKS **SOUTH...**

NOT TO SCALE!

EIGER 13,026' MÖNCH 13,449' JUNGFRAU 13,642' SCHILTHORN 9,748'

JUNG-FRAU-JOCH GIMMEL-WALD 4,593' BIRG 8,784'

TUNNEL KLEINE SCHEIDEGG 6,762' W. ALP

GRINDEL-WALD 3,393' GREAT HIKE MÜRREN 5,381'

MÄNN-LICHEN 7,317' STECHEL-BERG 3,025' NICE WALK

GRUND GRÜTSCHALP 4,879'

TO FIRST WENGEN 4,180' LAUTERBRUNNEN 2,612'

ISENFLUH

SCHYNIGE PLATTE 6,454' WILDERSWIL 1,916'

ISELT-WALD SPIEZ

TO LUZERN EAST WEST. TO BERN

LAKE BRIENZ LAKE THUN

BRIENZ INTER-LAKEN 1,860'

BALLENBERG OPEN-AIR MUSEUM DCH

PRIVATE RAIL - EURAIL NOT VALID --- BUS
OTHER RAIL - EURAIL VALID •••• BOAT
•—• MTN. LIFTS ····· TRAIL

than mailboxes. The songs of birds and brooks and the crunchy march of happy hikers constantly remind you why so many travelers say, "If Heaven isn't what it's cracked up to be, send me back to Gimmelwald."

Gimmelwald, an ignored station on the spectacular Schilthorn cable car, should be built to the hilt. But, led by a visionary schoolmaster, the farming community managed to reclassify its land as an "avalanche zone"—too dangerous for serious building projects. So while developers gnash their teeth, sturdy peasants continue to milk cows and make hay, thus surviving in a modern world only by the grace of a government that subsidizes such poor traditional industries.

Gimmelwald is a community in the rough. Take a walk—you can tour it in 15 minutes. Its two streets, a 700-year-old zig and zag, are decorated by drying laundry, hand-me-down tricycles, and hollowed stumps bursting proudly with geraniums. Little-boy cars are parked next to the tiny tank-tread cement mixers and mini-tractors necessary for taming this alpine environment. White-bearded elves smoke hand-carved pipes, and blond-braided children play "barn" instead of "house." Stones called *schindeln* sit like heavy checkers on old rooftops, awaiting nature's next move. While these stones protect the slate from the violent winter winds, today it's so quiet you can hear the cows ripping tufts of grass.

Notice the traditional log-cabin architecture. The numbers on the buildings are not addresses, but fire insurance numbers. The cute little hut near the station is for storing and aging cheese, not hostelers. In Catholic Swiss towns, the biggest building is the church. In Protestant towns, it's the school. Gimmelwald's biggest building is the school (two teachers share one job, 17 students, and a room that doubles as a chapel when the Protestant pastor makes his monthly visit).

There's nothing but air between Gimmelwald and the rock face of the Jungfrau nearly four miles away. Small avalanches across the valley look and sound like distant waterfalls. Kick a soccer ball wrong and it ends up a mile below on the Lauterbrunnen Valley floor.

In a Back Door–style hotel, you get more by spending less. Here, the shower's down the hall, and the Alps are in your lap.

Most Gimmelwalders have one of two last names: von Allmen or Feuz. To keep prescriptions and medical records straight, the doctor in nearby Lauterbrunnen goes by birth date first, then the patient's name.

The people of Gimmelwald systematically harvest the steep hillside. Entire families cut and gather every inch of hay as thoroughly as children of America's Great Depression once polished their dinner plates. After harvesting what the scythe can reach, they pull hay from nooks and crannies by hand.

Half a day is spent on steep rocks

harvesting what a machine can cut in two minutes on a flat field. It's tradition. It's like breathing. And there's one right way to do it.

To inhale the Alps and really hold it in, sleep high in Gimmelwald. Poor but pleasantly stuck in the past, the village has a creaky hotel, happy hostel, decent pension, and a couple of B&Bs.

Walter Mittler's Hotel Mittaghorn sits at the top end of Gimmelwald. The black-stained chalet has eight balconies and a few tables shaded by umbrellas on its tiny terrace. Everything comes with huge views. Sitting as if anchored by pitons into the steep, grassy hillside, the hotel is disturbed only by the cheery chatter of hikers and the two-stroke clatter of passing tractors.

Evening fun in Gimmelwald is found in the hostel (with lots of young Alp-aholic hikers eager to share information on the surrounding mountains) and, depending on Walter's mood, at Hotel Mittaghorn. If you're staying at Walter's, enjoy his simple supper and coffee schnapps. Then sit on the porch and watch the sun caress the mountaintops to sleep as the moon rises over the Jungfrau.

Starting early in the morning, the bright modern cable car swooshes by with 30 tourists gawking out the windows. In Gimmelwald, the modern world began in 1965 when it got the cable car. Before that, mothers ready to give birth had to hike an hour downhill to the valley floor for a ride into Interlaken. Many mothers didn't make it all the way to the hospital. Outside of Interlaken, a curve in the road is named for a Gimmelwald baby...born right there.

Today, the Schilthornbahn is the all-powerful lift that connects the valley floor with the mountain communities of Gimmelwald and Mürren on its way to the 10,000-foot Schilthorn summit. This artificial vein pumps life's essentials—mail, bread, skiers, hikers, school kids, coffins, hang gliders, and tourists—to and from each community.

From Gimmelwald, ride the cable car up to the peak of the Schilthorn, capped by a revolving restaurant called Piz Gloria ($92 round-trip, discounts early and late). Lifts go twice hourly, involve two transfers, and take 30 minutes. Watch the altitude meter go up, up, up.

For the most memorable breakfast around, ride the early cable car to the summit, where you'll find the restaurant and a thrilling 360-degree view. Sip your coffee slowly to enjoy one complete circle. Drop into the theater to see clips from the James Bond movie *On Her Majesty's Secret Service,* in which the restaurant is blown up. Then go outside for the real thrills. Frolic on the ridge. Watch hang gliders methodically set up and jump into airborne ecstasy.

While you can hike down from the summit, the first station below

Thrill-seeking hang gliders are a common sight on alpine peaks. Here, an absent-minded hang glider prepares for his last takeoff.

the summit, Birg, is the best jumping-off point for high-country hikes.

Two minutes from the Birg station, I'm completely alone—surrounded by a harsh and unforgiving alpine world. Anything alive is here only by the grace of nature. A black ballet of rocks is accompanied by cow bells and a distant river. Wisps of clouds are exclamation points. The Alps put you close to God. A day like today has Lutherans raising their hands and holy rollers doing cartwheels.

I make it to my target, a peak that stands dramatically high above Gimmelwald. After a steep descent, I step out of the forest at the top end of the village I call home. Walking over a pastel carpet of gold clover, bell flowers, milk kraut, and daisies, I'm surrounded by butterflies and cheered on by a vibrant chorus of grasshoppers, bees, and crickets.

The finish line is a bench that sits at the high end of Gimmelwald—one of my "savor Europe" depots. A great dimension of travel is finding the right spot and just sitting still. Crickets rattle congratulatory castanets, a river blurts out of a glacier, and Mürren crowns a bluff above me, keeping all the fancy tourists where they belong. An alpine farm that has intrigued me for years still sits high above the tree line, forever alone amid distant flecks of brown and white cows and goats.

Below me, the village schoolyard rumbles with children. Christian, the accordion player, who went up to the fields early this morning, chugs by on his mini-truck towing a wobbly wagonload of hay. His kids bounce like cartoon characters on top.

Enjoying this alone is fine. But sharing this bench with a new friend, with the sun of a daylong hike stored in your smiling faces, is even better.

SWITZERLAND

If you're interested in the alpine cream of Switzerland, it's best seen from nearby peaks and ridges (the Jungfrau, Kleine Scheidegg, or the Schilthorn). If you're looking for Heidi and an orchestra of cowbells in a Switzerland that you thought existed only in storybooks—take off your boots in Gimmelwald.

From Interlaken into the Jungfrau Region

When the 19th-century Romantics redefined mountains as something more than cold and troublesome obstacles, Interlaken became the original alpine resort. Ever since then, tourists have flocked to the Alps "because they're there." Interlaken's glory days are long gone, its elegant old hotels eclipsed by more jet-setting alpine resorts. Today, Interlaken's shops are filled with chocolate bars, Swiss Army knives, and sunburned backpackers.

I had always considered Interlaken overrated, but I came to understand that it's only a springboard for alpine adventures. Stop in Interlaken for shopping, banking, email, and telephone chores, and to pick up information on the region. Then head south into the Berner Oberland.

You have several options (see the map at the beginning of this chapter). Vagabonds who just dropped in on the overnight train can do a loop trip, going down Grindelwald Valley, over the Kleine Scheidegg ridge, and then into Lauterbrunnen. From there you can head on out by returning to Interlaken, or settle into Gimmelwald for the alpine cuddle after the climax. Those with more time (or less energy) go directly to the village of Gimmelwald (skipping Grindelwald) and explore the region from that home base.

Loop-trippers should get an early start and catch the private train from the Interlaken East station to Grindelwald (discounted with a Eurailpass or Eurail Selectpass; covered by the Swiss Pass railpass). Don't sleep in touristy Grindelwald, but take advantage of its well-informed

tourist information office and buy a first-class mountain picnic at its Co-op grocery. Then ascend by train into a wonderland of white peaks to Kleine Scheidegg, or even higher by gondola to Männlichen (show your pass at ticket windows for varying discounts for train and gondola). It's an easy one-hour walk from Männlichen down to Kleine Scheidegg.

Now you have successfully run the gauntlet of tourist traps and reached the ultimate. Before you towers Switzerland's mightiest mountain panorama. The Jungfrau, the Mönch, and the Eiger boldly proclaim that they are the greatest. You won't argue.

Like a saddle on the ridge, Kleine Scheidegg gives people something to hang onto. It has a lodge (with $50 dorm bunks) and an outdoor restaurant. People gather here to marvel at tiny rock climbers dangling from ropes halfway up the icy Eiger. You can splurge for the expensive ride from here to the towering Jungfraujoch ($110 round-trip from Kleine Scheidegg, discounts early and late)—expect crowds on sunny summer days, especially after a stretch of bad weather. The ride's impressive, but I couldn't have asked for more than the *Mona Lisa* of mountain views that I enjoyed from Kleine Scheidegg.

From Kleine Scheidegg, start your hike into the less-touristy Lauterbrunnen Valley. The hike is easy. My gear consisted only of shorts (watch the mountain sun), tennis shoes, a tourist brochure map, and a bib to catch the drool.

It's lunchtime as you hike into your own peaceful mountain world. Find a grassy perch, and your picnic will have an alpine ambience that no restaurant can match. Continuing downhill, you may well be all alone and singing to the rhythm of your happy footsteps. The gravelly walk gets steep in places, and you can abbreviate your hike by catching the train at one of two stations you'll pass along the way. As the scenery changes, new mountains replace the ones you've already seen. After two hours, you enter the car-free town of Wengen. Avoid the steep, dull hike from Wengen to Lauterbrunnen by taking the train down to the valley floor, where you can continue by bus and cable car to the village of Gimmelwald.

This is the scenic but very roundabout way to Gimmelwald. For a much more direct route, take the train from the Interlaken East station to Lauterbrunnen, transfer to the bus for Stechelberg, then ride the cable car up to Gimmelwald.

For more adventures in the Alps, turn to Chapter 70: Alpine Escapes.

*For good-value accommodations in **Gimmelwald**, try Hotel Mittaghorn (closed Nov-March, phone or email after April 1, tel. 033-855-1658, www .ricksteves.com/mittaghorn, mittaghorn@gmail.com), or Maria and Olle Eggimann's B&B (tel. 033-855-3575, oeggimann@bluewin.ch). For all the travel specifics, see the latest edition of Rick Steves' Switzerland.*

SWITZERLAND

EASTERN EUROPE

54. Czech Out Prague

Prague has always been historic. Now it's fun, too. No place in Europe has become so popular so quickly. And for good reason: The capital of the Czech Republic—the only Central European capital to escape the bombs of the last century's wars—is a people-friendly and entertaining showcase for Czech culture.

Prague is slinky with sumptuous Art Nouveau facades, offers tons of cheap Mozart and Vivaldi, and brews some of the best beer in Europe. It's an explosion of pent-up entrepreneurial energy jumping for joy after 40 years of communist rule. Its low prices will make your visit enjoyable and, with a few skills, nearly stress-free. From Munich, Berlin, or Vienna, it's roughly a five-hour train ride (day or overnight) to Prague...your train won't even stop at the border.

Praha, as residents call their town, is big, with 1.2 million people. For the quick visit, think of the town as small and focus on its relatively compact historic core. Prague is charming, safe,

Prague, the golden city of a hundred spires

Prague

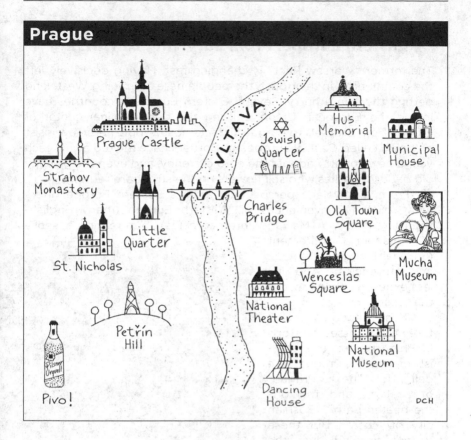

Prague Castle

Strahov Monastery

Little Quarter

St. Nicholas

Petřín Hill

Pivo!

VLTAVA

Charles Bridge

Jewish Quarter

Hus Memorial

Old Town Square

National Theater

Wenceslas Square

Dancing House

Municipal House

Mucha Museum

National Museum

DCH

EASTERN EUROPE

and ready to show you a good time.

Your Prague visit deserves at least two full days. With this much time, spend a morning seeing the castle and a morning in the Jewish Quarter—the only two chunks of sightseeing that demand any brainpower. Spend your afternoons strolling Charles Bridge and loitering around Old Town. Split your evenings between beer halls and classical concerts.

Prague Castle—which Czechs consider the biggest in Europe—has served as home to Czech rulers for more than a thousand years. The highlight is St. Vitus

A good guide gives meaning to a great city like Prague.

Eastern Europe: From Surviving to Thriving

The former "Warsaw Pact" is changing fast. Having decisively left the communists in their dust, the people here are racing West...and getting there in a hurry. Several Eastern European countries have joined the European Union, shifting the geographical center of Europe from Brussels to Prague. In fact, most people here now insist on being called *Central* Europeans. Borders have melted away, each year a new country adopts the euro currency, and even the grumpy old *babushki* ladies who sell flowers on the street are retiring.

From a traveler's perspective, today's Eastern Europe offers many of the conveniences of Western Europe (many English-speaking locals, ATMs, and Internet cafés), but retains a sense of pioneer excitement (unusual languages, foods, and currencies). And it's less expensive than most of the West.

This section covers three top sightseeing stops in this region: the tourist mecca of Prague, the delightful "next Prague" of Kraków, and the off-the-beaten-path Bosnian city of Mostar. But these destinations are just the beginning...use them as springboards for exploring a vast, beautiful, and diverse region.

Simmering in a Budapest thermal bath, surrounded by hedonistic Hungarians, is a quintessential Eastern European experience.

In **Hungary,** explore Eastern Europe's de facto "capital city," Budapest. Peel back the layers of history in this grand metropolis, home to ancient Romans, nomadic Magyars, conquering Ottomans,

Cathedral, where locals go to remember Saint Wenceslas, patron saint of the Czechs. This "good king" of Christmas-carol fame was not a king at all, but a wise, benevolent Duke of Bohemia. After being assassinated in 935, Wenceslas became a symbol of Czech nationalism. His tomb sits in an extremely fancy chapel.

Apart from the underwhelming Royal Palace, there's little else of importance to see in Prague Castle. Its lower end is the gimmicky Golden Lane—once lined with goldsmith shops, now filled with over-

reconquering Habsburgs, and modern-day Hungarian freedom fighters. Browse the truly great Great Market Hall, sampling some spicy paprika. Take in an inexpensive performance at the opulent Opera House, which gives Vienna's—just up the Danube—a run for its money. Relax by soaking with potbellied, Speedo-clad chess players under gorgeous Baroque domes at a thermal bath.

In **Croatia,** set sail on the shimmering Adriatic, to a remote island whose name you can't pronounce but whose wonders you'll never forget. Lie on a beach in the hot summer sun, listening to the lapping waves as a Venetian-style bell tower overhead clangs out the hour. Stroll on boardwalks through the Plitvice Lakes' waterfall wonderland. Ponder the fading scars of a recent war, and admire how skillfully the residents have revitalized their once-troubled region. Dine on a seafood feast and sip a glass of wine as you watch the sunset dip into the watery horizon.

In **Slovenia,** corkscrew your way up impossibly twisty mountain roads to panoramic vistas of cut-glass peaks. Sip a coffee at a sun-bathed outdoor café, and help the Slovenian college students at the next table polish their near-perfect English. Glide across an idyllic mountain lake to a church-topped island in the shadow of the Julian Alps. (For details, see Chapter 70: Alpine Escapes.)

On a recent visit to Eastern Europe, some of my favorite experiences came off the beaten path. At a humble vineyard buried deep in the Hungarian countryside, the proud vintner told me how this land had been in his family for generations, before being seized by the communists. The communist winemaking industry—interested in squeezing out quantity rather than quality—ruined his vines, but he's spent the last decade painstakingly restoring them to their former greatness. He poured me a generous taste, then threw his head back and taught me the tongue-twisting Hungarian "Cheers": *Egészségedre!* Sipping his full-bodied blend of red wines, I had to think he was off to a great start.

priced boutiques, galleries, cafés, and gawking tourists.

While the Golden Lane is a tourist trap, the Toy and Barbie Museum (nearby, at the bottom of the castle complex) is a treat. Its two entertaining floors of old toys and dolls are thoughtfully described in English. You'll see a century of teddy bears, 19th-century model train sets, and an incredible Barbie collection. Find the buxom 1959 first edition and you'll understand why these capitalistic sirens of material discontent weren't allowed here until 1989.

From the castle, the "King's Walk" leads into town. This ancient route of coronation processions, pedestrian-friendly and full of playful diversions, laces together most of Prague's essential sights. After being crowned in St. Vitus Cathedral, the new king would walk through the historic town, cross Charles Bridge, and finish at the Old Town Square. If he hurried, he'd be done in 20 minutes. Like the main drag in Venice between St. Mark's and the Rialto Bridge, this walk mesmerizes tourists. Use it as a spine, but venture off it—especially to eat.

Kicking off the King's Walk, you leave the castle following steep and cobbled Nerudova street towards the river. It's lined with old buildings still sporting the characteristic doorway signs (such as the lion, three violinists, and house of the golden suns) that served as street addresses. The surviving signs are carefully restored and protected by law. They represent the family name, the occupation, or the various passions of the people who once inhabited the houses. (If you were to replace your house number with a symbol, what would it be?) In 1770, in order to collect taxes more effectively, a court decree mandated the introduction of street numbers instead of these quaint house names. This neighborhood's many old noble palaces are now generally used as foreign embassies and offices of the Czech Parliament.

The much-loved Charles Bridge is my vote for Europe's most pleasant quarter-mile stroll. Commissioned by the Holy Roman Emperor Charles IV in the 1350s, its chorus line of time-blackened Baroque statues mix it up with street vendors and musicians. Be on the bridge when the sun is low for the best light, people-watching, and photo opportunities. (Although a multi-year restoration on the bridge means it may be partly covered with scaffolding during your visit, you can still walk the bridge's entire length.)

After crossing the bridge, follow the shop-lined street to the Old Town Square. The focal point for most visits, this has been a market square since the 11th century. Today, many of the old-time market stalls have been replaced by cafés, touristy horse buggies, and souvenir hawkers.

The square's centerpiece, the Hus memorial—unveiled

Prague's much-loved Charles Bridge will be undergoing a lengthy renovation over the next few years, but should remain open to pedestrians.

in 1915, 500 years after Jan Hus was burned—symbolizes the long struggle for Czech freedom. The statue of the Czech reformer stands tall, as he did against both Rome and the Habsburgs. Behind Hus, a mother with her children represents the ultimate rebirth of the Czech nation.

A few blocks past the Old Town Square stretches the centerpiece of urban, modern Prague: Wenceslas Square. The most dramatic moments in modern Czech history were played out on this stage. The Czechoslovak state was proclaimed here in 1918. In 1969, Jan Palach set himself on fire here to protest the puppet Soviet government. And the massive demonstrations here 20 years after his death led to the overthrow of the communist government. Czechs still remember the night in 1989 when they gathered, hundreds of thousands strong, filling the square. Jangling their key chains at the presidential palace, they chanted, "It's time to go now." Their message was heard, and the next morning they woke up a free nation.

Prague's Wenceslas Square: When there's a revolution, this is where the action is.

The great sights of Prague chronicle the struggle of the Czech people against the outside world. They also recall the struggles of the Jewish people within Czech society. I find Prague's Josefov the most interesting Jewish Quarter in Europe.

Two thousand years ago the Romans dispersed the Jews. But "time was their sanctuary which no army could destroy," as their culture survived in enclaves throughout the Western world. The main intersection of Prague's Jewish Quarter was the meeting point of two medieval trade routes. Jewish traders settled here in the 13th century and built a synagogue.

When the pope declared that Jews and Christians should not live together, this Jewish Quarter was walled in and became a ghetto. In the 16th and 17th centuries, Prague's ghetto—with 11,000 inhabitants—was one of the biggest in Europe.

Europe's Jews relied mainly on profits from lending money (forbidden to Christians) and community solidarity to survive. While their money protected them, it was often also a curse. Throughout Europe, when times got tough and Christian debts to the Jewish community

Pondering Jewish history

mounted, entire Jewish communities were evicted or killed.

In the 1780s, Emperor Josef II, motivated more by economic concerns than philanthropy, eased much of the discrimination against Jews. In 1852, the walls were torn down, and the neighborhood—named Josefov in honor of the emperor who provided this small measure of tolerance—was incorporated as a district of Prague.

In 1897, ramshackle Josefov was razed and replaced with a new modern town. This is what you'll see today: an attractive neighborhood of mostly Art Nouveau buildings, with a few surviving historic Jewish buildings.

By the 1930s, Prague's Jewish community was hugely successful. Yet of the 35,000 Jews living in the area in 1939, just 8,000 survived the Holocaust to see liberation in 1945. Strangely, the museums of the Jewish Quarter are, in part, the work of Hitler. He preserved parts of Josefov to be his "museum of the exterminated race." Seven sites (six synagogues and a cemetery) scattered over a three-block area make the tourists' Jewish Quarter. Each has a fascinating exhibit, and one ticket includes admission to all but one.

The Pinkas Synagogue, a site of Jewish worship for 400 years, is a poignant memorial to the victims of the Nazis. Its walls are covered with the handwritten names of 77,297 Czech Jews who were sent from here to gas chambers at Auschwitz and other camps. (You'll hear the somber reading of the names as you ponder this sad sight.) When the

communists moved in, they closed the synagogue and erased virtually everything. With freedom in 1989, the Pinkas Synagogue was reopened and all the names rewritten.

The Old Jewish Cemetery is the quarter's most photographed site. As you wander among 12,000 evocative tombstones, remember that from 1439 until 1787, this was

the only burial ground allowed for the Jews of Prague. Tombs were piled atop each other because of limited space, the sheer number of graves, and the Jewish belief that the body should not be moved once buried. With its many layers, the cemetery became a small plateau. And as things settled over time, the tombstones got crooked and mystically picturesque.

The "Old-New" Synagogue—"new" 700 years ago—has always been the most important synagogue and central building in Josefov. Standing like a bomb-hardened bunker, it feels as though it's survived plenty of hard times. Stairs take you down to the street level of the 13th century and into the Gothic interior. Built in 1270, it's the oldest synagogue in Central Europe.

Down the street from Josefov is the surreal sight of a giant metronome slowly ticking away. Locals know this marks the spot of a 100-foot-tall sculpture of Stalin—destroyed in 1962, a few years after Khrushchev revealed the communist tyrant's crimes in a "secret" speech.

It's hard to imagine the gray and bleak Prague of the communist era. Before 1989, the city was a wistful jumble of possibility. Cobbled lanes were shadowed by sooty, crusty buildings. Thick, dark timbers bridging narrow streets kept decrepit buildings from crumbling. Consumer goods were plain and uniform, stacked like Legos on thin shelves in shops where customers waited in line for a beat-up cabbage, tin of ham, or bottle of ersatz Coke. The Charles Bridge was as sooty as its statues, with no commerce except a few shady characters trying to change money. Hotels had two-tiered pricing: one for people of the Warsaw Pact nations and another (five or six

Before the fall of communism, Czech freedom-lovers found inspiration at the graffiti-covered wall dedicated to John Lennon—an icon of Western freedom in the 1980s. Authorities whitewashed it countless times, but the spirited graffiti kept coming back. Even today, after being independent since 1989, Czechs treasure their freedom and their Lennon wall.

times as expensive) for capitalists. This made the run-down Soviet-style hotels as expensive as a fine Western one for most tourists. At the train station, frightened but desperate characters would meet arriving foreigners to rent them a room in their flat. They were scrambling to get enough hard Western cash to buy batteries or Levis at one of the hard-currency stores. For more on this grim era, visit the Museum of Communism, described on page 580.

With capitalism came entrepreneurial con artists. There's no particular risk of violent crime, but green, rich tourists do get taken by con artists. Be on guard when changing money (even at banks) for bad arithmetic and inexplicable pauses while tellers count back your change. Understand the exact price before ordering at restaurants. Paying with cash is safer than using a credit card.

Taxis here are notorious rip-offs. Prague is walkable and also has fine public transportation, but if you prefer taxis, use only registered ones (marked with a company logo and phone number). My rule of thumb: Know the approximate local rate. If overcharged, pay what you think is fair, and walk away.

A newly affluent Prague has spiffed up its fine architecture. Prague is the best Art Nouveau town in Europe, with fun-loving facades gracing streets all over town. Art Nouveau, born in Paris, is "nouveau" because it wasn't inspired by Rome. It's neo-nothing...a fresh answer to all the revival styles of the later 19th century and an organic response to the Eiffel Tower art of the Industrial Age. The streets of Josefov, the Mucha window in the St. Vitus Cathedral, and Hotel Evropa on Wenceslas Square are just a few Art Nouveau highlights.

If you like Art Nouveau, you'll love the Mucha Museum—one of Europe's most enjoyable little galleries. I find the art of Alfons Mucha (MOO-kah, 1860–1939) insistently likeable. This popular artist's posters, filled with Czech symbols and expressing his people's ideals and aspirations, were patriotic banners arousing the national spirit. With the help of an abundant supply of slinky models, Mucha was a founding father of the Art Nouveau movement.

In the evening, Prague booms with live (and inexpensive) theater, opera, and classical, jazz, and pop music. You'll

As Eastern Europe races into the future, cities such as Prague are cleaning up their industries, giving elegant facades a face-lift, and replacing asphalt with charming cobbles and pedestrian zones.

choose from half a dozen classical "tourist" concerts daily in Prague's ornate Old Town halls and churches. The music is crowd-pleasing: Vivaldi, best of Mozart, pop arias, and works by local boys Anton Dvořák and Bedřich Smetana. Leafleteers are everywhere, handing out their announcements of the evening's events.

Even if Mozart himself were performing, many visitors would rather spend the evening at a Prague beer hall. *Pivo* (beer) is a frothy hit with tourists. After all, the Czechs invented Pilsner-style lager in nearby Plzeň, and the result, Pilsner Urquell, is on tap in many pubs. Budvar, another local beer, is popular with Anheuser-Busch's attorneys. Czechs are the world's most enthusiastic beer drinkers—adults drink an average of 80 gallons a year. In many Czech restaurants, a beer hits your table like a glass of water does in the United States. Be careful. *Pivo* for lunch has me sightseeing for the rest of the day on Czech knees. *Na zdraví* means "to your health" in Czech. After a few *pivos,* fun-loving Czechs stumble on their own words, raising their mugs and bellowing *"Nádraží"* (which means "train station").

*For good-value accommodations in **Prague**, try Hotel Julián (Elišky Peškové 11, Praha 5, tel. 257-311-150, reception tel. 257-311-145, www.julian.cz) or the Athos Travel room-booking service (tel. 241-440-571, www.a-prague .com). For all the travel specifics, see the latest edition of Rick Steves' Prague & the Czech Republic.*

55. Charming Kraków

The top stop in Poland is Kraków. Of all the Eastern European cities laying claim to the boast "the next Prague," Kraków is for real. And enjoying a drink on its marvelous Main Market Square, you'll know why. The biggest square in medieval Europe remains one of Europe's most gasp-worthy public spaces.

Knowing this is one of Europe's least expensive countries, I choose the fanciest café on Kraków's fanciest piece of real estate and order without even considering the price. Sinking deep into my chair and sipping deep into my drink, I ponder the bustle of Poland, two decades after it won its freedom.

Vast as it is, the square has a folksy intimacy. It bustles with street musicians, fragrant flower stalls, cotton-candy vendors, loitering teenagers, businesspeople commuting by bike, gawking tourists, and the lusty coos of pigeons. This square is where Kraków lives...and where visitors

Kraków

Street musicians play "The Star-Spangled Banner" for big spenders.

like me find themselves hanging out. To my left, activists protest Poland's EU membership. To my right, teens practice break-dancing moves.

The folk band—swaggering in their colorful peasant costumes—give me a private little concert. Feeling flush, I tip them royally. (Perhaps too royally. Be warned: A big tip gets you "The Star-Spangled Banner.")

Kraków is the Boston of Poland: a captivating old-fashioned city buzzing with history, intriguing sights, colorful eateries, and college students. Even though the country's political capital moved from here to Warsaw 400 years ago, Kraków remains Poland's cultural and intellectual center.

Flat and easy to navigate, Kraków is made for walking. A greenbelt called the Planty rings the Old Town, where the 13th-century protective walls and moat once stood (a great place for a stroll or bike ride).

With its diverse sights, Kraków can keep a speedy tourist busy for three days. Most sights are inside the Planty park, except for the historic Wawel Castle grounds and the Jewish quarter in Kazimierz. You'll want to side-trip to the notorious Auschwitz Concentration Camp. And most visitors also visit Wieliczka Salt Mine—my vote for the deepest art gallery in Europe.

Kraków grew wealthy from trade in the 12th century. Traders passing through were required to stop here for a few days and sell their wares cheap. Local merchants then sold those goods with big price hikes...and Kraków thrived. It became Poland's capital.

Poland's top tourist attraction promises to be "the next Prague." Tourism has brought Kraków prosperity—great restaurants, comfy hotels, and plenty of welcoming sights.

EU Enlargement and the "New Europe"

The Czech Republic, Slovakia, Poland, Hungary, Slovenia, and five other countries joined the European Union in 2004, with Bulgaria and Romania joining in 2007. Today, Croatia, the Republic of Macedonia, Turkey, and Iceland are also candidates for membership. (For a map of today's EU, see page 442.) Though EU membership—and investment—should ultimately benefit everybody, old members and new members have both had their doubts.

For example, new EU member Poland survived the communist era without collectivizing its small family farms. But now that they've joined the EU, collectivization is mandatory. Traditional Czech cuisine is also in jeopardy. EU hygiene standards dictate that cooked food can't be served more than two hours old. My Czech friend complained, "This makes many of our best dishes illegal." Czech specialties, often simmered, taste better the next day.

A wise Czech grandmother put it best. In her lifetime, she had lived in a country ruled from Vienna (Habsburgs), Berlin (Nazis), and Moscow (communists). She said, "Now that we're finally ruled from Prague, why would we want to turn our power over to Brussels?"

For their part, longstanding EU members have been skeptical about taking on more countries. Wealthy nations have already spent vast fortunes to improve the floundering economies of poorer member countries (such as Portugal, Greece, and Ireland). Most of the new members expect a similar financial-aid windfall, especially during these uncertain economic times. Also on the financial front, Westerners fret about an influx of cheap labor from the East. Finally, Western Europeans worry about their political power being diluted. In the "New Europe," Poland or the Czech Republic might emerge with a leading role.

As the "New Europe" takes shape, players on both sides will continue to define their new roles and seek compromise. So far, the general consensus in the East is that joining the European Union was the right move. In a few years, the Hungarians, Poles, Czechs, and their neighbors will all be working harder than ever and enjoying more coins jangling in their pockets...and they expect those coins will be euros.

Tatars invaded in 1241, destroying the city. Krakovians took this opportunity to rebuild their streets in a near-perfect grid around the spectacular Main Market Square. King Kazimierz the Great sparked Kraków's golden age in the 14th century. He established the university that still defines the city (and counts Copernicus and Pope John Paul II among its alumni).

But Kraków's power waned and the capital moved to Warsaw. Two centuries later, Poland was partitioned by neighboring powers. Warsaw ended up as a satellite of oppressive Moscow, and Kraków became a poor provincial backwater of Vienna. But despite Kraków's reduced prominence, Austria's comparatively liberal climate helped turn the city into a haven for intellectuals and progressives (including a young Russian revolutionary named Vladimir Ilyich Lenin).

Kraków emerged from World War II virtually unscathed. But when the communists took over, they decided to give intellectual (and potentially dissident) Kraków an injection of good Soviet values—in the form of heavy industry. They built Nowa Huta, an enormous steelworks on the city's outskirts, dooming the city to decades of smog. Thankfully, Kraków is now much cleaner than it was 15 years ago.

Entering through the main gate of the Old Town wall, past an outdoor gallery for struggling art students, you walk down Floriańska Street, passing one McDonald's worth a visit. When renovating this building, they discovered a Gothic cellar. They excavated it and added seating. Today, you can super-size your ambience by dining on a Big Mac and fries under a medieval McVault.

Got milk? Poland does. In milk bars, a throwback to the communist era, you can fill your tank cheaply.

Even better, keep your eyes open for a *bar mleczny* ("milk bar"). In the communist era, the government subsidized the food at these cafeterias to provide working-class Poles with an affordable meal out. The tradition continues, and today Poland still subsidizes your milk-bar meal. Prices are astoundingly low—soup for less than a dollar. And, while communist-era fare was gross, today's milk-bar cuisine is tastier. Just head to the counter, point to what you want, and get a quick and hearty meal for half the cost of McDonald's.

St. Mary's Church—overlooking the main square—marks the center of Kraków. From its taller tower (actually the city's watchtower), a bugler plays half a tune at the top of each hour. During the 1241 Tatar invasion, the story goes, a watchman in the tower saw the enemy approaching and sounded the alarm. Before he could finish the tune, an arrow pierced his throat—which is why even today, the music stops *subito* partway through. Today's buglers are firemen—serving as fire lookouts first...and musicians second.

Wawel (VAH-vehl) Hill towers over old Kraków. This hill, with its castle, cathedral, and complex of sights, is a symbol of Polish royalty and independence. It's sacred ground to every Pole, and the country's leading tourist attraction. Crowds and a ridiculously complex admissions system for the hill's many historic sights can be exasperating. Thankfully, for most non-Polish visitors, a stroll through the cathedral and around the castle grounds covers the site adequately and requires no tickets. Wawel's many museums are mildly interest-ing but skippable.

Wawel Cathedral is Poland's national church—its Westminster Abbey. The national mausoleum, it holds the tombs of Poland's most important rulers and his-torical figures. The interior is slath-ered in Baroque memorials and tombs. Everyone visits the tomb of Kazimierz the Great. But even Kazimierz is outdone by a black crucifix marking the relics of St. Jadwiga, the beloved 14th-century "king of Poland" (the sexist big-wigs of the day refused to call her "queen") who helped Christianize Lithuania and was sainted by John Paul II in 1997. All the candles flick-ering here indicate she's popular with Poles today.

A glass of wine and a salad with a serenade on Kraków's floodlit main square caps one of the best days Europe has to offer.

The Wawel Castle museums may be forgettable. But the complex has one "sight" which—while invisible—attracts travelers from around the world: chakra. Hindus believe the chakra is part of a powerful energy field that connects all living things. There are seven points on the surface of the earth where this chakra energy is most concentrated. These points include Jerusalem, Mecca, Rome...and Kraków's Wawel Hill. Look for peaceful people with their eyes closed. One thing's for sure: They're not thinking of Kazimierz the Great. The Wawel administration seems creeped out by all this. They've done what they can to discourage this ritual, but believers still gravitate from far and wide to hug the wall in the castle courtyard. (Just for fun, ask a Wawel tour guide about chakra and watch him squirm—they're forbidden to talk about it.)

A 20-minute walk beyond Wawel takes you to the historic center of Jewish Kraków, Kazimierz. After King Kazimierz the Great encouraged Jews to come to Poland in the 14th century, a large Jewish community settled in and around Kraków. According to legend, Kazimierz (the king) established Kazimierz (the village) for his favorite girlfriend—a Jewish woman named Ester—just outside the Kraków city walls. Kazimierz was an autonomous community, with its own Town Hall, market square, and city walls. By 1800, the walls came down, Kazimierz became part of Kraków, and the Jewish community flourished. By the start of World War II, 65,000 Jews lived in Kraków (mostly in Kazimierz), making up more than a quarter of the city's population. Only 6,000 Kraków Jews survived the war.

Today's Kraków has only about a hundred Jewish residents. Kazimierz still has an empty feeling, but the neighborhood has enjoyed a renaissance of Jewish culture lately following the popularity of *Schindler's List* (which takes place, and was partly filmed, in Kazimierz). The spirit of the Jewish tradition survives in the neighborhood's evocative synagogues, soulful cemeteries, and the lilting klezmer folk concerts put on by restaurants.

Kazimierz has two Jewish cemeteries, both more undiscovered and powerful than the famous one in Prague. Locals shop at plac Nowy's market stalls, a gritty factory-workers-on-lunch-break contrast to Kraków's touristy main square. Fans of Spielberg's Holocaust movie—and the compassionate Kraków businessman who did his creative best to save the lives of his Jewish workers—can see Schindler's actual factory, in the Podgórze district across the river from Kazimierz. The factory was recently converted into a museum to celebrate non-Jews who, like Schindler, risked their lives to save Holocaust victims.

Most of Kazimierz's Jews were killed at Auschwitz, a Nazi concentration camp in the Polish town of Oświęcim (a 70-minute drive west of Kraków). This is one of Europe's most moving sights and certainly the most important of all the Holocaust memorials. (For more on Auschwitz, see Chapter 72: Sobering Sites of Nazi Europe.)

Also near Kraków is the remarkable Wieliczka Salt Mine, which has been producing salt since 1250. Under Kazimierz the Great, one-third of Poland's income came from these precious deposits. Wieliczka miners spent much of their lives underground, rarely emerging into daylight. To pass the time, 19th-century miners began carving figures, chandeliers, and eventually even an entire chapel out of the salt.

The tour shows how the miners lived and worked (using horses that lived their whole lives underground, never seeing the light of day). It takes you through some impressive underground caverns, past subterranean lakes, and introduces you to some of the mine's many salt sculptures (including an army of salt elves and a life-size statue of this region's favorite son, Pope John Paul II). Your jaw will drop as you enter the enormous Chapel of the Blessed Kinga. Don't miss the extremely salty relief of the Last Supper.

A bright and fun generation of new young guides (with or without cars) all across Eastern Europe are proud to share their cities and cultures, making your visit especially meaningful.

Your walk finishes over 400 feet below the surface, where a traditional miners' lift hoists you back up to a sunlit world that seems particularly bright.

*For good-value accommodations in **Kraków**, splurge at one of the Donimirski Boutique Hotels (three swanky locations in or near the Old Town, www .donimirski.com), or sleep cheaper just off the Main Market Square at Pensjonat Trecius (ulica Św. Tomasza 18, tel. 012-421-2521, www.trecius .krakow.pl). For all the travel specifics, see the latest edition of* Rick Steves' Eastern Europe.

56. Off the Beaten Path in Bosnia-Herzegovina

Buffalo-Nickel Charm on a Road That Does Not Exist

Looking for a change of pace from Croatia's Dalmatian Coast, I drove from Dubrovnik into the city of Mostar, in Bosnia-Herzegovina. Almost everyone doing this trip takes the scenic coastal route. But, with a spirit of adventure, I took the back road instead: inland first, then looping north through the Serb part of Herzegovina.

Bosnia-Herzegovina's three main ethnic groups—Serbs, Croats, and Bosniaks—are descended from the same ancestors and speak closely related languages. The key distinction is that they practice different religions: Orthodox Christianity, Roman Catholicism, and Islam, respectively. For the most part, there's no way that a casual visitor can determine the religion or loyalties of the people just by looking at them. Studying the complex demographics of the former Yugoslavia, you gain a respect for the communist-era dictator Tito—the one man who could hold this place together peacefully. (To learn more about the conflicts in the former Yugoslavia, see www.ricksteves.com/yugo.)

Bosnia-Herzegovina is one nation, historically divided into two regions: Bosnia and Herzegovina. But the 1995 Dayton Peace Accords gerrymandered the country along other lines, giving a degree of autonomy to the area where Orthodox Serbs predominate. This "Republika Srpska" rings the core of Bosnia on three sides. When asked for driving tips, Croats—who, because of ongoing tensions with the Serbs, avoid this territory—insist that the road I want to take doesn't even exist. From the main Croatian coastal road just south of Dubrovnik, directional signs send you to the tiny Croatian border town...but ignore the large Serb city of Trebinje just beyond.

And yet, Trebinje more than exists...it is bustling and prosperous. As I enter the town, police with Ping-Pong paddle stop signs pull me over—you must drive with your headlights on at all hours. The "dumb tourist" routine gets me off the hook. I enjoy a vibrant market scene, and get cash at an ATM to buy some produce. (Even here—in perhaps the most remote place I've been in Europe—ATMs are plentiful.)

The Bosnian-Serb city of Trebinje enjoys a bright and busy Saturday market.

EASTERN EUROPE

Bosnia-Herzegovina's money is called the "convertible mark." I don't know if they are thrilled that their money is now convertible...but I remember a time when it wasn't. I stow a few Bosnian coins as souvenirs. They have the charm of Indian pennies and buffalo nickels. Some bills have Cyrillic lettering and Serb historical figures, while others use "our" alphabet and show Muslims or Croats. Like everything else in Bosnia-Herzegovina, the currency is a careful balancing act.

Later, after a two-hour drive on deserted roads through a rugged landscape, I arrive at the humble crossroads village of Nevesinje. Towns in this region all have a "café row," and Nevesinje is no exception. It's lunchtime, but as I walk through the town, I don't see a soul with any food on their plate—just drinks. Apparently locals eat (economically) at home, then enjoy an affordable coffee or drink at a café.

A cluttered little grocery—the woman behind the counter happy to make a sandwich—is my solution for a quick meal. The salami looks like Spam. I take my sandwich to an adjacent café and pay the equivalent of a US quarter for a cup of strong Turkish (or "Bosnian") coffee, with highly caffeinated mud in the bottom. Then I munch, drink, and watch the street scene.

Big men drive by in little beaters. High-school kids crowd around the window of the photography shop, which has just posted their class graduation photos. The girls on this cruising drag prove you don't need money to have style. Through a shop window, I see a newly engaged couple picking out a simple ring. One moment I see Nevesinje as very different from my hometown...but the next, it seems just the same.

Looking at the curiously overgrown ruined building across the street, I notice bricked-up, pointed Islamic arches, and realize it was once a mosque. In its backyard—a no-man's-land of bombed-out concrete and glass—a single half-knocked-over-turban-topped tombstone still manages to stand. The prayer niche inside, where no one prays anymore, faces an empty restaurant.

This charred mosque is a poignant reminder of more difficult times in Nevesinje...and of what has been lost.

After an hour's drive over a twisty mountain road, I cross into the Muslim-Croat part of Bosnia-Herzegovina, and arrive at the city of Mostar.

Mostar: Mending Broken Bridges

Mostar provided me with one of the richest travel experiences I've had in years. With jarring reminders of a recent war, but an inspiring resilience and a vibrant humanity, the city left me both exhilarated and exhausted.

Before the war, Mostar was famous for its 400-year-old, Turkish-style stone bridge. The Old Bridge's elegant, single-pointed arch—commissioned by the Ottoman Sultan Süleyman the Magnificent—was a symbol of Mostar's Muslim society, and of the town's status as the place where East met West in Europe.

Then, during the 1990s, Mostar became a poster child for the excesses

Mostar's symbol is its Old Bridge...with stoic grace and echoes of Turkey.

of the Bosnian war. First, the Croats and Bosniaks forced out the Serbs. Then they turned their guns on each other—staring each other down across a front line that ran through the middle of the city. Across the world, people wept when the pummeled Old Bridge—bombarded by Croat paramilitary artillery shells from the hilltop above—finally collapsed into the river.

Now, the bridge has been painstakingly rebuilt, and Mostar is thriving. As they have for generations, young men swan-dive from the bridge 75 feet down into the Neretva (which remains icy cold even in summer). Done both for the sake of tradition and to impress girls, this custom was carried on even during the time the destroyed bridge was temporarily replaced by a wooden one. On hot summer days, you'll see divers making a ruckus and collecting donations at the top of the bridge. They tease and tease, standing up on the railing and pretending they're about to jump...then getting down and asking for more money. Once they collect about $50, one of them will take the plunge.

The city's Bosniak core—where most visitors spend their time—offers an illuminating and unique glimpse of a culture that's both devoutly Muslim and fully European. Surrounding the Old Bridge is a

As if reaffirming their zest for life, young Mostarians plunge off their beloved Old Bridge into the chilly river below.

cobbled Old Town, which has been fully restored after the war. Here you can poke into several mosques, tour old-fashioned Turkish-style houses, shop your way through a bazaar of souvenir stands, and hear the call to prayer warbling across the rooftops.

Climbing up the hill from the Old Bridge is the lively, colorful Coppersmiths' Street—a shopping zone with the flavor of a Turkish bazaar: blue-and-white "evil eyes" (believed in the Turkish culture to keep bad spirits at bay), old Yugoslav army kitsch, and hammered-copper decorations (continuing the long tradition that gave the street its name).

I stop in at the Turkish-style Bišćević House. Dating from 1635, it's typical of old houses in Mostar, which mix Oriental style with Mediterranean features. It's surrounded by a high wall—protection from the sun's rays, from thieves...and from prying eyes. A fountain gently gurgles in the courtyard, enjoyed by the house's free-range pet turtles. Removing my shoes to enter the house, I climb a wooden staircase to the cool, shady, and airy living room. Privacy latticework allowed the women to peek down discreetly to see what was happening in the courtyard. At the back of the house is the gathering room. This space—designed in a circle so people could face each other, cross-legged, for a good conversation—has a dramatic view overlooking the Neretva. Heading back down to reclaim my shoes, I find a turtle clambering over them.

A few steps outside the touristy Old Town, burned-out husks of buildings and bullet holes everywhere are a constant reminder that the city is still recovering—physically and psychologically. In the back of my mind, I'm prodded by the chilling thought that, just a few years ago, these people—who make me a sandwich, direct me to a computer terminal in the cybercafé, stop for me when I cross the street, show off their paintings, and direct the church choir—were killing each other.

And yet, as in any conflict, most people here were innocent bystanders who felt trapped by an unwanted, unnecessary war. In fact, I didn't meet anyone in Mostar who called the war anything but a tragic mistake. And many are eager to share their lessons from living through those unthinkably difficult times.

I meet Alen, a thirtysomething Muslim who emigrated to Florida during the war, and is now back home in Mostar. Alen strolls with me through his hometown, offering an eyewitness account of its darkest hour. He points to a tree growing out the window of a bombed-out building. Seeming to speak as much about Mostar's people as its vegetation, he says, "It's a strange thing in nature: Figs can grow with almost no soil."

There are blackened ruins everywhere. When I ask why—after more than 15 years—the ruins still stand, Alen explains, "Confusion about who owns what. Surviving companies have no money. The bank of Yugoslavia, which held the mortgages, is now gone. No one will invest until it's clear who owns the buildings."

We visit a small cemetery congested with more than a hundred white-marble Muslim tombstones. Alen points out the dates. Everyone died in 1993, 1994, or 1995. This was a park before 1993. When the war heated up, snipers were a constant concern—they'd pick off anyone they saw walking down the street. Bodies were left for weeks along the main boulevard, which had become the front line. Mostar's cemeteries were too exposed, but this park was relatively safe from snipers. People buried their loved ones here...under cover of darkness.

New cemeteries in downtown Mostar are crammed with graves from a grotesque three-year period.

Alen says, "In those years, night was the time when we lived. We didn't walk...we ran. And we dressed in black. There was no electricity. If the Croat fighters didn't kill us with their bullets, they killed us with their rabble-rousing pop music. It was blasting from the Croat side of town."

The symbolism of the religious conflict is powerful. Ten minarets pierce Mostar's skyline like proud exclamation points. There, twice as tall as the tallest minaret, stands the Croats' new Catholic church spire. Standing on the reconstructed Old Bridge, I look at the hilltop high above the town, with its single, bold, and strongly floodlit cross. Alen says, "We Muslims believe that cross marks the spot from where they shelled this bridge...like a celebration."

Alen takes me to Masala Square ("Place for Prayer"), which is designed for big gatherings. Muslim groups meet here before departing to Mecca on the Hajj. But tonight, there's not a hint of prayer. It's prom night. The kids are out, and Bosnian hormones are sloshing everywhere. Being young and sexy is a great equalizer. With a beer, loud music, desirability, twinkling stars—and no war—your country's GDP doesn't really matter.

The next day, I decide to grab a lunch for my trip from Mostar back to Croatia. I stop at a tiny grocery store, where a woman I befriended the day before—a gorgeous person, sad to be living in a frustrating economy, and stiff from a piece of shrapnel in her back that doctors decided was safer left in—makes me a hearty ham sandwich. As she slices, I gather the rest of what will be a fine picnic meal on wheels.

As I sort through conflicting emotions on my way out of town, I drive over patched bomb craters in the pavement. In similarly war-torn Sarajevo, they've filled these scars with red concrete as memorials: "Sarajevo roses." Here they are black like the rest of the street—but knowing what they are, they show up red in my mind.

Despite the hardships of war—such as a chunk of shrapnel in the back—the resilient people of Mostar are putting their city and their lives back together.

*For good-value accommodations in **Mostar,** consider the simple, central Villa Fortuna B&B (tel. 036/552-197, fortuna_headoffice@bih.net.ba) or the Muslibegović House, a preserved traditional Turkish house (Osman Dikica 41, tel. 036/551-379, www.muslibegovichouse.com). For all the travel specifics, see the latest edition of* Rick Steves' Croatia & Slovenia.

57. Communist Sites in Eastern Europe

Until 1989, Eastern Europe was a foreboding place—a dark and gloomy corner of the "Evil Empire." Three decades ago, my Polish friends were taking in their windshield wipers at night. (If stolen, they were impossible to replace.) Bomb craters appeared in front of Bulgarian train stations...and no one talked about it. People ran their kitchen faucets so neighbors in their flimsy apartment flats couldn't hear them listening to Radio Free Europe. Teenagers were allowed one rock concert a year—which happened to be scheduled the same time as Easter Mass. And train conductors checked my ticket before slipping secretively with me into the bathroom to change money at black-market rates.

Happily, over the past 20 years, the people here have dropped the "Eastern" and are embracing the "European"...and they're not looking back. The obligatory grays and preachy reds of communism live on only in history books, museums, and cheesy theme restaurants. Freedom is a generation old, and—for better or for worse—McDonald's, MTV, and mobile phones are every bit as entrenched here as anywhere else in Europe. But the curious traveler can still uncover some time-travel communist sites—some kitschy and fun, others somber and moving.

Berlin, Germany

Berlin, once the western outpost of the Soviet Bloc, is filled with poignant memories of its communist days. And now that the city has been free and united for nearly two decades, there's a playful nostalgia—or "*Ost*-algia" (*Ost* is German for "east")—for what some consider happier times...back when "everybody had a job."

Today, theme eateries serve dreary food from the 1960s with a Cold War "ambience." Enjoying a creamy vanilla ice-cream sundae in eastern Berlin's Café Sibylle, I pondered the odd stone carving that hung overhead: an ear and half a moustache. The sundae, which comes with a shot of liquor, was the standard treat back then. And the ear and moustache are all that's left of what was the largest statue of Josef Stalin in Germany.

The café stands on what was the showpiece boulevard of communist Berlin. Its original buildings were completely leveled by the Soviet Army in 1945. When Stalin decided this main drag should be a showcase street, he had it rebuilt and named it Stalinallee. Today this street, lined with "workers' palaces"—apartment flats done in the bold "Stalin Gothic" style so common in Moscow in the 1950s—has been restored and renamed for Karl Marx. Socialist Realist reliefs on the buildings and lampposts celebrate triumphs of the working class.

One symbol of the old days still shines: Look at the old pedestrian lights, and you'll realize that at least some communists had a sense of humor. The perky red and green men—*Ampelmännchen*—were nearly replaced by far less jaunty Western signs. But after an uproar from "Ost-algic" residents, the East German signals have survived.

Little remains of the grandest souvenir of Cold War Berlin, the

The jaunty former East German traffic lights survive at the request of "Ost-algic" East Berliners.

infamous Berlin Wall. The 100-mile "Anti-Fascist Protective Rampart," as it was called by the East German government, was erected almost overnight in 1961 to stop the outward flow of people (three million leaked out between 1949 and 1961). Guides are quick with all the stats: The 13-foot-high Wall had a 16-foot tank ditch, a no-man's-land (or "death strip") that was 30–160 feet wide, and 300 sentry towers. During the Wall's 28 years, border guards fired 1,693 times and made 3,221 arrests, and there were 5,043 documented successful escapes (including 565 by East German guards).

The carnival atmosphere of those first years after the Wall fell is gone, but hawkers still sell "authentic" pieces of the Wall, flags of the DDR (East Germany), and military paraphernalia to gawking tourists. When it fell, the Wall was literally carried away by the euphoria. What managed to survive has been nearly devoured by persistent "Wall-peckers."

A low-key row of cobbles traces the Wall's former path around the city. A short stretch of the Wall survives at Zimmerstrasse. And a section at Bernauer Strasse (near the Nordbahnhof S-Bahn station) is part of the fascinating Berlin Wall Documentation Center.

The biggest surviving stretch of the Wall is the colorful East Side Gallery. Nicknamed "the world's longest outdoor art gallery," it stretches for nearly a mile and

Berlin's East Side Gallery: once a link in the imposing Wall...and now an art gallery

is covered with murals painted by artists from around the world. This segment of the Wall makes a poignant walk.

Checkpoint Charlie, the famous border checkpoint between the American and Soviet sectors, is long gone. But its memory is preserved by the Museum of the Wall at Checkpoint Charlie. During the Cold War, the House at Checkpoint Charlie stood defiantly—spitting distance from the border guards—showing off all the ingenious escapes over, under, and through the Wall. Today, while the drama is over and hunks of the Wall stand like victory scalps at its door, this museum still tells a gripping history—including those heady days when people-power tore down the Wall.

Budapest, Hungary

If communism was a religion during the Cold War, Budapest was Eastern Europe's sin city. Since Hungary's milder "goulash communism" allowed tourists from within the Soviet Bloc a taste of the decadent West, Budapest was famous for rock concerts, a sport shop selling Adidas, and the first McDonald's behind the Iron Curtain.

That McDonald's still stands, a few steps off the main pedestrian street, Váci utca. Munching a burger here, ponder that back then, there was nothing fast or cheap about Western "fast food." A Happy Meal was a splurge. People traveled here from other communist countries to wait in a line that stretched around the block for a burger and a Coke. Ronald McDonald stood on the street corner like a heretic prophet cheering on the downtrodden proletariat, while across the street, wannabe capitalists drooled over window displays featuring fancy tennis shoes that cost two months' wages.

The House of Terror is a sobering reminder of Hungary's "dual occupation"—first Nazis, then communists.

But just a generation earlier, Hungary was still as oppressive as its neighbors. And today, Budapest's House of Terror—long the headquarters of communist Hungary's secret police—documents a terrible story. When the communists moved into Budapest, their secret police took over the former Nazi headquarters. It was here that Hungarians suspected of being enemies of the state were given sham trials, tortured, and executed.

The museum's atrium features a Soviet tank and a vast wall covered with portraits of victims of this building. Exhibits cover gulag life, Socialist Realist art, and propaganda. Leaving the museum, you pass a chilling finale. The "wall of victimizers" is lined with photos of members and supporters of both the Nazi and communist secret police—many of whom are still living, and who were never brought to justice.

When regimes fall, so do their monuments. Just like statues of Saddam Hussein bit the dust in Baghdad, across Eastern Europe statues of Stalin, Lenin, and their local counterparts came crashing to the ground.

In Budapest, a clever entrepreneur gathered these stony reminders

This monument—in Budapest's Memento Park—represents a strong communist soldier racing into the future. But cynical Hungarians of the time had a different interpretation: a thermal-bath attendant running after a customer who forgot his towel.

of communist tyranny into a "Memento Park" where tourists flock to get a taste of the communist era. A visit here is a lesson in Socialist Realism, the art of communist Europe. Under the communists, creativity was discouraged. Art was acceptable only if it furthered the goals of the state. Aside from a few important figureheads, individuals didn't matter. Everyone was a cog in the machine—a strong and stoic automaton—an unquestioning servant of the nation.

Wandering through Budapest's Memento Park, you're entertained by a jumbled collection of once fearsome and now almost comical statues, seeming to preach their ideology to each other, as locals and tourists take funny photos mocking them. The gift shop hawks a fun parade of communist kitsch. On my last visit I picked up a CD featuring 20 patriotic songs—*The Greatest Hits of Communism*—and a Stalin vodka flask.

More Communist Sites

Many other places that suffered through communism have similar points of interest.

Prague, Czech Republic: On a thriving shopping street near the bottom of Prague's Wenceslas Square, wedged ironically between an American fast-food joint and a casino, stands the Museum of Communism. It re-creates slices of communist life—from a bland store counter to a typical classroom (where a poem on the chalkboard extols the virtues of the tractor).

The communist era left Eastern Europe with some decent public transportation, but ugly train stations were erected—like this one, in Prague. The low ceilings still make the individual feel like staying in line.

A few blocks away at the top of Wenceslas Square is a blocky building that housed Czechoslovakia's rubber-stamp Parliament back when they voted with Moscow. Between 1994 and 2008, this building was home to Radio Free Europe. After communism fell, RFE lost some of its funding and could no longer afford its Munich headquarters. In gratitude for its broadcasts—which had kept the people of Eastern Europe in touch with real news—the Czech government offered the building to RFE for one Czech koruna a year. Today, RFE has relocated, and this building's long interior can be viewed with a guided tour that takes you step-by-step through a fascinating stage of recent Czech—and journalistic—history.

Olomouc, Czech Republic: This appealing university town in Moravia (the eastern half of the Czech Republic) has a distinctive communist astronomical clock. Like Prague's famous clock, the one in Olomouc was intentionally destroyed by the Nazis in World War II. Today's version was rebuilt in 1953 by the communists—with their tacky flair for propaganda. This one-of-a-kind clock made in the Socialist Realist style is adorned with earnest chemists and heroic mothers rather than saints and Virgin Marys. High noon is marked by a proletarian parade, when, for six minutes, a mechanical conga line of milkmaids, clerks, blacksmiths, medics, and teachers are celebrated as the champions of everyday society. As with

any proper astronomical clock, there's a wheel with 365 saints, so you'll always know whose special day it is. But this clock comes with a Moscow-inspired bonus—red bands on the wheel splice in the birthdays of communist leaders, including Lenin and Stalin.

At Olomouc's astronomical clock, the white bands honor saints... while the dark bands trumpet communist bigwigs.

Gdańsk, Poland: Just a 20-minute walk from Gdańsk's colorful Hanseatic quarter are the dreary shipyards that Lech Wałęsa called the "cradle of freedom." Here the "Roads to Freedom" museum tells the story of the Solidarity movement of 1980, which started Eastern Europe's march to liberty. The engaging exhibit—housed in the very shipyards where the first labor strikes began—includes a replica of a sparsely stocked communist-era grocery store, the original list of 21

This monument—towering over the Gdańsk shipyard, where it inspired the birth of Solidarity—commemorates striking workers who were killed when the communist regime opened fire on them in 1970.

demands posted by the protestors, images of the newly minted Polish pope who inspired them, and plenty of bushy-mustachioed photos of the strike's leader, Lech Wałęsa. Wałęsa achieved rock-star status during the Gdańsk shipyard strikes, when—according to legend—the portly electrician hopped over a wall to become the leader of the protestors. He went on to become Poland's first post-communist president.

Warsaw, Poland: The Polish capital was devastated by World War II, then rebuilt largely by the Soviet regime. Towering over the seas of communist apartment blocks is the tallest building in Poland, the 760-foot Palace of Culture and Science. This massive skyscraper, dating from the early 1950s, was a "gift" from Stalin that the people of Warsaw couldn't refuse. Residents call it "Stalin's Penis" (using cruder terminology than that). Because it was to be "Soviet in substance, Polish in style," Soviet architects toured Poland to absorb local culture before starting the project. Since it's designed to show off the strong, grand-scale Soviet aesthetic and architectural skill, everything about the building is just plain big.

Tallinn, Estonia: In 2003, a wealthy Estonian-American opened a Museum of Estonia's Occupations. In the basement, between the toilets, stands an army of Soviet-era statues of communist leaders.

Any Town in Eastern Europe: Keep your eyes open for old communist-era loudspeakers. Locals remember growing up with these mouthpieces of government boasting

The harrowing, communist-style Palace of Culture and Science was a "gift" from Stalin to the people of Warsaw. (Talk about a white elephant.)

of successes ("This year, despite many efforts of sabotage on the part of certain individuals in service of imperialist goals, we have surpassed the planned output of steel by 195 percent"); calling people to action ("There will be no school tomorrow as all will join the farmers in the fields for an abundant harvest"); or quelling disturbances ("Some citizens may have heard about alien forces in our society taking advantage of this week's anniversary to spread unrest. This is to reassure you that the situation is firmly under control and nothing is happening. Nevertheless, for their own safety, we suggest all citizens stay home").

These days, as I walk through the streets of Eastern Europe, it occurs to me that Stalin—whose estate gets no royalties for all the postcards and vodka flasks featuring his mug—must be spinning in his communist grave.

For all the specifics, see the latest editions of Rick Steves' Budapest *or* Rick Steves' Eastern Europe.

GREAT BRITAIN

58. London: A Warm Look at a Cold City

I've spent more time in London than in any other European city. It lacks the grandeur of Rome, the warmth of Munich, and the elegance of Paris, but its history, traditions, people, markets, museums, and entertainment keep drawing me back.

London has changed dramatically in recent years, and many visitors are surprised to find how "un-English" it is. Whites are now a minority in major parts of this city that once symbolized white imperialism. Arabs have nearly bought out the area north of Hyde Park. Chinese take-outs outnumber fish-and-chips shops. Eastern Europeans pull pints in British pubs. Many hotels are run by people with foreign accents (who hire English chambermaids), while outlying suburbs are home to huge communities of Indians and Pakistanis. London is learning—sometimes fitfully—to live as a microcosm of its formerly vast empire.

London is a world in itself, a barrage on all the senses, an urban jungle sprawling over 600 square miles and teeming with eight

The London Eye towers over Big Ben.

London

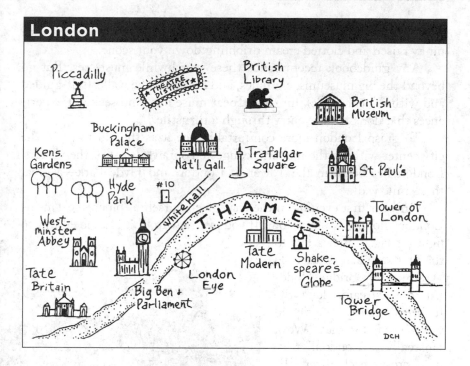

million people. As a first stop for many travelers, this huge city can be overwhelming. On my first visit I felt like Oliver Twist asking for more soup. Here are a few ideas to soften and warm this hard and cold city.

Have fun seeing the predictable biggies. Blow through the city on the open deck of a double-decker tour bus. Ogle the crown jewels in the Tower of London and see the Houses of Parliament in action. Cruise the Thames River, and take a spin on the London Eye. Hobnob with the tombstones in Westminster Abbey, and visit with Leonardo da Vinci, Botticelli, and Rembrandt in the National Gallery. Enjoy Shakespeare in a replica of the Globe Theatre, then marvel at a glitzy, fun musical at a modern-day theater. Whisper across the dome of St. Paul's Cathedral and rummage through our civilization's attic at the British Museum. Enjoy some of Europe's best people-watching at Covent Garden and snap

Have you tried London lately?

to at Buckingham Palace's Changing of the Guard. Sip your tea with pinky raised and clotted cream dribbling down your scone.

Any guidebook recommends these worthwhile must-sees. But go beyond the big museums, churches, and castles. Take walks (self-guided and with a local guide), hit the offbeat museums, and seek out experiences that don't require entry through a turnstile.

To grasp London more comfortably, see it as the old town in the city center without the modern, congested sprawl. Most of the visitors' London lies between the Tower of London and Hyde Park—a great three-mile walk.

On your first evening in the city, give yourself a "pinch-me-I'm-in-London" floodlit walking tour. If you just flew in, this is an ideal way to fight jet lag. Catch a bus to the first stop across (east of) Westminster Bridge. Side-trip downstream along the Jubilee Walkway for a capital view. Then, for that "Wow, I'm really in London!" feeling, cross back over the bridge to view the floodlit Houses of Parliament and Big Ben up close.

To thrill your loved ones (or stoke their envy), call home from a pay phone near Big Ben at about three minutes before the hour. As Big Ben chimes, stick the receiver outside the booth and prove you're in London: ding dong ding dong...dong ding ding dong. It's an audio postcard.

Then cross Whitehall, noticing the Winston Churchill statue in the park. (He's electrified to avoid the pigeon problem that stains so many other great statues.) Walk up Whitehall toward Trafalgar Square. Stop at the barricaded and guarded little Downing Street to see #10, home of the British prime minister. Chat with the bored bobby. From Trafalgar, walk to hopping Leicester Square and continue to youth-on-the-rampage Piccadilly, through safely sleazy Soho (north of Shaftesbury Avenue) up to Oxford Street. From Piccadilly or Oxford Circus you can taxi, bus, or subway home.

To nibble on London one historic snack at a time, take any of the focused two-hour walking tours of the city. For about $12, local historians take small groups through the London story, one entertaining page at a time. Choose from London's Plague, Dickens' London, Legal London, the Beatles in London, Jack the Ripper's London (which is the most popular, even though guides admit it's a lousy walk), Harry Potter's London, and many more. Some walks focus on the various "villages" of London, such as trendy Chelsea and leafy Hampstead.

The South Bank of the River Thames, rapidly becoming gentrified, is a thriving arts and cultural center. From Westminster Bridge to the Tower Bridge, the slick Jubilee Walkway is a trendy jogging, yuppie pub-crawling walk—lined with fun and off-beat sights. The London Eye observation wheel offers the city's highest public viewpoint (450 feet). Featuring modern art, the great Tate Modern on the South Bank is connected with the sedate St. Paul's Cathedral on the North Bank by the pedestrian Millennium Bridge. Skip the South Bank's outrageously amateurish, heavily promoted, and overpriced "London Dungeon," but consider Shakespeare's Globe Theatre and the Imperial War Museum.

For megatons of things military, the impressive Imperial War Museum covers the wars of the last century. You'll see heavy weaponry, love notes from the front, Vargas Girl pin-ups, Monty's Africa-campaign tank, and Schwarzkopf's Desert Storm uniform. Trace the development of the machine gun, watch footage of the first tank battles, and hold your breath through the gruesome "WWI trench experience." You can even buy WWII-era toys. The section on the Holocaust is one of the best on the subject anywhere. The museum doesn't glorify war, but chronicles the sweeping effects of humanity's most destructive century.

My favorite way to learn history is to stroll with a guide, as if beach-combing. You pick up obscure shards of a neighborhood's distant past, unlocking unexpected stories. On a bright, brisk January morning, I joined a guide, David Tucker, who runs a tour company called London Walks (www.walks.com).

From London Bridge, David pointed downriver past the Tower of London and said, "During the Second World War, Nazi bombers used the Thames as a guide on their nightly raids. When moonlit, they called it a 'silver ribbon of tin foil.' It led from the English Channel right to our mighty dockyards. Even with all the city lights carefully blacked out, those bombers easily found their targets. Neighborhoods on both banks of the river went up in flames. After the war, the business district on the North Bank was rebuilt, but the South Bank...it was long neglected."

Turning his back to St. Paul's Cathedral, he pointed to a vast complex of new buildings, displaying the recently restored, newly trendy South Bank, and continued, "Only now has the bombed-out South Bank been properly rebuilt. There's a real buzz in London about our South Bank."

We walked down to the beach. The Thames is a tidal river, and at low tide it's littered with history. Even today, many of the beaches are red with clay tiles from 500-year-old roofs. Picking up a chunky piece of tile worn oval by the centuries, with its telltale peg hole still clearly visible, the guide explained that these tiles were heavy, requiring large timbers for support. In the 16th century, when shipbuilding for the Royal Navy made these timbers more costly and rare, lighter slate tiles became the preferred roofing material. Over time, the heavy, red-clay tiles migrated from the rooftops to the riverbank...to the pockets of beachcombers like us.

Like kids on a scavenger hunt, we studied the pebbles. David picked up a chalky white tube to show me. It was the fragile stem of an 18th-century clay pipe. Back then, when tobacco was sold with disposable one-use pipes, used pipes were routinely tossed into the river. David tossed it down. Thinking, "King George may have sucked on this," I picked it up.

Climbing back to street level, we prowled through some fascinating relics of the South Bank neighborhood that survived both German bombs and urban renewal. Scaling steep stairs, we visited the Operating Theatre Museum, a crude surgical theater where amputations were performed in the early 1800s as medical students watched and learned. Down the street, the last surviving turret of the original London Bridge is the decorative centerpiece of an old hospital yard. We wandered through the still-bustling Borough Market to see farmers doing business with city shopkeepers.

Walking through this area put us through a time warp. David led us into a quiet courtyard, where we looked up at three sets of balconies climbing the front of an inn. He explained, "Courtyards like this provided struggling theater troupes—like young William Shakespeare's—with a captive audience."

Remember those roving troupes when you visit the Globe Theatre, a rebuilt version of the stage that eventually became their home. To see Shakespeare in a replica of the half-timbered, thatched theater for which he wrote his plays, attend a play at the Globe. This open-air, round theater does the plays as Shakespeare intended, with no

amplification ($8 to stand, $25–55 to sit, May–Oct, usually nightly, www .shakespeares-globe.org). The $8 "groundling" tickets—while open to rain—are the most fun. Playing the part of a crude peasant theatergoer, you can walk around, munch a picnic dinner, lean your elbows on the stage, and even interact with the actors. I've never enjoyed Shakespeare as much as here, performed as the Bard intended it...in the "wooden O." The theater is open to tour when there are no plays; the Shakespeare exhibit is worthwhile (and open even during afternoon plays).

Cheap Globe Theatre tip: Plays are long. Many groundlings, who are allowed to come and go as they please, leave before the end. Peasants with culture hang out an hour before the finish and beg or buy a ticket off someone leaving early.

Shakespeare is just the first act here in the world's best theater city. Choose from top musicals, comedies, thrillers, sex farces, and more. Over the years I've enjoyed *Harvey,* starring Jimmy Stewart; *The King and I,* with Yul Brynner; *My Fair Lady; A Chorus Line; Cats; Starlight Express; Les Misérables;* and *Chicago.* Performances are nightly except Sunday, usually with one matinee a week. Matinees are cheaper and rarely sell out. Ticket prices are comparable to New York, ranging from about $10 to $90. Most theaters are marked on London tourist maps and cluster in the Piccadilly–Trafalgar area.

Unless you want this year's smash hit, getting a ticket is easy. The *London Theatre Guide* and the *Entertainment Guide* (free at any hotel or tourist office) list everything in town. From home, it's easy to check www .officiallondontheatre.co.uk or www.theatremonkey.com for the latest on what's currently playing in London. Once you've decided on a show, call the theater directly, ask about seats and available dates, and buy a ticket with your credit card. Arrive about 30 minutes before the show starts to pick up your ticket and to avoid lines.

For a booking fee, you can reserve online. Most theater websites link you to a preferred ticket vendor, usually www.ticketmaster.co.uk or www.seetickets.com. Keith Prowse Ticketing is also handy by phone or online (US tel. 800-669-8687, London toll tel. 0844-209-0382, www .keithprowse.com).

Ticket agencies, which charge a standard 25 percent booking fee, are scalpers with an address. Agencies are worthwhile only if a show you've just got to see is sold out at the box office. Many ticket agencies speculate, scarfing up hot tickets, in order to make a killing after the show is otherwise sold out. US booking agencies get their tickets from another agency, adding to your expense by involving yet another middleman. You'll stand a good chance of saving money by simply calling the box office directly to book your tickets (international phone calls are cheap, and credit cards make booking a snap).

Cheap theater tricks: Most theaters offer cheap returned tickets, standing-room, matinee, and senior or student standby deals. These "concessions" are indicated with a "conc" or "s" in the listings. Picking up a late return can get you a great seat at a cheap-seat price. Even if a show is "sold out," there's usually a way to get a seat. Call the theater box office and ask how. The famous half-price "tkts" booth at Leicester (pronounced "Lester") Square sells discounted tickets for top-price seats to shows on the push list the day of the show only ($5 service charge per ticket, Mon–Sat 10:00 a.m.–7:00 p.m., Sun 11:00 p.m.–4:00 p.m., matinee tickets from noon, lines often form early, lists of shows at www.tkts.co.uk).

I buy the second-cheapest tickets directly from the theater box office. Many theaters are so small that there's hardly a bad seat. After the lights go down, "scooting up" is less than a capital offense.

If your theatergoing puts you in a literary frame of mind, visit the British Library. While the library contains 180 miles of bookshelves filling London's deepest basement, two beautiful rooms filled with state-of-the-art glass display cases show you the printed treasures of our civilization. You'll see ancient maps; early gospels on papyrus; illuminated manuscripts from the early Middle Ages; the Gutenberg Bible; the Magna Carta; pages from Leonardo's notebooks; original writing by the titans of English literature, from Chaucer and Shakespeare to Dickens and Wordsworth; and music manuscripts from Beethoven to the Beatles.

On Sunday, enjoy an hour of craziness at Speaker's Corner in Hyde Park. By noon, there are usually several soapbox speakers, screamers, singers, communists, or comics performing to the crowd of onlookers. "The grassroots of democracy" is actually a holdover from when the gallows stood here and the criminal was allowed to say just about anything he wanted to before he swung. I dare you to raise your voice and gather a crowd—it's easy to do. If you catch the London double-decker bus tour from Speaker's Corner Sunday at

10 a.m., you'll return at noon for the prime-time action.

Kew Gardens are lively and open daily. Cruise the Thames or ride the Tube to London's favorite gardens for plants galore and a breezy

respite from the city. While the Royal Botanic Gardens of Kew are, for most visitors, a delightful opportunity to wander among 33,000 different types of plants, they are also a hardworking organization committed to understanding and preserving the botanical diversity of our planet. Garden lovers could spend days exploring Kew's 300 acres.

For a quick visit, spend a fragrant hour wandering through three buildings: the Palm House, a humid Victorian world of iron, glass, and tropical plants built in 1844; a Waterlily House that Monet would swim for; and the Princess of Wales Conservatory, a modern greenhouse with many different climate zones growing countless cacti and bug-munching carnivorous plants. Then climb up to the Rhizotron and Xstrata Treetop Walkway, a 200-yard-long scenic steel catwalk that puts you high in the canopy 60 feet above the ground.

Antiques buffs, people-watchers, and folks who brake for garage sales love to haggle at London's street markets. There's good early-morning market activity somewhere every day of the week. There are markets for fish, fruit, used cars, antiques, clothing, and on and on. Portobello Road (Mon–Wed and Fri–Sat 8 a.m.–6:30 p.m., closes at 1 p.m. Thu, closed Sun) and Camden Lock (daily 10 a.m.–6 p.m.) are just two of the many colorful markets that offer great browsing. But don't expect great prices. These days, the only people getting a steal at London's markets are the pickpockets.

No visit to London is complete without enjoying a pint in a woody pub. Pubs are an integral part of English culture. You'll find all kinds, each with its own personality. Taste the different beers. If you don't know what to order, ask the bartender for a half pint of his

or her favorite. Real ale, pumped by hand from the basement (look for the longest handles on the bar), is every connoisseur's choice. For a basic American-type beer, ask for a lager. Teetotalers can get lemon-lime soda pop by asking for a "lemonade." Children are welcome in most pubs but will not be served alcohol until they are 18. Order some pub grub and talk to the people. Enjoy a public house. By getting beyond the bobbies and beefeaters—by meeting the people—you see London take on a personality you can't capture on a postcard.

*For good-value accommodations in London's **Victoria Station neighborhood**, try Luna Simone Hotel (47 Belgrave Road, tel. 020/7834-5897, www.luna simonehotel.com). In **South Kensington**, stay at the Aster House (hotelesque splurge, 3 Sumner Place, tel. 020/7581-5888, www.asterhouse.com). Near **Kensington Palace**, consider the London Vicarage Hotel (10 Vicarage Gate, tel. 020/7229-4030, www.londonvicaragehotel.com). For all the travel specifics, see this year's edition of* Rick Steves' London, Rick Steves' England, *or* Rick Steves' Great Britain.

59. Bath: England at Its Elegant and Frivolous Best

Two hundred years ago, this city of 85,000 was the Hollywood of Britain. Today, the former trendsetter of Georgian England invites you to take the 90-minute train ride from London and sample its aristocratic charms. If ever a city enjoyed looking in the mirror, Bath's the one. It has more "government-listed" or protected buildings per capita than any town in England. The entire city, built of the creamy warm-tone limestone called "Bath stone," beams in its cover-girl complexion.

An architectural chorus line, Bath is a triumph of the Georgian (British for "Neoclassical") style, with buildings as competitively elegant as the society they once housed. If you look carefully, you'll see false windows built in the name of balance (but not used, in the name of tax avoidance) and classical columns that supported only Georgian egos. Two centuries ago, rich women wore

Bath: Georgian on my mind

GREAT BRITAIN

Bath

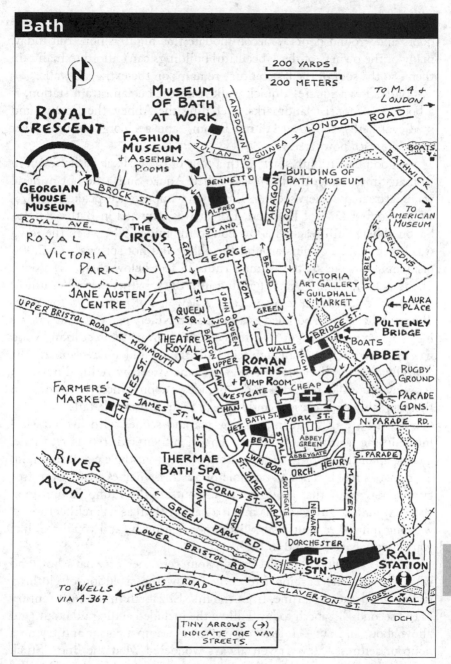

200 YARDS
200 METERS

N

TO M-4 &
LONDON

ROYAL
CRESCENT

MUSEUM
OF BATH
AT WORK

FASHION
MUSEUM
& ASSEMBLY
ROOMS

LONDON ROAD

BOATS

GEORGIAN
HOUSE
MUSEUM

BROCK ST.

THE
CIRCUS

LANSDOWN ROAD

JULIAN

BENNETT

GUINEA

PARAGON

WALCOT

BATHWICK

BUILDING OF
BATH MUSEUM

TO
AMERICAN
MUSEUM

ROYAL AVE.

ALFRED

ST. AND.

HEN. GDNS.

ROYAL
VICTORIA
PARK

GAY ST.

GEORGE

MILSOM

BROAD

HENRIETTA ST.

JANE AUSTEN
CENTRE

UPPER BRISTOL ROAD

MONMOUTH ST.

THEATRE
ROYAL

JOHN

QUEEN
SQ.

WOOD

QUEEN

GREEN

BARTON

WALLS

VICTORIA
ART GALLERY
& GUILDHALL
MARKET

BRIDGE ST.

HIGH

LAURA
PLACE

PULTENEY
BRIDGE

BOATS

ABBEY

FARMERS'
MARKET

CHARLES ST.

JAMES ST. W.

UPPER
BOROUGH

WESTGATE

CHAN.

HET.

BATH ST.

BEAU.

STALL

ROMAN
BATHS
+ PUMP ROOM

CHEAP

YORK ST.

ABBEY
GREEN

ABBEYGATE

N. PARADE RD.

S. PARADE

i

RUGBY
GROUND

PARADE
GDNS.

THERMAE
BATH SPA

ST. JAMES PARADE

AVON ST.

CORN

ST.

AMB.

LWR. BOR.

SOUTHGATE

ORCH.

HENRY

MANVERS ST.

RIVER
AVON

GREEN PARK RD.

NEWARK

DORCHESTER

BUS
STN

RAIL
STATION

i

LOWER BRISTOL RD.

TO WELLS
VIA A-367

WELLS ROAD

CLAVERTON ST.

ROSS.

CANAL

DCH

TINY ARROWS (→)
INDICATE ONE WAY
STREETS.

feathered hats atop three-foot hairdos, and the very rich stretched their doors and ground floors to accommodate this high fashion. But today, many of the owners of these beautiful buildings can't afford to maintain them, so the soot of the last century remains on the extra-tall walls.

Bath's town square, a quick walk from the bus and train station, is a bouquet of tourist landmarks, including the Abbey, the Roman and medieval baths, the royal "Pump Room," and a Georgian flute player complete with powdered wig.

A good day in Bath starts with a tour of the historic baths. Even in Roman times, when the town was called Aquae Sulis, the hot mineral water attracted society's elite. The town's importance peaked in 973, when the first king of England, Edgar, was crowned in Bath's Anglo-Saxon abbey. Bath reached a low ebb in the mid-1600s, when the town was just a huddle of huts around the abbey and hot springs with 3,000 residents oblivious to the Roman ruins 18 feet below their dirt floors. Then, in 1687, Queen Mary, fighting infertility, bathed here. Within 10 months she gave birth to a son...and a new age of popularity for Bath. The revitalized town boomed as a spa resort. Ninety percent of the buildings you see today are from the 18th century. Local architect John Wood was inspired by the Italian architect Palladio to build a "new Rome." The town bloomed in the Neoclassical style, and streets were lined not with scrawny sidewalks but with wide "parades," upon which the women in their stylishly wide dresses could spread their fashionable tails.

For a taste of aristocracy, enjoy tea and scones with live classical music in the nearby Pump Room. For an authentic, if repulsive, finale, have a sip of the awfully curative Bath water from the elegant fountain. To make as much sense as possible of all this fanciness, catch the free city walking tour that leaves from just outside the Pump Room door. Bath's volunteer guides are as much a part of Bath as its architecture. A walking tour gives your visit a little more intimacy, and you'll feel like you actually have a friend in Bath.

In the afternoon, stroll through four centuries of what's hot (and what's not) in the Fashion Museum. Follow the evolution of clothing styles, one decade at a time, from the first Elizabeth in the 16th century to the second Elizabeth today. Follow the included audioguide tour, and allow about an hour—unless you pause to lace up a corset and try on a hoop underdress. Haven't you always wondered what the line, "Stuck a feather in his cap and called it macaroni," from "Yankee Doodle" means? You'll find the answer (and a lot more) in Bath—one town whose narcissism is certainly justified.

*For good-value accommodations in **Bath**, try Brocks Guest House (32 Brock St., tel. 01225/338-374, www.brocksguesthouse.co.uk) or the cheaper 14 Raby Place (14 Raby Place, tel. 01225/465-120). For all the travel specifics, see this year's edition of* Rick Steves' England *or* Rick Steves' Great Britain.

60. York: Vikings, Bygone Lifestyles, and England's Top Church

Historians run around York like kids in a candy shop. But the city is so fascinating that even nonhistorians find themselves exploring the past with the same delight they'd give a fun-house hall of mirrors.

York is 200 miles north of London (just two hours by train). For a practical introduction to the city, start your visit by taking one of the free, entertaining, and informative guided walking tours (leaving morning, afternoon, and summer evenings from the tourist office). To keep the day open for museums and shopping and enjoy a quieter tour (with a splash of ghostly gore), take the evening walk. The excellent guides are likeably chatty and opinionated. By the end of the walk, you'll know the latest York city gossip, several ghost stories, and what architectural "monstrosity" the "insensitive" city planners are about to inflict on the public.

With this introductory tour under your belt, you're getting the hang

York's massive Minster

of York and its history. Just as a Boy Scout counts the rings in a tree, you can count the ages of York by the different bricks in the city wall: Roman on the bottom, then Danish, Norman, and the "new" addition—from the 14th century.

The pride of the half-timbered town center is the medieval butchers' street called the Shambles, with its rusty old hooks hiding under the eaves. Six hundred years ago, bloody hunks of meat hung here, dripping into the gutter that still marks the middle of the lane. This slaughterhouse of commercial activity gave our language a new word. What was once a "shambles" is now ye olde tourist shopping mall.

York's four major sights—the York Castle Museum, the Jorvik Viking Centre, the best-in-Europe National Railway Museum, and the

York

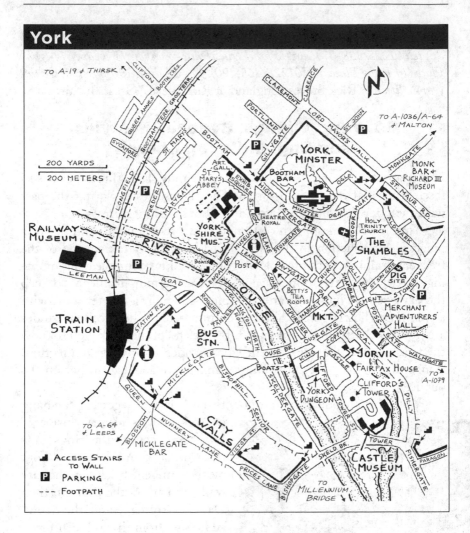

To A-19 & Thirsk

200 YARDS
200 METERS

RAILWAY MUSEUM

RIVER OUSE

LEEMAN

TRAIN STATION

STATION RD.

BUS STN.

MICKLEGATE

QUEEN ST.

TO A-64 & LEEDS

MICKLEGATE BAR

CITY WALLS

NUNNERY LANE

PRICES LANE

TO MILLENNIUM BRIDGE

BISHOPGATE

VICTOR ST.

SENIOR

BISHOPHILL

TANNER ROW

WELLINGTON NORTH ST.

ROUGIER ST.

Boats

OUSE BR.

SKELDERGATE

KING ST.

YORK DUNGEON

CLIFFORD ST.

SKELD. BR.

CASTLE MUSEUM

TOWER ST.

CLIFFORD'S TOWER

FISHERGATE

PARAGON

TO A-1079

FAIRFAX HOUSE

JORVIK

CLAREMONT CLARENCE

PORTLAND

GILLYGATE

LORD MAYOR'S WALK

ST. JOHN

TO A-1036/A-64 & MALTON

CLIFTON BOOTH CRES.

QUEEN ANNE'S GROS. TERR.

SYCAMORE BOOTHAM TERR. ST. MARYS

LONGFIELD FREDERIC EARLS

MARYGATE

BOOTHAM

ST. MARY'S ABBEY

ART GALL. EXHIB. SQUARE

HIGH PETERGATE

BOOTHAM BAR

YORK MINSTER

DEAN

OGLE

MINSTER YD.

GOODRAMGATE

MONK BAR & RICHARD III MUSEUM

MONKGATE

ST. MAUR RD.

ALDWARK

HOLY TRINITY CHURCH

THE SHAMBLES

DIG SITE

STONEBOW

MERCHANT ADVENTURERS' HALL

FOSS

PICCA.

WALMGATE

DILLY

YORKSHIRE MUS.

THEATRE ROYAL

MUSEUM ST.

BLAKE ST.

STONEGATE

LOW PET.

LENDAL BR.

Post

CONEY ST.

DAVYGATE

CHURCH ST.

SPURRIERGATE

MARKET ST.

PARLIAMENT ST.

PAVEMENT

COLLIER.

SHAMBLES

FOSSGATE

COPPERGATE

OUSEGATE

BETTY'S TEA ROOMS

MKT.

ACCESS STAIRS TO WALL

P PARKING

- - - FOOTPATH

huge and historic York Minster cathedral—can keep a speedy sightseer busy for two days.

Charles Dickens would feel right at home in York's Castle Museum. English memorabilia from the 18th and 19th centuries are cleverly displayed in a huge collection of craft shops, old stores, living rooms, and other intimate glimpses of those bygone days.

As towns were being modernized in the 1930s, the museum's founder, Dr. Kirk, collected entire shops and reassembled them here. In Kirkgate, the museum's most popular section, you can wander through a Lincolnshire butcher's shop, Bath bakery, coppersmith's shop, toy shop, and barbershop.

The shops are actually stocked with the merchandise of the day.

Fiddling around old York

Eavesdrop on English grannies as they reminisce their way through the museum's displays. The general store is loaded with groceries and candy, and the sports shop has everything you'd need for a game of 19th-century archery, cricket, skittles, or tennis. Anyone for "whiff-whaff" (Ping-Pong)? In the confectionery, Dr. Kirk beams you into a mouth-watering world of "spice pigs," "togo bullets," "hum bugs," and "conversation lozenges."

In the period rooms, three centuries of Yorkshire living rooms and clothing fashions paint a cozy picture of life centered around the hearth. Ah, a peat fire warming a huge brass kettle while the aroma of freshly baked bread soaks into the heavy, open-beamed ceilings. After walking through the evolution of romantic valentines and unromantic billy clubs, you can trace the development of early home lighting—from simple waxy sticks to the age of electricity. An early electric heater has a small plaque explaining, "How to light an electric fire: Switch it on!"

Dr. Kirk's "memorable collection of bygones" is the closest thing in Europe to a time-tunnel experience, except perhaps for the Jorvik Viking Centre just down the street.

A thousand years ago, York was a thriving Viking settlement called Jorvik (YOR-vik). While only traces are left of most Viking settlements, Jorvik is an archaeologist's bonanza, the best-preserved Viking city ever excavated.

If you sailed the "Pirates of the Caribbean" north several latitudes and back in time 1,000 years, you'd have Jorvik. More a ride than a museum, this exhibit drapes the abundant harvest of this dig in Disney cleverness. You'll ride a little people-mover for 20 minutes through the re-created Viking street of Coppergate. It's the year 975, and you're in the village of Jorvik. Slowly glide through the reconstructed village. Everything—sights, sounds, even smells—has been carefully re-created. You experience a Viking village. Next, your time-traveling train rolls you through the actual excavation site, past the actual remains that inspired the reconstructed village. Stubs of buildings, piles of charred wood, broken pottery—a time-crushed echo of a once-thriving town. Everything is true to the dig—even the faces of the models are derived by computer from skulls dug up here.

Your ride ends at a gallery filled with artifacts from every aspect of Viking life: clothing, cooking, weapons, clever locks, jewelry, even children's games. The gift shop—the traditional finale of any English museum—capitalizes nicely on your newly developed fascination with Vikings in England (www.vikingjorvik.com).

Innovative 20 years ago, Jorvik and its cousins all over England seem tired and gimmicky today. For straightforward Viking artifacts, beautifully explained and set in historical context with no crowds at all, tour the nearby Yorkshire Museum (www.yorkshiremuseum.org.uk).

York's thunderous National Railway Museum shows 200 illustrious years of British railroad history. Fanning out from a grand roundhouse is an array of historic cars and engines, including Queen Victoria's lavish royal car and the very first "stagecoaches on rails." Even spouses of train buffs will find the exhibits on dining cars, post cars, Pullman cars, and vintage train posters interesting.

York's Minster, or cathedral, is the largest Gothic church north of the Alps. Henry VIII, in his self-serving religious fervor, destroyed nearly everything that was Catholic—except the great York Minster. Henry needed a northern capital for his Anglican church.

The Minster is a brilliant example of how the High Middle Ages were far from dark. The Great East Window, the size of a tennis court, is only one of the art treasures explained in the free hour-long tours given throughout the day. The church's undercroft gives you a chance to climb down, archaeologically and physically, through the centuries to see the roots of the much smaller but still huge Norman church (built in A.D. 1100) that stood on this spot and, below that, the Roman excavations. Constantine was proclaimed Roman emperor here in A.D. 306. The undercroft also gives you a look at the modern concrete and stainless steel save-the-church foundations.

To fully experience the cathedral, go for an evensong service (no offering plates, no sermon; Mon–Sat at 5:15 p.m., Sun at 4 p.m., sometimes no services mid-July–Aug). Arrive early and ask to be seated in the choir. You're in the middle of a spiritual Oz as 40 boys sing psalms—a red-and-white-robed pillow of praise, raised up by the powerful pipe organ. You feel as if you have elephant-size ears, as the beautifully carved choir stalls—functioning as giant sound scoops—magnify the thunderous, trumpeting pipes. If you're lucky, the organist will run a spiritual musical victory lap as the congregation breaks up. Thank God for York. Amen.

*For good-value accommodations in **York**, try Airden House (1 St. Mary's, tel. 01904/638-915, www.airdenhouse.co.uk) or The Sycamore (19 Sycamore Place, tel. 01904/624-712, www.thesycamore.co.uk). For all the travel specifics, see this year's edition of* Rick Steves' England *or* Rick Steves' Great Britain.

61. Blackpool: Britain's Coney Island

Blackpool is England's tacky, glittering city of fun. But it's ignored by American guidebooks. Located on the coast north of Liverpool, with a six-mile beach promenade, it's the private playground of North England's Flo and Andy Capps.

When I told Brits I was Blackpool-bound, their expressions soured and they asked, "Oh, God, why?" Because it's the ears-pierced-while-you-wait, tipsy-toupee place that widows and workers go to year after year to escape. Tacky, yes. Lowbrow, OK. But it's as English as can be, and that's what I'm after. Give yourself a vacation from your sightseeing vacation. Spend a day just "muckin' about" in Blackpool.

Blackpool is dominated by the Blackpool Tower—a giant amusement center that seems to grunt, "Have fun." You pay about $25 to get in, and after that the fun is free. Work your way up through layer after layer of noisy entertainment: circus, bug zone, space world, dinosaur center, aquarium, and the silly house of horrors. Have a coffee break in the elegant ballroom festooned with golden oldies barely dancing to barely live music. The finale at the tip of this 500-foot-tall symbol of Blackpool is a smashing view, especially at sunset.

Hop a vintage trolley car to survey Blackpool's beach promenade.

British people flock to Blackpool to soak up the seaside resort's atmosphere.

The cars, which rattle constantly up and down the waterfront, are more fun than driving. Each of the three amusement piers has its own personality. Are you feeling sedate (north pier), young and frisky (central pier), or like a cowboy dragging a wagon full of children (south pier)?

Stroll the Promenade. A million greedy doors try every trick to get you inside. Huge

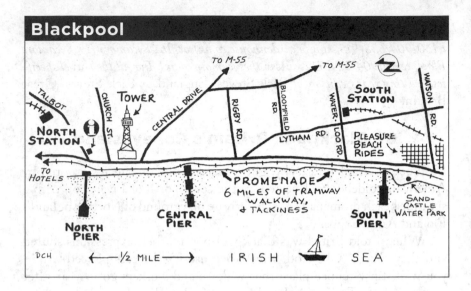

Blackpool

arcade halls advertise free toilets and broadcast bingo numbers into the streets. The randy wind machine under a wax Marilyn Monroe blows at a steady gale, and the smell of fries, tobacco, and sugared popcorn billows everywhere. Milk comes in raspberry or banana in this land where people under incredibly bad wigs look normal. I was told that I mustn't leave without having my fortune told by a Gypsy spiritualist, but, at $10 per palm, I'll read them myself.

Don't miss an evening at an old-time variety show. Blackpool always has a few razzle-dazzle music, dancing-girl, racy-humor, magic, and tumbling shows ($12–48 tickets at the door). I enjoy the "old-time music hall" shows. The shows are corny—neither hip nor polished—but it's fascinating to be surrounded by hundreds of partying British seniors, swooning again and waving their hankies to the predictable beat. Busloads of happy widows come from all corners of North England to giggle at racy jokes. A perennial favorite is *Funny Girls,* a burlesque-in-drag show that delights footballers and grannies alike.

Blackpool's "Illuminations" light up the night every September and October. Blackpool (the first city in England to switch on electric streetlights, in 1879) stretches its season by illuminating its six miles of waterfront with countless blinking and twinkling lights. The American inside me kept saying, "I've seen bigger and I've seen better," but I filled his mouth with cotton candy and just had some simple fun like everyone else on my specially decorated tram.

For a fun forest of amusements, Blackpool Pleasure Beach is tops. These 42 acres of rides (more than 125, including "the best selection

Liverpool's Magical Mystery Tour

About an hour south of Blackpool is Liverpool, with the gentrified Albert Dock harborfront featuring the city's top museums, a cheap hotel, vast parking, and plenty of Beatles lore.

Die-hard fans may want to pay homage at John and Paul's boyhood homes—both restored circa 1950s (must visit with a National Trust Tour, 2 hours, $27, reservations recommended, tel. 0151/233-2457 or tel. 0151/427-7231, www.nationaltrust.org .uk/main/w-the_beatles.htm). Or try the less in-depth Beatles "Magical Mystery" bus tour, which hits the lads' homes (exteriors only), Penny Lane, and so on. The tourist information office has specifics on the big bus that goes daily (also two hours). For something more extensive, fun, and intimate, consider a three-hour minibus Beatles tour with Phil Hughes. It's longer because it includes information on historic Liverpool as well as the Beatles stuff (www.tourliverpool.co.uk).

The "sights" each tour covers are basically houses where the Fab Four grew up, places they performed, and spots made famous by the lyrics of their hits ("Penny Lane," "Strawberry Fields," the Eleanor Rigby graveyard, etc.). While perfectly boring to non-fans, enthusiasts will enjoy listening to the commentary while seeing the shelter in the middle of the roundabout, the fire station with the clean machine, and the barber who shaves another customer. It's still in my ears and in my eyes.

of white-knuckle rides in Europe"), ice-skating shows, cabarets, and amusements attract seven million people a year, making Pleasure Beach one of England's most popular attractions. Its roller coasters include the Pepsi Max Big One, among the world's highest (235 feet), fastest (85 mph), and least likely to have me on board.

For me, Blackpool's top sight is its people. You'll see England here like nowhere else. Grab someone's hand and a big baton of "rock" (rock candy), and stroll. Ponder the thought of actually retiring here and spending your last years dog-paddling through

British people imagining sunshine at the beach in Blackpool

this urban cesspool of fun, wearing plaid pants and a bad toupee.

Blackpool is a scary thing to recommend. Maybe I overrate it. Many people (ignoring the "50 million flies can't all be wrong" logic) think I do. If you're not into kitsch and greasy spoons (especially if you're a nature lover and the weather happens to be good), skip Blackpool and spend more time in nearby North Wales or England's Lake District. But if you're traveling with kids—or still are one yourself—visit Blackpool, Britain's fun puddle: where every Englishman goes, but none will admit it.

*For good-value accommodations in **Blackpool**, try Beechcliffe Private Hotel (16 Shaftesbury Ave., tel. 01253/353-075, www.beechcliffe.co.uk). For all the travel specifics, see this year's edition of* Rick Steves' England *or* Rick Steves' Great Britain.

62. The Cotswold Villages: Inventors of Quaint

The Cotswold region, a 25-by-90-mile chunk of Gloucestershire, is a sightseeing treat: crisscrossed with hedgerows, raisined with storybook villages, and sprinkled with sheep.

As with many fairy-tale regions of Europe, the present-day beauty of the Cotswolds was the result of an economic disaster. Wool was a huge industry in medieval England, and the Cotswold sheep grew it best. Wool money built lovely towns and palatial houses as the region prospered. Local "wool"

It's hard to go wrong in the Cotswolds.

churches are called "cathedrals" for their scale and wealth. Stained-glass slogans say things like "I thank my God and ever shall, it is the sheep hath paid for all."

With the rise of cotton and the Industrial Revolution, the wool industry collapsed, mothballing the Cotswold towns into a depressed time warp. Today visitors enjoy a harmonious blend of man and nature: the most pristine of English countrysides decorated with time-passed villages, gracefully dilapidated homes of an impoverished nobility, tell-me-a-story stone fences, and "kissing gates" you wouldn't want to experience alone. Appreciated by throngs of 21st-century romantics, the Cotswolds are enjoying new prosperity.

Towns are small, and everyone seems to know everyone. The area is provincial, yet ever so polite, and chatty residents commonly rescue themselves from a gossipy tangent by saying, "It's all very... ummm...yyya."

The north Cotswolds are best. Two of the region's coziest towns, Chipping Campden and Stow-on-the-Wold, are eight and four miles, respectively, from Moreton-in-Marsh, which has the best

public transportation connections. Any of these three towns makes a fine home base for your exploration of the thatch-happiest of Cotswold villages and walks.

Chipping Campden is just touristy enough to be convenient. This market town, once the home of the richest Cotswold wool merchants, has some incredibly beautiful thatched roofs. Both the great British historian G. M. Trevelyan and I call Chipping Campden's High Street the finest in England.

Walk the full length of High Street (like most market towns, wide enough for plenty of sheep business on market days). On one end, you'll find impressively thatched homes. Walking north on High Street, you'll pass the 17th-century Market Hall, the wavy roof of the first great wool mansion, a fine and free memorial garden, and, finally, the town's famous 15th-century Perpendicular Gothic "wool" church.

Stow-on-the-Wold has become a crowded tourist town, but most visitors are day-trippers, so nights, even in summer, are peaceful. Stow has no real sights other than the town itself, some good pubs, antiques stores, and cute shops draped seductively around a big town square. The tourist office sells a handy walking-tour brochure called *Town Trail*. A visit to Stow is not complete until you've locked your partner in the stocks on the green.

Moreton-in-Marsh, an easy home base for those without a car, is like Stow or Chipping Campden without the touristic sugar. Rather than gift and antiques shops, you'll find streets lined with real shops: ironmongers selling cottage name-plates and carpet shops strewn with the remarkable patterns that decorate

Imprisoned by the charm of the Cotswolds

B&B floors. A shin-kickin' traditional market of 100-plus stalls fills High Street each Tuesday as it has for the last 400 years. The Cotswolds have an economy outside of tourism, and you'll feel it in Moreton.

Stanway, Stanton, and Snowshill, between Stow and Chipping Campden, are my nominations for the cutest Cotswold villages. Like marshmallows in hot chocolate, they nestle side by side—awaiting your arrival.

Stanway, while not much of a village, is notable for its manor house. The Earl of Wemyss, whose family tree charts relatives back to 1202, opens his melancholy home and grounds to visitors just two days a week in the summer ($10, June–Aug house open and 300-foot-tall fountain flows Tue and Thu 2–5 p.m., tel. 01386/584-469, www.stanwayfountain .co.uk). The 14th-century tithe barn predates the manor and was originally where monks, in the days before money, would accept one-tenth of whatever the peasants produced. Peek inside—this is a great hall for village hoedowns.

While the tithe barn is no longer used to greet motley peasants with their feudal "rents," the lord still gets rent from his vast landholdings. The place feels like a time warp. Stepping into the obviously

The Earl of Wemyss opens his quirky and fascinating manor house to the public and personally greets his guests.

lived-in palace, you're free to wander pretty much as you like, but keep in mind that a family lives here.

Ask the ticket-taker (inside) to demonstrate the spinning rent-collection table. In the great hall, marvel at the one-piece oak shuffle-board table and the 1780 Chippendale exercise chair (half an hour of bouncing on this was considered good for the liver).

The manor dogs have their own cutely painted "family tree," but the earl admits that his current dog, C. J., is "all character and no breeding." The place has a story to tell. And so do the docents stationed in each room—modern-day peasants who, even without family trees, probably have relatives going back just as far in this village. Really. Talk to these people. Probe. Learn what you can about this side of England.

Stanway and neighboring Stanton are separated by a great oak forest and grazing land with parallel waves actually echoing the furrows plowed by medieval farmers. Let someone else drive so you can hang

out the window under a canopy of oaks as you pass stone walls and sheep.

In **Stanton,** flowers trumpet, door knockers shine, and slate shingles clap: a rooting section cheering visitors up the town's main street. The church, which dates back to the ninth century, betrays a pagan past. Stanton is at the intersection of two lines (called ley lines) connecting prehistoric sites. Churches such as Stanton's, built on a pagan holy ground, are dedicated to St. Michael. You'll see his well-worn figure above the door as you enter. Inside, above the capitals in the nave, find the pagan symbols for the moon and the sun. But it's Son worship that's long established, and the list of rectors goes back to 1269. Finger the back pew grooves, worn away by sheepdog leashes. A man's sheepdog accompanied him everywhere.

Snowshill, another nearly edible little bundle of cuteness, has a photogenic triangular square with a fine pub at its base. Snowshill Manor is a dark and mysterious old palace filled with the lifetime collection of the long-gone Charles Paget Wade. It's one big, musty celebration of craftsmanship, from finely carved spinning wheels to frightening samurai armor to tiny elaborate figurines carved by long-forgotten prisoners from the bones of meat served at dinner. Taking seriously his family motto, "Let Nothing Perish," he dedicated his life and fortune to preserving

If you'd rather be riding, rent a horse.

things finely crafted. The house (whose management made me promise not to promote it as an eccentric collector's pile of curiosities) really shows off Mr. Wade's ability to recognize and acquire fine examples of craftsmanship. It's all very...ummm...yyya.

The Cotswolds are walkers' country. The English love to walk the peaceful footpaths that shepherds walked back when "polyester" meant two girls. They vigorously defend their age-old right to free passage. Once a year, the Rambling Society organizes a "Mass Trespass," when each of England's 87,000 miles of public footpaths is walked. By assuring each path is used at least once a year, they stop landlords from putting up fences. Most of the land is privately owned and fenced in, but you're welcome (and legally entitled) to pass through, using the various sheep-stopping steps, gates, and turnstiles provided at each stone wall.

After a well-planned visit, you'll remember everything about the Cotswolds—the walks, churches, pubs, B&Bs, thatched roofs, gates, tourist offices, and even the sheep—as quaint.

*For good-value accommodations in **Chipping Campden,** try Sandalwood House B&B (Back Ends, tel. 01386/840-091); in **Stow-on-the-Wold,** Cross Keys Cottage (Park Street, tel. 01451/831-128); and in **Moreton-in-Marsh,** Treetops B&B (London Road, tel. 01608/651-036, www.treetopscotswolds .co.uk). For all the travel specifics, see this year's edition of* Rick Steves' England *or* Rick Steves' Great Britain.

63. Mysterious Britain

Stonehenge, Holy Grail, Avalon, Loch Ness...there's a mysterious side of Britain steeped in lies, legends, and at least a little truth. Haunted ghost walks and Nessie the Monster stories are profitable tourist gimmicks. But the cultural soil that gives us Beowulf, Shakespeare, and "God Save the Queen" is fertilized with a murky story that goes back to 3000 B.C., predating Egypt's first pyramids.

As today's sightseers zip from castle to pub, they pass countless stone

Mysterious Britain

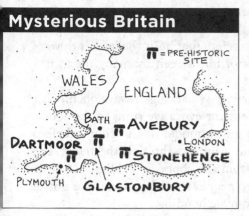

circles, forgotten tombs, man-made hills, and figures carved into hillsides whose stories will never be fully understood. Certain traveling druids skip the beefeater tours and zero right in on this side of Britain. With a little background, even the skeptic can appreciate Britain's historic aura.

Britain is crisscrossed by lines connecting prehistoric Stonehenge-type sights. Apparently prehistoric tribes intentionally built sites along this huge network of "ley" lines, which some think may have functioned together as a cosmic relay or circuit.

Glastonbury, two hours west of London and located on England's most powerful ley line, gurgles with a thought-provoking mix of history and mystery. As you climb the Glastonbury Tor, notice the remains of the labyrinth that made the hill a challenge to climb 5,000 years ago.

In A.D. 37, Joseph of Arimathea—Jesus' wealthy uncle—brought vessels containing the blood and sweat of Jesus to Glastonbury, and with them, Christianity to England. (Joseph's visit is plausible—long before Christ, residents traded lead to merchants from the Levant.) While this story is "proven" by fourth-century writings and accepted by the Church, the King-Arthur-and-the-Holy-Grail legends it inspired are not.

Those medieval tales came when England needed a morale-boosting folk hero to inspire its people during a war with France. They pointed to the ancient Celtic sanctuary at Glastonbury as proof of the greatness of the fifth-century warlord, Arthur. In 1911, his supposed remains (along with those of Queen Guinevere) were dug up from the abbey garden, and Glastonbury became woven into the Arthurian legends. Reburied in the abbey choir, their gravesite is a shrine today. Many think the Grail trail ends at the bottom of the Chalice Well, a natural spring at the base of Glastonbury Tor.

In the 16th century, Henry VIII, on his church-destroying rampage, wrecked the powerful Glastonbury Abbey. For emphasis, he hung and quartered the abbot, sending the parts of his body on four national tours...at the same time. While that was it for the abbot, two centuries later Glastonbury rebounded. In an 18th-century tourism campaign, thousands signed affidavits stating that water from the Chalice Well healed them, and once again Glastonbury was on the tourist map.

Today, Glastonbury and its tor are a center for searchers, too creepy for the mainstream church, but just right for those looking for a place to recharge their crystals. Since the society that built the labyrinth worshipped a mother goddess, the hill, or tor, is seen by many today as a Mother Goddess symbol.

After climbing the tor (great view, easy parking, always open), visit the Chalice Well at its base. Then tour the evocative ruins of the abbey, with its informative visitor's center and a model of the church before Henry got to it. Don't leave without a browse through the town. The Rainbow's End café (two minutes from the abbey at 17 High Street) is a fine place for salads and New Age people-watching. Read the notice board for the latest on midwives and male bonding.

From Glastonbury, as you drive across southern England, you'll see giant figures carved on hillsides. The white chalk cliffs of Dover stretch across the south of England, and almost anywhere you dig you hit chalk. While most of the giant fig-

Cerne Abbas Giant: "Maidens can still be seen leaping over his willy."

ures are creations of 18th- and 19th-century humanists reacting against the coldness of the Industrial Age, three Celtic figures (the Long Man of Wilmington, the White Horse of Uffington, and the Cerne Abbas Giant) have, as far as history is concerned, always been there.

The Cerne Abbas Giant is armed with a big club and an erection. For centuries, people fighting infertility would sleep on Cerne Abbas. And, as my English friend explained, "Maidens can still be seen leaping over his willy."

Stonehenge, England's most famous stone circle, is an hour's drive from Glastonbury. Built in phases between 3000 and 1000 B.C. with huge stones brought all the way from Wales or Ireland, it still functions as a remarkably accurate celestial calendar. A study of more than 300 similar circles in Britain found that each was designed to calculate the movement of the sun, moon, and stars, and to predict eclipses in order to help early societies know when to plant, harvest, and party. Even in modern times, as the summer solstice sun sets in just the right slot at Stonehenge, pagans boogie. Modern-day tourists and druids are kept

Stonehenge is surrounded by a rope. This is as close as you'll get.

at a distance by a fence, but if you're driving, Stonehenge is just off the highway and worth a stop ($11). Even a free look from the road is impressive.

Why didn't the builders of Stonehenge use what seem like perfectly adequate stones nearby? There's no doubt that the particular "blue stones" used in parts of Stonehenge were found only in (and therefore brought from) Wales or Ireland. Think about the ley lines. Ponder the fact that many experts accept none of the explanations of how these giant stones were transported. Then imagine congregations gathering here 4,000 years ago, raising thought levels, creating a powerful life force transmitted along the ley lines. Maybe a particular kind of stone was essential for maximum energy transmission. Maybe the stones were levitated here. Maybe psychics really do create powerful vibes. Maybe not. It's as unbelievable as electricity used to be.

The nearby stone circle at **Avebury,** 16 times the size of Stonehenge, is one-sixteenth as touristy. You're free to wander among 100 stones,

ditches, mounds, and curious patterns from the past, as well as the village of Avebury, which grew up in the middle of this 1,400-foot-wide Neolithic circle.

Spend some time at Avebury. Take the mile-long walk around the circle. Visit the fine little archaeology museum and pleasant Circle

Restaurant next to the National Trust store. The Red Lion Pub (also within the circle) has good, inexpensive pub grub. As you leave, notice the pyramid-shaped, 130-foot-high Silbury Hill. This man-made mound of chalk, nearly 5,000 years old, is a reminder that you've only scratched the surface of Britain's fascinating prehistoric and religious landscape.

A fine way to mix Neolithic wonders and nature is to explore one of England's many turnstile-free moors. You can get lost in these stark and sparsely populated time-passed commons, which have changed over the centuries about as much as the longhaired sheep that seem to gnaw on moss in their sleep. Directions are difficult to keep. It's cold and gloomy, as nature rises like a slow tide against human constructions. A crumpled castle loses itself in lush overgrowth. A church grows shorter as tall weeds eat at the stone crosses and tilted tombstones.

Dartmoor is the wildest moor—a wonderland of green and powerfully quiet rolling hills in the southwest, near the tourist centers of Devon and Cornwall. Crossed by only two or three main roads, most of the area is either unused or shared by its 30,000 villagers as a common grazing land—a tradition since feudal days. Dartmoor is best toured by car, but it can be explored by bike, rental horse, thumb, or foot. Bus service is meager. Several national park centers provide maps and information. Settle into a small-town B&B or hostel. This is one of England's most remote corners—and it feels that way.

Dartmoor, with more Bronze Age stone circles and huts than any other chunk of England, is perfect for those who dream of enjoying their own private Stonehenge sans barbed wire, police officers, parking lots, tourists, and port-a-loos. Ordnance Survey maps show the moor peppered with bits of England's mysterious past. Down Tor and Gidleigh are especially thought-provoking.

Word of the wonders lurking just a bit deeper into the moors tempted me away from my B&B in Gidleigh. Venturing in, I sank into the powerful, mystical moorland. Climbing over a hill, surrounded by hateful but sleeping towers of ragged granite, I was swallowed up. Hills followed hills followed hills—green growing gray in the murk.

Where was that 4,000-year-old circle of stone? I wandered in a world of greenery, eerie wind, white rocks, and birds singing but unseen. Then the stones appeared, frozen in a forever game of statue-maker. For endless centuries they had waited patiently, still and silent, for me to come.

I sat on a fallen stone as my imagination ran wild, pondering the people who roamed England so long before written history documented their story. Grabbing the moment, I took out my journal. The moor, the distant town, the chill, this circle of stones. I dipped my pen into the cry of the birds to write.

For good-value accommodations in **Dartmoor,** *try St. Johns West B&B (in Murchington, near Chagford, tel. 01647/432-468, http://stjohnswest.cjb.net, johnwwest@btinternet.com). For all the travel specifics, see this year's edition of* Rick Steves' England.

IRELAND

64. The Dingle Peninsula: A Gaelic Bike Ride

Be forewarned: Ireland is seductive. In many areas, traditions are strong and stress is a foreign word. I fell in love with the friendliest land this side of Sicily. It all happened in the *Gaeltacht*—an area of traditional culture where the government protects the old Irish ways. Shaded green on many maps, this cultural region is fragmented into geographical areas that fringe the west coast of the Emerald Isle. *Gaeltacht* means a place where Irish (or Gaelic) is spoken. But Irish culture is more than just the ancient language. You'll find it tilling the rocky fields, singing in the pubs, and lingering in the pride of the small-town preschool that brags "all Irish." Signposts are in Irish only, with many in the old Irish letter-ing. If your map is in English...good luck. Modern Irish yuppies report that the old Irish language is cool and on the rise.

The Dingle Peninsula—green, rugged, and untouched—is my favorite *Gaeltacht*. (The government recently tried to officially rename it with its Gaelic handle, An Daingean—until local merchants loudly complained that it was ruining Dingle's well-established "brand." But you'll still see *An Daingean* signs here.) While the big tour buses clog the neighboring Ring of Kerry before heading east to kiss the Blarney Stone, in Dingle it still feels like the fish and the farm actually matter. Forty fishing boats sail from Dingle. And a nostalgic whiff of peat continues to fill its nighttime streets, offering visitors an escape into pure Ireland. For more than 25 years, my Irish dreams have been set here, on this sparse but lush peninsula where residents are fond of saying, "The next parish is Boston."

Of the peninsula's 14,000 residents, 1,900 live in Dingle town. Its few streets, lined with ramshackle but gaily painted shops and pubs, run up from a rain-stung harbor. During the day, teenagers—already working on ruddy beer-glow cheeks—roll kegs up the streets and into the pubs in preparation for another tin-whistle night.

Fishing once dominated Dingle, and the town's only visitors were students of old Irish ways. Then, in 1970, the movie *Ryan's Daughter* introduced the world to Dingle. The trickle of its fans has grown to a flood, as word has spread of its musical, historical, gastronomical, and scenic charms—not to mention Fungie the friendly dolphin, who hangs out in the harbor.

The Dingle Peninsula Circle—By Bike or Car

The Dingle Peninsula is 10 miles wide and 41 miles long, from Tralee to Slea Head (Ceann Sleibhe in Gaelic). The top of its mountainous spine

Enjoy the Emerald Isle on two wheels.

is Mount Brandon—at 3,120 feet, the fourth-tallest peak in Ireland. While only tiny villages lie west of Dingle town, the peninsula is home to half a million sheep. The weather on this distant tip of Ireland is often misty, foggy, and rainy. Good and bad weather blow by in a steady meteorological parade. With stops, the 30-mile circuit (go with the traffic, clockwise) takes five hours by bike or three hours by car.

Leaving Dingle town, it becomes clear that the peninsula is an open-air museum. It's littered with monuments reminding visitors that the town has been the choice of Bronze Age settlers, Dark Age monks, English landlords, and Hollywood directors. In the front yard of the Milestone B&B is an ancient border marker that has stood there since the time of the Celts—one of more than 2,000 stony pieces in the puzzle of prehistoric life here.

Across the bay, the manor house of Lord Ventry is surrounded by palms, magnolias, fuchsias, and fancy flora introduced to Dingle by the Englishman who once owned the peninsula. His legacy—thanks only to

Dingle: Before Tourism and After

I love envisioning towns the way they were before tourism and the modern world brought prosperity. Dingle town, on the once-bleak southwest tip of Ireland, is now more upscale. Ireland, long one of Europe's poorest corners, became one of its richest during the "Celtic Tiger" economic boom from the mid-1990s to the mid-2000s (though the recent economic downturn has hit it hard). These days, towns are painted a rainbow of pastels (which tourists think are traditional), and residents no longer make soil from sand and seaweed in order to grow their potatoes.

the mild, Gulf Stream–protected weather—is the fuchsias that line the peninsula roads. And just down the road, locals point to the little blue house that once kept Tom Cruise and Nicole Kidman cozy during the filming of *Far and Away*.

Near a two-room schoolhouse, a street sign warns *Taisteal go Mall*—slow down. Near the playground, students hide out in circular remains of a late Stone Age ring fort. In 500 B.C., it was a petty Celtic chieftain's headquarters—a stone-and-earth stockade filled with little stone houses. So many of these ring forts survived the centuries because of superstitious beliefs that they were "fairy forts."

In the little town of Ventry (Ceann Tra'), talk with the chatty Irish you'll meet along the roadside. I once met an elfish, black-clad old man here. When I asked if he was born here, he breathed deeply and said, "No, 'twas about six miles down the road." When I told him where I was from, a faraway smile filled his eyes as he looked out to sea and sighed, "Aye, the shores of Americay."

The wet sod of Dingle is soaked with medieval history. In the dark-

IRELAND

Dingle Peninsula

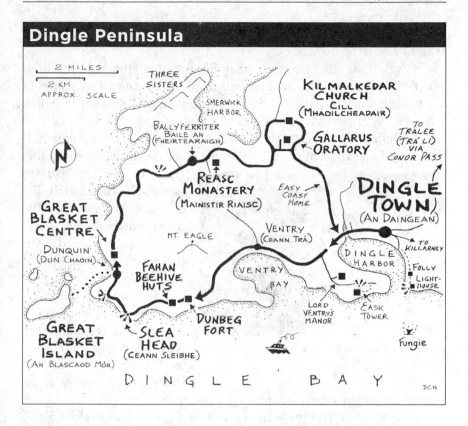

est depths of the Dark Ages, when literate life almost died in Europe, peace-loving, bookwormish monks fled the chaos of the Continent and its barbarian raids. They sailed to this drizzly fringe of the known world and lived their monastic lives in lonely stone igloos or "beehive huts," which you'll see dotting the landscape.

Several groups of these mysterious huts, called *clochans*, line the road. Built without mortar by seventh-century monks, these huts take you back. Climb into one. You're all alone, surrounded by dank mist and the realization that it was these monks who kept literacy alive in Europe. To give you an idea of their importance,

The Irish seem to have all the time in the world to share craic *(conversation) with you.*

Charlemagne, who ruled much of Europe in the year 800, imported Irish monks to be his scribes.

It was from this peninsula that St. Brendan, the semi-mythical priest-explorer, is said to have set sail in the sixth century in search of a legendary western paradise. Some think he beat Columbus to North America...by almost a thousand years!

Rounding Slea Head, the point in Europe closest to America, the rugged coastline offers smashing views of deadly black-rock cliffs and the distant Blasket Islands (Na Blascaodai). The crashing surf races in like white horses, while long-haired sheep—bored with the weather, distant boats, and the lush countryside—couldn't care less.

Ireland's top attraction—the friendliest people in Europe

Just off the road you'll see the scant remains of the scant home that was burned by the movie-star equivalent of Lord Ventry as he evicted his potato-eating tenants in the movie *Far and Away.*

Even without Hollywood, this is a bleak and godforsaken place. Sand and seaweed heaped on the clay eventually became soil. The land created was marginal, just barely growing potatoes. Ragged patches of this reclaimed land climb the hillsides. Rocks were moved and piled into fences.

Stacks of history can be read into the stones. From the air, Ireland looks like alligator skin—a maze of stone fences. With unrivaled colonial finesse, the British required Irish families to divide their land among all heirs. This doomed even the largest estates to fragmentation, shrinking lots to sizes just large enough to starve a family. Ultimately, of course, the land ended up in the possession of British absentee landlords. The tiny rock-fenced lots that carve up the treeless landscape remind the farmers of the structural poverty that shaped their history. And weary farmers have never bothered with gates. Even today they take a hunk of wall down, let their sheep pass, and stack the rocks again.

Study the highest fields, untouched since the planting of 1845, when the potatoes never matured and rotted in the ground. You can still see the vertical ridges of the potato beds—a reminder of that year's Great Potato Famine, which eventually, through starvation or emigration, cut Ireland's population by one-quarter.

Take your time at the Gallarus Oratory (c. A.D. 700)—the sight-seeing highlight of your peninsula tour. One of Ireland's best-preserved early Christian churches, its shape is reminiscent of an upturned boat. Its watertight dry-stone walls have sheltered travelers and pilgrims for 1,300 years.

From the oratory, continue up the rugged one-lane road to the crest of the hill, then coast back into Dingle—hungry, thirsty, and ready for...

The enduring Gallarus Oratory

Dingle Pubs

With 40 pubs for its 1,900 people, Dingle is a pub-crawl waiting to happen. Even if you're not into pubs, give these a whirl. The town is renowned among traditional musicians as a place to get work ("€50 cash a day plus drink"). There's music every night and rarely a cover charge. The scene is a decent mix of locals, Americans, and Germans. While two pubs—the Small Bridge Bar (An Droichead Beag) and O'Flaherty's—are the most famous for their good beer and folk music, make a point to wander the town and follow your ear.

On a Dingle evening, follow your ear to a music-filled pub.

When you say "a beer, please" in an Irish pub, you'll get a pint of "the tall blonde in the black dress"—Guinness. If you want a small beer, ask for a half pint. Never rush your bartender when he's pouring a Guinness. It takes time—almost sacred time. If you don't normally like Guinness, try it in Ireland; it doesn't travel well and is better in its homeland. Murphy's is a very good Guinness-like stout, but a bit smoother and milder.

The Irish government passed a law in 2004 making all pubs and restaurants in the Republic smoke-free; Northern Ireland followed in 2007. (Hotels, however, can still have designated smoking rooms.) Smokers now take their pints outside, turning alleys into covered smoking patios. An incredulous Irishman responded to the law by saying, "What will they do next? Ban drinking in pubs? We'll never get to heaven if we don't die."

In an Irish pub, you're a guest on your first night; after that, you're a regular. Women traveling alone need not worry—you'll become part of the pub family in no time.

It's a tradition to buy your table a round, and then for each person to reciprocate. If an Irishman buys you a drink, thank him by saying, *"Go raibh maith agat"* (guh-rev-mah-a-gut). Offer him a toast in Irish— *"Slainte!"* (slahn-chuh). A good excuse for a conversation is to ask to be taught a few words of Irish. You've got a room full of native speakers who will remind you that every year, 10 languages go extinct. They'd love to teach you a few words of their favorite language.

Craic (pronounced "crack") is the art of conversation—the sport that accompanies drinking in a pub. People are there to talk. Join in. Ireland—small as it is—has many dialects. People from Cork (the big city of Ireland's south coast) are famous for talking very fast (and in a squeaky voice)...so fast that some even seem to talk in letters alone. Those from Kerry are famous for being a bit out of it. One joke goes that when the stupidest man in county Cork moved to county Kerry, it raised the average IQ in both areas.

Traditional Irish Music

Traditional music is alive and popular in pubs throughout Ireland. "Sessions" (musical evenings) may be planned and advertised or impromptu. Traditionally, musicians just congregate and play. There's generally a fiddle, flute or tin whistle, guitar, *bodhrán* (goat-skin drum), and maybe an accordion. Things usually get going around 9:30 or 10 p.m. "Last call" (last chance to order a drink before closing) is around "half eleven" (11:30 p.m.), sometimes later on weekends.

The *bodhrán* is played with two hands: one wielding a small two-headed club and the other stretching the skin to change the tone and pitch. The wind and string instruments embellish melody lines with lots of improvised ornamentation. Occasionally the fast-paced music will stop, and one person will sing a lament in a slightly nasal style called *shan nos* (Gaelic for "old style"). This is the one time when the entire pub will stop to listen, as sad lyrics fill the room. Stories—ranging from struggles

Irish pubs—a blur of banjo pickin', flute tootin', great beer, and new friends

against English rule to tragic love songs—are always heartfelt. Spend a lament studying the faces in the crowd.

The music comes in sets of three songs. Whoever happens to be leading determines the next song, only as the song the group is playing is about to be finished. If he wants to pass on the decision, it's done with eye contact and a nod.

A session can be magic, or it can be lifeless. If the chemistry is right, it's one of the great Irish experiences. The music churns intensely while the group casually enjoys exploring each others' musical styles. The drummer dodges the fiddler's playful bow. Sipping their pints, they skillfully maintain a faint but steady buzz. The floor on the musicians' platform is stomped paintfree, and barmaids scurry artfully through the commotion, gathering towers of empty, cream-crusted glasses. With knees up and heads down, the music goes round and round. Make yourself right at home, "playing the boot" (tapping your foot) under the table in time with the music.

Great Blasket Island (An Blascoad Mór)

Great Blasket (An Blascoad Mór in Gaelic), a rugged, uninhabited island off the tip of Dingle Peninsula, seems particularly close to the soul of Ireland. Its population, once as many as 160 people, dwindled until the last handful of residents was moved by the government to the mainland in 1953. These people were one of the most traditional Irish communities of the 20th century—symbols of an antique culture. They had a special closeness to their island, combined with a knack for vivid storytelling. From this poor, primitive, but proud fishing and farming community came three writers of international repute whose works—basically tales of

Ghost town on Great Blasket Island

life on the island—are translated into many languages. In shops all over the peninsula, you'll find *Peig* (by Peig Sayers), *Twenty Years A-Growing* (Maurice O'Sullivan), and *The Islandman* (Tomás O'Crohan).

Today, Great Blasket is a grassy three-mile poem, overrun with memories. With fat rabbits, ruffled sheep, abandoned stone homes, and a handful of seals, it's ideal for windblown but thoughtful walks.

A ferry runs hourly, depending on weather and demand, from Dunquin, at the tip of the Dingle Peninsula, to Great Blasket (April–Sept 10:30 a.m.–2:30 p.m.). A scenic, 2.5-hour Blasket Island circuit cruise leaves from Dunquin Harbor. Boats also depart from Dingle town several times a day.

Before visiting the islands, stop at the state-of-the-art Great Blasket Centre (Ionad An Blascaod Mór, on Dingle Peninsula facing the islands, tel. 066/915-6444). This center creatively gives visitors the best possible look at the heritage, language, literature, life, and times of Blasket islanders. See the fine video, hear the sounds, read the poems, browse through old photos, and then gaze out the big windows at those rugged islands and imagine. Even if you never got past limericks, the poetry of these people—so pure and close to each other and nature—is an inspiration.

For good-value accommodations in **Dingle,** *try Bambury's Guesthouse (Mail Road, tel. 066/915-1244, www.bamburysguesthouse.com, info@bamburys guesthouse.com) or the simpler Sra'd Eoin House (John Street, tel. 066/915-1409, www.sraideoinbnb.com, sraideoinhouse@hotmail.com). For all the travel specifics, see this year's edition of* Rick Steves' Ireland.

65. Northern Ireland and Belfast

Ireland is a split island still struggling with questions left over from its stint as a British colony. While the island won its independence back in the 1920s, the predominantly Protestant northern section opted to stick with its Pope-ophobic partners in London. While somewhere between a headache and a tragedy for locals, this adds up to some fascinating travel opportunities for you and me. And recent history has given everyone some good, solid reasons to be hopeful.

With so many people working so hard to bring Ireland together, a browse through Belfast will give you more faith in people than despair over headlines. There's a guarded optimism as creative grassroots efforts to grow peace are taking hold.

Make your visit to Ireland complete by including Northern Ireland. This is a British-controlled six-county section of a nine-county area

With this Union Jack bulldog street mural, a Belfast Protestant neighborhood makes its Unionist feelings pit-bull-clear.

called Ulster. It offers the tourist a very different but still very Irish world. The British-ruled counties of Northern Ireland, long a secret enjoyed and toured mainly by the country's own inhabitants, are finally being recognized by international travelers.

Of course, people are being killed in Northern Ireland—but not as many as in any major American city. Car accidents kill more Northern Irish than do bombs or guns. With common sense, travel in this area is safe. No American has ever died in "the Troubles," and travelers give Northern Ireland rave reviews.

Include Belfast in your Irish travel plans. Here's an itinerary that will introduce you to this capital city and Ireland's best open-air folk museum. At the same time, you'll meet some of the friendliest people in Europe and learn firsthand about their struggle.

Belfast

Seventeenth-century Belfast was only a village. With the influx, or "plantation," of Scottish and English settlers, Belfast boomed, spurred by the success of the linen, rope-making, and shipbuilding industries. The Industrial Revolution took root with a vengeance. While the rest of Ireland remained rural, Belfast earned its nickname, "Old Smoke," when many of the brick buildings you'll see today were built. The year 1888 marked the birth of modern Belfast. After Queen Victoria granted city status to this town of 300,000, citizens built its centerpiece, City Hall.

Belfast is the birthplace of the *Titanic*...and many other ships that didn't sink. Two huge, mustard-colored cranes (the biggest in the world, nicknamed Samson and Goliath) rise like skyscrapers above the harbor. They stand idle now, but serve as a reminder of this town's former ship-building might.

Today, investments from south of the border—the Republic of Ireland—are injecting quiet optimism into the dejected shipyards where the *Titanic* was built, developing the historic Titanic Quarter. Cranes are building condos along the rejuvenated Lagan riverfront.

It feels like a new morning in Belfast. It's hard to believe that the bright and bustling pedestrian center was once a subdued, traffic-free

Belfast

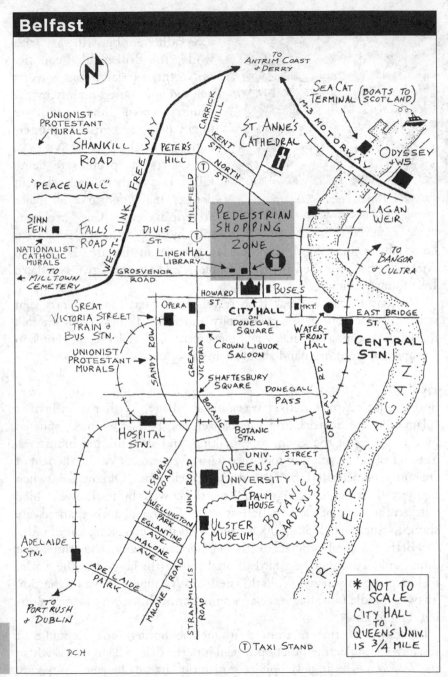

security zone. Now there's no hint of security checks, once a tiresome daily routine. These days both Catholics and Protestants are rooting for the Belfast Giants ice-hockey team, one of many reasons to live together peacefully.

Still, it's a fragile peace and a tenuous hope. Mean-spirited murals, hateful bonfires built a month before they're actually burned, and pubs with security gates are reminders that the island is split...and 800,000 Protestant Unionists prefer it that way.

A visit to Belfast is easy from Dublin. Consider this plan for the most interesting Dublin–Belfast day trip: With the handy two-hour Dublin–Belfast train ($54 "day-return" tickets, more on Fri and Sun), you can leave Dublin early and catch the Belfast City Hall tour at 11 a.m. After browsing through the pedestrian zone, ride a shared black taxi (see below) through the Falls Road neighborhood. At 3 p.m., head out to the Ulster Folk and Transport Museum in Cultra. Picnic on the evening train back to Dublin.

The well-organized day-tripper will get a taste of both Belfast's Industrial Age glory and its recent Troubles. It will be a happy day when the sectarian neighborhoods of Belfast have nothing to be sectarian about. For a look at a couple of the original home bases of the Troubles, explore the working-class neighborhoods of Falls Road (Catholic) and Shankill Road or Sandy Row (Protestant).

At the intersection of Castle and King Streets, you'll find the Castle Junction Car Park. This nine-story parking garage's basement (entrance on King Street) is filled with old black cabs—and the only Irish-language signs in downtown Belfast. These shared black cabs efficiently shuttle residents from outlying neighborhoods up and down the Falls Road and to the city center. All cabs go up the Falls Road to Milltown Cemetery, passing lots of murals and the headquarters of Sinn Fein (the Irish Republican Army's political wing). Sit in front and talk to the cabbie. Easy-to-flag-down cabs run every minute or so in each direction on Falls Road. Forty trained cabbies also do one-hour tours (www.taxitrax.com).

At the Milltown Cemetery, walk past all the Gaelic crosses down to the far right-hand corner (closest to the highway), where the IRA Roll of Honor is set apart from the thousands

Murals reinforce political walls.

of other graves by little green railings. They are treated like fallen soldiers. Notice the memorial to Bobby Sands and nine other hunger strikers. They starved themselves to death in the nearby Maze prison in 1981, protesting for political prisoner status as opposed to terrorist criminal treatment. The prison closed in 2000.

The Sinn Fein office and bookstore are near the bottom of Falls Road. The bookstore is worth a look. Page through books featuring color photos of the political murals that decorate the buildings. Money raised here supports the families of deceased IRA members.

A sad corrugated structure called the Peace Wall runs a block or so north of the Falls Road (along Cupar Way), separating the Catholics from the Protestants in the Shankill Road area. This is just one of 17 such walls in Belfast.

While you can ride a shared black cab through the Protestant Shankill Road area (leave from North Street near the intersection with Millfield Road), the easiest way to get a dose of the Unionist side is to walk Sandy Row—a working-class-Protestant street behind the Hotel Europa (said to be Europe's most-bombed hotel). From Hotel Europa, walk a block down Glengall Street, then turn left for a 10-minute walk along a working-class Protestant street. A stop in the Unionist memorabilia shop, a pub, or one of the many cheap eateries here may give you an opportunity to talk to a local. You'll see a few murals filled with Unionist symbolism. The mural depicting William of Orange's victory over the Catholic King James II (Battle of the Boyne, 1690) stirs Unionist hearts.

Children march in a Protestant Orange parade: Political differences are taught at an early age.

Most of Ireland has grown disillusioned with the violence wrought by the IRA and the Protestants' Ulster Volunteer Force (UVF). They are now seen by many as having evolved into rival groups of gangsters who actually work together, Mafia-style, to run free and wild in their established territories. Maybe the solution can be found in the mellowness of Ulster retirement homes, where old "Papishes" with their rosaries and old "Prods" with their prayer books sit side by side talking to the same heavenly father. But that kind

IRELAND

of peace is elusive. An Ulster Protestant on holiday in England once told me with a weary sigh, "Tomorrow I go back to my tribe."

For a trip into a cozier age, take the eight-mile train ride to the 180-acre Ulster Folk and Transport Museum at Cultra. The Folk Museum is an open-air collection of 34 reconstructed buildings from all over the nine counties of Ulster, designed to showcase the region's traditional lifestyles. After wandering through the old town site (church, print shop, schoolhouse, humble Belfast row home, and so on), you'll head into the country to nip into cottages, farmhouses, and mills. Many houses are warmed by peat fires and friendly attendants. The museum can be dull or vibrant, depending upon your ability to chat with the people staffing each building.

The adjacent Transport Museum (downhill, over the road from the folk museum) traces the evolution of transportation from its beginning 7,500 years ago, when someone first decided to load up an ox, and continues to the present, with an interesting exhibit on the sinking of the Belfast-made *Titanic*. In the next two buildings, you roll through the history of bikes, cars, and trains. The car section goes from the first car in Ireland (an 1898 Benz), through the "Cortina Culture" of the 1960s, to the adventures of John DeLorean (with a 1981 model of his car).

Speeding on the train back to Dublin, gazing at the peaceful and lush Irish countryside while pondering DeLorean, the *Titanic*, and the Troubles, your illusion of a fairy-tale Europe has been muddled. Belfast is a bracing dose of reality.

*For good-value accommodations in **Belfast**, try Malone Guest House (80 Malone Road, tel. 028/9066-9565, www.maloneguesthousebelfast.co.uk, maloneguesthousebelfast@yahoo.co.uk) or Jurys Inn (Fisherwick Place, tel. 028/9053-3500, www.jurysinns.com, jurysinnbelfast@jurysinn.com). For all the travel specifics, see this year's edition of Rick Steves' Ireland.*

SCANDINAVIA

66. Norway in a Nutshell: Oslo and the Fjords

Oslo is the smallest and least earthshaking of the Nordic capitals, but this brisk little city is a scenic *smörgåsbord* of history, sights, art, and Nordic fun. As an added bonus, you'll be inspired by a city that simply has its act together. Add on a "Norway in a Nutshell" excursion over the mountains and to the fjords, and this is potentially one of Europe's best three-day packages of sightseeing thrills.

I am always struck by how peaceful Oslo feels. A congestion fee keeps most cars out of the town center, while a tunnel takes nearly all the rest under the city. The old train station facing the fjord boat landing is now the Nobel Peace Prize Center, which explains the unique vision of Alfred Nobel: the inventor of dynamite who dedicated his fortune to the celebration of peace-makers. The brick City Hall—where the prize is awarded— towers high above the harbor action. On every visit, matching memories from my childhood trips here, I see a weather-beaten sailor standing at the

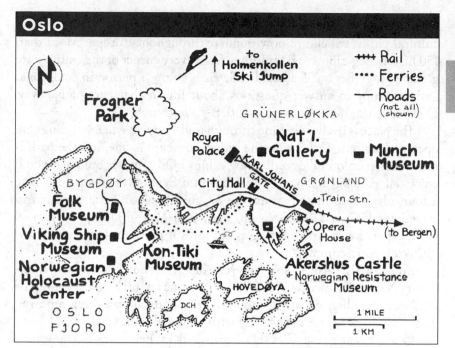

Oslo

to
↑ Holmenkollen
Ski Jump

╋╋╋╋ Rail
•••• Ferries
— Roads (not all shown)

Frogner
Park

GRÜNERLØKKA

Royal
Palace

Nat'l.
■ Gallery

■ Munch
Museum

KARL JOHANS GATE

City Hall

GRØNLAND

BYGDØY

← Train Stn.

Folk
Museum

Viking Ship
Museum

Opera
House

(to Bergen)

Kon-Tiki
Museum

Norwegian
Holocaust
Center

Akershus Castle
+ Norwegian Resistance
Museum

HOVEDØYA

OSLO
FJORD

DCH

1 MILE

1 KM

stern of his boat, hoping to sell the last of the shrimp he caught before sunrise.

On May 17, Norway's national holiday, Oslo bursts with flags, bands, parades, and pride. Blond toddlers are dressed up in colorful ribbons, traditional pewter buckles, and wool. But Oslo—surrounded by forests, near mountains, and on a fjord—has plenty to offer the visitor year-round.

Oslo's most popular sights tell an exciting story of Viking spirit. From the City Hall, hop the ferry for the 10-minute ride to Bygdøy. This cluster of sights reflects the Norwegian mastery of the sea. Some of Scandinavia's best-preserved Viking ships are on display here. Rape, pillage, and plunder were the rage 1,000 years ago in Norway. There was a time when much of a frightened Western Europe closed every prayer with, "And deliver us from the Vikings, amen." Gazing up at the prow of one of those sleek, time-stained vessels, you can almost hear the shrieks and smell the armpits of those redheads on the rampage.

Nearby, Thor Heyerdahl's balsa raft, *Kon-Tiki*, and the polar ship *Fram* illustrate Viking energy channeled in more productive directions. The *Fram*, serving both Nansen and Amundsen, ventured farther north and south than any other ship.

Just a harpoon toss away is Oslo's huge open-air Norwegian Folk

Museum. The Scandinavians were leaders in the development of these cultural parks, which are now popular throughout Europe. More than 150 historic log cabins and buildings from every corner of the country are gathered together on 35 acres. Inside each house, a person in traditional garb is happy to answer questions about life in that part of Norway. Don't miss the 1,000-year-old wooden-stave church.

The place is lively only June through mid-August, when buildings are open and staffed. (Otherwise the indoor museum is fine, but the park is just a walk past lots of locked-up log cabins.) On summer Sundays, you'll enjoy folk dancing at 2 p.m. (mid-May–mid-Sept only). If you don't take a tour, glean information from the $2 guidebook and the informative attendants ($17, or $13 off-season, daily mid-May–mid-Sept 10 a.m.–6 p.m.; off-season daily 11 a.m.–3 p.m., until 4 p.m. on weekends; www.norskfolke.museum.no).

You can also visit Oslo's 700-year-old Akershus Fortress. Its fascinating Nazi-resistance museum shows how one country's spirit cannot be crushed, regardless of how thoroughly it's occupied by a foreign power. The castle itself is interesting only with a guided tour.

Oslo's avant-garde City Hall, finished in 1950, was a communal effort of Norway's greatest artists and designers. Tour the interior. More than 2,000 square yards of bold, colorful murals are a journey through the collective mind of modern Norway. City halls, rather than churches, are the dominant buildings in this your-government-loves-you northern corner of Europe. The main hall of the City Hall actually feels like a temple to good government—the altar-like mural celebrates "work, play, and civic administration." Each December, the Nobel Peace Prize is awarded in this room.

Norway has given the world two outstanding modern artists: Edvard Munch (pronounced "monk") and Gustav Vigeland. Oslo's Munch Museum is a joy. It's small, displaying an impressive collection of one man's work, rather than numbing you with art by countless artists from countless periods. You leave the Munch Museum feeling like you've learned something about one artist, his culture, and his particular artistic "ism"—expressionism. Happily, Munch's

Norwegian art in Oslo's Frogner Park

famous *Scream,* stolen from this museum in 2004, was recovered two years later. You can see another version of *Scream* at Oslo's centrally located National Gallery.

Thirty years of Gustav Vigeland's creativity—in the form of 192 bronze and granite sculptures—are featured at Oslo's Frogner Park. The centerpiece is the 46-foot-tall totem pole of tangled bodies known as the *Monolith of Life.* This, along with the neighboring Vigeland Museum, is a must on any list of Oslo sights.

When the sun's out, all of Oslo's parks are packed. Norwegians are avid sun-worshippers, and a common ailment here is *"solsting"* (a fun twist on sunburn). American visitors will notice a lot of nudity: topless women and naked kids. Scandinavia has a casual approach to nudity. (I'm not talking just mixed saunas. Many Americans are amazed at what's on prime-time TV here.) Parents let their kids run naked in city parks and fountains. It's really no big deal. My friend tells me, "If you ever end up in a Norwegian hospital and need an X-ray, I hope you're not modest. Women strip to the waist and are casually sent from the doctor's office down the hall past the waiting public to the X-ray room. No one notices...no one cares." Norwegians are quick to point out the irony that while America goes into a tizzy over a goofy "wardrobe malfunction," or a president who had a hard time keeping his zipper up, it's the US that statistically has the biggest problem with sex-related crimes.

While traditional Oslo sightseeing is contained in the monumental and classically Norwegian city center, a short walk takes you to the city's two trendy multiethnic zones: Grünerløkka and Grønland.

Grünerløkka—with its funky shops, old hippies, and bohemian cafes—is the Greenwich Village of Oslo. In the 19th century, it was a planned working-class neighborhood. As the factories faded, the low rents attracted artistic types. They injected a creative and edgy ambience to the district which, in turn, attracted young professionals looking to spice up their lives. Eventually the prices will rise too high, and the creative types who gave the area its color in the first place will be forced out. Today, Grünerløkka is still enjoying the alternative crowd...but its bohemian days are numbered.

Bordering Grünerløkka is Oslo's rough-and-tumble immigrant zone—a stretch of a street called Grønland. It's a hit with locals and tourists because this is where Turks, Indians, Pakistanis, and the rest of Oslo's growing immigrant community congregate. Over a quarter of the city's residents are not ethnic Norwegians. These new Norwegians provide a much-needed and generally appreciated labor force.

Oslo's entrepreneurial immigrants also have opened wonderful ethnic restaurants—literally adding spice to the otherwise pretty drab local cuisine. Colorful greengrocers' carts spill onto sidewalks, and the various kebabs and spicy *borek*—about $3 to go—make the cheapest meals in town. Dueling tandoori restaurants actually offer meals for under $15—unheard of in Oslo, which has been called Europe's most expensive city. I'll buy that. Norwegians cope with the high cost of dining out with the *engangsgrill* ("one-time grill"). These foil grills—which cost about $4 at a supermarket—are all the rage. On balmy evenings, the city is perfumed with the smoky fragrance of one-time grills as the parks fill up with Norwegians eating out on the cheap.

Without relatives, life in Oslo on a budget is possible only if you have a good guidebook and take advantage of money-saving options. Budget tricks like picnicking and sleeping in private homes offer the most exciting savings in this most expensive city.

One Day for the Fjords?

If you go to Oslo and don't get out to the fjords, you should have your passport revoked. Norway's greatest claim to scenic fame is its deep

Norway's Sognefjord

and lush fjords. Sognefjord, Norway's longest (120 miles) and deepest (more than a mile), is tops. Anything but Sognefjord is, at best, foreplay. This is it: the ultimate natural thrill Norway has to offer.

For the best one-day look at fjords, do "Norway in a Nutshell." This series of well-organized train, ferry, and bus connections lays this most beautiful fjord country before you on a scenic platter. Ambitious and energetic travelers can see the whole shebang in a day; with more time or less energy, consider an overnight in Bergen (or along the fjord).

Every morning, northern Europe's most spectacular train ride leaves Oslo at about 8 a.m. for Bergen. Cameras smoke as this train roars over Norway's mountainous spine. The barren, windswept heaths, glaciers, deep forests, countless lakes, and a few rugged ski resorts create a harsh beauty. The railroad is an amazing engineering feat. Completed in 1909, it's 300 miles long and peaks at 4,266 feet—which, at this Alaskan latitude, is far above the tree line. You'll go under 18 miles of snow sheds,

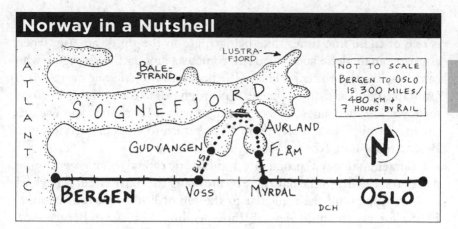

Norway in a Nutshell

ATLANTIC

SOGNEFJORD

LUSTRA-FJORD

BALESTRAND.

NOT TO SCALE
BERGEN TO OSLO
IS 300 MILES/
480 KM +
7 HOURS BY RAIL

AURLAND
FLÅM
GUDVANGEN
BUS

BERGEN   VOSS   MYRDAL   OSLO
DCH

over 300 bridges, and through 200 tunnels in just less than seven hours (about $220 one-way, second-class railpass-holders pay $10 to reserve, reservations required; in peak season—July through mid-August—book several weeks in advance).

At Myrdal, a 12-mile spur line ($40 one-way, or $25 with a railpass) drops you 2,800 breathtaking feet in 55 minutes to the village of Flåm on Sognefjord. This is a party train. The engineer even stops the train for photographs at a particularly picturesque waterfall.

While most "Norway in a Nutshell" tourists zip immediately from the train onto the scenic fjord boat in Flåm, those with time enjoy an overnight stop on the fjord.

Flåm is a handy tourist depot with several simple hotels. Aurland, a few miles north of Flåm, is more of a town. It's famous for producing some of Norway's sweetest *geitost*—goat cheese. Aurland has as many goats as people (1,900). Nearly every train arriving in Flåm connects with a bus or boat to Aurland, also on Sognefjord. While nearby Bergen is famous for its rain—more than six feet a year—Sognefjord is a relative sun belt, with only two feet of rain a year.

The train from Myrdal to Flåm is quite scenic, but the ride doesn't do the view justice. For the best single-day activity from Flåm, take the train to Berekvam (halfway back up to Myrdal), then hike or bike (rentable from the Flåm tourist office) the gravelly construction road back down to Flåm. Bring a picnic and extra camera batteries.

From Flåm, "Nutshellers" catch the most scenic of fjord cruises. Sightseeing boats leave throughout the day ($40 one-way, discounts with a student card). For 90 minutes, camera-clicking tourists scurry on the drool-stained deck like nervous roosters, scratching fitfully for a photo to catch the magic. Waterfalls turn the black-rock cliffs into a bridal fair.

You can nearly reach out and touch the sheer, towering walls. The ride is one of those fine times, like being high on the tip of an Alp, when a warm camaraderie spontaneously combusts among the strangers who came together for the experience. The boat takes you up one narrow arm (Aurlandsfjord) and down the next (Nærøyfjord) to the nothing-to-stop-for town of Gudvangen, where waiting buses ($13) shuttle you back to the main train line at Voss. From Voss, return to Oslo or carry on into Bergen for a short evening visit.

Bergen, Norway's second city and historic capital, is an entertaining place. You can finish the day there by browsing the touristy but fun wharf area, or zipping up the funicular to the top of 1,000-foot-tall "Mount" Fløyen for city and fjord views, before spending the night in Bergen—or, for maximum efficiency, catching the overnight train back to Oslo. Back in Oslo's station, as you yawn and stretch and rummage around for a cup of morning coffee, it'll hit you: You were gone for 24 hours, experienced the fjord wonder of Europe, and saw Bergen to boot.

For good-value accommodations in **Oslo,** *try Thon City Hotel Stefan (Rosenkrantz Gate 1, tel. 23 31 55 00, www.thonhotels.no/stefan) or Oslo Budget Hotel (Prinsens Gate 6, tel. 22 41 36 10, www.budgethotel.no). Sleep cozy near the palace at Ellingsen's Pensjonat (Holtegata 25, tel. 22 60 03 59, www .ellingsenspensjonat.no). For all the travel specifics, see the latest edition of* Rick Steves' Scandinavia.

67. Ærø: Denmark's Ship-in-a-Bottle Island

Few visitors to Scandinavia even notice Ærø, a sleepy, 6-by-22-mile island on the southern edge of Denmark. Ærø has a salty charm. Its tombstones are carved with such sentiments as: "Here lies Christian Hansen at anchor with his wife. He'll not weigh until he stands before God." It's a peaceful and homey island, where baskets of new potatoes sit in front of farmhouses—for sale on the honor system.

Ærø's capital, Ærøskøbing, makes a fine home base. Temple Fielding called it "one of five places in the world that you must see." Many Danes agree,

Main Street, Ærøskøbing

SCANDINAVIA

washing up on the cobbled main drag in waves with the landing of each ferry. The town's preservation is mandated by law.

Ærøskøbing is a town-in-a-bottle kind of place. Wander down lanes right out of the 1680s, when the town was the wealthy home port to more than 100 windjammers. The post office dates to 1749, and cast-iron gaslights still shine each evening. Windjammers gone, the harbor now caters to German and Danish holiday yachts. On midnight low tides, you can almost hear the crabs playing cards.

The Hammerich House, full of old junk, is a 1900s garage sale of a museum open daily in summer. The "Bottle Peter" museum on Smedegade is a fascinating house with a fleet of more

A warm and traditional welcome awaits you at an old-fashioned Danish country inn.

than 750 different bottled ships. Old Peter Jacobsen died in 1960 (and is probably buried in a glass bottle), leaving a lifetime of his tedious little creations for visitors to squint and marvel at.

Touring Ærø by car is like sampling chocolates with a snow shovel. Much better to enjoy a breezy 18-mile tour of Ærø's subtle charms by bike. Borrow a bike from your hotel or rent one from the Pilebækkens Cykler at the top of town. On Ærø, there are no deposits and no locks. If you start in the morning, you could be home in time for a hearty lunch.

Ærø's "night watchman" offers spirited tours of his quaint little burg.

Ready? Leave Ærøskøbing west on the road to Vrå, going past many of the U-shaped farms that are typical of this island. The three sides block the wind and are used for storing cows, hay, and people. *Gaard* (farm) shows up in many surnames. Bike along the coast in the protection of the dike, which turned the once-salty swampland to your left into farmable land. Pedal past a sleek

Denmark's Ærø Island Bike Ride

modern windmill and Borgnæs, a pleasant cluster of mostly modern summer cottages. (At this point, bikers with one-speeds can shortcut directly to Vindeballe.)

After passing a secluded beach, climb uphill over the island's summit to Bregninge. Unless you're tired of thatched and half-timbered cottages, turn right and roll through Denmark's "second-longest village" to the church. Peek inside. Then roll back through Bregninge, head a mile down the main road to Vindeballe, and take the Vodrup turnoff to the right.

A road leads downhill to dead-end at an ancient site on a rugged bluff called Vodrup Klint. If I were a pagan, I'd stop here to worship. Savor the sea, the wind, and the chilling view.

Backtrack and pedal to Tranderup, past a lovely farm and a potato stand. At the old town of Olde, you'll hit the main road. Turn right toward

Store Rise—marked by its church spire in the distance. Just behind the church is a 6,000-year-old Neolithic burial place, the Langdysse (Long Dolmen) Tingstedet. Hunker down. Ærø once had more than 200 of these. Only 13 survive.

Inside the Store Rise church, notice the little ships hanging in the nave, the fine 12th-century altarpiece, and Martin Luther in the stern making sure everything's theologically shipshape.

Continue down the main road passing the church. Consider a stop at the micro-brewery, built on the site of an 1884 dairy. Wing by the hopeful forest of modern windmills whirring on your right and continue to Dunkær.

For the homestretch, take the small road, signed Lille Rise, past the topless windmill. Except for "Lille Rise," it's all downhill as you coast home past great sea views to Ærøskøbing.

After a power tour of big-city Scandinavia, Ærø offers a perfect time-passed island on which to wind down, enjoy the seagulls, and pedal a bike into the essence of Denmark. After a break in this cobbled world you may understand the sailors who, after the invention of steam-driven boat propellers, decided that building ships in bottles was more their style.

For good-value accommodations in Ærø, try Pension Vestergade 44 (Vestergade 44, tel. 62 52 22 98, www.vestergade44.com) or Det Lille Hotel (Smedegade 33, tel. 62 52 23 00, www.det-lille-hotel.dk). For all the travel specifics—including a more thorough description of the bike ride—see the latest edition of Rick Steves' Scandinavia.

THROUGHOUT EUROPE

68. Offbeat Europe

No one planning a trip to Europe needs to be reminded to see Big Ben and the Leaning Tower. But did you know that you can spelunk the sewers of Paris, quaff homebrewed beer with German monks, or ski in Scotland in summer? It's these unexpected experiences that are often the most memorable part of a trip. Here are a few that I've especially enjoyed writing home about.

Salzburg's Super-Soaker Prince: Salzburg's 17th-century Hellbrunn Castle entertains with a garden full of trick fountains and tour guides sadistically soaking tourists. At the touch of a button, paths (and pedestrians) get doused and benches turn into fountains. It's silly fun, especially with kids on a sunny day ($13, closed Nov–March, www.hellbrunn.at).

Belgium's Little Squirt: For more dribbling diversions, stop by Brussels' *Manneken-Pis*, a statue of a young boy urinating, and the irreverent mascot of this great Belgian city. You'll find this little squirt three blocks off the main

Belgium's little squirt

Offbeat Europe

▲ = LUGE

square, La Grand Place. He'll probably be aiming through some clever outfit—by tradition, costumes for the lad are sent to Brussels from around the world. Go figure. Cases displaying scores of these colorful get-ups are on display in Brussels' City Museum.

Frankfurt's Red Light Towers: Near Frankfurt's central station, people killing time between trains can visit one of 20 "Eros Towers"—each a five-story brothel filled with hookers. Frankfurt's prostitutes, who are legal and taxed, note that business varies with the theme of the trade show at the nearby convention center. While Frankfurt's annual auto show is boom time, hookers complain that the world's largest annual book fair is a complete bust. (No, I'm not a customer.) Beware—drug addicts and pushy barkers make this neighborhood feel unsafe after dark.

Europe's Skinniest Park: Paris' skinny, two-mile-long Promenade Plantée Park is a narrow garden walk on a viaduct once used for train tracks. The elevated park, which cuts through lots of modern condos, gives a fun peek into the workaday lives of Parisians today. Staircases lead to the street level, where artsy, offbeat shops (whose rent is subsidized by the city government) fill the viaduct's arches. The park runs

A sliver of a park slices through downtown Paris.

from place de la Bastille, along avenue Daumesnil to Saint-Mandé.

Skiing in Edinburgh: If you'd rather be skiing, the Midlothian Ski Centre, just outside Edinburgh, has an artificial brush-skiing hill with a chairlift, two main slopes, two bunny slopes, and a jump

Boning Up on Europe's Relics

Centuries ago, relics were an important focus of worship. These holy relics, often bones, were the "ruby slippers" of the medieval age.

Cappuccin monks have a thought-provoking habit of hanging their dead brothers out to dry for all to see...for ever and ever, amen.

They gave you power—got your prayers answered and helped you win wars—and ultimately helped you get back to your eternal Kansas.

The bones of monks were venerated, and sometimes even artistically arranged in crypts and chapels. In **Rome's** Cappuccin Crypt, hundreds of skeletons decorate the walls to the delight—or disgust—of the always wide-eyed visitor. The crypt offers unusual ideas in home decorating, as well as a chance to pick up a few of Rome's most interesting postcards. A similar Cappuccin Crypt is a highlight of many visits to **Palermo** in Sicily. In **Évora,** Portugal, osteophiles make a pilgrimage to the macabre "House of Bones" chapel at the Church of St. Francis, lined with the bones of thousands of monks.

Overcrowding in cemeteries has prompted unusual solutions. Austria's tiny town of **Hallstatt** is crammed between a mountain and a lake. Space is so limited that bones get only 12 peaceful buried years in the church cemetery before making way for the newly dead. The result is a fascinating chapel of bones in the cemetery. Each skull is lovingly named, dated, and decorated, with the men getting ivy, and the women, roses. Hallstatt stopped this practice

(www.midlothian.gov.uk). You can rent your gear from local shops. While you're actually skiing over what seems like a million toothbrushes, it feels like snow skiing on a slushy day. It's open nearly year-round (probably closed when it snows). Beware: Doctors are used to treating an ailment called "Hillend Thumb"—digits dislocated when people fall and get tangled in the brush.

The Tide Went Out and Never Came Back: Holland is twice as big today as it was 300 years ago. Why? Because the Dutch have been

Head to Hallstatt's Bone Chapel.

in the 1960s, about the same time the Catholic Church began permitting cremation.

Kutná Hora's ossuary, an hour by train from Prague, is decorated with the bones of 40,000 people, many of them plague victims. The monks who stacked these bones 400 years ago wanted viewers to remember that the earthly church is a community of both the living and the dead. Later bone-stackers were more into design than theology—creating, for instance, a chandelier made with every bone in the human body.

Some cities, such as Paris and Rome, have catacombs. Many cities opened up a little extra space by de-boning graveyards, which used to surround medieval churches. During the French Revolution, **Paris** experienced a great church cemetery land grab. Skeletons of countless Parisians were dug up and carefully stacked along miles of tunnels beneath the city.

Seekers of the macabre can bone up on Europe's more obscure ossuaries, but any tourist will stumble onto bones and relics. Whether in a church, chapel, or underground tunnel in Europe, you might be surprised by who's looking at you, kid.

Kutná Hora's ossuary, decorated Early Ghoulish

"reclaiming" land from the sea using dikes and windmill-powered pumps. During the process, many tiny islands—home to traditional fishing villages—were stranded high and dry in the middle of Dutch farmland. The fishing village of Schokland, once on an island in the Zuider Zee, is one such village. The village has a now-useless lighthouse, and you can walk right up to a buoy that once bobbed in the harbor. A bent and rusty propeller from a WWII English bomber ornaments the village square...a reminder that when farmers first tilled their new soil, they

Pyramid power in Rome

uncovered more than just muck and mollusks.

Roman Pyramid: You don't need to go to Egypt to see an ancient pyramid. Standing 90 feet tall, Rome's pyramid was built in 12 B.C. as a tomb for the Roman Gaius Cestius, after the Cleopatra and Mark Antony scandal brought exotic Egyptian styles into vogue. Later the pyramid was incorporated into Rome's city wall.

Rome's Fake Dome: Rome's St. Ignazio church (near the Pantheon) is a riot of Baroque illusions. As you walk into the church, admire the dome. Keeping your eyes on the dome, walk under and past it. It's false. When the church was built, a nearby monastery didn't want its light blocked by a huge dome, so the flat roof was instead skillfully painted to look like a dome.

The Original Ice Man: The South Tirol Museum of Archaeology in Bolzano, Italy, is an excellent museum. It features "Ötzi the Ice Man," a 5,000-year-old body found frozen with his gear in a glacier by some German tourists in 1991. With the help of informative displays and a great audioguide, you'll learn about life in this prehistoric period way before ATMs. You'll see a convincing reconstruction of Ötzi, and yes, you will actually get to see the man himself—lying peacefully inside a specially built freezer ($13, www.iceman.it).

Tourists get a chilly reception from this reproduction of Bolzano's Ötzi the Ice Man.

Choco-Sightseeing: Along with its rich culture, Europe is loved for its delicious chocolate. All day long, rivers of molten chocolate work their way through factories into small foil packages. While chocolate factories generally give tours only to clients or groups, many have museums, showrooms, video presentations, and free tasting rooms where visitors are welcome. Chocoholics love the Imhoff Chocolate Museum in Köln. Their self-proclaimed "Mmmuseum" takes you on a well-described-in-English tour from the origin of the cocoa bean to the finished product. You can see displays on the culture of chocolate and watch treats trundle down the conveyor belt in the functioning chocolate factory, the museum's highlight. The top floor's exhibit of chocolate advertising is fun. Sample sweets from the chocolate fountain, or take some home from the fragrant choc-full gift shop ($11, www.schokoladen museum.de).

Skinny-Dipping in Downtown Munich: Munich's Central Park, the Englischer Garten, offers a variety of offbeat things to explore. Up to 300,000 residents commune with nature here on a hot summer day...many of them buck naked. Nudism, denoted by the code letters "F.K.K." (Freikörperkultur, free body culture), is perfectly legal and widely practiced here. It's quite a spectacle to most Americans (they're the ones riding their bikes into the river and trees).

Munich's English Garden offers more than nude sunbathing. Surfers "hang ten" in the rapids of the city's little river.

Well-Fed Geese: At various farms in France's Dordogne region, you can watch *la gavage:* farmers force-feeding geese to fatten up their livers for the local specialty, foie gras. In a kind of peaceful, mesmerizing trance, the farmer rhythmically grabs a goose by the neck, pulls him under his leg and stretches him up, slides a tube down to the belly, and fills it with corn. He pulls the trigger to squirt the corn, slowly slides the tube up the neck and out, holds the beak shut for a few seconds, lets that goose go, and grabs the next. As their livers swell, the geese take on a special shape—like they're waddling around with a full diaper under their feathers (a mouthwatering symbol for foie gras fanatics). While some people consider this treatment inhumane, the

Foie gras in the making

farmers have their own perspective: The free-range geese are calm, in no pain, and have an expandable liver and no gag reflex. They ask: Are these geese really any worse off than the many hormone-fed farm animals slaughtered after living in cages?

Monk Brewers: Imagine a fine Bavarian Baroque church at a monastery that serves hearty food and perhaps the country's best beer, in a carnival setting full of partying Germans. That's the Andechs monastery, crouching happily between two lakes at the foot of the Alps, just south of Munich. Come ready to eat tender chunks of pork, huge soft pretzels, spiraled white radishes, and savory sauerkraut, and to drink Andecher monk-made beer—so good that it would almost make celibacy tolerable. Everything is served in medieval portions; two people can split a meal. Andechs has a fine picnic center offering first-class views and second-class prices (tel. 08152/3760). From Munich without a car, take the S-5 train to Herrsching and catch a sporadic shuttle bus, taxi, or hike three miles. Don't leave before strolling up to see the church.

A Swiss Urban River Promenade: In Bern, join the merchants, students, and carp in a lunchtime float down the Aare River. The Bernese, proud of their health and their clean river, have a wet tradition. On hot summer days, they hike upstream and float back down to the excellent (and free) riverside baths and pools *(Aarebad)* just below the Parliament building. While the locals make it look easy, this can be dangerous—the current is swift. If you miss the last pole,

If you miss the last pole, you're history.

you're history. If the river is a bit much, you're welcome to enjoy just the pools, and watch this fast-flowing fun from the sidelines.

Paris' Historic Sewers: In Paris, the Sewer Tour takes you along a few hundred yards of an underground water tunnel, lined with interesting displays, well-described in English, that explain the evolution of the world's longest sewer system. Flush hard: If you lined up Paris' sewers end to end, they would reach beyond Istanbul ($6, closed Thu–Fri, located where pont de l'Alma greets the Left Bank).

The Peat Spas of Třeboň: The small Czech town of Třeboň is famous for its spa, where people come from near and far to soak in peat. Immersed in a *One Flew Over the Cuckoo's Nest* ambience, patrons are

ushered to a changing cubicle, strip naked, then climb into a big steel tub. The peat muck only flows at the top of the hour, when the attendant pulls a plug and you quickly disappear under a rising sea of dark-brown peat broth...like a gurgling sawdust soup. When finished, you shower and lie face-down (in what feels like a nurse's office with a pile of dirty sheets stacked in the corner) for a vigorous massage. You walk out with your shirt stuck to your skin by a mucky massage cream...wondering what soaking in that peat soup was supposed to accomplish.

Swiss Military Readiness: Travelers marvel at how Swiss engineers have conquered their Alps with the world's most-expensive-per-mile road system. But no one designs a Swiss bridge or tunnel without designing its destruction. Each comes with built-in explosives so that, in the event of an invasion, the entire country can be blasted into a mountain fortress. When driving, notice ranks of tank barriers lined up like giant Tic-Tacs along strategic roadsides. As you approach each summit, look for the explosive patches ominously checkering the roads.

In Switzerland, fake barns hide guns and underground shelters.

But the Swiss are realizing that the cost of maintaining their strategic defense initiative is no longer justified. In fact, many of the country's 15,000 secret underground military installations are being decommissioned, and some are being opened to the public as museums.

The Fortress Fürigen Museum of War History offers a rare glimpse into Swiss military preparedness. This little country dug some 20,000 bunkers into the sides of the Alps—and the Festung Fürigen, built during World War II, is one of the few open to the public. Tour the kitchen, hospital, dorms, and machine-gun nests ($5, April–Oct open to public on weekends, tel. 041-618-7522). It's in Stansstad on Lake Luzern, a 15-minute train ride from Luzern.

Ride the Luge: The *Sommerrodelbahn* is one of the most exhilarating alpine experiences. Speed demons spend entire summer days riding chairlifts up in order to "luge" down the concrete bobsled courses on oversize skateboards. You sit with a brake stick between your legs. Push to go fast. Pull to stop. Luge courses are normally open daily in the summer 9 a.m. to 5 p.m., and each ride costs $5–10. The course banks on the corners, and even a first-timer can go very, very fast. Most are careful on their first run and really rip on their second. To avoid a slow-healing souvenir, keep both hands on your stick. You'll rumble, windblown and smile-creased, across the finish line with one thought on your mind— "Do it again!"

You've got several luge options. In the French mountain resort of Chamonix, at the base of Mount Blanc, two concrete courses run side by side (the slow one marked by a tortoise and the fast one marked by a hare). In Austria, south of Salzburg on the road to Hallstatt, you'll pass two metal courses: one near Wolfgangsee (scenic with grand lake views) and one at Fuschlsee (half as long and cheaper).

In Germany and Austria, near "Mad" King Ludwig's Neuschwanstein Castle, you'll find two courses. One is in Austria, just beyond Biberwier (under Zugspitze, Germany's tallest mountain); the Biberwier Sommerrodelbahn is the longest in Austria at 4,000 feet. And just a mile from Neuschwanstein is Germany's Tegelberg course—because it's metal rather than concrete, it's often open when the other course has closed at the least sprinkle of rain.

Head for the hills, or go underground. Anywhere in Europe, the offbeat sights are a fun way to get some distance from the crowds and lighten up a heavy-duty museum itinerary.

69. The Flavors of Europe

In my quest to experience Europe as the locals do—intimately and on all fronts—I make a point to eat well. In a given year, I'm lectured by a Belgian woman who tells me that the guts are the absolute best part of a crab. I crunch into the cartilage of a prized plate of pigs' ears on a back street in Madrid. And I pay a ransom for barnacles, gathered at great risk by teams of divers off the coast of Galicia in northwest Spain. (How do you eat barnacles? With a simple twist, rip, and bite.) Eating well wherever I go, I find my budget survives and my trip is always the better for it. While each country vies for my favor, France and Italy contribute most to my noticeably expanding waistline.

To fully enjoy the art of eating in France, my daughter Jackie and I decide to take an all-day class with a renowned Parisian cook. We prowl

through the market with her, gather the needed ingredients, cook it all up in her kitchen, and (of course) devour the delicious fruits of our labor...all spiced with lots of tips, philosophy, and attitude.

When it comes to cuisine, there's no false modesty among French chefs. Our chef cooks with strong principles: "In France, we love fat because fat is where the flavor is...never cook with a wine you wouldn't drink...in America, you just don't have a great leek culture...it's always a good thing to let your meat rest, you know...water is the friend of the enemy...pat your pears."

Wandering with her from shop to shop and through a bustling market, we learn plenty: Baking and pastry are separate arts; a chef can't do both well. (Go to a *boulangerie* for bread, and a *patisserie* for pastry.) Fish shops need to indicate how the fish was caught: *pêché en* means fished rather than farmed; *élevé en* is "raised" on a fish farm. Poultry sold with the head attached is a sign of freshness.

My favorite discovery: a bottle of Fleur de Sel, the top crust of hand-harvested sea salt (generally from Brittany). This grappa of salt—which you sprinkle by the pinch—is $10 very well spent.

After Jackie flies home, I continue my dogged quest for great-yet-affordable taste treats on the road—this time by working on the restaurant listings in my Paris guidebook.

Restaurateurs dazzle me with their cooking: gizzard salads, made of fresh greens with rich kidneys and gizzards; crêpes, where something magic happens to Emmentaler cheese when it's cooked in all that butter; escargot, with a hot plate to keep the sauce steamy for dipping the crunchy bread into the garlic.

I experience high-class eating with Dominique—as fragile and elegant as her petite restaurant—who forces me to empathize with those force-fed geese by force-feeding *me* the foie gras. And I enjoy quality food at budget prices in a Greek restaurant with plastic tables. I ask, "Do you have yogurt with honey?" They say, "Sure, we're Greek," and bring me a bowl that takes me straight to Santorini.

In Paris, you can't escape the desserts: the ritual cracking of the caramelized crust of a crème brûlée...the tangy peach sorbet drenched in liqueur that you lap up like a thirsty puppy...and plates of pastel mini-macaroons (pistachio, rose, mint, or raspberry) served with tea at the palatial Laudrée café on the Champs-Elysées.

I'm not a food sophisticate, but I love people—especially cooks—who love their work. Monsieur Isaac, the self-proclaimed "ace of falafels" in the Jewish Quarter, brags, "I've got the biggest pita on the street...and I fill it up!"

When I head south to Italy, it seems the entire country is singing, *"Mangia, mangia."* In the rugged Riviera villages of the Cinque Terre, people are famously passionate about their food. In Vernazza, Giovanni makes pasta. "I like the pasta too much," he says, holding a belly far bigger than mine.

Alessandro has clearly found his niche. Rolling his cart into Vernazza for the weekly market as he has every Tuesday for 23 years, he sells porcini mushrooms, dried cod, and sturdy parmesan cheese to Vernazzan shoppers who've proudly never set foot in a big city mall.

Valerio, a waiter in my favorite Riviera restaurant, is evangelical about the beauties of anchovies. Knowing I want to teach Americans the wonders of Italian anchovies, he brings me a plate with the little fish prepared four ways and says, "It's not harsh and cured in salt like yours in America. I know, people in America say, 'Pizza—but hold the anchovies.' Our anchovies were swimming yesterday—they are fresh. Taste this."

Further south and far from the sea, the Tuscan landscape is dotted with *agriturismos*. These traditional family farms rent out spare rooms to make ends meet—and to show off Italy's knack for fine country living. Signora Gori, who runs a noble old farm, takes me on a walk through her estate. As a horrendous chorus of squeals comes from a rustic slaughter-house on the horizon, she says, "This is our little Beirut." But the view is lush, pristine, and tranquil.

Taking me into a room dominated by a stainless steel table piled with red sides of pork, she declares, "And here we make the prosciutto." Burly men in aprons squeeze the blood out of hunks of meat the size

of dancing partners. Then they cake the ham in salt to begin a curing process that takes months. While the salt helps cure the meat, a coating of pepper seals it. In spooky but great-smelling rooms, racks of hanging hams age. A man, dressed and acting like a veterinarian, tests each ham by sticking it with a horse-bone needle and giving it a sniff.

Passing a sty dominated by a giant pig nicknamed Pastenetto ("the little pastry"), Signora Gori escorts me into the next barn, where fluffy white lambs jump to wobbly attention in their hay. Backlit, it's a dreamy, almost biblical scene. Picking up a baby lamb, she explains, "We use unpasteurized milk in making the pecorino cheese. This is allowed but only with strict health safeguards. I must really know our sheep."

This close-to-the-land-and-animals food production is part of Italy's Slow Food movement (www.slowfood.it). Advocates believe there's more to life than increasing its speed. They produce and serve food in the time honored way. It may be more labor-intensive and expensive, but it's tastier and—just as important—connects consumers more directly with their food. They know who made it and how.

On the far side of the farm, the son empties his last bucket of purple grapes into the dump truck, and it—in turn—unloads into a grinder that munches through the bunches. The machine spits stems one way and juice (with mangled grapes) the other. Following that promising little river into the cellar, we're surrounded by tall vats of aging grape juice. My guide jokes that while making wine is labor-intensive, right now the grapes are doing all the work. And as they ferment, we head home to dinner.

Around a long, rustic table polished by many decades of feasting, the entire Gori family—three generations surrounded by heirlooms from many more—gathers and welcomes their American guest. It's a classic Tuscan table: simplicity, a sense of harmony, no hurry, and a glass of fine red wine.

A key word for your Tuscan travels is *corposo*—full-bodied. Lifting the elegant glass to my lips, I sip, while enjoying the pride in the eyes of a family so comfortably and happily rooted in their heritage and cultural soil. Entirely satisfied, I say, *"Corposo."* They say, *"Si, bravo."*

As I dip my bread in extra-virgin olive oil and savor a slice of their prosciutto, my friends explain that great wine goes best with simple food. With each bite and every sip, I better understand the art of Tuscan living—and why I'll always hunger to return to Europe.

70. Alpine Escapes

Even those who know a Rocky Mountain high find something special about the Alps. In the Alps, nature and civilization mix it up comfortably, as if man and mountain shared the same crib.

Imagine walking to the long, legato tones of an alpenhorn. Then, just when you need it most, there's a mechanical lift to whisk you silently and effortlessly—if not cheaply—to the top of that staggering ridge or peak, where your partner can snap a photo of you looking ruggedly triumphant. You'll pass happy yodelers, sturdy grannies, and dirndl'd moms with apple-cheeked kids.

While the most famous corners are now solidly in the domain of tour groups, much of the best alpine charm is folded away in no-name valleys, often just over the ridge from the Holiday Inns and the slap-dancing stage shows.

Here are a few places that will make your alpine adventures more than a scenic hike.

Log-Cabin Villages: Both Switzerland and Austria have isolated log-cabin villages, smothered with alpine goodness, set in a flower-speckled world of serene slopes, lazy cows, and musical breezes. While both Taveyanne and Fallerschein are barely accessible by car, they're worth circling on the map if you suspect you may have been Kit Carson in a previous life.

The village of Taveyanne is in the French-speaking part of Switzerland, two miles off the road from Col de la Croix to Villars (or take the footpath from Villars). It's just a jumble of log cabins and snoozing cows stranded all alone at 5,000 feet. The only business in town is the Refuge de Taveyanne, where the Siebenthal family serves hearty meals—great fondue and a delicious *croute au fromage avec oeuf*—in a prize-winning, rustic setting. Who needs electricity? There's a huge charred fireplace with a cannibal-size cauldron, a prehistoric cash register, low-beamed ceilings, and well-hung ornamental cowbells. For a memorable experience—and

Alpine Escapes

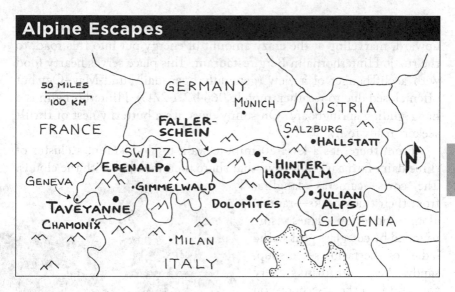

the only rentable beds in the village—rent one of five mattresses in their primitive loft (accessed by an outdoor ladder, bathroom outside, $15/person, open May–Oct, closed Mon and Tue except July–Aug, tel. 024-498-1947).

You can hike...or frolic...from France to Slovenia and never come out of the Alps.

The similarly remote village of Fallerschein is in western Austria, south of Reutte. Thunderstorms roll down its valley as if it were God's bowling alley. But the blissfully simple pint-size church on the high ground seems to promise that this huddle of houses will remain standing. The people sitting on benches are Austrian vacationers or clandestine lovers who've rented cabins. Fallerschein is notorious as a hideaway for those having affairs. The town is 4,000 feet high at the end of a one-mile road near Namlos, on the Berwang road south of Reutte, in Austria's Tirol.

Hinterhornalm over Gnadenwald: The same mountains that put Innsbruck on the vacation map surround Hall. For a lazy look at life in the high Alps around these towns, drive up to 5,000-foot Hinterhornalm and walk to a remote working farm.

Begin your ascent in Gnadenwald, a chalet-filled village sandwiched between Hall and its Alps. Pay $7 at the toll hut, then wind your way upward, marveling at the crazy amount of energy put into this road, to the rustic Hinterhornalm Berg restaurant. This place serves hearty food with a cliffhanger of a view (generally open daily mid-May–Oct but often closed due to weather, mobile 0664/211-2745). Hinterhornalm is a hang-gliding springboard. On sunny days, it's a butterfly nest of thrill-seekers ready to fly.

From there, it's a level 20-minute walk to Walderalm, a cluster of three dairy farms with 70 cows that share their meadow with the clouds. The cows—cameras dangling from their thick necks—ramble along ridge-top lanes surrounded by cut-glass peaks. The ladies of the farms serve soup, sandwiches, and drinks (very fresh milk in the afternoon) on rough plank tables. Below you spreads the Inn River Valley and, in the distance, tourist-filled Innsbruck.

A firsthand look at fairy-tale alpine culture is just a hike away at Walderalm, near Gnadenwald.

Ebenalp in Appenzell: Switzerland's Appenzell is a region whose forte is cow culture rather than staggering peaks. Its only famous peak, Säntis, is a modest 8,200 feet high. For a fun angle on alpine culture, go five miles south of Appenzell town to Wasserauen and ride the lift to the top of nearby Ebenalp ($27 round-trip). From its summit, enjoy a sweeping view of a major chunk of Switzerland. Then hike down about 15 minutes to a prehistoric cave home (its tiny museum is always open). Wander in and through until you reach a narrow, sunny ledge. Perched here is the Wildkirchli, a 400-year-old cave church that housed hermit monks from 1658 to 1853. Also clinging precariously to the cliffside is Berggasthaus Aescher. This rugged guest house, originally built to accommodate those who came here to pray with a hermit monk, now bunks hikers communing with nature.

Rather than sleep in the unmemorable town of Appenzell, stay in the Berggasthaus Aescher ($40/dorm bed, includes breakfast and comforter, no sheets required or provided, Family Knechtle-Wyss, 12 min by steep trail below top of lift, closed Nov–April, tel. 071-799-1142, www.aescher-ai.ch). This old house has only rainwater and no shower. The goats live inside a neighboring hut. The Berggasthaus is sometimes quiet and sometimes festive (locals party until the wee hours on weekends). While Saturdays can be packed with more hikers than mattresses, you'll usually get a small woody dorm to yourself.

The hut is actually built onto the cliffside; the back wall is rock. Study this alpine architecture—and geology—from the toilet. Sip your coffee on the deck, behind a curtain of water dripping from the gnarled overhang a hundred yards above. Leave a note in the guest book, which goes back 60 years.

From this perch, cows look like dandruff littering meadows on the far side of the valley. In the distance, below Säntis, an hour's walk away, is the alpine lake Seealpsee and Wasserauen. Only the hang gliders, like neon jellyfish, tag your world as 21st-century.

A Swiss cliff-hanger of a hideaway: Berggasthaus Aescher on Ebenalp

Slovenia's Julian Alps: Tiny, undiscovered Slovenia (part of Yugoslavia until 1992) offers fine alpine scenery with a Slavic twist. The northwestern corner of Slovenia is crowned by the Julian Alps, which are laced with hiking paths, blanketed in a deep forest, and speckled with ski resorts and vacation chalets. Beyond every ridge is a peaceful alpine village nestled around a quaint Baroque steeple.

Visiting Lake Bled's picturesque island is a must. Hire a traditional *pletna* boat to row you out to the island, which is capped by a super-cute church. Ninety-eight steps lead from the dock up to the Church of the Assumption on top. Grooms prove themselves "fit for marriage" by carrying their brides all the way up.

The single best day in the Julian Alps is spent driving up and over the breathtaking Vršič (vur-SHEECH) Pass and back down via the Soča (SOH-chah) River Valley. There are 50 hairpin turns—24 on the way up, 26 on the way back down—each one numbered and labeled with the altitude in meters. Curling on twisty roads between the peaks, visitors enjoy stunning high-mountain scenery, thought-provoking World War I sights, and charming hamlets.

A humble little Orthodox chapel at switchback #8 honors the 10,000 Russian POWs who built this road during World War I. In 1916, an avalanche thundered down the mountains, killing hundreds of workers. The chapel was built where the final casualty was found.

The road crests at just over 5,000 feet, where a mountain hut offers stunning alpine views. Twisting back down the other side of the mountains, the road deposits drivers in the valley of the Soča River. The Soča—with water somehow both crystal clear and spectacularly turquoise—is a mecca for kayakers and other whitewater adventurers, who call it "Adrenaline Valley."

Beautiful as it is, the Soča Valley saw some of the fiercest fighting of World War I. Known as the Soča Front—or the Isonzo Front in Italian—the million casualties here gave it the nickname "Valley of the Cemeteries." The fighting here between the Italian and Austro-Hungarian armies was waged not in the valleys, but at the tops of the mountains.

The valley's World War I sights are concentrated in the humble village of Kobarid. This town was immortalized by Ernest Hemingway, who drove a Red Cross ambulance nearby (and later wrote about Kobarid in *A Farewell to Arms*).

Kobarid's excellent museum offers a haunting look at the tragedy of the Soča Front. The tasteful exhibits, with a pacifist tone, focus not on the guns and heroes, but on the big picture of the front and on the stories of the common people who fought and died here.

For a powerful finale to your museum visit, head up to the hilltop just above town. Built in Fascist style under Mussolini (in 1938), this octagonal pyramid holds the remains of 7,014 Italian soldiers. Names are listed alphabetically, along with mass graves for more than 1,700 unknown soldiers *(militi ignoti)*.

Only Slovenia combines alpine thrills, World War I history, and Slavic culture...all within yodeling distance of Austria and Italy.

Italy's Dolomites: Italy's own stretch of Alps is just over the border from Slovenia's. For all the details, turn to Chapter 39: North Italy Choices: Milan, Lakes, or Mountains.

...And More Alps: For even more high-mountain thrills, see Chapter 48: From France to Italy over Mont Blanc; Chapter 52:

Hallstatt, in Austria's Commune-with-Nature Lake District; and Chapter 53: Gimmelwald: For the Swiss Alps in Your Lap.

71. Dungeons and Dragons: Europe's Nine Most Medieval Castle Experiences

Castles excite Americans. Medieval fortresses are rotting away on hilltops from Ireland to Israel, from Sweden to Spain, lining the Loire and guarding harbors throughout the Mediterranean. From the west coast of Portugal to the crusader city of Rhodes, you'll find castle thrills lurking in every direction.

Europe's Best Castles

Most of Europe's castles have been discovered, but some are forgotten, unblemished by entrance fees, postcard racks, and coffee shops, and ignored by guidebooks. Since they're free, nobody promotes them. The aggressive traveler finds them by tapping local sources, such as the town tourist office and the friendly manager of your hotel or pension.

Stroll inside the ramparts to see what life was really like in those places your childhood bedtime tales reserved for fairy princesses and Prince Charmings. Life in the Middle Ages was actually a lot like the people: nasty, brutish, and short. In cities, there was some measure of safety and security, but the countryside was the domain of outlaw bands of "merry men," who invaded farms and villages to fill their pockets and satisfy their thirst for violence. In those days, the difference between robbers and armies was only a matter of "how big."

Most countryside castles began not as palaces for princes, but as armored bunkers for landowners, protecting their harvest, hired hands, and any foolhardy traveler who might pass through (some castles also "protected" key roads and rivers, extorting tolls from all who passed).

A real castle had all the romance of a fallout shelter. Sure, it had a lofty tower or two, but only to spot trespassers and to give attackers second thoughts. When the bad guys came knocking, a negotiated ransom was the typical outcome—not a swashbuckling battle.

In the 17th and 18th centuries, large-scale European wars made these castles handy tactical tools. But for the most part, they became obsolete against ever-growing armies and cannons (and between wars, better law enforcement made the countryside safer). Most castles fell into ruin, used as quarries to build more practical things.

Suddenly, in the late 19th century, everything changed. Under the Prussian leadership of Bismarck, the Germanic cluster of mini-states quickly came together as a single powerful nation. There was a great surge in German nationalism, and a popular obsession with "roots," both real and Romantic. Wagner's fairy-tale operas and King Ludwig II's re-created castles epitomized the new German "pop history," which was rewritten to express the ideal spirit of German-ness instead of its grim reality. Modern tourism took root during this same time. So there was not only a patriotic spirit, but also an economic incentive behind the "reinterpreting" of castles in a Romantic style. A few short decades later, Walt Disney made the fairy-tale castle his trademark, and ("authentic" or not) the rest is history.

What travelers see today is a muddle of Middle Age bunker mentality and 150-year-old Romantic renovation...which also happens to be real. While confusing, this weird mix makes for great sightseeing.

Visiting Europe can overwhelm you with too many castles to tour in too little time. To help you prioritize, here are my favorites: nine medieval castles—some forgotten, some discovered—where the winds of the past really howl.

Carcassonne, France

Before me lies Carcassonne, the perfect medieval city. Like a fish that everyone thought was extinct, Europe's greatest Romanesque fortress-city somehow survives.

Medieval Carcassonne is a 13th-century world of towers, turrets, and cobblestone alleys. It's a walled city and Camelot's castle rolled into one, frosted with too many day-tripping tourists. At 10 a.m., the salespeople stand at the doors of their main-street shops, their gauntlet of tacky temptations poised and ready for their daily ration of customers. But

Best stormed early or late

an empty Carcassonne rattles in the early morning or late-afternoon breeze. Enjoy the town early or late. Spend the night.

I was supposed to be gone yesterday, but it's sundown and here I sit—imprisoned by choice—curled in a cranny on top of the wall. The moat is one foot over and 100 feet down. Happy little weeds and moss upholster my throne. The wind blows away many of the sounds of today, and my imagination "medievals" me.

Twelve hundred years ago, Charlemagne stood below with his troops, besieging the town for several years. As the legend goes, just as food was running out, a cunning townswoman had a great idea. She fed the town's last bits of grain to the last pig and tossed him over the wall. Splat. Charlemagne's restless forces, amazed that the town still had enough food to throw fat party pigs over the wall, decided they'd never succeed in starving the people out. They ended the siege, and the city was saved. Today, the walls that stopped Charlemagne open wide for visitors.

Warwick Castle, England

From Land's End to John O'Groats, I searched for the best castle in Britain. I found it. With a lush, green, grassy moat and fairy-tale fortifications, Warwick Castle will entertain you from dungeon to lookout

Warwick Castle—for kings and queens of any age

(www.warwick-castle.co.uk). Standing inside the castle gate, you can see the mound where the original Norman castle of 1068 stood. Under this mound (or motte), the wooden stockade (bailey) defined the courtyard as the castle walls do today. The castle is a 14th- and 15th-century fortified shell holding an 18th- and 19th-century royal residence surrounded by dandy gardens, landscaped by Lancelot "Capability" Brown in the 1750s.

There's something for every taste—an educational armory, a terrible torture chamber, a knight in shining armor on a horse that rotates with a merry band of musical jesters, a Madame Tussauds re-creation of a royal weekend party with an 1898 game of statue-maker, a queenly garden, and a peacock-patrolled, picnic-perfect park. The great hall and staterooms are the sumptuous highlights. The "King Maker" exhibit (it's 1471 and the townsfolk are getting ready for battle...) is highly promoted but not quite as good as a Disney ride. Be warned: The tower is a one-way, no-backing-out, 250-step climb offering a view not worth a heart attack. Even with its crowds of modern-day barbarians and its robber-baron entry fee ($29), Warwick's worthwhile.

Eltz Castle, Germany

Burg Eltz is my favorite castle in all of Europe. Lurking in a mysterious forest, it's furnished throughout as it was 500 years ago. Thanks to smart

Eltz Castle, near Cochem, on Germany's Mosel River

diplomacy and clever marriages, Burg Eltz was never destroyed. It's been in the Eltz family for 850 years.

The first *burg* (castle) on the Elz creek was built in the 12th century to protect a trade route. By about 1490, the castle looked like it does today: the homes of three big landlord families gathered around a tiny courtyard within one formidable fortification. Today, the excellent 45-minute tour winds you through two of those homes (the third is the caretaker's residence). The elderly countess of Eltz traces her family back 33 generations; you'll see a photo of her family. She enjoys flowers, and has had the castle's public rooms adorned with grand floral arrangements every week for the last 40 years.

It was a comfortable castle for its day: 80 rooms made cozy by 40 fireplaces and wall-hanging tapestries. Its 20 toilets were automatically flushed by a rain drain. The delightful chapel is on a lower floor. Even though "no one should live above God," this chapel's placement was acceptable because its altar fills a bay window (with nothing built over it), that floods the delicate Gothic space with light. The three families met—working out common problems as if sharing a condo—in the large "conference room." A carved jester and a rose look down on the big table, reminding those who gathered that they were free to discuss anything ("fool's freedom"—jesters could say anything to the king), but nothing discussed could leave the room (the "rose of silence").

Burg Eltz is between Koblenz and Cochem, about an hour's drive from the Rhine River. The only way to see the inside of the castle is with a 45-minute tour (in English, included with $11 admission ticket, www .burg-eltz.de).

Rheinfels Castle, Germany's Rhineland

Sitting like a dead pit bull above St. Goar, this mightiest of Rhine castles rumbles with ghosts from its hard-fought past. Burg Rheinfels (built in 1245) withstood a siege of 28,000 French troops in 1692. But in 1797, the French Revolutionary army destroyed it.

Rheinfels was huge. Once the biggest castle on the Rhine, it spent the 19th century as a quarry. So today, while still mighty, it's only a small fraction of its original size. This hollow but interesting shell offers your single best hands-on ruined-castle experience on the river.

Even in ruins, Rheinfels is mighty.

A highlight of your Rheinfels experience may be meeting Günther—"the last knight of Rheinfels"—who greets visitors at the turnstile and is a wealth of information.

The massive Rheinfels was the only Rhineland castle to withstand Louis XIV's assault during the 17th century. For centuries, the place was self-sufficient and ready for a siege. Circling the central courtyard, you'd find a bakery, pharmacy, herb garden, animals, brewery, well, and livestock. During peacetime, about 500 people lived here; during a siege, there could be more than 4,000.

Any proper castle was prepared to survive a six-month siege. With 4,000 people, that's a lot of provisions. The count owned the surrounding farmland. Farmers—in return for the lord's protection—got to keep 20 percent of their production. Later, in more liberal feudal times, the nobility let them keep 40 percent. (Today, the German government leaves workers with 60 percent after taxes...and provides a few more services.)

Hike around the castle perimeter. Notice the smartly placed crossbow-arrow slit. Thoop...you're dead. While you're lying there, notice the fine stonework and the chutes high above. Uh-oh...boiling oil...now you're toast.

To protect their castle, the Rheinfellas cleverly booby-trapped the land just outside their walls by building tunnels topped by thin slate roofs and packed with explosives. By detonating the explosives when under attack, they could kill hundreds of approaching invaders. In 1626, a handful of underground Protestant Germans blew 300 Catholic Spaniards to (they assumed) hell.

You're welcome to wander through a set of never-blown-up tunnels. But be warned: It's completely black, unmarked, and with confusing dead-ends. The ground is generally muddy. Assuming you make no wrong turns, it's a 200-yard-long adventure, never letting you walk taller than a deep crouch. It cannot be done without a light (bring a flashlight or candles, available from Günther at the turnstile).

A door blasted through the castle wall takes you to the small, barren prison. You walk through a door prisoners only dreamed of 400 years ago. (They came and went through the little square hole in the ceiling.) The holes in the walls supported timbers that thoughtfully gave as many as 15 miserable residents something to sit on to keep them out of the filthy slop that gathered on the floor. Twice a day, they were given bread and water. Some prisoners actually survived for more than two years in this dark hole. While the town could torture and execute, the castle had permission only to imprison criminals in these dungeons. According to town records, the two men who spent the most time down here—2.5 years each—died within three weeks of regaining their freedom. Perhaps after a diet of bread and water, feasting on meat and wine was just too much.

Germany's Rhine River is filled with castle-crowned hills. These can be enjoyed conveniently by train, car, or boat. The best 50-mile stretch is between Koblenz and Mainz. The best one-hour cruise is from St. Goar to Bacharach.

Château de Chillon, Switzerland

Set romantically at the edge of Lake Geneva near Montreux, this wonderfully preserved 13th-century castle is worth a side-trip from anywhere in southwest Switzerland. Château de Chillon (shee-yon) has never been damaged or destroyed—it's always been inhabited and maintained. Its oldest fortifications date to the 11th century, and the castle was expanded by the Savoy family in the 13th century, when this became a prime location—at a crossroads of a major trade route between England, France, and Rome. It was the Savoys' fortress and residence, with four big halls (a major status symbol) and impractically large lakeview windows (their powerful navy could defend against possible attack by sea).

When the Bernese invaded in 1536, the castle was conquered in just two days, and the new governor made Château de Chillon his residence (and a Counter-Reformation prison). Inspired by the Revolution in Paris, the French-speaking people on Lake Geneva finally kicked out their German speaking Bernese oppressors in 1798. The castle became—and remains—the property of the Canton of Vaud. It has been used as an armory, a warehouse, a prison, a hospital, and a tourist attraction. Rousseau's writings first drew attention to the castle, inspiring visits by Romantics such as Lord Byron and Victor Hugo, plus

Shimmering Château de Chillon

other notables including Dickens, Goethe, and Hemingway.

Attack the castle by ferry (free with a Eurailpass or the Swiss Pass railpass, but it uses up a travel day). Follow the English brochure, which takes you on a self-guided tour through fascinatingly furnished rooms (www.chillon.ch). The dank dungeon, mean weapons, and 700-year-old toilets will excite even the dullest travel partner.

Reifenstein Castle, Italy

For an incredibly medieval kick in the pants, get off the autobahn one hour south of Innsbruck at the Italian town of Vipiteno (called "Sterzing" by residents who prefer German). With her time-pocked sister just opposite, Reifenstein Castle bottled up this strategic valley leading to the easiest way to cross the Alps.

Reifenstein offers castle connoisseurs the best-preserved medieval-castle interior I've ever seen. Take a tour (open Easter–October, three tours daily Saturday–Thursday, closed Fri, tel. 0472-765-879). You'll discover the mossy past as you learn how the cistern collected water, how drunken lords managed to get their keys into the keyholes, and how prisoners were

Rugged Reifenstein Castle

left to rot in the dungeon (you'll look down the typical only-way-out hole in the ceiling). In the only surviving original knights' sleeping quarters (rough-hewn plank boxes lined with hay), you'll see how knights spent their nights. Lancelot would cry a lot.

Moorish Ruins of Sintra, Portugal

The desolate ruins of a 1,200-year-old Moorish castle overlook the sea and the town of Sintra, just west of Lisbon. Ignored by most of the tour-ists who flock to the glitzy Pena Palace (capping a neighboring hilltop), the ruins of Sintra offer a reminder of the centuries-long struggle between Muslim Moorish forces and Christian European forces for the control of Iberia. From 711 until 1492, major parts of Iberia (Spain and Portugal) were occupied by the Moors. Contrary to the sig-nificance that Americans place on the year 1492, Europeans remember the date as the year the Moors were finally booted back into Africa. For most,

Run with the winds of the past in Europe's countless ruined castles. Here in Portugal, with a little imagination, you're under attack over a thousand years ago.

these ruins are simply a medieval funtasia of scramble-up-and-down-the-ramparts delights and atmospheric picnic perches with vast Atlantic views in an enchanted forest. With a little imagination, it's A.D. 800, and you're under attack.

Castle Day: Neuschwanstein (Bavaria) and the Ehrenberg Ruins (Reutte in Tirol)

Three of my favorite castles—two famous, one unknown—can be seen in one busy day. "Castle Day" takes you to Germany's Disney-like Neuschwanstein Castle, the more stately Hohenschwangau Castle at its foot, and the much older Ehrenberg Ruins across the Austrian border in Reutte.

Make the Austrian town of Reutte your home base. (It's just over the German border, three Alp-happy hours by train west of Innsbruck.)

From Reutte, catch the early bus across the border to touristy Füssen, the German town nearest Neuschwanstein. (Planning ahead, note the times buses return to Reutte.) From Füssen, you can walk, pedal a rented bike, or ride a bus a couple of miles to Neuschwanstein.

Neuschwanstein is the greatest of King Ludwig II's fairy-tale castles. His extravagance and Romanticism earned this Bavarian king the title "Mad" King Ludwig...and an early death. His castle is one of Europe's most popular attractions.

You can reserve by calling 08362/930-830 (no later than 6 p.m. on the previous day) or by visiting www.ticket-center -hohenschwangau.de ($13 for one castle, $24 for both, plus $3 per person per castle for the reservation fee). If you don't book ahead, arrive by 8 a.m. to buy a ticket—you'll likely be touring soon after. Your ticket lists appointed times for you to visit Ludwig's boyhood home, Hohenschwangau Castle, and then the neighboring Neuschwanstein on the hill. If you arrive late, you'll spend a couple of hours in the ticket line and may find all tours booked.

Hohenschwangau Castle, where Ludwig grew up, offers a good look at his life. Like its more famous neighbor, it takes about an hour to tour. Afterward, head up the hill to Ludwig's castle in the air.

Neuschwanstein Castle, which is about as old as the Eiffel Tower, is a textbook example of 19th-century Romanticism. After the Middle Ages ended, people disparagingly named that era "Gothic," or barbarian. Then, all of a sudden, in the 1800s it was hip to be square, and neo-Gothic became the rage. Throughout Europe, old castles were restored and new ones built—

Some of Europe's most popular attractions, such as "Mad" Ludwig's castles, sell tickets with entry times. If you don't reserve ahead or arrive early, you'll risk not getting in at all.

wallpapered with chivalry. King Ludwig II put his medieval fantasy on the hilltop not for defensive reasons, but simply because he liked the view.

The lavish interior, covered with damsels in distress, dragons, and knights in gleaming armor, is enchanting. (A little knowledge of Wagner's operas goes a long way in bringing these stories to life.) Ludwig had great taste—for a mad king. Read up on this political misfit—a poetic hippie king in

"Mad" King Ludwig's Neuschwanstein Castle

the realpolitik age of Bismarck. After Bavarians complained about the money Ludwig spent on castles, the 40-year-old king was found dead in a lake under suspicious circumstances, ending work on his medieval fantasy-come-true. After the tour, climb farther up the hill to Mary's Bridge for the best view of this crazy yet elegant castle.

This is a busy day. By lunchtime, catch the bus back to Reutte and get ready for a completely different castle experience.

Pack a picnic and your camera, and with the help of some directions, walk 30 minutes out of town to the brooding Ehrenberg Ruins. You'll see a small hill crowned by a ruined castle.

The Kleine Schloss ("small castle") is really ruined but wonderfully free of anything from the 21st century—except for a fine view of Reutte sleeping peacefully in the valley below.

Standing like a conqueror on a broken piece of wall, imagine how proud Count Meinrad II of Tirol (who built the castle in 1290) would be to know that his castle repelled 16,000 Swedish soldiers in the defense of Catholicism in 1632. When cloaked in a cloud shroud, you can peer into the spooky mist and almost see medieval knights in distress and damsels in shining armor. Grab a sword fern, shake your hair free, and unfetter that imagination.

Recently the ruins have been the focus of an exciting project, spearheaded by Armin Walch and funded in part by the European Union. Walch—the Indiana Jones of Tirolean archaeologists—has excavated an "ensemble" of four castles. Once the largest complex in the region, its purpose was to defend Tirol against Bavaria and northern Europe.

The "toll fort" on the valley floor—which levied duties along the ancient Via Claudia in Roman times—is flanked by Ehrenberg and a sister castle (Fort Claudia) on the opposite side. After locals rained cannon balls on Ehrenberg from the bluff above it, a much bigger castle was built higher up. Over the centuries it became completely overgrown and concealed. Today, the trees have been shaved away, the ruin has been excavated, and Ehrenberg is visible once again.

This is part of a huge project to create a European Castle Museum, using hands-on exhibits and a multimedia theater to show off 500 years of military architecture in one sweep (www.ehrenberg.at).

The brooding Ehrenberg Ruins

The European Union has stepped in to help fund the project because it promotes the heritage of a region (Tirol) rather than a nation. The EU's vision for Europe's future is to help create a continent of "regions" rather than nations.

You can see Ehrenberg's castle reconstructed on Reutte's restaurant walls. Ask at your hotel where you can find a folk evening full of slap-dancing and yodel foolery. A hot, hearty dinner and an evening of Tirolean entertainment is a fitting way to raise the drawbridge on your memorable "Castle Day."

*For good-value accommodations in **Carcassonne**, try Hôtel le Montmorency annex (just outside La Cité and behind Hôtel du Château at 2 rue Camille Saint-Saëns, tel. 04 68 11 96 70, www.lemontmorency.com); in **St. Goar**, Hotel am Markt (Am Markt 1, tel. 06741/1689, www.hotel-am-markt -sankt-goar.de); in **Reutte**, Moserhof Hotel (Planseestrasse 44, in nearby Breitenwang, tel. 05672/62020, www.hotel-moserhof.at); and in **Füssen**, Altstadthotel zum Hechten (Ritterstrasse 6, tel. 08362/91600, www.hotel -hechten.com). For all the travel specifics, see this year's editions of the pertinent Rick Steves' country guides.*

72. Sobering Sites of Nazi Europe

Fondue, nutcrackers, Monet, Big Ben...gas chambers. A trip to once-upon-a-time Europe can be a fairy tale. It can also help tell the story of Europe's 20th-century fascist nightmare. While few travelers go to Europe to dwell on the horrors of Nazism, most people value visiting the memorials of fascism's reign of terror and honoring the wish of its survivors—"Never forget." These

Memorial at the Dachau concentration camp

sites are committed to making the point that intolerance and fascism are still alive and strong. Their message: Fascism can emerge from its loony fringe if we get complacent and think the horrors of Hitler could never happen again.

Why are these sites worth a bit of your vacation? Because you can learn from them. Genocide is as recent as conflicts in Yugoslavia, Rwanda, and Sudan. Even today, Machiavellian politicians can hijack great nations, artfully manipulating fear, patriotism, and mass media to accomplish their aggressive agendas.

Concentration Camps

The most sobering of all Nazi sites are concentration and extermination camps. Of the many concentration-camp memorials in Europe, the most moving is Auschwitz-Birkenau (near Kraków, Poland). Three others are also evocative and convenient to visit: Dachau (just outside Munich), Mauthausen (between Vienna and Salzburg), and Terezín (near Prague).

No sight in all of Europe is as powerful as **Auschwitz-Birkenau** (www.auschwitz.org.pl). This Nazi concentration camp in the Polish town of Oświęcim (a 70-min drive west of Kraków) was the site of the systematic murder of more than a million innocent people.

Auschwitz was the biggest, most notorious concentration camp in the Nazi system...strategically located in the heart of Jewish Europe. Since the Middle Ages, Poland was known for its tolerance of Jews. By the beginning of World War II, Poland had Europe's largest concentration of Jews: 3.5 million. During the Holocaust, the Nazis murdered

Nazi Sites

4.5 million Jews in Poland (many brought in from other countries). Today, only a few thousand Jews live in all of Poland.

A visit to Auschwitz is obligatory for Polish students. You'll often see Israeli high school groups walking through the grounds waving their Star of David flags. Many people, including Germans, leave flowers and messages. One of the messages reads: "Nations who forget their own history are sentenced to live it again."

There are two camps: Auschwitz I and Auschwitz II (better known as Birkenau). Most visitors begin at Auschwitz I. After seeing a grippingly graphic video, you cross under the notorious gate with the cruel message *Arbeit Macht Frei* ("Work sets you free") and into the rows of barracks—each containing an exhibit.

People being transported here, thinking they were going to a new homeland, were encouraged to bring luggage. After they were killed, everything of value was plundered by the Nazis. In these barracks, room after room is literally full to the ceiling of prisoners' personal effects: eyeglasses; fine Jewish prayer shawls; crutches and prosthetic limbs; shoes; suitcases; and even human hair.

The "Death Block," from which nobody ever left alive, is particularly evocative. The Starvation Cell held prisoners selected to starve to death when a fellow prisoner escaped. The Dark Cell, crammed with 30 people at a time, had only a small window for ventilation. If it became

"Work sets you free."

covered with snow, the prisoners suffocated.

Seven hundred people at a time could be gassed in the Auschwitz crematorium. This wasn't efficient enough for the Nazis, so they built a far bigger death camp two miles away. From Auschwitz, a shuttle bus takes visitors to part two of their visit: Birkenau.

At first sight, it's clear: Birkenau is all about the efficient mass production of death. It held 100,000 prisoners and could cremate 16,000 a day. From the top of the guard tower, survey the staggering scope of Birkenau: a few wooden barracks housing exhibits, and a vast field of chimneys—all that remains of the other barracks—stretching nearly as far as the eye can see.

Train tracks lead through the middle of the camp to the dividing platform, where a Nazi doctor would evaluate each prisoner. If he pointed right, the prisoner was sentenced to death, and trudged—unknowingly— to the gas chamber. If he pointed left, the person would be registered and generally worked to death. It was here that families from all over Europe were torn apart forever.

Beyond the dividing platform, the tracks arrive at the finale of this wrenching visit: the ruins of the gas chambers and crematoria. As they entered the undressing rooms, people were given numbered lockers, conned into thinking they were coming back. (The Nazis didn't want a panic.) Then they piled into the "shower room," where they were murdered with poison gas. Their bodies were then burned in one of four giant crematoria. Finally, their ashes were dumped into a ghostly lake.

Birkenau: remembering the Holocaust's mass production of death

The Auschwitz crematoria were destroyed by the Nazis as the Soviet army approached, leaving today's haunting ruins. The Soviets arrived on January 27, 1945, and the nightmare of Auschwitz was over. The Polish parliament quickly voted to turn these grounds into a museum, so that the world would understand, and never forget, the horror of what happened here.

Dachau, near Munich, is a much tamer concentration-camp experience (closed Mon, www.kz-gedenkstaette-dachau.de). While some visitors complain that Dachau is too "prettied-up," it gives a powerful look at how these camps worked. Built in 1933, this first Nazi concentration camp offers a compelling voice from our recent, grisly past, warning and pleading "Never Again"—the memorial's theme. On arrival, pick up the mini-guide and check when the next documentary film in English will be shown. The museum, the movie, the chilling camp-inspired art, the reconstructed barracks, the gas chambers, the cremation ovens, and the memorial shrines will chisel into you the hidden meaning of fascism.

Mauthausen town sits cute and prim on the romantic Danube at the start of the very scenic trip downstream to Vienna. But nearby, atop a now-still quarry, linger the memories of a horrible slave-labor camp. Mauthausen is a solemn place of meditation and continuous mourning. Fresh flowers adorn yellowed photos of lost loved ones. The home country of each victim has erected a gripping monument. You'll find yourself in an artistic gallery of grief, resting on a foundation of Never Forget. Retrace the steep and treacherous steps of the camp's inmates—the "stairway of death" *(Todesstiege)*—to and from the quarry where they worked themselves to death. Mauthausen offers an English booklet, a free audioguide, an English movie, and a painful but necessary museum (www.mauthausen-memorial.at).

Just outside of Prague is **Terezin** concentration camp (Theresienstadt in German, www.pamatnik-terezin.cz). This particularly insidious place was dolled up as a model camp for Red Cross inspection purposes. Inmates put out their own newspaper, and the children put on cute plays. But after the camp passed its inspection, life returned to slave labor and death. Ponder the touching collection of Jewish children's art, also on display in the Pinkas Synagogue in Prague's Jewish Quarter.

You can also visit **Sachsenhausen** near Berlin (www.gedenkstaette -sachsenhausen.de), **Buchenwald** near Weimar (www.buchenwald.de), and many others.

Germany and Austria

Since destruction and death are fascist fortes, only relatively insignificant bits and pieces of Hitler's Germany survive. But as time passes, today's Germans are increasingly aware of the need to remember the horrors that began in their country.

Hitler got his start—and had his strongest support—in the beer halls of **Munich.** The **Munich City Museum** (Münchner Stadtmuseum) traces the origin and development of Nazism. To uncover Nazi sites in Munich, take the **Hitler and the Third Reich walking tour** by Radius Tours (www.radiustours.com). Ironically, we have the Nazis to thank for the accuracy of Munich's postwar reconstruction. When Allied bombings were imminent, Nazi photographers documented Munich's great architecture—allowing it to be rebuilt exactly as it was after the war.

Berlin, now that its Wall is history, is giving its Nazi chapter a little more attention. Most original Nazi sites are hidden. To help you find them, take the **Infamous Third Reich Sites walking tour** by Berlin Walks (www.berlinwalks.com). But don't even bother looking for "Hitler's Bunker"—it's long gone.

Berlin has several Nazi-related museums and memorials. The **Topography of Terror** exhibit illustrates SS tactics (in the ruins of the former SS/Gestapo headquarters, near what was Checkpoint Charlie). The adjacent four small "mountains" are made from the rubble of the bombed-out city. The chilling **Book Burning Monument** commemorates the 20,000 books that were burned on Berlin's Bebelplatz at the order of the Nazis. Glance into the glass floor in the middle of the square (on Unter den Linden) to see a huge underground room with empty shelves. The gripping **Käthe Kollwitz Museum** is filled with art inspired by the horrors of Berlin's Nazi experience. Berlin's **New Synagogue** was burned on Kristallnacht in 1938, but has since been restored. The excellent **Jewish Museum Berlin,** which focuses on Jewish culture, was designed by the American architect Daniel Libeskind. The zigzag shape of the zinc-walled building is pierced by voids, symbolic of the irreplaceable cultural loss caused by the Holocaust (www.juedisches-museum-berlin .de). In nearby **Wannsee** (near Potsdam), you can tour the house where Hitler's cronies came up with the "Final Solution" of the Holocaust (www.ghwk.de).

There was resistance to Hitler even in Berlin. In front of the glass-domed **Reichstag** is a row of slate slabs imbedded in the ground memorializing the 96 politicians who were murdered and persecuted because their politics didn't agree with Chancellor Hitler's. Near the Kulturforum museums is a former military headquarters (Bendlerblock) where conspir-

As Hitler consolidated his power in the 1930s, he arrested 96 members of the German Parliament who opposed him. He sent them to concentration camps, where most perished. This monument, outside the renovated Reichstag where they once worked, is their memorial.

ators plotted an ill-fated attempt to assassinate Hitler—and where they were also shot for the crime. It's now the site of the **German Resistance Memorial** (Gedenkstätte Deutscher Widerstand, free audioguide available). Just outside the city is the **Plötzensee Prison,** where Nazi enemies were imprisoned and executed (www.gedenkstaette-ploetzensee.de).

Berlin's **Memorial to the Murdered Jews of Europe** consists of 2,711 gravestone-like pillars. Completed in 2005, it is the first formal German government-sponsored Holocaust memorial. It's controversial for the focus—just Jews. The government promises to build memorials to the other groups targeted by Hitler. The pillars are made of hollow concrete, each chemically coated for easy removal of graffiti. The number of pillars, symbolic of nothing, is simply how many fit on the provided land. Is it a labyrinth...symbolic cemetery...intentionally disorienting? The meaning is entirely up to the visitor. Beneath the field of concrete pillars is the state-of-the-art information center. This studies the Nazi system of extermination, humanizes the victims, traces stories of individual families and collects vivid personal accounts, and lists 200 different places of genocide. The memorial's location—where the Berlin Wall once stood—is coincidental. It's just a place where lots of people can easily experience it. The bunker of Nazi propagandist Joseph Goebbels was discovered during the work and left buried (under the northeast corner of the memorial). Hitler's bunker is just 200 yards away, under a nondescript parking lot. Such Nazi sites are intentionally left hidden to discourage neo-Nazi elements from turning them into shrines (www.stiftung-denkmal.de).

Berlin's Memorial to the Murdered Jews of Europe is a moving monument to one of history's greatest tragedies.

In Nürnberg, the ghosts of Hitler's showy propaganda rallies still rustle in the **Rally Grounds** (now Dutzendteich Park), down the Great Road, and through the Congress Hall. The north wing of the hall houses the Nazi Documentation Center, with a "Fascination and Terror" exhibit that examines the causes and consequences of the Nazi phenomenon (www.museen.nuernberg.de). Across town is the **Nürnberg Trials Courtroom**—where high-ranking Nazi officers answered to an international tribunal after the war ended.

The town of **Berchtesgaden,** near the Austrian border, is any German's choice for a great mountain hideaway—including Hitler's. The remains of Hitler's Obersalzberg headquarters, with its extensive tunnel system and Nazi Documentation Center, will interest WWII buffs (www.ober salzberg.de).

Hitler's Eagle's Nest, high above Berchtesgaden, is a fascinating bit of Bavaria and an easy side-trip from Salzburg.

Just north of Trier in the town of Irrel is the **Westwall Museum,** with tourable bunkers that made up part of the Nazis' supposedly impenetrable western fortification (closed in winter, www.westwall -museum.de).

On Vienna's Judenplatz, you'll find the **Austrian Holocaust Memorial**—a library turned inside-out to remind visitors that each victim had a story. Nearby is the **Judenplatz Museum,** displaying the ruins of a forgotten 14th-century synagogue unearthed during the memorial's construction (www.jmw.at).

The Netherlands and Scandinavia

In Amsterdam, **Anne Frank's House** gives the cold, mind-boggling statistics of Nazi cruelty some much-needed intimacy by telling the heartbreaking story of a young girl who became one of those statistics. Even bah-humbug types who are dragged in because it's raining and their spouses read the diary find themselves caught up in Anne's story (www.annefrank.org).

The small town of Haarlem, 20 minutes by train from Amsterdam, has its own Anne Frank–type story. Touring a cozy apartment above a clock shop just off the busy market square, you'll see **Corrie Ten Boom's "Hiding Place."** The sight was popularized by an inspirational book and movie about this woman and her family's experience hiding Jews from Nazis. Tipped off by an informant, Nazis raided their house but didn't find the Jews, who were hiding behind a wall in Corrie's bedroom. Because the Nazis found a suspiciously large number of ration coupons, they sent the Ten Boom family to a concentration camp. Only Corrie survived (www.corrietenboom.com).

Amsterdam's **Dutch Theater,** which was used as an assembly hall for local Jews destined for Nazi concentration camps, is a powerful memorial. On the wall, 6,700 family names represent the 104,000 Dutch Jews deported and killed by the Nazis. The nearby **Jewish History Museum**—four historic synagogues joined together by steel and glass to make one modern complex—tells the story and struggles of Judaism through the ages (www.jhm.nl).

While Hitler controlled Europe, each country had a courageous, if small, resistance movement. All over Europe you'll find streets and squares named after the martyrs of the resistance. Any history buff or champion of the underdog will be inspired by the patriotism documented in Europe's Nazi-resistance museums—the most extensive is Amsterdam's **Dutch Resistance Museum.** You'll see propaganda movie clips, study a forged ID card under a magnifying glass, and read of ingenious, daring efforts to hide Jews from the Germans (www.verzetsmuseum.org).

The **Museum of Deportation and the Resistance** in Mechelen, Belgium, is fascinating (www.cicb.be), as are resistance museums in **Copenhagen** (www.frihedsmuseet.dk) and **Oslo** (www.mil.no/felles /nhm). Oslo's **Norwegian Holocaust Center** is actually located in the former home of Nazi collaborator Vidkun Quisling (www.hlsenteret.no).

Poland

Poland was hit harder by World War II than any other country—more than six million Poles died, half of them Jews. But the Poles—Jewish or not—did not go quietly. Monuments around the capital city remember their valiant, though eventually unsuccessful, uprisings.

In 1940 and 1941, a million and a half Jews were moved into a ghetto in Warsaw. By 1943, only a tenth of the ghetto's Jews survived—the rest had died from disease or been shipped to concentration camps. The survivors staged the **Ghetto Uprising** against their Nazi oppressors, but almost all of them were eventually killed in the fighting, captured and executed, or sent to concentration camps. Today the former ghetto— leveled during the war—has been rebuilt as a dull residential zone, but a few monuments scattered around the area honor the uprising's heroes. The new Museum of the History of Polish Jews is slated to open here in 2012 (www.jewishmuseum.org.pl).

A year after the Ghetto Uprising, as the Soviet army approached, a Polish resistance army staged the **1944 Warsaw Uprising** against the Nazis, which resulted in the deaths of nearly a quarter of a million Warsaw civilians. Both of these events are depicted in the Oscar-winning film *The Pianist.* Today, you can still visit the neighborhoods and landmarks where these brave uprisings began. A high-tech museum about the 1944 Uprising tells the story eloquently (www.1944.pl).

The real Oskar Schindler—hero of the film *Schindler's List*—lived and worked in the Polish city of Kraków. Fans of the film can visit Schindler's factory (near the Kraków–Zabłocie train station), which has been converted into a museum (www.mhk.pl). The Jarden Bookshop, located in Kraków's Jewish Quarter, offers *Schindler's List* tours (www.jarden.pl).

The Czech Republic

After completing his "final solution," Hitler had hoped to build a grand museum of the "decadent" Jewish culture in Prague. Today, the museums and synagogues of **Prague's Jewish Quarter** (Josefov), containing artifacts the Nazis assembled from that city's once-thriving Jewish community, stand together as a persistently unforgettable memorial (see Chapter 54: Czech Out Prague).

France

Paris commemorates the 200,000 French victims of Hitler's camps with the **Memorial de la Déportation.** Walking through this evocative park, on the tip of the Ile de la Cité just behind Notre-Dame, is like entering a work of art. Walk down the claustrophobic stairs into a world of concrete, iron bars, water, and sky. Inside the structure, the eternal flame, triangular niches containing soil from various concentration camps, and powerful quotes will etch the message into your mind. Then gaze at the 200,000 crystals—one for each person who perished.

Rivaling Auschwitz as the most moving sight of all is the martyred village of **Oradour-sur-Glane,** in central France (www.oradour.org). This town, 15 miles northwest of Limoges, was machine-gunned and burned in 1944 by Nazi SS troops. Seeking revenge for the killing of one of their officers, they left 642 men, women, and children dead in a blackened crust of a town under a silent blanket of ashes.

The poignant ruins of Oradour-sur-Glane—scorched sewing machines, pots, pans, bikes, and cars—have been preserved as an eternal reminder of the reality of war. When you visit, you'll see the simple sign that greets every pilgrim who enters: *Souviens-toi*...remember.

EAST MEDITERRANEAN

73. Peloponnesian Highlights: Overlooked Greece

The Peloponnesian Peninsula stretches southwest from Athens. Studded with antiquities, this land of ancient Olympia, Corinth, and Sparta offers plenty of fun in the eternal Greek sun, with pleasant fishing villages, sandy beaches, bathtub-warm water, and none of the tourist crowds that plague the much-scrambled-after Greek Isles.

Nafplio and Its Historic Side-Trips

The charming Peloponnesian port town of Nafplio is small, cozy, and strollable. Though it has plenty of tourism, Nafplio is both elegant and proud. It's a must-see on any Greek visit because of its historical importance (the first capital of an independent Greece), its accessibility from Athens (an easy 2.5-hour drive or bus ride), and its handy location as a home base for touring the ancient sites at Mycenae and Epidavros (both described later). Nafplio has great pensions, appealing restaurants, a thriving evening scene, inviting beaches nearby, and a good balance of local life and tourist convenience.

Nafplio's harbor is guarded by three castles: one on a small island, another just above the old town, and a third capping a tall cliff above the city. All three are wonderfully floodlit at night. Just looking from the town up to its highest castle makes you need a tall iced tea.

But this old Venetian outpost, built in the days when Venice was

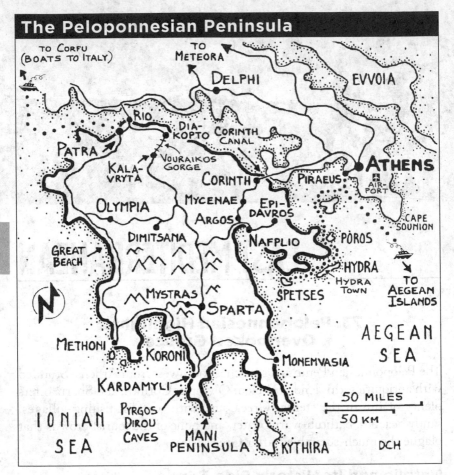

The Peloponnesian Peninsula

the economic ruler of Europe, is the best-preserved castle of its kind in Greece and well worth the climb. (A fun Nafplio pastime is asking various residents exactly how many steps there are. Most estimates fall between 850 and 1,000, but you'll never hear the same answer twice.) From the highest ramparts, you can see several islands and look deep into the mountainous interior of the Peloponnese. Below you lies an enticing beach.

This is a rough land with

Nafplio's castle towers over the town.

simple wines. A local vintner told me there's no such thing as a $50 bottle of fine Greek wine. I asked him, "What if I want to spend $30?" He said, "You can buy three $10 bottles." With dinner, I like to order the infamous resin-flavored *retsina* wine. It makes you want to sling a patch over one eye and say, "Arghh." The first glass is like drinking wood. The third glass is dangerous: It starts to taste good. If you drink any more, you'll smell like it the entire next day.

With its new affluence and a new generation of winemakers (many of them trained abroad), Greece is getting better at wine. More than 300 native varietals are now grown in Greece's wine regions. But like many locals, I often skip the wine and go for a cold beer, or the cloudy, anise-flavored ouzo. Supposedly invented by monks on Mount Athos, it's worth a try even if you don't like the flavor.

After a few days in Greece, you become a connoisseur of the Greek salad, appreciating the wonderful tomatoes, rich feta cheese, and olive-oil drenching. If a tourist complains about Greek food, they'll usually say something like, "It was fish with heads and the same salads every day." I like tiny fish with heads—squeeze lemon luxuriously all over them, and eat everything but the wispy little tails. Greece has specialties that are good and memorable—often both.

Epidavros, 18 miles east of Nafplio, has an underwhelming museum, forgettable ruins...and the most magnificent theater of the ancient world.

Epidavros' state-of-the-art acoustics

It was built nearly 2,500 years ago to seat 15,000. Today, it's kept busy reviving the greatest plays of antiquity. You can catch performances of ancient Greek comedies and tragedies on weekends from June through August. Try to see Epidavros either early or late in the day. The theater's marvelous acoustics are best enjoyed in near-solitude. Sitting in the most distant seat as your partner stands on the stage, you can practically hear the *retsina* rumbling in her stomach.

Thirty minutes north of Nafplio are the ruins of **Mycenae,** with a fine museum. This was the capital of the Mycenaeans, who won the Trojan War and dominated Greece 1,000 years before the Acropolis and other Golden Age Greek sights. As you tour this fascinating fortified citadel, imagine that the Mycenaeans were as mysterious to Socrates and

First Stop: Athens

Wherever you go all over the world (Mexico City, Dublin, Turkey, Egypt...you name it), it's smart to bone up on history and art in the capital city's big museum before tackling the ruins that dot the countryside. Athens is no exception. The Greek capital is big and crowded...but its "big three" sights are must-sees: the stunning Acropolis (with its showpiece Parthenon); the Ancient Agora just below; and the remarkable National Archaeological Museum.

Far and away the world's best collection of ancient Greek art, the National Archaeological Museum takes you chronologically from 7000 B.C. to A.D. 500, through beautifully displayed and well-described exhibits (and in air-conditioned comfort). Take this museum as seriously as you can, as if cramming

In Athens' National Archaeological Museum, you'll see textbook examples of lifelike, graceful Golden Age Greek art—such as Poseidon of Artemision (who's missing his trident).

for a big test. Trace the evolution of Greek art, study a guidebook, take a guided tour, and examine the ancient lifestyles painted on the vases.

Finally, after gaining a rudimentary knowledge of Greek art here, head for the hills—prepared to resurrect all that B.C. rubble.

Plato as those guys are to us. The classical Greeks marveled at the huge stones and workmanship of the Mycenaean ruins. They figured that only a race of giants (Cyclopes) could build with such colossal rocks...and called it "cyclopean" architecture.

Visitors today can gape at the Lion's Gate, peer into a deep ancient cistern, and explore the giant *tholos* tomb. The tomb, built in 1500 B.C., stands like a huge stone igloo, with a smooth subterranean dome almost 50 feet wide and more than 40 feet tall. The most important Mycenaean artifacts, like the golden "Mask of Agamemnon," are in the National Archaeological Museum in Athens.

Olympia

Visiting ancient Olympia is a Peloponnesian pilgrimage for modern tourists. Olympia's once-majestic temple columns—toppled like a tower of checkers by an earth-quake—are as evocative (with the help of the excellent museum) as anything from ancient times.

On your mark, get set...go!

Olympia was a mecca of ancient Greek religion—its greatest sanctuary and one of its most important places of worship. Ancient Greeks came here only every four years, during the religious festival that featured the Olympic Games. The original Olympic Games were more than an athletic festival. They served a political purpose: to develop a Panhellenic ("cross-Greek") identity. Every four years, wars between bickering Greeks were halted for a sacred one-month truce, and leading citizens from all corners would assemble here. Athletes, who were usually aristocratic youth, would stay here to train for months. There were no losers...except those who quit and cheated. Drinking animal blood—the Red Bull of the day—was forbidden. Official urine drinkers tested for this ancient equivalent of steroids.

Today, modern visitors just can't resist lining up on that original starting block from the first Olympic Games in 776 B.C.

The Mani Peninsula and Southern Peloponnesian Coast

The deserted hill town of Vathia is typical of the desolate Mani Peninsula.

The Mani Peninsula—the southern tip of mainland Greece (in fact, of the entire Continent, east of Spain)—feels like the end of the road. It's stark and sparse. If Greece had an OK Corral, this is where it would be. The awe-inspiring, fortified ghost- and hill-town of Vathia is vendetta-ville—it seems everyone lived in a fort and sat in corners looking outward for danger.

Today, Mani's population is a tiny fraction of what it once was. Many of its former residents either fled the country for the promise of faraway lands like America, or were killed in the violent bickering that seems to be a tradition.

Only goats thrive here. While mountains edged with abandoned terraces hint that farming was once more extensive, olives have been the only Mani export for the last two centuries.

In the days of old, people hid out tucked in the folds of the mountains, far from the coast and marauding pirate ships. Empty, ghostly hill towns clamber barnacle-like up distant ridges and are fortified for threats from both without and within. Cisterns that once sustained hardy communities by catching pure rainwater are now mucky green puddles that would turn a goat's stomach. The farther south you go, the bleaker conditions become. And yet, many Mani towns feature sumptuous, old, fresco-slathered churches...pockets of brightness that survive in this otherwise parched land.

The tragic history and rugged landscape provide an evocative backdrop—making hedonism on the Mani coast all the more hedonistic. **Kardamyli,** a humble beach town, has a "Bali in a dust storm" charm. This handy base for exploring the Mani Peninsula works like a stun gun on your momentum. On my last trip, I could have stayed here for days, just eating well and hanging out. It's the kind of place where travelers plan their day around the sunset.

Stepping out of my room and onto the shady veranda, I bonked my head on a lemon. Then, strolling to the taverna on the beach, I enjoyed memories of a long-ago Mani dinner: Settling my chair into the sand under a bare and dangling lamp at sunset, preparing to eat an octopus, I had enjoyed a faint but refreshing spritzing. Looking around for the source of the mist, I saw a tough young Greek in a swimsuit the size of a rat's hammock tenderizing a poor octopus to death by whipping it like a wet rag, over and over, on a big flat rock. The octopus would be featured that night on someone's dinner plate—but not mine.

Twenty years later, I settled in at Lela's Taverna under a leafy canopy. Light bulbs still swung in the breeze—but, no longer naked, they were dressed in gourd lampshades. Lela, bent and cloaked in black, scurried as a fleeting rainstorm drove a few people inside. In a land where "everybody's grandma is the best cook," ancient Lela is appreciated for how she gives her *tzatziki* a fun kick, and for the special way she marinates her olives.

I sat under an eave enjoying the view. I've always loved gazing into the misty Mediterranean, knowing the next land is Africa. Inky waves churned as a red sun set. The light morphed, as it does each evening, from solar to incandescent.

More treats line the coast east of the Mani Peninsula. **Monemvasia,** a Gibraltar-like rock with a Crusader-style stone town at its base, has ruins all across its Masada-like summit. It's connected by a causeway to the mainland. Reaching the summit of Monemvasia is a key experience on any Peloponnesian visit.

Although it's famous and "on the way," skip **Mystras.** Yes, it was once the cultural capital of the Byzantine Empire, but today there's just not much to see. Mystras spills down a mountain over the town and the scant ancient ruins of **Sparta.** Sparta—where mothers famously told their sons to "come home with your shield...

Monemvasia is one of the most striking sights of Greece.

or on it"—is a classic example of how little a militaristic society leaves as a legacy for the future.

Cockcrow on Hydra

Probably the best small town in this part of Greece is just offshore from the Peloponnesian Peninsula. Hydra—less than two hours south of Athens by hydrofoil—offers the ideal "Greek island" experience, without a long journey across the Aegean.

Hydra has one real town, no real roads, no cars, and not even any bikes. Zippy water taxis whisk you from the quaint little harbor to isolated beaches and tavernas. Sure-footed beasts of burden laden with everything from sandbags and bathtubs to bottled water climb stepped lanes. Behind each mule-train

Mules take the place of cars on Hydra.

toils a human pooper-scooper; I imagine picking up after your beast is required. On Hydra, a traffic jam is three donkeys and a fisherman.

The island once had plenty of spring water. But today Hydra's very hard water is shipped in from the mainland. No wonder showering (lathering and rinsing) is such an odd, frustrating experience.

The island is a land of tiny cats, tired burros, and roosters with big egos. While it's generally quiet, dawn teaches visitors the exact meaning of "cockcrow." The end of night is marked with much more than a distant cock-a-doodle-doo: It's a dissonant chorus of cat fights, burro honks, and what sounds like roll call at an asylum for crazed roosters. After the animal population gets that out of its system, the island slumbers a little longer.

Tourists wash ashore with the many private and public boats that come and go, but few venture beyond the harborfront. I decided to head uphill, and my small detour became a delightful little odyssey. While I had no intention of anything more than a lazy stroll, one inviting lane after another drew me up, up, up to the top of the town. Here, shabby homes enjoyed grand views, tired burros ambled along untethered, and island life trudged on, oblivious to tourism.

Over the crest, I followed a paved riverbed (primed for the flash floods that fill village cisterns each winter) down to the remote harbor hamlet of Kaminia—where 20 tough little fishing boats jostled within a breakwater. Children jumped fearlessly from rock to rock to the end of the jetty, ignoring an old man rhythmically casting his line.

A rickety woven-straw chair and a tipsy little table were positioned just right overlooking the harbor. The heavy reddening sun commanded, "Sit." I did, sipping ouzo and observing a sea busy with taxi boats, the "flying dolphin" hydrofoils that connect this oasis with Athens, freighters—like castles of rust—lumbering slowly along the horizon, and a cruise ship anchored like it hadn't moved in weeks.

Ouzo, my anise-flavored drink of choice on this trip, and the plastic baggie of pistachios purchased back in town were a perfect complement to the setting sun. Blue and white fishing boats jived with the chop. I'd swear the cats—small, numerous as the human residents of this island,

A sunset laced with ouzo...classic Greece

To Greece or Not to Greece?

Some travelers think they can squeeze Greece into a few days at the end of a trip through Europe. But if that's all the time you've got, I question the sanity of investing a lot of effort, money, and stress just to spend a couple of days in huge, polluted Athens and take a quick trip to an island—especially when you consider that 500 years before Christ, southern Italy was called "Magna Graecia" (Greater Greece). You can find excellent Greek ruins at Paestum, just south of Naples.

But with more time, Greece merits a visit. In the summer, Greece is the most touristed, least explored country in Europe. It seems that nearly all of its visitors are in a few places, while the rest of the country casually goes about its traditional business.

You'll get to Greece fastest by flying. Popular budget air carriers such as easyJet (www.easyjet.com) offer cheap flights from various European cities. For more on these and other low-cost flight options, see "Flying Within Europe" in Chapter 9: Flying. If you're beginning or ending your multi-country trip in Greece, it's especially smart to consider an "open jaw" flight plan (flying into one city and out of another).

Italy used to be the tourist's launch pad for Greece. But by car or train, it takes two days of solid travel to get from Rome to Athens, and two days to get back. By boat, it's a long overnight trip (Eurail covers Ancona or Bari, Italy, to Patra, Greece, on Superfast Line, www.superfast.com; and gets you a 30–50 percent discount from Brindisi, Italy, to Patra, Greece, on Hellenic Mediterranean Lines, www.ferries.gr/hml; also see www.youra.com/intlferries).

and oh so feminine—were watching the setting sun with me. An old man flipped his worry beads, backlit by the golden glitter on the harbor. Three men walked by, each reminding me of Spiro Agnew.

As darkness settled at Kodylenia's Taverna, my waiter—who returned here to his family's homeland after spending 20 years in New Jersey, where he "never took a nap"—brought a candle for my table. The soft Greek lounge music tumbling out of the kitchen mixed everything like an audio swizzle stick. I glanced over my shoulder to the coastal lane home...thankfully, it was lamp-lit.

Walking home, under a ridge lined with derelict windmills, I tried to envision Hydra before electricity, when spring water flowed and the community was powered by both wind and burros. At the edge of town I passed the Sunset Bar, filled with noisy cruise-ship tourists, and was

Where Greece Meets Turkey

Athens and the Peloponnese are a fine place to begin your Greek vacation. But to mix in some cultural variety, go to Turkey. It's closer than you might think: Historic rivals Greece and Turkey practically flow into each other in the eastern Aegean. The Greek isles of Sámos, Rhodes, and Kos are each connected daily by boat to Turkey. This short boat ride gives you more of a cultural change than the flight from the US to Athens.

Leaving Greece via Sámos offers a look at one of my favorite Greek islands and drops you in Kuşadasi, a pleasant place to enter Turkey and a 20-minute drive from Ephesus (both described next in Chapter 74: Turkey's Hot).

Sámos—green, mountainous, diverse, and friendly—has tourist crowds, but not as bad as other Greek islands. Bus transportation on the island is fine. And it's cheap to crisscross Sámos on your own moped. Pounding over potholes, dodging trucks, stopping to gaze across the sea at the hills of Turkey, and being spanked happily by the prickly wind and Greek sun, you will find that a moped ride around Sámos is exhilarating.

The tourist map shows plenty of obscure sights on Sámos. Gambling that the Spiliani monastery was worth the detour, I traded potholes for gravel and wound my way up the hill. The road ended at a tiny church overlooking the sunburned island. Behind the church was the mouth of a cave, with whitewashed columns carved like teeth into the rock. I wandered into the drippy, dank darkness, cool and quiet as another world. Sitting still, I could almost hear the drip-by-drip growth of the stalagmites and the purr of my brain. The only motion was the slight flicker of slender candles. I was ready to venture out of Christendom and into Islam.

thankful I'd taken the uphill lane when I left my hotel that morning. Locals, proud of the extravagant yachts moored for the night, like to tell of movie stars who make regular visits. But the island is so quiet that, by midnight, all the high-rollers seem to be back on board watching movies. Sitting on a ferry cleat the size of a stool, I scanned the harbor—big flat-screen TVs flickered from every other yacht.

Back in Hydra town, I observed the pleasant evening routine of strolling and socializing. Dice clattered on dozens of backgammon boards, entrepreneurial dogs and soccer-goal-oriented children busied themselves, and a tethered goat chewed on something inedible in its low-profile corner. From the other end of town came the happy music of a christening party. Dancing women filled the building, while their

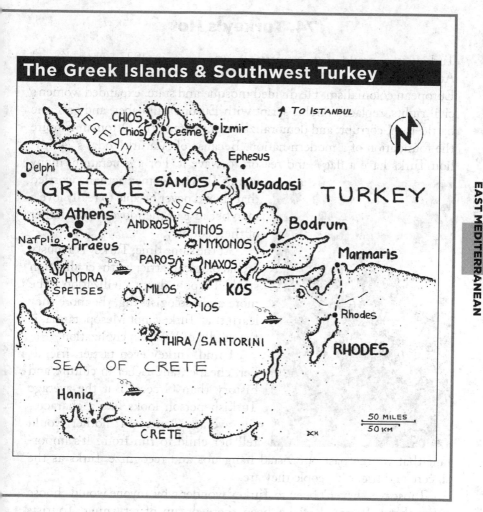

The Greek Islands & Southwest Turkey

children mimicked them in the street. Farther down, two elderly, black-clad women sat like tired dogs on the curb.

Succumbing to the lure of the pastry shop, I sat down for our day-end ritual: honey-soaked baklava. I told the cook I was American. "Oh," he said, shaking his head with sadness and pity, "you work too hard."

I answered, "Right. But not today."

*For good-value accommodations in **Hydra**, try Hotel Leto (Hydra Town, tel. 22980-53385, www.letohydra.gr) or the smaller Alkionides Pension (Hydra Town, tel. 22980-54055, www.alkionidespension.com). For all the travel specifics, see the most recent edition of Rick Steves' Athens & the Peloponnese.*

74. Turkey's Hot

Turkey is a proud new country. It was born in 1923, when Kemal Atatürk, the father of modern Turkey, rescued it from the buffet line of European colonialism. He divided mosque and state, expanded women's civil rights, replaced Arabic script with Europe's alphabet, and gave the battle-torn, corrupt, and demoralized remnants of the Ottoman Empire the foundation of a modern nation. Because of Atatürk, today's 74 million Turks have a flag—and reason to wave it. For a generation, many young Turkish women actually worried that they'd never be able to really love a man because of their love for the father of their country.

At the same time, Turkey is a musty archaeological attic, with civilization stacked upon dusty civilization. The more archaeologists dig, the more they learn that Turkey, not Mesopotamia, is the cradle of Western civilization.

I find Turkey even tastier, friendlier, cheaper, and richer in culture and history than Greece. But the average Turkish person looks like a character the average American mother would tell her child to run from. It's important that we see past our visual hang-ups and recognize Turks as the sincere and friendly people they are.

Those who haven't been to Turkey wonder why anyone would choose to go there. Those who have been there dream of returning. Tourists are learning that the image of the "terrible Turk" is false, created to a great degree by the country's unfriendly neighbors. Turks are quick to remind visitors that, surrounded by Syria, Iraq, Iran, Georgia, Bulgaria, and Greece, they're not exactly living in Mr. Rogers' neighborhood.

Many visitors are put off by Turkey's "rifles on every corner" image. Turkey is not a police state. Its NATO commitment is to maintain nearly a million-man army. Except far to the east, where this million-man army is dealing with Kurdish separatists, these soldiers have little to do but "patrol" and "guard"—basically, loiter in uniform.

Today's Turkey is on the move. It's looking West and getting there. Eager to join the European Union, Turkey has pushed to modernize—its widespread Internet access, mobile phones, and slick bus system rival the status of many EU members. I once had a forgotten plane ticket express-mailed across the country in 24 hours, for $5. Only half of Turkey's 42,000 villages had electricity in 1980. Now they all do. Does all this modernization threaten the beautiful things that make Turkish culture so Turkish? An old village woman assured me, "We can survive TV and tourism because we have deep and strong cultural roots."

English is widely spoken, and tourism is booming. Even the Turkish lira has been reborn. In 2005, a new Turkish lira went into circulation, trimming off six zeroes; and in 2009, the currency started sporting a fresh new look. Now $1 is worth about 1.50 liras...and tourists can leave their calculators at home.

Travel in Turkey is relatively cheap. Vagabonds order high on menus. And buses, which offer none of the romantic chaos of earlier years, take travelers anywhere in the country nearly any time for as little as $5 an hour.

Turkey knows it's on the fence between the rising wealth and power of an ever-more-united Europe and a forever-fragile-and-messy Middle East. Turks recognize the threat of the rising tide of Islamic fundamentalism, and, while the country is 99 percent Muslim, most want little to do with the Iranian-style rule that steadily blows the dust of religious discontent over their border. But fundamentalists are making inroads, and as these men walk by with veiled women in tow, modern-minded Turks grumble—a bit nervously.

Two months after the first Gulf War, I enjoyed my ninth trip through Turkey, this time with 22 travel partners and a Turkish co-guide. We had a life-changing 15 days together, enjoyed a level-headed look at Islam, took a peek at a hardworking developing country with its act impressively together, and learned how our mass media can wrongly shape America's assessment of faraway lands. No survey was necessary to know that we all brought home a better understanding of our world. But a survey did show that 14 people bought carpets (mostly less than $1,000, one for $3,000), eight people had diarrhea (seven for less than two days, one for six days), and nine of us learned to play backgammon well enough to challenge a Turk in a smoky teahouse. For the price of a Big Mac, we bought tea for 20 new friends, played backgammon until the smoke didn't bother us, and rocked to the pulse of Turkey. Oh, those tiny handmade dice...cockeyed dots in a land where time is not money.

Turkey reshuffles your cards. A beautiful girl is called a pistachio. A person with a beautiful heart but an ugly face is called a Maltese plum—the ugliest fruit you'll ever enjoy. Much of Turkey is scrambling into the modern Western world, but the Turkish way of life is painted onto this land with indelible cultural ink. If you're able to put your guidebook aside and follow your wanderlust, you'll still find sleepy goats playing Bambi on rocks that overlook a nomad's black tent. High above on the hillside, the lone but happy song of the goatherd's flute plays golden oldies. His wife bakes bread and minds the children, knowing her man is near.

Turkey is like abstract art, a riveting movie without a plot, a melody of people, culture, and landscape that you just can't seem to stop whistling.

Güzelyurt—Cappadocia Without Tourists

Cappadocia is rightly famous as the most bizarre and fascinating bit of central Turkey that accepts credit cards. The most exciting discovery I made on my last trip was a town on the edge of Cappadocia called Güzelyurt.

Güzelyurt means "beautiful land." The town is a harmonious blend of cultures, history, architecture, and religions. Walk down streets that residents from 3,000 years ago might recognize, past homes carved into the rocks, enjoying friendly greetings of *"merhaba."* Scowling sheepdogs, caged behind 10-foot-high rookeries, give the scene just enough tension.

Walk to a viewpoint at the far side of town, toward the snowy slopes of the Fuji-like volcano (Mt. Hasan) that rules the horizon. Before you is a lush and living gorge. The cliff rising from the gorge is stacked with building styles: Upon the 1,600-year-old church sit troglodyte caves, Selcuk arches, and Ottoman facades. And on the horizon gleams the tin dome of the 20th-century mosque, with its twin minarets giving you a constant visual call to prayer. The honey that holds this architectural baklava together is people.

Put your camera away, shut your mouth, and sit silently amidst the sounds of 1000 B.C. Children play, birds chirp, roosters crow, shepherds chase goats, and mothers cackle. (Ignore that distant motorbike.)

Below you, sleeping in the greens and browns of this land of simple living, is the church of St. Gregorius. Built in 385, it's thought by Gregorian fans to be the birthplace of church music, specifically the Gregorian chant. Its single minaret indicates that it's preserved as a mosque today in a valley where people call God "Allah."

Who needs three-star sights and tourist information offices? In Güzelyurt, we dropped by the City Hall. The mayor scampered across town to arrange a lunch for us in his home. He welcomed us Christians, explaining, "We believe in the four books"—his way of saying, "It doesn't matter what you call him, as long as you call him." He showed us the

names of his Greek Christian friends, kept as safe and sacred as good friends could be in his most precious and holy possession, the family Quran bag.

The lady of the house made tea. Overlapping carpets gave the place a cozy bug-in-a-rug feeling. As the lady cranked up the music, we all began to dance like charmed snakes until our fingers could snap no more. A small girl showed me a handful of almonds and said, "Buy dem." *Badem* is Turkish for almond, and this was her gift to me. Enjoying her munchies, I reciprocated with a handful of Pop Rocks. As the tiny candies exploded in her mouth, her surprised eyes became even more beautiful.

The town's name is spelled proudly across its volcanic backdrop. The black bust of Atatürk seems to loom just as high over the small market square. The streets are alive with the relaxed click of victorious *tavla* (backgammon) pieces. The men of the town, who seem to be enjoying one eternal cigarette break, proudly make a point not to stare at the stare-worthy American visitors searching for postcards in a town with no tourism.

Güzelyurt, in central Turkey, is a short bus ride from Aksaray. It's near the Ihlara Valley, famous for its five-mile hike through a lush valley of poplar groves, eagles, vultures, and early Christian churches.

Belisirma, near Güzelyurt, is even more remote. With a population of "100 homes," Belisirma zigzags down to its river, which rushes through a poplar forest past the tiny Belisirma Walley Wellkome Camping (one bungalow). A group of bangled women in lush purple wash their laundry in the river under the watchful eyes of men who seem to have only a ceremonial function. Children on donkeys offer to show off the troglo-dyte church carved into the hill just past the long, narrow farm plots. A lady, her face framed in the dangling jewelry of her shawl, her net worth hanging in gold around her neck, points to my postcard, a picture of a little girl holding a baby sheep. The girl is her niece. They call the card "Two Lambs."

14 Days in Turkey

Turkey offers the most enjoyable culture shock within striking distance of Europe. But it's a rich brew, and, for most, two weeks is enough for a good first look. Here's my recommendation for the best two-week visit

14 Days in Turkey

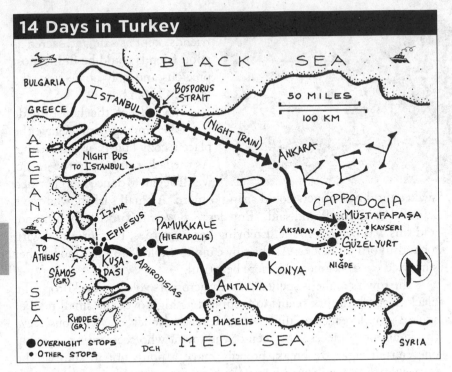

to Turkey. (This plan is tried and tested, as it's the route our guided tours follow.)

Flying to Istanbul is about as tough as flying to Paris. When planning your trip, remember that flying "open jaw" into Istanbul and home from Athens can make for a diverse and efficient itinerary.

Spend your first two days in Istanbul. Take a taxi from the airport to the old Roman racetrack called the Hippodrome, near the Blue Mosque in the Sultanahmet district, where you'll find several decent hotels and hostels.

For an easygoing first evening, walk over to the Blue Mosque and enjoy the park. Spend the next day doing the historic biggies: Topkapı Palace, Blue Mosque, and the Hagia Sophia (Aya Sofya) church. The latter was completed in 537, when Istanbul was called

Impressive from the outside, Istanbul's Blue Mosque is named for the deeply hued tiles inside.

Constantinople and was the leading city in Christendom. It was the largest dome in Europe until Brunelleschi built Florence's great dome in the Renaissance, almost a thousand years later.

Bone up on Anatolian folk life in the Turkish and Islamic Arts Museum (next to the Hippodrome), then taxi to the bustling New District (Beyoğlu) for dinner in the Nevizade Sokak restaurant arcade, where Istanbul's beautiful people and tourists alike enjoy the funky elegance. If you like baklava, stroll the district's main drag, İstiklal Street, in search of a pastry shop. From the heartbeat of modern Istanbul, Taksim Square, catch a cab home. A less touristy dinner option is the Ortaköy district, in the shadow of the Bosphorus bridge.

The next morning, browse the bustling Grand Bazaar and Spice Market. After lunch, take an intercontinental cruise up the Bosphorus. If you disembark in "Asian" Istanbul (the part of the city that lies east of the Bosphorus), you can taxi quickly to the station to catch your over-night train to Ankara.

This gets you to the country's capital by 8 a.m. As you munch feta cheese, olives, tomatoes, and cucumbers for breakfast in the dining car, it dawns on you that you're far from home.

Ankara has two blockbuster sights. The Museum of Anatolian Civilizations is a prerequisite for meaningful explorations of the ancient ruins that litter the Turkish countryside. The Atatürk Mausoleum shines a light on the recent and dramatic birth of modern Turkey and gives you an appreciation of the country's love of its version of George Washington. For a happening scene, a great view, and a look at modern Turkey, ride to the top of the Ankara tower.

From Ankara, it's a four-hour bus ride to exotic and evocative Cappadocia, an eroded wonderland of cave dwellings that go back to the early Christian days, when the faithful fled persecution by hiding in Cappadocian caves. Cappadocia gives you a time-tunnel experience, with its horse carts, strangely eroded mini-Matterhorns (called "fairy chimneys"), traditional crafts, and labyrinthine underground cities. Don't miss the Back Door town of Güzelyurt (described earlier).

From mysterious Cappadocia, cross the Anatolian Plateau to Konya, the most conservative and orthodox Muslim city in Turkey, home of the Mevlevi order and the whirling dervishes. The dance of the dervish connects a giving god with our world. One hand is gracefully raised, and the other is a loving spout as the dervish whirls faster and faster in a trance the modern American attention span would be hard-pressed to understand.

Then follow the steps of St. Paul over the Taurus Mountains to the

Islam in a Pistachio Shell

Five times a day, God enjoys a global wave as the call to prayer sweeps from the Philippines to Morocco to the US at the speed of the sun. The muezzin chants, "There is only one God, and Muhammad is his prophet."

Islam is the fastest-growing religion on Earth. Unbiased listings place Muhammad above Jesus on rankings of all-time most influential people. For us to understand Islam by studying Osama bin Laden and al-Qaeda would be like a Turk understanding Christianity by studying Timothy McVeigh and the Ku Klux Klan.

Traveling in an Islamic country is an opportunity to better understand this religion. Just as it helps to know about spires, feudalism, and the saints to comprehend your European sightseeing, a few basics on Islam help make your sightseeing in Muslim countries more meaningful.

The Islamic equivalent of the Christian bell tower is the minaret, which the muezzin climbs to chant the call to prayer. In a kind of architectural

Muslims in modern-day Turkey—a mix of East and West.

Darwinism, the minarets have shrunk as calls to prayer have been electronically amplified; their height is no longer so necessary—or worth the expense. Many small, modern mosques have one tin mini-minaret about as awesome as my little toe.

Worshippers pray toward Mecca, which, from Turkey, is roughly in the same direction as Jerusalem, but not quite. In Istanbul, Hagia Sophia was built 1,400 years ago as a church, its altar niche facing Jerusalem. Since it became an out-of sync-with-Mecca mosque, the Muslim focus-of-prayers niche is to the side of what was the altar.

A mosque is a shoes-off place. Non-Muslims are welcome to drop in. The small stairway that seems to go nowhere is symbolic of the growth of Islam (Muhammad had to stand higher and higher to talk to his growing following). Today every mosque has one of these as a kind of pulpit. No priest ever stands on the top stair, which is symbolically reserved for Muhammad.

The "five pillars" of Islam are the core tenets of the faith, basic to an understanding of a religious force that is bound to fill our headlines for years to come. Followers of Islam should:

1. Say and believe, "There is no other God but Allah, and Muhammad is his Prophet."
2. Pray five times a day. Modern Muslims explain that it's important to wash, exercise, stretch, and think of God. The ritual of Muslim prayer works this into every day—five times.
3. Give to the poor (one-fortieth of your wealth, if you are not in debt).
4. Fast during daylight hours through the month of Ramadan. Fasting is a great social equalizer and helps everyone to feel the hunger of the poor.
5. Make a pilgrimage to Mecca. Muslims who can afford it, and who are physically able, are required to go on a pilgrimage (hajj) to the sacred sites in Mecca and Medina at least once in their lifetime. This is interpreted by some Muslims as a command to travel. Muhammad said, "Don't tell me how educated you are, tell me how much you've traveled."

Prayer services in a mosque are segregated; women worship in back, men in front. For the same reason I might find it hard to concentrate on inner peace in a yoga class full of women, Muslim men decided prayer would go better without the enjoyable but problematic distraction of bent-over women between them and Mecca. How Muslims can have more than one wife is a bigamistery to many. While polygamy is illegal (and has never been practiced by most folks) in Turkey, Islam does allow a man to have as many wives as he can love and care for equally (up to four). This originated as Muhammad's pragmatic answer to the problem of too many unattached women caused by the deaths of so many men in the frequent wars of his day. Religious wars have been as common in Islam as they have been in Christendom.

These basics are a simplistic but honest attempt by a non-Muslim to help travelers from the Christian West understand a very rich but often misunderstood culture that is worthy of our respect. These days, religious extremists can polarize entire populations. And those who profit from the related strife—either from weapons sales, or by turning serious news into light entertainment just to sell more advertisements—are clever at riding the bloody coattails of any religious conflict. Therefore, we need all the understanding we can muster.

Exotic terrain, ornery transport...Cappadocia

Mediterranean resort of Antalya. You can hire a *gulet* (a Turkish yacht) to sail the Mediterranean coast to your choice of several beachside attractions. After a free day on the beach, travel inland to explore the ruins of Aphrodisias and its excellent museum.

Nearby is Pamukkale, a touristy village and Turkey's premier mineral spa. Soak among broken ancient columns in a mineral spring atop the white cliff, terraced with acres and acres of steamy mineral pools. Watch frisky sparrows hop through a kaleidoscope of white birdbaths.

For the final leg of your two-week swing through Turkey, head west to the coastal resort of Kuşadası. Nearby is my favorite ancient site, the ruins of Ephesus. For a relaxing finale, take a Turkish *hamam* (bath with massage) in Kuşadası before flying back to Istanbul from nearby İzmir or catching the daily boat to the entertaining island of Sámos in Greece (see the "Where Greece Meets Turkey" sidebar on page 682). Boats and planes take travelers from Sámos to other Greek islands and on to Athens.

Some Hints to Make Turkey Easier

Good information is rare here, especially in the East. Bring a good guidebook from home. Take advantage of my book, *Rick Steves' Istanbul*, or Lonely Planet's guidebook to Turkey. Maps are easy to get in Turkey and useful to have.

Eat carefully. Find a cafeteria-style restaurant and point. Choose your food personally by tasting and pointing to what you like. Joke around with the cooks. They'll love you for it. The bottled water, soft drinks, *chai* (tea), and coffee are cheap and generally safe. Watermelons are a great source of safe liquid. If you order a glass of tea, your waiter will be happy to "process" your melon, giving it to you peeled and in little chunks on a big plate.

Learn to play backgammon before you visit Turkey. Backgammon, the national pastime, is played by all the men in this part of the world. Join in (women, too). It's a great way to instantly become a contributing member of the teahouse scene.

Really get away from it all. Catch a *dolmuş* (a shared van or taxi) into the middle of nowhere. Get off at a small village. If the bus driver thinks you must be mistaken or lost to be getting off there, you've found the right place. Explore the town, befriend the children, trade national dance lessons. Act like an old friend returning after a 10-year absence, and you'll be treated like one.

You'll be stared at all day long. Preserve your sanity with a sense of humor. Joke with the Turks. Talk to them, even if there's no hope of communication. One afternoon, in the town of Erciş, I was waiting for a bus and writing in my journal. A dozen people gathered around me, staring with intense curiosity. I felt that they needed entertainment. I sang the Hoagy Carmichael classic, "Huggin' and Chalkin'." When the bus came, I danced my way on board, waving goodbye to the cheering fans. From then on, my singing entertained most of eastern Turkey.

Make invitations happen and accept them boldly. While explor-

Greek and Turkish travel agencies are more helpful than they look.

ing villages with no tourism, I loiter near the property of a large family. Very often the patriarch, proud to have a foreign visitor, will invite me to join him cross-legged on his large, bright carpet in the shade. The women of the household bring tea, then peer at us from around a distant corner. Shake hands, jabber away in English, play show and tell, pass around photos from home, take photos of the family, and get their addresses so you can mail them copies. They'll always remember your visit. And so will you.

*For good-value accommodations in **Istanbul**, consider Aya Sofya Pensions SC (along Soğukçeşme Sokak, tel. 0212/513-3660, www.ayasofyapensions .com) or Germir Palace Hotel SC (Cumhuriyet Caddesi 7, tel. 0212/361-1110, www.germirpalas.com). In **Güzelyurt**, try Hotel Karballa (Çarşı içi, tel.*

*382/451-2103, www.karballahotel.com, info@karballahotel.com) or Kadir's Antique Gelveri Houses (Yukarı Mahalle Aksaray 37, tel. 382/451-2021, www.kadirshouses.com, antiquegelverihouses@gmail.com). In **Kuşadasi**, consider Grand Oder Otel (Atatürk Bulvari Girsi Yat Limani Karsisi, tel. 256/618-1690, www.onderotel.com, info@onderotel.com). In **Sámos** (Greece), try Hotel Sámos (11 The. Sofouli, tel. 22730-283-778, www.samoshotel.gr, hotsamos@otenet.gr). For more about Turkey, see the latest edition of* Rick Steves' Istanbul.

75. Istanbul Déjà Vu

When I was in my 20s, I finished eight European trips in a row in Turkey. I didn't plan it that way—it was the natural finale, the subconscious cherry on top of every year's travel adventures. Recently, realizing

I hadn't set foot in Istanbul for nearly a decade, I made a point to return to the city where East meets West. The comforting similarities and jarring differences between today's Istanbul, and the Istanbul I remember, filled the trip both with nostalgia and with vivid examples of how change is sweeping the planet.

The moment I stepped off my plane, I remembered how much I enjoy this country. Marveling at the efficiency of Istanbul's Atatürk Airport, I popped onto the street and into a yellow *taksi*. Seeing the welcoming grin of the unshaven driver who greeted me with a *"Merhaba,"* I just blurted out, *"Çok güzel."* I forgot I remembered the phrase. It just came to me—like a baby shouts for joy. I was back in Turkey, and it was "very beautiful" indeed. My first hours in Turkey were filled with similar déjà vu moments like no travel homecoming I could remember.

As the *taksi* turned off the highway and into the tangled lanes of the tourist zone—just below the Blue Mosque—all the tourist-friendly businesses still lined up, providing a backdrop for their chorus line of barkers shouting, "Yes, Mister!"

I looked at the dirty kids in the streets and remembered a rougher time, when kids like these would earn small change by hanging out the passenger door of ramshackle vans. They'd yell "Topkapı, Topkapı, Topkapı" (or whichever neighborhood was the destination) in a scramble to pick up passengers in the shared minibuses called *dolmuş*. (The *dolmuş*—a wild cross between a taxi, a bus, and a kidnapping vehicle—is literally and appropriately translated as "stuffed").

While Turkey's new affluence has nearly killed the *dolmuş*, the echoes of the boys hollering from the vans bounced happily in my memory: "Aksaray, Aksaray, Aksaray...Sultanahmet, Sultanahmet, Sultanahmet." I remembered my favorite call was for the train station's neighborhood: "Sirkeci, Sirkeci, Sirkeci" (SEER-kay-jee).

Istanbul, now with a population of almost 15 million, is thriving. The city is poignantly littered both with remnants of grand (if eventually corrupt) empires, and with living, breathing reminders of the harsh reality of life in the developing world. Sipping my tea, I watched old men shuffle by, carrying nothing but walking as if still bent under the towering loads they had carried all of their human-beast-of-burden lives.

And yet, this ancient city is striding into the future. During my visit, everyone was buzzing about the upcoming completion of the new tunnel

under the Bosphorus, which will give a million commuters in the Asian suburbs of Istanbul an easy train link to their places of work in Europe. This tunnel is emblematic of modern Turkey's commitment to connecting East and West, just as Istanbul bridges Asia and Europe. I also see it as a concrete example of how parts of the developing world are emerging as economic dynamos.

Stepping out of my shoes, I entered the vast and turquoise (and therefore not-quite-rightly-named) Blue Mosque. Hoping for another déjà vu, I didn't get it. Something was missing. Yes...gone was the smell of countless sweaty socks, knees, palms, and foreheads soaked into the ancient carpet upon which worshippers did their quite physical prayer workouts. Sure enough, the Blue Mosque had a fresh new carpet—with a subtle design that keeps worshippers organized in the same way that lined paper tames printed letters.

The prayer service let out, and a sea of Turks surged for the door. Being caught up in a crush of locals—where the only way to get any personal space is to look up—is a connecting-with-humanity ritual for me. I seek out these opportunities. It's the closest I'll ever come to experiencing the exhilaration of body-surfing above a mosh pit. Going outside with the worshipping flow, I scanned the dark sky. That scene—one I had forgotten was so breathtaking—played for me again: hard-pumping seagulls powering through the humid air in a black sky, surging into the light as they crossed in front of floodlit minarets.

Walking down to the Golden Horn inlet and Istanbul's churning waterfront, I crossed the new Galata Bridge, which made me miss the dismantled and shipped-out old Galata Bridge—so crusty with life's struggles. Feeling a wistful nostalgia, I thought of how all societies morph with the push and pull of the times.

Istanbul's new Galata Bridge retains the lively spirit of the old one, with a lower level for eateries, pedestrians, and fishermen.

But then I realized that, while the old bridge is gone, the new one has been engulfed with the same vibrant street life—boys casting their lines, old men sucking on water pipes, and sesame-seed bread rings filling cloudy glass-windowed carts. It reminded me how stubborn cultural inertia can be.

On the sloppy adjacent harborfront, the venerable "fish and bread boats" were still rocking in the constant chop of the busy harbor. In a humbler day, they were 20-foot-long open dinghies—rough boats with battered car tires for fenders—with open fires for grilling fish, literally fresh off the boat. For a few coins, the fishermen would bury a big white fillet in a hunk of fluffy white bread, wrap it in newsprint, and I was on my way...dining out on fish.

In recent years, the fish and bread boats had been shut down—they had no license. After a popular uproar, they came back. They're a bit more hygienic, no longer using newspaper for wrapping, but still rocking in the waves and slamming out fresh fish.

Wandering under stiletto minarets, I listened as a hardworking loudspeaker—lashed to the minaret as if to a religious crow's nest—belted out a call to prayer. Noticing the twinkling lights strung up in honor of the holy month of Ramadan, I thought, "Charming—they've draped Christmas lights between the minarets." (A Turk might come to my house and say, "Charming—he's draped Ramadan lights on his Christmas tree.") I marveled at the multigenerational conviviality at the Hippodrome—that long, oblong plaza still shaped like a chariot racecourse, as it was 18 centuries ago. Precocious children high-fived me and tried out their only English phrase: "What is your name?" Just to enjoy their quizzical look, I'd say, "Seven o'clock." As I struggle to understand their society, I guess my mischievous streak wanted them to deal with a little confusion as well.

In Turkey, I have more personal rituals than in other countries. I cap my days with a bowl of *sütlaç*. That's rice pudding with a sprinkle of cinnamon—still served in a square and shiny stainless steel bowl with a matching spoon, not much bigger than a gelato sampler.

And I don't let a day go by in Turkey without enjoying a teahouse game of backgammon with a

It's enlightening to visit a place where you are the cultural spectacle.

stranger. Boards have become less characteristic; they're now cheap and mass-produced, almost disposable. Today's dice—plastic and perfect—make me miss the tiny handmade "bones" of the 20th century, with their disobedient dots. But some things never change. To test a fun cultural quirk, I tossed my dice and paused. As I remembered, a bystander moved for me. When it comes to backgammon, there's one right way...and everybody knows it. And in Turkey, perhaps as a result of its ruthless history, when starting a new game, the winner of the last game goes first.

With each backgammon game, I think of one of my most precious possessions back home: an old-time, hand-hewn, inlaid backgammon board, with rusty little hinges held in place by hasty tacks, and soft, white wood worn deeper than the harder, dark wood. Twenty years after taking that backgammon board home, I open it and still smell the tobacco, tea, and soul of a traditional Turkish community. There's almost nothing in my world that is worn or has been enjoyed long enough to absorb the smells of my life and community. It's a reminder to me of the cost of modernity. And when the feel and smell of my old backgammon board takes me back to Turkey, I'm reminded how, in the face of all that modernity, the endangered though resilient charm of traditional cultures is something to value.

Today in Turkey, the people—like those dots on the modern dice—

line up better. The weave of a mosque carpet provides direction. There's a seat for everyone, as the *dolmuş* are no longer so stuffed. Fez sales to tourists are way down, but scarf wear by local women (a symbol of traditional Muslim identity) is way up. Each of my déjà vu moments shows a society confronting powerful forces of change while also wanting to stay the same.

For good-value accommodations in **Istanbul,** *consider Uyan Hotel SC (Utangaç Sokak 25, tel. 0212/516-4892 or 0212/518-9255, www.uyanhotel .com) or İstiklal Suite Home SC (İstiklal Caddesi 45, tel. 0212/245-0772, www.istanbulsuite.com). Other Istanbul accommodations are listed on page 693. For all the travel specifics, see the most recent edition of* Rick Steves' Istanbul.

76. Eastern Turkey

Istanbul and the western Turkish coast—while still fascinating, cheap, and eager to please—are moving toward European-style mainstream

tourism. For the most cultural thrills, head east. Tour inland Anatolia with abandon, using Ankara as a springboard. From here, buses transport you to the region, culture, and era of your choice.

Find a town that has yet to master the business of tourism, like Kastamonu (5 hours northeast of Ankara). The business hotel where I stayed was cheap ($20 doubles) and comfortable, but not slick. I handed a postcard to the boy at the desk, hoping he could mail it for me. He looked it over a couple of times on both sides, complimented me, and politely handed it back. As I left, he raised his right hand like a cigar-store Indian and said, "Hello." While changing money, I was spotted by the bank manager, who invited me into his office for tea. Since I was his first American customer, he wanted to celebrate.

Outside, a gaggle of men wearing grays, blacks, and browns were shuffling quietly down the street. A casket floated over them as each man jostled to the front to pay his respects by "giving it a shoulder."

Turkey is a land of ceremonies. Rather than relying on a list of

Eastern Turkey

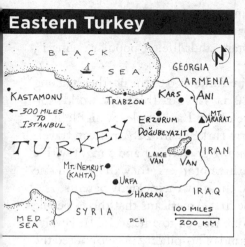

festivals, travel with sharp eyes, flexibility, and some knowledge of the folk culture. Life here is punctuated with colorful, meaningful events. As the dust from the funeral procession clears, you may see a proud eight-year-old boy dressed like a prince or a sultan. The boy is celebrating his circumcision, a rite of passage that some claim is an echo of the days of matriarchal Amazon rule, when entry into the priesthood required c-c-c-castration. This is a great day for the boy and his family. Turks call it the "happiest wedding"—because there are no in-laws.

Having an interpreter helps you explore and mingle with meaning, but it's not required. Many older Turks speak German. The friendliness of Turkey is legendary among those who have traveled beyond the cruise ports. While relatively few small-town Turks speak English, their eagerness to help makes the language barrier look much less formidable.

Enjoy jabbering with the people you meet. If Turkish sounds tough to you, remember, it's the same in reverse. Certain sounds, like our "th," are tricky. My friend Ruth was entertained by the tortured attempts Turks made at pronouncing her name: "Woooott." Any English-speaking Turk can remember spending long hours looking into the mirror, slowly enunciating: "This and these are hard to say. I think about them every day. My mouth and my teeth, I think you see, help me say them easily."

In Turkey, you don't need museums—they're living in the streets.

Throughout Turkey, travelers cringe at the sight of ugly, unfinished construction that scars nearly every town with rusty tangles of steel rebar waiting to reinforce future concrete walls. But in Turkey, unfinished buildings are family savings accounts. Inflation here can be ruinous. Anyone in need of a hedge against inflation keeps a building under construction. Whenever there's a little extra cash, rather than watch it evaporate in the bank, Ahmed will invest in the next stage of construction. It's the goal of any Turkish parent to provide each child with a house or apartment with which to start adult life. A popular saying is, "Rebar holds the family together."

If you're looking for a rain forest in Turkey, go to the northeast, along the Black Sea coast, where it rains 320 days a year. This is the world's top hazelnut-producing region and home of the Laz people. A highlight of one tour (which I led through Eastern Turkey with 22 American travelers and a Turkish co-guide) was spending an evening and a night with a Laz family. Actually the families of three brothers, they all lived in one large three-layered house provided to them by their elderly parents.

The people in our group were the first Americans that the 16 people who lived there had ever seen. We were treated to a feast. In Turkey, it's next to impossible to turn down this kind of hospitality. As we praised the stuffed peppers, members of our group discreetly passed Pepto-Bismol tablets around under the table. (The pouring tea didn't quite mask the sound of ripping cellophane.)

After dinner, we paid our respects to the grandma. Looking like a veiled angel in white, she and her family knew she would soon succumb to her cancer. But for now, she was overjoyed to see such a happy evening filling her family's home.

When we wondered about having an extended family under one roof, one of the sons said, "If a day goes by when we don't see each other, we are very sad." To assure harmony in the family, the three brothers married three sisters from another family. They also assured us that entertaining our group of 22 was no problem. If we weren't there, they'd have had as many of their neighbors in.

No Turkish gathering is complete without dancing, and anyone who can snap fingers and swing a hula hoop can be comfortable on the living-room dance floor of new Turkish friends. Two aunts, deaf and mute from meningitis, brought the house down with their shoulders fluttering like butterflies. We danced and talked with four generations until after midnight.

Stepping into the late-night breeze, I noticed that what had seemed to be a forested hillside was now a spangled banner of lights shining through windows, each representing a "Third World" home filled with as many "family values" as the one we were a part of that night. So much for my stereotypical image of fanatical Muslim hordes. Before we left the next morning, our friends tossed a gunnysack of hazelnuts into our bus.

For decades, this eastern end of Turkey's Black Sea coast was a dead end, butting up against the closed border of Soviet Georgia. But today the former USSR is ringed by sprawling "Russian markets" rather than foreboding guard posts.

From Finland to Turkey, we found boxy Lada automobiles overloaded with the lowest class of garage-sale junk, careening toward the nearest border on a desperate mission to scrape together a little hard cash. In the Turkish coastal town of Trabzon, 300 yards of motley tarps and blankets displayed grandpa's tools, pink and yellow "champagnski," Caspian caviar (the blue lid is best), battered samovars, fur hats, and nightmarish Rube Goldbergian electrical gadgetry. A Georgian babushka lady with a linebacker's build, caked-on makeup, and bleached-blonde hair offered us a wide selection of Soviet pins, garish plastic flowers, and practically worthless ruble coins.

To satisfy my group's strange appetite for godforsaken border crossings, we drove out to the Georgian border. No one knew if we could cross or not. As far as the Turkish official was concerned, "No problem." We were escorted through the mud, past pushcarts bound for flea markets and huge trucks mired in red tape. In this strange economic no-man's-land, the relative prosperity of Muslim Turkey was clear. Just a prayer call away from Georgia, a sharp little Turkish mosque with an exclamation-point minaret seemed to holler, "You sorry losers, let us help you onto our boat." Young Georgian soldiers with hardly a button on their uniforms checked identity cards, as those who qualified squeezed past the barbed wire and through the barely open gate. A soldier told us we couldn't pass. In search of a second opinion, we fetched an officer who said, "Visa no, problem"—a negative that, for a second, I misinterpreted as a positive.

Driving inland from the Black Sea under 10,000-foot peaks, our bus crawled up onto the burnt, barren, 5,000-foot-high Anatolian plateau to Erzurum, the main city of Eastern Turkey (24 hours by bus from Istanbul). Life is hard here. Blood feuds, a holdover from feudal justice under the Ottomans, are a leading cause of imprisonment. Winters are below-zero killers. Villages spread out onto the plateau like brown weeds, each with the same economy: ducks, dung, and hay.

But Allah has given this land some pleasant surprises. The parched plain hides lush valleys where rooftops sport colorful patches of sundried apricots, where shepherd children still play the eagle-bone flute, and where teenage boys prefer girls who dress modestly. And you can crack the sweet, thin-skinned hazelnuts with your teeth.

Entering a village, we passed under a banner announcing, "No love is better than the love for your land and your nation." Another ducks, dung, and hay town, it took us warmly into its callused hands. Each house wore a tall hat of hay—food for the cattle and insulation for the winter. Mountains of cow pies were neatly stacked and promised warmth and cooking fuel for the six months of snowed-in winter that was on its way. A man with a donkey cart wheeled us through town. Veiled mothers strained to look through our video camera's viewfinder to see their children's mugging faces. The town's annually elected policeman bragged that he keeps the place safe from terrorists. Children scampered around women beating raw wool with sticks—a rainbow of browns that would one day be woven into a carpet to soften a stone sofa, warm up a mud-brick wall, or serve as a daughter's dowry.

Driving east from Erzurum, we set our sights on 17,000-foot Mount Ararat, which is in the part of Turkey inhabited by Kurds. Villages growing between ancient rivers of lava expertly milk the land for a subsistence living. After a quick reread of the flood story in Genesis, I realized this powerful, sun-drenched, windswept land had changed little since Noah docked.

On a ridge high above our bus, I could make out the figure of a lone man silhouetted against a bright blue sky waving at us. A few years ago, he could have been a guerrilla. Once a deadly internal conflict, Turkey's fight with its persistent Kurdish insurgency has pretty much died down in the last decade. But the turmoil in Iraq—and the prospect that those Kurds could form an autonomous nation—has reignited this prickly issue. One thing is for sure: Turkey does not want to share a border with an independent Kurdistan.

When I got up early the next morning to see the sunrise over Mount Ararat, I could make out a long convoy of Turkish army vehicles. It reminded me that these days it takes more than 40 days of rain to fix things. Our world is a complicated place in which the nightly news is just a shadow play of reality. To give it depth, you need to travel.

For the entire script of my Eastern Turkey public television program, check out www.ricksteves.com/tv.

77. The Treasures of Luxor, Egypt

Egypt seems distant and, to many, frightening. The constant hustle ruins the experience for softer tourists—if you're looking for quaint and charming, look elsewhere. But Egyptians are extremely friendly and genuinely happy to see you; you will hear "Welcome to Egypt" often (for some, it's the only English words they know). And the sightseeing and cultural thrills are among the best on earth.

With my travel spirit flapping happily in the breeze, I pedal through Luxor on my rented one-speed, catching the cool shade and leaving the stifling heat with the pesky *baksheesh*—beggar kids—in the dusty distance.

Choosing the "local ferry" over the "tourist ferry," I'm surrounded by farmers rather than sightseers. As the sun rises, reddening the tomb-filled mountains, I pedal south along the West Bank of the Nile. The noisy crush of tourists is gone. The strip of riverbank hotels back in Luxor is faint and silent. I'm alone in Egypt: a lush brown and green world of reeds, sugarcane, date palms, mud huts, and a village world amazingly apart from what the average tourist sees.

An irrigation ditch leads me into the village of Elbairat. Here, I am truly big news on two wheels. People scurry, grabbing their families to see the American who chose them over King Tut. I'm sure somewhere in the Egyptian babble were the words, "My house is your house." They would have given me the Key to the Village, but there were no locks.

Elbairat is a poor village with a thriving but extremely simple farm economy. A little girl balances a headful of grass—heading home with a salad for the family water buffalo. A proud woman takes me on a tour of her mud-brick home, complete with a no-fly pantry filled with chickens and pigeons.

This is the real Egypt...how the majority of Egypt's 81 million people live. So close to all the tourists, yet rarely seen.

Start your Egyptian experience in the urban jungle of Cairo, which enjoys a chaotic energy. With each visit, I stay at the Windsor Hotel (www .windsorcairo.com). Stepping into the ramshackle elevator most recently, I asked the boy who ran it if he spoke English. He said, "Up and down." I said, "Up." He babied the collapsing door to close it, turned the brass crank to send us up, and expertly stopped us within an inch of the well-worn second-floor lobby, where even people who don't write feel like writers.

One of the more interesting ways to see Egypt

Across the street, the neighborhood gang sat in robes sucking lazy water pipes called *shishas* (a.k.a. hookahs or hubbly-bubblies). With everyone wearing what looked like hospital robes, playing backgammon and dominoes with pipes stuck in their mouths like oxygen tubes, and clearly going nowhere in a hurry, it seemed like some strange outdoor hospital game room. For about a buck, the smoke boy brought me one of the big free-standing pipes and fired up some apple-flavored tobacco.

For an authentic immersion in Cairo's cultural blast furnace, hire a taxi and cruise through the teeming, poor neighborhood called "Old Cairo." Adventuresome types can roll down the windows, crank up the Egyptian pop on the radio, lean out, and give pedestrians high fives as you glide by. Others may simply want to pray (with your eyes open).

The issue with Cairo traffic is not so much speed as the lack of turn signals, the constantly honking horns, and the absence—or complete ignorance—of any traffic rules. All together, it makes for an indelible travel memory. You are in the midst of what feels like a junkyard of cars come to life, vans packed with people, donkeys pulling cartloads of onions, motorcycles with three or more people squeezed on, and caftan-clad pedestrians weaving through the vehicles to cross the street. You're experiencing Cairo at its colorful and noisy best...and worst.

Then head for Luxor. Plenty of cheap flights from Cairo are available on Egyptair (www.egyptair.com). But the overnight train ride from Cairo to Luxor is posh and scenic, a fun experience in itself. A deluxe air-conditioned sleeping car provides comfortable two-bed compartments, fresh linen, a wash basin, dinner, and a wake-up service (www.egyptrail.gov.eg).

On top of the "village-by-bike" thrills, Luxor is a delight. The East Bank offers two famous sites: Karnak (with the Temples of Amun, Mut, and Khonsu, one mile north of Luxor) and the Temple of Luxor, which dominates Luxor town.

To the ancient Egyptians, the world was a lush green ribbon cutting north and south through the desert. It was only logical to live on the East Bank, where the sun rises, and bury your dead on the West Bank, where the sun is buried each evening. Therefore, all the tombs, pyramids, and funerary art in Egypt are on the West Bank.

Directly across the Nile from Luxor is the Temple of Queen Hatshepsut, Deir el-Medina, Ramesseum, Colossi of Memnon, and the Valleys of the Kings, Queens, and Nobles. Be selective. You'll become jaded sooner than you think. (Before you trek too far, buy tickets for all the sites you plan to visit at the Central Ticket Office just beyond the Colossi of Memnon.)

Luxor town itself has plenty to offer. Explore the tourist market. Pick up an inexpensive, custom-made caftan *(galabaya)* and have your name sewn on in arty Arabic. In the spice market, breathe deeply the heavy

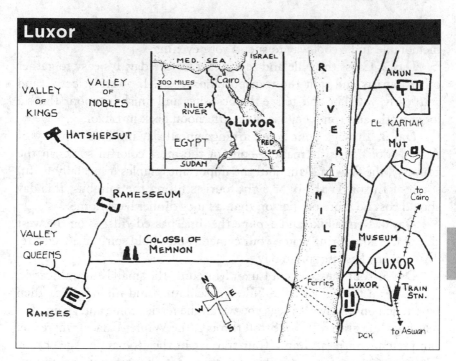

Luxor

scents of cinnamon, cardamom pods, and chilies. North of the temple are the more traditional souks (markets). Behind the newly built Hilton Luxor, shops (with less-pushy vendors) sell a wide array of scarves. Here you'll find even more colorful storefront food shops—including bakers selling warm-from-ancient-stone-ovens breads and pastries. I found the merchants who pester the tourists at the tombs across the Nile had the best prices on handicrafts and instant antiques. A trip out to the camel market is always fun—and you can pick up a camel for half the US price.

Five Days in Luxor

For me, five days in a mid-size European city is asking for boredom. But Luxor (pop. 375,000) fills five days like no other place its size.

Day 1. Your overnight train from Cairo arrives around 5 a.m. If it's too early to check in, leave your bags at a hotel, telling them you'll return later to inspect the room. Hop a horse carriage to be at the temples at Karnak when they open, while it's still cool. (These comfortable early hours should never be wasted.) Check into a hotel by midmorning. Explore Luxor town. Enjoy a felucca ride on the Nile at sunset. If you decide to go to the Karnak sound-and-light show after dark, be sure to select a time when it's broadcast in your language. The show is a little cheesy and packed with big tour groups, but seeing the temple at night is memorable and a cool way to spend your evening.

Day 2. Cross the Nile and rent a taxi for the day. It's easy to gather other tourists and split the transportation costs. If you're selective and start early, you'll be able to see the best sites and finish by noon. That's a lot of work, and you'll enjoy a quiet afternoon back in Luxor.

Day 3. Through your hotel, arrange an all-day minibus trip to visit Aswan (don't miss its market—one of the most colorful souks in the country), the Aswan Dam, and the important temples (especially Edfu) south of Luxor. With six or eight tourists filling the minibus, this day should cost no more per person than a fancy dinner back home.

Day 4. Rent a bike and explore the time-passed villages on the west side of the Nile. Bring water, your camera, and a bold spirit of adventure. This was my best Egyptian day.

Day 5. Tour the excellent Luxor Museum. The small Mummification Museum on the bank of the Nile is fascinating and informative. Then have lunch on the riverbank as you watch the ferries come and go and the feluccas glide gracefully by. Stroll through the Winter Palace, where you can pretend you're a Grand Tour traveler in the Romantic Age. Enjoy Luxor town and take advantage of the great shopping opportunities. Catch the quick flight or overnight train back to Cairo.

In the cool months (peak season), it's wise to make hotel reservations. Off-season, in the sweltering summer heat, plenty of rooms sit vacant. Air-conditioning is found in moderately priced hotels. Budget hotels with a private shower, fan, and balcony offer doubles for about $30. A cot in the youth hostel costs $5. But Egypt is not a place where you should save money at the expense of comfort and health. For under $150, you'll get a double room with a buffet breakfast in a First World resort–type hotel with an elitist pool and a pharaoh's complement of servants. (Consider the riverside Sofitel Winter Palace Hotel; the new section is less atmospheric but half the price of the historic old palace; from the US, dial 011-20-95-238-0425, www.sofitel.com, h1661@sofitel.com.)

Eat well and carefully. With the terrible heat, your body requires lots of liquid. Bottled water is cheap and plentiful, as are soft drinks. Or try a glass of the local specialty: beautiful ruby-red hibiscus tea called *karkade* (served hot or chilled). It was said to be the favorite of pharaohs. Watermelons, which can be cooled in your hotel's refrigerator, are thirst-quenching. Choose a clean restaurant. Hotels generally have restaurants comparable to their class and price range.

To survive the high temperatures, try to schedule your sightseeing day from 5 a.m. (or when you hear the morning prayers on the city loudspeakers commence) until noon. The summer heat, which they say can melt car tires to the asphalt, is unbearable and dangerous after noon. Those early morning hours are prime time: The temperature is comfortable, the light is crisp and fresh, and the Egyptian tourist hustlers are still sleeping. Spend afternoons in the shade. And celebrate the spectacular Nile sunsets.

Carry water and wear a white hat (on sale there). An Egypt guidebook (those by Lonely Planet and Rough Guide work well) is a shield that shows unwanted human guides that you need no help.

Stay on the budgetary defense. No tip will ever be enough. Tip what you believe is fair by local standards and ignore the inevitable plea for more. Consider carrying candies, cheap ballpoint pens, or little gifts for the myriad children constantly screaming *"Baksheesh!"* ("Give me a gift!") Hoard small change in a special pocket so you'll have tip money readily available. Getting change back from your large bill is tough.

Transportation in and around Luxor is a treat. The taxis are horse-drawn carriages. These are a delight, and posted taxi prices make it unnecessary to haggle over the cost (although it is customary to leave a tip). The locals' ferry crosses the Nile from dawn until late at night and costs only pennies.

Travel on the West Bank by donkey, bike, or automobile taxi. You can rent donkeys for the romantic approach to the tombs and temples of West Thebes—but be warned: Sun melts the romance fast. Bikes work for the cheap and hardy—the ride up to the Valley of the Kings is especially tough going. A taxi is the quickest and most comfortable way to explore. When split among four, a taxi for the "day" (6 a.m. to noon) is reasonable. Save money by assembling a tour group at your hotel. You'll enjoy the quick meet-you-at-the-ferry-landing service and adequately cover Luxor's West Bank sights.

Cruise on the Nile in a felucca, the traditional sailboat, for just a few dollars an hour. Lounging like Cleopatra in the cool beauty of a Nile sunset is a romantic way to end the day and start the night.

Lounging on a felucca as the sun sets on the Nile

APPENDIX

Contents

Sample Routes

After years of designing bus tours, brainstorming with my guides, and helping travelers plan their itineraries, I've come up with some fun and efficient three-week plans. These itineraries are fast but realistic if you plan well and travel smart. They're roughly the routes our guided bus tours follow, and are also the routes covered in my various country guidebooks.

Great Britain in 22 Days

While this three-week itinerary is designed to be done by car, it can be done by train and bus or, better yet, with a BritRail & Drive Pass (best car days: Cotswolds, North Wales, Lake District, Scottish Highlands, Hadrian's Wall). For three weeks without a car, I'd probably cut back on the recommended sights with the most frustrating public transportation (South and North Wales, Ironbridge Gorge, and the Scottish

Highlands). Lacing together the cities by train is very slick. With more time, everything is workable without a car.

Day 1: Arrive in London, catch bus to Bath. Get over your jet lag in Bath (3 nights).

Day 2: Enjoy Bath.

Day 3: Pick up your rental car and day-trip to the stone circle at Avebury and the towns of Wells and Glastonbury.

Day 4: Visit South Wales, including St. Fagans Museum and Tintern Abbey. Head for the Cotswolds and sleep in Chipping Campden (2 nights).

Day 5: Explore the Cotswolds and Blenheim Palace.

Day 6: Visit Stratford, Warwick Castle, and Coventry. Sleep in Ironbridge Gorge (1 night).

Day 7: Explore Ironbridge Gorge, then head to North Wales. If the Welsh medieval banquet is going on at Ruthin Castle, enjoy the banquet and sleep in Ruthin; otherwise, sleep in Conwy (2 nights).

Day 8: Enjoy the highlights of North Wales.

Day 9: Stop by Liverpool to enjoy Beatles sights, then head to Britain's tacky but fun "Coney Island," Blackpool (1 night).

Day 10: Explore the southern Lake District, home-basing in the Keswick area (2 nights).

Day 11: Tour the northern Lake District.

Day 12: Drive up the west coast of Scotland, overnighting in Oban (1 night).

Day 13: Explore the scenic Scottish Highlands, looking for the Loch Ness monster. End your day in Edinburgh (3 nights).

Day 14: Another Highlands adventure, or begin touring Edinburgh.

Day 15: More time in Edinburgh.

Day 16: Visit Hadrian's Wall and the Beamish Museum, arriving in Durham in time for an evensong at the cathedral (1 night).

Day 17: Explore the North York Moors, winding up in York. Turn in your car and check into your hotel (2 nights).

Day 18: Enjoy York.

Day 19: Take an early train to London and begin exploring the city (3 nights).

Day 20: Enjoy London.

Day 21: More time in London.

Day 22: Fly home.

Ireland in 23 Days

This three-week itinerary is designed to be done by car, although most of it can be done by train and bus. For three weeks without a car, spend

your first three nights in Dublin using buses and taxis. Cut back on the recommended sights with the most frustrating public transportation (Ring of Kerry, Valley of the Boyne, Connemara, and Counties Mayo, Wexford, and Donegal). You can book day tours by bus for some of these areas through local tourist offices. For at least two people traveling together, taxis—while expensive—can work in a pinch if the bus schedule doesn't fit your plans (i.e., Cork to Kinsale, Dublin to Trim). If you have time for only one idyllic peninsula on your trip, I'd suggest the Dingle Peninsula over the Ring of Kerry.

Day 1: Fly into Dublin, pick up your rental car, and visit the ancient Glendalough monastic settlement in the Wicklow Mountains. Sleep in Kilkenny (2 nights).

Day 2: Explore Kilkenny, with a side-trip to the Rock of Cashel.

Day 3: Move on to Waterford. Sleep in Waterford (2 nights).

Day 4: Visit County Wexford sights (Hook Head Lighthouse, Kennedy Homestead, *Dunbrody* Famine Ship, Irish National Heritage Park).

Day 5: Drive to Cobh, explore the town, then continue on to Kinsale (2 nights).

Day 6: Enjoy Kinsale.

Day 7: Visit Muckross House and Farms, then move on to Kenmare (1 night).

Day 8: Tour the Ring of Kerry, ending in Dingle (3 nights).

Day 9: Drive or bike the Dingle Peninsula loop.

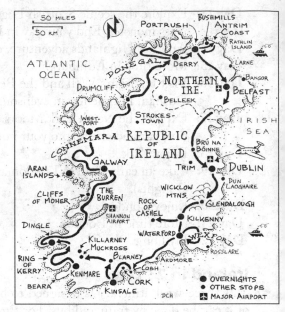

Day 10: Make a day trip out to the Blasket Islands or relax in Dingle (this is a good laundry/rest day).

Day 11: Head north to Galway, stopping along the way at the dramatic Cliffs of Moher. Explore the Burren region and enjoy the Dunguaire Castle medieval banquet in Kinvarra before settling down in Galway (2 nights).

Day 12: Spend the day in Galway.

Day 13: Take a boat out to the Aran Islands, where you'll sleep (1 night).

Day 14: Tour the wild Connemara area and County Mayo, winding up in Westport (1 night).

Day 15: Drive to Northern Ireland, ending in Derry (2 nights).

Day 16: Side-trip to Donegal.

Day 17: Enjoy Derry, then drive to Portrush (2 nights).

Day 18: Explore the Antrim Coast.

Day 19: Head into Belfast and explore Northern Ireland's capital (1 night).

Day 20: Drive to the Valley of the Boyne sights, then on to Dublin. Drop off your car and check into your hotel or B&B (3 nights).

Day 21: Enjoy Dublin.

Day 22: More time in Dublin.

Day 23: Fly home.

APPENDIX

France in 22 Days

This itinerary is designed to be done by car, but works by train with liberal use of buses, mini-van tours, and taxis. A France Flexipass with nine train days works well. A France Rail & Drive Pass is another good option a car is especially efficient in Normandy, the Dordogne, and Provence. If you have only two weeks, do your Paris sightseeing at the start of your trip, skip Honfleur, and fly home from Nice. *Bonne route!*

Day 1: Fly into Paris, pick up your car, visit Giverny and Honfleur, and overnight in Honfleur (1 night). Save Paris sightseeing for the end of your trip.

Day 2: Spend today at D-Day sights: Arromanches, American Cemetery, and Pointe du Hoc (and Caen Memorial Museum, if time allows). Dinner and overnight in Bayeux (1 night).

Day 3: Visit the Bayeux tapestry and church, then go to Mont St. Michel. Sleep on Mont St. Michel (1 night).

Day 4: Spend your morning on Mont St. Michel, then head for châteaux country in the Loire Valley. Tour Chambord, then stay in Amboise (2 nights).

Day 5: Do a day-trip, touring Chenonceaux and Cheverny or Chaumont. Save time at the end of the day for Amboise and its sights.

Day 6: Head south to the Dordogne region, stopping at Oradour-sur-Glane en route. End in your choice of Dordogne villages, where you'll sleep (2 nights).

Day 7: Browse the town and market of Sarlat and tour the Font-de-Gaume cave.

Day 8: Head to the Languedoc region, have lunch in Puycelci or Albi, and spend the evening in Carcassonne (1 night).

Day 9: Enjoy a morning in Carcassonne, then on to Provence with a stop at the Pont du Gard aqueduct. Stay in Arles (2 nights).

Day 10: All day for Arles and Les Baux.

Day 11: Visit Avignon or a Provençal hill town such as Roussillon, then depart for the Riviera, staying in Nice or Villefranche-sur-Mer (2 nights).

Day 12: Sightsee in Nice and Monaco.

Day 13: Make the long drive north to the Alps, and sleep in Chamonix (2 nights).

Day 14: With clear weather, do the mountain lifts up to Aiguille du Midi and beyond.

Day 15: Devote another half-day to the Alps (in Chamonix or Annecy). Then head for Burgundy, ending in Beaune for a wine-tasting. Sleep in Beaune (1 night).

Day 16: Spend the morning in Beaune, then move on to Colmar (2 nights).

Day 17: Enjoy Colmar and the Route du Vin villages.

Day 18: Return to Paris, visiting Verdun and Reims en route. Collapse in your Paris hotel (4 nights).

Day 19: Sightsee Paris.

Day 20: More time in Paris.

Day 21: Finish up your sightseeing in Paris, and consider side-tripping to Versailles.

Day 22: Fly home.

Scandinavia in 22 Days

This itinerary, designed to be done by car, can also be done by public transportation (train, bus, and boat). Doing this itinerary by train is most efficient with a little reworking: I'd go overnight whenever possible on any train ride six or more hours long. Streamline by doing North Zealand, Odense, and Ærø as a three-day side-

trip from Copenhagen. Take the overnight train from Copenhagen to Stockholm (via Malmö), skipping Växjö and Kalmar. The Bergen/Setesdal/Århus/Copenhagen leg is possible on public transit, but Setesdal (between Bergen and Kristiansand) is not worth the trouble if you don't have a car. Consider flying out of Bergen.

Day 1: Arrive in Copenhagen (3 nights).

Day 2: Sightsee Copenhagen.

Day 3: More time in Copenhagen.

Day 4: Head through North Zealand and into Sweden. Spend the night in Växjö (1 night).

Day 5: Explore Växjö, then continue through Glass Country to Kalmar, where you'll sleep (1 night).

Day 6: Continue on to Stockholm (2 nights).

Day 7: Sightsee Stockholm.

Day 8: All day in Stockholm, then take the night boat to Helsinki.

Day 9: Enjoy the day in Helsinki before returning to Stockholm on the night boat.

Day 10: Head to the town of Uppsala, then on to Oslo (3 nights).

Day 11: Sightsee Oslo.

Day 12: More time for Oslo.

Day 13: Go north to Lillehammer, in the Gudbrandsdal Valley. Sleep in the Jotunheimen area (1 night).

Day 14: Explore the Jotunheimen Mountains and head for the fjords. Sleep in the Lustrafjord area or Aurland (1 night).

Day 15: Gawk at the Sognefjord, taking the "Norway in a Nutshell" route to Bergen (2 nights).

Day 16: Spend the day in Bergen.

Day 17: Take the long drive south through the Setesdal Valley to Kristiansand (1 night).

Day 18: Catch the boat to Denmark, where you'll explore Jutland, stopping in Århus and Legoland. Sleep in Århus or near Legoland in Billund (1 night).

Day 19: Continue south to the salty island of Ærø, where you'll sleep in the village of Ærøskøbing (2 nights).

Day 20: Enjoy Ærø.

Day 21: Head back north to Copenhagen, via Odense (Hans Christian Andersen House) and Roskilde (Viking ships).

Day 22: Fly home.

Spain and Portugal in 22 Days

While this itinerary is designed to be done by car, it works by train

Granada's Alhambra is a Moorish masterpiece.

and bus. For three weeks without a car, I'd simplify it by starting in Barcelona and finishing in Lisbon. From Barcelona, fly or take the speedy AVE train to Madrid (see Toledo, Segovia, and El Escorial as side-trips); take the early, direct train from Madrid to Granada (leaving at about 9:05 a.m.); bus along Costa del Sol to Tarifa (day-trip to Morocco); bus to Arcos de la Frontera, Sevilla, and Algarve; and take the train to Lisbon. This skips Salamanca, Coimbra, and Nazaré, and assumes you'll fly "open jaw" into Barcelona and out of Lisbon. If you're taking the train from Lisbon

back to Madrid, you can sightsee your way in three days (via Coimbra and Salamanca), or simply catch the night train straight to Madrid.

Day 1: Arrive in Barcelona (2 nights).

Day 2: Enjoy Barcelona's sights.

Day 3: Sightsee Barcelona, then take afternoon AVE train (or flight) to Madrid (2 nights).

Day 4: Sightsee Madrid.

Day 5: Pick up your rental car and drive to El Escorial palace and Franco's monumental Valley of the Fallen on your way to

Segovia (1 night).

Day 6: Sightsee Segovia before driving to Salamanca (1 night).

Day 7: See the sights in Salamanca, then cross the Portuguese border and head for Coimbra (2 nights).

Day 8: All day for Coimbra.

Day 9: Visit Batalha and/or Fátima en route to Nazaré for the afternoon and night (1 night).

Day 10: Sightsee Nazaré, then visit Belém on the way into Lisbon (2 nights).

Day 11: All day for Lisbon.

Day 12: Morning in Lisbon, then head to Portugal's south coast, the Algarve. Sleep in Salema (2 nights).

Day 13: Enjoy a beach day, and consider a side-trip to Cape Sagres.

Day 14: Head east across the Spanish border to Sevilla (2 nights).

Day 15: All day for Sevilla. Consider a flamenco show tonight.

Day 16: Follow Andalucía's Route of White Villages to the hill town Arcos de la Frontera (1 night).

Day 17: See Arcos, then head south to Jerez (sherry bodegas and horse shows), and on to Tarifa (2 nights).

Day 18: Use Tarifa as a home base for a day trip into Morocco.

Day 19: Visit Gibraltar and drive to Granada (2 nights).

Day 20: All day to enjoy Granada and visit the Alhambra.

Day 21: Leave early and drive through La Mancha to Toledo (1–2 nights).

Day 22: Spend the day in Toledo. Sleep again in Toledo or move on to Madrid for another overnight or a late flight home.

Germany, Austria, and Switzerland in 23 Days

Although this itinerary is designed to be done by car, you can do it by train with minor modifications. If traveling by train, sleep in Füssen rather than Reutte, sleep on the train from Vienna to Zürich on your way to the Swiss Alps (skipping Hall and Appenzell), skip French-speaking Switzerland, skip the Black Forest, and add two days in Berlin, connecting it with night trains.

Overlooking the Rhine

Day 1: Arrive in Frankfurt, pick up your car, and drive to Rothenburg (2 nights).

Day 2: Sightsee the medieval walled town of Rothenburg.

Day 3: Drive along the Romantic Road route to Reutte, Austria (2 nights).

Day 4: Using Reutte as a home base, spend the day at castles near Füssen and other sights in Bavaria.

Day 5: Drive to Munich and begin exploring the city (2 nights).

Day 6: All day in Munich.

Day 7: Drive over the Austrian border to Salzburg and see the town (1 night).

Day 8: Tour the *Sound of Music* country, the Salzkammergut Lake District. Spend the night in tiny Hallstatt (1 night).

Day 9: Visit Mauthausen Concentration Camp and follow the Danube into Vienna (3 nights).

Day 10: All day to enjoy Vienna.

Day 11: Another day for Vienna.

Day 12: Make the long drive into Switzerland, ending in the Swiss village of Appenzell. Sleep in Appenzell or in the mountain hut at Ebenalp (1 night).

Day 13: Drive west to the Berner Oberland, and stay in the high-altitude village of Gimmelwald (2 nights).

Day 14: Enjoy a free day in the Alps, with great hikes and spectacular views.

Day 15: Spend some time in Bern, then drive west to Murten (2 nights).

Day 16: Using Murten as a home base, day-trip south through the French Swiss countryside to Lake Geneva.

Day 17: Drive to the Black Forest, spending the night in the village of Staufen (1 night).

Day 18: Tour the Black Forest on your way north to Baden-Baden (2 nights).

Day 19: Relax and soak in the baths at Baden-Baden.

Day 20: Drive to the Rhine, take a river cruise, and visit some castles. Sleep in the riverside town of Bacharach (1–2 nights).

Day 21: Explore the Mosel Valley, including one of Europe's best castles: Burg Eltz. Return to spend the night in Bacharach, or sleep in the cute Mosel village of Beilstein.

Day 22: More time on the Rhine, or visit Köln and/or Frankfurt. To extend your trip, take a night train to Berlin.

Day 23: Fly home (or enjoy some time in Berlin).

Best of Italy in 22 Days

This trip is best by car, but works fine by rail with a few modifications. For the longer segments served by faster trains, you can either buy reserved

tickets through a US travel agent, or pick them up upon arrival in Italy. Pay as you go for short, unreserved runs, such as Milan to Varenna or the hops between villages in the Cinque Terre. In the Dolomites, consider basing yourself in Bolzano. From Venice, go directly to the Cinque Terre, then do Florence and Siena. A car is efficient in the hill towns of Tuscany and Umbria, but a headache elsewhere. Sorrento is a good home base for Naples and the Amalfi Coast. Skip Paestum unless you love Greek ruins. To save Venice for last, start in Milan and see everything but Venice on the way south, then sleep through everything you've already seen by catching the night train from Naples or Rome to Venice. This saves you a day and gives you an early arrival in Venice.

Day 1: Arrive in Milan (1 night).

Day 2: Pick up your rental car and drive to Lake Como. Sleep in Varenna (2 nights).

Day 3: Enjoy romantic Lake Como.

Day 4: Drive to the Dolomites with a three-hour stop in Verona. Sleep in the alpine town of Castelrotto (2 nights).

Day 5: Explore the Dolomites (hikes, lifts, mountain bikes, horseback riding).

Day 6: Drive to Venice (2 nights).

Day 7: All day for Venice.

Day 8: Head to Italy's art capital, Florence (2 nights).

Day 9: Spend the day sightseeing in Florence.

Day 10: Go to the Cinque Terre, on the Italian Riviera, and set up in the village of Vernazza (2 nights).

Day 11: All day to enjoy the Cinque Terre (great beaches and hikes).

Day 12: Drive to Siena via Pisa (2 nights).

Day 13: Sightsee Siena.

Day 14: Free time to explore Tuscany and Umbria. Sleep in the hill town or *agriturismo* of your choice (2 nights). Assisi and Orvieto are good options.

Day 15: More free time in Tuscany and Umbria.

Day 16: Drive early to the Amalfi Coast. Sleep in Sorrento (3 nights).

Day 17: Spend the day sightseeing in Sorrento, with a side-trip to Pompeii.

Day 18: Using Sorrento as a home base, day-trip to Paestum via the Amalfi Coast.

Day 19: Drive to Rome, drop off your rental car, and explore Italy's capital (3 nights).

Day 20: Enjoy Rome.

Day 21: More time for Rome.

Day 22: Finish up your sightseeing in Rome, and fly home.

The Best of Western Europe in 23 Days

This far-reaching itinerary makes most sense by train; a Eurail Global Pass for 21 consecutive days is a good fit. Taking two night trains avoids two long travel days. The day trips from Munich to Salzburg and from Florence to Siena keep the hotel situation streamlined and take advantage of excellent public transportation services. With your railpass, the Rhine cruise is covered, and you get a discount on the Romantic Road bus that runs Frankfurt–

Rothenburg–Füssen–Munich (though the train is preferable, entirely covered, and faster). While the route can be done by car (with certain adjustments), this plan is heavy on big cities, where cars are worthless and expensive to park.

Day 1: Arrive at Amsterdam's Schiphol airport, and stay in the nearby town of Haarlem (2 nights).

Day 2: Using Haarlem as a home base, day-trip to Amsterdam.

Day 3: Cross the German border to the Rhine River Valley. Explore the quaint riverside town of Bacharach (2 nights).

Day 4: Cruise the best stretch of the Rhine (between Bacharach and St. Goar), then tour St. Goar's Rheinfels Castle. Return to Bacharach by train.

Day 5: Take the train to Rothenburg and sightsee (1 night).

Day 6: After a morning in Rothenburg, take the Romantic Road bus to Munich (1 night).

Day 7: Spend the day in Munich, or consider day trips: a bus tour to "Mad" King Ludwig's fairy-tale castles, or a train from Munich to Salzburg (1.5 hours each way). Take a night train to Venice.

Day 8: All day to enjoy Venice (1 night).

Day 9: Head from Venice to Florence (3 nights).

Day 10: Spend the day in Florence's museums.

Day 11: Using Florence as a home base, side-trip to Siena.

Day 12: Head for Rome (3 nights).

Day 13: Sightsee Rome.

Day 14: More time in Rome.

Day 15: Take the train to the Cinque Terre and set up in the village of Vernazza (2 nights).

Day 16: Today's a "vacation from your vacation" in the Cinque Terre. Hit the beach or hike the Riviera trails.

Day 17: Train into the Swiss Alps, and sleep in the mountain town of Gimmelwald (3 nights).

Day 18: Alps Appreciation Day: Spend the day enjoying the hiking and high-mountain scenery.

Day 19: More time in the Alps. If the weather's bad, side-trip to Bern or Luzern.

Day 20: Take a morning train from Interlaken to Paris (3 nights), then spend the afternoon sightseeing.

Day 21: All day for Paris.

Day 22: More time in Paris, maybe with a day trip to Versailles.

Day 23: Fly home.

The Best of Eastern Europe in 22 Days

This ambitious, once-over-lightly, far-reaching itinerary works best by public transportation. Most of the time, you'll take the train. There are a few exceptions: Bled and Ljubljana are better connected by bus. To get from Bled to Plitvice, take the bus to Ljubljana, the train to Zagreb, and then the bus to Plitvice. To get from Plitvice to the coast, take the bus to Split. The Dalmatian Coast destinations are connected to each other by boat or bus (no trains). No single railpass covers all of the trains, but point-to-point tickets are cheap to buy as you go.

The massive Hungarian Parliament watches over Budapest from the bank of the Danube.

By car, this itinerary is exhausting, with lots of long road days. It makes more sense to connect long-distance destinations by night train (e.g., Prague to Kraków) and then strategically rent cars for a day or two in areas that offer inviting day-trip destinations difficult to reach by public transit (e.g., the Czech or Slovenian countryside).

Day 1: Arrive in Prague and begin sightseeing (2 nights).

Day 2: All day in Prague.

Day 3: All day for more Prague. Take a night train to Kraków.

Day 4: Arrive in Kraków and check into your hotel (2 nights). Spend the day sightseeing in Kraków.

Day 5: Using Kraków as a home base, day-trip to Auschwitz.

Day 6: Finish up in Kraków, maybe including a side-trip to Wieliczka Salt Mine. Then take the overnight train (via

Füzesabony) to the charming Hungarian town of Eger (1–2 nights); if the Eger night train is not available, take the night train to Budapest instead, and continue to Eger in the morning.

Day 7: Spend the day enjoying Eger.

Day 8: Take the train to Budapest, check into your hotel, and begin sightseeing (3 nights).

Day 9: All day in Budapest.

Day 10: More time in Budapest.

Day 11: Catch the direct nine-hour train to Ljubljana, Slovenia, where you'll sleep (no night-train option, 2 nights).

Day 12: Spend the day touring Ljubljana.

Day 13: Go to Lake Bled and explore the lake and surrounding mountains. Sleep in the town of Bled (2 nights).

Day 14: Rent a car for a day trip around the Julian Alps.

Day 15: Cross into Croatia to Zagreb for a few hours of sightseeing, then take an early-evening bus to Plitvice Lakes National Park. Sleep in a Plitvice hotel (1 night).

Day 16: Spend the morning hiking the waterfall wonderlands of Plitvice, then take an afternoon bus to the Dalmatian Coast. Sleep in Split (2 nights).

Day 17: Sightsee Split.

Day 18: Island-hop by boat to Hvar, then to the island town of Korčula, where you'll sleep (2 nights).

Day 19: Spend the day relaxing in Korčula.

Day 20: Take the boat or bus to Dubrovnik, and check into your hotel (2 nights).

Day 21: All day for exploring Dubrovnik.

Day 22: Fly home.

Greece (Athens and the Peloponnese) in 15 Days

This itinerary works best by car. To stretch this plan to three weeks, visit the mysterious monastery-topped stone formations at Meteora, or spend more time on your choice of Greek isles.

Day 1: Arrive in Athens and begin sightseeing (3 nights).

Day 2: Sightsee in Athens.

Day 3: More time in Athens.

Day 4: Take the boat to Hydra (2 nights).

Day 5: Sightsee in Hydra.

Day 6: Take boat back to Athens, pick up your rental car, and drive to Delphi (1 night).

Day 7: Sightsee in Delphi, then drive to Olympia (1 night).

Day 8: Sightsee in Olympia, then drive to Kardamyli (2 nights).

Day 9: Relax in Kardamyli.

Day 10: Take the Mani Peninsula loop drive, then continue on to Monemvasia (2 nights).

Day 11: Sightsee in Monemvasia.

Day 12: Explore Mycenae en route to Nafplio (2 nights).

Day 13: Sightsee in Nafplio and take a side-trip to Epidavros.

Day 14: Return to Athens (1 night), where you'll drop off the rental car.

Day 15: Fly home (or go off in search of your favorite Greek island).

The Whirlwind Tour: Europe's Best Two-Month Trip

Let's assume you have two months, plenty of energy, and a desire to see as much of Europe as is reasonable. Fly into London and travel around Europe with a two-month Eurail Global Pass. You'll spend two months on the Continent and use any remaining time in Great Britain, before

Europe's Best Two-Month Trip

or after you start your railpass (because Eurailpasses don't cover Great Britain). Budgeting about $1,450 for a two-month first-class Eurailpass, $120 a day for room and board, and about $20 a day for sightseeing and entertainment, the entire trip will cost about $9,850 per person. (This does not include airfare—generally $1,000–1,500.) It can be done. Rookies on a budget do it all the time—often for less.

If I were planning my first European trip and wanted to see as much as I comfortably could in two months (and I had the experience I now have to help me plan), this is the trip I'd take. I have to admit, I itch just thinking about this itinerary.

Several of these destinations are included in this book's "Back Doors" section. In these cases, I've noted which chapter you can turn to for more details and accommodations suggestions. For one fat book covering many of the stops mentioned below, consider this year's *Rick Steves' Best of Europe* guidebook.

London and Side-Trips—5 days

London is Europe's great entertainer; it's wonderfully historic. Culturally milder than the Continent, it's the best starting point for a European adventure. The English speak English, but their accents will give you the sensation of understanding a foreign language.

From London's airports, you'll find easy train or subway access to the hotels. To get your bearings, catch a "hop-on, hop-off" orientation bus tour (departs every 20 min) from the park in front of Victoria Station. Give the London Eye a spin and tour the spiffed-up British Museum. Every day will be busy and each night filled with a play and a pub. For more on London, see Chapter 58.

Spend your remaining time in the English countryside: Bath (see Chapter 59), the Cotswolds (see Chapter 62), York (see Chapter 60), and the university city of Cambridge. But the Continent beckons. Paris is less than three hours away by Eurostar train (at least 15 trains/day). Cheaper seats can sell fast. To save money, order your tickets up to six months ahead (www.ricksteves.com/eurostar). If you'll be ending your trip in London, plan for your return: Reserve the accommodations of your choice and get tickets to a hot play.

Paris—3 days

Ascend the Eiffel Tower to survey a Paris studded with architectural gems and historical one-of-a-kinds. You'll recognize the Louvre, Notre-Dame, the Arc de Triomphe, Sacré-Cœur, and much more.

Take a walk covering Paris' biggies. From the Latin Quarter, head to Notre-Dame, the Deportation Monument to Nazi victims, and Sainte-Chapelle. Cross the Seine over the famous Pont Neuf. Walk by the Louvre, through the Tuileries Gardens, and up the avenue des Champs-Elysées to the Arc de Triomphe.

Be sure to experience the Louvre, Orsay Museum (Impressionism), Rodin Museum (*The Thinker* and *The Kiss*), Napoleon's Tomb, a jazz club, and Latin Quarter nightlife. Spend an evening in Montmartre soaking in the spiritual waters of the Sacré-Cœur and browsing among the tacky shops and artists of the place du Tertre. Pick up the *Pariscope* entertainment guide. Most museums are

Paris' Eye-ful Tower

closed on Monday or Tuesday.

Learn the Paris Métro (subway)—it's fast, easy, and cheap. Ask your hotelier to recommend a small family-owned restaurant for dinner. For more on Paris, see Chapter 46.

Side-trip to Europe's greatest palace, Louis XIV's Versailles (take the RER-C train to the end of the line: Versailles R.G.). Another great side-trip is the city of Chartres, with its wonderful Gothic cathedral (cathedral tours by historian Malcolm Miller Mon–Sat at noon and 2:45 p.m., no tours last half of Aug and Jan–Feb).

Start your Eurailpass when you leave Paris. Take the overnight train to Madrid (14 hours), or take a detour...

Loire Valley—2 days

On the way to Spain, explore the dreamy châteaux of the Loire Valley. Make Amboise your headquarters. Stay at the luxurious Le Manoir les Minimes (34 quai Charles Guinot, tel. 02 47 30 40 40, www.manoirles minimes.com) or the half-timbered Hôtel le Blason (11 place Richelieu, tel. 02 47 23 22 41, www.leblason.fr), or enjoy bed and breakfast at L'Iris des Marais with the engaging Katia Frain (14 quai des Marais, tel. 02 47 30 46 51, www.irisdesmarais.com). Consider an all-day bus tour of the châteaux. For the simplest approach to château sightseeing, skip the Loire and see Vaux-le-Vicomte, the epitome of a French château, just a 45-minute side-trip from Paris.

Madrid—2 days

On arrival, reserve your train out. Reservations are required on long trains in Spain and on all trains when using a railpass.

Take a taxi or the subway to Puerto del Sol to find a central hotel. Try Hotel Europa (just off Puerta del Sol, Calle del Carmen 4, tel. 915-212-900, www.hoteleuropa.net) or Hostal Acapulco (Calle de la Salud 13, fourth floor, tel. 915-311-945, hostal_acapulco@yahoo.es).

Bullfights, shopping, and museums will fill your sunny days. Madrid's three essential sights are the Prado Museum (Goya, El Greco, Velázquez, Bosch), Reina Sofía (Picasso's *Guernica*), and the Royal Palace (one of Europe's most lavish interiors). Bullfights are on Sundays and holidays throughout the summer (check at hotel, buy tickets at arena). Tourists and pickpockets alike enjoy El Rastro, a huge flea market that sprawls every Sunday.

From Madrid, side-trip to Toledo (30 min by AVE train, or about an hour by bus or shared taxi).

Toledo—1 day

Save a day for this perfectly preserved historic capital, home of
El Greco and his masterpieces.
Back in Madrid, take the night
train to Lisbon (about 10 hours).
Night trains make sense for long
distances in Iberia, and there is
no daytime train to Lisbon. But
remember, domestic shuttle flights
cost less than $100.

*Toledo: Spain's historic capital and
El Greco's hometown*

Lisbon—2 days

Lisbon, Portugal's friendly capi-
tal, can keep a visitor busy for days. Its highlight is the Alfama. This
salty old sailors' quarter is a photographer's delight. You'll feel rich here
in Europe's bargain basement (see Chapter 42).

Side-trip to Sintra for its eclectic Pena Palace and mysterious ruined
Moorish castle. Circle south for a stop on Portugal's south coast, the
Algarve (train from Lisbon to Lagos, about 3.5–4.5 hours).

Algarve—2 days

Settle down in Salema, the best beach village on the south coast of
Portugal (see Chapter 43). Cross into Andalucía for flamenco, hill towns,
and Sevilla.

Sevilla and Andalucía—3 days

After strolling the *paseo* of Sevilla, the city of flamenco, sleep at Hotel
Amadeus (lovingly decorated with a music motif, Calle Farnesio 6, tel.
954-501-443, www.hotelamadeussevilla.com), or the homey Pensión
Córdoba (Farnesio 12, tel. 954-227-498, www.pensioncordoba.com).
Then head for the hills and explore Andalucía's Route of the White
Villages. Arcos de la Frontera is a good home base (see Chapter 44).
From Sevilla, ride the speedy AVE train back to Madrid. Fly or catch
the speedy AVE day train (or slower night train) to Barcelona.

Barcelona—2 days

Tour the Picasso Museum, relax, shop, and explore the Gothic Quarter.
Stay at the simple Hotel Jardí (Plaça Sant Josep Oriol 1, tel. 933-015-
900, www.hoteljardi-barcelona.com) or the palatial but affordable
Hotel Granvía (Gran Via de les Corts Catalanes 642, tel. 933-181-900,

www.nnhotels.com). Catch a train to Arles, France (about 8 hours with 2 transfers).

Provence or French Riviera—2 days

Your best home base for Provence is Arles (Hôtel Régence, 5 rue Marius Jouveau, tel. 04 90 96 39 85, www.hotel-regence.com). Tour the Papal Palace in Avignon and ramble among Roman ruins in Nîmes (nearby Pont du Gard bridge) and Arles (amphitheater).

Most of the Riviera is crowded, expensive, and stressful, but if you're set on a Riviera beach, Nice is where the jet set lies on rocks. Tour Nice's great Chagall Museum and stay at B&B Nice Home Sweet Home (35 rue Rossini, mobile 06 19 66 03 63, www.nicehomesweethome.com). Then dive into intense Italy.

Cinque Terre—2 days

The Cinque Terre is the best of Italy's Riviera. You will find pure Italy in these five sleepy, traffic-free little villages between Genoa and Pisa. Although it's becoming more well-known, the Cinque Terre remains the ultimate Italian coastal paradise (see Chapter 37).

As you finish a day-long Riviera hike, your home village, Vernazza, comes into view.

Florence—1 day

Florence is steeped in history and art. Europe's Renaissance art capital is packed in the summer but worth the headaches. Reserve ahead at the Uffizi Gallery from the US online at www.b-ticket.com/b-ticket /Uffizi or by phone by calling 011-39-055-294-883 (or ask your hotelier to reserve it for you when you book your room). Stay at Casa Rabatti (cheap, homey, near station, Via San Zanobi 48 black, tel. 055-212-393, casa rabatti@inwind.it), Hotel Accademia (elegant, marbled, more expensive, Via Faenza 7, tel. 055-293-451, www.hotelaccademiafirenze.com), or Soggiorno Battistero (mid-range, next door to the Baptistery, Piazza San Giovanni 1, tel. 055-295-143, www.soggiornobattistero.it).

Hill Towns of Tuscany and Umbria—2 days

This is where dreams of Italy are fulfilled. Visit Siena and Civita di Bagnoregio (see Chapter 38).

Rome—3 days

Devote your first day to classical Rome: Tour the Colosseum, Forum, Capitol Hill (and its museum), and Pantheon. Linger away the evening at Piazza Navona. Chocolate *tartufo* ice cream is mandatory.

For your second day, visit Vatican City. Tour the Vatican Museum and Sistine Chapel; take the back exit out of the Sistine Chapel to get directly into St. Peter's Basilica (avoiding the line). Climb to the top of the dome for a grand view. Take advantage of the Vatican's post office, which is better than Italy's. Picnickers will find a great open-air produce market three blocks before the Vatican Museum entrance.

Spend your third morning at Ostia Antica, ancient Rome's seaport (like Pompeii, but just a subway ride away from Rome). In downtown Rome, visit Piazza Barberini for its Bernini fountain and Cappuccin crypt (thousands of bones in the first church up Via Veneto). In the early evening, join Romans doing the "Dolce Vita stroll" from Piazza del Popolo to the Spanish Steps. Have dinner on Campo de' Fiori. Explore Trastevere, where yesterday's Rome lives out a nostalgic retirement.

Stay near the Vatican Museum at Hotel Alimandi Tunisi (Via Tunisi 8, tel. 06-3972-3941, toll-free Italian tel. 800-122-121, www.alimandi.it) or near the train station at Hotel Oceania (Via Firenze 38, 3rd floor, tel. 06-482-4696, www.hoteloceania.it). Take a train to Venice (about 5–8 hours, or an overnight train).

Venice—2 days

Cruise the colorful canals of Venice. Grab a front seat on boat #2 for an introductory tour down the Grand Canal. Stay near the Rialto Bridge at Albergo Guerrato (Calle drio la Scimia 240a, tel. 041-528-5927, www.pensioneguerrato.it) or near St. Mark's Square at Hotel Campiello (Castello 4647, tel. 041-520-5764, www.hcampiello.it). The Accademia Gallery showcases the best Venetian art. Tour the Doge's Palace and St. Mark's, and catch the view from the Campanile bell tower. Then wander, leave the tourists, and get as lost as possible. Don't worry—you're on an island,

In Venice, it's fun to get lost.

and you can't get off. Catch the night train to Vienna (about 11.5 hours).

Extras You May Want to Add

More England—Bath, York, Cambridge, and the Cotswolds
Ireland—Dublin, Dingle Peninsula
Scotland—Edinburgh, St. Andrews, the Highlands, Isle of Skye
French Alps—Chamonix, Aiguille du Midi
Belgium—Bruges, Brussels
Poland—Kraków, Warsaw, Gdańsk
Hungary—Budapest, Eger, Pecs, Sopron
Slovenia—Lake Bled, Julian Alps, Ljubljana
Croatia—Dubrovnik and the Dalmatian Coast, Plitvice Lakes National Park, Rovinj and Istria
Spain's South Coast and Morocco
Southern Italy—Naples and the Amalfi Coast
Greece—Athens, the Peloponnese, the islands
Russia—St. Petersburg, Moscow (visa required in advance)
Visiting, resting, and a little necessary slack for laundry and post-cards
Travel days to avoid sleeping on the train

Vienna—2 days

Savor the elegance of Habsburg Vienna, Paris' eastern rival. This grand capital of the mighty Austrian Empire is rich in art history and Old World charm. Stay at tidy Pension Hargita (Andreasgasse 1, tel. 01/526-1928, www.hargita.at) or the classier Pension Suzanne (near Opera, Walfischgasse 4, tel. 01/513-2507, www.pension-suzanne.at). Side-trip east for a look at Prague (4.5 hours by train).

Prague—2 days

Prague, a magnificently preserved city, is a happening place and the easiest first excursion into Eastern Europe (see Chapter 54).

Salzburg—1 day

Mozart's gone, but you'll find his chocolate balls everywhere. Baroque Salzburg, with its music festival and *Sound of Music* delights, is touristy in a way most love. Sleep cheap at Institute St. Sebastian (Linzergasse 41, tel. 0662/871-386, www.st-sebastian-salzburg.at) or pricier at Gasthaus zur Goldenen Ente (Goldgasse 10, tel. 0662/845-622, www.ente.at).

Surrounded by Austria's Ehrenberg ruins

Tirol and Bavaria—2 days

Tour "Mad" King Ludwig's fairy-tale castle at Neuschwanstein (reserve in advance to avoid waiting in line, www .ticket-center-hohenschwangau.de) and Bavaria's heavenly Wieskirche. Visit the Tirolean town of Reutte and its hill-crowning ruined castles. Running along the overgrown ramparts of the Ehrenberg ruins, your imagination works itself loose, and suddenly you're notching up your crossbow and ducking flaming arrows (see Chapter 71).

Switzerland—3 days

Pray for sun. For the best of the Swiss Alps, establish a home base in Switzerland's rugged Berner Oberland, south of Interlaken. The traffic-free and quiet village of Gimmelwald above the Lauterbrunnen Valley is everything an Alp-lover could possibly want (see Chapter 53).

Switzerland's best big city is Bern and best small town is Murten. The country is crisscrossed with unforgettably scenic train rides. Be careful: Mixing sunshine and a full dose of alpine beauty can be intoxicating.

King of the Alps, high above Gimmelwald

Munich—2 days

Munich, the capital of Bavaria, has a great palace, museums, and the world's best street singers. But they probably won't be good enough to keep you out of the beer halls. You'll find huge mugs of beer, bigger pretzels, and even bigger beer maids. The Hofbräuhaus is the most famous (near Marienplatz in the old town center). Good places to stay include Hotel Münchner Kindl (simple, in old center,

Munich's thriving Marienplatz

Damenstiftstrasse 16, tel. 089/264-349, www.hotel-muenchner-kindl.de) and Hotel Monaco (tucked inside the fifth floor of a nondescript building two blocks from the station at Schillerstrasse 9, tel. 089/545-9940, www.hotel-monaco.de). Take the train to Rothenburg (2.5–3 hours).

Rothenburg and the Romantic Road—1 day

The always-popular queen of quaint German towns, Rothenburg, lies in the heart of medieval Germany (see Chapter 51). Then head for the Rhine.

Rhine/Mosel River Valleys and Köln—2 days

Take a Rhine cruise (covered by the German Pass or any Eurailpass that includes Germany) from Bingen to Koblenz to enjoy a parade of old castles. The best hour of the cruise is from Bacharach to St. Goar. In St. Goar, hike up to the Rheinfels castle (see Chapter 71). Stay in Bacharach at Hotel Kranenturm (Langstrasse 30, tel. 06743/1308, www.kranenturm.com) or up at the Castle Youth Hostel (Jugendherberge Stahleck, tel. 06743/1266, www.diejugendherbergen.de, $25 beds) with panoramic Rhine views.

Cruise along the sleepy Mosel Valley and tour Cochem's castle, Trier's Roman ruins, and the impressive medieval castle Burg Eltz (see Chapter 71). Then go to Germany's capital, ever-vibrant Berlin (a 4.5-hour train ride from Köln).

Berlin—2 days

Berlin, capital of a united Germany, with its great art and stunning Reichstag dome, is worth two busy days. For accommodations, try homey Pension Peters (Kantstrasse 146, tel. 030/3150-3944, www.pension-peters -berlin.de) or the classy Hotel Astoria (Fasanenstrasse 2, tel. 030/312-4067, www.hotelastoria.de). Then take the train from Berlin to Copenhagen (about 6.5 hours by day; or take the longer night train-plus-ferry via Malmö, Sweden).

Climb Berlin's Reichstag dome.

Copenhagen—1 day

Finish your continental experience with a blitz tour of the capitals of Scandinavia: Copenhagen, Stockholm, and Oslo. To save money and time, avoid expensive hotels by sleeping on trains and ferries. From Malmö, Sweden (near Copenhagen), you can take an overnight train to Stockholm or Oslo, and from Copenhagen you can reach Oslo on an overnight cruise.

Leave your bags at the Copenhagen train station. Tour the city during the day and spend the evening at Tivoli, just across the street from the train station. Catch a night train to Stockholm (via Malmö, no night train on Saturdays, about 8 hours; otherwise hourly on the x2000 high-speed train, 5.5 hours). If you'd like to stay overnight in Copenhagen, try a comfortable B&B (such as Puk and Holger De la Cour's home, Amaliegade 34, fourth floor, tel. 33 12 04 68, mobile 23 72 96 45, www.delacour-bed-and-breakfast.eu).

Stockholm—2 days

With its ruddy mix of islands, canals, and wooded parks, Stockholm is a charmer, studded with fine sights: the 17th-century *Vasa* warship, Europe's best open-air folk museum at Skansen, and a gas-lamped old town. Sleep in the elegant Norrmalm neighborhood at the Stureparkens Gästvåning (Sturegatan 58, tel. 08/662-7230, www.stureparkens.nu) or on the centrally located island of Gamla Stan at the Rica Hotel Gamla Stan (Lilla Nygatan 25, tel. 08/723-7250, www.rica.se). Catch the late-afternoon train to Oslo (6–8 hours; night train may run in summer).

Oslo—1 day

After a busy day wandering through Viking ships, the *Kon-Tiki*, and the Nazi Resistance Museum, and climbing the ski jump for a commanding view of the city and its fjord, you'll be famished. It's red-nosed Rudolph with lingonberries for dinner (see Chapter 66).

Scenic Train, Fjord Country, and Bergen—2 days

For the best look at the mountainous fjord country of west Norway, do "Norway in a Nutshell," a combination of spectacular train, boat, and bus rides (see Chapter 66). Catch the morning train from Oslo over the spine of Norway to

Bergen. You can do the Nutshell in a day, but you'll have more fjord fjun if you stay overnight near Flåm in Aurland at the funky Vangsgården Guest House (tel. 57 63 35 80, www.vangsgaarden.no). Enjoy a day in salty Bergen. Stay downtown at Guest House Skiven (good budget rooms, Skivebakken 17, tel. 55 31 30 30, www.skiven.no), or catch the night train back to Oslo (about 7 hours, no night train on Saturday).

Oslo—1 day

Take a second day in Oslo. There's plenty to do. Hop an overnight cruise back to Copenhagen (16 hours).

Copenhagen—1 day

Another day in Copenhagen. *Smörgåsbords*, Viking *lur* horns, and healthy, smiling blondes are the memories you'll pack on the night train south to Amsterdam (about 16 hours).

Amsterdam—2 days

Amsterdam is a study in contrast: Prostitutes shimmy in the Red Light District while marijuana smoke wafts from coffeeshops, all against a backdrop of 17th-century buildings and elegant canals (see Chapter

50). If you prefer a small town home base, consider day-tripping into Amsterdam from nearby Haarlem (Hotel Amadeus Haarlem, Grote Markt 10, tel. 023/532-4530, www .amadeus-hotel.com; or the homey bed-and-breakfast House de Kiefte, Coornhertstraat 3, tel. 023/532-2980, mobile 06-5474-5272, housedekiefte @gmx.net). You'll discover great side-trips in all directions.

After touring crazy Amsterdam and biking through the tulips, you can get to England via a cheap flight (1 hour), the train (4.5 hours via the Chunnel), or boat (about 11 hours). Or, easier still, consider avoiding the return to London by flying out of Amsterdam (arrange this "open jaw" flight before you leave home).

Final Thoughts

This 61-day Whirlwind Tour is just a sampler. There's plenty more to see, but I can't imagine a better first two months in Europe. The itinerary includes opportunities for several nights on trains or ferries. This could save you hundreds of dollars in hotel costs, and also frees up your days for doing more interesting things than sitting on a train or boat.

A Eurailpass is good for two calendar months (e.g., May 15 through midnight July 14). If you validate when you leave Paris and expire (the Eurailpass, not you) on arrival in Amsterdam, you'll spend 53 days, leaving eight days of railpass time to slow down or add options.

Bon voyage!

Travel with Rick Steves Without Leaving Home

Whether you're preparing for your trip, or simply looking to do a little armchair travel, consider joining me on my public television series and my public radio show.

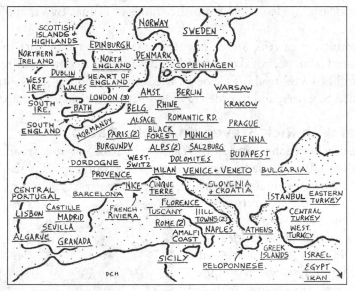

Rick Steves' Europe on Public Television

Our television series, *Rick Steves' Europe,* airs in high definition on more than 300 public television stations across the United States. We've

Producer/director Simon Griffith, cameraman Karel Bauer, writer/host Rick Steves, and David—working together to bring the best of Europe home to you on public television.

filmed more than 100 episodes altogether, covering Europe from top to bottom—from Ireland to Egypt, and from Helsinki to Portugal's south coast—with a new season of 11 shows premiering in late 2010. We've also produced two one-hour specials: *Rick Steves' European Christmas* (celebrating family holiday traditions in seven different European cultures) and *Rick Steves' Iran* (made in the hope of humanizing that proud if perplexing nation of 70 million people).

To see a particular TV show whenever the travel bug bites, you can get our 80 most up-to-date episodes on DVD (up to 8 regional shows per DVD, or the entire series in a 40-hour boxed set that includes specials such as *Rick Steves' Iran*). You can also watch the shows at www.hulu.com. If you'd prefer to view shorter segments, you can download free "vodcasts" (video clips) from the shows at iTunes (www.apple.com/itunes).

Production of *Rick Steves' Europe* is made possible in part through the generous support of American Airlines (www.aa.com) and Bread for the World (www.bread.org). For all the scripts, shooting news, streaming video bloopers, and to order DVDs, visit www.ricksteves.com/tv.

Travel with Rick Steves on Public Radio

My weekly hour-long radio show, *Travel with Rick Steves*, is broadcast by more than 130 public radio stations around the country and is also available as a free on-demand podcast.

It's a great opportunity to hear a wide variety of experts and authors explain what tickles their travel fancy. My guests—who pack their interviews with practical travel tips—have included guidebook authors, travel writers, accomplished naturalists and adventure travelers, experts on art and photography, foodies and flight crews, and local tour guides to take us to around the world. We've met a French philosopher, an Irish member of the British House of Lords, a Masai community leader, and even the Princess of Norway. From France to the Four Corners, from Tuscany to Tanzania, from Dubrovnik to Dubai, from Germany to the Galapagos Islands—plus tips on French food, Italian wine, the geography of bliss, travel budget tricks, and lots more—there's information for any itinerary.

The show also provides a venue for our enthusiastic and well-traveled community of listening Road Scholars to ask questions and share tips.

Even if you're not planning a trip to a particular destination, *Travel with Rick Steves* will bring you a flavor of places near and far, and stimulate your imagination—taking you on a vicarious journey.

Literally hundreds of hours of interviews are organized by country and available for free at my website. My hope: that you can pack them along on your MP3 player so they can bring added understanding and joy to your travels (as they do mine). To make that easy for you to do, try Rick Steves Audio Europe, which puts all of my audio information in one easy place to download to your MP3 player or smartphone. It's free whether you access it at www.ricksteves.com or in iTunes.

For a list of radio stations carrying the show, upcoming topics, and details on how to join in the conversation yourself, see www.ricksteves .com/radio.

Rick's readers—his Road Scholars—have a wealth of travel information to share. For thousands of great hot-out-of-the-rucksack tips on more than 100 different travel topics, visit our Graffiti Wall at www.ricksteves.com/graffiti. Thanks to all those who take the time to share their travel intelligence. Here is a sampling of travelers' tips from the packing, shoes, flying, senior savvy, scams, communicating, and chocoholic sections of the Graffiti Wall.

Packing: Creative Extras

■ Xerox copies of the mug-shot page of my passport for when a hotel or bank needs to have my passport.

■ Sarong: A large piece of lightweight material, it can be used as a quick-drying towel, blanket, pillow, etc.

■ Extra pair of insoles: For when shoes get wet. Overnight, I pulled the insoles out of the pair I wore and let the shoes and insoles air out. A second pair of insoles is much lighter than a second pair of shoes.

■ Inflatable hangers: Clothes dry faster.

■ The two most useful medicines: Tylenol is a general analgesic and helps reduce fatigue. Benadryl is a great sedative and sleep aid.

■ Small suction cups with hooks: To hang a toiletry bag from the mirror in small bathrooms and to dangle money belt from the youth-hostel shower wall.

■ Ladies—two words: Fem Wipes. Cleansing towelettes (Summer's Eve, Massengill) individually wrapped

like Handi-Wipes...great for freshening up—and removing pigeon doo.

■ Half a tennis ball works as a stopper in any sink!

■ Earplugs for the night the hostel gets rowdy!

■ Small plastic baggie: To save theater stubs, train tickets, subway tickets, and all kinds of other tiny souvenirs.

■ Dental floss or fishing line: Strong, versatile, waterproof, nearly weightless. Tied backpack together when it broke, doubled as a shoelace, etc.

■ "Freshette," a feminine standup urinary aide, tel. 800-542-5580, www.freshette.com.

■ Sleep machine/alarm clock: In noisy hotel rooms, the sleep machine (which emits various soothing sounds) is a true godsend.

■ Local CDs: We rented a car, and in each country we visited we bought CDs of traditional music. We'd be driving down German side roads, passing maypoles, and listening to tubas.

■ Comfy slippers: If your feet aren't happy, YOU aren't happy. Pamper them!

■ A portable motion-detector alarm ($30 from Radio Shack): Place near the hotel door or window. If someone moves the door or window, the motion sensor emits a high-pitched sound similar to a fire alarm.

■ If you have a fancy camera, a little black electrician's tape across the brand name discourages thieves. What appears to be a generic camera is almost worthless to those who regularly "hunt" Canon, Leica, Nikon, and so on.

■ I "cinch-tied" the opening of my backpack to make it less accessible for would-be thieves (punched holes in the band at the top of the bag and ran an extendable cable lock through the holes, pulled it tight, and locked it).

■ Fake hair: My thin, sweaty hair looks fabulous with Revlon's fake hair (Spare Hair). Of many styles, my favorite is a "scrunchie" of curled hair on an elastic band. I pull my hair back in a modified pony tail with some hair sticking up out of the elastic band like a bun, bobby pin the loose end of the pony tail around this, then use the Spare Hair scrunchie around the bun twice, and it looks like I've spent hours curling my hair. It takes about 15 minutes to do. I can go days with only washing my bangs.

■ A headlight instead of a flashlight. Better for reading in bed. Frees your hands if needed.

■ Post-It notes to flag guidebooks.

■ Women, pack some yeast infection cream or Monistat one-day suppositories—difficult to find in some countries.

■ Body Shop's "Peppermint Cooling Foot Spray" and "Peppermint Cooling Foot Lotion" in small, travel-size bottles: Soothe tired, aching feet.

■ Tiny musical instrument: If you can play a harmonica, the spoons, the bones, or another tiny instrument, bring it. Playing music can break the ice, start friendships, and even earn you a free meal!

■ Pillowcase: To put your backpack/travel bag in while you sleep on it on an overnight train. It's another obstacle thieves must overcome. Also, set up the Coke-can warning system on your compartment door (a few pennies in an empty can).

■ Put extra camera lenses in a thick ankle sock. You can toss them in your daypack without worrying about damage and they take up less room than bulky lens cases.

■ Pack a picture of your home town and a small map to locate it.

■ Tie something distinctive, like a ribbon, to your luggage handle for quick spotting at airport carousels.

■ Mailing tubes: To collect prints and posters, also handy for small items and breakables. A very thin placemat from a favorite Paris restaurant made it home safely this way and is now framed and hanging in my home.

■ Ziploc bags: To store the second half of that huge café sandwich.

■ Digital voice recorder: A great way to catch the waves, traffic, sounds in the cafés, and more. I send audio files to friends via the Internet, with digital photos.

■ Combo journal/scrapbook: Buy a fancy (lightweight) journal and take colored pens and a glue stick. As you write each day, add creative touches by sketching in color, paste in museum tickets, or even cut/paste local brochures, etc.

■ Vitamin B6: Makes your blood undesirable to mosquitoes. You have to take it for a few days before it works. Also, a couple of years ago I bought a neat little gadget at Babies-R-Us that keeps mosquitoes away. It's designed for babies (who are too young for bug-spray), but works for anyone! This magical red, plastic ladybug clips onto your clothing...or diapers.

Shoes: Walking Softly

■ My Ecco Gore-Tex hiking shoes scrambled thru Scottish Highlands and County Kerry, muddy bogs, wet grass, and muck, not to mention cobbled medieval rambles. Excellent grip. It's not a heavy shoe. The waterproofing is a good idea.

■ Last year I took a pair of Merrell men's walking shoes to Italy. The best part is they are an oxford-type lace-up shoe, but with a cross-training-type sole. We used them for light jogging before breakfast, all-day sightseeing, and for dining out in dressy evening restaurants. They're great shoes if you only want to bring one pair.

■ I've had great luck with any shoes made by Montrail. The soles are specifically designed to handle the added weight of, say, a backpack. You can find them at most outdoor stores.

■ I've loved my Dr. Martens since my punk-rock years in the early '80s and have yet to find a more comfortable walking shoe. However, these shoes have about a two-week breaking-in period, during which they're pretty darn stiff and uncomfortable.

■ I picked up a pair of Campers about a month before going to Rome, and I was very pleased. They are light, comfortable, and stylish. In fact, many an Italian foot was shod exactly like mine.

■ I took one pair of Rockport Pro Walkers to Europe for two weeks, and they were wonderful. Comfortable and stylish, they went with everything. With only one pair of shoes, I was careful to shake a little foot powder into them every night to keep them from smelling too bad.

■ Hush Puppies work for me. A cloudburst in Siena soaked me and my shoes. They dried out and looked as good as new. Mine are roomy enough for thick socks, which helps for long walks. The smooth black leather looks great with a little touching up. I wear orthotics and they fit fine in the shoes. I carry a lightweight pair of flip-flops for showering and wearing around my hotels or B&Bs.

■ I bought a pair of Ecco shoes three and a half years ago. They kept me comfortable and dry during a three-month European backpacking trip—not easy in the Swiss Alps! I am now a tour guide, and for two years these shoes have been the only ones I've used to pound the cobblestones.

■ I purchased a pair of Mephisto Diva boots (workboot styling) for $67 at the Chaussures Magfred shoe store on the rue Cler in Paris (back here in the States they cost $295!). My feet really like these boots! I got great shoes, and a great souvenir from France that I can wear anytime.

■ I have tried several different brands, but always come back to Dansko. I have traveled to Europe on several occasions and have worn the sandals and/or the clogs without any problems. You can purchase discounted Dansko footwear with slight imperfections at www.danskooutlet .com.

■ I traveled Europe for six weeks this spring with an 18-pound backpack and one pair of shoes: Teva Hydro Rodiums. They were great for everything—walking, hiking, whatever. They're light, breathable, and dry very quickly. No socks necessary, either, unless it's cold.

■ I've worn Birkenstock Arizonas for years. They have one type with a padded sole that is really comfortable for standing and walking. They have microfiber straps, and the Birk clerk said the shoes were originally designed for diabetics. Translation: No blisters. Bonus with Birks: They

slip off easily to allow a few minutes of barefooted bliss.

■ I've been searching for the perfect travel shoes. For me, they must meet four criteria: 1) won't look too goofy with khakis; 2) won't look too goofy with shorts; 3) provide enough comfort and support to walk all day; and 4) preferably waterproof. I finally found a shoe to meet all four requirements: Rockports. Mine are nubuck leather, waterproof, and comfortable. And I don't feel like a dork when wearing shorts.

■ As a doctor who treats foot and ankle problems, here are a few tips: Buy quality, break them in first, get used to walking before you go (maybe you'll discover that foot problem before you leave and have it treated here), take along some Advil or other pain reliever, and consider the use of prescription orthotics. They will make your foot do what you hope the "right" shoe will do—but often doesn't.

■ I find that a good pair of hiking shoes (low-cut, lightweight boots) can be more supportive than most shoes. A hiking shoe with a nylon or steel shank (sole stiffener) and some ankle support can take most of the load off your feet when you're walking on cobblestones or hard pavement.

■ As a physical therapist, I would recommend taking two pairs of shoes with good socks. If you are on your feet a lot, simply changing shoes every eight hours prevents foot discomfort.

■ I just came back from 10 days in London and Paris. I saw bowling shoes everywhere, on both men and women. And the matching handbags look like bowling-ball bags. Who'd have thought that if I'd brought my ugly bowling shoes I'd be trendy while walking in Trafalgar Square or strolling the Champs-Elysées?

■ I travel frequently to London and Paris, often in winter. I wear Ecco shoes and couldn't be happier. Even though they're rubber-soled, I always pack a pair of Tingely Moccasin Stretch Storm Rubbers in case it rains. They look like shoes and really keep a rainy day from becoming soggy.

■ If your feet still hurt after a long day tramping around, regardless of your shoes, try this: Put about four inches of cold water in the tub, sit on the side, and put your bare feet in the water. The cold water will numb your aching feet and help reduce swelling. You could also stick your bare feet in any other cold water, like a stream.

■ If you're prone to blisters, try this: Use your underarm antiperspirant on your feet. I'll use it on my heel, arch, toes, and on the top of my foot. Blisters come from heat, heat comes from friction, and the body's response is sweat. Antiperspirant saves your socks and your feet. Remember to use antiperspirant, not deodorant. If you use deodorant, you'll just have nice-smelling blisters.

■ After two trips to Europe that were uncomfortable for my feet, I've finally found a solution. I switched to more technical socks. Good socks are as important as good walking shoes. Use a pair of light running socks that are blended (not 100 percent cotton) and designed to wick away moisture.

■ SmartWool makes a great sock. They keep your feet relatively dry and odor free.

■ What does Rick wear? Mephistos are comfy for my Stateside needs. But for all the walking I do in Europe, I need something sturdier. For many years I wore Rockport Walkers, but now I'm really into the warmth and solid support of my Eccos.

Flying Smart

■ Can't get enough frequent-flyer miles to take your whole family to Europe? Use your US award to get your family to a busy airport such as Newark/New York, Washington DC, or Miami, where there are cheap departures. Using half the frequent-flyer miles we'd need to get to Europe, we got free flights to Newark, where our $300 round-trip tickets to London were less than half of what we'd pay from Colorado. Extra bonus: We got a long layover on the East Coast and spent a week with family there on the way to Europe.

■ With earplugs known as Earplanes, I overcame my problems with ear air-pressure equalization during flights.

■ For the flight over, take earplugs, ski socks, and a large water bottle (fill it at a drinking fountain after you go through airport security). Once the plane takes off, remove your shoes and put on the warm socks. Rather than constantly bugging flight attendants for water, you'll have your own supply.

■ On long flights with small kids, bring a tiny flashlight. The light will quiet a crying toddler.

Senior Savvy

■ Get as much knowledge as possible about your hotel/hostel/room etc. before you leave. Being able to plan how to get to your accommodations is a necessity. For example, staying in castles may be adventurous or romantic, but don't forget that they're built on high points (like mountains or really big hills). Make sure that you know how you're going to get to the top, whether by taxi, bus, etc. You don't want to carry your heavy backpack and a roll-along up a dirt trail with lots of steps. Research your accommodations or suffer.

■ Remember that hostels frequently have bunk beds. You may get a top bunk. If you have problems getting up to it, politely ask if someone will change with you. Most of the time one of the young people will oblige. Buy them a drink in the bar or a bottle of water to show your appreciation.

■ Now that we are seniors, endless stairs are not as enjoyable as they once were. We visit Paris often, buy a transit pass, use the bus system exclusively, and eliminate all of those Métro stairs. A large system map is posted at most bus stops, and a pocket map is available at Métro ticket booths (a magnifying glass is helpful with the small print). We make a point of never being in a hurry (we're on vacation), so waiting at a bus stop is no problem. Another advantage of the Paris bus is being able to see the street life and neighborhoods (not seen on the Métro).

■ On our last trip to Germany, I noticed that discounts are available on most of the boat trips on the Rhine and the Bodensee—on certain days. If you are staying in a departure city such as Rudesheim or Friedrichshafen for several days, schedule your excursion for a discounted day. You can probably check online ahead of time. These trips are a wonderful way to relax. We slap on the sunscreen, stake out a good seat on the sundeck, and sip our wine as we drift past the villages and castles. It's as good as a day-long spa treatment!

■ At 69, I am now an "older traveler." Compared with being a "younger traveler" as I was in 1969, things have improved for me. In general, Europeans respect older people. Although nobody gives me their seat on the Métro (yet), I have noticed that younger people gladly engage with me in conversation and seem interested in me as a person. I recommend that senior travelers stay in hostels occasionally. The ones I've been in welcome people of all ages. You have an opportunity to meet people of different nationalities and ages.

■ London is a very good deal for the over-60 crowd. Ask for the senior rate at museums, theaters, and so on. In quite a few places, we got reduced rates and, in several, admission was free. You will have to show proof of age.

■ On our last trip to Europe, we smiled and politely asked if the establishment offered a senior discount, even when it was not posted that one was available. In nearly every instance we got one. Sometimes it saved us as much as half price. Don't be afraid to ask, but remember to smile.

■ We just returned from a wonderful trip to Germany with my 79-year-old mother-in-law. It soon became apparent that she was having trouble realizing the fact that we "weren't in Kansas anymore." My tip to seniors: Please keep an open mind. Your hotel accommodations may not provide washcloths, Kleenex, or more than one wastebasket. If you don't expect things to be like they are in the States, you'll have a much better time and so will your traveling companions.

■ My wife and I, both seniors, took a tour of Spain, Morocco, and Portugal. After the long transatlantic flight and a day of riding in the bus, my wife's ankles swelled up appreciably. According to the tour guide, this is not unusual. She had my wife keep her legs high the next two nights (by putting a bolster pillow under the foot end of the mattress) and drinking lots of water both days. The swelling was gone by the second day. Moral: Drink lots of water on the way over and during each day!

■ For peace of mind, compile a checklist of all the things you need to do to get your house ready before leaving on vacation. Then, check off the items and take the list with you. This way there is no worrying, "Did I turn off the stove?"

■ People who wear hearing aids should bring spare batteries along and not plan to purchase them in Europe. I thought I had taken enough batteries, but my hearing aids quit near the end of our trip. I went to pharmacies but no one had what I needed, nor did they know where I might purchase that particular size. Finally I discovered the last set in the bottom of my toiletries bag. Otherwise I would have missed lots of sounds our last week.

■ Carry a small notebook to write down things to remember: train reservations to be made, events you want to record later in your journal, and so on.

■ Those of us over-60s traveling by train in Great Britain can take advantage of their Senior Railcard—buy online or from a station agent for £26 (valid for one year, www.senior-railcard.co.uk). The 33 percent savings on most rail fares quickly justifies the cost.

■ At 65+ with bad backs, we hired a taxi in Sorrento to take us sightseeing in Positano, Amalfi, and Ravello, a $300 splurge that was worth every cent.

■ My partner and I stayed in a "youth" hostel for the first time by Lake Como and thought we'd be the oldest people there. Not so! This was the wonderful La Primula hostel near Menaggio, Italy, which offers a spectacular view of the lake while you're dining on great food on their outdoor patio. At our table was a 60-ish couple from Sydney and a 79-year-old British woman who was backpacking alone through Europe! All three were a delight, but especially the backpacker, who said she stays in hostels for the evening company.

■ Most major museums have loaner wheelchairs available, and you'll find this information on their websites. (If they don't mention it, call or email to ask them.) Also, be sure to request, in advance, assistance at the airport. This is a free service that airlines are happy to provide.

■ We have found that many museums in Europe do have elevators even though they have no sign telling about them. Just ask! You will be taken to a small, carefully hidden elevator, and most often escorted to your floor.

■ Seniors in Belgium (over 65 and departing after 9 a.m.) get a huge discount on train fares.

■ Seniors, before traveling outside the US, make sure your travel insurance covers air-ambulance evacuation. I traveled with my 92-year-old father and he became very ill. We had to evacuate him by air ambulance and it cost me $10,000. Thankfully he's fine now. But we could have saved so much anguish if we had been prepared.

■ I traveled for a month in Italy with my 65-year-old mother. We stayed in hotels located as centrally as possible to the sights we wanted to see, and broke most of our days into two parts (with at least an hour of feet-up time after lunch). We were happy to splurge on cabs from the train station to the hotel (easier than hauling your own luggage up and down stairs in the subway or bus, and not terribly expensive). We had an extremely enjoyable trip by not trying to fit too much into each day and enjoying people-watching from cafés when our feet were tired.

■ I went on a trip with a piece of small luggage that also converts into a backpack. I'm in good shape, walk every day, and watch what I eat, but I'm 64 and the backpack eventually made my shoulders ache. The pain lasted for several months. I will use wheeled luggage from now on.

Tourist Scams

■ Just got back from Rome, and the only problem was just me being stupid and inexperienced. But, I learned my lesson! When we first arrived, we got a taxi from the Termini station (without getting a quote ahead of time). When we arrived, the price was €28 (crazy amount!) I was surprised, but I handed him two €20 bills. He took them and then showed me two fives as if that's all I handed him. I had just arrived and was very confused, so I paid the difference and realized what happened right after he drove off. After that, I asked every taxi driver for a cost before I got in and carried smaller bills.

■ While in Barcelona, we stopped our car (a new Renault with French plates) to look at something, and a man on a scooter rode up and asked for directions. While we were talking to him, his partner apparently slit our rear tire with a knife. Several blocks later I pulled over to change the flat tire, and the same two men arrived—disguised with motorbike helmets—to give directions to a "tire shop" just around the corner. I had the trunk lid open to access the spare tire, thus limiting my view into the interior of the car. While the first man was trying to convince me to go with him to the tire shop, the other man was in the car and going through our stuff, including my wife's purse. A local woman on a balcony started screaming at the two thieves; I closed the trunk lid, started shouting and waving the tire wrench, and the two of them dropped the purse and ran off. When I returned the car, I mentioned to the agent that we had been to Barcelona, and he said, "Did you have your tires slit?"

■ High tourist areas like around Sacré-Cœur in Paris and the Spanish Steps in Rome have rip-off artists that will try to make "friendship" bracelets right on your arm. I didn't have problems with these people because I totally ignored them. However, some of my friends didn't listen to my advice and ended up having to buy the bracelets.

■ Pickpockets in Europe's larger cities sometimes dress like business-men. I observed a pickpocket rush onto a subway train car in Rome just as the doors were closing. He was dressed very nicely, as if he was just getting off work. He had his sport coat draped over one arm, and was holding a newspaper in the other. As my husband and I were close to the doors, I observed this man's fingers working the zipper on the woman's handbag just next to me! I looked up, made eye contact with him, and he gave me a "LOOK" that was meant to frighten me. The moral of the story: You need to be watching your surroundings, not just for people that "look" like they might steal from you, but at everyone! Pickpockets have adapted, and will continue.

■ A scam that seems prevalent in Paris (we encountered it three times there) is for a person to "find" a ring on the ground and then ask if it is yours. He then remarks that it is gold and offers to sell it to you. The rings are placed on the ground ahead of time. If you buy it, you'll soon find out that the gold ring that you paid 50 euros for was actually worth 50 cents. Beware of people coming to you asking if you dropped your wallet, ring, or anything else that they "found and picked up." They will offer you the item in exchange for money.

■ When I was in Vienna, my friend and I wanted to buy tickets to that evening's opera. We were walking around Stephensdom and were approached by a rather official-looking lady in a long velvet cape who was selling opera tickets. There were at least eight more of these people walking around in the square, all were selling tickets. She spoke perfect English and said she worked for the opera house and that they sold tickets in the square to help shorten the lines at the box office. She had a clipboard complete with seating chart of the opera house. We bought what we thought were very good seats at a reasonable price, and were given a receipt along with the tickets. Later that night, we were very sadly turned away—the opera had in fact been sold out for a month. We were told by the box office employees that the people in capes often sell fake tickets to tourists. They warned us that the only safe place to purchase tickets was from the box office. Unfortunately, it was too late for us, and we were out about $200.

■ Our change for dinner at a Bolzano restaurant should have been around €6. We received what certainly looked like three €2 coins. Normally we would have just pocketed the change, but I was in the process of collecting a set of euro coins from each country we traveled to, so I examined the coins to see which country they came from. These coins looked really strange. They turned out to be 500-lira coins, which of course aren't worth anything but look amazingly like a €2 coin. We called the waitress right

back and showed them to her. She just shrugged her shoulders, took them back and gave us euros instead. She didn't even try to pretend that she wasn't the one that gave them to us. So watch your money.

■ We experienced the "lost leather jacket salesman" scam in Rome last November. Luckily, I had read Rick's Graffiti Wall and knew about it. My husband, ever ready for a story to tell the grandkids, played along with the guy, showing him how to get to the train station and giving him a map. He gave us two "leather" jackets as a thank you. Then he asked for money for gas. I pulled out a €5 note and told him that was all we had. After several minutes of me trying to give back the jackets and him insisting that we must have more money, he gave up and drove away. I now have two vinyl jackets and a great story to tell. We saw those same jackets in the flea markets for €8 each, so we think we scammed the scam artist!

■ The only "scam" we encountered was the Value-Added Tax refund system. In order to request a VAT refund, you have to get your paperwork stamped at the departure airport after you have gone through immigration. In Rome, we were told the VAT refund office was in another terminal, even though we were in the international departure terminal, so it would be better to get the stamp in Munich, where we connected. In Munich, only one person knew where the office was, and she said it was closed most of the afternoon. So there was no way to get this stamp before we left, and there's no refund without the stamp. When I asked the Lufthansa rep about this, she said it happens all the time. I'd rather give the money to some poor kid pickpocketing than the EU taxman.

■ In Budapest, you will see attractive women walking up and down Váci utca. They are not prostitutes. They approach young men, pull out a map, and pretend they're Eastern European tourists looking for directions, then ask you to have a drink with them at a nightclub. Just say no—otherwise they'll take you to a bar where the only access is via elevator and the Cokes are $20 apiece. Of course, they'll order Cognac. While we were not victims, I did meet a Brit who paid £100 for three drinks.

■ My husband gave me a strange look as we stood on a very crowded car near the exit of the Paris Métro. A 14-year-old boy was picking his back pocket. We were wearing money belts and were not worried because we wanted to see the boy's expression when he finally discovered the phrase book in the pocket he thought was a wallet. It was priceless—he was so disappointed. He even let it slip back down into the pocket. Guess it's all part of the European experience, as Rick says. We could hardly keep from laughing out loud.

■ Having traveled extensively through Europe (and currently living there), I have found that a few minutes of pre-planning will save you the stress of using a potentially crooked

taxi from airports and train stations to your hotel or tourist destination: Ask your hotel when you book your room! They will tell you a range of what it should cost. Write it down and show it to the cabbie before you get in. Only agree to the ride once the price is set, and don't get out and/or pay until you are clearly where you need to be. It seems so obvious and only takes a few seconds, but it is well worth it. Flying completely blind leaves you stuck behind a language barrier arguing over fees for crossing bridges, having multiple people, etc.

■ Watch out for the shell game, like Rick says! I was waiting for a friend and I saw people gathered around nearby. I went over and watched for a while. It looked so easy. It looked like even the tourists were winning. I was finding the ball every time, so I decided to play once. I thought for sure I knew where it was, but it wasn't there, of course. The people in the crowd kept urging me to get my money back by playing again. I shouldn't have listened to them. I lost again, of course! Never even get close to those games. I wasn't going to play, but I did—and it cost me!

■ In Eastern Europe, watch out for vendors giving change in the wrong currency. I was in a rush and the vendor in the Prague train station gave me Hungarian bills as change, instead of Czech currency. Since I was unfamiliar with the currency, I didn't recognize it until much later.

■ In Rome, avoid the young men who carry around roses. They work on flattery and hand roses to women (often young or "beautiful") while dishing out a load of compliments. One such man literally gave me a dozen such roses and shoved them in my hands despite my disapproval, then he turned to my husband and demanded money for them (and he would not allow me to put them back into his hands after I had repeatedly said I did not want any). I got wise and started literally shoving these men out of my way whenever I noticed them approaching.

■ In St. Petersburg there are kiosks throughout the city selling tickets to various theater and cultural events. The tickets are legitimate, but if the agent offers to sell you special "reduced price tickets," don't go for it. These tickets are valid only for Russian citizens, or foreigners with a student or work visa. Thanks to the craftiness of our hostess, we were still able to use the tickets. But, if you want to avoid the embarrassment of being turned away at the door, your best bet is simply to buy your tickets at the theater box office and pay the full non-citizen price. Even this price is still far cheaper than for comparable entertainment in the US.

■ At a well-known, very touristy, upscale coffee shop in Vienna, we had a check for about €14. The stiff, robot-like waiter took our €20 bill and promptly disappeared. After we tracked him down and insisted on getting change, he threw €2 on our table and walked away. I will visit less touristy places from now on.

■ While visiting gravesites at the Père-Lachaise Cemetery in Paris, my girlfriend and I were "befriended" by a very knowledgeable gentleman at Chopin's grave. He told us he worked there and seemed pleased that we spoke some French. He was quite friendly and said, "I'll show you a shortcut to Jim Morrison's grave." Well, an hour later, and quite frankly after an excellent tour of not only the well-known graves but also little-known facts, he led us outside of the cemetery to "Jim Morrison's favorite café." At this point, we knew it wasn't free, and we offered him €5. He was obviously upset and asked for more "for his family." I said I was sorry and I wished he had been up front about the cost. We could tell he was going to start a scene so we said "sorry" again and high-tailed it out of there. After sharing my story with others I've learned of other "friendly tour" scams that have actually ended quite violently. I consider the €5 a very inexpensive education.

■ On my last trip, two men claimed they were police and flashed IDs (and quickly put them away), then asked for my identification with the casual afterthought, "Passport is okay." I said, "Hold up your ID so I can read it carefully." The men looked shocked, then became abusive. I said, "I am now going to scream at the top of my lungs for a real policeman. Would you like to wait and talk to him?" They ran away. This type of scam always takes place away from crowds and out of sight of uniformed policemen. Never be afraid to scream loudly for assistance. I did that once on a bus (yes, #64 in Roma). I screamed *"Aiuto! Ladro!"* ("Help! Thief!"), and the Italians on the bus almost killed the poor thief, shoving her off the bus.

■ My husband and I arrived at Paris' Gare du Nord train station in the early evening and proceeded to read the map to find out how to get to our hotel via the Métro. One guy came up and advised us to buy tickets from the ticket machine. When we were at the machine trying to read the French, another guy came out and "helped" us to buy tickets. Later, what was supposed to be a three-day ticket turned out to be a one-way, single-use ticket. We paid him €48, the price shown on the ticket machine, but he must have cancelled the transaction and bought us the single-trip ticket instead.

■ In Paris, at a boutique across the street from the Louvre, the shop owner presented me with a receipt for €25 for my two T-shirts, but gave me a receipt for €250 to sign for the credit-card purchase. When I called him on it, he claimed it was a mistake. I have no doubt that it was intentional, so consider yourself warned, keep track of your decimals, and watch what you sign.

■ When we visited France—mainly in Paris—we as Americans started wondering why we were getting quarters in our pockets from change. We finally figured it out when we realized that the €1 coin is the same

size as the American quarter. I finally caught on after we bought tickets at a Métro station and realized that the cashier had made this exchange. What a bundle she must be making!

■ Be warned when buying from street artists. A lot of the "original" artwork (mostly the watercolors) is actually just printed by computer on watercolor paper.

■ Beware of letting your round-trip tickets out of sight on the overnight train from Kraków to Prague (or any other Eastern European routes, for that matter). The "conductor" took my round-trip ticket as I got into the *couchette* and assured me that I'd get it back in the morning. Come morning, he said he gave it to me, then later said he put it in my *couchette*. Then he went through the motions of looking in his pockets, but I was screwed. My round-trip ticket was gone and he'd likely sell it for the 25 bucks it was worth. If possible, get a round-trip ticket that is physically two separate pieces of paper, and then only give the conductor the one necessary for that leg of the trip.

■ On a Sunday in Barcelona, I was going from the Picasso Museum to the Palau de la Música Catalana. In order to get there as quickly as possible I headed through one of the side streets—a big mistake! I vaguely noticed three young men standing off to the side. Everything happened very fast. One came in front of me, snatched my travel purse—which I carry across one shoulder and round my neck—with enough force to break the tough strap. He took off down an alley. Fortunately, I lost little of real value because I wear a money belt. The incident made me more conscious of keeping to the more frequented streets.

■ When traveling, use ATMs only when the bank is open. An ATM machine ate our card, and when we went back to the bank in the morning, we found out that it was missing. There were charges already made before we could cancel the card. Train stations and airports often have the best ATMs, with lots of people around to help.

■ We were targeted on the Via Nationale in Rome. As we walked six short blocks from the train station to our hotel, a passerby pointed to my wife's back. We were shocked to see her entire back covered with some kind of whitish brown substance. The man, dressed in a business suit, held his nose, pointed to the sky (birds), and quickly offered a tissue to help us clean up. As we took his tissue and set our backpack on the ground to get more tissue out, another guy swooped in, grabbed the backpack, and started to quickly move away. Fortunately I saw him do it, took three quick steps right at him and yelled. He set the backpack down and took off. What were we thinking? Birds? A poop that size would have needed to come from the largest prehistoric bird known to man.

■ On the way to the airport on the Paris RER, we encountered people working in groups asking for signatures on a petition to help the disabled. They were very aggressive and shoved the petition on my lap and over my bag. They unzipped the bag and tried to pick it, but I protested very loudly.

Communication: Connecting with Locals

■ Sincere admiration opens doors. Admiring someone's dog/cat/flowers/ motorcycle/garden/whatever is a great way to start a conversation.

■ Meet friendly locals in the Czech Republic by attending a hockey game. I am a 26-year-old woman who turned loneliness into lots of fun this way. I'm planning my second solo trip for October, and the hockey arena will be my first stop!

■ When you're on a train, make conversation. Many Europeans want to practice English as much as you may want to practice their native language.

■ One night in Paris, we noticed a hundred or so people on the Pont Neuf, so we checked it out. Locals our age were just hanging out drinking beer, wine, Coke—even smoking pot. Everyone was simply relaxing. My wife and I found a nice spot to sit (Notre-Dame ahead, Eiffel Tower behind), bought a few beers from a vendor, and hung out until well past 1 a.m. No police and no trouble, just a lot of fun.

■ If you're traveling with a skate-board-loving kid, take skateboard/ surfer-type stickers for them to give to new friends.

■ Make eye contact. After a week in Rome, I hadn't really met a soul. So I thought about it—and I realized that I hadn't actually looked at anyone! Being a big-city dweller, I was in the habit of avoiding eye contact with people on the streets. That evening, I made plenty of eye contact, and within an hour I was having the time of my life with new friends at a nearby trattoria!

■ Irish nightlife centers around the pubs. To meet locals, arrive a bit early to snag a big table with several extra chairs. As the night gets busier, people always ask to share the table. Every time I've tried this, I've met a fun montage of great people.

■ A couple of tips: Eat by yourself in busy restaurants. You may be seated at a table of locals with an empty chair, or they may come and sit by you. And fake ignorance. Even if you know the answer, just ask that cute German girl a question. It could lead to a long conversation.

■ When I'm taking public transportation, I like to engage people by asking simple questions (like making sure I'm on the right train, or where to get off), which signals to locals that I'm a traveler looking to connect.

■ The easiest way to meet locals is to be where they are. They're not watching the 10:10 a.m. bell-ringing festival or prowling through souvenir shops. They're living their normal lives: the guy at the car wash, people at the town pool. Visitors are always welcome for a buck or two. Just wander the shopping area of any little town and strike up conversations.

■ Don't be so stuck on your schedule that you miss out on once-in-a-lifetime opportunities. We had just parked our car in a small German town, and a kindly gentleman walking by made a comment about the tight squeeze and how lucky we were to find a place. In chatting with him, we learned that he had served with Rommel in North Africa. Our schedule was suffering, so we said our good-byes. Later it dawned on me that I had missed the chance to discuss real history with a participant. I was too concerned with my plans to take the time to buy the guy a beer, so I missed out on an experience I can never recapture.

■ Pictures of grandchildren are great icebreakers!

■ If you belong to a service club like Kiwanis or Rotary, check the Internet for club meetings.

■ Just as you want to meet local folks when abroad, look kindly on foreign travelers in the United States. They just might be looking for the same kind of experience.

■ Everywhere I've traveled a polite, genuine smile is the best icebreaker.

■ Attending church services can be a great way to meet people. Neighborhood churches (rather than famous cathedrals and huge "downtown" churches) are the best, since visitors are less common there, and people go out of their way to make you feel welcome. Many have a welcoming coffee-and-cookies time after Mass.

■ Try second-class seating on trains. You'll find lively locals instead of stuffy businessmen and American tourists.

■ Track down your European roots! The highlight of my recent European adventure was visiting my Italian relatives—a truly priceless experience. Four months before I left for Europe, I sent my relatives a brief letter. I introduced myself, let them know when I would be in Italy, and told them I would be interested in meeting them. They quickly responded, offering me a ride from the nearest train station and a place to stay. They met me at the station in Trento and brought me to their small village north of the city. I was the only tourist in town, and all 500 inhabitants of the village (many of them my relatives) seemed as excited to meet me as I was honored to meet them.

■ While in Germany, be sure to visit one of the many thermal baths that are found in just about any large town. These places are only frequented by Germans. If you have the courage, pay a bit extra and visit the saunas. Clothing inside a sauna is not optional—it's forbidden! And in most places, men and women sauna together. How's that for an icebreaker?

■ I have just returned from St. Petersburg, Russia. This was my first-ever trip out of the country. I handed out pencils (with pictures of American dollar bills) and candy to the children. I was the talk of the town. I found the people to be very appreciative of me, the dorky American tourist from a small farm town, thanks to candy and funny-looking pencils.

■ Don't know anyone in your destination? You might just make contact over the Internet. Last fall I visited Croatia. Before going I posted to an Internet travel bulletin board while doing research for my trip. A Croatian journalist responded to several of my posts. He gave me lots of good ideas, and when I asked about getting to some of the more remote places in Istria, he responded that he would love to show me his country. I was a little wary about meeting him—but I knew the minute I met him that everything was okay. My new online pal drove me around Istria and showed me things few tourists see.

■ I collect little pins from places I've been and display them on my favorite travel hat. When I'm on the road, the hat gets piles of attention. People comment, want to look at it closely, and ask which pin was from my home city. I bring a few pins from my home, which I give as gifts to new friends.

■ I volunteer for my sheriff's office, and I've recently started collecting police-uniform patches. On my last trip I took several patches from home to swap with law-enforcement agencies. Everywhere I went, I visited the police, who were glad to swap patches. I built my collection and I made a lot of new friends!

■ Try to speak their language. After a seemingly futile attempt to communicate in French, many of the locals would laugh and switch to English and we were fine. The French appreciated our efforts (and we learned as we went).

■ We made personal business cards on our computer and passed these out to people we met as we traveled. Today we still receive email from folks we met. It's great to be remembered and to still keep in touch.

■ Find a good international pen-pal website (I used Penpal International at http://ppi.searchy.net) and meet people from all over the world. Now I have places to go and people to see next time I'm in Europe.

■ Rick's 3-in-1 German, Italian, and French phrase book was my best friend during a recent three-month adventure throughout Europe. I quickly learned that one of the most important phrases was, "Which is your favorite dish/cheese/wine/etc.?" By asking this in restaurants and open-air markets, it shows an interest in the menu and respect for the waiter or vendor and his opinion. The usual result: a great dish, and friendly conversation to boot.

■ Join a club, seek out weekend soccer teams, go to town meetings, visit public swimming pools, shop in small markets, attend school concerts and sporting events, go to nightclubs, attend personal appearances and book-signings in bookstores, track down travel slide shows, go to church, use public transportation, use barbers/hairdressers, buy from small

vintners—there are many low-key ways to meet locals. Be courteous, inquisitive, and willing to participate when appropriate. Show people you are interested in them and their lives, not just the tourist traps, and your trip suddenly becomes more meaningful.

■ One of the best ways to meet people is to bring children with you! We took our two kids for two months around Europe. We did something we would never do in the States, and it worked like a charm: We bribed them. We told them if someone told us how well-behaved or polite they were, they would get the equivalent of $3. We didn't realize how great our kids could be! They discovered right away that saying "please" and "thank you" in the local language, smiling, and saying "good day," earned them a smile and a pat on the head. The money actually became a secondary reward, and they worked harder at learning how to say foreign words and making connections with people than we did.

■ Before a trip overseas, go to your chamber of commerce/hospitality association/tourist board, and they will usually give you small flags or lapel pins of your state to give away to friends you make in your travels.

■ I break barriers by complimenting people and stating (in the native language) when I like something. In a restaurant in Croatia, I saw the cook and said, *"Dobro"*—Croatian for "good." Soon the entire staff was smiling at me, and when I left an hour later I felt more like a friend than just another tourist.

■ The best thing I did to strike up conversation with locals was to sew my state flag's patch to my pack. So many people of all nationalities asked me what it was.

■ Along with "please" and "thank you" it is really useful to learn to say, in the local language, "You have a beautiful country. We are having a wonderful time." Say it over and over. You will be happy and so will everyone else.

■ I notice that whenever I attempt a few words of the native language, the people I'm speaking to are always more open and willing to share great "insider" information with me.

■ Food is truly universal, so if possible, I ask questions about what I'm eating, how it's made, if it's a personal favorite, and so on. People appreciate my genuine interest in their food and cultures and seem delighted to explain the "special ingredient" that makes their dish so good. A great souvenir is bringing the recipe of a favorite place home.

■ In Germany, I shared a bench along the river with an older German lady. We sat in silence for a few minutes until three very good-looking men jogged past on the path. I looked at her, looked at the guys, raised my eyebrows, and said, "Yummm." She laughed, nodded her head, and the ice was broken. We had a fun chat and agreed to meet again the next day. When I showed up, she had brought a German dessert to share with me.

■ Wherever you go, do something local—like a flea market. This is a great way to mingle with residents (and see what they shop for).

■ Before a recent trip to Paris, I accidentally stuck a picture of my dog in the book I was reading. When we got to our hotel, the picture fell out, and I instantly learned I had a great conversation-starter. For the rest of the trip, I was showing off my dog like a proud parent. Love of animals is an international language!

■ Here's one good way to meet people in England: Ask to photograph their dogs! All last summer in England I was on a self-appointed mission to photograph as many Jack Russell terriers as I could. Dog owners love to show off their dogs, demonstrate their best tricks, and tell stories.

■ With four of us traveling together, we knew we were at a disadvantage when it came to "mingling with the locals." To make sure that we did get to have stories to relate over dinner, we separated several times during the day.

■ Remember, the locals you meet are individuals, not tourist attractions who cease to exist when you put away your camera.

Chocoholics Unite

■ Cadbury chocolate bars are awesome. The Dairy Milk, Crunchie, and Wispa bars are fantastic. Also, when in London, try the hot chocolate—tastes just like a liquid Dairy Milk bar.

■ After many years of Swiss-chocolate adoration, I now bow to the Belgians. They are the masters.

■ The best chocolate is in Germany. I lived in Germany for 12 years and couldn't get enough of their chocolate. Milka and Ritter Sport are great! The Kinder Überaschung (Kid's Surprise) eggs are very popular. Also, during Christmas they come out with Advent calendars that have chocolate hidden behind the flip-open door for each day. Eating those made the wait bearable. In London, visit Charbonnel et Walker, 28 Old Bond Street, near Kensington, for the best chocolates anywhere.

■ My favorite European chocolate: Ritter Sport. It's German, but it's sold all over Europe. Ritter Sport is a square bar that comes in a million varieties. My favorite is praline (dark blue wrapper).

■ One word: Sprungli, Zürich, Bahnhofstrasse...OK, that was three words, but when in Zürich, go to the Sprungli shop on Bahnhofstrasse and enjoy...mmmm...makes my mouth water just thinking about it.

■ We did the equivalent of a pub crawl in Bruges and sampled truffles at all the small chocolate shops. By noon we were on a major sugar buzz.

■ Once I met a man on a plane who told me he was the chocolate taster for Hershey's and his job was to travel the world tasting chocolate. His favorite? Belgian.

■ Did you know they put the equivalent of 1.5 cups of milk into every huge Cadbury Dairy Milk bar? At last, a palatable solution to the specter of osteoporosis!

■ A good friend from Brussels explained that "Mary's" had the best chocolate in Brussels (and thus the world). He noted that there are two stores of every type, which are appointed by the King. One is a large, commercial place (Godiva in this case) and one is a small place, where the King actually buys his goods. Mary's is that place.

■ If you are a chocoholic, then you must tour the Cadbury factory (train to Birmingham, then train to Bournville, then a 10-min walk, www.cadburyworld.co.uk). Upon entering, you're greeted with the most heavenly smell, a lively tour, and an entire chocolate bar! As you munch, you walk through the history of chocolate.

■ Try the hot chocolate in Paris to truly experience it the way it was meant to be. The best place is Angelina near the Louvre, across from the Tuileries on rue de Rivoli. Order the Africain, a pot of liquid pleasure. We loved Angelina so much that we named our cat after it.

■ After two trips to Paris, walking everywhere and tasting along the way, we've found our favorite chocolatier. It's Puyricard (on avenue Rapp in the seventh arrondissement).

■ The chocolate factory alone is reason enough to visit Köln, Germany. They offer tours with a history of chocolate-making and a great look at all the machines in action.

These are just the tip of the iceberg. To read many more—and contribute—visit www.ricksteves.com/graffiti.

European Weather

The following climate chart can be helpful in planning your itinerary, although I have never found European weather to be particularly predictable. The first line shows the average daily high, the second line is the average daily low, and the third line shows the average number of days with no rain.

	J	F	M	A	M	J	J	A	S	O	N	D
AUSTRIA • Vienna												
	34°	38°	47°	58°	67°	73°	76°	75°	68°	56°	45°	37°
	25°	28°	30°	42°	50°	56°	60°	59°	53°	44°	37°	30°
	16	17	18	17	18	16	18	18	20	18	16	16
BELGIUM • Brussels												
	40°	44°	51°	58°	65°	72°	73°	72°	69°	60°	48°	42°
	30°	32°	36°	41°	46°	52°	54°	54°	51°	45°	38°	32°
	10	11	14	12	15	15	14	13	17	14	10	12
CROATIA • Dubrovnik												
	53°	55°	58°	63°	70°	78°	83°	82°	77°	69°	62°	56°
	42°	43°	57°	52°	58°	65°	69°	69°	64°	57°	51°	46°
	18	15	20	20	21	24	27	28	23	20	14	16
CZECH REPUBLIC • Prague												
	31°	34°	44°	54°	64°	70°	73°	72°	65°	53°	42°	34°
	23°	24°	30°	38°	46°	52°	55°	55°	49°	41°	33°	27°
	18	17	21	19	18	18	18	19	20	18	18	18
DENMARK • Copenhagen												
	37°	37°	42°	51°	60°	66°	70°	69°	64°	55°	46°	41°
	29°	28°	31°	37°	45°	51°	56°	56°	51°	44°	38°	33°
	14	15	19	18	20	18	17	16	14	14	11	12
EGYPT • Cairo												
	65°	69°	75°	83°	91°	95°	96°	95°	90°	86°	78°	68°
	47°	48°	52°	57°	63°	68°	70°	71°	68°	65°	58°	50°
	30	27	30	30	31	30	31	31	30	31	29	30
FINLAND • Helsinki												
	26°	25°	32°	44°	56°	66°	71°	68°	59°	47°	37°	31°
	17°	15°	20°	30°	40°	49°	55°	53°	46°	37°	30°	23°
	11	10	17	17	19	17	17	16	16	13	11	11
FRANCE • Paris												
	43°	45°	54°	60°	68°	73°	76°	75°	70°	60°	50°	44°
	34°	34°	39°	43°	49°	55°	58°	58°	53°	46°	40°	36°
	14	14	19	17	19	18	19	18	17	18	15	15

	J	F	M	A	M	J	J	A	S	O	N	D
FRANCE • Nice												
	50°	53°	59°	64°	71°	79°	84°	83°	77°	68°	58°	52°
	35°	36°	41°	46°	52°	58°	63°	63°	58°	51°	43°	37°
	23	22	24	23	23	26	29	26	24	23	21	21
GERMANY • Munich												
	35°	38°	48°	56°	64°	70°	74°	73°	67°	56°	44°	36°
	23°	23°	30°	38°	45°	51°	55°	54°	48°	40°	33°	26°
	15	12	18	15	16	13	15	15	17	18	15	16
GREAT BRITAIN • London												
	43°	44°	50°	56°	62°	69°	71°	71°	65°	58°	50°	45°
	36°	36°	38°	42°	47°	53°	56°	56°	52°	46°	42°	38°
	16	15	20	18	19	19	19	20	17	18	15	16
GREECE • Athens												
	55°	57°	60°	68°	77°	86°	92°	92°	84°	75°	66°	58°
	44°	44°	46°	52°	61°	68°	73°	73°	67°	60°	53°	47°
	15	17	20	21	23	26	29	28	26	23	18	16
HUNGARY • Budapest												
	34°	39°	50°	62°	71°	78°	82°	81°	74°	61°	47°	39°
	25°	28°	35°	44°	52°	58°	62°	60°	53°	44°	38°	30°
	18	16	20	19	18	17	21	22	23	21	16	18
IRELAND • Dublin												
	46°	47°	51°	55°	60°	65°	67°	67°	63°	57°	51°	47°
	34°	35°	37°	39°	43°	48°	52°	51°	48°	43°	39°	37°
	18	18	21	19	21	19	18	19	18	20	18	17
ITALY • Rome												
	52°	55°	59°	66°	74°	82°	87°	86°	79°	71°	61°	55°
	40°	42°	45°	50°	56°	63°	67°	67°	62°	55°	49°	44°
	13	19	23	24	26	26	30	29	25	23	19	21
ITALY • Palermo, Sicily												
	60°	62°	63°	68°	74°	81°	85°	86°	83°	77°	71°	64°
	46°	47°	48°	52°	58°	64°	69°	70°	66°	60°	54°	49°
	19	20	23	24	28	28	31	29	26	23	22	21
MOROCCO • Marrakech												
	65°	68°	74°	79°	84°	92°	101°	100°	92°	83°	73°	66°
	40°	43°	48°	52°	57°	62°	67°	68°	63°	57°	49°	42°
	24	23	25	24	29	29	30	30	27	27	27	24
NETHERLANDS • Amsterdam												
	40°	42°	49°	56°	64°	70°	72°	71°	67°	57°	48°	42°
	31°	31°	34°	40°	46°	51°	55°	55°	50°	44°	38°	33°
	9	9	15	14	17	16	14	13	11	11	9	10

How Europe Compares to North America

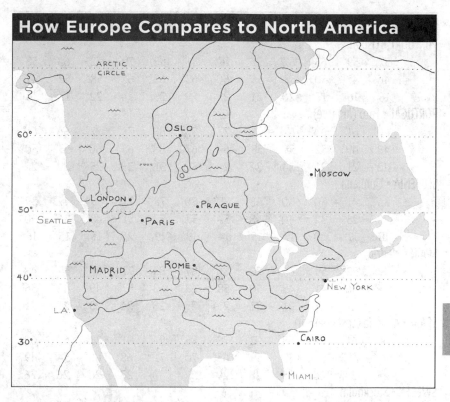

Wondering what clothes to pack? Europe and North America share the same latitudes and a similar climate. This map shows Europe superimposed over North America (shaded) with latitude lines. Use the map as a general weather guide. For example, London and Canada's Vancouver are located at a similar latitude and are both near the sea, so you can assume their climates are nearly the same. But you can't go by latitude alone. Rome and New York City should have similar weather, but Rome is hotter because it's surrounded by the warm Mediterranean. Inland areas have colder winters, so Prague can get as chilly as Minneapolis. Elevation affects climate as well. For more info, see the climate chart here and www.weatherbase.com. Bon voyage!

	J	F	M	A	M	J	J	A	S	O	N	D
NORWAY • Oslo												
	28°	30°	39°	50°	61°	68°	72°	70°	60°	48°	38°	32°
	19°	19°	25°	34°	43°	50°	55°	53°	46°	38°	31°	25°
	16	16	22	19	21	17	16	17	16	17	14	14
POLAND • Kraków												
	32°	34°	45°	55°	67°	72°	76°	73°	66°	56°	44°	37°
	22°	22°	30°	38°	48°	54°	58°	56°	49°	42°	33°	28°
	15	13	19	15	19	15	15	16	18	17	15	15

	J	F	M	A	M	J	J	A	S	O	N	D
PORTUGAL • Lisbon												
	57°	59°	63°	67°	71°	77°	81°	82°	79°	72°	63°	58°
	46°	47°	50°	53°	55°	60°	63°	63°	62°	58°	52°	47°
	16	16	17	20	21	25	29	29	24	22	17	16
PORTUGAL • Faro (Algarve)												
	60°	61°	64°	67°	71°	77°	83°	83°	78°	72°	66°	61°
	48°	49°	52°	55°	58°	64°	67°	68°	65°	60°	55°	50°
	22	21	21	24	27	29	31	31	29	25	22	22
SLOVENIA • Ljubljana												
	36°	41°	50°	60°	68°	75°	80°	78°	71°	59°	47°	39°
	25°	25°	32°	40°	48°	54°	57°	57°	51°	43°	36°	30°
	18	17	20	17	15	14	19	19	20	17	15	16
SPAIN • Madrid												
	47°	52°	59°	65°	70°	80°	87°	85°	77°	65°	55°	48°
	35°	36°	41°	45°	50°	58°	63°	63°	57°	49°	42°	36°
	23	21	21	21	21	25	29	28	24	23	21	21
SPAIN • Almería (Costa del Sol)												
	60°	61°	64°	68°	72°	78°	83°	84°	81°	73°	67°	62°
	46°	47°	51°	55°	59°	65°	70°	71°	68°	60°	54°	49°
	25	24	26	25	28	29	31	30	27	26	26	26
SWEDEN • Stockholm												
	30°	30°	37°	47°	58°	67°	71°	68°	60°	49°	40°	35°
	26°	25°	29°	37°	45°	53°	57°	56°	50°	43°	37°	32°
	15	14	21	19	20	17	18	17	16	16	14	14
SWITZERLAND • Geneva												
	38°	42°	51°	59°	66°	73°	77°	76°	69°	58°	47°	40°
	29°	30°	36°	42°	49°	55°	58°	58°	53°	44°	37°	31°
	20	19	22	21	20	19	22	20	20	21	19	21
TURKEY • Istanbul												
	46°	47°	51°	60°	69°	77°	82°	82°	76°	68°	59°	51°
	37°	36°	38°	45°	53°	60°	65°	66°	61°	55°	48°	41°
	13	14	17	21	23	24	27	27	23	20	16	13

Metric Conversion

1 inch	=	25 millimeters	1 ounce	=	28 grams
1 foot	=	0.3 meter	1 pound	=	0.45 kilogram
1 yard	=	0.9 meter	Temp. (°F)	=	9/5 °C + 32
1 mile	=	1.6 kilometers	1 kilogram	=	2.2 pounds
1 sq. yd.	=	0.8 square meter	1 kilometer	=	0.62 mile
1 acre	=	0.4 hectare	1 centimeter	=	0.4 inch
1 quart	=	0.95 liter	1 meter	=	39.4 inches

INDEX

MAP INDEX

Audio Europe

Free mobile app (and podcast)

With the **Rick Steves Audio Europe** app, your iPhone or smartphone becomes a powerful travel tool.

This exciting app organizes Rick's entire audio library by country—giving you a playlist of all his audio walking tours, radio interviews, and travel tips for wherever you're going in Europe.

Let the experts Rick interviews enrich your understanding. Let Rick's self-guided tours amplify your guidebook. With Rick in your ear, Europe gets even better.

Thanks Facebook fans for submitting photos while on location! From top: John Kuijper in Florence, Brenda Mamer with her mother in Rome, Angel Capobianco in London, and Alyssa Passey with her friend in Paris.

Find out more at ricksteves.com/audioeurope

ricksteves.com

turn your travel dreams into affordable reality

▶ Free Audio Tours & Travel Newsletter

Get your nose out of this guide book and focus on what you'll be seeing with Rick's free audio tours of the greatest sights in Paris, London, Rome, Florence and Venice.

Subscribe to our free Travel News e-newsletter, and get monthly articles from Rick on what's happening in Europe.

▶ Great Gear from Rick's Travel Store

Pack light and right—on a budget—with Rick's custom-designed carry-on bags, roll-aboards, day packs, travel accessories, guidebooks, journals, maps and DVDs of his TV shows.

130 Fourth Avenue North, PO Box 2009 • Edmonds, WA 98020 USA
Phone: (425) 771-8303 • Fax: (425) 771-0833 • www.ricksteves.com

Rick Steves

www.ricksteves.com

EUROPE GUIDES

Best of Europe
Eastern Europe
Europe Through the Back Door

COUNTRY GUIDES

Croatia & Slovenia
England
France
Germany
Great Britain
Ireland
Italy
Portugal
Scandinavia
Spain
Switzerland

CITY & REGIONAL GUIDES

Amsterdam, Bruges & Brussels
Athens & the Peloponnese
Budapest
Florence & Tuscany
Istanbul
London
Paris
Prague & the Czech Republic
Provence & the French Riviera
Rome
Venice
Vienna, Salzburg & Tirol

SNAPSHOT GUIDES

Barcelona
Berlin
Bruges & Brussels
Copenhagen & the Best of
  Denmark
Dublin
Dubrovnik
Hill Towns of Central Italy
Italy's Cinque Terre
Krakow, Warsaw & Gdansk
Lisbon
Madrid & Toledo
Munich, Bavaria & Salzburg
Naples & the Amalfi Coast
Northern Ireland
Norway
Scotland
Sevilla, Granada & Southern Spain
Stockholm

TRAVEL CULTURE

Europe 101
European Christmas
Postcards from Europe
Travel as a Political Act

Rick Steves' EUROPE THROUGH THE BACK DOOR — The Travel Skills Handbook — 2011

Rick Steves' BEST OF EUROPE — 2011

Rick Steves' ITALY — with foldout color MAP — 2011

Rick Steves' PARIS — 2011

Rick Steves guidebooks are published by Avalon Travel,
a member of the Perseus Books Group.

NOW AVAILABLE:
eBOOKS, APPS & BLU-RAY

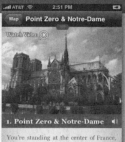

eBOOKS

Most guides available as eBooks
   from Amazon, Barnes & Noble,
   Apple iBook and Sony eReader,
   beginning January 2011

RICK STEVES' EUROPE DVDs

Austria & the Alps
Eastern Europe, Israel & Egypt
England & Wales Europe
European Travel Skills & Specials
France
Germany, Benelux & More
Greece & Turkey
Iran
Ireland & Scotland
Italy's Cities
Italy's Countryside
Rick Steves' European Christmas
Scandinavia
Spain & Portugal

BLU-RAY

Celtic Charms
Eastern Europe Favorites
European Christmas
Italy Through the Back Door
Surprising Cities of Europe

PHRASE BOOKS & DICTIONARIES

French
French, Italian & German
German
Italian
Portuguese
Spanish

JOURNALS

Rick Steves' Pocket Travel Journal
Rick Steves' Travel Journal

APPS

Rick Steves' Ancient Rome Tour
Rick Steves' Historic Paris Walk
Rick Steves' Louvre Tour
Rick Steves' Orsay Museum Tour
Rick Steves' St. Peter's Basilica Tour
Rick Steves' Versailles

PLANNING MAPS

Britain, Ireland & London
Europe
France & Paris
Germany, Austria & Switzerland
Ireland
Italy
Spain & Portugal

Rick Steves books and DVDs are available at bookstores
and through online booksellers.

Credits

Contributor

Cameron Hewitt has researched, written for, and edited the last nine edi-

tions of *Europe Through the Back Door*. He has researched various guidebooks and led tours for Rick Steves' travel company since 2000. While he's visited almost every European country, his favorite area is Central and Eastern Europe, where he co-authors Rick Steves' guidebooks on Eastern Europe, Croatia & Slovenia, and Budapest. When he's not traveling, Cameron lives in Seattle with his wife Shawna.

Panorama Images

	Photographer
Getting Started	
Paris	Rick Steves
Planning Your Itinerary	
Florence, Italy	Rick Steves
Transportation	
Railway in Switzerland	Rick Steves
Money	
Money Montage	David C. Hoerlein
Sleeping and Eating	
Casa Rabatti, Florence	Rick Steves
Travel Savvy	
The Tube, London	ETBD staff
Special Concerns	
Civita, Italy	Rick Steves
Perspectives	
Turkey	Rick Steves
Italy	
Vernazza, Cinque Terre	Rick Steves
Portugal, Spain, and Morocco	
Lisbon	Rick Steves
France	
Eiffel Tower	Carol Ries
Belgium and the Netherlands	
Bruges	Rick Steves
Germany, Austria, and Switzerland	
Rothenburg, Germany	Rick Steves
Eastern Europe	
Prague, Czech Republic	Rick Steves
Great Britain	
Parliament, London	Rick Steves
Ireland	
Blasket Islands	Pat O'Connor
Scandinavia	
Frogner Park, Oslo	David C. Hoerlein
Throughout Europe	
Tegelberg Luge, Bavaria	Dominic Bonuccelli
East Mediterranean	
Nafplio, Greece	Carol Ries

How Was Your Trip?

If you enjoyed a successful trip with the help of this book and would like to share your discoveries, please fill out the survey at www.ricksteves.com /feedback. Thanks in advance for your feedback—it helps a lot. We're all in the same traveler's school of hard knocks...and it's OK to compare notes. Your feedback helps us improve this book for future travelers!

For our latest travel tips, tap into our information-packed website: www.ricksteves.com. For any updates to this book, check www.ricksteves .com/update.

Europe Through the Back Door is more than Rick Steves. All 70 of us are pooling our travel experience and working hard to help you enjoy the trip of a lifetime!

Acknowledgments

Danke to Cameron Hewitt for his travel savvy, editing, and commitment to excellence. *Dank u wel* to Risa Laib for managing my guidebook series so lovingly. And *grazie* to the following for sharing their knowledge in their fields of travel expertise: Dave Hoerlein (artful maps, public-transit tips); Wide World Books & Maps (guidebooks, www.wideworldtravelstore.com); Brooke Burdick (Internet skills and electronics); Joan Robinson and Ann Neel (women's packing tips); Kent Corrick (travel insurance); Elizabeth Holmes (travel agents, overseas flights, www.elizabethholmes.com); the staff at Rail Europe (train travel); Alfred Celentano at Europe by Car and Gary Koenig at Auto Europe (car rental and leasing); Rick Seaney at Farecompare.com (air travel); Chad Cashion at Bank of America (money); Katherine Widing and Richard Walters (biking); Alan Spira, M.D., and Craig Karpilow, M.D. (health for travelers); Arlan Blodgett and Stewart Hopkins (photography); Deanna Russell and Brad McEwen (tours); Susan Sygall and Ken Plattner (travelers with disabilities); Jennifer Hauseman (gay travelers); Audrey Edwards and Leiane Cooke (travelers of color); and Jane Klausen (the European Union).

Merci for support from my entire well-traveled staff at ETBD, including Gene Openshaw, Steve Smith, Rich Sorensen, and in particular, Anne Kirchner for keeping things in order while I'm both in and out. *Spasiba* also to Pat Larson, Sandie Nisbet, and John Givens at Small World Productions for introducing so many travelers to this book through our original public television series, *Travels in Europe with Rick Steves*. *Muchas gracias* to Simon Griffith for directing and producing our current *Rick Steves' Europe* television series with such passion and artistry.

Finally, *tusen takk* to my parents for dragging me to Europe when I didn't want to go.

Avalon Travel
a member of the Perseus Books Group
1700 Fourth Street
Berkeley, CA 94710

For a complete list of Rick Steves' guidebooks, see page 19.

Printed in the USA by Worzalla.
First printing August 2010

For the latest on Rick's lectures, guidebooks, tours, public television series, and public radio show, contact Europe Through the Back Door, Box 2009, Edmonds, WA 98020, tel. 425/771-8303, fax 425/771-0833, www.ricksteves .com, rick@ricksteves.com.

ISBN 978-1-59880-655-7
ISSN 1096-794X

Europe Through the Back Door Reviewing Editors: Cameron Hewitt, Jennifer Madison Davis
ETBD Editors and Researchers: Tom Griffin, Gretchen Strauch, Cathy McDonald
ETBD Managing Editor: Risa Laib
Additional Writing: Cameron Hewitt
Avalon Travel Senior Editor and Series Manager: Madhu Prasher
Avalon Travel Project Editor: Kelly Lydick
Copy Editor: Patrick Collins
Proofreader: Nikki Ioakimedes
Indexer: Stephen Callahan
Production and Typesetting: McGuire Barber Design
Cover Design: Kimberly Glyder Design
Graphic Content Director: Laura VanDeventer
Maps & Graphics: David C. Hoerlein, Laura VanDeventer, Lauren Mills, Barb Geisler, Mike Morgenfeld, Brice Ticen
Cover Photo: Hallstatt, Austria © David C. Hoerlein
Front Matter Color Photos: p. i, Bruges Canal © Dominic Bonuccelli
Photography: Rick Steves, Dominic Bonuccelli, David C. Hoerlein, Cameron Hewitt, Jennifer Madison Davis, Lauren Mills, Laura VanDeventer, Pat O'Connor, Rich Sorensen, Robyn Cronin, Ragen Van Sewell, Jane Klausen, Bruce Van Deventer, Carol Ries, Sonja Groset, Jennifer Hauseman, Mike Potter, Robert Wright, Anna Conley (p. 62), Allen Shoemaker (p. 231), Benjamin Shoemaker (p. 242), Ron Haas (p. 268), Marcella Benson (p. 383), Rachel Worthman (p. 391), Lizanne Fowler (p. 397), John Adkins (p. 403), Randy Ratzlaff (p. 478 & 484)